My Double Life 1

This Dark Wood

A Journey into Light

Episodes and Pattern in a Writer's Life

CW00835810

First published by O-Books, 2015
O-Books is an imprint of John Hunt Publishing Ltd., Laurel House, Station Approach,
Alresford, Hants, SO24 9JH, UK
office1@jhpbooks.net
www.johnhuntpublishing.com

For distributor details and how to order please visit the 'Ordering' section on our website.

Text copyright: Nicholas Hagger 2015

ISBN: 978 1 84694 5904 8

All rights reserved. Except for brief quotations in critical articles or reviews, no part of this book may be
reproduced in any manner without prior written permission from the publishers.

The rights of Nicholas Hagger as author have been asserted in accordance with the Copyright, Designs and
Patents Act 1988.

A CIP catalogue record for this book is available from the British Library.

Design: Stuart Davies

Printed and bound by CPI Group (UK) Ltd, Croydon, CR0 4YY

We operate a distinctive and ethical publishing philosophy in all areas of
our business, from our global network of authors to production and
worldwide distribution.

My Double Life 1

This Dark Wood

A Journey into Light

Episodes and Pattern in a Writer's Life

Nicholas Hagger

BOOKS

Winchester, UK
Washington, USA

Books Published by Nicholas Hagger

The Fire and the Stones
Selected Poems
The Universe and the Light
A White Radiance
A Mystic Way
Awakening to the Light
A Spade Fresh with Mud
The Warlords
Overlord
A Smell of Leaves and Summer
The Tragedy of Prince Tudor
The One and the Many
Wheeling Bats and a Harvest Moon
The Warm Glow of the Monastery Courtyard
The Syndicate
The Secret History of the West
The Light of Civilization
Classical Odes
Overlord, one-volume edition
Collected Poems 1958 – 2005
Collected Verse Plays
Collected Stories
The Secret Founding of America
The Last Tourist in Iran
The Rise and Fall of Civilizations
The New Philosophy of Universalism
The Libyan Revolution
Armageddon
The World Government
The Secret American Dream
A New Philosophy of Literature
A View of Epping Forest
My Double Life 2: A Rainbow over the Hills

"Our structure is very beautiful. DNA can be thought of roughly as a very long chain with flat bits sticking out.... The beauty of our model is that the shape of it is such that only these pairs can go together."[1]

Francis Crick, Letter to his 12-year-old son on the
double-helix structure of DNA, 19 March 1953

'Double' (adj): "consisting of two, usually equal parts"; "having twice the usual size, quantity or strength"; "having two different roles or interpretations" (*Concise Oxford Dictionary*). And: "consisting of two combined"; "forming a pair, coupled"; "acting in two ways at different times" (*Shorter Oxford English Dictionary*).

"Quod me nutrit me destruit."
"That which feeds me destroys me."
Inscribed on a 1585 portrait thought to be of Marlowe, echoing words in Ovid's *Tristia* (3.3.73–74) which adorn the statue of Ovid in Tomis: "*Hic ego qui iaceo tenerorum lusor amorum/ingenio perii Naso poeta meo*"; "Here I lie, who played with tender loves,/Naso the poet, killed by my own talent [or temperament]".

*

The vision of unity

Graeco-Roman bronze of the Titan Atlas holding the unified world, showing Africa misshapen (in accordance with the geographical knowledge of the Graeco-Roman time), by a sculptor who grasped that the earth is round.

This Dark Wood
"I woke to find myself in a dark wood,
Where the right road was wholly lost and gone."

Dante, *Inferno*, I, 1–3
(trans. by Dorothy Sayers)

"For forty years I have schooled myself... to write an epic which begins 'In the Dark Forest', crosses the purgatory of human error, and ends in the light and *'fra i maestri di color che sanno'* ['among the masters of those who know']."

Ezra Pound, *An Introduction to the Economic Nature of the United States* (reprinted in Ezra Pound, *Selected Prose, 1909–1965*)

"Essex reared me through war, now holds my bones.
I, lost in this Dark Wood, trod ancient stones
And found Light on the Way, am now content
My works – deeds, words – should be my monument....
Peep behind the universe for the One:
Behind each shadow reigns a glorious Sun."

Nicholas Hagger, 'Epitaphs', *Collected Poems*

*

To Asa Briggs, author of *Secret Days*, who urged me to write this account of my Cold-War activities in October 1978 and who will understand why I delayed 35 years; and to my family, for whom this time has always been something of a mystery, and especially to my children and grandchildren.

CONTENTS

Table of Contents

Summary of the story through section headings

Prologue: The Path and Pattern

The path through a dark wood. *My Double Life* belongs to a *genre* of transformation. Pattern: life as a succession of episodes. Pairs of opposites; concept of time. The cone-like self: a pine cone's scales, pairs of opposites. A spruce cone has at least 42 pairs of scales or opposites. Fibonacci spirals, 13 counter-clockwise and 8 clockwise. The double helix, two entwined spirals. The structure of *My Double Life*: successive episodes. *My Double Life 1* as the first 15 of 42 episodes and pairs of opposites. Inclusion of my intelligence work – Sir John Masterman, Asa Briggs. Personal pattern: the story of my quest for Reality, the One. To what extent was the path of my life subject to chance, choice or destiny? Universal pattern: the pattern of the path of my life reflects a universal pattern.

Part One: Quest for the One

1. Origins

My inherited DNA. My parents' marriage. My mother's family: Broadleys and Hardings. Rev. Benjamin Broadley and the Navy. Hannah Comfort (Mrs. Burton) owned a school. Charles Harding wrote for *The Times*. George Broadley I's tailor's business and marriage to Elsie Harding. Tom Broadley I and the RFC. Broadley Brothers, death of George Broadley I of cancer in 1926. George Broadley II corners the family business. Provision for Norah. Dwindling of family business. My father's family: Haggers and Osbornes. The Haggers of Therfield, Hertfordshire. Possible descent from the Haggers of Bourn, Cambridgeshire: Carolus Haggar of Brugge (Bruges) moved to Chelmsford, Essex c.1366; Bourn Hall completed by John Hagger, c.1602. Is there a link between Therfield and Bourn Haggers? The Osbornes. Origin of Hagger name.

2. The Call

Episode 1: Family and War
Wartime childhood. In London: Norbury and Caterham. Gwen Broad. Evacuation to East Grinstead: St Anton and Beecholme. Move to Loughton: 52 Brooklyn Avenue. I attend Essex House School. German bombs blow out

our windows. I attend Oaklands School, Trap's Hill – Froebel and Nature. V-1 and V-2 rockets. Oaklands School moves to Albion Hill. Brother and grand-father. I hear Churchill speak at Loughton war memorial in 1945. Move to Journey's End. My sixth birthday.

Episode 2: Nature and School
Awareness of Nature. William Addison. Nature walks, Bird Diary. Life at Journey's End and Oaklands. Sunday school: Methodist church. Interview with Dr James at Chigwell School. Epping Forest. Foreign coins and stamps. Iron-Age forts, Roman coin and garden. Oneness with frosty stars. Chinese coins: eternity. Illnesses: latent tuberculosis, meningitis, tonsillitis. Entrance exam to Chigwell School: newts. Gradual shutting-out of Nature. I start at Chigwell School. Grange Court. Speech Day: Bernard Howard. Dentist: Howard Carter's brother. Folkestone. Chigwell: 17th-century Big School. Cricket captain. Festival of Britain. Churchill comes to Loughton in 1951. Capt. W.E. Johns. Death of the King. Butterflies. Classics. I collect Roman and Greek coins. Love for literature: Julius Caesar, very early writing. In Normandy: Le Home-sur-la-Mer, D-Day beaches. I meet Montgomery. Oaklands School: dance. 'O'-level: letter to Capt. W.E. Johns and his reply. Dream of 'O'-level Greek set-books paper. Merrow: oneness of the universe.

Episode 3: Archaeology and Politics
Taken from literature to classics. Interest in archaeology. Tutankhamen. Cricket and Cornish megaliths. Greek antiquities: British School of Archaeology at Athens. Roman dig: sewer at Chester. Interest in USSR: I see Bulganin and Khrushchev. Suez crisis and corps camp. I attend key Suez debate: support for Suez invasion. Exiles from Hungarian Uprising. Local elections: count. The Angry Young Men: Colin Wilson. Sir Oswald Mosley. Entrance exam to Oxford: Sir John Masterman and Corinthian coin.

Episode 4: Literature and Law
Call to be a poet in March 1957. In Italy and Sicily with David Hoppit. A week in a Loughton solicitors' office. Motor cycle side-cars and cricket for Buckhurst Hill. Solicitors' articles in London. Vision of my future in Loughton library. Practical philosophy lectures on non-dualism. Colin Wilson talks in coffee-house. Research into European literature, walks with John Ezard. Ken Campbell. Alex Comfort. London lunch-times. John Biggs-Davison MP, article on nuclear weapons. Rejection of the Law, research into Existentialism. Rejection of the Church, path to Reality through literature. The Royal Court. Colin Wilson, Stuart Holroyd and Sparticans. In Greece with Alan Magnus: sleeping in Kazantzakis's study, jumping to catch the train. Starting at Oxford: Worcester College – Ricky Herbert, Kingsley

3. The Journey: Awakening

early Universalism. Unrest at the University of Baghdad: 3B. Freedom of speech. Babylon. Kaseem "immortal" tyrant. The poor. Students: fight on campus, death of student and my alibi for a girl student. Chief of Secret Police becomes Dean of College and purges students. Students in prison in zoo cages. President of University proposed for execution. My Secret Police file. Exit visa: leaving Iraqi dictatorship.

Episode 7: Vitalism and Mechanism
London: brain and soul, research into brain function – the physiological basis of thinking, mechanistic view of mind. Birth of daughter, Nadia. Death of Kaseem. Father's brain haemorrhage. George MacBeth and B.S. Johnson. I apply to British Council for a lectureship in Japan. Work in Dulwich Park as gardener, and vitalism. Gardener in three schools. Offered lectureship in Japan. Work in library. Father's third stroke, death and funeral. W.B. Emery and the Great Pyramid. Getting off to Japan: flat. Visit to Dick Paul in Palmerston's lounge, Carlton Gardens. Experience of the One by Strawberry Hill pond – vitalism and soul triumph over mechanism.

Episode 8: The Absolute and Scepticism
Arrival in Japan. Discovery that I am a Visiting Foreign Professor – first since William Empson. Tokyo University of Education, teaching in Empson's room. James Kirkup. E.W.F. Tomlin, Representative of the British Council in Japan, friend of Eliot. Tokyo University of Education and Keio University. Modern and traditional Japan. Brian Buchanan's house in Nobe. Poems: 'The Expatriate', 'The Seventeenth-Century Pilgrim'. Thomas Fitzsimmons. Meeting with Junzaburo Nishiwaki. *Diaries*. Earthquake. Tomlin and the Absolute: metaphysical philosopher. With Anthony Powell. With Edmund Blunden. Work at the Bank of Japan. Tom Fitzsimmons and self-unification. Kamakura. Nobe: horseshoe valleys. To Zen with Haga: in Ichikawa city meditation centre, timeless Being. Koganji temple: beginning of First Mystic Life (20 July 1964–18 October 1965). Course in Hakone, and shrines. Metaphysical theme. Climbing Mount Fuji: clean senses. In Hiroshima: nun. World history: Toynbee. The One in Nobe. Arrival of Frank Tuohy. Tuohy and Wittgenstein. In Kyoto and Nara: the Absolute of the Zen Stone Garden. Poetry: *The Early Education and Making of a Mystic*, 'The Silence'. Death of grandmother. Freeman, 'The Silence' and Modernism. Chinese atomic bomb: Leon Stover. I become tutor to Prince Hitachi: world history. Bank of Japan and loan. At Zen Engakuji temple in Kitakamakura with Tuohy – centipede. At Gora: creative will. Dinner with Prince and Princess Hitachi: Imperial ancestors in nesting-boxes, Shinto *kami*. Trine and the infinite. Second visit to Kyoto and Nara, with Bank of Japan: Stone Garden again. Tribute to Eliot. Centre-shift. Inner images. Nishiwaki and the Absolute: the wisdom of the

Part Two: Path through a Dark Wood

4. Way of Loss: Dark Night of the Soul, the Purgative Way

Episode 10: Establishment and Revolution
Living in Loughton, teaching current affairs to Japanese in London. 17-March Grosvenor-Square demonstration against Vietnam war. Soviet invasion of Czechoslovakia, student revolution in France. At 'Free Greece' demonstration. Prospect of lecturing in Libya. Drink with Biggs-Davison at the Commons. Concern over Caroline's brother Richard's marriage. 21-July Grosvenor-Square demonstration against Vietnam war. Leaving to lecture at the University of Libya, Tripoli: multiplicity. Drive through France and Tunisia: Carthage. Tripoli. To Sabratha with Col. Ben Nagy. *The Daily News*: Chatter and Ansari. To Leptis Magna with Ben Nagy: talk of revolution to eliminate poverty and increase the flow of Libyan oil to the West. Tripoli: meeting with Libyan ministers and intellectuals, a pro-Western *coup* – Ben Nagy and Shukri Ghanem. King Idris. Journalism: I write articles for *The Daily News* as 'the Barbary Gipsy'. Ministers: the Minister for Petroleum. With Angus Wilson. Chief of Police, Col. Ali Shilabi, gatecrashes a gathering of *coup* ministers. Ansari accused of being an Egyptian spy. Recruited to the SIS by Andrew Mackenzie. In T.E. Lawrence's footsteps.

Episode 11: Liberation and Tyranny
Party for faction of pro-Western *coup* at the Minister of Health's farm. Meeting with Andrew Mackenzie: scenario of *coup*. Party at the King's farm. Omar and Abdulaziz al-Shalhi. Envelope. Meeting with Viktor. Visit to Djerba, and American couple: Ben Nagy meets Col. Saad eddin Bushwerib of Libyan army, who is to carry out *coup*. London. Meetings with Keith Priest and Melissa, and John Harrow. Interview with Dr Muntasser, Libyan Ambassador to UK. Back to Tripoli: dinners with Beshir al-Muntasser, news that the pro-Western *coup* has been set for 5 September. I am an eyewitness of Gaddafi's *coup* of 1 September 1969; Viktor. Ansari says my article on Libyan-British relations triggered the 1-September *coup*. Two last articles for *The Daily News*, blocking intervention. Hostages. Circumventing prohibition. *The Daily News* closed, I am set up by Ansari and taken to radio station. Censor: now followed by fawn Volkswagen. Egyptian origin of Gaddafi's *coup*: how Gaddafi's *coup* happened. King was to abdicate on 2 September. Gaddafi read my article on Libyan-British relations. How the *coup* was organised. Gaddafi mimicked the 5-September pro-Western *coup*. Egypt behind Gaddafi's *coup*. Bushwerib now Libyan Ambassador to Egypt. Gaddafi's perspective.

5. Transformation: the Illuminative Way

Episode 13: Ambassador and Journalism
Return to UK. With Ezra Pound in Rapallo. Geneva. London: reunions. I take a room in 13 Egerton Gardens, London SW3. Journalism on Libya: articles for *The Times* and *The Sunday Telegraph*. London poets. Poetry Revolution to restore grand themes, seriousness, prophecy and vision: three visits to John Heath-Stubbs; Ted Hughes. Letter from Donald Maitland, now Heath's Press Secretary. I meet Andrew Mackenzie in Trafalgar Square and through Maitland become Edward Heath's 'unofficial Ambassador' to representatives of African liberation movements. I am to defend the West against Soviet and Chinese Cold-War expansion in Africa and pursue link with Chinese. Visit to Africa Bureau: meeting Africans. Visits to representatives of African liberation movements. My three-column article in *The Times* on World Council of Churches' grants to African liberation movements – first mention of UNITA in *The Times*. Meeting with Andrew MacKenzie in Trafalgar Square: new terms. UNITA. New controller, Martin Rowley: more articles for *The Times*. George MacBeth. Purgation: detachment and renunciation. Agreement to divorce to protect access. Mike Marshment plans a trek into Angola to include Jean-Paul Sartre and me. More articles, room searched, papers strewn. Jorge Sangumba, UNITA's Foreign Secretary, and trek with Sartre. Jorge says he will introduce me to the Chinese Chargé. Visit to Angola disallowed. Cover job in ESN school in Greenwich: Riverway. Jorge asks Edgar Snow to arrange for me to interview Mao. Jorge to introduce a Chinese First Secretary. Attack on my car. Jorge urges me to obtain Portuguese war *communiqués*, as does Polly Gaster; and wants to introduce the editor of *Hsinhua* News Agency. Martin Rowley introduces me to a China expert. I meet Chinese First Secretary, Chang Chi-hsiang, expert on liberation movements, with Jorge. Exposed to the KGB: news that Viktor has shown Czech intelligence/KGB my signed receipt – I am now operating openly like James Bond. Divorce: legally protected access. Hostile surveillance: Egerton Gardens filled with police. Pussy-cat, Portuguese linguist, becomes housekeeper at 13 Egerton Gardens. Pussy-cat controls incoming calls, cleans and cooks – and bugs my room. I become a coach-driver for Riverway outings. John Ezard's interview: "John Ezard of MI5." Targeting Chinese: with four China experts in Harrods' Way In, six Chinese targets. Interviewing Africans. 'Portugal's African War': I am paid for *The Times* article not used. New controller, James Appleton.

Episode 14: Illumination and Nationalism
Mystic and artist Margaret Riley at 13 Egerton Gardens. Pottery pyramid of chains. One direction. Dinner with Toynbee's granddaughter. Poetry of

sleep in a Chinese camp. Mikumi National Park: lion and *tsetse*. I run out of money. Return home, reflect on increase in British influence. My disenchantment. Grumbling. Aftermath of Tanzania. Exposure and review. Test of intuition. Switched from Africa to India and Japan against my wishes. I rediscover my poetic spring. Vastation experiences. The unity of the universe. I turn against intelligence work. Cornwall: with Colin Wilson, D.S. Savage. Threat to expose me. Leak? New teaching job by Clapham Common. Last Riverway outings with ESN boys: signal-box, hospital mortuary, Windsor and the Royal family, St Paul's and Michael Horovitz. Row between MI6 and MI5. "Never see your daughter again": I am asked to sign that I will not see my daughter again. Discontinuing: I leave the SIS. The real reason. Balanced view. SIS judgement wrong. No contact with SIS since 1973. The vision of unity: first inklings of a neo-Baroque movement. Out of the dark wood with a vision.

Epilogue: View of the Path – Episodes and Memories, Pattern and Unity

Pattern and unity in a life. Pattern and symmetry as design: life as a succession of episodes and memories, and pairs of opposites. Pattern of transformation in 15 episodes and pairs of opposites: personal episodes and memories, pattern and unity – double helix. Pattern of progression and regression (+A + −A): transformation to a vision of the unity of the universe. Pattern and unity in all lives. Pattern of transformation in all lives: all lives have episodes and opposites and have the potential to progress towards vision of the unity of the universe. A pre-ordained path? Free will + chance = Providential destiny; works like seeds of a spruce cone. The unity of each being. Universal episodes and memories, pattern and unity in all lives – analogy of a spruce cone; the unity of Being. The structure of all human experience.

The Rainbow Portrait of Elizabeth I holding a rainbow, painted in the last year of her reign (c.1602, attributed to Isaac Oliver). The Queen is wearing an orange cloak decorated with eyes, ears and mouths, a sign that she sees and hears everything through her intelligence agents. (*See* p.112.) On her left sleeve is a jewelled serpent. She holds a rainbow in her right hand and the Latin inscription on the painting, '*Non sine sole iris*', translates as 'No rainbow without the sun'.

Sketch for a portrait of Nicholas Hagger by Stuart Davies

"The unexamined life is not worth living."
Socrates, in Plato, *Apology*, 38a

Prologue: The Path and Pattern

"Without Contraries is no progression. Attraction and Repulsion, Reason and Energy, Love and Hate, are necessary to Human existence."

Blake, 'The Marriage of Heaven and Hell', c.1793

My Double Life presents my life in two volumes: 'a life in two slices'. I led a double life in several senses. From early on I developed an everyday social life that found employment as a lecturer and kept a family; and an adventurous life that approached the One in literary works and quested in the Middle and Far East. From my mid-twenties I was living at social and metaphysical levels and experienced a First Mystic Life. Then I took on my secret work and lived the double life of an undercover intelligence agent, during which I experienced illumination and a Second Mystic Life. Later still I was a teacher, and then a Principal of schools and employer, while writing books. Like many Geminis I had twins within my mind.

Each of the two volumes of *My Double Life* tells of a dual life. I sometimes think I was ladled a double helping for I crammed so much experience into my life that I seem to have lived two lives within the span of one lifetime. This impression has been redoubled by the diversity of my work life – looking back, I seem to have had several professions – and by the variety of the literary *genres* and forms in which I have written. Yet I was always aware that I had an underlying single life that lived in harmony with the oneness of the universe.

The path through a dark wood
My Double Life *belongs to a* genre *of transformation*
My Double Life 1: This Dark Wood narrates a personal journey along a perilous path through a "dark wood": the influences, belief systems, ideological conflicts and political causes of the 20th century. As I progressed along the Mystic Way I came to understand that I could not reach the goal of my quest – Reality, the One – until I had undergone a transformation, a metamorphosis: a centre-shift after purgation from sensual attachments, followed by illumination, which I had sought in Zen temples in Japan and which burst upon me inconveniently in 1971 when I was grappling with secret work. This profound experience changed my way of seeing, and I found that I now instinctively saw the universe as a unity behind all the differences. *My Double Life 1: This Dark Wood* describes the changes in my circumstances that led to this experience, which I came to see as universal –

Universalist. Its sequel *My Double Life 2: A Rainbow over the Hills* completes the story of the transformation and development in my life and thinking during a remarkable odyssey that led me from Oxford materialism to the metaphysical outlook of my literary, philosophical and historical works.

During my journey I had four Mystic Lives in all. The first two of these can be dated from the chronological list of experiences of the Light (*see* Appendix 1, p.489). There are 16 experiences of the Light in *My Double Life 1: This Dark Wood* and 77 in *My Double Life 2: A Rainbow over the Hills*, a total of 93 experiences of the Light, each of which is documented from *Diaries* written at the time. Between the First and Second Mystic Lives I endured a Dark Night of the Soul, and between my Second and Third Mystic Lives I experienced the first part of my Dark Night of the Spirit, in which I was fed new powers. *My Double Life 1: This Dark Wood* ends near the beginning of this Dark Night. In *My Double Life 2: A Rainbow over the Hills* the story continues, and between my Third and Fourth Mystic Lives I experienced the second part of my Dark Night of the Spirit in which I was confronted with ordeals. My Unitive Life began after my Fourth Mystic Life.

My Double Life belongs to a literature of transformation, a tradition of 'process works' that began with Ovid's *Metamorphoses*, continued with St Augustine's *Confessions*, Bunyan's *Pilgrim's Progress* and the Continental *Bildungsroman*s (novels about early life and development) – Crébillon fils' *The Wayward Head and Heart*, Goethe's *Wilhelm Meisters Lehrjahre*, Constant's *Adolphe* and Hesse's *Demian* and *Siddhartha*; and reached new heights in Wordsworth's *Prelude* and T.E. Lawrence's account of his life as a British intelligence agent, *Seven Pillars of Wisdom*.

In *A New Philosophy of Literature* I identified the metaphysical and secular aspects of the fundamental theme of world literature that can be found in the literature of every culture since the *Epic of Gilgamesh*, c.2,600BC: the quest for metaphysical Reality, the One; and condemnation of social follies and vices. *This Dark Wood* is a quest for the One, and I encounter many follies and vices on the way.

Pattern: life as a succession of episodes
Pairs of opposites; concept of time
I covered some of the ground of *My Double Life 1* and 2 from a different angle in *A Mystic Way* (1994), which showed how my life influenced my poems.

My Double Life 1 and 2 incorporates, revises and updates *A Mystic Way* while retaining its concern to catch the cumulative process of my thinking and avoid imposing a present construct on past experience. In the two new volumes I have deliberately followed the wording of passages in *A Mystic Way* that have not been updated or presented from a new angle, preferring to retain the original account and (as they incorporate the earlier work) I have generally not referred to pages of *A Mystic Way* in the Notes and References.

In *A Mystic Way* I brought a philosophical principle to my treatment of time. Time cannot be seen; only its effects can be detected as a succession of events. In *A Mystic Way* I stated that "time is a succession of events" and that "the present is added cumulatively to the past so that new layers are endlessly added to previous layers".[1]

I have since developed that concept of time. In *My Double Life 1* and *2* I focus on a life, and time, in terms of successive episodes. I see that I lived my life in a succession of episodes. Time is now an episodic succession of events: a succession of events within an episode – and, indeed, a succession of episodes. And as time progresses, memories of successive episodes are continuously stored in layers within the memory.

An 'episode', according to the *Concise Oxford Dictionary*, is "one event or a group of events as part of a sequence", "an incident or set of incidents in a narrative". I have come to see that in each episode of my experience, on each stage of my path, the "group of events" or "set of incidents" consisted of pairs of 'contraries'. In each episode within my narrative there was a pair of conflicting sequences of events or opposites. That meant that in each episode I was living a kind of 'double life'.

The episodes inspired my memories. As I journeyed from episode to episode, memories of successive pairs of conflicting sequences of events – pairs of opposites – formed round my self. In my earliest episode the two conflicting sequences of events were imposed on my self and stored in my memory. As I grew older I found myself living through a new episode in which a second pair of conflicting sequences of events superimposed itself as a new layer on my self and my memory. And as I grew older still I lived through a new episode in which a third pair of opposites superimposed itself as a new layer on my self and my memory. And so on. Most episodes do not begin and end abruptly. Their opposites grow out of the previous episode and fade during the next episode.

I have come to see that the pattern of my life – its "repeated decorative design" (*Concise Oxford Dictionary*) – can be found in my progression through these episodes, these pairs of opposites and memories which formed – accreted – round my self, each of which controlled my life for a period of time. Tracing my progress through these episodes – these successive pairs of opposites, these sequences of events within episodes – reveals how I found my particular path and journeyed up it to this particular sloping hill.

This view of a life as a succession of episodes of conflicting sequences of events (and the layered memories of successive pairs of opposites that formed on my self) is in harmony with the view of the universe I expressed in my books. These see the universe as a unity that reconciles pairs of opposites or contradictions: day and night, spring and autumn, life and death. In a *saké* (rice-wine) bar in Tokyo in 1965 I asked the Japanese poet Junzaburo Nishiwaki (a contemporary of Eliot's) for a distillation of the wisdom of the East. He wrote on a business reply card now framed on my study wall, "+A + −A = 0, great nothing". (*See* p.186.) He explained to me that the universe is a unity that reconciles all contradictions, that the One combines day and night, life and death. I brought this Eastern idea back from Japan. Each pair of opposites – of conflicting sequences of events that form memories on my self – in different periods of my life is a "+A + −A" that reflects Eastern thinking.

The cone-like self: a pine cone's scales, pairs of opposites
I have come to see the layered memories of successive episodes that formed round my self, and the origin of my literary, historical and philosophical works, in terms of the image of a cone borne by an evergreen conifer: a pine, spruce, yew, cedar, cypress, larch or redwood tree.

I first made this association in August 2011. I was reflecting on how at every stage of my growth my life has been an accumulation of successive pairs of contradictions when I travelled from Cornwall to stay on Dartmoor, at Gidleigh Park. I was shown to my room and sat in the window looking down at the river that gushed through boulders beyond the lawn and rushed headlong like the course of a life. I noticed dark humps of woods beyond it. On the window-sill between me and the open window was a bowl of pine cones.

I picked one out and examined its open arms or 'scales'. I realised it was a female seed-bearing cone that shed seeds when the scales opened, and opened and closed in response to the weather. I realised the cone would one day be significant. A bowl of pine cones was an image for something, but I had not yet fathomed what. I wondered if it was an image for clusters or sequences of events. I brought the cone back with me and placed it on my desk.

Several months passed. Then, sitting in this window and looking out over this dark wood from this hill, I ruminated again on the pattern of a life, of episodes and memories, and on the structure of the self; and found myself again holding the pine cone. I examined it and realised that each scale or arm was one of a pair. A cone is formed of pairs of scales. They are in layers that are arranged in two spirals. I was holding a double-spiral structure consisting of layers of pairs of opposites, whorls around an axis. It was a perfect image for the concept of a life that I had been forming: successive episodes with pairs of contradictions, memories of which formed round the self.

A spruce cone has at least 42 pairs of scales or opposites

I have a conifer in my Essex front garden. It is a Norway spruce (*picea abies*), the species of Christmas tree donated each winter by the people of Norway and erected in Trafalgar Square. I wandered outside and picked up a five-inch-long spruce cone that was lying on the ground. (Once I might have called it a 'fir-cone' but that generic description is scientifically inaccurate as spruces and firs are different species of conifer.) Its scales were closed but as I examined it I found the same principle applied: the scales were in pairs of opposites, layer upon layer from bottom to top. I counted in zigzag up each of the two spirals and reckoned there were about 42 layers of scales. I brought it in and laid it on my desk. I knew the hard scales protected seeds that grew beneath them. During the next two days the scales opened and deposited small winged seeds. I put the spruce cone and the seeds in a small box, and within a few days it had shed more than 130 seeds.

I now intuitively grasped that the structure of the self is similar to the structure of a conifer's female cone. From childhood onwards we progress along a path through episodes, and as our cone-like self experiences and remembers our path in our memory we grow layers of scale-like pairs of opposites: memories of conflicting pairs of sequences of events, contraries, each of which is an expression of the Eastern $+A + -A = 0$. Beneath each scale of a conifer cone are two ovules which develop into seeds. The scales at the base and top of the cone are sterile, without seeds. I grasped that as we grow a new layered episode of a pair of opposites we at the same time grow the seeds of our own creativity.

I knew that the analogy of the conifer cone should not be taken too literally. Conifer cones have two seeds per scale, i.e. four seeds per layered pair of opposites. It does not follow that a fully-grown self living to about 105 with 42 layers and pairs of opposites, and therefore 84 'scales', has exactly 168 seeds or projects. But I intuitively felt that the principle of seeds being produced from beneath layers and pairs of scales does apply to the self, that the germs of potential creative works and projects are produced from beneath layers of memories of pairs of opposites based on episodes with conflicting pairs of sequences of events, even though the number of creative works and projects achieved differs from the number of seeds in a cone.

Fibonacci spirals, 13 counter-clockwise and 8 clockwise

My thinking was carried forward in January 2012. My wife had a locally well-known naturalist and environmentalist[2] to lunch. I produced the small box containing the two cones and the deposit of seeds. I remarked on the pairs of opposite scales. As she handled the cones the environmentalist said, "Of course, they're spirals. It's the Fibonacci sequence. It determines their form." Her remark dropped into my mind like a stone. I did some research.

As in many growing things, from the base of a cone spirals whirl upwards in two opposite directions. There is a double set of spirals, one going in a clockwise direction and one in a counter-clockwise direction. In a fully-grown pine cone there are 13 counter-clockwise spirals and 8 clockwise spirals, a total of 21 spirals. In all cones these conflicting spirals go in the same differing directions. In a fully-grown spruce cone the same applies. The number of these spirals is determined by the sequence of numbers named after Leonardo of Pisa, who was known as Fibonacci and who in 1202, in his *Liber Abaci*, introduced the sequence (which was already known in Indian mathematics) to the West: 0, 1, 1, 2, 3, 5, 8, 13, 21, 34, 55, 89, 144, 233, 377 and so on. The first two numbers are 0 and 1, and each subsequent number is the sum of the previous two.

If we divide each number (e.g. 13) by the number that precedes it in the sequence (e.g. 8) it gives a value of approximately 1.6180339, the golden ratio or mean which is represented by the Greek letter *phi*. To successors of the early-13th-century Fibonacci such as Leonardo da Vinci this was the ratio of beauty. Thus the perfect face contains this figure of design proportion – the width of the mouth is 1.618 times the width of the nose, for example – whereas in a lopsided, unbeautiful face this is not the case. The same is true of the proportion of the limbs of the body. Each finger bone is 1.618 times the length of the preceding finger bone, and the distance from elbow to wrist is 1.618 times the distance from wrist to fingertip. The distance from belly button (or navel) to the soles of the feet is 1.618 times the distance from the top of the head to the belly button, and ideal height is 1.618 times the distance from shoulder to fingertip. Fibonacci saw a mechanism in Nature that implements proportion. He did not say how or why the drive or thrust within Nature spurs the DNA to reproduce this ratio.

Sunflowers by and large obey the Fibonacci sequence of numbers. Different types of sunflower have 55 spirals (34 clockwise, 21 counter-clockwise), 89 (55 clockwise, 34 counter-clockwise) or in the case of very large sunflowers even 233 (144 clockwise, 89 counter-clockwise). The counter-clockwise spirals appear to limit their growth to accord with the golden ratio. The arrangement of the Fibonacci numbers maximises the number of seeds that can be packed into a seed head. Spiralling growth is found in the leaf arrangements, stems and branches of other plants, in their petals and seedheads, and in the whorl of a nautilus shell. It is found in the growth of many flowers and fruits, the uncurling of fern fronds, and the positioning of branches on tree-trunks as well as in the growth of mollusc shells. Plant cells turn at 0.618 of a revolution (222.5 degrees) to maximise space, forming spirals. Not all plants obey the Fibonacci sequence. For example, corn grows in straight lines.

I was startled to discover that Alan Turing, the father of computer science who helped break the Enigma code at Bletchley Park, spent two years working on the Fibonacci numbers in sunflowers to understand how plants grow. He wrote a paper on form in biology in 1951 and devised a theory to explain why Fibonacci sequences appear in sunflowers and plants, but before the theory could be tested he died after biting an apple injected with cyanide in 1954. A Turing's Sunflowers project led by the Museum of Science and Industry in Manchester in 2012 analysed sunflower specimens sent by 12,000 people in seven countries and found that of 557 heads analysed, 458 (82%) had their rows arranged in Fibonacci spiral patterns, and that of the rest 33 had patterns based on the Lucas series, a modified Fibonacci sequence that begins with 2 and 1 and proceeds on the same basis (3, 4, 7, 11, 18, 29 and so on).[3]

Looking at my spruce cone again, I realised that the cones are imbricate – arranged so as to overlap each other like fish scales (or roof tiles) to protect seeds. I saw that the scales are different sizes and that their ends are curled up to different extents so that when the scales are closed the ends fully protect the seeds above from predators and rain. (A cone closes if soaked in water.) Sequoia cones, including those of redwood trees, the tallest trees on earth, feel heat from fires. They wait until fire threatens the seeds before scattering them, probably because in primeval times, long before the advent of man, lightning strikes started forest fires. Such intricate organisation and ordering was truly wonderful, and I marvelled that the DNA instructs each spruce scale to grow to a precise specification that differs from that of all the other scales.

I was again struck by the 8 clockwise and 13 counter-clockwise spirals. They twist in opposite directions, the spirals are also opposites, their own +A (i.e. 8) + −A (i.e. 13) = 0. I dwelt on the image and concept of a self as spirals of memories of experiences. I saw mind as clockwise and counter-clockwise spirals of sequences of memories of experiences.[4]

I sensed that the whole intricate structure of the self consists of pairs of opposite memories of experience. That is to say, I sensed that each episode passes into our memory as a pair of opposite sequences of events, and that within each opposite are subsets of further sequences of events. And that each memory may be within a pair of 'scales' that is simultaneously stored within two opposite spirals and has an essential part in the whole.

I grasped that each episode in a life could be shown as a pair of opposite experiences, and that a self could be shown as spirals of sequences of memories of experiences. In each of my pairs of opposites, one half of the pair would be part of a spiral on one side of the cone of the self, and the other half of the pair would be part of an opposite spiral on the other side of the cone of the self. Just as one can look at a cone as pairs of scales, as clockwise spirals and as counter-clockwise spirals, so one can look at a self as pairs of opposites, as clockwise spirals and as counter-clockwise spirals of memories, all winding up to the cone-shaped self's present outlook at its top. For our earliest memories are at the cone-shaped self's base, and our most recent are in our present episode, towards the top.

The double helix, two entwined spirals
It is worth pointing out that if my memories of the pairs of opposites within the episodes of my double life are held within two entwined spirals that formed round my self, then they resemble the pairs of opposites within the double helix, or two entwined spirals, of DNA. (*See* below.) If this is so, then human memory and inheritance can be seen to follow the same process, pattern and law: another confirmation of the unity between human consciousness and biological Nature.

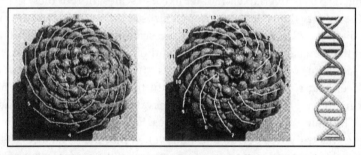

8 clockwise (left) and 13 counter-clockwise (middle) spirals of a pine cone; and (right) diagram of the double helix of DNA showing two ribbon-like (phosphate-sugar) chains with horizontal rods connecting pairs of bases or opposites that hold the chains together

The structure of My Double Life: *successive episodes* – My Double Life 1 *as the first 15 of 42 episodes and pairs of opposites*
Through such musings I arrived at the form of *My Double Life*. I realised that I had been confirmed in my thinking about its structure. I could see 30 episodes along the path of my life so far, of which the first 15 are covered in *My Double Life 1: This Dark Wood*, ending with the end of my career in intelligence. I have structured *This Dark Wood* round the first 15 of the 30 layered episodes I have lived through. They begin on p.22. In each of the numbered episodes in my life there was a pair of conflicting sequences of events that are reflected in the title of the section devoted to each episode. Each episode, or rather each conflicting sequence of events within the pair, is also a layer of memories stored within my self. I shall consider the pattern of these 15 episodes in the Epilogue. The remaining 15, and a review of all 30, can be found in *My Double Life 2: A Rainbow over the Hills*.

These 30 episodes – so far, and the 42 episodes of my fully-grown self if

I live to be 105 and the average length of an episode is 2.5 years – can be seen as having a linear chronological progression from episode 1 to episode 30 and eventually to episode 42, and we shall see that the pairs of opposites have their own progression within their double helix. (*See* p.474.)

I sensed that as my finished life – if it achieves its full span – will have 42 layers and pairs of opposites, I have just completed the 30th layer, and the 31st–42nd layers are still in the future.

Inclusion of my intelligence work – Sir John Masterman, Asa Briggs

"I said, 'I will watch how I behave, and not let my tongue lead me into sin; I will keep a muzzle on my mouth as long as the wicked man is near me.' I stayed dumb, silent, speechless."

Psalm 39, Jerusalem Bible

When I discussed my experiences in Libya with the historian (Lord) Asa Briggs, Provost of Worcester College, Oxford in October 1978 and told him what I had been doing immediately before and during Gaddafi's *coup* as an intelligence agent, he told me very strongly, "You must write a book about your experiences. You have told me something I have often wondered about and did not know, you must write it down. You have just explained how the West came to accept the Gaddafi Revolution. I have not seen this written anywhere else. You must write the *full* story. It is of historical importance." He followed this up with a letter: "I feel that you ought to write up your experience, and I am sure that it would be of very wide interest."[5]

I did not know that he had worked in Bletchley Park for two years from early summer 1943 to May 1945 and that he would write his own account, *Secret Days* (which would be published in 2011 when he was 90). Nor did I know that my Provost when I was at Worcester College, Sir John Masterman, had been Chairman of the Twenty Committee ('XX Committee') during the Second World War and in charge of the 'double-cross system' that turned German agents round and duped German intelligence into believing that D-Day would take place in the Pas de Calais rather than Normandy. I did not know that the account he wrote immediately after the war in 1945 was walled round with silence in the UK until it was finally published as *The Double-Cross System in the War of 1939 to 1945* in the US in 1972. (*See* p.119.) Without realising it until later on, I came through a college that has a strong tradition – as Masterman and Briggs demonstrated – of publishing accounts of individual dealings with intelligence. In response to Asa Briggs' 1978 urgings I brought out *The Libyan Revolution* in 2009, which told only half the story: the events I lived through in Libya in 1968–1970. I have now fully acceded to Briggs' 1978 urgings and (35 years late) here include the whole story of my four years of intelligence work from May 1969 to the summer of 1973.

As to the merit of such secret work, Masterman and Briggs had the advantage of working against the murderous Nazis. All agree that it was splendid to decode Enigma, make D-Day a success and stand up to the Nazis during the war against Hitler. Collecting information on the expansionist Soviet Union and China in Africa, a continent in which Nelson Mandela struggled against *apartheid* in South Africa in the 1950s and Smith's UDI (Unilateral Declaration of Independence) in Rhodesia alienated the world in the 1960s, seems on the face of it a less clear-cut case, especially as liberal opinion supported the struggle of the Africans. Nevertheless there was still a real strategic prospect that the Soviet Union would invade Western Europe, and standing up to post-Stalinist Soviet expansion in Europe and Africa during the Cold War and to Maoist Chinese expansion in troubled African states such as Tanzania was as vital to British interests in the 1970s as standing up to Nazi expansion was in the late 1930s and 1940s.

Standing up to Gaddafi's Libya is a more clear-cut case as at a very early stage after his 1969 *coup* Gaddafi began to fund and arm international terrorist groups, including the IRA, and opposing Gaddafi meant opposing terrorism. Those who endangered themelves to defend the West against terrorism in the early days of Gaddafi's tyranny have been dismayed by claims in the press that after 2004 the British intelligence services allied with Gaddafi; systematically targeted Libyan dissidents and opponents of Gaddafi living in Britain and worked to send them back to Gaddafi for detention and torture,[6] betraying the risky work carried out a generation earlier by anti-Gaddafi intelligence agents.

My book *The Libyan Revolution*, which presented Gaddafi in a less than flattering light as a despot, may have been caught up in an operation to implement this policy that included walling books round with silence. The generation of Masterman and Briggs would have been astounded if the British intelligence services had suddenly taken Hitler's side towards the end of the war, delivered his opponents to him for detention and torture and impeded books that were unenthusiastic about him, yet the operation to assist Gaddafi after 2004 is just as astonishing. Something went badly wrong with the West's response to Gaddafi's attempt to acquire weapons of mass destruction in the first decade of the 21st century. Now Gaddafi has fallen, the Libyan part of this record speaks for a generation that stood up to Gaddafi immediately after his *coup* and is a contribution to undoing the betrayal of 2004.

On his opening page Asa Briggs gives three reasons for writing *Secret Days*: his duty to contribute a personal memoir to the collective Bletchley-Park inheritance while he has time to record it; his duty as a historian to recall his own experiences in perspective, which he considers to be of importance; and his wish to answer the question as to why a historian should work in Bletchley Park. Similar considerations apply to my reasons for including my four years with the SIS in this account. I feel I have a duty to contribute a personal memoir to the SIS inheritance; I have a duty to recall my own experiences in perspective, which I consider to be of importance; and I want to answer the question as to how I came to work for the SIS. I have weighed my contribution in a measured way and have taken other considerations into account. I believe it is in the public interest that I should leave behind an appropriate record of my experiences during that long-ago time.

Although it is more than 40 years since I discontinued my intelligence work and we are now in a different era, I have adhered to the principles of disclosure and have not named members of the Secret Intelligence Service I had dealings with, who are referred to by Christian names and surnames other than their own to protect their anonymity. I have not revealed full details of the operations that involved me. I have borne in mind that in much of my intelligence work I was sharing what I was already doing – after the event. I have waited until Gaddafi's death before saying what I was really doing in Libya, and I have waited for a clear 40 years to elapse before writing about aspects of the Cold War, during which time the world has changed, the Cold War has ended and most of the participants have died, including the leaders Edward Heath, Leonid Brezhnev and Mao Zedong. The pre-internet methods that applied in my day may now look antiquated, but there is historical merit in telling what happened, as Asa Briggs was quick to see in 1978. Members of the armed forces are able to refer to their 'war record'. I have judged that the time is now right for me to refer to my 'secret-war record'.

I have another reason for writing this work: to make clear key events in my life which members of my family have found baffling. Some of these events have been reflected without explanation in my literary work. Some of my poems, including a few in *The Gates of Hell* sequence, cannot be fully understood without an understanding of the pressures of coping with the dangers of an agent's life and their role in triggering the break-up of my first marriage. Furthermore, my progress from nationalism to Universalism in my literary, historical and philosophical works cannot be fully understood without a grasp of the significance of my four years of being instructed to think nationalistically and of my disturbing discovery that I was working not just for my country but within a latent, self-interested New World Order (*see* pp.414–415). For 40 years I have kept silent about these events. In the words of the version of *Psalm* 39 quoted above, I kept a muzzle on my mouth and stayed dumb. Now that I am in the year of my 75th birthday it is time to set the record straight about events that began 45 years ago.

I believe that my inclusion of my intelligence work for the first time in *My Double Life 1: This Dark Wood* enables me to present the full extent of the darkness within my Dantean wood, which at times was as impenetrable as Conrad's "heart of darkness". It is important to me to bring out that my illumination burst upon me and left me reeling during a month when in the London streets outside I was being tailed by surveillance squads: a combination of two extremes that could not be more opposite. I believe that the contrast between my intelligence work and my early mystical life makes my narrative unique and that the inclusion of my intelligence work makes *My Double Life 1: This Dark Wood* a unique contribution to the *genre* of transformation. There is not another work like it in this *genre*: T.E. Lawrence left his intelligence links out of *Seven Pillars of Wisdom*. Although opening to the mystic Light and operating as a latter-day James Bond are extreme experiences, and at opposite extremes, I believe this account of my perilous path through a dark wood has a universal resonance.

Personal pattern: the story of my quest for Reality, the One
This Double Life tells the story of my quest and its pattern. It is not a conventional autobiography that describes the progress of a social ego but rather an objective narrative that focuses on my personal quest, an epic journey available to all wayfarers. In the later parts of my story I have frequently quoted from my *Diaries* as they were written immediately after the events described and give 'at-the-time' authenticity to my recollection. 'At-the-time' wording bypasses fallible memory and inadvertent embellishing-in-hindsight. It adds vividness by recapturing with precision long-forgotten details relating to the day on which events happened, and reproduces how events struck me at the time. My aim has been to get as close to the original experience in the moment as is possible at such a distance, and my method has enabled me to achieve a fidelity to the moment which many memoirs that look back over decades fail to achieve. The moments all belong to a process, and my double life is a 'process life'. My *Diaries* add immediacy and bring the past alive in the dynamic, baroque, process-led Universalist manner. I have sourced the quotations from my *Diaries* so that my memoir has the flavour of being evidential and objective as well as vividly detailed and 'at the time'.

My personal quest led me into a transformation (or metamorphosis) that began on the other side of the world. The episodes (or successive conflicting sequences of events) along my path were reflected in layered memories which contain my projects and indicate the structure of my self and the pattern of my life. Just as a cone sheds its seeds, so our layered memories contain seed-like projects we shed while we are alive. My layered memories contain my seed-like projects, my works, most of which I have already shed (or spread before humankind).

To what extent was the path of my life subject to chance, choice or destiny?
My narrative in the two volumes of *My Double Life* is objective because its main focus is not on me but on objective aspects of my quest: my path, the pattern of my life and the development of Universalism. It subordinates my personal, individual experiences to the objective presentation of a universal quest. My narrative describes events that seem to be chosen by free will; or seem to happen by chance; or seem to fulfil a destiny. All my experiences (+A + –A) were useful and essential to the shape of my life when viewed as a whole, and they too fulfilled a destiny. 'Destiny' is what is predetermined and fated to happen to a particular person. There is no place for the concept of destiny in a materialist world that is governed solely by chance, accident and coincidence. The concept of destiny is only meaningful if Providence presides over our path. An objective narrative of my quest will bring out the interconnection between free will, chance and destiny.

Universal pattern: the pattern of the path of my life reflects a universal pattern
In *My Double Life 1: This Dark Wood* I have tried to identify the pattern behind my experiences and how I remember them. The content of my personal, individual experience is unique as is everyone else's, but I regard the structure of my experience, of episodes that are remembered in layers within the self, as being universal. This work suggests that the principles that underlie my individual experience and everybody's experience are universal principles.

Besides describing a personal, individual journey *This Dark Wood* is a universal work that reflects the experiences and development of many young people. The objective pattern of the path I set out is a universal one, and there *is* a universal pattern of experience. The pattern of the path of my life reflects a universal pattern.

So *My Double Life 1: This Dark Wood* focuses on the relationship between the personal, individual and local on the one hand and the universal on the other hand; on personal and universal pattern; on the episodic structure of all experience; and on my developing awareness that the universe is a unity. It is therefore a Universalist work. As with all my works, it came with an urgency and effortlessness that sometimes seemed inspired: I completed the research and writing in seven months (from 14 January to 14 August 2012). I have to thank my PA Ingrid Kirk for her role in enabling me to complete this work so quickly.

So much for the principles behind the pattern and structure of *My Double Life*. I can now proceed to the origins of my double life.

PART ONE

Quest for the One

"There was but one duty for a grown man; it was to seek a way to himself, to become resolute within, to grope his way forward wherever that might lead him. The discovery shook me profoundly.... I had often toyed with pictures of the future, dreamed of roles which might be assigned to me – as a poet, maybe, or prophet.... All that was futile. I was not there to write poetry, to preach...; neither I nor any other man was there for that purpose. They were only incidental things. There was only one true vocation for everybody – to find the way to himself."

Hermann Hesse, *Demian*

CHAPTER 1

Origins

Locations: Yorkshire, Sussex, Cambridgeshire, Hertfordshire, London

"Every gift of noble origin
Is breathed upon by Hope's perpetual breath."
Wordsworth, 'These times strike monied
worldlings with dismay' (1803)

My inherited DNA
In a sense my path – and my double life – began before I was born, in the
DNA I inherited from my ancestors. Some aspects of my quest and the 30
episodes of my life and writings can be traced back to the influences of
earlier generations on the family tree on which I budded and grew.

My parents' marriage
My father, Cyril Hagger, had his early schooling in Barnet. *His* father
worked in Canada sawing trees at some time, and he may have been away
during my father's early years. Probably when he was eleven, in 1917, my
father won a place at a Bluecoat school that was based on Christ's Hospital,
a charitable institution for bright students from poor backgrounds. The
original Bluecoat School was founded by Edward VI in 1552 in the former
Grey Friars monastery in Newgate Street, London, which had been confiscated by Henry VIII. It relocated to the Horsham area in 1902, when its
branch in Hertford (not far from Barnet) was closed to boys. Scholarships to
Bluecoat schools were provided by livery companies and councils, and
there was clearly a link between my father's school in Barnet and the
Bluecoat school he attended, probably through the East Barnet Valley Urban
District Council which would have sent local boys to the Hertford site until
1902. Bluecoat boys wore a Tudor uniform: a blue frock coat and yellow
stockings with white bands. My mother often mentioned my father's
attendance at "the Bluecoat School" but my father spoke little of it except to
say it was so cold in his dormitory that sometimes he had to break ice to
wash.

When he was 14, in 1920, my father contracted polio – it is thought from
a swimming pool. He lost the use of his breathing muscles and, although he
never referred to it, seems to have spent two years in an iron lung as my
mother said on more than one occasion. An iron lung was then an airtight

wooden box with motor-driven bellows and bladder that pulled in and expelled air, forcing his lungs to 'breathe'. (His head was out of the box.) The cost of this treatment, if indeed it happened, seems to have been borne by his Bluecoat school's charitable foundation, in whose care he was being schooled. The iron lung would have had the same effect on my father that being in a plaster cast for a year had on Sir Alex Douglas-Home: it would have made him very determined. Having overcome polio, he felt there was nothing that could not be achieved. Despite walking with a limp, he got himself qualified in accounting, wrapping himself in a blanket to study in his unheated room, and in 1925 began a career in local government with East Barnet Valley Urban District Council (renamed East Barnet Urban District Council in 1935) that must have seemed impossible when he was 14. He said more than once that in 1925 there was a shortage of jobs and local government was the only employer that would employ 'an invalid'; and that he had to be significantly better than the competition to make up for his disability. In 1931 he became accountancy assistant to Mitcham Borough Council.

Both my parents were musical. My mother, Norah Broadley, was a violinist from Sussex. She gave more than a dozen violin recitals in East Grinstead and London between 1932 and 1938.[1] My father sang. (He may have begun singing to strengthen his lungs after polio.) He was a member of the Royal Choral Society and sang as a tenor in the Fleet Street Choir. He once sang the *Messiah* at the Royal Albert Hall. My parents met on a train at Paddington Station, where I often caught a train to Cornwall.

I inherited my father's determination, and his natural aptitude for

figures. (Also, perhaps, an instinctive warmth towards the Tudor time.) My parents' music came out in me as poetry.

My father married my mother at the Methodist church in East Grinstead on 28 August 1937. A local newspaper report[2] states that my mother was given away by her brother George Broadley II and "wore a dress of ivory satin, cut on classical lines, with train. She also wore a veil lent by her mother and wreath of orange

Norah Broadley, Nicholas's mother, playing her violin in the 1930s; and Nicholas's parents Cyril Hagger and Norah Broadley on their wedding day in 1937

blossom." The second hymn was 'He who would valiant be/'Gainst all disaster', which reflected my father's early struggle with polio, and his determination "to be a pilgrim". The pianist who accompanied her during her recitals, Walter Crapps, played the organ. The reception was held at Felbridge Place Hotel, and the honeymoon was in Switzerland.

My father had already bought "their future residence", 20 Fairview Road, Norbury, so they could be near his work at Mitcham Town Hall. He very soon owned other properties. In 1938 he bought 52 and 54 Westfield Road, Cheam, and he soon owned two more properties.

I inherited (or acquired) his property-managing skills along with my mother's.

My mother's family: Broadleys and Hardings

My mother's family were Broadleys and Hardings, and I inherited traits from several of them.

Rev. Benjamin Broadley and the Navy

My mother's paternal great-grandfather was the Yorkshire-based shoemaker John Broadley I who was born at Wakefield, Yorkshire c.1800. He married Ann and had four children, who were all born in Ackworth.

My mother's paternal grandfather was their fourth child, the Rev. Benjamin Broadley,[3] an itinerant Methodist minister born in 1833 who served in different parts of the UK and had been a Naval chaplain ('Chaplain to the Fleet') in India and Malta.

From him I inherited some of my desire to travel abroad and find out about foreign cultures, and to quest for truth.

The Rev. Benjamin Broadley married Charlotte Harrison,[4] who had money of

Rev. Benjamin Broadley (born 1833), Nicholas's great-grandfather in 1892; and Hannah Burton, née Comfort (born 1813, Nicholas's great-great-grandmother who owned a school and lived to be 101)

her own which was invested for her children.[5] They had five surviving children including John Broadley II (born in 1867)[6] and George Broadley I (born in 1870), my mother's father.

Hannah Comfort (Mrs. Burton) owned a school

My mother's maternal great-grandmother, Hannah Comfort, was born in 1813. She was the daughter of Humphrey Comfort and Sarah Nelham, who was born in 1776 (and whose sampler, dated 1786, embroidered when she was 10, hung on my Aunt Margaret's wall).[7] They had eight children including Hannah. Hannah married James Burton. In a plated brown photo I believe to have been taken in 1864 Hannah sits in a white bonnet, her hair in buns on either side and wearing spectacles, and her long crinolined dress stretches to the chequered floor. Her husband was killed in 1870 when he fell out of a buggy (a horse-drawn, two-wheeled vehicle) on London Bridge, and eight years afterwards she started a girls' school in Croydon at 65. She taught there until she was 85 and owned it until she died aged 101 in 1914. (My mother was the youngest guest at her 100th birthday party and was given a Queen Anne table, which I now have, that was split in the middle after Frank Burton, her grandson, played leap-frog over it and fell. I also have Hannah's warming-pan.)

Hannah's life spanned from the end of Napoleon to the First World War. I have her brass warming-pan (for live coals) hanging by its long handle on my kitchen wall. Inside is a short genealogy, written by my aunt Margaret, beginning with Sarah Nelham and ending with my name and date of birth.

From Hannah I inherited my interest in running schools.

Charles Harding wrote for The Times

Hannah had eight children, including Sarah Ann Burton (born in 1844), who presumably helped her mother in the school. In 1864 Sarah seems to have married Charles Harding (born in 1846). I have brown-plated, presumably wedding, photos of both Sarah and her husband Charles taken in 1864 when Charles was 18 and Sarah 20. Charles stands beside a large urn in a wing-collar and tie, wearing a knee-length coat. Charles was a civil servant and Fellow of the Royal Geographical Society. He was linked to the War Office, was an expert on marine currents and wrote weather reports for newspapers, in particular on meteorology for *The Times*. I have his two barometers in my hall.

Charles and Sarah Harding lived in Tulse Hill – I found my way to nearby West Dulwich – and then at 65 Holmewood Gardens, near Christchurch Road, Streatham. It would have been in Streatham that when nineteen their daughter Elsie, my grandmother (who was born in 1874), acquired a brown-plated photo of the pianist, composer and later statesman Paderewski, who visited London in 1891. She has written her name on the back, 'Elsie G. Harding, Oct 3rd 1893'.

From Charles and Sarah Harding I inherited an instinctive connection with *The Times* and my interest in the modern equivalent of Victorian meteorology, the universe.

George Broadley I's tailor's business and marriage to Elsie Harding
Both John II and George Broadley I came south and together set up a tailor's business, Broadley Brothers, in Bromley in 1893.[8] They had each been given £500 as capital by their mother, who wanted all her four sons to own their own shop.[9] In 1896 George Herbert Broadley – he was named after the English Metaphysical poet George Herbert – stood on Victoria Station, wondering where he should open his own business. On a notice-board he saw 'East Grinstead', liked the sound of the name, and, following his intuition, caught a train there and after seeing a 'To Let' board founded the East Grinstead branch of the business at 14th-century premises: 38 & 40 High Street, which he leased.[10] George (my grandfather) was now based there in Sussex.

I inherited a good intuitive business sense from him and an instinctive bent for founding institutions.

Two years after he opened the East-Grinstead branch of Broadley Brothers, in 1898 George Broadley I married Elsie Harding. (I have the silver teapots engraved with a 'B' they were given as a wedding present.) They had met at Brixton Hill Methodist church and at first lived above the East-Grinstead shop. Their eldest son Tom I climbed out onto the parapet for a dare and, alarmed, they moved to Fairmead, Lewes Road, and then to 212 London Road. In 1907 they bought Lonsdale House, Lingfield Road for £750, with a mortgage of £600 from the East Grinstead and Mutual Building Society.[11] In 1910 they owned one of the first two cars in East Grinstead, a second-hand Talbot. By now they were a prominent East-Grinstead Methodist family. They had two sons and three daughters, including my mother Norah and my aunt Margaret.

Nicholas's maternal grandparents George Broadley I (died 1926) and Elsie Harding with Norah (right) and Flo; and their son, Flight Lieutenant Tom Broadley I in 1918, just before he was killed in action

Tom Broadley I and the RFC
Their eldest son, Tom Broadley I had been born in 1899 and educated at City of London School. The first human flight of 1903 amazed his generation, and the daredevils yearned to fly. Overstating his age, he volunteered to join

the Royal Flying Corps during the First World War and received 25s. a day. He was not supposed to fly until he was 18 but the RFC were so desperate for pilots that they allowed him to fly while he was 17. On 1 April 1918 the RFC was absorbed into the Royal Air Force. On 15 September 1918, just before the end of the war, Tom's Bristol Fighter was shot down over enemy lines in France, probably on a reconnaissance (i.e. spying) mission to pinpoint the whereabouts of German troops so there could be follow-up attacks. He was reported missing, presumed killed, and it was only in 2000 that his grave was located on the Commonwealth War Graves Commission's website: grave E20 in Chili Trench Cemetery at Gavrelle, Pas de Calais, France. I have his wings in my study.

From him I inherited a tendency to volunteer for daredevil activities overseas.

Broadley Brothers, death of George Broadley I of cancer in 1926
George Broadley I had expanded the family business. In addition to the branches of Broadley Brothers at Bromley (opened by John II in 1893) and East Grinstead (opened by George in 1896), new branches opened under George in Haywards Heath in 1900 (which was managed by one of the East Grinstead staff, Sidney Alfred Moon), in Horsham in 1907 (although that branch closed in 1915), in Hove and briefly in Eastbourne.

Towards the end of the First World War George Broadley I bought a War Bond, which financed the Government's war effort, and three months later had a win. This provided the capital for a business in Eastbourne, and he bought Coombers in Seaside, intending to leave it to his son George Broadley II, who worked in the shop for a while. The previous owner Coomber continued to live in a flat over the shop and every afternoon during the hot summer of 1919 sat in the back garden in a deck-chair under a mulberry tree, regretting that he had sold. He decided to buy the business back and he offered ten times what he had sold it for. As part of the deal he handed over 2 Bakewell Road, Eastbourne, where George Broadley I allowed his in-laws, the Hardings, to live rent-free.[12]

In 1925 George Broadley I bought Daledene in Lewes Road, East Grinstead, at auction for £2,300, intending to sell it at a profit. In the same year he was diagnosed with cancer of the oesophagus. His daughter Margaret, who had become a nurse at the London Hospital in 1923 and who would in due course rise to become first a Sister and then an Assistant Matron, was the first to notice his cancer on the beach at Tenby. There is a poignant photo of the two standing together on that beach at the very moment she realised his condition.

Suspecting that he had not long to live, and not wanting to leave Elsie with two properties, he sold Lonsdale House, the more saleable of the two, and he and Elsie moved into Daledene for his last months.[13] He was given a lead cure, which was thought to be an effective way of dealing with cancer in those days. However, the lead poison killed him in November 1926. (My aunt Margaret, his daughter, told me that as she and the family sat round his bed expecting each breath to be his last, he suddenly rose up and cried out, "Tom," and then died: "Tom was waiting for him.")[14] His death certificate[15] gives as the cause of death "Carcinoma of oesaphagus accelerated by injections of collosol lead for the purposes of treatment. Misadventure. No PM [i.e. *Post-Mortem*]."

George Broadley II corners the family business
Under the terms of his will,[16] his two trustees and executors, his widow Elsie and son George II, were to administer the estate until 20 February 1931. George I's 75% share of the profits of the Haywards Heath business went to his widow Elsie, and it would be at her discretion as to whether to leave his capital share in the business or remove it. (Soon afterwards the Haywards Heath business was sold to Moon, the managing partner who owned 25% with an option to purchase, and retained the name "Broadleys".) His widow was to have all the profits from the East Grinstead business and 75% of the profits of the Hove business plus £70 per month. George II would have no profits from the East Grinstead business but 25% of the profits from the Hove business and £500 per annum.

After 20 February 1931 (the "settlement date") the two trustees had authority to increase or diminish the Hove business, and George II was given authority to buy the business for £3,000, which could take the form of a loan to him at 7%, to be paid off at £250 per payment. The two trustees were instructed to continue to hold the East Grinstead business, and George II would be allowed to offer to buy the business at a price to be agreed (subject to valuation) by Elsie. George I's widow Elsie was to have the remainder of the estate. Its net value after probate was £16,734.18s.7d. (in 2011 value in excess of £797,000).[17]

Clause 8 of his will states: "It is my wish that, my said son being herein sufficiently provided for, my said wife shall maintain and provide for my daughters in equal shares, but this expression of my wish shall not impose any obligation or create a trust in favour of my daughters."

The will was clear. East Grinstead could be sold to George II if Elsie agreed, but as George II was sufficiently provided for already, the proceeds should provide for Elsie's three daughters (one of whom was my mother) in equal shares. It was my grandfather's wish in principle (although there was no obligation in case profits collapsed) that my mother and her two sisters should each end up with a third of the East Grinstead business or its cash equivalent.

What the will envisaged did not happen for after 20 February 1931 George II persuaded his co-trustee Elsie to sell the East Grinstead business to him and with it 75% of the profits. Elsie would retain 25% of the profits.[18] According to his daughter Margaret, Elsie had not even signed a cheque before her husband died, and George II "ground her down on Thursdays" at their weekly trustee meeting on the running of the business.[19] To buy the Hove and East Grinstead businesses George II agreed to make payments of £250 per annum. These were made for 21 years up to 1952, and there were no payments for some years during the Second World War. Until 1952 George had a half share, his wife Lucy a quarter share and Elsie, my grand-mother, was left with a quarter share of the East Grinstead profits.[20] George Broadley II had thus cornered the East Grinstead family business and restricted the amount available for his three sisters. For many years it was a mystery as to why this happened in 1931, but the will makes it clear that the cornering was triggered by the "settlement date".

The will mentions three businesses: East Grinstead, Haywards Heath and Hove. Horsham and Eastbourne had been and gone. George II opened new branches of Broadley Brothers in Portslade and Worthing. In 1938–1939 George II acquired a derelict business at Worthing, then taking about £5 a week, and this was sold when it was clear that only the taxman was benefiting. Branches opened in Folkestone and Dover under John II and his successors.[21]

Elsie was persuaded (as a patriotic gesture) to invest her savings from the estate, from George II's payments and from her quarter share of the profits, in War Loan, which fell in value and in interest rate (from 5% to 3.5%). In July 1940 she bought £725.15s.2d War 3.5% Loan Deed stock at $96^3/_{16}$ for £698.1s.9d.[22] I later found out from George I's wife Lucy (see p.206) that a bank manager advised George I to invest his repayments to Elsie in 100% War Loan.[23] When this slumped to 80% he advised Elsie to sell and reinvest in a building society but she did not heed his advice. The slump in War Loan continued and as a result Elsie lost most of her savings.

My father had also patriotically invested in War Loan and had also lost most of his savings when the Government reduced War Loan's worth. He was bitter about this for the rest of his life.

George II blamed his mother's unwise investment while citing his father's good fortune with a War Bond in the First World War. Elsie's three daughters considered that he had wrested control of what their father had intended for them, by sharp practice. My aunt Margaret ("Argie") told me in 1992: "George did his mother. Lucy pushed. My mother used to dread George coming. My father's will left it all to my mother, but with the condition that there should be provision for his daughters. George had three-quarters of the business for £5,250."[24]

I often heard this as a boy, and I had a deep-seated resolve to 'get the family business back' by starting a new business that would replace the East Grinstead business my mother and therefore I had been excluded from. My aunt Argie told me in 1992: "You are the only one who has got the business back. The others haven't."[25] I knew from an early age that I would have to earn my own living before I could do this. What happened in 1931 was a context for my seeking to get on by going abroad, and for that part of the story of *My Double Life 1: This Dark Wood.*

Provision for Norah

Despite her bad experience with War Loan my grandmother continued to have a prosperous lifestyle. She left Daledene in 1935 and moved to St Anton, Maypole Road, East Grinstead opposite Lord and Lady Stamp. The house was named after a holiday she had in St Anton, Austria the previous year. My mother, Norah, moved with her.

Despite Elsie's straitened circumstances my mother owned three houses in the 1930s: Pentire, Blackwell Road, East Grinstead, which she bought in 1936;[26] and 15 and 17 Moat Road, East Grinstead, which she had from 1937 to 1948. She eventually owned the house the Hardings occupied in Eastbourne, 2 Bakewell Road.[27] These houses must have come from Elsie's implementing of my grandfather's wish to provide for his daughters, either from her savings or from George II's annual payments. There was some provision for his daughters, but not to the extent that my grandfather's will envisaged.

My mother was from an affluent business family, and from her I inherited some of my intuitive understanding of property.

Dwindling of family business

The trading accounts for the business for the year to 20 February 1949 show that the profit for the year was £2,493.15s.9d, half of which went to George, a quarter to Lucy and a quarter to my grandmother, whose drawings were £365.9s.0d.[28] George II bought the adjoining premises to expand. When he died in 1964 , the business was run by Tom II, who ran up a huge overdraft in 1970 to renovate the building. He died in 1971. His brother John V took over and soon afterwards bought the freehold for 38–40 High Street from the Percy Dixon Trust for £4,000.[29]

Two branches of the family had founded the family business in the 1890s, and though they had endured much had been shed over the years. George II's descendants sold the Bromley business soon after John II's youngest son Harold died in 1987. The Folkestone business is still run as Broadley Brothers by a grandson of John II, Eric Broadley (son of Fred), and his son. The Dover business, opened by John II's family, has long since disappeared. Of the businesses on my grandfather's side of the family, the Hove and Portslade businesses were closed and leased out to a coffee-house and estate agent in 2001, and the freeholds could be sold when the leases came to an end; and only East Grinstead survives. The descendants of George II have continued to run East Grinstead, first Tom II's son Christopher Broadley (who left to join the Navy full-time in Portsmouth in 1999 but retained a quarter share) and then John V's son Simon Broadley, who runs it with his wife and four staff (and has a quarter share, the other two shares having been owned by the widows of Tom II and John V).

The mighty family business with several branches that had spanned Sussex and Kent during the Edwardian and Georgian times had now dwindled to one branch, and in a time when viable profits are made from chains of 20 or 30 shops its trading volume was relatively small. It is said that when Christopher and Simon retire the business will pass out of the family. There will then be the freehold of the East Grinstead building to lease or sell (along with the freehold of the Hove and Portslade buildings). What to my mother and two aunts had seemed a fortune in the 1920s had faded into a relatively modest asset at the end of our Elizabethan era.

My father's family: Haggers and Osbornes
The Haggers of Therfield, Hertfordshire

My father's family were Haggers and Osbornes. My father's father (my grandfather) was born in Victoria Road, East Barnet, Herts (according to his birth certificate of 1873), and he lived in East Barnet (according to his 1899 marriage certificate)[30] and, after a spell in Walthamstow where my father was born[31] at 76 Macdonald Road in 1906, in New Barnet. He was living at 12 Park Road, New Barnet in 1933[32] and I visited him at (I believe) 40A Station Road, New Barnet, where he was living after the Second World War. (The house is still standing but has been taken over by the Raphael Property

Trust.) He is variously described as a 'carpenter' (on his own and his son's marriage certificate),[33] as a 'builder' (on my father's marriage certificate)[34] and as a 'master builder' (in reports of his death on 2 May 1959). He had worked in Canada, sawing trees.

From him I may have inherited my instinctive understanding of trees.

His family can be traced back to a line of rural farmers and agricultural workers of Therfield, Hertfordshire going back to William Hagger, who was born in 1650.[35] He often told my father that they were descended from the Haggers who were lords of the manor near Cambridge.

Nicholas's paternal grandparents Willoughby Thomas Hagger and Elizabeth Osborne in 1937

Possible descent from the Haggers of Bourn, Cambridgeshire: Carolus Haggar of Brugge (Bruges) moved to Chelmsford, Essex c.1366; Bourn Hall completed by John Hagger, c.1602

My father's family was not affluent in recent years but may have flourished in the Elizabethan Age. His branch of the family looked back to the Bourn Haggers: the Haggers (or Hagars) who came from Essex c.1550 and became lords of the manor in Bourn, Cambridgeshire.

There were interchangeable spellings of 'Hagger', which could be spelt 'Haggar' or 'Hagar' during the Tudor time, and my research shows that these 'Haggers' seem to have come from Brugge (or Bruges) in Flanders c.1366[36] (twenty years after Edward III's defeat of the French at Crécy). They may have fled from the plague epidemic in the Low Countries of 1360–1364.[37] They settled in Chelmsford, where Carolus Haggar married Anne Morys in 1414/15. His son John Haggar I married Isabella Butcher and produced John Haggar II, who married a Foredam and lived in Heydon, near Royston in Hertfordshire (which some sources locate in Essex and others in Cambridgeshire).[38] His son John Haggar III married Constance Bell. He was said to own the manor of Burwash before 1550[39] and bought the manor called Ragons or Dives (names of previous owners) in 1554.[40] He later acquired the manor of St George in Bourn. By the time of his death in 1589 he therefore owned the manors of Riggesby, Burwash and St George in Bourn and had begun building Bourn Hall. He had now added 800 acres to the estate, and the Haggers were now the largest wool growers in Cambridgeshire.[41]

In the later medieval time an incoming tenant could achieve a low rent by undertaking to pay a lump sum up front, known as a fine. I have ten documents in both Latin and English and dated between 1554 and 1594 regarding fines. The first spells the landlord's name 'Haggar', and the next nine 'Hagger'.

His son John Hagar IV married Frances Peyton of Isleham (who gave a chalice to the local church in 1569). He completed the building of Bourn Hall, a U-shaped three-sided courtyard house, in 1602. A rainwater head (i.e. box over a drainpipe in the guttering) on the south-east front still bears the date 1602 and the initials H with I F below it (Iohannes, Latin for John, and Frances Hagar). The family became armigerous in 1605.[42] The Hagar arms could be blazoned (i.e. painted) "*Or* [i.e. golden] on a bend [i.e. a diagonal stripe from top right to bottom left of a shield] sable [i.e. black] three lions passant [i.e. walking with three paws on the ground and the right forepaw raised] argent [i.e. silver, white] of the field" and a crest could be blazoned "On a mount [i.e. background, setting] *vert* [i.e. green], a talbot [i.e. a hound or hunting-dog with long hanging ears, heavy jaws and great powers of scent] passant or [i.e. *d'or*, golden], collared and lined gules [i.e.

red], the line tied in a bundle trailing".[43]

In everyday, rather than heraldic, English, the arms could show on a gold background a black diagonal stripe with three silver lions walking with their front paw raised, and the crest could show on a green background a hound with its front paw raised, wearing a golden collar and trailing a red lead (or leash). Printed sources suggest that the beast in the crest should be blazoned "A hound scenting *or* [i.e. gold]".[44] Taken literally, the crest could show a golden hound scenting, but there may be a veiled suggestion that the Hagars scented – pursued – gold. The arms were in a window in Bourn church until William Dowsing was commissioned and salaried by the Puritan Government to destroy popish images in churches throughout Suffolk and Cambridgeshire in the 1640s, perhaps including the Hagar Arms. John Hagar IV died in 1616/17 and was buried in Bourn.

His son Robert Hagar I had a younger brother John Hagar who died in 1616. Robert married Anne Benedick and died in 1652 aged 57.

His son John Hagar V lived to a great age. He was still lord of the manor after 1693 and died in 1706. By his first marriage to Elizabeth Archer of Royston he had a son Robert Hagar II, who died in 1710 leaving no issue. By his second marriage to Frances Russell he had several children, including his third son John Hagar VI, Admiral John Garrit Hagar, who was born in 1681 and became Vice Admiral of the White Squadron. He married Anne, the heiress daughter of Sir John Hewet[45] at Waresley, Hunts, which is eight miles from Bourn, and moved there in c.1727.

It has been said that if the Hagger arms survived Dowsing's iconoclasm, Admiral Hagar removed the window bearing the arms from Bourn church and took it with him when he left. He sold the Bourn estate in 1733 to move to Waresley.[46] He died in February 1747/8, leaving a son John Hewet Hagar (technically John Hagar VII) who was born in 1725, and seven other children, including Robert Hagar, vicar of Hawnes, Bedfordshire, who died in 1767.

There are reports of Haggers (including one of Robert Haggar II's children) being Quakers. There was a Quaker burial-ground of Haggers, which I once found on the bend of a country road between Audley End and Royston.

In 1998 I visited Bourn church (the church of St Helen and St Mary), which is near the Hall, and found the tomb slabs in the floor of four Hagars: John V, Robert II, John V's wife Frances (*née* Russell) and their daughter Frances, who had all died between 1706 and 1727 according to the dates on the floor. I was shown a Communion chalice presented by John Hagar IV's wife Frances Peyton in 1569, and a Communion salver (bread dish) given by Frances Hagar (*née* Russell) in 1694/5. I could imagine these silver treasures standing near the Hagar window with three lions passant.

Is there a link between Therfield and Bourn Haggers?

My father was often told by his father that our Therfield-based family descended from the Bourn Haggers. It is not clear at what date the Bourn Haggers and the Therfield Haggers were linked, but there is a strong presumption that there *was* a link as the two families were only 13 miles apart in a rural setting with few nearby towns. This presumption is shared by the Hagg*r One Name Study begun in 2003 and dedicated to proving that all the bearers of all the spellings of the Hagger name belong to one 'tribe'. One would expect the link to be before the beginning of the 17th century as there were few males after then who could have founded a new line.

It is possible that a brother of Carolus Haggar[47] or of one of the first four John Haggars married and relocated to Therfield and founded a branch of the family there which eventually produced William Hagger and the Richard Haggars of Therfield who spanned from c.1650 to 1850. In 1605 John Haggar III's youngest brother George married Joan King at Bourn church,[48] and had a son Thomas, who was baptised at Bourn church, in 1606. Perhaps the descendants of this line included the two George Haggers who were born in Therfield in 1747 and 1761. Also in 1605 John Haggar III's other brother William (born 1559) married Katherine Hitch, and they do not show on Bourn records after that date. If there was a link between the Bourn and Therfield Haggers it is likely to have been before 1684 when the first recorded Therfield Hagger marriage took place.

After the sale of Bourn Hall in 1733 the Bourn Haggers (or Hagars) followed the example of Admiral Hagar, left Bourn, and dispersed. Bourn Haggers may well have joined the Hagger farmers already established (since 1684) at Therfield 13 miles away. The Bourn and Therfield Haggers were from different social classes, and any Bourn Haggers joining the Therfield Haggers would soon have found that they had gone down in the world.

In short, although I cannot be completely sure that my grandfather was right in repeatedly claiming that we were descended from the Bourn Haggers, circumstantial evidence suggests there is a strong possibility. On the strength of that strong possibility I was asked to open the Bourn fête in 2000 as a descendant of John Haggar III and John Hagar IV. I was given a tour of Bourn Hall, which is now an infertility clinic for test-tube babies, and saw the 1602 guttering bearing John Hagar IV's initials.

From the Bourn Haggers I may have inherited my instinctive connection with historic houses and interest in the Admiralty; and also my interest in the Quaker Inner Light.

The Osbornes

Little is known of the family of my father's mother, the Osbornes, although all my father's male descendants have Osborne as a middle name.

My father's mother, Elizabeth Emma Osborne, was the daughter of Samuel Osborne, who is described as a 'shoemaker' (according to her marriage certificate).[49] She was born in 1873 in Port Vale, Bengeo, Hertfordshire to a journeyman carpenter (according to her birth certificate) and before she married she was living at 96 Macdonald Road, Walthamstow (according to her marriage certificate).[50] My father was born in Walthamstow according to his 1906 birth certificate (which does not give a postal address), possibly at 96 Macdonald Road.[51] (I detect symmetry. She was living in Walthamstow and my father came to work in Loughton, near Walthamstow.)

In her eighties she was a distant softly-spoken figure with white hair and a very wrinkled face I wrote to as 'Nana'. Only two photos of her have survived. They show a slim waif of an old lady in a long dress and a hat standing by her white-haired husband. In one her face is veiled by a wide hat, and in the other her face is partly obliterated by a shaft of light that has leaked into the film.

Origin of Hagger name

The name 'Hagger' has roots in four languages. In Latin it is rooted in *'agger'*, 'a rampart' (or defensive wall). In Old English, *'haeg-gar'* means 'hedge-warrior'. In Middle English, it was related to *'hacgard'* and the Yorkshire *'hagar'*, 'wild, untamed man' and possibly to *haggen*, 'to cut or chop', indicating woodcutter. In Old Norse, *'hagr'* means 'fit' or 'ready'. It has often been said that some Haggers look like Vikings and are numerous in East Anglia, a Viking stronghold. They may have come from the Danish Aggersborg,[52] possibly via Viking Normandy and nearby Bruges.

If that is so I also inherited from my father's side the old Viking sense of 'adventuring' (or plundering) abroad.

A DNA[53] test I commissioned focused on the last 500 years and showed that the Haggers are most likely to have originated within the native population of Germany c.1500. This may provide some confirmation for my link to the origin of the Bourn Haggers in Bruges c.1366. Bruges was then on the fringe of the German Holy Roman Empire.

The test also focused on interactions over hundreds or thousands of years and showed that the Haggers' 'world region match' was North-West Europe, but that the Mediterranean, Aegean and East Europe came close. It showed that my closest global relations are Caucasians from the US and Australia. The European sub-regions where my DNA is most common are, in descending order, Germanic, Italian, Belgic and Ashkenazic. These findings applied to many different ancestors and times.

The test suggested a link with German Saxons 1,500 years back; a link with Greece, Italy and Spain 2,500 years back; and a link with the Near East and the Caucasus (where the Indo-European Kurgans originated) 3,000 years back. Over 6,000 years back my ancestors may have been Indo-European Kurgans, who spread from the Russian steppes via the Urals, Scythia and Thrace to the Caucasus c.4,000BC and spread to Danubian Europe c.3,500BC, then to the Aegean and the Adriatic. Over many genera-tions my ancestors may at different times have been Romans, Anglo-Saxons and perhaps Vikings (the Northmen who settled in Normandy, not that far from Bruges). There may have been additional Roman, Anglo-Saxon and Viking influences through my ancestors on my maternal side, the Broadleys and Hardings.

From the Broadleys, Hardings and Haggers I inherited an instinctive bent for: 'adventuring' abroad, volunteering for dangerous activities, Nonconformism, Inner Light, writing, poetry (musical writing), business, property-management, running schools, love of forests and interest in the universe.

Within the conflicting sides of what I inherited from my ancestral influ-ences – risky adventuring and inner inspiration – can be found the origins of my double life, which would be precipitated by a call.

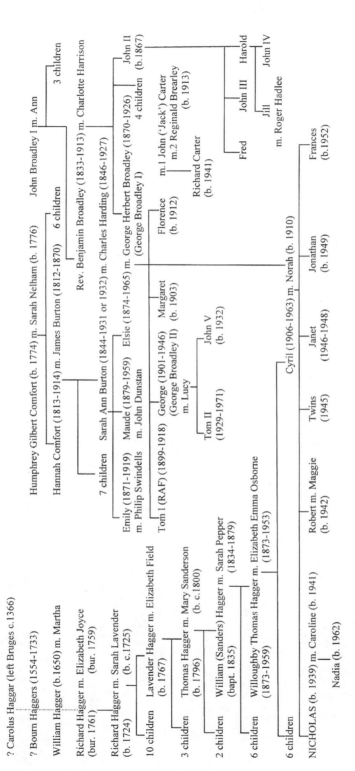

The Hagger family to 1974

19

CHAPTER 2

The Call

'Bildungsroman', "a novel dealing with one person's early life and development".

Concise Oxford Dictionary

As I gaze on the green fields I lay in as a child and see them in my mind's eye filled with golden buttercups, and walk on the sands of Cornish beaches where I ran as a child and which I return to some school holidays, I am filled with a sense of a pattern. My beginning is very much present in my life now, and there seems an inevitability about my progress from an ordinary boy to the man I am.

Listening to the drone of bees in the summer forsythia in my childhood garden which is full of the echoes of little people I knew, I have a sense that we are bees of the invisible, to use Rilke's words. I set out from my hive in the morning and found a Way I always instinctively knew was there. My path has led me through Nature and the central idea of civilizations to an understanding of the universe. Mine was a seeking generation, and I sought the meaning of life in sunlight and shadow. Gazing at a frog in my lily pond, aware of the mud and the glorious flower in the sun, I feel the pattern has a mysterious meaning.

I lived my early years near Epping Forest. The curved sweep of its trees clad the rim of an incomplete crater whose sloping sides formed the seven hills of Loughton, at the foot of which I came and went. Lush-green in spring, sere-green in summer, yellow-red in autumn and bare-bough-black in winter, the Forest prinked and loomed on the horizon as I journeyed to and from school and towards my future. Forest places were among the earliest places I knew: the cricket field, the High-Road pond and the Iron-Age Loughton Camp.

Gazing down at the sweep of the Forest at dusk from the crater's other side I glimpse Queen Elizabeth's hunting lodge, Connaught Water and High Beach spire half-hidden in the dark wood below me. From this sloping hill I know where these places are but down there, immersed in the wood, I would find them hard to locate. As the light fades I realise that when I first became aware of myself I was lost in a dark wood within my mind and, like a wayfarer, took the path that would lead to the person I am and to the pattern that my life now has.

Like Dante, I woke to find myself in a dark wood and had to find the path I was meant to follow. I was in confusion as I tried to find the direction that was right for me. I realised quite early that the path I found myself on would not lead me to where I needed to be. I seemed to have taken a wrong turning and was unsure where I was heading. I stumbled onwards, passing tracks on either side that might lead me astray. There was no clear way forward.

Now, from this hill, I can see so clearly. Looking at this dark wood that stretches to the twilit skyline, in my deepest memory I can pinpoint the path I struggled to find. I can see the pattern in my life. I see that from quite early I was on a quest for a reality quite different from that of everyday life. At first I had glimpses without fully understanding what I was seeing. Eventually I came to grasp that I was seeking the One, the unity behind and within the universe that can only be known by the deepest part of oneself, and that I would have to undergo a transformation within my self if I was to find it. I did not know that I had set out on a universal Mystic Way.

From time to time I heard a call (more a summons than an invitation) and knew within in what direction I should be heading. It was painful, getting myself on to the path that was right for me. I now see my path as a response to an early call. Then I made a telephone call that would make my direction harder to find.

Episode 1:

Family and War

Years: 1939–1945
Locations: London; East Grinstead; Loughton

"Fair seed-time had my soul, and I grew up
Fostered alike by beauty and by fear."
Wordsworth, *The Prelude*, bk 1, lines 301–302

Wartime childhood
The first episode in my life (and layer of memories on my self) began with my birth and was dominated by two conflicting social influences: the safety of my family, a strong influence in my very early years, and the outbreak and dangers of the Second World War.

Family: London and East Grinstead

It can be estimated that I was conceived around 29 August 1938 when (as Goebbels' diaries make clear) Hitler had already planned the Second World War, a month before the signing of the Munich Agreement. I came into a hostile world with a message of peace that would take decades to unfold: a Universalist message of the common basis of humanity.[1]

I was born in Mary Northcliffe ward in the London Hospital, for which my aunt worked as a nurse, on 22 May 1939 when the British Empire was intact and war was looming. (As I was born within the sound of the bells of St Mary-le-Bow, Cheapside, which could be heard in the London Hospital on a quiet night, I was technically a Cockney.) I was two weeks late, weighed 8lbs 5ozs and had a mop of hair. The Princess Royal visited when I was four days old, and I was presented and gripped her finger. I have receipts[2] showing that on 24 May my father paid £5.10s towards the cost of maintaining my mother in hospital for a week and £7.17.2d on 7 June for maintaining her in hospital for a further ten days.

In London: Norbury and Caterham

We went to live in Norbury at the house my parents had bought (20 Fairview Road). My mother recorded my progress in her Baby book, and I now read that I smiled at four weeks. I was christened at Streatham Methodist church at six weeks, on 2 July. There is a photo in the photo albums of me being held by my father. I am wearing the long Victorian christening robe my grandmother wore at her christening. I now have this.

Nicholas held by his father at his christening at six weeks, 2 July 1939

Gwen Broad

A friend of my grandmother's, the artist Gwen Broad, was present. She had lived near St Austell in Cornwall. When she married Nanscawen her mother sold the house in St Austell and bought Hill Place, a 1296 farm in East Grinstead. She and her husband arrived in East Grinstead in 1919 and became close friends of George I and my grandmother, Elsie. They all visited Stratford-upon-Avon together in 1924.

Gwen Broad wrote me a letter dated 2 July 1939 which hangs on my wall along with pencil drawings of her medieval farmhouse. The letter says:

To Dear Little Nicholas, With every good wish for a life filled with love and usefulness. Your Dawn has commenced in sunshine, may the eventide have just sufficient clouds to make a glorious sunset! With love from Your Mother and Father's friend, Gwen M. Broad.

The sunshine did not last long. War loomed, and in August I was taken to stay at St Anton in Maypole Road, East Grinstead with my grandmother. Photos in the albums show me in the large garden in a pram. When war broke out I stayed on at my grandmother's with my mother while my father lived in digs at 32 Tooting Bec Gardens, Streatham to be near his work. He attended Streatham Methodist church. In November my father bought Goscar, 284 Croydon Road, Caterham, Surrey and we moved there in December. My father let the Norbury property.[3]

Evacuation to East Grinstead: St Anton and Beecholme
On a Sunday in May 1940 Caterham was bombed. Terror from the air threatened my family idyll. It was clear that London was going to be blitzed, and I was evacuated back to the safety of East Grinstead in Sussex with my mother and grandmother. There is a photo of me sitting on a rug on the lawn in May 1940 looking intensely up at my aunt Margaret.

Nicholas and his aunt Argie, Margaret Broadley, by the lily pond at St Anton, East Grinstead in May 1940; and Nicholas holding tennis-ball in the East Grinstead doorway, November 1940

The rest of 1940 I lived in that large brick house in Maypole Road. In June I was crawling and in July tottering and toddling. I remember the long back garden very clearly. It had a crazy-paving path under a rose-covered arbour walk alongside a lawn. It led to a rose-clad pergola with a trellis on either side and a pool with rushes that I sat near on a rug that hot summer. I can see a hedge nearby and a lot of shrubs and trees. Towards the bottom of the garden there was a greenhouse, and beyond it a shed where Percy the gardener could be found. I watched in fascination as he spun the wheel of his knife-grinder faster and faster so it made a rhythmic beat as he sharpened his tools. When I was older I scooted down the path on a yellow scooter to see Percy.

I remember the inside of the house very clearly. We had our meals at the back, sitting at a table by the window. A gong boomed for mealtimes – the same gong now hangs in my hall – and Lily, our maid in a cap, brought my lunch from the kitchen which was visible when she opened the distant door. In the front room there were toy soldiers, Canadian Mounties and Scottish bagpipers, and Boer-War and First-World-War wagons with cloth awnings.

There were coloured matches on the mantelpiece. In the hall a clock chimed each quarter and struck each hour – I have it now in my dining-room. All these early family memories have the force of images, but most of all I remember the sunshine on the back table during those early wartime months.

The war did not reach East Grinstead. There are photos in the albums of me in a pram and strapped into my wooden high chair in the fresh air. The high chair is low down for the base cleverly collapsed back on itself for one side to turn into a table, and the whole thing was now on wheels. My grandmother is in some of the photos. She was known as 'Ga-ga' until the end of her life after my babyish attempt to say "Grannie". There are photos of me standing, holding on to or leaning on a small table in July and walking unsteadily in a coat in early September. In November I am standing holding a tennis-ball in my right hand. In other photos I am standing holding a pail and a watering-can beside a herbaceous border whose flowers are taller than me.

In April 1941 my mother had a miscarriage.[4] In late 1941 she was expecting another child and we moved to nearby Beecholme in Cranston Road, East Grinstead. An envelope 'On His Majesty's Service' from the Collector of Taxes addressed to my father there has survived. It is postmarked 4 February 1942. Beecholme was semi-detached with one front room, and there was a cellar window just visible above the earth at the front. My mother told me there were frogs in the cellar.

My mother gave birth prematurely to my brother Robert on 27 March 1942, and Beecholme was the first home he knew. I remember standing in the window of the front room and watching my father go to work, presumably to travel to Mitcham after a weekend with us. As he limped down the front path and turned left I saw his balding head beyond a hedge (which has long since disappeared). I can see him raise his stick as a form of waving. On the back lawn there was a conifer, I believe a pine tree. It seemed to be of great height and cast its shadow across the lawn. My mother loosely referred to its cones as 'fir-cones'. I revisited the back garden when older and was shocked to see that my enormous pine tree had been felled.

My aunt Margaret interrupted her nursing to come down some weekends, and that spring she always took me for a walk down the Lewes Road towards Ashurst Wood. We turned off Imberhorn Lane to a small wood on the right through which there was a right of way. It was full of primroses and fenced off and a farmyard gate had "Shut This Gate" written on it. My aunt, who was called 'Argie' for the rest of her life after my babyish attempt to say "Margaret", called it "Shut-This-Gate Wood". I would run knee-deep in primroses and remember being blissfully happy. That wood was a Paradise far removed from war.

War: Loughton and bombs

I first became aware of the war after my father began a new job in Loughton, Essex, as chief accountant in the treasurer's department of the Chigwell Urban District Council. He lived in digs to be near his work from November 1942 to March 1943, when my mother, my brother and I moved to a rented semi-detached house, 52 Brooklyn Avenue in Loughton.

Move to Loughton: 52 Brooklyn Avenue

The house had a long garden at the end of which flowed Loughton Brook. This was the fourth time my parents had moved house (excluding the year my mother and I spent at my grandmother's house): I had moved from Norbury to Caterham, to Beecholme in East Grinstead and now Brooklyn Avenue, Loughton.

I can remember sitting in a high chair in the kitchen, still three, or just four, and looking at an enormous map of Europe which covered the whole wall. It was crowded with names of places and filled with pins with different coloured heads. These marked the front lines in battles my father followed on the 'wireless'. I remember rocking my high chair backwards and forwards and looking at a fly-paper dangling from a lampshade. It was sticky, and flies settled on it, drawn by its smell, and found themselves stuck on its arsenic. I can see my giantess of a mother coming from the kitchen carrying a round bowl with rabbits round its edge and putting it down on the tray of my high chair.

I can also remember sitting in my pram outside the General Post Office (now The Last Post free house). In East Grinstead a lot of people knew us and I had smiled at everyone. In Loughton I did not know anybody, and according to my mother I asked by our front gate while she was pushing Robert in his pram, "Could we meet someone to smile at?"

Our outings to the High Road were mostly connected with collecting our rations. Because food was imported and there were problems with shipping we all had a limited weekly food allowance. We collected our ration books from the Ministry of Food's Food Office on the corner of High Beech Road and at Williams near The Drive, the retailer we were registered with, coupons were cut out in return for the ration we were each allocated: 4 ozs of cheese a week, 1 egg (2 for children), sugar, bacon, meat and bread.

We had moved into the path of the German bombers – we were now living in Prime Minister Winston Churchill's constituency – and one night in March 1943 war invaded our family life: there was a tremendous crash and all our windows blew in. I sat on the stairs, excited. There were air raids every night, generally when I was tucked up in bed. The police siren would start up and wail, and in the early days my father would take me downstairs and we would sit under the kitchen table to protect us if the upper storey collapsed. Later we sheltered in an indoor Morrison shelter in the corner of our sitting-room, an iron 'cage' about three feet high introduced in 1941 and named after the Home Secretary and Minister of Home Security Herbert Morrison.

Every night my father would sit by my bed and tell me a never-ending story about Peter and his dog, and I was pleased when there was an air raid as he would continue the story. Air raids meant double story. Sometimes my mother told us a story about my brother and me climbing up a rainbow and speaking to Thor on his thundercloud. She wrote the story up, and I have a typed copy of her short work, *The Rainbow Children*. My feeling for Old Norse saga began at this time. She also read us books by Beatrix Potter. My favourites were *Peter Rabbit* and *Jeremy Fisher*, and I loved the trout's dive and the butterfly sandwich.

After some time we all became used to the bombing and we stayed in bed. I sometimes asked my father what would happen if a bomb landed on our house, and he said with a shrug, "If that happens we'll all go together. There's nothing we can do about it." Every night we had to say our prayers: The Lord's Prayer followed by "God bless" and then a list of a dozen named relatives. By now prayers had become a fervent wish that all my family would survive the terror that could strike without warning from the skies, the nightmare brought by war.

Somehow at an early age I learned to live with the danger and threat of impending death. I would sometimes lie in bed, a stone hot-water bottle near my feet in winter, listening for Lopping Hall's four-faced clock to strike the hour, and hear the police siren rev up for its wail and hold my breath as distant explosions happened. Living through a bombing raid was a bit like living through a thunderstorm: I held my breath and hoped the thunder would stay far away and that the lightning would not destroy our house or hit me.

I attend Essex House School

In May 1943[5] my parents sent me to school at Essex House. My only surviving report is for the spring term 1944. The report is headed 'Essex House, Kindergarten and Preparatory School, Woodford Green & Loughton'. The Loughton site, which I attended, was a house at 258 High Road, that was pulled down in 1958 to make way for a utilitarian building that now includes a restaurant. It was run by the Miss Huntleys, who were missionaries. My report states that my Form Mistress was Mary A. Huntley and the Head Mistress Janet M. Huntley. I remember hardly anything of my time there, but my report has me "very interested" in story and states "Has made a good beginning" in writing. In reading I was "beginning to recognise and match words". My General Report was: "Nicholas took a keen and intelligent interest in all that was going on."

German bombs blow out our windows
In March 1944 the war again smashed into our family life. One late afternoon my father said I could go with him to the Post Office. It was nearly dark as

he shut the front door and we walked down the path to the front gate. The police siren began revving up to wail an alarm, and suddenly there was a white flash and – I can see it so vividly now – for an instant everything was lit up as bright as day. Then there was a rattle, a clatter and a crash and the glass fell out of the windows (again). I can see my father turn back from the gate and limp hurriedly towards the house without saying a word, and I jumped excitedly up and down and chanted, "A bomb, a bomb."

The photo albums show me standing near the blown-out windows of the garage with my brother. A string of German bombs had fallen in the Forest, and six fell on the cricket field 200 yards away, gouging out a crater in the corner where

Nicholas (left) and his brother Robert under blown-out windows of garage at 52 Brooklyn Avenue, March 1944

Trap's Hill joins the High Road. Essex House was damaged and for the last few days of the spring term classes were relocated to the Methodist church hall, a short walk away.

I attend Oaklands School, Trap's Hill – Froebel and Nature
I was now taken away from Essex House as the Loughton site was closed and the school continued at its Woodford-Green site. I started at Oaklands School,[6] which was based in a Regency house (since pulled down) at 363 High Road, Loughton, across the road and nearer to the cricket field on the corner of Trap's Hill. It too had been damaged by the German bombs, and the first day of the summer term that April I was back in the Methodist church hall, which briefly acted as a refuge for bombed-out Oaklands children.

Oaklands School had been founded in 1937 by Miss Elizabeth Lord, who had trained at the Froebel Educational Institute along with her colleague Miss Mabel Reid.[7] During her training Miss Lord had stayed with friends of her mother's, the two Miss Butlers of 86 Spring Grove, Loughton. She had taught at Oakland House School, 86 Shooters Hill Road, Blackheath for 15 years, near a school in Blackheath where my wife, who would succeed her, was teaching when I met her. Miss Lord loved her teaching and the children so much that she wanted her own Oakland House, and one of the Miss Butlers provided the funding for her to start her own school. Even though it had no oak-trees the new school was called Oaklands because of the school in Blackheath. (I see a symmetry between an Oakland House in Blackheath and an Oaklands in Loughton, and successive Heads coming from Blackheath to Loughton.)

Miss Lord once told me that the school opened with one pupil who was made to troop through the school's front door, out of the back door, and round to the front door again many times to give the impression that a lot of pupils were arriving. Friedrich Froebel's ideas permeated the new school: closeness to Nature, discovery through observation and approaching the unity of the universe. (For Froebel, who died in 1852, unity within diversity was the spiritual principle of God.) The uniform was green with a badge showing an oak-tree.

Rear of the school 1939

Old Oaklands School, 363 High Road, Loughton, front (during war) and back (1939)

Oaklands soon reopened. I remember the green gate and standing in assembly on the first-floor landing near the Nature table, where there were tadpoles in an aquarium. We sang 'We plough the fields and scatter' and 'All things bright and beautiful', and the school song, 'A Little Song of Life' by Lizette Woodworth Reese which began 'Glad that I live am I' and included the lines: "After the sun the rain;/After the rain the sun;/This is the way of life,/Till the work be done." At the back there was a walled garden with a tufty lawn on which we played at break while the teachers drank tea on the veranda.

When the police siren wailed we were led to a Morrison shelter, a rusty iron 'cage' about three feet high which stood in the grounds. (Outside shelters were usually dug-in Anderson shelters covered with earth and grass, but this was a Morrison shelter with mesh sides that you could look through.) Inside there was a rug and we lay on our fronts with a book and peered through the mesh for planes, puffs of smoke and parachutes floating down. A boy called Robin Fowler lay beside me and for a sweet I swapped a brown Japanese banknote showing a herd of cattle, which I still have. His mother, Mrs. Fowler, often walked me back to my house in Brooklyn Avenue, and I remember one of my shoelaces coming undone before we had reached my gate. I was too young to tie my own laces, and Mrs. Fowler propped her bicycle, which she had been pushing, against a tree and tied my lace for me.

V-1 and V-2 rockets

In June 1944 the first V-1 pilotless doodle-bug rocket landed in our part of Britain, Hitler's retaliation for D-Day. We could hear the sound of the engines, and we soon learned that when an engine cut out the flying bomb would explode within ten seconds. I remember lying in bed in Brooklyn Avenue, cowering under my eiderdown and listening to a drone cut out and waiting and counting in quiet terror, hoping it would not land on our house, and hearing a distant boom. I lay in bed during the summer evenings of 1944 and tried to fathom why Hitler wanted to kill us with his dreadful weapons, a deep-seated question that would surface again in *The Warlords* and *Overlord*, my writings about the war.

Between June and the following March over 9,500 V-1 rockets were fired at south-east Britain. I continued to attend Oaklands School and we all carried on as if we were not under rocket attack. The teachers bravely created an illusion of normality within the ever-present threat of terror from the skies.

In August 1944 my family went on holiday to escape the V-1s for a couple of weeks. The south-coast was prohibited because it was still a military zone following the invasion of D-Day, so we went to Ilfracombe, Devon. The beach toll was 1d per person. I can see the grey beach in a rocky bay and my father lying in the sea wearing a striped one-piece bathing costume with straps over his shoulders. The weather was atrocious and when we poured coffee from our thermos into a cup the wind blew the coffee away so it did not reach the cup. We all slept in one guest-room bedroom, and I can see myself sitting in a cot in the corner of our room turning the pages of *The Naughty Ninepins*, an Edwardian (1910) book with pictures every other page that was later a favourite with my children.

In September 1944 the V-1s were tailing off, although they continued until the following March. Now the first V-2 rockets landed. Their approach was silent. The first we heard was a bang. More than 1,400 landed in south-east Britain between September and March, further Nazi retaliation for the

Allied invasion as US and British troops fought their way towards Berlin. During this time we lived fatalistically, hoping we would not be suddenly obliterated without warning, assuming that we would survive, aware of the danger that could annihilate our houses and wipe out our families at any time. During those months I learned that life is ephemeral and that death can strike now, a deep-rooted perception that adds intensity to everyday observation.

Oaklands School moves to Albion Hill

That same September of 1944 Oaklands School moved from the corner of Trap's Hill to its present site in Albion Hill, Loughton. It was risky to plan to move a school before D-Day when the outcome of the war was uncertain and V-1s threatened from the air. Miss Lord probably had no choice as the lease ran out and the leaseholder may have wanted to sell the site to a developer planning to build shops. The grounds of the new Oaklands had oak-trees.

I moved with the school. I remember the sea of buttercups in the main field and the huge oak reputed to be 800 years old: now the oak-tree on the school badge. We sat under that tree pretending to smoke acorn pipes. Brown acorns crunched underfoot. In the overhanging bushes at the bottom of the main field there was a camp. Older boys turned it into an army headquarters, and nearby there was a pretend concentration camp. I was captured one break and guarded, a broken branch blocking my escape. The sentries prevented me from rejoining my playing friends. So we re-enacted in play the grim scenes some had seen in the cinema of conditions in Belsen and similar camps.

Family at end of war
Brother and grandfather

That autumn my mother often made tea on the lawn at the back of the house in Brooklyn Avenue. There were greengages in the garden with lantern-like fruit. The photo albums show me holding a spade in the garden. In the next garden Freddie Durrant, the beetle-browed owner of the local shoe shop (Durrant's opposite Lopping Hall) mowed the lawn at weekends, and my brother peered through the fence and called peremptorily, "Dumma, Dumma, Bobbie 'lower" ('Durrant, Durrant, pick Robert a flower'). Sometimes Robert and I played cricket on the concrete slope between the gateway and the garage. Once my brother said he did not want to play and I complained to a passing policeman, who came in and persuaded Robert to bat in front of the garage doors while I bowled.

About this time I was invited to tea with school friends at some of the large local houses, including Ripley Grange, the mock-Tudor house of

Pelham Clark, son of the architect Charles Clark; a large house off Golding's Hill, the house of Justin Lindy, son of the architect Kenneth Lindy who exhibited designs for the rebuilding of the City of London in 1944; and Warren Hill House (later Warren Hall), the house of the Lusty family, makers of Lloyd-loom woven furniture.

In the winter of 1944 my grandfather (Willoughby Thomas Hagger, 'Grandpa') came to stay. I recollect him vividly. He had white hair and a white moustache, and looked like Lloyd George. He had had a finger chopped off in a Canadian sawmill (which sawed tree-trunks into planks and boards). He went for a walk to the shops on his own in thick fog, and had not returned by lunch-time. I was sent out to find him. I found him lying on the edge of the kerb under a lamppost further down Brooklyn Avenue, on the High-Road side of its junction with Churchfields. He had fallen and cut his head. I helped him up and led him home and helped my mother clean his bloodstained brow. When the fog lifted we drove him back to his flat on the first floor of (I believe) 40A Station Road, New Barnet. It had a black fire-escape at the back. I remember sitting in a dimly-lit old-fashioned room with Victorian and Edwardian furniture, where his wife, my grandmother, was a shadowy figure in the background.

I hear Churchill speak at Loughton war memorial in 1945
My mother was pregnant at the time. On 12 April 1945 she gave birth to twins, Katherine and Mary. They were both sickly, and she was still in hospital when the victorious wartime Prime Minister, Winston Churchill, toured his constituency. He began in Woodford and came to Loughton.

He spoke on King's Green, standing on a step of the war memorial facing the cricket field, with Mrs. Churchill at his side. I was there, in the care of Mr and Mrs. Allwood, the Methodist minister and his wife, who took me while my father visited my mother in hospital. It was a drizzly day, and I stood very close to Churchill. The war was over and there was rejoicing, and the 1945 general election had been called. He congratulated his constituents on surviving flying bombs and rockets, and said that if he was called away during the election (a reference to the Potsdam conference, for which he was about to leave) Mrs. Churchill would take his place in the constituency.

Churchill speaking in Loughton in 1945, with Nicholas out of view (bottom left)

At Potsdam Churchill heard that he had lost the general election. He had been rejected by the British people after defeating the Nazis, and he flew home and was replaced by Clement Atlee. My contact with

Churchill days before his rejection made a profound impact on me, which came out in *The Warlords* and *Overlord*.

Move to Journey's End

I now learned that we were to move for the fifth time since I was born, to Journey's End in Station Road, Loughton. (Again I detect symmetry: my grandfather lived in Station Road, New Barnet, and now my father was to live in Station Road, Loughton.) It was an 1870s double-fronted house with two green gables facing the front and another to one side, a green porch, a green gate with 'Journey's End' on the top and a row of green lime-trees on either side behind the fence. On the fence to the right of the gate was a board saying 'Private'. My father had a short walk to work at the Council Offices in Old Station Road, which I could see from the window of the bedroom I shared with my brother. At the back there was a lawn with a pear-tree in the middle, and another pear-tree and an apple-tree near the fence.

Journey's End, Loughton as it used to be

There were redcurrant, raspberry and gooseberry bushes.

We rented the house from the Maitlands, the lords of the manor of Loughton until their departure to Lincolnshire. One of the lords of the manor had been the Rev. J.W. Maitland who enclosed tracts of the Forest and prosecuted Thomas Willingale for exercising his lopping rights.[8] Lopping Hall was given to the people of Loughton by the Corporation of London to make amends for the removal of their right to lop wood in the nearby Forest in the early 1880s.[9] Although we were not to move in until July the Maitlands allowed my mother to use the kitchen and back garden for my sixth birthday party, four days after my birthday on Saturday 26 May. My mother had been discharged from hospital but had to leave the poorly twins there.

My sixth birthday

I have a vivid recollection of a hot, sunny day and long tables set out in a U and covered with white tablecloths near the central pear-tree on the lawn, and some twenty Oaklands children sitting on chairs and eating a sumptuous spread which my mother had somehow provided despite rationing. I was sitting at the cross table near redcurrant bushes and I can see my mother, just out of hospital, standing the other side of my table as one of the helpers spilt damson jam with round damsons in it on the white tablecloth. I can see my mother in a summer dress scraping the damson jam with a knife and rubbing salt on the stain with a white napkin. It is so vivid I can almost reach out and help her rub salt on the stain.

I did not know it, but one of my twin sisters, Katherine, had died on the previous Saturday, 19 May, and the other, Mary, would die on the very day of my party, 26 May.[10] My mother, rubbing salt into the stain, was in fact grieving for Katherine and resigned to the imminent loss of Mary, a sorrow she bore without showing it. My twin sisters had lived for five weeks and six weeks respectively.

It must have been a day or two later that I was called into my father's study at Brooklyn Avenue. With excellent psychology he told me in a very adult way and asked me if I would help him tell my younger brother. I felt important as I helped him explain that they had both reached their brief journey's end and died.

The deaths were a devastating blow to my parents. They would lose two more children in the coming years, but this double loss affected both of them. My mother's faith was tested but she responded by framing some words from Joseph Henry Shorthouse's *John Inglesant*: "Nothing but the infinite Pity is sufficient for the infinite pathos of human life." My father had always been a stoic, having had polio when he was 14 and having lived through the unemployment and war of the 1930s, and now he became even more stoical.

With the end of the war and the death of my twin sisters around the time of my sixth birthday the first episode of my life came to an end.

Episode 2:

Nature and School

Years: 1945–1954
Locations: Loughton; Chigwell

"Come forth into the light of things,
Let Nature be your teacher."
Wordsworth, 'The Tables Turned'

The next episode in my life consisted of two conflicting influences on my growth: Nature and school.

Nature: Oaklands Paradise
That summer I studied a map of the world and grasped that a quarter of the world's land mass was pink because it belonged to the British Empire. I was very proud of belonging to a nation that ruled a quarter of the world and had defeated Hitler.

Awareness of Nature
I was very aware of Nature. My drawing book, dated 22 May 1945 (the date of my sixth birthday), shows that I had drawn seven six-spot burnets, two kingfishers, a dragonfly, a snake and several newts, frogs and tadpoles – along with British warplanes and flags.

William Addison
I had received a five-shilling book token for my sixth birthday. I took it to Addison's Bookshop, and William Addison, who had just finished his *Epping Forest, Its Literary and Historical Associations* (his first book of many on Epping Forest), clerical in a dark suit, white shirt and tie, guided me to a shelf of *Observer's Books,* and encouraged me to choose *The Observer's Book of Trees.*

Nature walks, Bird Diary
The Oaklands fields were inspirational to us six-year-olds. We were taken for Nature walks in the grounds by Mabel Reid. She eventually became Miss Lord's business partner – from September 1947 she owned two-fifths of Oaklands' new Albion-Hill site to Miss Lord's three-fifths[1] – and was very influential in implementing Froebel's closeness to Nature, direct observation and awareness of the unity of the universe. She took us pond-dipping and we studied the aquarium outside Miss Lord's study door for the life cycle of caddis, dragonfly larvae, frog-spawn, tadpoles and newts. We went into the Forest to the Strawberry Hill pond and came away with Canadian pondweed, and we caught sticklebacks. She taught us about birds. We were encouraged to create bird tables at home, feed birds and keep a Bird Diary. We learned about flowers and the prehistoric plants at the bottom of the main field. I have not been Froebel-trained but from an early age I was on an instinctive quest to perceive the unity of the universe because on Nature walks through direct observation I was imbued with the life cycle of all creatures and their interaction with the whole of creation. And so when I came to preside over Oaklands I instinctively carried forward Froebel's way of looking.

Life at Journey's End and Oaklands
Nature was still central after we moved into Journey's End in July. I carried

a large model of a grey battleship round to my new home, which was empty. During the war it had been occupied by the ARP (Air Raid Protection, founded in 1935) and the WVS (Women's Voluntary Service, founded in 1938), and cut telephone wires poked out of the skirting above bare boards and green lino in most rooms.

We lived in the nursery, downstairs at the back. There were steps down into the primitive red-and-black-tiled kitchen, and through a separate door there was a larder kept cool by mesh over an open window frame. (We had no fridge or freezer until 1948. Milk and butter were stored in the cellar or stood in water. The butter was always soft, and there was a risk of catching TB from milk. We shopped every day and the Sunday joint lasted most of the week. It was kept under a gauze meat-cover to keep off flies, and the dripping was eaten with bread.)

My brother and I shared the large bedroom under the back gable. We had single beds and a gas fire, and we often went to sleep with the landing light on listening for the Lopping-Hall clock to strike the hour. Sometimes music floated up from downstairs. My father would play the piano in the dining-room and sing in his quavering tenor voice, "And fairies are flying" or (from Elgar's *The Dream of Gerontius*) "And carefully I dip thee in the lake". Sometimes my mother played Vivaldi's or Mendelssohn's violin concerto, which drifted beautifully upstairs and wafted us off to sleep. After nine months of listening for strident sirens and thunderous V-1 or V-2 rockets it was a delight to go to sleep to safe, harmonious chords.

That summer holidays we spent long days in the Journey's-End garden, often having tea on the sunny lawn. I helped my father dig the flower-bed by the back fence and forked up a bit of iron. I asked what it was, and my father laughed and said, "It's a bit of shrapnel." I had dug up a fragment of a wartime bomb or shell. My brother Robert and I took turns to wear a First-World-War leather airman's helmet with protruding ear sockets. This had belonged to my uncle Tom, who was killed in 1918. As a joke he had written the name of his grandfather, 'Chas [i.e. Charles] Harding' in ink on the inside. Allowed back on the south coast now that the war was over, we went to Bognor in August, and stayed with a Mrs. Bolt at 26 Glamis Street. When we returned we helped my father pick apples and pears, dodging the wasps settling on windfalls, and carried them down to the cellar where we stored them in tiers separated by newspaper. We ate them throughout the autumn and winter.

That autumn we fell into a pattern. After a cooked breakfast of fried bread, bacon and a fried egg we walked to school or sometimes took a double-decker bus. We took off our green caps, blazers and satchels and hung them on pegs by the window nearest to the gate. We ran out to climb in the jungle gym, a wooden structure below Miss Lord's study window. The back of the school was covered in ivy. We played at break, often in the main field, which was full of buttercups and hawthorn. There were foxes' lairs, badgers' sets and rabbit holes, and there were squirrels.

Because my parents were musical I had piano lessons in some breaks. While my classmates were hunting for conkers, or crouching over worms or an insect that had lost a wing I sat with Kathleen Goldie (who was soon to die of TB) learning "All Cows Eat Grass" and "Every Good Boy Deserves Fun", following her finger pointing at the music and wishing I could be out with Nature. It was soon clear that I did not have my parents' bent for music, and to their disappointment I discontinued my piano lessons.

New Oaklands School, Albion Hill, Loughton, school photograph with Nicholas as a pupil (inset), 1946

But I had some facility with words. I loved reading and was taught to write in Marion-Richardson-style handwriting. I had a strong sense of rhythm, and my parents' music came out in me as a love of poetry. We read poems about Nature. I copied out Christina Rossetti's 'Who has seen the wind?' and Blake's 'The sun does arise' (from 'The

New Oaklands, back and side view

Ecchoing Green') and 'Little lamb, who made thee?' (for each of which I earned a red star). I read and chanted chunks of Longfellow's *Hiawatha*, whose rhythms I loved:

By the shores of Gitchee Gumee,
By the shining Big-Sea-Water,
Stood the wigwam of Nokomis,
Daughter of the moon, Nokomis.
Dark behind it rose the forest,
Rose the black and gloomy pine-trees
Rose the firs with cones upon them....

(I was thinking about fir-cones when I was six.) We acted out scenes from *Hiawatha*. We bought dyed feathers from a shop at the foot of Church Hill and became Red-Indian Hiawathas and squaws by poking a feather into a headband.

We were encouraged to observe Nature. I walked home for lunch and met my father, who also came back for lunch, hopping and limping by his stick, bald and smiling. We ate in the nursery, looking out of the window at the bird table on the lawn, and I kept my Bird Diary going. I recorded each new species of bird I saw and where I had seen it: on our rubbish dump or on the garden fence.

After lunch I returned to school, sometimes on the red double-decker bus (no. 20). Once, wearing short trousers and probably aged six, I stood on the open bus platform gripping the white hand-pole with my football boots tied together round my neck, and rang the bell once as the bus sped to the Request Stop by The Crescent. The driver ignored my request to stop and sped on. I panicked, jumped, hit the ground and slithered in the direction of the bus, and my football boots clattered on the High Road. I lay crying with badly grazed knees and elbows opposite Albion Hill, down which a lady hurried to my assistance. I can see her advancing now, her hair was done up in a grey bun. "The bus didn't stop," I blubbed. It was feared I had fractured my skull, but I had not. One day I would buy Oaklands School and control the traffic in Albion Hill, and I sometimes wonder if my leap from the bus was Providence's way of nudging me to bring my future destiny to my attention.

At school we did a lot of drawing, which sharpened my observation: scenes from *Hiawatha* with tents and Red-Indian feathers, and symbols of British might in the form of planes and ships.

In the evenings we all had supper at the nursery table. My father sometimes had bread, dripping and cheese. In the early winter we all sat round the coal fire (the only form of heat in the nursery), holding out our hands to the glowing coals and feeling their warmth on our cheeks. Christmas was magical. Holly with red berries hung above the mirror over the nursery fireplace, and two paper chains made of linked ovals of paper ran diagonally from corner to corner under the nursery ceiling, crossing over in the middle near the central light. On Christmas Day my brother and I found presents stacked round two farmhouse chairs in the nursery. They were wrapped in paper covered with holly, red berries and glitter like snow. A 1920s cardboard Father Christmas in red holding a small Christmas tree was propped up on the breakfast table. The Christmas cake had half a dozen small china Edwardian bandsmen on it, one beating a drum. In the evenings my father filled hot-water bottles, holding one after another casually over the red-and-black-tiled kitchen floor, bravely indifferent to a possible splash-back from the scalding water.

Sunday school: Methodist church

Every Sunday, when I would rather be out in Nature, we put on our Sunday suits and walked to the Methodist church, a 1903 neo-Gothic building. We sat in long wooden pews on a long strip of carpet. At the end of each pew there was a tray on the floor and each pew had a holder for umbrellas. There was a round clock on the left-hand wall with Roman numerals, and time passed very slowly between XI and XII. After twenty minutes children filed down to the front to go to children's church Sunday school in the hall behind the altar which had accommodated the bombed-out children of Essex House and Oaklands.

One month they rehearsed a short play based on the traditional 18th-century song that was popular in colonial America, "Soldier, soldier, will you marry me,/With your musket, fife and drum?" I played the soldier. I was dressed up and stood on the stage (beneath a drooping wire hanging down with curtains at either end) before a packed audience. There was a chest, and a girl kept opening the lid and giving me a garment, which I had to put on. After putting on a hat, a coat and two boots I was offered "pants" (i.e. trousers) to put on over what I was wearing. I lost interest and wandered off stage, and was guided back on.

Another time I sang Dryden's "Fairest isle, all isles excelling" in a children's church eisteddfod. I also sang Shakespeare's "When daisies pied, and violets blue". These songs fed my love of poetry. The church congregation had a galaxy of vivid characters who I have described elsewhere.[2]

Interview with Dr James at Chigwell School

I was very happy at Oaklands. I loved the structured learning within the context of Nature. When we ran out to play we were surrounded by trees and were aware of the birds and berries of the seasons.

My parents now resolved to send me to Chigwell School. In early 1946 I was taken for an interview with the Head, Dr James. (He left soon afterwards to become High Master of St Paul's and in due course Head Master of Harrow.) I can see him sitting behind his desk, wearing a suit and waistcoat.

In March 1946 he wrote my parents three letters[3] regarding my admission in September 1947, one of which says that Chigwell offered "a number of places annually" to Essex County Council under the Direct Grant scheme which had just begun.

Epping Forest

I now became much more aware of Epping Forest. It was never far away as we came and went for Loughton nestled in a three-sided crater and dense forest covered the rim to the east and was visible at the end of several roads, sullen in winter and cheerful in summer. There were hills at each end of Loughton, and from the upstairs of Oaklands School at one end and from the wooden seat above the sloping cricket field at the other end Loughton seemed to be a clearing in the Forest, as it was in the 19th century, with the Roding valley across fields to the west.

My brother and I were drawn towards the Forest at the end of our road. My aunt Argie described "the lure of the Forest". She took us for walks when she visited from the London Hospital and crossed us over the High Road into Forest Road. Soon we started running towards the Forest as if our blood was drawn by the moon.

My brother and I sometimes walked along Nursery Road to the Stubbles, an open clearing of heath surrounded by scrub and Forest. Its knee-high grass was filled with purple-and-green grasshoppers that swung and hopped. There were wild flowers and butterflies – cabbage whites, meadow browns and azure blue – and dragonflies skimmed and hovered round the pond. There were brambles, gorse and berries, and the Forest sloped down to a stream. Sometimes we fished in the stream at the end of Forest Road and caught sticklebacks and minnows in home-made nets made from a cane, a round piece of wire and sewn-together flour bags. We carried a jamjar filled with water, its lid punctured by holes to allow our catch to breathe. One Good Friday we strayed into a bog near the end of Forest Road and returned home with our sandals caked with clay.

In April my aunt Argie arranged for us to see Queen Mary at the back of the London Hospital. The banks of daffodils made a great impression on me. They were in full bloom and magnificent. I remember standing amid a crowd watching the Queen walking distantly with an obsequious entourage, and being spellbound by the hundreds of daffodils dancing in the breeze.

In the summer term Mabel Reid took us to Strawberry Hill and we fished in the inner of the two ponds, opposite a fallen beech, and found dragonfly larvae and caddis, newts and tadpoles. In class we drew Canadian pondweed and water violets and all the seeds of the Forest flowers and trees, and fungi, observing details with precision. On Nature walks in the Forest we listened to the songs of the willow warbler and wren, and sometimes heard a nightingale. Knowing my interest in Nature, my parents bought at auction a specimen cabinet with 12 drawers of butterflies, moths and beetles (which over the years disintegrated into dust) and two old glass cases of birds' eggs, which I still have in my study.

Foreign coins and stamps

I was becoming a collector, and I now became a collector of coins. I was invited to tea with a classmate, the daughter of the bank manager of Barclays, Loughton, who lived in the bank building in the High Road that is still in use. After tea I was taken to the foreign-currency room. There was a pile of foreign coins that was knee-high in relation to my knees at that age. The manager said I could take two handfuls and keep as many coins as I could hold. I plunged in my hands and carried two heaps to the wall. Out spilled onto the floor African coins with holes in them, Indian coins shaped like diamonds and serrated Arab coins. There were rupees, piastres and mills.

When I returned home I put my two handfuls in an olive-green cashbox with compartments that my father found for me, and I still have them to this day. Coins encouraged me to look up the countries they came from in my atlas, and I became more aware of geography and history.

I now started collecting stamps. My father started me off with a second-hand album. I swapped stamps at school and soon I had triangular and diamond-shaped stamps from exotic places, and stamps that showed views of remote islands in the British Empire with a king's head in the right-hand corner.

Collecting coins and stamps taught me to catalogue a chronological sequence and to give the world a semblance of order. My labelled stamp album and coin collection anticipated my *Collected Poems* and *Collected Stories*.

Iron-Age forts, Roman coin and garden

The Forest had two Iron-Age forts that had been fought over by the Trinovantes and Catuvellauni: Ambresbury Banks, which was linked to Suetonius Paulinus's defeat of Boudicca in 61; and Loughton Camp.[4] From Strawberry Hill we walked under the supervision of Mabel Reid down a dip and up a slope, scuffling leaves, and cut into the Forest to earthen walls in a beech wood: all that remained of Loughton Camp. We imagined the Romans storming up the slope to capture the fort and re-enacted the battle with sticks and lay dead in last autumn's yellow-brown brittle beech leaves. Loughton Camp first stirred my sense of history and my life-long interest in the Romans. In History lessons we drew an ancient English camp and village, a Roman house and amphitheatre, Caesar and a Roman soldier,

Hadrian's Wall and Augustine, "the preacher from Rome".

It must have been about this time that, walking back from school, I crossed the High Road and stood by the red pillar-box and watched a mechanical digger dig into the sloping wasteland by the top of The Crescent and saw something gleam and fall. When it was safe, I tiptoed on the wild grass and retrieved it from the clay. It was a bronze-looking Roman coin. I carried it home and when I had washed off the mud I could see a head on the front and an eagle on the back. Some years later I took it to Seaby's in London and was told that the head was of Caracalla. In 2013 Professor Chris Howgego, keeper of the Ashmolean's Heberden coin room, identified the head as belonging to Elagabalus and the coin as colonial coinage from Antioch. (It had a Greek delta, the fourth letter of the Greek alphabet, and epsilon on the back which he thought stood for "of the 4 eparchies", the 4 provinces of Roman Syria of which Antioch was the head.)[5] He reckoned that a Roman soldier in Syria posted to Britannia brought it with him, traded it and that it changed hands until it came into the possession of the person who dropped it near Oaklands School. In later life my finding a coin of value so near Oaklands seemed symbolic, and I wonder if even at this young age I was being nudged by Providence into understanding that Oaklands had been earmarked to provide me with a livelihood.

In the summer of 1946 I was in touch with Nature in the garden at Journey's End. It was full of spiders and I often found a stag beetle. A hedgehog sometimes crossed the lawn. Honeysuckle trailed from a wall. It was always full of bees. Ivy climbed a fence by the clothes-post. There were roses and Michaelmas daisies. I found a lime-hawk moth among the leaves on the lime-trees in the front garden. I helped pick gooseberries and redcurrants, peas and runner beans. I helped dig the beds, careful not to spear earthworms with the fork or to tread on snails like the ones that lived in our pail. Each day I put bacon rind on the bird table and then sat in the nursery window and noted the birds that came, looking some up in *The Observer's Book of Birds*. We were rewarded with red stars that could accumulate into a gold-star prize. I won a gold-star prize for my Bird Diary: *The Hedge I Know*. Even the names my father mentioned over the nursery table suggested Nature and the Forest: Gale and Willingale (two of his colleagues) and Digweed (the undertaker). I quickly became a woodlander, alert to the changing colour of leaves, knowing the different kinds of tree and their fruit, knowing about wild flowers and of course Forest ponds, knowing the haunts and habitats of birds, butterflies, moths and flowers. Loughton was a community and in the High Road a couple of dozen people said "Good morning" to me.

I grew with the seasons, I lived in the rhythm of the days and months. There were glorious summer mornings when the sky over the Council

Offices was a brilliant blue. There were still evenings of almost unbearable beauty when the family sat out in deck-chairs, watching the gnats dance and listening to the blackbirds' piping. When I went to sleep the shadows of the branches of the pear-tree on the lawn were projected onto my bedroom wall by a street light, and when the wind blew the shadows moved. As a result I have always needed to live near trees.

My mother was pregnant again. My brother and I returned to Bognor and again stayed at 26 Glamis Street, this time with my grandmother and my aunt Argie. My letters home reveal that I caught 26 crabs at Aldwick and lots of shrimps and found an empty whelk shell. (I found one in Japan that I included in my poem 'The Silence'.) My interest in Nature now extended to rock pools.

In October 1946 my little sister Janet was born. She had a hole in her heart and when she came home she was permanently flushed and in discomfort, often in pain. Nothing could be done for her. She cried a lot, and when she went to sleep we tiptoed about for if she woke she would be awake and in discomfort for several hours.

Oneness with frosty stars
One day I was invited to have tea after school at my classmate Michael Rogers' house at 24 Ollards Grove, Loughton (where Mark Liell, the local solicitor and then Mabel Reid had previously lived). After tea it was dark and we ran out to a large shed that stood towards the end of the garden, on the right. It was a clear night and already frosty, and I was taken aback by the brilliance of the stars. I am now back in my infant self looking up at the stars full of wonder, and there was a oneness between the stars and me.

Chinese coins: eternity
About this time I took an interest in my mother's round work-basket in which she stored her cotton reels and needles. It had at least ten old Chinese coins sewn on the top. Each had a square hole with Chinese ideograms round it, and on one side there were the four gates of a Buddhist *stupa* (or shrine), a symbol of Heaven that incorporated *yin* and *yang*. She kindly cut some off for me to have. I did not realise that the central hole symbolised eternity, but after the night full of stars my young head was full of the universe and I was close to thinking about where the stars had come from: an embryonic concept of eternity.

Illnesses: latent tuberculosis, meningitis, tonsillitis
That winter I was not well. I had a bad cough I could not get rid of and when I was older X-rays revealed white spots on my lungs (a band of atelectasis) that confirmed I had had latent pulmonary tuberculosis (TB). TB has now

been eradicated and it is not widely appreciated that at the end of the war it was still possible to catch TB. (The consultant who found the white spots said he thought my latent TB came from milk.) I weathered my bout but it left me with an enduring problem with my lungs.

The winter of 1946–1947 was very severe and bitter, and there were snowdrifts ten feet deep. In January I had acute earache. My mother kept me in bed but one night in February my earache got worse and I was almost screaming with pain. I was rushed to the London Hospital in a white ambulance in almost unbearable pain. The bell rang non-stop like a fire-alarm. I could hear it lying in the back of the ambulance, and I can still hear it now. I had suspected meningitis and mastoid inflammation, and responded to a new drug, penicillin, which had only just been mass-produced. Many years later a hearing expert I consulted proved on an audiometer that I suffer sensory neural loss in the middle of my right ear between my outer ear and my brain, and concluded that the pain I felt in the ambulance was in fact meningitis, caused by my tubercular chest infection. This meningitis was eating away part of the bone and progressing towards the brain. As a result I now have some nerve deafness. The hearing expert said that if I had not been given penicillin I would have died. The penicillin saved my life.

In hospital I had my tonsils out. As I came round a nurse thrust the spout of a white teapot between my lips to make me drink. I convalesced in Buxton Ward under an ear-nose-and-throat specialist. Buxton Ward was a children's ward and there were boxes of cigarette cards: complete sets of sea fish, fresh-water fish and birds. There was also a complete set of small creatures, including harvest mice and newts. All the illustrations of Nature's creatures were very exact and precise. I passed a week doing jigsaw puzzles and studying the pictures on the cigarette cards. When I returned to school I discovered that some of the other pupils had some of the cigarette cards I had seen, and by swapping I began to collect cigarette cards as well as coins and stamps.

My illness brought me closer to my father. I watched him hold the brown kettle that had boiled on the stove and pour boiling water into a hot-water bottle as my boyish eyes wonderingly took in his indifference to a possible scalding splash on his own skin. He crouched by my bed, which was now in the front upstairs room nearest Lopping Hall. He told me the Americans would send a rocket to the moon, which captured my imagination. I now took an interest in the moon. He took my brother and me to the Stubbles and we all played football on the heath with the Forest on two sides. We were the only people there. I was goalie between two posts marked by clothes, and leaning on his stick he swung his good leg and toe-punted the ball high over my head. When we returned home we talked in his bedroom. Suddenly he said, "You won't want to know me when you're older. It's natural, all children think like that." I said, "I will always be close to you." It was inconceivable that I might one day disagree with him.

Entrance exam to Chigwell School: newts
Spring arrived and I was now well enough to sit the entrance exam for Chigwell School. It took place on a warm Saturday afternoon in New Hall and was supervised by the legendary Arnold Fellows ('A.F.'), a giant man from the Edwardian and First-World-War eras with a shock of white hair. We sat in rows facing Top Field. I was about fourth from the front and slightly to the left of centre. I cannot recall the maths paper – there must have been one – but have a vivid recollection of the English composition paper. There were two questions: 'The London Clapham Omnibus'; and 'Newts'. I did not know that an omnibus was a bus, I had never heard of Clapham and did not know that there is a plaque to the inventor of the bus, George Shillibeer, in the parish church of St Mary, Chigwell, which is why A.F. had chosen the title. I wrote on newts. I had often observed them in the Oaklands aquarium, and I had drawn them: the great-crested newt with a speckled yellow-orange underbelly and ridged dragon-like back; the palmate newt; and the common or smooth newt. I wrote about their little, barely-webbed hands and feet and how they resemble lizards, and I covered their life cycle and habits. I got into Chigwell on my knowledge of newts – on my love of Nature.

My last term at Oaklands was full of sunshine. The summer of 1947 was baking. There was a water shortage, and I remember the 'water cart', a horse-drawn enormous cylinder like a beer barrel on its side with a tap, stopping outside Journey's End and we ran out and filled jugs with water and carried them with steady hands back into the house.

I was counting the days to starting at Chigwell. Perhaps to escape the water shortage, in August we stayed at Folkestone (in 4 Julian Road) with my cousin Richard, the son of my mother's sister Flo whose marriage had not survived the war. My father came down for a day and took me by bus to Canterbury to see Denis Compton, who in 1947 scored 18 centuries and 3,816 runs. We sat in sunshine by the green cricket field and the large tree within the boundary but it was the social activities of the cricket I was absorbed in, not Nature. Middlesex were batting and with sun dazzling from car windscreens Compton came in at no. 4 and made 106. I can see him brushing back his tousled hair and dancing down the wicket to hit the leg-spinner over his head, risking being stumped. "There he goes again," my father said each time he charged down the wicket. When he reached 100 he put his bat up and mopped his brow and the moment passed into my memory as an image outside time, full of bravado.

That day the Middlesex team was captained by R.W.V. Robins, whose son would insure my historic house in the future, and included F.G. Mann, whose nephew would be my publisher for the best part of a decade. Looking back, I wonder if I was not just watching Compton's century but was also being shown two families whose help I would need one day.

In those days cricketers were remote. They featured on cigarette cards and the only contact with them was to get their autograph. Several boys at the ground had autograph albums, and I asked my father if I could have one and now began collecting autographs.

School: Chigwell and shutting-out of Nature
Faced with the cost of my starting at a new school in a new uniform and with new sportswear and looking to increase his income, at some point in 1947 my father bought from the Church Commissioners the lease of a London property, 6 Warrington Gardens, W9 (now demolished). I expect he funded the purchase from the sale of my mother's houses in Moat Road, East Grinstead. The property consisted of single rooms that were let to overseas visitors. My father installed our domestic help and her husband as managers of the property, and he went up to London every Friday to collect rents.

I start at Chigwell School
I started at Chigwell School on a misty day in September 1947. I travelled by steam train with my mother, who put her bicycle in the guard's van and pushed it from Chigwell station to the school with my kitbag (packed with my sports clothes) in the basket on the handlebars. We turned into the quadrangle in front of the early-17th-century Big School and looked for someone to tell us where I should go. I was the youngest boy in the school, aged eight, and a bigger boy led us to a changing-room where I had to padlock my kitbag to a peg. The bigger boy told me that the chapel was still closed due to war damage, and he led me to New Hall. I found myself sitting on a bench with much older boys.

I had actually lost my way into morning prayers for the senior school, and there was a lot of Church-of-England kneeling down and standing again. At the end of prayers I plucked up the courage to ask where I should be. I found myself standing in short trousers before long-trousered Bernard Williams, a praefect who was more than 10 years older than me and later (according to *The Times*) the most brilliant moral philosopher of his time. Williams took pity on my plight and treated me kindly, probably the oldest boy in the school helping the definitely youngest boy in the school. (I would later thank him for this kindness when he was Provost of King's College, Cambridge.) I was then taken to Hainault House and joined boys of my own age and sat at the empty desk.

That first break I bought a sticky bun with chocolate on top from the tuck shop for 2d. A boy came and pleaded "Treat-o" (i.e. "Can I have a bite of your bun?") and I had not the faintest idea what he meant. Boys were playing conkers and marbles, strange games with their own language rooted in the Napoleonic wars which I had not encountered before. I got through the hurly-burly of lunch-time and in the afternoon we had an art lesson in which our teacher asked who had the glue. At Oaklands we had been taught to be helpful to teachers. We always helped Mabel Reid during her Nature walks. I pointed to the desk where the glue was. The teacher said to the boy sitting at the desk, "You must return it when you've finished with it," and that was the end of the matter. But after school I learned that my new school believed in concealing things from teachers. "You're a sneak," an older boy said to me as I put my satchel on my back and prepared to leave. Being the youngest boy in the school I had been picked on by the class bully, who was using the whereabouts of the glue for his own sadistic ends. As I edged towards the door he said, "You're a sneak. Come on everybody, chase the sneak." I ran for it, and they ran after me calling, "Sneak, sneak." I ran past the church and down the hill, and only paused when I no longer heard their footsteps. Then I walked to the station and caught a steam train.

My paradisal close relationship with Nature had been shattered. I had suffered the mob torment Shelley encountered at Eton, which his classmates named "Shelley-baits". I had been chased into solitude and felt an outsider. Any illusions I had about my new school were now in smithereens. Its rough-and-tumble vied with Tom Brown's schooldays at Rugby school. I realised that no more would pupils and staff have Nature walks and look on each other as friends. Those cosy days had gone, now pupils and staff were at war. I soon learned that half the class cribbed and cheated, copying each other's homework first thing in the morning and copying each other's class work behind the teacher's back during lessons. There was a deep conflict between the boys and the Establishment, which handed out a hundred lines, imposed detentions or in extreme cases wielded the cane.

My unpropitious start made me resolve to do well in the lessons and beat the lot of them. I did not trust any of them. I applied myself to my work and did everything asked of me. To give them their due they soon forgot about the glue. I settled in and my report for the Easter term 1948 showed that although I was still the youngest boy in the Junior School I came first in all subjects except French, in which I came third.[6] I was first in English, Maths, History, Scripture and Geography. Nature Study/Science was ungraded, but in the summer term I came first in that too,[7] and was awarded the form prize for the year. Doing all the homework and competing for marks locked me into a new social structure and took me further away from Nature.

But there was sadness during this year. In March 1948 my little sister Janet died from the incurable hole in her heart. We had always tiptoed past her pram in the hall because if she woke she might cry for two hours from the pain round her heart. It was a merciful release but another blow to my parents.

I was caught up in more social activity that summer. My mother was soon pregnant again, and in early September I spent a week away from my parents with my aunt Argie at the Lawns Hotel, Hove. I remember working the lift and I can recall a gong sounding for meal times. We visited Broadley Brothers, Hove during our stay, and my uncle George Broadley II drove us to the Devil's Dyke. (On another occasion my mother took me to visit my grandmother in East Grinstead, and I was taken to Broadley Brothers, East Grinstead, and was bought a raincoat from the family shop.)

Grange Court
In September 1948 my class moved down to the 17th- or early-18th-century Grange Court, which had opened as a war memorial to the 50 Old Chigwellians who had fallen in two world wars. To reach it, we walked down the road from the main school. It had a wide central passage and staircase, at the foot of which Arnold Fellows (A.F.) had his study. We had assembly in this passage, off which was my classroom. Discipline was strict and in some assemblies A.F. called a boy out for poor work, walking with his hands in his pockets or not wearing a cap and marched him into his study. Through the open door we could hear the crack of the cane and the boy would walk back pale and near to tears. A.F. had a kind side. He taught us English parsing with a pile of sixpences on his desk, and if a boy answered a question correctly he would flick a sixpence. If the boy caught it he could keep it.

Through such punitive examples and rewards an invisible disciplinary structure hung above us in the air. It seemed as real as the walls and roof of Grange Court and came between us and Nature. When we played 'king-he' outside at break (a game in which boys avoided having a tennis-ball thrown at them to turn them into 'hes') the invisible structure of the game took all our attention and there was little awareness left of the grass, the trees and the cycle of the seasons. We were in Nature, but our awareness was elsewhere.

In February 1949 my little brother Jonathan was born. Between February and May 1949 my father bought Journey's End from the Maitland family for £600, and he immediately had builders in to improve the accommodation for a growing family.

In the summer of 1949 A.F. began teaching us Latin, whose grammar further removed us from Nature, and the organisational and social activity of cricket. In the nets he would remove a penknife from his trouser pocket, stick the blade into the pitch on a good length and bowl off breaks, and as often as not knock the handle of the penknife back. In our practice games if a boy played a bad shot A.F. would take his bat from him, bend him over and whack him with the bat. I played in my first match at Forest School for the Under-12, although just

Extract from Chigwell School photograph, showing Nicholas (front row, centre), 1949

ten. One of our team was absent, and I was picked to replace him and batted at number 11. A.F. had demonstrated the cross-batted pull shot, swivelling with bent knees. Receiving a short ball, I did what A.F. had taught us and scored 4 to the short boundary at square leg, where A.F. was umpiring. He called, "Good shot," the only time I ever heard an umpire intervene loudly in a partisan way during a cricket match. Practising cricket, repetitively playing strokes to improve my skills, now began to fill my spare time.

Speech Day: Bernard Howard
At Speech Day I collected the form prize I had won the previous year. I received it from Henry Willink,[8] Minister of Health in the UK's wartime Coalition Government and then Master of Magdalene College, Cambridge. (The vote of thanks at the end was made by Bernard Howard, owner of Fir Bank until 1929, the house that was renamed Oaklands in 1944. He looked at me as I shook Willink's hand in short trousers, unaware that I would one day own the house he had owned.)[9]

The book (rebound in ribbed binding by the school) was on butterflies. By choosing this book I was asserting and reaffirming Nature amid the class's anti-teacher spirit which was illustrated that morning when, in the Chigwell parish church, we knelt in prayer in our suits and one of my class-mates produced marbles and flicked two of them under the pew before him, and as they rolled had to crawl under the pew to retrieve them. (In later life I would employ his wife.) I kept my interest in Nature alive by entering a poetry recital prize in the Swallow Room. I stood under the dome and recited a poem, Clare's 'The Yellowhammer'. I believe I won.

Dentist: Howard Carter's brother
Now I began to be interested in archaeology. My imagination was stirred by ancient Egypt. My dentist, who had a surgery in Loughton's High Road, Dr Carter, was the brother of the Egyptian archaeologist Howard Carter (who features later in my story). Dr Carter examined my teeth and found some

drilling to do. To relax me he told me how his brother found Tutankhamen's tomb and how he entered a room and saw "wonderful things". He interrupted his story to drill my tooth, keeping me in suspense. Then he told me about the curse: "To whomsoever shall disturb these remains, death shall come on wingèd wings". He used ancient Egypt as a form of pain control. (It must have been he who gassed me to extract a tooth, and I can still remember coming round with the room spinning again and again. I do not recall that he told me about Osiris in the Underworld on that occasion.) I now began reading about Egypt, which took me further away from Nature and my natural surroundings.

Folkestone

In the spring of 1950 my brother Robert and I were packed off to stay with our cousin Richard in Folkestone while my parents concentrated on our new brother, Jonathan. Organisation and arrangements were now imposed on Nature. Every morning we ran round Kingsnorth Gardens and played cricket and football there. We then went back and played cricket in the garden, sometimes hitting the ball into a jungle of runner beans. Each day we took the bus to the sandy beach and wandered along the promenade above concrete arches down on the beach.

We passed entertainers, and it was there that I discovered Rex D'Alston, a 'prophet' with long hair who sat and poked smouldering potash and theatrically pronounced on what he saw, proclaiming in a loud, declamatory voice: "God – is – dead." My aunt Flo tried to move us on for his challenging assertion conflicted with what Mr Baker had preached in the church she took us to. But I was fascinated and hung back and read on a propped-up board press cuttings of how he had cycled round Folkestone blindfolded and found a watch that had been hidden by the mayor. He had strange powers and he saw my interest and addressed me, raking his potash, "Do you hear? God – is – dead." Looking back, I have a strange feeling that he was a kind of John the Baptist who was preparing the way for something I would do that would remedy the contemporary perception of the death of God.

We were taken to visit my aunt Lucy who had purloined our inheritance, above the Hove Broadley Brothers' shop. We also visited my grandmother in East Grinstead and were taken to visit her sister, Aunt Maude, who wore her hair in a cottage-loaf bun. She lived at Lenthorne, 29 Crescent Road, East Grinstead, with her companion, the bespectacled Miss Walter, and a smelly dog, Cheekah, that yapped at us and snapped at our ankles. Aunt Maude had not been lucky in love; her husband, John Dunstan, had died of cancer in 1912, aged 32, and her cousin Lewis Burton had fallen in love with her. He was drowned off Australia, and it was said that he had been eaten by a shark. Her house was like a Victorian junk shop and she had a stuffed crocodile and an armadillo shell. Aunt Maude said that my brother and I could have these one day, but a few years later her mind went and she invited the baker in to help himself to whatever he wanted and he left with my choice, the crocodile. My brother did receive the armadillo, which has a firm, rounded shell.

In the summer we stayed with my cousin again. Channel swimmers swam up and down the open-air swimming-pool in goggles, and we watched them train. They stayed in the guest-houses in Marine Crescent and we stopped them for autographs as they came and went: their enormous trainer Sam Rocket, and Mari Hassan Hamad, who I believe won the race from Dover to Cap Gris-Nez and back. Covered in grease, they waded ashore in France and then turned round and swam back through the night with only a small boat to keep them company. Monitoring the movements of the Channel swimmers further removed me from Nature for my attention was more on the swimmers' organisation of their training than on the waves and the boiling surf. This was symptomatic of the phase I was in, which was more engaged with social habits and practices than with Nature.

Cricket played an important part in our lives. Back in Essex my brother and I played cricket in the garden, bowling from an upturned pail near the back door at a wicket (the swing-seat turned on end) that stood before the shed doors (the wicketkeeper). The flower-beds were fielders and hitting the ball onto any flower-bed without bouncing first was out caught. We kept a running tally of the ever-changing score, and again the organisational aspect of our games partially blinded us to Nature and the changing of the seasons. At the weekends we walked to watch cricket at Loughton cricket field or on a field with a small wooden grandstand the other side of the station subway.

We listened to Test matches on the radio, and in my first experience of black-and-white television that June (while delivering a message to a master who lived next to the school) I glimpsed G.H.G. Doggart batting in a white cap for England against the West Indies.

Chigwell: 17th-century Big School

In September 1950 I moved from Grange Court to Big School, and had some lessons in Big School One, which was in the original part of the 1629 school and had been William Penn's classroom. It had been the Latin School in a time when Chigwell School included both Latin and English wings. The classroom still had a 17th-century feel about it, and sitting beneath the bust of the school's founder, Archbishop Harsnett, in Latin classes I came to love the 17th-century ambience, which stayed with me and coloured my interest in the Metaphysical poets. Latin proses and unseen translations further turned my awareness away from the outside world and into books.

I continued to attend the Methodist church every Sunday, and it too turned my mind to accurate work. In October I copied out Bunyan's 17th-century hymn, "He who would valiant be" (which had been sung at my parents' wedding), in my immaculate, babyish hand for a Methodist handwriting competition, and won first prize.

Cricket captain

The next spring, 1951, I was in the London Hospital under an ear-nose-and-throat consultant, Charles Keogh, and had my sinuses washed out. In hospital I submitted to a new routine of timings that controlled my attention. That summer there were more social activities as I did my school work and played cricket.

I must have shown leadership skills and appeared responsible for I was now captain of the Under-12s at cricket,[10] and between 1951 and 1955 I was captain of the Under-12, Under-13½, Under-15 and Under-16 cricket teams[11] and also football teams. My new responsibility brought with it a new system that controlled my awareness. I had a say in who was in the team, greeted the opposing captain, tossed the coin and made the decision as to whether to bat or field at cricket and whether to choose end or kick-off at football. Our enthusiasm for football had been enhanced by the arrival at Chigwell of John Dutchman as new Geography master. He played football for the amateur team Pegasus (an ex-Oxbridge team) which had just reached the 1951 Amateur Cup Final at Wembley (where my father had taken us to watch the Amateur Cup Final of 1947). He gave us free tickets to watch. There was a crowd of 100,000, and we cheered him on. Pegasus won 2–1, the first goal coming from a cross by Dutchman and a diving header.[12]

Sport – cricket, football and cross-country running – took place against a backdrop of Nature, but my captain's calculations involving the weather, assessment of the pitch, batting order, who to bowl, field placing, half-time team-talk, marking, strategy, how to win and so on effectively shut Nature out. We were close to the grass when we dived to stop a ball at cricket or when we performed a sliding tackle at football or pounded along the edges of ploughed fields in cross-country, but we were too involved in the social, human complexities of the sport to appreciate our natural surroundings and observe keenly with an undistracted eye. During my four years of being a captain my soul lay unawakened as I developed my rational, social ego through my ball skills, my running and my homework.

During those four years I took our team to play on the grounds of well-known independent schools, including Alleyn's School. The Head of Alleyn's in my time (from 1952 onwards) was Francis Cammaerts, the wartime controller of the British spy Christine Granville, who dramatically rescued him and two other men shortly before they were due to be executed in France. Looking back I find it haunting that the ex-wartime Special Operations Executive spy might have stood on the boundary and watched me bat as if a pointer to my future direction. For in a sense I would follow his path and then become a Head.

Festival of Britain
In July 1951 I saw Princess Elizabeth arrive to open a camping and sports area at Grange Farm, Chigwell School's labour. I stood very near the future Queen as she was greeted outside Grange Farm.

Focusing on the future was another way of removing us from the present. In the summer of 1951 we had our holiday at Westcliff and then went to the Festival of Britain: Britain showcasing itself to the world after a time of post-war austerity. Watching black-and-white film of the Festival now, I think how dreary it all looked but at the time it was exciting and futuristic. We went to the Dome of Discovery and the seemingly unsupported Skylon and marvelled at the Royal Festival Hall, and sensed that Britain had a wonderful future. I entered a church essay competition, 'A visit to London in AD2000', and recorded that I went to Lord's to see "England v. the Rest of the United States of Europe". I had no doubt at the age of 12 that Churchill's Zurich speech of 1946 would result in a United States of Europe.

Churchill comes to Loughton in 1951
I was aware of politics now, and I came face to face with Churchill that October. Churchill came to Loughton to speak in the hall of the Loughton High School for Girls (now Roding Valley High School) during the 1951 general election. The school was a short walk from Journey's End, and I stood on the top step. His car arrived, he stepped out, bent over his stick in a black coat with a black hat. I stopped him as he was about to enter the building and held out my autograph album, and he beamed at me and signed 'W. Churchill'. That contact reinforced the impression he made on me just before Potsdam and cumulatively shaped an image of him that I would draw on in *The Warlords* and *Overlord*.

Capt. W.E. Johns
I now began reading heavily, which further removed me from my surroundings. In January 1952 we went to the Schoolboys' Exhibition at Olympia. I bought a Letts' Schoolboys' Diary and made daily entries (that, it has to be said, were pretty pedestrian) throughout 1952. We went again in 1953 and I bought another Schoolboys' Diary and wrote entries during the first two-thirds of 1953, recording events such as homework, my cleaning of

corps equipment, cricket results and the books I was reading. There was always a children's author at the Schoolboys' Exhibition: in 1952 the author was Capt. W.E. Johns, author of the Biggles books, and in January 1953 I would meet both Anthony Buckeridge and Enid Blyton.

I had a short chat with Johns and he signed my autograph album "Best wishes, W.E. Johns". I did not then know that he had personally turned down T.E. Lawrence when Lawrence applied to join the RAF under the name of Shaw on 30 August 1922. He had checked with Somerset House and found that there was no record of Shaw's birth. Later he was forced to accept him, and Lawrence admitted his identity to him while waiting for a train to Uxbridge.[13] (Lawrence later became one of my heroes: he was a British intelligence agent who risked his life for his country, led a revolt against the Ottoman Empire and asked profound questions about the meaning of life.)

I had read a number of the Biggles books already but I now borrowed more. I borrowed them one at a time from the shelves of the penny library in the High Road, Loughton, which was a couple of doors down from Lopping Hall. The shelves were on wheels and were often parked on the pavement. On one occasion I announced to the family that I had borrowed *Biggles, Secret Agent*. At the time I did not know the word 'agent' and I pronounced it 'aggent' (with a 'g' rather than a 'j'). My reading took me further away from Nature. It created an imaginary world of human activity and further separated me from the immediacy of my surroundings.

Death of the King

Now State events took our minds away from Nature. In February 1952 King George VI died. I remember hearing news of the King's death in Chigwell School's lobby, an old part of the school where we helped ourselves to one of the third-of-a-pint bottles of free milk that were in a crate there. (Gulping the milk always made my eyes ache for a while.) Under an old etching of William Penn among the American Indians in what became Pennsylvania, the Rev. Whitford, a Scripture master, excitedly told a group of milk-drinkers about the lying-in-state and funeral, and the coming coronation. He said that after Princess Elizabeth acceded to the throne as Elizabeth II there might be a new Elizabethan Age. He had sadistically smacked us on the back of our thighs when we did not play football hard enough in the snow and he had demonstrated God's care by whacking anyone who crossed him with a Bunsen-burner tube in the science lab, but now he was our friend, exploring the implications of the coming Age.

The next month, in March 1952, my sister Frances was born. She was a twin but her brother died. This was my fourth brother or sister to have died that I knew about, but years later my mother said she had lost *six* children. There was a miscarriage between me and my brother Robert, in 1941, but I do not know when the sixth child died. Perhaps it was before I was born. My mother remained religious and accepted the deaths as God's will. My father never went to church now. He had become more sombre. He gardened on Sundays, and more than once he came in and said, "I've been looking at the worms, trying to understand how life works."

After church every Sunday my brother and I visited my grandmother, who had moved from East Grinstead to 20 Brook Road, Loughton, opposite what was then the public library. She lived there with my aunt Argie and we sat in huge armchairs and told them about our week. Sometimes they had their neighbours in and I was invited to join them for a game of pit: a card game devised by the psychic Edgar Cayce (who features later), first sold in 1904 and inspired by the US Corn Exchange. It recreated outcry bidding for commodities (such as wheat, barley and corn), and my grandmother saw its competitive spirit as transmitting her husband's business approach to her grandchildren.

Butterflies
My contact with Nature now turned scientific as I was encouraged to develop the eye of a lepidopterist. For my birthday in May 1952 my parents gave me a butterfly net, which I took to the Stubbles. I caught azure blues, peacocks, small tortoiseshells and red admirals, and tipped them into a jar with leaves on which they could feed. Its lid was punctured with breathing-holes. They also gave me a killing-jar without holes in the lid, with ammonia soaked in cotton wool, and a tin of relaxing fluid to make it easier to mount them when they were dead. I preferred to keep my captured butterflies alive and study them and then release them rather than kill them so cruelly.

Nature and school: writing and classics
School was still my main reality. My birthday had fallen on a half-day holiday for Ascension Day and I went from school with three classmates and my brother to watch a cricket match, Essex v Surrey, in which Doug Insole (who features later) scored 124.

Soon afterwards an incident took place that I still vividly recall. In those pre-health-and-safety days, boys were expected to help get a classroom ready for the next lesson, another system that shackled our minds. Big School was divided into two classrooms by a partition, and when the partition had to be drawn across to make two rooms, a couple of boys were told to tug. On 16 June 1952 the folded-back partition would not budge. Requested by our Latin master, Godfrey Stott, I put my fingers in and tugged, and it suddenly straightened, too quickly for me to withdraw my fingers. As the folded doors turned into a wall my right index finger was squashed in the join with a sickening crack. When the worried master had opened the doors my finger was numb and my nail had been torn from the bottom skin and was cocked up. I was taken to a doctor in the school shooting-brake. He pierced the nail with a needle and declared that the finger was not broken. But ever since then that finger has not been straight, and I believe it *was* broken. Today the finger would be X-rayed, but in those days a doctor gave an opinion and after that we 'got on with it'. I believe I was still wearing a finger-stall during our annual holiday at the Garston Hotel, Paignton in Devon.

Back at school for the autumn term, life was an endless round of lessons, matches, homework and sorting stamps, social activities I recorded daily in my Schoolboys' Diary. We had no television (which was not yet widespread) and we spent most evenings reading. I loved reading and my main social activity each week was to choose a book for bedtime reading at the public library opposite my grandmother's house. On Sundays we listened to a classic serialised on the radio such as *Oliver Twist* or *The Forsyte Saga*. Listening to literature on the radio stimulated my imagination and I visualised Bill Sikes clubbing Nancy to death in my mind's eye more hauntingly when I heard it on the radio than when I later watched it on television.

I collect Roman and Greek coins

I was now more absorbed in the past than aware in the present. I was extremely interested in the Romans, who were tantalisingly elusive as I read about them in Latin. I read Lloyd Douglas's *The Robe*. Electrification made it possible for us to travel to London by tube on our own during the holidays, and somehow I discovered B.A. Seaby's, a coin dealers then in Audley House, 11 Margaret Street behind Oxford Street. Several times I climbed the stairs and spent an afternoon rummaging in the reject boxes, which contained coins of Roman emperors and Greek city-states with minor blemishes for 6d, a few of which I could afford out of my saved-up pocket money each time I went. I picked out the coins I thought I would have and gave them to old Mr Seaby, a grey-haired man of about 75 who peered at each coin through his jeweller's eye *loupe* (the magnifying glass that fits in the eye socket) and gutturally identified the emperor: "Ow-goo-stus" (Augustus), or "Tee-bare-ius" (Tiberius). I went back regularly and for two years spent much of my pocket money in building up a collection of all Roman emperors and Greek city-states, which I still have. I loved to handle portraits of Julius Caesar, especially when I was reading (and making my own translation[14] of) Tacitus's *Caesar at Alexandria* in Big School One, but coins of Caesar were never rejects and it was only in adult life that I could afford two or three silver coins with his face on them. I fell in love with, and bought for 10/6d., a female goddess's head on a silver drachma from Chalcis

Euboea, which looked perfect.

Soon I knew more about the empires of 1st-century-AD Rome and 5th-century-BC Athens than I did about the 20th-century British Empire. The portraits on the coins were the closest I could get to how the Roman historical figures looked, and it gave me pleasure to handle images of their faces as I delved into the classical period. Ancient coins have an individual beauty like poems, and my collection of coins was to me then what a collection of my poems is to me now.

Love for literature: Julius Caesar, very early writing

That winter was foggy and sulphurous yellow smog nuzzled against the old gas lamps near Loughton station, where I walked every Saturday late afternoon to buy my father a newspaper, *The Evening Standard*, so he could read the football reports. I can hear the news-vendor crying in the smog "*Star, News* or *Standard*, all the latest results" and "Paper Late".

My health was not robust, and towards the end of March I was in bed for ten days with flu, which turned into pharyngitis. I returned to school just in time to act in *Julius Caesar*. I was a messenger, and had to rush up some steps to the stage and deliver four lines. (I think of Eliot's 'The Love Song of J. Alfred Prufrock': "No! I am not Prince Hamlet, nor was meant to be;/Am an attendant lord.") I was also in the crowd as one of the mob. We were roused by Antony's speech and attacked Cinna the poet.

I had learned chunks of *Julius Caesar* during the rehearsals and I loved literature. We had read Coleridge's 'The Ancient Mariner' in class and I was drunk with the language. On Sunday mornings I stayed in bed and read a hundred pages of a book before going downstairs to my mother's hot sausage pie with marmite. Before Christmas I had been listening to a series on the radio, *The Lost Planet*, and before I was ill I had begun writing a story about my own idea of a lost planet. I abandoned it after a couple of weeks, but this story and my daily diary entry were the first signs that I might one day write books.

In the Easter holidays of 1953, when I was still 13, I began to write a novel. It came out of the story and was influenced by the radio programme *Journey into Space*. It was about a journey to the moon and later to a planet called Holacanthus and was a cross between H.G. Wells' *The First Men in the Moon* and *Gulliver's Travels*. It had a realistic beginning and I researched details about the universe in the local library, where Miss Attwood, who lived next door to Journey's End, worked. She helped me find the right books. I carried this novel on in the summer holidays.

In Normandy: Le Home-sur-la-Mer, D-Day beaches

Now French became another discipline that removed me from my surroundings. In September I went to France after our annual holiday at Bembridge in the Isle of Wight. My mother had had a succession of *au pairs* to help with the children. I stayed in Paris with the family of her first *au pair*, Michèle Maurel, for a couple of days and remember sipping an ice-cold Coca Cola late at night in the dark Champs-Élysées. Then we went to their holiday home in the Calvados district of Normandy for a week. It was at Le Home-sur-la-Mer, near Cabourg and not far from the D-Day beaches. The house was almost on the beach, which was generally deserted, especially in the evenings, and there was half a mile of sand at low tide. It formed part of D-Day's Sword beach. It was hot, and our six-course suppers, when ten of us sat round a table, always began with the carrying-in of an enormous tureen. On two evenings this was filled with a thick mush which they told me was sorrel, a reddish wild plant. When cooked, it looked like beans and I hated its taste but had to eat it. I borrowed a bicycle and cycled around the surrounding countryside and went shrimping. I spoke French all the time and became a Francophile. I particularly relished the torpor after lunch when the family sat in deck-chairs and refused to do anything until their lunch had been satisfactorily digested.

Michèle's father drove me to the port of Ouistreham, and showed me Sword beach, where the British had landed and fought their way to Pegasus Bridge, and Caen, so that I could see where Montgomery was bogged down after D-Day. It was just over nine years after D-Day but many of the beaches still had war defences on them, and in places the clearing-up still remained to be done. I absorbed the atmosphere of D-Day, which was to come out in *Overlord*.

I meet Montgomery
This served me well when on 18 October 1953 Field Marshal Montgomery visited Chigwell School and I was chosen to meet him after chapel. The previous week Godfrey Stott had set us a prose about Caesar to turn into Latin, and we were told to write 'Caesar' as 'Montegomerius'. A dozen of us found Montgomery sitting on a garden bench with his back to the chapel, wearing mufti and looking across Top Field. I told him I had just been to the D-Day beaches and he looked at me and nodded. Then we all accompanied him to New Hall and he stood with his back to the stage, on our level, and gave us an inspirational talk. A thin, dartingly alive man with a pointed nose, he told us that we were the nation's future leaders, and that as a commander of two million men in the last war he believed it was a commander's first duty to gain the trust and confidence of his men and demand integrity, courage and enthusiasm. "If you can win their hearts," he said, "then there is nothing you cannot do." He told us the story of El Alamein and said, "And I went through the Germans at El Alamein," and he

paused for effect and made a sawing movement with his right hand, "like a knife going through butter." (Many years later I drew on my memory of this encounter in *The Warlords* and *Overlord*.)

Oaklands School: dance
Now another system was imposed on me: I was taught to dance. My mother had fixed up for me to go to the house of an instructress, and I was taught to waltz, quickstep, foxtrot, and samba in the course of several weeks. An arrangement was then made for me to attend a dance to try out my new skills. It was held at Oaklands School in the assembly hall. There was a live band on the low stage and a Master of Ceremonies. The boys were in black tie and the girls – a number of whom were ex-Oaklanders – sat on chairs all round the walls. I politely danced with some of my former classmates until about 9.30 p.m., and then suddenly had an overpowering urge to escape the charade of 'wallflowers' and be alone. It was the same feeling I had had when I was a soldier on the stage and walked off. I quietly slipped out and walked home.

My mother was shocked at my early arrival: "Why are you so early? Go back. You must go back." And so, as when I was a soldier, I was pushed back 'on stage'. I slipped back into Oaklands without comment and stayed to the end but I did not enjoy the evening. I had suffered from adolescent shyness and was not completely sure what to say.

I now grasped that my parents had my life planned out. My father had sometimes said, "One day you will be a lawyer, and you'll have your own solicitor's office and can become an MP." To this scenario could now be added, 'And you will marry an ex-Oaklands girl and live happily ever after with social standing.' I was supposed to be cementing relationships with my ex-classmates, not slipping away from them to be on my own.

Ours was a very provincial life, and not much happened in the evenings. Occasionally there was an outing to London. There was a Methodist church Fellowship visit to *The Boy Friend* at the Victorian Wyndhams theatre, which had a Louis-XVI interior. I sat directly behind the Labour politician Hugh Gaitskell. Our group leader pointed him out and tapped him on his shoulder. Gaitskell turned round, and, believing I had tapped him, asked me if I was enjoying the show. He then signed my programme.

'O' level: letter to Capt. W.E. Johns and his reply
For Christmas my father bought me G.O. Sayles' *The Medieval Foundations of England*, which my History master said I should read. My father saw it as outlining the foundations of our legal system. At the time it seemed very abstract and turgid for a standard work, but although I did not realise it then, it contained my spiritual foundations: the progress of the spiritual life

during the Anglo-Saxon, Norman and medieval times.

I was in my 'O'-level year, and at Christmas I was still writing my novel. I had filled several exercise books and announced to my startled parents that I would be a writer. Having lived through the unemployment of the 1930s, my parents wanted me to pass my exams, study Law and get a secure job with a company like Shell and then consider going into politics. To my parents, writing was on a par with music: to be done as a hobby, not as a living.

Alarmed, my parents persuaded me to write to Capt. W.E. Johns, author of the Biggles books, on the strength of the chat I had had with him at the Schoolboys' Exhibition and ask his advice as to whether I should be writing a novel during my 'O'-level year. On 24 February 1954 Johns wrote back from Park House, Hampton Court: "I think you should get your exams over before you try writing a story. You can't do both at once."[15] I took his advice. But my first juvenilia put me in touch with the universe, and began my thinking about the universe which continues to this day.

Dream of 'O'-level Greek set-books paper

I now became aware of hidden powers that Nature had given us. My 'O' levels loomed. We read Euripides' *Alcestis* in Greek and learned chunks. I was not confident in my translations from this set book and from Thucydides' book 4. During my sleep the night before the Greek set-books exam I dreamt I saw the paper. I woke with the four passages I would have to translate still in my mind and hastily found them in the texts and prepared them before breakfast. When I went into the exam and turned the paper it was as I had seen. All four passages were there.

When I recounted this to my aunt Argie she told me that she had had a similar experience when she took her London Matriculation in 1921. She had dreamt that she had seen the first two or three questions of her History paper, and had discussed them with a friend over breakfast and the questions were just as she had seen. My experience left me with a sense that the mind has powers we have barely begun to understand.

With 'O' levels over, I returned to my writing. We had our annual holiday at Westgate, in a hotel on the front between Margate and Herne Bay. Several days were very wet and the rain lashed in from the sea. I wrote as the rain beat on the roof and lashed the high windows, and I felt at peace as if I had contacted my future self.

Merrow: oneness of the universe

Later my brother and I stayed with my cousin Richard, who had moved from Folkestone to Merrow near Guildford. He now lived at 31 Holford Road near the North Downs. We often ran up to the stretch of the downs that formed a golf course at the end of the road. The first tee overlooked a kind of valley. There was rough down to the bottom and then a sloping fairway up to the green.

It was in the rough under the first tee that I had my first mystical experience and became aware of the unity of the universe. It was really a kind of pantheistic experience. One day was immensely hot. I was alone and collapsed into the rough and lay among wild flowers and sedge under the blue sky and suddenly realised that everything around me was alive. There were azure blues and meadow browns in the rough all round me and time stopped and I had a tremendous sense of the oneness of the universe, which I can recall to this day and have never forgotten.

I believe I saw Nature through my soul that day. I was back engaging with Nature as I had at Oaklands as a boy. Lying in the rough, I was still, I gazed with the eye of an embryonic poet and sensed a reality beyond the everyday mundane things. The universe was a place of great beauty, and it was thrillingly alive, full of crawling, flying things. I was taken back to the time I was surprised by frosty stars in Ollards Grove, Loughton.

That day marked an early stirring – if not an awakening – of something within me, an awareness of physical beauty. The timelessness in the rough had come as a call to be in touch with the underlying harmony of the universe. I knew then very clearly that Nature should be my guide.

Episode 3:

Archaeology and Politics

Years: 1954–1956
Locations: Loughton; Chigwell; Stratford-upon-Avon; Marazion; Chester; Castlemartin; Llandudno

"Never was any desolation more sublime and lovely. The perpendicular wall of ruin is cloven into steep ravines filled up with flowering shrubs, whose thick twisted roots are knotted in the rifts of the stones."
Shelley, letter to Peacock, 23 March 1819; of the Baths of Caracalla in which he wrote *Prometheus Unbound*, part 2

A new episode began with my growing and conflicting interest in archaeology and politics, both of which I now see were necessary to put me on my future path.

Taken from literature to classics: interest in archaeology

I was now in fact extremely interested in literature. My mother arranged for me to go to Stratford-upon-Avon for a few days and stay with a friend of hers, who went to work. I had to stay out all day and, being somewhat shy, welcomed my own company. I visited Shakespeare's birthplace and Anne Hathaway's cottage and spent many hours sitting near the Avon. Those days by the Avon cemented my love of Shakespeare that had begun with *Julius Caesar*. I saw *Othello* at the New Shakespeare Memorial Theatre (since pulled down). I had passed my 'O' levels. I had achieved 89 per cent for English Literature – Shakespeare's *Macbeth* (which I virtually knew by heart) and Chaucer's *Prologue* – and I was hoping to study English Literature at 'A' level. But in June I had collected the form prize for the year, and the Headmaster, Mr Thompson, wanted me for his classical sixth, and my wish to read the poets – which I knew within myself I had to – was overruled.

Wanting me to read Law at university, my father had persuaded me to choose James's *Introduction to English Law* as my prize. He talked of getting me articled to London solicitors. He saw the Latin side of classics as dovetailing with the Law.

The next two years of 'A' level immersed me in Latin, Greek and Ancient History, which I loved. I had a very good classical education. We sat in the library (then the Swallow Room) at a long table on chairs with mitres on their backs, seated on frayed blue cushions. The scrapes each time we moved our chairs echoed up into the dome.

Swallow Room Library, 1956, with Nicholas second from right

We read a lot of Plato, and thought about his invisible reality or being, *to on*, which made we want to be a philosopher. I can trace my philosophical works back to this time. We sometimes had classes in the room adjoining the Tuck Shop, over the door of which Greek lettering proclaimed *phrontisterion*, 'thinking-shop', and more Greek lettering exhorted *meden agan*, 'nothing too much', a Delphic maxim sometimes attributed to Solon and seen by Aristotle, who developed it into his doctrine of the mean. (The Greek lettering has since been removed.) In the library we read some of the *New Testament* in Greek. We read the epic poets Homer and Virgil, and I can trace my two epic poems back to this time. We read the poetic dramatists Aeschylus, Sophocles (*Oedipus Tyrannus*) and Euripides. The poets Ovid, Horace and Catullus I had already encountered, and the materialist philosophers Democritus and Lucretius. I can trace my verse plays and poems back to these influences. We read Tacitus and Thucydides, two wonderful historians who made we want to be a historian, and we covered the history of Greece to just after the Peloponnesian war and the history of Rome to the end of the Republic. I can trace my books on world history back to this time. In my mind I was already on my way to working within, perhaps writing within, literature, philosophy and history.

Archaeology: Greek, Roman, Egyptian
I had begun thinking about military and political systems, reactionaries and revolutionaries, the causes of the wars and the conflicts between Rome and Carthage, Athens and Sparta. I related these conflicts to the First and Second World Wars and to the British Empire under Churchill (who was Prime Minister until April 1955), and I can trace my growing political awareness back to this Churchillian time. Soon I had gone back into prehistory and was making my own maps of sites in Minoan Crete. We were all taken to hear a live lecture in London by Michael Ventris on the Minoan script, Linear B. I read the Greek myths and spent weekends compiling charts of all the Greek gods and of the Roman emperors, and the idea took hold that I should become an archaeologist and write about ancient civilizations. This work prepared me for my study of 25 civilizations.

For pleasure I read Robert Graves' *I, Claudius* and *Claudius the God*. Standing in the Chigwell dining-hall I described my enjoyment of these two books to my neighbour as we waited for grace before sitting down. The glass tumblers for our water were by our laid places, and one suddenly exploded, disintegrating into tiny pieces. A boy opposite me said very excitedly to me, "It was your voice that did that. Voices can penetrate glass if they resonate in the right way." I now became half-aware that I possessed strange powers, but I attributed the shattering of the glass to the passion in my voice as I warmed to my Roman theme.

My interest in archaeology soon included ancient Egypt. An eccentric Chigwell Latin-and-Greek master, George Harvey ("Spider") Webb lived in a caravan in the school grounds. He taught us to carry a book with us wherever we went: "You can read all Latin and Greek literature in the original on the tops of buses." We thought he had already done this as he never prepared his lessons and heard our prepared translation unseen but always knew the meanings of the most difficult words. He had married a millionairess ice dancer and had got through her £2 million fortune. The last vestiges disappeared when he bought a boat owned by George Dawson at auction and sent a sixth-former to bid while he attended a staff meeting. The sixth-former bought the wrong boat. After that he lived on his own in the caravan.

Tutankhamen

He kept the book-loft, and, rooting round for classical texts, I came across a glass case of Egyptian figurines. I said, "Sir, do you want these?"

"No," he said, "they have Tutankhamen's curse on them. They came from Tutankhamen's tomb. When I was in Egypt in 1922 I took them from Howard Carter when he wasn't looking. They were lying on the sand." I recalled how Howard Carter's dentist brother had told me stories about Tutankhamen. "They have brought me nothing but ill luck. If you are not superstitious you can have them." I said, "Oh, thank you sir," and, holding the glass case carefully, ran down the stairs and across the school to the cycle-shed and put it in my saddle-bag and later cycled carefully home.

What I had was a perfect wooden *shabti* (or *shawabti*) of Tutankhamen, two wooden effigies of gods (one of Horus), many small figures of gods with animal heads and a figure of Osiris. Some years later I took the effigy of Tutankhamen to the British Museum and the expert there pronounced it genuine but said the crucial gold lettering had rubbed off the black bitumen at the back. Now I made lists of all the Egyptian Pharaohs and reflected on the symmetry of my listening to Dr Carter's stories in the dentist's chair and being given his brother's Egyptian figurines in the book-loft.

Cricket and Cornish megaliths

At the end of the war my father had taken me to Loughton cricket field to sit on a wooden seat (a couple of planks on two short uprights) and watch cricket. On one occasion I had returned with more than forty gnat bites. I now found I was playing there. I had joined Buckhurst Hill Cricket Club in June 1955, having been proposed by a neighbour and seconded by Alan Lavers, the ex-Essex cricketer who was captain of the 1st XI. Soon afterwards I was invited to play for Alan Lavers' XI against Loughton on the Thursday of Loughton's cricket week.

There was a huge crowd, with people sitting five deep all round the ground as happened on a summer Saturday in those pre-television days. Loughton batted first on a sweltering day and made over 200. We went in just before tea and almost immediately we were 4 for 2. Batting at no. 4, I faced a fast bowler who charged in down the slope from the Trap's-Hill end. I hit him for a boundary, doubling our score, and there was applause all round the ground. He charged in again, the ball whistled towards me, and trying to deflect it to leg I spooned a 'leading-edge' catch which he took, diving, to thunderous applause. I had made my debut as a club cricketer and it had been a natural progression from playing cricket at Chigwell to playing on a wider stage.

My adolescent shyness had grown into a pre-poetic sensitivity, and I was now most at my ease when I lived in the past. In the summer of 1955 my parents drove via Stonehenge to Exeter, where we stayed at the Great Western Hotel, and then had our annual holiday near St Michael's Mount. We stayed at a house in Marazion across the road from the sea: Trevarthian (since turned into flats). My brother and I slept in a large book-lined room that opened onto the veranda and looked onto a lawn with small palm trees. For my bedtime reading I found a book on Marshal Voroshilov and the Communist Revolution. This carried forward my interest in modern Russian history, and in politics. I can trace my later opposition to the Soviet Union back to this time.

I dived into Cornwall's past. I hired a bicycle and pedalled off into the narrow Cornish lanes and found a megalithic chamber tomb in a deserted field. I parked my bike, climbed a stile over a stone wall, found the entrance and entered the tomb, and suddenly my archaeological interest had extended to British history. I cycled round the Cornish lanes with an ordnance survey map looking for every stone circle or ancient monument, and tried to imagine the people who built them. My parents sat for many hours on the beach opposite St Michael's Mount, and I appeared at lunchtime for our picnic and at supper-time for our evening meal, but otherwise I roamed through Nature and steeped myself in the past. My interest in archaeology had reconnected me to Nature, and I observed the flowers and the birds as I sought out each monument.

That winter I tried to take my younger brother to watch a football match at Fulham, and when the match was cancelled because of fog I took him to the British Museum instead and showed him some of the treasures of past civilizations. I had even managed to turn an outing to football into archaeology.

Greek antiquities: British School of Archaeology at Athens
Soon I was writing letters to the Archaeological Correspondent of *The Times* about Troy, to which he replied at length, and to the British School of Archaeology at Athens, who invited me to hear Sinclair Hood on the excavations at Knossos, with Sir Mortimer Wheeler in the chair. This took place in the rooms of the British Academy in Burlington Gardens, London, and from the audience Leonard Cottrell asked a question and made a comment. I wondered at being so close to the author of *The Bull of Minos*, which I had just read. A fortnight later I heard Hood speak again, with Sir Leonard Woolley in the chair.

Roman dig: sewer at Chester
Through the Council for British Archaeology I subscribed to the Calendar of Excavations, and was invited to join a dig at Chester.

In April 1956 I took a train from Euston to Chester and stayed in a hotel in Chester's Bridge Street. I joined an excavation in its second week to establish whether I should choose the career of an archaeologist. Two narrow trenches had already been dug, and I was given a trowel and a brush and, squatting uncomfortably in the bottom of each trench in turn between bits of Roman brick, probed and prised and gouged and found a lot of Roman tiles and several Roman nails. Soon the other volunteers were asked to start a third trench, and I worked with them while they ran into a belt of glass in a medieval robbers' trench (an area where medieval robbers had destroyed Roman remains and left their own coloured glass). The digging was beginning to pall, and was, quite frankly, becoming boring. I was already disenchanted when Mr Thompson, the curator of the Grosvenor Museum, slipped while clambering between trenches and knocked down half of two Roman buttresses I had dug out. In the course of taking photographs, the experts pronounced that I had been squatting in a *cloaca* – a Roman sewer – and that the tiles and nails had been thrown down there deliberately to get rid of them. The idea that I had been excavating a sewer did not appeal, and I rapidly lost interest in the dig – and in becoming an archaeologist.

The next day I was "unwell" and spent the morning by the River Dee. The weather was glorious, the sun shone, there was a blue sky and the weir frothed while I lay on the bank. In the afternoon I took a bus to Llangollen through beautiful moorland scenery.

Politics: Suez
Now contemporary history – contemporary politics – inspired me.

Interest in USSR: I see Bulganin and Khrushchev
I came home early and, my interest in the USSR having been spurred by the book on Voroshilov that I had found in Cornwall, went straight from Euston to Downing Street in time to see the new leaders of the Soviet Union, Bulganin and Khrushchev, arrive for a meeting with Anthony Eden, who had just taken over from Churchill as Prime Minister. By the time I observed the round, ebullient, balding Khrushchev and the gravely-bearded, white-haired Bulganin outside number 10 I had somehow ceased to consider archaeology as a career and had taken up a new interest in politics.

This new interest was semi-dormant during the summer term as I worked hard revising for my 'A' level exams and coping with a family setback. My brother Robert had been diagnosed as a diabetic in March, on his fourteenth birthday after months of unquenchable thirst when he would run to the kitchen tap and drink two or three glasses of cold water. He had been stabilised and put on insulin, and was learning to cope with a diet that involved weighing portions of food on small scales. The diagnosis was a further blow to my parents, who had already lost six children, and my father in particular became more melancholy and stoical.

I played cricket for the school 1st eleven, under the captaincy of Alan Hurd (who later played for Essex and for the Gentlemen of England). I had some good innings. I remember 42 against the Headmaster's XI on a brilliant day with a blue sky. Alan Lavers, who had seconded me for Buckhurst Hill and picked me to play on Loughton cricket field, was bowling for the Headmaster's XI. Sometimes when I went out to bat I felt I would do badly, and I did. Sometimes I went out to bat knowing I would do well, and I did. This was one of those days I felt confident. I thrashed Lavers to the boundary twice in an over, and after the second four he stood arms akimbo in the middle of the pitch and said, "Nicholas, you can't do that, that was a good-length ball." I said, "I've done it, and watch out or I'll do it again." But my best innings of the season was by far and away the 27 I scored at Bancroft's on the pitch surrounded by school buildings on their dismal, drizzly Visitation Day. Bancroft's had made 109 and I opened the batting for Chigwell, and I could not put a foot wrong. I felt almost godlike. Wickets fell the other end, and we were 65–6 at the close. But each run of my 27 was middled and struck firmly, and I could have had double that score but for brilliant fielding.

Suez crisis and corps camp
My new interest in politics was stoked up by Suez. On 26 July 1956 Col. Nasser seized the Suez canal, and throughout the coming months it seemed that I might be called up to take part in impending military action. I saw the Suez crisis in terms of challenges to the Athenian and Roman Empires, which had to be put down if the empires were to survive. Every day I took cuttings from *The Daily Telegraph*, which my parents took, and assembled my cuttings in a large album. I began a lifelong habit of taking cuttings from the daily newspapers.

It is easy to think of fighting when you are in uniform. Every Monday for two or three years I had taken part in the Combined Cadet Force (CCF), wearing itchy khaki, belt and gaiters and parading with a rifle, and had risen to be a Lance-Corporal. The company commander in those days was a boy who later married Alan Lavers' daughter. I found the CCF fairly boring, and can recall classroom sessions on how to strip a Bren gun, a procedure brilliantly caught by Henry Reed in his poem 'Lessons of the War' which begins "Today we have naming of parts". I was in Signals, and for Cert A (i.e. Certificate A) had to learn about the handset (the Don Mark V).

The annual corps camp that August was at Castlemartin, near Pembroke in South Wales. It was extremely wet, and we walked on, and slept on, duckboards of the kind that had formed paths through the mud in the trenches of the First World War. We were on a hill and the water poured underneath our duckboards as we tried to sleep, oozing up between the wooden slats and soaking our sleeping-bags even though we were under canvas. We walked to the NAAFI tent for our breakfast and collected a packed lunch and then we marched out into the countryside and fought a never-ending war, occasionally ducking along hedgerows, moving in on the 'enemy' and firing blanks, but usually digging ourselves in and making as little contact with the enemy as the British troops made with the Germans in the Great War. At one point we were dug in near an orchard of crab-apple-trees, and we balanced crab-apple windfalls on the end of our rifles and fired them in the air. They rose in a parabola and rained around the officer in charge, who took a dim view of our bored antics.

I soon tired of these war-games, and the first sunny day I reported for my sandwiches and then gave my platoon the slip and went absent without leave. Doubling up, I ran along a hedgerow, my rifle in one hand and my packed lunch in the other. I dodged the crossfire and at the end of a valley ran up a hill and came out on top of cliffs 200 feet high, where I was safe from all sniper fire. I saw the sparkling blue sea beneath me, and Stack Rocks. I tore off my tie and itchy shirt, tugged off my boots and gaiters and my khaki trousers and collapsed in my pants on the springy turf and spent an idyllic day sunbathing, gazing across the Rocks beneath me at the sea and eating my sandwiches. I felt at one with Nature, and it was only towards sundown that I reluctantly put my itchy clothes back on and threaded my way back through the closing stages of the battle to my platoon, in time to march home.

A fortnight later I was devouring the politics of the international crisis. I was back in Wales as our annual holiday was at Llandudno. We stayed at the Hydro Hotel where I heard that I had passed my three 'A' levels and had done sufficiently well to win a County Major Scholarship if I passed the entrance exam into a university (the system then). I still needed classics and archaeology to get into university. My brother and I walked up and down Snowdon, and we all drove to Conway Castle and across the Menai Bridge to Anglesey. Each evening I sat in the hotel's glass veranda and made maps and drawings of Roman ruins. I took extensive cuttings about Suez and stuck them in my album of press clippings. I had a complete record of the Suez crisis, and I used to say, "If I'm going to be drafted, I want to know what I'm dying for." I felt I was treading in my uncle Tom's footsteps, and that just as he had joined the RFC and been killed at 19 so it was possible that

I would be called up to fight against Nasser (who features later) and be killed at 18 or 19.

Back in Essex, my growing interest in politics led me to write to our MP, John Biggs-Davison, Churchill's successor, to ask for a ticket to one of the Suez debates. Biggs-Davison (a free right-wing spirit who was to become known as a Suez rebel) later sent me a ticket to the Strangers' Gallery for the debate on 12 September when Eden unveiled a three-power plan for a Suez Users' Association. It was the beginning of the collusion which led to the Suez debacle, and Nasser swiftly described it as a provocation.

I attend Suez debate: support for Suez invasion
In the House of Commons I was completely absorbed. I can see Eden, tall, grey and elegant, standing at the dispatch-box, speaking (it seemed) for approaching an hour to a packed House, Churchill sitting on the front bench a few places down from him, and Gaitskell (who had spoken to me in the Wyndham's theatre) replying. Later I went into the corridor and found groups of MPs debating heatedly. I interjected in one group and found myself the focal point of attention. I was on the side of the British Empire and Churchill. The Suez Canal had been the Empire's lifeline to India, and had been carved through the desert during 70 years of British rule. I was on the side of the British imperial mission which had had a beneficial, progressive effect in civilising backward peoples. "If you kick someone's ankle often enough they will retaliate," I said. "That's not a fair parallel," snapped a grey-haired Labour MP. And I was attacked and defended by people speaking at the same time, heatedly shouting each other down, and I came away feeling involved, a participant. I had made contact with our leaders. This was what my father's dream envisaged for me: to use my legal qualification to become an MP.

My interest in politics filtered down to a local level. From the Loughton Methodist church pulpit, the minister, a dour, severe northerner, Mr Grant, who had a parting down the middle and spectacles, preached sermon after sermon on the wickedness of the Government's Suez policy. His sermons were more political than religious, and, angry at his one-sidedness which ignored crucial threads in my cuttings and defending the position of Churchill and the Empire, I wrote a letter under a pseudonym, 'Tiberius', saying so and refuting his position (and his ministership), and sent it to the local newspaper, *The West Essex Gazette*. The letter was printed very prominently and my parents were mildly horrified: my father said, "It's always a mistake to rush into print." Poor Mr Grant suffered what almost amounted to a nervous breakdown and left the district soon afterwards.

In early November Anglo-French forces bombarded Suez while Israel marched on Egypt. Soon afterwards the Chigwell School Debating Society had a debate on Suez. The Chigwell School Debating Society was reputed to have had a higher standard than the Oxford Union in the 1940s and early 1950s, when budding Professors like John Boardman and Bernard Williams took part. It still had a high standard, and I proposed the motion for the Government, and John Ezard (later of *The Guardian*) spoke against the Government. The debate was held in the packed library or Swallow Room, and I mustered the most support and won. I cycled home with John Ezard afterwards, listening to his complaints that the result was unfair and that he had won the argument, and sticking to my guns. So began a life-long friendship despite our conflicting political attitudes.

Exiles from Hungarian Uprising
My interest in politics was fired up by the failure of the Hungarian Uprising in November 1956. Soon after it was crushed by Soviet tanks a party of Hungarian refugees was brought to Grange Farm, next to Chigwell School, for temporary accommodation. I remember standing next to a young Hungarian in his twenties dressed in shabby clothes and wearing a cap, who put his hand in his trouser pocket and held out a handful of Hungarian coins for us to have as they were no longer any good to him. I held coins in each hand, and was reminded of how I scooped two handfuls from the mound of coins in Barclays' bank.

Local elections: count
About this time my father got me on the count for local and general elections. The count took place at a polling-station, and I was generally paired with Mr Digweed, the undertaker (who had often featured in my father's lunch-time talk across the nursery table). We sat and made piles of crosses while the candidates toured with rosettes, anxiously comparing the height of our piles.

The Angry Young Men: Colin Wilson
In the autumn of 1956 my parents bought a black-and-white television to make my newly-diabetic brother's lot more pleasant. The family watched it in the dark downstairs while I worked upstairs in my room. I then went downstairs and joined them about 10.30 p.m. Most of the programmes were light entertainment: police files, comedians and the Palladium, but on one occasion all the Angry Young Men, the new phenomenon of the mid-1950s, were interviewed together sitting at a long table and speaking in turn, including Colin Wilson, Stuart Holroyd and Ken Tynan. I was extremely interested in their political stance: in why they were angry at the traditions that had served British society so well through two world wars and a mighty Empire.

Sir Oswald Mosley

A boy at school was interested in the activities of Sir Oswald Mosley and his Union Party which anticipated a United States of Europe. He persuaded several of us to hear him speak in Trafalgar Square. This mini-Hitler's supporters wore black shirts in the 1930s, but now they wore white shirts and beat drums. We stood under Mosley as, standing on a plinth in a smart suit, he addressed us on a policy (support for Europe) which was then revolutionary but now has the support of all the political parties.

Greek archaeology

That winter as I prepared for the entrance exam to Oxford I swung back to archaeology. Every Sunday evening my brother and I sat in the sitting-room on our own and from 7.30, listening to Victor Silvester's ballroom dancing (generally a selection of waltzes and foxtrots), I prepared by way of revision enormous family trees of all the Roman emperors and Greek gods and heroes, on scrolls that could be rolled up, and made several maps and drawings of Mycenae and of Minoan sites in Crete. In the course of these evenings I found a mistake in Robert Graves's *Greek Myths*, a reference to Diomedes at the time of the Trojan War and another reference several hundred years later. I showed it to Webb, the master who had given me the Tutankhamen figurine, in the Chigwell lobby one break, thinking I had misunderstood, and he roared with laughter, confirming that Graves had made Diomedes several hundred years old. "He makes it up," he said, "he's bound to make mistakes." My faith in books was severely shaken by this episode, and after that I was wary, wondering if authors had got things right, and I accepted nothing uncritically.

Entrance exam to Oxford: Sir John Masterman and Corinthian coin

In December 1956 I went up to Oxford and took the entrance exam in classics for a cluster of colleges that included Worcester College with a view to reading Law (at my father's wish). The one consolation was that I might go into politics. We sat papers morning and afternoon for four days, with interviews some evenings. There were 100 of us sitting for 4 places – only 5 per cent of the population went to university in those days – and many were from schools such as Eton and looked very confident and sophisticated, and I thought I stood no chance. We sat in Worcester College's dining-hall, which was dingily lit with high windows, and we wrote in our own shadows in 19th-century conditions. In the general paper the first question asked if epic is less sophisticated than other forms of poetry, and I was able to use the extensive work I had done on Homer. In the essay paper there was a question on the political parties, which I answered with my new-found political enthusiasm.

But it was my archaeology that made an impact. On the Friday evening there was a *viva voce* with the Provost and 15 fellows, the entire teaching fellows of the college, who sat behind a very long table. The Provost was Sir John Masterman, a gaunt, gentle, slow, deliberate, elderly Edwardian with brushed-back hair and 1910 cricket fields in his face, and it was later hard to believe that during the Second World War he was in charge of the double-cross system[1] that turned German agents around and sent them back into Germany with misinformation about D-Day so that Hitler would strengthen his defences round Calais rather than Normandy.

In due course I was asked for my hobbies.

"Collecting Roman and Greek coins," I said.

"Oh," said the Senior Tutor, A.N. Bryan-Brown, who had been a fellow since 1922 and as Public Orator made speeches in Latin on official occasions, a formidable, tall, upright, balding man with wispy grey hair round his ears, "and what do you know about the coins of Corinth?"

Some years earlier I had actually swapped (I seem to recollect) a sweet and a biscuit for a tiny copper Corinthian coin owned by David Hoppit (later Property Correspondent of *The Daily Telegraph*). (Hoppit's recollection is that I gave him a fossil, an ammonite, rather than a sweet and a biscuit. He may have been right: perhaps I swapped my sweet and biscuit for the fossil, and then the fossil for the coin.) I described how "one particular coin" had a winged horse – Pegasos – on the front and a trident on the back.

"It *can't* have," said Bryan-Brown. "There *isn't* such a Corinthian coin."

"Well," I said, "it *has* – I've got it."

That settled the matter, and there was considerable amusement, indeed laughter, among the dons on the other side of the table as I had stood my ground and argued on equal terms with the Senior Tutor in an area in which he was deemed to be expert. I am sure that when they checked through the 100 candidates after we had all gone home, the thing that made me stand out from the other 99 young men was the Corinthian coin. Bryan-Brown commented in writing to my Headmaster that my Latin prose had shown "patches of purple", a reference to the purple robe worn by a Roman Emperor. His suggestion that my prose had patches that could have been written by a Roman Emperor was praise indeed.

I have often wondered if there was something Providential about Hoppit's placing in my hand that coin which turned out to be an entrance token to Oxford.

Episode 4:

Literature and Law

Years: 1956–1959
Locations: Loughton; London; Oxford; Italy; Sicily; Greece
Works: *A Well of Truth*

"The friends that have it I do wrong
Whenever I remake a song,
Should know what issue is at stake:
It is myself that I remake."
W.B. Yeats, *Collected Works*, p.551 (1908)

I now came to a fork in my path and had to choose between Literature and Law. This new episode presented a stark choice between two conflicting directions.

Literature: poetry and Italy
Having heard to my astonishment that I had got into Oxford, but would have to wait a year and a half before going up even though I would be exempted from National Service, my father was anxious that I should commence legal articles, and it was arranged that I would leave school at Easter. I was pleased at the prospect of leaving school. I did not need to improve in classics, and during the spring term of 1957 I felt unmotivated. I had achieved my goal.

Call to be a poet in March 1957
We post-Oxford-entrance classicists were encouraged to attend lessons in English Literature, and during those last few weeks I read Donne and Coleridge. Suddenly, with stunning abruptness, the enthusiasm I had had for literature over two years previously returned. I remember sitting on a garden bench in Lower Field one gloriously sunny morning in March as my school-days were drawing to a close, near a hawthorn hedge that adjoined what was Dr Pratt's and has been more recently Lord Sugar's garden. For pleasure I was reading the *Faber Book of Modern Verse*, and reading Hopkins' 'Wreck of the *Deutschland*' I thrilled to the language and took my eye off the book in the warm sun and knew that I was going to be a poet. I again felt a call to reflect the unity of the universe that was so evident that March

morning, in original works of my own. (I detect symmetry, for the call came as I was reading a poem about the wreck of the ship, *Deutschland* in 1957, and, as if responding to the circumstances of the call as much as to the call itself, nearly 40 years later my first poetic epic, *Overlord*, would be about the wreck of *Deutschland*, Germany.)

In Italy and Sicily with David Hoppit

My new love of literature was reinforced during a visit to archaeological Italy. I slipped away from Chigwell just as I had slipped away from the war games at corps camp. I withdrew without anyone noticing I had gone. My visit to Italy soon afterwards was an archaeological holiday. I youth-hostelled with David Hoppit, who had given me the Corinthian coin that got me into Oxford. He wore shorts and had an enormous rucksack on his back. I had planned the itinerary.

We went to Rome and saw all the ruins, the catacombs and the Sistine Chapel. We went to Horace's villa at Licenza in the Sabine Hills about 22 miles north-east of Rome and I found Horace's "*fons Bandusiae*", his Bandusian spring, nearby and cupped my hands in the limpid, clear stream and sipped the water and imagined Maecenas giving Horace this estate in the mid-30s BC. Then we went to Naples and visited Pompeii and Herculaneum and climbed Mt Vesuvius. On the way down, striding and skidding down through the powdery ash, I fell off. I flew through the air and landed on my arms, grazing my elbows. We went to Sorrento and Capri. Then we bought a pilgrims' ticket to Sicily. This was especially cheap as it required us to visit the weeping madonna in Syracuse as pilgrims.

On the way to Sicily we got off the train at Paestum to see the Greek temples of Poseidon and Hera. In those days the Temple of Hera was not fenced off, and we spent the night in our sleeping-bags near the altar, under the stars. I was desperately ill and David looked after me admirably. He now says that I nearly died, and it is possible that my blood was infected with the Vesuvian ash. We were on our own and had to wait at least a day until my retching had stopped.

We caught another train to Sicily and made our way to the cathedral in Syracuse. We stared with repelled curiosity at the wax-like face of the statue of the Virgin Mary, which was reputed to have shed actual tears. Then we got our pilgrims' tickets stamped by a man who sat at a table near the cathedral door. The stamping validated them for the return journey.

We were most unlikely pilgrims. We had a wonderful time in Catania. The Youth Hostel was full but we were allowed to sleep in sleeping-bags on the marble floor. We went to the Blue Grotto and up Mt Etna. The next day Lorenzo, the warden of the Catania Youth Hostel, swam with us – we both trod on sea urchins and spikes broke off in the soles of my feet and were as painful as splinters – and then he took us out in a small rowing-boat. At dusk he sang on the silky, silver-blue water "*Santa Lucia*" in a rich tenor. (St Lucia was a martyr in Syracuse during the Diocletian persecutions of AD304 and is the patron saint of Syracuse.) Suddenly Etna spurted red behind his balding head. It erupted the day after our ascent. The fountaining red lava lit the twilit sky and continued after dark.

We returned to Rome, and visited the Vatican, where we encountered a group of girls from a local convent school, the Ilford Ursuline, guarded by nuns with folded arms. Among them was David Hoppit's future wife. I detect symmetry. His coin changed my life, and my itinerary brought him within feet of the woman who would change his life.

Nature blended with literature in archaeological Rome. I was steeped in Roman and Greek ruins, but Rome's literary echoes fascinated me: the house where Keats lived by the Spanish steps, and Keats' grave in the Protestant cemetery near Porta San Paolo with its sad inscription about his own transience: "Here lies one whose name was writ in water." In Sicily I had spent a whole afternoon sitting by the sea, watching the waves come in and murmuring Keats' "It keeps eternal whisperings around". In Rome I sensed the ghosts of Shelley, who wrote 'Adonais' on the death of Keats, and of Byron. I loved Roman archaeology, but now I was haunted by Romantic literature and longed to read the works of all the Romantic poets.

On the way home the train stopped in northern Italy near a 'cactus tree', a prickly pear. I climbed down from our stationary carriage and in burning heat pulled off a cactus pad, brought it back in my rucksack and planted it in a pot. For years afterwards there was a small prickly pear at Journey's End several pads high with red buds. This hardy cactus reminded me of the freedom of spirit I found that spring in Italy and Sicily.

A week in a Loughton solicitors' office

When I returned to Essex the Law closed in on me. My father put me in Mark Liell's office in Attwater & Liell, Loughton for a week to see if I liked the Law. I sat at a desk with my back to his back and listened to the work he did and found it boring. I read Chester Wilmot's *Struggle for Europe* in every available moment while Mark Liell sat hunched over his desk. At one point he asked what I was reading, and I showed him. He said, "Not bad." I did not enthuse about the Law, but more importantly from my father's point of view I did not say it was impossible, and in the course of May and June articles were arranged with a London firm.

Motor cycle side-cars and cricket for Buckhurst Hill

I had to find work for a couple of months before beginning in the Law. There were no office jobs going for such a short time, and little work was available. I took a job near Loughton bus garage at the top of Rectory Lane, making motor cycle side-cars for 3 shillings an hour within a small firm of about ten working men. We were in a corrugated-iron hangar, which I believe is now occupied by a car-repair business I sometimes visit. I hated it. I had nothing in common with any of the people there, although they were mostly very decent towards me. From 8 a.m. to 5 p.m. I sawed struts of wood, riveted them together and passed them to Joe, who hammered metal round them. The finished side-cars looked flimsy and liable to buckle at the slightest impact, and I resolved never to travel in a side-car. That June was baking and the heat on the corrugated-iron roof was unbearable. At morning-, lunch- and tea-breaks I read snatches of Keats and Shelley and returned to my Italian reality, but it was difficult to be alone and *Music While You Work* was on the radio all day. My first experience of the world of work was my idea of hell. I found myself actually looking forward to the Law. However, this experience stood me in good stead when I came to be an employer.

The one thing that kept me going was cricket every Saturday. I was picked to play for Buckhurst Hill 1st eleven under Alan Lavers. Our opening game was at Westcliff, who had two county bowlers, Harold Crabtree and Colin Griffiths. I had a dream debut. Buckhurst Hill batted first, and out of our 121–7 I scored 40, the highest score, sharing a partnership with Alan Lavers. Westcliff beat us by 6 wickets, but my place was guaranteed for the rest of that season. Our home games were played on Buckhurst Hill's 'top ground' where spectators often sat four deep round the boundary on a Saturday afternoon in those pre-television days. There was a main road just beyond one of the waist-high boundary fences and we batsmen competed to hit a four that would bounce and hit a passing red double-decker bus.

Buckhurst Hill now wanted me to play on Sundays and brought me into conflict with my mother, who as the granddaughter of a Methodist minister had been brought up with strict Lord's Day observance, which meant following the Puritan Sunday and abstaining from organised games. She begged me not to play, but I answered her objections and went ahead. My season ended during cricket week in August, when, watched by Alan Hurd on the boundary, Tony Durley (an Essex player) and I had a long partnership of over 100, he scoring 85 and I scoring 31, which nearly saved the game for Buckhurst Hill.

Not all my innings were that glorious. Generally after I was out I would sit in the pavilion, half-watching the cricket, and read Keats, Shelley and Byron. Alan Lavers told me that I should be concentrating on my team-mates' performance. But I had poetry within me and felt that so long as I kept glancing up I should be allowed to read on a Saturday afternoon. Years later I read with delight that J.M. Brearley, captain of England, read Tolstoy after an early Test dismissal, apparently without being told off. My boundary reading put my Chigwell classics master Webb's advice into practice, that I should carry a book in my pocket at all times.

Law: London solicitors
Solicitors' articles in London

It was a tremendous relief to leave the motor cycle side-car factory at the end of June and start my articles with Gregory, Rowcliffe & Co. at 1 Bedford Row, London WC1. I travelled by tube. I received no pay; on the contrary, my father had to pay 50 guineas a year for four years so that I could be a free office boy for the firm. The Georgian building in Bedford Row was grimy, with windows that were never cleaned.

There were six partners, and I was articled to Francis Fortescue-Brickdale (a sleek, stylish silver-haired, shy man), but spent my time with Peter Pierrepont (a large man with a domed head, spectacles and a pleasing smile who died in 1989). I sat at a desk by a window looking out on Bedford Row, and he called "Miss Watts" to bring his secretary running from the next room to sit and take dictation in shorthand. He flicked rubber bands about his office, elongating them into catapults and then letting go, and was irreverent about the Law. Opposite me sat a clerk, Mr Marsh, who wore spectacles and had stick-out teeth. He said nothing all day, burying himself in immensely lengthy tax computations, but when tea arrived he would say, "Ah, tea, delicious tea," always the same words. Elsewhere the office was full of creatures from another age: deaf old Dorrit was as Dickensian as his name, and there were two other old men in the Ledger Department who wrote with their noses close to their ledgers. Bob, the foetal, whey-faced office boy (who, unlike me, got paid) had a twisted grin and reminded me of Uriah Heep.

The Law I did was incredibly tedious. It was wills, marriage settlements and estates. It was all to do with tidying up after death. Clients would ring up, some of them lords, and sometimes I would take messages. Sometimes I was an errand boy to counsel at his chambers in the Law Courts. The way of life of clients had nothing to do with the literature I was discovering: the plays of John Osborne and Samuel Beckett, the novels of Hemingway and poems of Milton. I hated it. I toyed with writing a play: I began one called *Syme in his Window* and another called *Pachomius*, which was about a flood that wiped out a community of desert mystics. (The idea came from nowhere.) I read Hemingway or Milton on the tube home, and back in my room I felt discontented, trapped in a subject I did not want to do.

During the summer evenings I learned to drive in my aunt Argie's Mayflower and passed my test in my father's A70, but even while driving I was filled with latent resentment.

Vision of my future in Loughton library
I still went to the public library in Brook Road every week. It stood to the left of the double gates in what is now Roding Valley High School's grounds. One late summer evening, there was a glorious sunset that washed through the windows and bathed the floor. I was standing between shelves and suddenly saw my own shadow stretch out a long way before me on the floor and I had a glimpse of my future, of the person I might become, a giant out in the future who had achieved wisdom and to whose wisdom I had to ascend and with whom I would be united if I created myself, or recreated myself, along Existentialist lines. It was a moment in which I was aware of my destiny, of what I had to work towards and will into being, and it left a profound effect on me. I had glimpsed the direction of the path that would lead me towards this future self, a literary direction, and in my long poem 'The Silence' my Shadow appears as an image of the wise man I should become and of the knowledge I should acquire.

Practical philosophy lectures on non-dualism
I resolved to take steps to improve my knowledge and work towards my Shadow. One evening, waiting for a tube at Chancery Lane station on the way home from Bedford Row, I saw a poster: PHILOSOPHY. It advertised a course of lectures at the London School of Economic Science in the Haymarket. Not knowing that one day I would be a philosopher, I was moved to write down the telephone number, and I enrolled the next day. It was a course of 12 lectures, each of which was repeated by different lecturers every night of the week after work. I soon gathered that they were lectures in practical philosophy or wisdom, in what is now known as the Advaita system (non-dualism, founded by Sankara): the Indian road to enlightenment. There was a strong emphasis on practical or experiential wisdom and the *Upanisads*, and Gurdjieff was mentioned with approval quite regularly. Much was made of the need for greater awareness and attention, and we were set exercises to heighten our awareness during the coming week.

European literature
Colin Wilson talks in coffee-house
My soul was beginning to awaken. In the second week of the course I went to the Haymarket coffee-house to kill time before the lecture began, and on the table in front of me saw a printed Christmas-card-like notice about a forthcoming visit the author Colin Wilson (who had become a dishwasher at the Haymarket coffee-house in January 1955)[1] was making to the nearby Fleet Street coffee-house. I had read about *The Outsider* (and how overnight he had come from obscurity to be hailed as a genius), and now *Religion and*

78

the Rebel was about to come out. One evening after work I went alone to hear him.

There were probably fifty standing in a small area near the entrance, and there was a leather chair on which he stood. Young, wearing thin spectacles and a polo-necked sweater, he appeared assured and inwardly confident, not nervous at all. He had read everything and he could not have been much older than 25. After his message about how our civilization was in spiritual decay someone asked him, "What's your view of how life began?"

He replied, "I see it as breaking through like a leak in a dam."

"Isn't that naïve?"

"Well, if it's naïve then Shaw and T.E. Hulme and Bergson held that view and so they're naïve." And then he was onto the next question, riding the criticism with considerable aplomb.

I was impressed, and I inwardly knew that one day I would know him and stay with him, and be as assured about the universe as he was. He was outside all disciplines, he was a role model: a writer who reflected on the meaning of life. He declared, "I think of myself as a genius," and he made the idea of genius accessible and attainable in the present rather than a quality to be found only in the dead.

Research into European literature, walks with John Ezard
The next day I went to Holborn library at lunch-time and Loughton library in the evening and I borrowed books by a number of authors Colin Wilson had mentioned. The lectures on practical philosophy took on an added importance, and soon my bedroom was filled with books. I was now reading *The Outsider* and many of the books it discussed. One Saturday afternoon John Ezard (my opponent in the debate on Suez) called to see if I would go for a walk in the Forest. He was shown up to my bedroom, and he surveyed the books on the counterpaned bed and said, "Do you realise you've got the best books of Western civilization here?" There were about twenty books, including Dante, Shakespeare, Kierkegaard, Dostoevsky, Blake, Hesse, Goethe, Camus, Sartre and Eliot; the *Bhagavad-Gita*, the *Upanisads* and the *Bible*. Alongside these was Hitler's *Mein Kampf*, which my father had urged me to read along with Dostoevsky, and which I recall reading on a warm day in the Journey's-End garden, not realising that I was already preparing for my first poetic epic, *Overlord*. We walked in the Forest and discussed our reading, and he threw in new books I had not come across, such as the poems of Yeats and the plays of O'Neill. I took Eliot's *Selected Poems* with me on the tube each day and read it until the cover nearly fell off, and then I went to Loughton library and found books on what the poems meant and I read them. On one of my visits to the library my father accompanied me, hopping and limping along Brook Road with

his orange-brown stick, and I remember explaining on the way home that I had chosen Joad's *God and Evil* because "the most important thing in life is to know why we're here".

That autumn and winter my room at the firm of solicitors became a kind of reading-room. I moved down to the Trust Department next to Mr Rowcliffe's front-facing room ("the holy of holies") where the completely bald, moustached senior partner sat motionless at a leather desk, a cigarette between his lips with an inch of drooping ash that trembled each time he gave a quiet cough. There he signed letters until his poised and elegant secretary, Miss Watts, announced that his taxi had arrived.

In my large room at the back I sat at a desk near three managing clerks. I was in front of Mr Sidney Davis, who dictated letters fluently, hand-clicking a Dictaphone. On the other side of the room sat a blotchy, red-headed drunkard called Smith, and the other side from Mr Davis sat B.C. Janes, who played truant to play minor-counties cricket for Buckinghamshire. (Janes got away with it until he made 141 not out and banner headlines on the back page of the *Evening News*, which Mr Rowcliffe read. Janes was called in and given a very severe warning.) Much of my time was spent in dipping into the books I had found. From Holborn library I found William James's *The Varieties of Religious Experience* and Pascal. From Loughton library, Tolstoy and Mann.

At a time when English literature was turning provincial I had opened fully to the Continental influences, and had little time for the Law. In the train home I read T.E. Hulme and Bergson. In the long winter evenings, sitting in front of the gas fire in my bedroom, I read the four main novels by Dostoevsky: *Crime and Punishment, The Brothers Karamazov, The Possessed* and *The Idiot*; and I lived Raskolnikov, Ivan, Stavrogin, Kirilov and Myshkin.

Ken Campbell

My spare time was given to literature. One Saturday afternoon shortly before Christmas John Ezard took me to see a *matinée* of a pantomime in Ilford with Ken Campbell, who had just won a school essay prize for an essay on O'Neill. The play was knockabout, but afterwards we went back with the director and main actor, a man called Jimmy, to the converted signal-box in which he lived. We sat on the floor near levers which had survived the conversion, and I remember Jimmy saying that according to F.C. Lucas the three key concepts of criticism were taste, discrimination and judgement. (Campbell went on to become an actor and a director.) Shortly afterwards Ezard, Campbell and I went up to London and found the Partisan coffee-house, where Angry Young Men were known to hang out, and played chess there on the chequered tables. Just to sit in the Partisan was to make an Angry statement and to appear an Angry Young Man.

Alex Comfort
One afternoon Ezard called on me and took me to the nearby house of Alex Comfort, whom he knew. There I met the lean, bespectacled poet, who extended a withered arm and hand, which I shook. We sat with his son, a short-trousered boy, and watched *Quatermass* on black-and-white television, during which his wife appeared. Later Comfort left home and later still wrote *The Joy of Sex*.

London lunch-times
The lunch-times when I did not go to Holborn library I went to Lincoln's Inn Fields and listened to the speakers at the 'speakers' corner' there. Sometimes Allen and Drabble, two of the three other articled clerks in my firm, would walk by. They wore pinstripes and bowler-hats, unlike me, already dressing as solicitors, and looked down their noses at me for listening to the arguments from the soapboxes and for sometimes joining in.

At the Law Courts, queuing to register to be a solicitor, I met up with a Jewish boy who was also going to study Law at Worcester College, Alan Magnus (later a solicitor for the National Coal Board). He was in articles in a firm in Fleet Street, and some lunch-times he invited me to the Fleet Street Jazz Club to hear Kenny Ball. He jived superbly, and he taught me to jive and took me to Chris Barber's (in Oxford Street) and to Cy Laurie's (in Windmill Street, near Piccadilly). Some evenings we went to a coffee bar in Soho, the Macabre, and I many times sat drinking coffee there to the background music of 'Magic Moments' and 'Diana'.

John Biggs-Davison MP, article on nuclear weapons
In provincial Loughton there was nothing to do in the evenings save read or walk with John Ezard, and following my contact with my MP John Biggs-Davison (who had sent me a ticket to the Commons Suez debate) I was persuaded to join the Young Conservatives who met every Friday evening at the Hideaway café in the parade of shops near the site of the old Oaklands. The Chairman of the Young Conservatives wore a bow-tie, and each week there was a speaker. On one occasion it was the young Peter Walker (later a Minister), who spoke impressively without notes. On another occasion it was John Silberrad, a barrister who lived locally. At question time I praised the Angry Young Men for their questioning of society (as reformers), and Silberrad said, "Well, there's an angry young man," and everyone laughed. Both Walker and Silberrad feature later in my story, and I detect a pattern. There were plenty of girls (mostly secretaries), and regular dances and social events between the meetings, and Biggs-Davison suggested that I should revive a magazine, *Right Wheel*.

I had borrowed Robert Carew Hunt's *The Theory and Practice of*

Communism from the local library and had read it while travelling to and from London. It turned me against Communism, and I was now firmly anti-Communist. I did not know that Carew Hunt (also Carew-Hunt) had been recruited to the Secret Intelligence Service by Philby to deal with North and South America and prepare background papers on Communism.[2] The book had shaped my view of Communism's approach to nuclear weapons and confirmed that I was on Churchill's side, right of centre, in my attitude to international events, a view confirmed by my reading of Guy Wint[3] and Peter Calvocoressi, *Middle East Crisis* on Suez. For the first issue of *Right Wheel* I wrote a long article on nuclear weapons.[4] (*See* p.494.) Looking back at it now I can see the interest my article might have aroused in shadowy British Cold-War circles.

In February 1958 my article came to the attention of Biggs-Davison. In March he sent me a note saying that the editorial was "extremely well written"[5] and in May he wrote, "You have done well to grasp the nettle of nuclear weapons."[6] His support meant that I went up to Oxford as a right-winger with an Angry questioning of society, rather than as a left-winger like most of my contemporaries.

Rejection of the Law, research into Existentialism

In early 1958 I studied the Trust Accounts and Bookkeeping part of the Law Society's Solicitors Intermediate exams. It was hard, gruelling work which I did not enjoy as it left me less time for reading literature. I took a Gibson and Weldon correspondence course, which was based on Roland's *Trust Accounts* and Carter's *Bookkeeping for Solicitors*. I took the exam in March and passed.

The bookkeeping I had mastered served me well when many years later I found myself doing the bookkeeping for my own business. But at the time I was alarmed that the Law was closing in on me. Wondering if the Law could be more interesting abroad than in England, in April I visited the Public Schools Appointments Bureau to find out what jobs would be available in the Law for a solicitor working abroad. I was told I could be a colonial judge. This did not appeal.

Work at the firm of solicitors was now even more boring, and the following typed communication, which has somehow survived, still makes me cringe: "Mr Hagger, Estate of the late Lady Baker. Will you please prepare a Corrective Affidavit showing back tax and sur-tax and penalties as agreed with the Inland Revenue, £5,000. PWP. 22/4/58.[7] I cringed, for what did it mean? Why was the Affidavit necessary, let alone important? I was just not interested in what was agreed with Inland Revenue. I had the ability and the skill to keep Trust accounts and books, but there were more urgent things to think about than a late lady's tax problems and Corrective Affidavits.

I knew I had a choice to make. That was brought home to me soon afterwards. One night as I travelled home the tube stuck in a tunnel and there was an eerie silence and a voice spoke my name: "Nick Hagger." I turned and realised I was standing near Hughes, who used to sit next to me in the Latin class in the Swallow Room under the dome. (He was the least prepared of us, and our Head, Thompson, who took us for Latin sensed this. Lesson after lesson he strode with clicking heels towards the library in his gown and called before he reached the open door, "Fire away, Hughes," and Hughes would have to begin translating the passages we had prepared for homework.) Hughes was holding Sartre's essay *Existentialism is a Humanism*, which he showed me. "It's about freedom," he said. "I'm in an office I hate, and I wish I could be free." He spoke as if my deeper self was speaking.

When I got home I went straight to Loughton library. The book was not in stock but I ordered it. When it came I read it two or three times and mulled over the free choice which might shape the person I wanted to become.

Rejection of the Church, path to Reality through literature
Around this time I moved further away from the Church. The Methodist minister who had been appointed to replace Mr Grant was spending the first year of his tenure in the US. His stand-in from autumn 1957 had been an American, Ralph Bickford, a swarthy, simian, bespectacled small man who was in England for just a year. One morning in church he leant over the pulpit and told the children, "You know, I don't believe in Hell."

I was asked to take him to a football match, which he wanted to experience. I took him to watch Leyton Orient. We stood behind one of the goals, leaning on an iron crash barrier. I explained the rules.

On the way home he told me in a sombre, almost despairing voice that church services had become mechanical for him, that he was going through the motions and had lost his faith. He told me had been diagnosed as a diabetic and that he would start treatment in America. Some months after he left it was announced that he had died of undiagnosed diabetes.

I was sure he had chosen to do nothing out of metaphysical despair. I thought he should have recognised that the quest for Reality, the One, was outside the Church. I believed that the path to Reality lay through literature.

The Royal Court
The Royal Court theatre was the focal point of the 1956 movement in drama. I went to the Royal Court several times in 1958 and sat in the cheapest seats at the top and saw new-wave plays. In the interval George Devine, white-haired and bow-tied, would be about, and afterwards I went next door to the pub. There, after John Osborne's *Epitaph for George Dillon* I met Robert

Stephens, the actor who played the lead. There too I encountered Patrick Magee, an actor in Beckett's *Waiting for Godot*, who told me that Beckett had told him, "Two thieves were crucified next to Christ. That both were damned do not presume, that both were saved do not despair." Beckett was saying little more than that he did not know whether the thieves were saved. However, at the time I was concerned to find a purpose to life, and this sceptical sentiment had resonance.

My reading had gone on apace: Shaw, James, Rilke, Nietzsche, Kafka, D.H. Lawrence, Turgenev and Joyce. I kept a pocketbook and headed pages 'Plays', 'Novels' and 'Poetry', and listed authors and works as soon as I had read them. I now needed to discuss these books.

Colin Wilson, Stuart Holroyd and Sparticans

In May, in a Sartrean free choice, I wrote to Colin Wilson, asking to meet him. He replied from Old Walls, Bodrugan Farm, Mevagissey in Cornwall, saying that he could not meet me until September.[8] I wrote back in June, sending him (as only a very young man can) a long letter reminding him that he claimed to stand for religious Existentialism and asking him for his view of the purpose of life.[9]

Colin Wilson wrote back in June referring me to Stuart Holroyd, the author of *Emergence from Chaos*, a fellow Angry Young Man, giving me his phone number.[10] I met Stuart Holroyd outside the Dominion theatre, Tottenham Court Road. He was a small, quiet, intensely-serious young man in a jacket and a checked shirt with the top button done up and no tie. He had an Existentialist bent. I talked at great length with him in a Soho coffee bar. I had read *Declaration* (a book of essays by a number of Angry Young Men), and I discussed the Angry Young Men with him. I met him again. We had dinner at the Star Bar in Soho, a small Indian restaurant. I remember saying to him, "We don't want anything to do with any system, the individual alone is important," and Holroyd asked me to repeat this. He then thought about it and nodded in approval. We went on to see Eliot's *The Elder Statesman*. Holroyd invited me to join the Sparticans.

The Sparticans were a newly-formed, London-based group that sought to change society in accordance with the views of the Angry Young Men. At the end of June I attended a meeting of the Sparticans. About thirty young left-wing men and women sat angrily in a square in a room in London (37 Howitt Road, NW3), and although Colin Wilson was not there, Bill Hopkins and Stuart Holroyd had a lot to say about what needed to be done to change society. I came away with a George Hay, who on the tube handed me a leaflet saying "Spartica is a map for the lost". The next day he wrote me a letter telling me that full membership was 5s. a month, payable to Greta Detloff, the Treasurer (whose phone number was the same as Stuart Holroyd's), and asking me (as there was no HQ or source of revenue) if I could run off some membership forms on the Young Conservatives' duplicator?

That summer of 1958 I was torn between reformist and Conservative influences, between the questioning, revolutionary Angry Sparticans who wanted to change society and human nature and ban the nuclear deterrent and who looked to Colin Wilson; and the socialising Young Conservatives who wanted to perpetuate tradition and retain the nuclear deterrent and who looked to John Biggs-Davison. From now on I gave expression to these two apparently conflicting sides of my nature: the Existentialism I then associated with Colin Wilson and the views of the right-wing Establishment I then associated with the independent and well-read Suez rebel, Biggs-Davison, Churchill's successor.

At the end of July, to my intense relief, I finished my year in the firm of solicitors. Brickdale took me out to lunch, and then I was temporarily free, although I was still stuck with the Law.

In Greece with Alan Magnus: sleeping in Kazantzakis's study, jumping to catch the train

In August, still in love with Greek history, I went to Greece. John Ezard, saying goodbye, enjoined me: "Come back an artist." I travelled with Alan Magnus (who was also to read Law at Worcester College). We joined a party from Chigwell School for the three days' train journey through Yugoslavia to north Greece – paying our share of the party ticket reduced our travel cost – and then left the party and went off on our own, hitchhiking and youth-hostelling with sleeping-bags and a Primus stove for six weeks, during which we grew beards. We visited Thermopylae, Mt Parnassus (which we went up), Delphi and Mt Helicon, Thebes, Thespiae and the Vale of the Muses and then spent three days based in Athens visiting the Athenian ruins. We went to Sounion (where I sat where Byron sat) and Marathon. I encountered Stephen Medcalf (who had been at Chigwell) on the bus and we visited Marathon together, not knowing that he would often call on me at Oxford. It was unbearably hot – there was a heat wave in the Sahara and it was 130°F in the shade – and a siesta was obligatory. I wrote: "The sun clings to each part of the body like a vice, and the breeze is like a draft from an oven."[11]

We went to Dafni (Daphnae) where in the groves adjoining the monastery there was a wine festival and we were allowed to wander among the trees and to sample any of 36 different Greek wines as many times as we liked. After a Dionysian evening we fell asleep in one of the groves.

We went to Eleusis and then set off round the Peloponnese and visited Megara, Corinth (where I slept in the Temple of Apollo), Patras, Olympia, Pylos and Sphacteria (where I walked up the path Cleon took), Kalamai,

Tripolis (where we had a bath for 2/6d), Argos, Nafplia (Nauplion), Epidavros (Epidaurus, where we slept alongside the ancient stone theatre and went out onto the stage at 7 a.m. and with no one else in view tested the amazing acoustics, listening to each other's whispers), Tiryns and Mycenae – sheer Paradise for one who knew the history of these places. On hillsides all round the Peloponnese we saw the huge letters OXI ("*ochi*"), "no" to British Prime Minister Macmillan's plan for Cyprus. I did not know that I would come face to face with Col. Grivas, the implementer of the 'No'.

At the end of August we were back in Athens. We took a boat from Piraeus to Crete. We sat on deck with black-clad women, goats and sheep, and many were sick. In Crete we berthed at Iraklion and slept on a barge. The next day I visited the Minoan palace at Knossos and the palaces at Gourna and at Phaestos. The palace at Phaestos was a flat stone base surrounded by mountains. There was a visitors' book in a guest-house nearby and, repelled by some of the other tourists with their trappings of wealth, I wrote, "Being is more important than having."

In the evening we encountered a Cretan who led us to a small museum not far from the sea. It was fully furnished and it turned out to be the house of Kazantzakis (the author of *Zorba the Greek* who once attended Bergson's lectures and who had died the previous October). We were allowed to sleep in our sleeping-bags on the carpet of his study – again events had put me in touch with a writer as if to draw attention to what I should be doing – and I can remember standing near his high-backed writing-chair and going out onto his veranda and standing in his garden by lush, exotic banana fronds the next morning.

After three days in Crete we took the boat to Rhodes, and having seen the island, including Lindos, we took a caique (a light Levantine boat with a sail) to Turkey, intending to make our way to Istanbul. The caique was running arms and we put in on a deserted shore, where boxes were hastily unloaded. We established that the nearest bank was two days away at Izmir, so we returned with the caique. There was a tremendous storm and the boat was swamped by huge waves and we had to bail out. (I later wrote a story based on this experience, 'A Gun-Runner in Danger'.) After our return to Rhodes we took a coach to the Valley of the Butterflies. Our guide threw a stone at a tree, disturbing thousands of camouflaged butterflies whose brown upper wings concealed red-orange underwings. They slept on the bark and when they all flew up the air was filled with a swarm of red wings.

We went on to Mykonos via Kos and Patmos. We were rowed ashore and found a small whitewashed old house for 2/6d a night. Donkeys brayed outside and we breakfasted on the front on bread, butter and honey. The sea was a very deep blue-indigo and very choppy, and we took a small boat across to the island of Delos, the old Athenian treasury.

Back in Athens we met up with the party from Chigwell and travelled back on the party ticket. At Belgrade station I left the train with one of the school party, Ion Alexis Will. We left our passports and luggage on the train and went to a station café for coffee and fell into conversation about Tito with a Yugoslav student. I looked up and saw our train receding slowly down the platform, green flags crossed at the back and a soldier with a rifle standing guard on the observation platform below them. I let out a yell and leapt up. In a flash I realised the danger of being without money or a passport in a Communist country. I set off in pursuit with Will puffing behind me. He was rather podgy and fell back. The guard levelled his gun at me, and Mr Croft, the master in charge appeared beside him on the observation platform with Alan Magnus and several of the party who, despite the armed soldier, began shouting encouragement. I ran the race of my life, and as I reached the end of the platform pulled level with the end of the train. Steps led up to the observation platform. "I can make it," I shouted back at Will, "what should I do?"

"Jump," shouted Mr Croft and Alan Magnus and the boys, who were crowding round the guard and his gun, "jump."

"Jump," Will shouted puffing and panting behind me, "you go on."

I jumped and caught the handle and landed on the bottom step up to the observation platform at the very moment the train accelerated and as I looked back Will was already fifty yards away at the end of the station platform, a forlorn figure in shirt and shorts without passport or money. I resumed my seat in the carriage and recovered my breath while Mr Croft reassured me that I had done the right thing.

Will was arrested and spent a week in a Yugoslav prison. There was an international incident. His case was front-page news and his father had to send him money and a new train ticket to get home. Strangely, Will turned up at Worcester College, Oxford a year after me. (Years later, in 1974, Ken Campbell co-wrote a play, *The Great Caper*, with him. I do not know if the 'caper' was influenced by my 'jump'.)

I often thought of that jump. I had jumped, I had acted, I had changed my future. If I had not jumped I would have been in a worse situation. I grasped that my jump was a lesson that I should apply in my own life. That jump became symbolic of an existential choice. I longed to jump from the station platform of the Law and catch the train of Literature.

Law at Oxford
Starting at Oxford: Worcester College – Ricky Herbert, Kingsley Shorter, discussions on European literature; Brian Bond
In October I went up to Oxford, the first member in my family to go to university. I lived in a downstairs back bedsit, which had an electricity

meter, at 20 Worcester Place, a small terraced late-19th-century house with steps up to the front door, round the corner from Worcester College. Alan Magnus and four other undergraduates also had rooms in the building, and a grumbling landlady lived in the basement. I discovered that Magnus and I had a joint tutorial together with our tutor A.B. Brown, an urbane, owlish man with spectacles who smoked cigars.

Worcester College had been founded in 1714 by a Worcestershire man, Sir Thomas Cookes. It had a blackened *façade* and high-up clock, and high railings, but beyond the porters' lodge and cloisters there was an imposing

lawn. On the right, looking down at the lawned quadrangle was an 18th-century 'terrace' with staircase accommodation, and on the left were the older medieval 'cottages', where the 19th-century writer Thomas De Quincey had a room. The cottages had been part of Gloucester College, which was founded as a college for

Worcester College, quadrangle and lawn, terrace (including staircase 5) on left

Benedictine monks in 1283 and after the dissolution had passed into Gloucester Hall c.1560 and had survived the 18th-century building of Worcester College. Beyond it, the other side of a wall, were the gardens. In the 18th century money did not run to building on the fourth side of the quadrangle.

I saw the Worcester College tradition as being predominantly 18th-century – social-rationalist, elegant and Augustan – on a medieval base that included 14th-century mysticism. I can trace my neo-Baroque poetry back to this combination.

In the late 1950s many of the undergraduates wore cavalry twill, ties and sweaters, not jeans. Gowns were worn in hall and in tutorials. We went into college (wearing gowns) for meals in hall and for tutorials, at which Magnus and I read our essays in turn. The first essay I read had a literary style and Magnus's was a string of points. Brown said, "From the point of view of what the Law requires, Hagger should be more like Magnus, and Magnus should be more like Hagger."

But I did not want to jettison my literary feel, that was the trouble. Poring over the cases of Criminal Law, over Roman Law and the History of the English Judicial System, I kept thinking of the books I might be reading – books about the meaning of life and the purpose of the universe, about individuals rather than systems, subjects more interesting than offences against property and possession such as the law of larceny as applied to windfalls and R v Cunningham (1957); the umpteen tedious rights in Justinian's code; and the hundred and assize courts and '*nisi prius*' jurisdiction.

I threw myself into college life. I was asked to play football for the college and attended various societies, including the Union debates, at one of which, after much agonising, I voted against unilateral nuclear disarmament and defeated the motion 291 to 290 by free choice. But I still had a lot of time alone, and especially around tea-time I would sit on my bed in my room and ponder, sometimes playing my record-player, and the conviction grew that just as I had jumped from the Belgrade platform onto the train so I should jump from the Law into a more congenial subject.

I now saw Oxford as a faintly depressing place: a modern city filled with gloomy and decaying colleges and blackened stone, and an emptiness filled with the braying upper-class accents of undergraduates in cavalry twill, moneyed young men from privileged homes with snobbish attitudes. Within this Oxford was another, of a few undergraduates eager to read all European literature and to relate to all knowledge, interested outside their subject, valuing learning for its own sake and talking with intellectual passion. Perhaps this second Oxford disappeared in the course of the 1980s when a Thatcherite emphasis on the market made undergraduates acutely aware of unemployment and choose subjects that would lead to secure jobs.

Very early on I saw a long-haired young man in a suede jacket and instantly recognised him from the pub next to the Royal Court. He told me he had been living very near Sloane Square, and had often been in that pub. Again I detected a pattern. Ricky Herbert and I became close friends. We teamed up with an older mature student, Kingsley Shorter (later a Russian interpreter at the UN). They both read Modern Languages, and soon we were meeting for coffee at the Playhouse up the road or going back to Ricky's room in college, and I was hearing about Huysmans' *A rebours* (*Against Nature*) and Stendhal's *Le Rouge et le Noir* (*The Red and the Black*), and discussing the pre-Existentialist outlooks of Des Esseintes and Julien Sorel.

How real our literary heroes were to us. They had the force of vivid living people we knew. I very swiftly declared myself an Existentialist and developed a philosophy of free act which (like jumping for the train in Belgrade) could affect one's life. "You're free," I used to urge them, "you can go up to anybody and say anything. Only social convention, your own nature (your fear of embarrassment) and habit hold you back." As a result of conversations such as these (which generally took place over coffee) I was thought of as an Existentialist, and was identified with the free act. And I was given opportunities to put my thinking into practice at the parties and jiving sessions I attended in the Union cellars. I met several girls, as did Alan Magnus, whereas Ricky and Kingsley and some of the others tended to hold back as spectators. Ricky's hero was Dostoevsky's Underground Man, and he used to speak very amusingly of his view of life "from under the floorboards".

My discussions with Ricky and Kingsley widened to include German and Russian as well as French literature. Kingsley's friend Perry Anderson (later a Marxist essayist and editor of the *New Left Review*) was reading Russian Literature and spoke excitedly about Bazarov in Turgenev's *Fathers and Sons*. Little by little the idea began to grow that I, who stood for the free act, was absurdly bound by the Law, and that I should break free from Law by exercising my freedom. Incongruously (as incongruously as being an Angry Young Man and a Young Conservative at the same time, believing in keeping the best and changing the worst) at this time besides being a radical Existentialist, I was a traditional sportsman and played several games of football for the college as inside left. We wore chocolate and pink and played in the college grounds beyond the lake. Our captain was Brian Bond, a historian (later a military historian who worked with Basil Liddell Hart). He used to call out from behind me, "Come on Woggins" (meaning 'Worcester College'), and when occasionally I scored, "Oh, well played."

Choosing Literature
Negotiations to change from Law to English Language and Literature
Literature called to me upstairs at 20 Worcester Place. I sometimes climbed the stairs and looked in on David Pitman, the younger brother of Robert Pitman of *The Sunday Express*, whose wife Pat Pitman was writing *Encyclopedia of Murder* with Colin Wilson. He was reading Milton's *Paradise Lost* and struggling with Anglo-Saxon grammar. He told me about his tutor, the very young Christopher Ricks, and although I was steeped in French, German and Russian literature I was aware that I was not fluent in the European languages. Slowly my old desire to do English Literature at 'A' level resurfaced. I was not keen on the idea of learning Anglo-Saxon grammar but the writers ahead in the English course – the poets Donne, Coleridge and Tennyson – had all looked at life and made their definitive statements about it. I wanted to absorb their wisdom in preparation for a task I felt would take me abroad and for a destiny linked with poetry which I instinctively knew was ahead. Deep down I knew that to be a poet and convey the purpose of life and my vision of Reality I had to study the poetic tradition, although my calling, writing poems in the future, would never earn me a living.

When I returned to Loughton for the Christmas vacation I raised the issue with my parents. I said, "One should be allowed to decide that one doesn't want to spend 40 years of one's life doing something one doesn't want to be doing." Moulded by the unemployment of the 1930s, they felt I should continue with the Law, that a BA solicitor would have the world at his feet and could go into politics like Biggs-Davison or go into Shell. But in the evenings I went to a local pub, The Holly Bush (later Hollybush), and drank with John Ezard, who was now reading English at Cambridge and our conversations revolved around different authors and their interpretation of life, and I knew within that I had to change to English Literature. Sometimes we went up to London and visited the bookshops in Charing Cross Road. We bought all William Golding's books, including *Free Fall*, at Foyles.

I move lodgings

Back in Worcester Place our landlady was being difficult. Her grumblings had turned into accusations, demands to know which of us undergraduates had trodden mud on the stairs, left the bathroom in disorder, and so on. (It must have been difficult for her to tolerate half a dozen grown men tramping through her house in all weathers.) A room had become vacant in the Riding Stables just opposite the college as a Tanganyikan Pita-Kabisa (who liked to be known as 'Peter' and features later in my story, *see* p.413) had to leave. I made a free choice, agreed to take his place, piled all my belongings into a supermarket trolley I borrowed from the college and pushed them round the corner to my new room.

It was now time to make a choice about the Law. After agonising for several days I raised the prospect of a change with both Brown (my Law tutor), who said I would do very well if I stayed with the Law, and Christopher Ricks (the English tutor), who lived next door to the Riding Stables.

Christopher Ricks

Ricks had me to his house and questioned me, his vigorous eyes searchingly bright under his young bulbous forehead. He pointed out that the course was called English Language and Literature and included a linguistic side (Old English and Middle English), and that it ended in 1860. He said that the Anglo-Saxon should not be too much of a problem as I would only have to learn enough of the language to translate passages. There would be no specific questions on the grammar as in Mods. He asked what I thought of Pasternak's *Dr Zhivago* and when I said, "It's in the grand Dostoevskian tradition," he said, "I would have thought it's in the grand Tolstoyan tradition." I explained that I was thinking of *The Possessed*. We discussed Colin Wilson, and he said scathingly, "I shall die without having read Colin Wilson's latest book. It's regrettable, but there we are." Ricks had a great ability to use irony to state an attitude. He said, "Your motives for changing would be mine if I were in your position."

At the end of February I wrote to my parents, saying that Brown and Ricks would be happy for me to switch if the County, Gregory, Rowcliffe and they were happy. I expected deferment from National Service to be confirmed. It had been announced that National Service was to end in 1962. I wrote, "I have in the next two weeks to make a decision which you may consider wrong." I then waited for a reply.

Experience of the One by Worcester College lake
The reply came in early March,[12] an envelope in my father's handwriting in the H pigeon-hole in the porters' lodge near the entrance to Worcester College. I found it before breakfast and took it down past the cottages to the college lake, sat on a stone seat near the arched gate and opened it, my destiny as a future poet at stake. It was a glorious sunny morning and no one was about. I was completely alone. My father's letter was dated 1.3.59 and I read:

> Dear Nicholas, I have read your letter, and from what you say it does appear that you are almost persuaded to make the change in studies you contemplated in the vac and over which we had so much discussion. There is really very little for me to say for a decision of this nature must be personal to you…. What it really means is that you have found the Law dull and unsatisfying.

It was a four-page letter but as soon as I grasped that I was being given his consent, a sense of freedom and tremendous exhilaration welled up in me. I felt a tremendous elation, and as I looked up at the lake, with trees reflected in it and a trace of cloud from a higher world still, everything blended and I had a profound feeling that *I* was the lake and the lake was in *me*. I seemed

Worcester College lake; and the stone seat where Nicholas read the letter from his father and then had a mystical experience in early March 1959

to grow in stature, I felt I had always existed. I was filled with a great power. I felt I had rejected a future as a lawyer and could now progress towards my future as a poet and the power filled me with a conviction, a certainty, that this would happen. The power was in the universe. Later, having returned to my room without going into the hall for breakfast, I wondered at the power of my mind which could suddenly become the universe.

My free act in jumping from Law to Literature had put me in charge of my destiny. I was in direct contact with my soul, and instinctively knew within that I had been faithful to a call from my future direction, a call I dimly heard but could not decipher. I was convinced that I was now on the right path.

Episode 5:

Wisdom and Intelligence

Years: 1959–1961
Locations: Oxford; Loughton; Paris; Spain; Yugoslavia; Greece
Works: *A Well of Truth*
Initiative: encounter with Col. Grivas

"Wisdom is the principal thing; therefore get wisdom: and with all thy getting get understanding."

Proverbs 4.7

In my next episode I pursued Reality to achieve wisdom, but found my pursuit in conflict with intelligence in both its dazzling and more sinister meanings. Looking back, I believe the choice I made placed me on the path to Reality.

Wisdom: Reality and hedonism
'Wisdom' is "having experience and knowledge and the power of applying them critically or practically" (*Concise Oxford Dictionary*). To me that meant experience and knowledge of Reality, which I came to associate with the wisdom of the East, and the power of applying them practically.

I heard the call to Reality again that April. In the Easter vacation I went to Paris on my own.

I read Milton in Paris
I found a room in the Latin Quarter, near St-Germain-des-Prés. It cost me 12/6d a night, and I ate well at a self-service restaurant nearby. I spent many hours sitting in the park of the Île Saint-Louis in the middle of the Seine, reading (at Ricks's request, to catch up with what the other English under-graduates had been doing for two terms) Milton's *Paradise Lost* in its entirety and revelling in each Homeric simile. This work prepared me for *Overlord* and *Armageddon*, my two poetic epics that lay ahead. I pored over *King Lear* and other Elizabethan plays, on which there was to be a 'collection' (exam) on the first day of the new term. As I read I thought about Milton's God and Lear's heath, and, seeking wisdom, was already on a quest for Reality, the One.

I visit Jean-Paul Sartre
I also took in European culture. I visited the Louvre and Michèle Maurel in her Paris flat, and I went to the cinema some afternoons and saw Dostoevsky's *Idiot* in French. And I reread Sartre's *Existentialism is a Humanism*.

I visited Sartre. I had found that his apartment was in the Rue Napoleon, got in to the block and climbed the stairs. In a free act I rang his doorbell, and the great man came to the door, dressed in a formal suit and tie, and squinted at me through his spectacles. On the landing I had a short conver-sation with him in French, explaining that I would like to discuss freedom with him. I had questions to ask about M. Roquentin in *La Nausée* and about *Existentialism is a Humanism*. His reply in French seemed courteous enough, but it was couched in language that I did not fully understand and explained that he was about to leave for an engagement. I withdrew, overjoyed at having had contact with such a proponent of free choice.

Christopher Ricks: my preference for mystical literature
Back in Oxford I embarked on doing English Language and Literature in two years instead of three (or five counting the two years of 'A' level I had missed). I did my collection on *King Lear* and Shakespeare's contemporaries in the hall and did better than any of my year "without having read any English" as Christopher Ricks put it.

I had my first tutorial with Ricks. It was a hot day and we left his room in the 13th-century cottages, walked into the gardens and sat on a wooden bench. He asked me what literature I liked.

I said, "Mystical literature, for example Blake and Wordsworth." I meant literature that approaches Reality.

He said, "I shall teach you to like social satire."

He stood for the 18th-century college tradition of social reality and intelligence. I was open to the new influence, but in retrospect that first exchange summed up our different approaches. For him as an atheist reality was social whereas I was on a quest for a hidden Reality. Throughout the next two years he spoke warmly of the verbal, social approach of the Augustans and social satirists, emphasising intelligence, whereas I defended the more mystical approach. And although in due course I was glad to read Dryden and Pope, my taste did not change in any way; rather, it deepened.

I worked hard on Shakespeare and his contemporaries, and enjoyed reading Marlowe, especially *Dr Faustus* and Faustus's pact with Mephistophilis to exchange his soul for power, honour, influence, prosperity and fame. I was absorbed in Middleton (to whose work Ricks brought a fresh, verbal approach, demonstrating that certain key words were ambiguous and that Beatrice and De Flores understand different meanings and misunderstand each other). I relished his intelligence. However, I had a less inspiring tutor for Anglo-Saxon, and although I enjoyed studying Anglo-Saxon literature in translation and attended lectures by J.R.R. Tolkien (who spoke almost inaudibly in an uninspiring tone) I struggled with learning enough of the Anglo-Saxon language to be able to translate passages into English, having missed the groundwork the others had done while I was studying Law. I had to learn Anglo-Saxon as thoroughly as I had learned Latin – there *were* tests on Anglo-Saxon grammar – and I resented the drudgery and found it boring and unnec-essary. I was interested in the Old English origins of current words but failed to see the point of mastering the dead language of Old English merely to translate *Beowulf* in an exam. I resented the time I was expected to devote to such a futile pursuit when there were such interesting books to read and discuss.

The 'Randolph Set'
Some lunch-times and most early evenings I went with Ricky and Kingsley to the Randolph, a hotel at the top of Beaumont Street where the 'Randolph Set' met. There were always literary discussions going on. Ian Flintoff, the Shakespearean actor (and later Labour supporter), virtually lived there. He sat from opening time to closing time, always accompanied by newspaper men, including Rex from *The Daily Express*, and half a dozen on the fringe of films. I spent many hours going more deeply into French, German and Russian literature, discussing the writings of authors such as Sartre. I was instinctively putting myself through an internationalist syllabus (which I would later think of as Universalist) that included all the European masters and did not then exist. We were interested in literature that took us towards Reality.

Michael Horovitz and 'Medusa'

The Randolph was a base for Bohemians. They were actually also semi-Beatniks. The Beat poets – 'Beat' being short for 'Beatitude' – had conducted the latest literary movement (much of it from the apartment of Kenneth Rexroth, who features later in my story) and proclaimed approaching Reality through drugs. We dressed daringly and were sometimes joined by Michael Horovitz and David Sladen, two *avant-garde*-ist Beatnik-followers.

Horovitz published *New Departures*, a very *avant-garde* magazine, and at his parties in Hinksey marijuana was passed round and Horovitz would himself write a poem. I saw him write one poem influenced by Ginsberg's *Howl* that was 375 lines long (many lines comprising only one word) in about four minutes, a practice I did not consider poetry, not even *avant-garde* poetry, but rather stream of consciousness – or spontaneous self-expression. I did not believe that Reality could be approached by getting high.

It must have been at the same party that I encountered David Sladen, sitting on the top of an armchair on a landing with his back to the stairwell, holding forth to four young men who were listening intently. He was making a case for solipsism, the philosophical view that only one's self exists or can be known. He inadvertently dropped his cigarette down the inside of the armchair, and smoke began to rise round his feet. Acknowledging the existence of fire outside himself, which destroyed his own argument, he leapt from the back of the chair and ran while his captive audience put out the fire.

On another occasion Horovitz held a poetry event, I believe in the Oxford Playhouse coffee bar. About forty of us sat cross-legged on the floor and various poets recited from memory. Near the end Horovitz asked publicly whether I had a poem to recite, and I read 'Medusa', one of my early poems which I had typed out. I now wonder whether Providence was giving me a nudge through him.

Abandon, apparition of grandfather at time of his death

That summer I was drunk with excess of freedom. I worked every morning and most afternoons and often went out in the evenings. There were several parties and I got drunk several times and lived by excess, as if testing for myself by the breach of it Aristotle's *meden agan* ('nothing too much') which was inscribed over the door of the Greek room by the Tuck Shop at Chigwell. Ricky used to take a relatively harmless stimulant, Preludin, which was passed round to heighten consciousness. In the evenings I led an abandoned life, living for the moment, taking pleasure in alcohol, reeling back to the Riding Stables and knowing that the hedonism was a waste of time and futile. I stayed on the edge of their riotous living and retained my self-discipline.

One night, 2 May 1959, however, the senselessness and futility of their way of life appalled me, and I had a nagging feeling that Anglo-Saxon grammar was as dull as Law, that I had jumped out of the frying-pan into the fire. I returned to the Riding Stables depressed and, full of self-recrimination, toyed with the idea of hanging myself. There was a high window beneath the 20-foot-high ceiling, and not intending to do anything I drunkenly experimented, rigged up a noose from rope that had secured my trunk and stood on a chair and contemplated throwing it over a bar that protruded from the high window. I did throw it over the bar and the rope was long enough for me to hold the two ends in my hands.

Suddenly, quite distinctly, my grandfather (who as a boy I had rescued in fog) appeared in the corner of the room and lifted a hand as if to stop me. I can still see him, white-haired and stooping, his hand up. Then he vanished. I was shaken. I put the rope away and went to bed. The next day I heard he had died on 2 May[1] about the time I saw him.

Arnold Wesker, Woodrow Wyatt

That summer term I attended a number of meetings, including a large gathering in the Randolph for the kitchen-sink dramatist Arnold Wesker. He arrived casually dressed and stood with his back to a wall while we in his audience stood or sat in three long rows on the carpet. After an informal talk he was asked, "What is socialism?" He replied "Brotherhood" to tumultuous applause.

I attended the commem (commemoration ball) at the college. I hired a dinner-jacket and remember Woodrow Wyatt, a prominent television commentator with immaculately groomed black hair, who had been an undergraduate at the college, arriving in bow-tie and two or three of the tutors lying drunk in the corner of a marquee about 4 in the morning.

Arnold Fellows

But an Old Chigwellian's sherry party in early June in Merton gave me the most pleasure as I found A.F. standing by the mantelpiece. He told me he would be retiring in 1960 and would live in Barnes. "I've never had a house," he said, "I've always lived in the school or Grange Court." He had heard that I had changed to English Language and Literature and he asked me what I would do. Without hesitation I said I would be a writer, to which, without hesitation, he (the author of *The Wayfarer's Companion*) replied in a touching show of support for his former pupil: "Whatever you write, send it to me. I may not understand it, but I will proofread it for you and make sure it's in accurate English." I never took him up on this generous offer and caring involvement. In 1965 he married a French woman, and died soon afterwards, and it was affectionately suggested by more than one Old

Chigwellian that the French woman had worn him out.

I went back to Loughton at the start of the summer vacation. I found that while I was away my family had switched their allegiance from Methodism to Church of England to fit in with attendance at chapel in Chigwell School, leaving my aunt Argie to be the sole bearer of her parents' Methodist banner.

Return to Oaklands School
In early August I walked up to Oaklands one evening at dusk, slipped through the High-Road gate, sat in the summer hut (where the Garden Room now is) and looked out at the main field where I had spent my childhood among buttercups. I reflected on my progress since that time. It was as if a guardian angel, having steered me away from Law to English Literature, was bringing me face to face with a future task and destiny, showing me what was ahead. It grew dark, and I sat on, pondering my childhood and what the future held as a mist rose and blotted out the stars.

In Spain with John Ezard: itinerant
Almost immediately afterwards I left England to hitchhike round Spain for six weeks. I intuitively sensed that I would have experiences as a wandering itinerant that would take me towards wisdom and Reality. I travelled to Paris with Fred Young, a stocky, crew-cut undergraduate who wore a black shirt and dark glasses and modelled himself on Marcek in *Ashes and Diamonds*, and John Ezard, witness of my flight from Law, who was now somewhat vague, unco-ordinated and shambolic but, like Ricks, embodied an acute intelligence I often found helpful.

A French international footballer gave us all a lift from Paris to the Spanish Costa Brava. He drove his fast car all night and I remember him getting out near the Pyrenees at dawn and admiring the view of hills and a valley. Fred Young got a lift to south Spain on his own, and Ezard and I stayed in Barcelona. We saw a bullfight and then spent three days hitching to Valencia.

Totendanz
At Cambrils (outside Tarragona) we slept by the sea. We were awoken at dawn by seven black-coated figures holding hands and wearing black capes and hats. They were performing a *Totendanz* (dance of death) on the seashore. It was very similar to the *Totendanz* at the end of Ingmar Bergman's *The Seventh Seal*, and they passed within a couple of feet of us. I was more curious than frightened that they might carry us off to our deaths.

In Valencia we slept on a traffic roundabout and then pushed on to Malaga to catch the *fiesta*. We encountered Fred Young standing beside a road. In Malaga we all slept on the beach, and the rats were as large as cats.

At dawn, waking in my sleeping-bag, I saw them slinking low against the skyline and then scurrying off into the shadows. Fred Young then went off on his own again.

Meeting with Ernest Hemingway
Steeped in Hemingway's books, including *The Sun Also Rises*, Ezard and I followed the *fiesta*. We pushed on to Coin, a mountain village about 40 kms outside Malaga, to catch the *fiesta* there. The main street was lit with fairy lights and thronged with people and dancers. There were many stalls and there was much to drink. We met an American who gave us a card saying 'Angus Ward, former US Ambassador to Spain' and declared, "I'm Angus Ward. I'll put you up. I'll meet you at my house. Buzz at the gate." He then disappeared. Locals told us after dark that Señor Ward lived high on the hill in great security, as one might expect of an ex-ambassador to the US.

We climbed away from the *fiesta* up into the mountains and came to the twilit walled enclosure and rang the gate buzzer. Señor Ward came to the gate, wearing shorts. He was getting on for 60 and slightly balding. It was not the man who had given us the card. He took the card and said he did not know the man who had sent us. "I'm afraid you've been the victim of a trick. All I can suggest is that you sleep on the hillside here. It's warm, you'll be all right." The man who gave us the card must have had a grudge against the former US ambassador.

We laid our sleeping-bags among the wild flowers in the grass on the dark, sloping hillside above the lights of Coin. We wriggled into them and lay back, and the stars were brilliantly bright. They were moving and squirming and squirting "like a tray of live winkles" (as I described them in a story I later wrote of this title). The whole universe was alive, and I saw hundreds of shooting stars before I fell asleep. It was the end of the dog days, but to me the experience had a mystical force, reinforcing the idea that the universe was vital rather than mechanistic and that it had manifested from an invisible, hidden Reality.

We returned to Malaga, which was hot and stank after the mountain air. We saw another bullfight, at which Chicuelo II was slightly gored. Ernest Hemingway, the American writer, was sitting one row from the front in a maroon shirt, silver-bearded, and someone told us that he could be found in the evenings at the Miramar Hotel, Malaga. We went on to the bar there, passing Danny Kaye who was singing into a microphone near a band in the humid grounds, and sure enough Hemingway was standing in the air-conditioned cool with a drink in his hand, listening intently to a couple of men, watching with deep, sensitive eyes. Ezard and I lurked nearby, and when there was an opportunity I told Hemingway that I wanted to be a writer – he nodded barely perceptibly – and that we had been to the bullfight. He gave me his full attention and drawled very gently, "There's a *mano a mano* ['hand-to-hand'] tomorrow. Ordonez and Dominguin. You must see that. It will be the best bullfight of the year." I did not know that he had been following the rivalry between the no. 1 and the no. 2 bullfighters all summer and was writing *A Moveable Feast* about it. Kenneth Tynan, the drama critic, was sitting drinking Scotch about ten feet away, and he too (he later told us) was in Malaga for the *mano a mano*.

I stood beside Hemingway, a big, gentle man, recalling the Nick Adams short stories and Lt. Henry and Krebs and his other heroes and the collapse of values after the First World War which he had so memorably reflected, my mind too full of individual questions about his work to ask any one question that would have priority over the others. A man pushed in on our conversation and asked, "Tell me, Mr Hemingway, don't you feel the bulls of today aren't as big as they were some years ago?" Hemingway turned and gazed at him with his sensitive eyes and slowly took 300 pesetas from his pocket and slapped the three notes into the man's hand and said, "Go and buy yourself a book on bull-fighting, you stupid bastard." I was taken aback, for the man who had been so gentle to us had suddenly turned aggressive, and while I adjusted to my surprise a woman came up and said flattering things about his work, to which Hemingway quietly said one word (meaning 'Flatterer') which is not aired in polite society. I could see that Hemingway belonged to everybody. He was a public institution, and everyone went and spoke to him and he reacted with sympathetic understanding or honest (intolerant, exasperated) irritation depending on the person, holding up a mirror to their own nature as perhaps all great men do.

We turned away from Hemingway. Our contact was slight but real enough for me to feel that I could relate the man to his stories as in the case of my slight conversation with Sartre. Those few minutes made a lasting impression on me so that when I heard, sitting in a pub at the end of Smart's Lane, Loughton, one lunch-time in July 1961 that Hemingway had put a shotgun barrel into his mouth and shot himself after being diagnosed with hypertension (actually depression and anxiety requiring electric shock treatment), I felt genuinely sad, as though a friend had died.

Mano a mano: *Dominguin gored, Ordonez*
The *mano a mano* was the next day, a Friday evening. We queued for tickets before the sun got up that morning and we entered the stadium as the cool began to set in after the day's heat. We sat in the second row back. The summer-long rivalry between Ordonez and Dominguin had boiled up into a climax. Dominguin went first and was followed by Ordonez. Both killed their bulls.

Then Dominguin had his second bull. It was huge and very lively. It charged and thudded into the wooden barricade just below us. Dominguin did a series of passes, not moving his feet at all, and again and again the crowd roared *"Olé"* and there was deafening applause at the end. Haughtily, almost contemptuously, Dominguin threw down his sword and cape, turned his back on the bull and knelt down just beneath us and facing us, his ams in the air, all caution thrown aside in a breathtaking display of courage as he displayed his mastery.

But the bull had not surrendered. It charged and tossed him and he flew through the air. It charged again and gored him in his side, rolling him over and over. The crowd screamed and leapt to its feet. Matadors (including Ordonez) ran out and flapped their capes to distract the bull, turning it round and round on itself. Slowly Dominguin was helped to his feet, blood oozing through his tunic down one side. He waved the matadors away. His white face was twisted with pain but he recovered his hat, sword and cape and, just as still and poised as before, executed a whole series of brilliant passes to more *"Olés"* and thunderous applause, and then completed a perfect kill, plunging his sword over the bull's horns and turning his back dismissively as the bull moved its head from side to side and sank to its knees. Then proudly, stiffly, his pale face still twisted in agony, he walked to the side of the ring below us, unaided – and collapsed, the side of his tunic stained red.

The crowd was on its feet again, roaring, and as I stood on my seat so see over the heads I saw Hemingway waving his arms. (He was also in the second row back, further round the ring.) This *mano a mano* would be the climax of his book. Dominguin was lifted onto a stretcher and taken to hospital. Ordonez had won the *mano a mano*, but Dominguin had won the glory.

The next day I saw Ordonez. We had taken to sleeping on the beach at Torremolinos, 14 kms away from Malaga. We hitchhiked out from Malaga at night and back in for the next evening. In the late afternoon we were standing beside the road and a huge car (I believe a Rolls-Royce) slowed down. In the front seat sat Hercules ("Hercy") Belville, a very fastidious, mannered Oxford undergraduate I had met several times in the Randolph. (He later became a film producer and director, worked with Polanski for 14 years and died in 2009.) In the back sat Ordonez. Belville waved to me. He could see we were hitchhiking but he drove on, not stopping to allow us to scramble in alongside Ordonez and plant our dusty clothes on his plush back seat. (He received his comeuppance: not long after he was very badly injured in a car crash.)

Reading Metaphysical poets
From the hot dry south of Spain we hitchhiked north to San Sebastian

through dusty, central Spain. By the side of the road I read the Penguin anthology, *The Metaphysical Poets* (selected by Helen Gardner), which was on my list of vacation work. I can see myself squatting in an arid hilly landscape, the road stretching in each direction and no trees, reading Donne, Marvell, Herbert and some of the more minor Metaphysical poets, and discussing the Metaphysical world view with John Ezard. This prepared me for my first *Selected Poems*, titled *A Metaphysical's Way of Fire*. The Reality for which I was questing was in the poems, not in Spain. I enlarged on how the perspective of these poets differed from that of the secular poets who wrote about social reality today. I associated these poets with Eliot's religious outlook and their questioning of values with the questioning of the more worldly heroes of Sartre and Hemingway. I was groping towards wisdom: a vision of an invisible Reality which Coleridge and Shelley knew.

Wisdom and intelligence: poetry and Existentialist self-remaking

Back in England I worked for collections on Old and Middle English texts, including *Beowulf* and *Gawain and the Green Knight*. I bregrudged the time spent on mastering the grammar of these dead languages, and pored over Chaucer, Spenser, Skelton, the Silver poets of the Renaissance, the 17th-century poets, Restoration drama and a first look at the Augustans.

Room on staircase 5

That autumn I lived in college in the 18th-century terrace: in room 9 on staircase 5. (Eliot had famously read 'The Waste Land' aloud in room 6 on that staircase on 4 February 1928.)[2] The sitting-room had Regency-striped curtains and overlooked the gardens at the back. There was a small bedroom off it with a bowl for a jug of water which the 'scout' (servant) brought before breakfast. I spent the morning at lectures or at the Bodleian library or Radcliffe Camera, where I often looked at the spiral staircase, and the afternoons working in my room, leaving the evening free for going out or, when one of my weekly essays approached, going into the college library and drawing together all the books I had read to write my essay.

The tutorial in Literature was one-to-one. I would go to Ricks's book-lined room in the cottages, sit and read my essay aloud. He would make verbal comments which I noted down and we discussed issues arising from his response to what I had written (which was generally favourable). Sometimes we discussed his latest book review for *The Sunday Times*. Then he would set me my next essay and rattle off from memory a reading list of about twenty books or journals, while I scribbled them all down. He carried all the references to PMLA (Publication of the Modern Languages Association) and RES (Review of English Studies) in his head, and was never wrong.

He was very sharp. One day, at a time when an undergraduate publication was running a survey of undergraduates' views of their dons, he greeted me: "We dons have decided to run our own survey of the undergraduates, and so I am going to begin, 'Mr Hagger came in with his usual disarming smile and sat down confidently to read me his essay, which as usual he had completed.'" I laughed at the fluent charm and rapid nimbleness of his greeting.

In Ricks's tutorials, intelligence ruled. The English language, Old English and Middle English classes involved groups of 6 to 12 of us, although there were some tutorials which we attended in pairs. We had Tittensaw for Old English, a pallid, slow, dreamy young man who looked 17 and was in complete contrast to Ricks, who was a live wire, always fidgeting and never still, and poised to strike with a rapidly delivered and highly articulate view which I found very stimulating. I now found the chunks of Old English and Middle English language that we had to translate for exam purposes of even more questionable interest than Law.

I always got something from any poet we read. Spenser's *Fairie Queene* left me cold, but I loved his *'Prothalamion'* and *'Epithalamion'*. Wyatt and Surrey seemed forbidding, but I loved looking for evidence of Wyatt's affair with Anne Boleyn and relating his sonnets to the event which may have led to his execution. I also loved Donne's 'Aire and Angels' and Marvell's 'The Garden'. Through my reading of 17th-century literature I first encountered the mysterious Light which was in the work of every minor poet of the time but which never seemed to be mentioned in modern critical books or 20th-century authors except in fleeting references by Eliot. During my second year in college I wrote my essays at night in the college library. I climbed the spiral staircase opposite the porters' lodge, stayed up all night writing an essay and would go to bed at dawn with a profound satisfaction and go to sleep listening to the birds singing. I would wake two hours later in time for my tutorial.

I sensed that Reality could be found among the Metaphysical poets I had read in Spain but had not fully recognised the significance of the Light. I was still a prophet of freedom and (having jumped from Law to English Literature) emphasised breaking away from past habits and choosing oneself in a decisive existential leap or jump.

Ricky Herbert jumps into the canal
One night I found Ricky in the Gloucester Arms. He had had a few drinks and as we walked back to the college he praised one of his favourite characters in literature, the hero of Goncharov's *Oblomov* who slothfully takes to his bed and asks why anyone should be interested in current affairs. Like Stolz in that novel I urged him to put aside his false attitude. We were

crossing a bridge over the canal that runs near Worcester College – it must have been Hythe Bridge – and I urged him to define himself in terms of one definitive, Raskolnikovian act. I said, recalling how I jumped and just caught the departing train in Belgrade station, "You can stand on the side of the bridge and jump into the water to prove that you are free. To choose to do something in breach of habit as an *'act gratuit'* and jump to reject all Oblomovian sloth – that is a demonstration of freedom."

It was dark, and to my astonishment without a word Ricky did as I said. Still wearing his suede jacket, he got up on the iron top of the bridge and casually jumped. He disappeared. I bent over and heard a terrific splash at least 20 feet below and saw white froth and foam in the moonlit dark. Then there was silence.

"Ricky?" I called.

There was a sploosh and, rising like a river god from the stagnant water, Ricky waded, dripping moonlight, to an iron ladder and climbed up the sheer stone wall and stood, dripping from head to toe, and said, "I'm free."

"Bravo," I congratulated him. "You've demonstrated your freedom in a way that will never be forgotten." One or two passers-by stopped and looked at us oddly with a mixture of curiosity and suspicion.

We headed for the nearby college. Still dripping, Ricky squelched through the lodge. Evans, the porter, called "Good night, sir" to us, and Ricky called casually, "Good night, Evans." Evans stared in disbelief.

News of what Ricky had done soon spread. My reputation as the philosopher of freedom was enhanced. John Gretton, a fellow under-graduate, asked me to play Camus' Caligula at the Playhouse for the college Buskins, but in the event they put on *Two Gentlemen of Verona* instead.

I bundle Peter O'Toole over the Worcester College gate
Intelligence featured in another situation that term which symmetrically also included the Gloucester Arms and jumping. I looked into the Gloucester Arms in mid-evening to see if Ricky was around and found myself talking to a young and bearded Peter O'Toole. He was sitting with his chauffeur waiting for his wife Sian Phillips to finish her performance at the Playhouse. He told me he was currently playing Shylock at Stratford-upon-Avon and we discussed his interpretation of the part. He said he had a bottle of vodka and asked if he could come back to my room to drink it. (This was in his drunken period before *Lawrence of Arabia*.)

I took him back to my room along with the chauffeur, who produced two bottles of vodka. I found a copy of *The Merchant of Venice* and for the next three hours we had an increasingly drunken interpretation of just about every line of the play, O'Toole stressing feeling, I stressing the intelligent, academic side with some historical nuances that he was not aware of.

Suddenly I looked at my watch and saw that it was midnight, long after the theatre had finished and the college gates were closed. I explained that I had to get them to climb out of the grounds without being caught.

I got them down to the bottom of the staircase and then O'Toole started declaiming chunks of Shylock at the top of his voice. He broke away from me and lurched down to the basement. I found him trying to pee in the Law library. He said he disliked lawyers and had a good mind to burn the Law library down. I got him to the washroom toilets next door and then propelled him back up a floor and out into the gardens at the back, stressing the need for silence.

As we approached the rear gate in the dark there was a scraping noise and we retreated into bushes. Someone had run at the nine-foot-high gate from outside and was climbing. Fingers and then a bespectacled head appeared over the top in the dark, an ankle swung over and a man jumped down our side wearing a dinner-jacket and black tie. "'How like a fawning publican he looks!/I hate him for he is a Christian,'" bellowed O'Toole in his Shylock voice, and, hands out and terrified, Mr Campbell, the History tutor, rushed off towards the terrace through the dark.

Then the chauffeur and I tried to push the completely-drunk O'Toole over the nine-foot gate. We took a leg each and heaved upwards. Still reciting Shylock, O'Toole was bent double over the gate. We took a foot each and heaved up again. For a few seconds O'Toole lay horizontally on top of the gate declaiming Shylock. Then he disappeared.

We heaved ourselves up to look over and saw O'Toole lying on the pavement the other side, having fallen nine feet. He picked himself up and wandered in a zig-zag direction still reciting Shylock, while I gave the chauffeur a leg-up and then pulled myself up to see the chauffeur running after O'Toole in the direction of the Playhouse. The next time I saw O'Toole was 50 years later on a cruise. (*See My Double Life 2: A Rainbow over the Hills.*)

Interdisciplinary coffee

Now that 'my year' was living in college there were regular invitations, issued at the end of lunch in hall, to have after-lunch coffee in an under-graduate's rooms, and I often found myself in a group of seven in which everyone was studying a different subject. I found being with students of philosophy, history and Continental and Russian literature stimulating, and I tracked down and familiarised myself with the works they mentioned. I spent long hours reading outside my subject. Much of my time at Oxford was a time of exploration and discovery. Instinctively I had already grasped that breadth was as important as depth. The discussions were cross-disciplinary and often debated truth, and my Universalism may have had its roots in these collegiate gatherings, which I found immensely valuable.

Now I see such groupings as one of the most valuable aspects of the collegiate system.

Social satire
At Christmas I worked for the Post Office, delivering Christmas mail in Loughton. I read the 18th-century Augustans: the excessively rationalistic Johnson, Swift, Dryden and Pope, and wrote on "social satire". On Christmas Eve I drank with John Ezard in The Holly Bush and regarded the other drinkers satirically, applying Augustan principles to their apparent way of life. I measured them against an ideal Reality. Amid the decorations and paper hats, the party atmosphere and raucous laughter there was an obvious lack of awareness of the true meaning of Christmas.

I visit Colin Wilson and D.S. Savage in Cornwall
In January 1960 I took a train down to Cornwall for a few days. From St Austell station I found my way to Colin Wilson's house on a sloping cliff with a distant view of the sea: Tetherdown, Gorran Haven. Standing by the front door was the young bespectacled, eager man who had spoken so fluently and confidently in the Fleet Street coffee-house. He had written *The Age of Defeat*, which was widely discussed among the undergraduates. He invited me in, and I sat on the large sofa in a spacious book-lined room and found him very welcoming for someone who was public property. I was able to hold forth about some of the writers I was studying, and we discussed the writers he was writing about – the Beats – and metaphysics: Reality. He said he could not put me up because his parents were occupying the chalet, but he rang D.S. Savage, the literary critic (author of *The Withered Branch*) who lived in Mevagissey.

I was put up at the Lawns Hotel, a guest-house Savage kept (later called Hollies House). A grave, Russian-looking man with greased dark hair and a well-groomed beard, Savage despised Colin Wilson's popularity – he was particularly scathing about *Ritual in the Dark* – and I gathered I was something of an ambassador between the two households. Savage reverentially produced a suitcase and showed me the unpublished essays of the deceased Catholic E.F.F. Hill, which he was trying to publish and valued more highly than Wilson's work.

The next day at lunch-time Colin Wilson met me at The Ship, Mevagissey (which has since been burned down and replaced by a restaurant). He bought all the fishermen a drink and when he was there all eyes were upon him. He drove me back to Tetherdown, and I spent the afternoon talking with him. After dark we walked outside under the stars, and he denied that he was a Fascist (as someone had suggested) and when I mentioned hitch-hiking in Spain told me how much he had enjoyed hitchhiking in France, reading Plato and not really minding if he got a lift.

He was extremely open about experiences he had had in the spirit of an Existentialist philosopher, and always sought to relate particular experiences he shared to a general truth, a trait I liked and admired. I remember him describing an intimate experience he had had. It was refreshing that such experiences could be shared objectively for the Existentialist conclusions that could be drawn. Such conversations suggested that *all* experience is the currency of philosophy, that nothing should be held back, that the philosopher had a total commitment to understanding experience. I warmed to him, and after he dropped me back at Savage's felt uncomfortable listening to Savage's withering comments about his lack of talent as a novelist.

I visited Colin Wilson again the next day and sat with him. After I left I walked down to the sea and took a bus and found Old Walls, the house to which he had fled at the beginning of his Outsider's exile in Cornwall and from which I had received his first letter to me.

W.H. Auden, William Empson and J.I.M. Stewart

Back at Oxford I began writing poems; or rather, I felt the urge to write poems and was discontented with what came out. I wanted to be a poet, and I heard a creased-faced W.H. Auden recite some of his poems from memory – he completely dried in the middle of 'The Willow-wren and the Stare' – and on another occasion Theodore Roethke read his poems. Christopher Ricks, a self-described Empsonian, invited the poet William Empson, author of *Some Versions of Pastoral* and *Seven Types of Ambiguity*, to chat to us, which he did, bespectacled and bearded in a long room in college with a rectangle of desks. I attended a series of lectures on Yeats given by J.I.M. Stewart (*alias* Michael Innes) even though Yeats was not on the syllabus, for I needed to get to grips with Yeats as part of my remaking of myself as a poet. I was haunted by Yeats's lines, which seemed to apply to me:

> The friends that have it I do wrong
> Whenever I remake a song,
> Should know what issue is at stake:
> It is myself that I remake.

Coming out of Schools, where the lectures took place, one Tuesday morning about 11.15 I had a strong glimpse into the future. In my mind's eye I saw a small harbour where I knew I would one day write poetry. I wondered if it was in Ireland, but I now know it was in Charlestown, a few miles from Colin Wilson's house, where I have had a second home since 1987 and written many of my poems.

I often saw Auden wandering in the High Street, for he was Professor of Poetry at Oxford University. I attended one of his lectures in Schools. It was packed. There were over 700 present, and I was standing outside a first-floor balcony, looking down on Auden as he talked about Shakespeare's *The Tempest* (a lecture which formed part of *The Dyer's Hand*). I did not know that one day Ricks would become Professor of Poetry and that I would have tea with him before walking across the road to Schools to sit in comfort and hear him speak.

Visit to John Ezard in Cambridge, Ian McKellen

In March I visited Cambridge and sat with John Ezard in his rooms at St Catherine's. A quiet man was present, Ezard's room-mate Ian McKellen (later Sir Ian McKellen, a distinguished actor).

That Easter Ezard and I resumed our walks in Epping Forest. We used to meet on the open Forest land near the stream off Staple's Road. One day I picked him up in my father's A70 and we drove to Audley End and followed a signpost to Royston in search of the graveyard of Haggers my father had often mentioned. I followed several hunches until, on a corner, in a place I have not since been able to find, I came across a small church and churchyard. Walking among the graves and peering at the tombstones, I saw a number of Haggers. (*See* pp.13–15.)

One night we left The Holly Bush and walked up to Strawberry Hill when it was misty, and Ezard quoted Coleridge's 'Christabel': "'Is the night chilly and dark?/The night is chilly but not dark.'" A week later we walked to Strawberry Hill again, and this time he quoted Coleridge's 'Dejection: an Ode': "'I see, not feel how beautiful they are.'" He told me, "That's how I feel. I'm numb within. I've lost the power to respond to Nature with feeling." We are all removed from Nature by social and educational systems, but he reacted drastically to his plight. Shortly afterwards I heard he had left his college and been admitted to Fulbourn Hospital in Cambridge to have electric-shock treatment. Our walks had come to an end.

Ricky Herbert: the path of De Quincey

That Easter I read Defoe, Richardson and Fielding, and wrote an essay on the 18th-century novel. It was a fine spring and I sat in the garden at Journey's End, sometimes on the wooden bench near the ivy and sometimes in a deck-chair near the pear-tree on the lawn. I also read the Romantic poets, and returned to Wordsworth, Coleridge, Keats, Shelley and Byron, seeing them with more mature eyes through the critical intelligence but still fascinated by their search for Reality. I spent as much time reading Kingsley Shorter's copy of Rilke's *Duino Elegies* and comparing French and German Romanticism with the English Romantic poets.

In the summer of 1960 I watched Ricky's slow disintegration. A young man called Graham Wallis had appeared in college. He had no money and no possessions except for his filthy clothes, and for a couple of weeks he slept in people's rooms (mainly Ricky's). He was on drugs and professed to know some of the American Beats, and the conversation revolved round the experience of beatitude. He borrowed my copy of Dostoevsky's *The Idiot* and when he returned it the white parts of the cover had turned grubby brown.

Then one hot summer's day he became too daring and sunbathed on the main lawn. There was a sprinkler on, and, peeling off some of his clothes, he had a public wash and shower. He was challenged and apprehended by a porter, removed from the college and banned from re-entry.

But he had introduced a drug pedlar, a swarthy young man with an impeccably upper-class accent, who arrived in college with marijuana and several, including Ricky, would smoke it in the room next to mine. Kingsley was not drawn in. He had returned to Subud and went off to sit and meditate, waiting "for an experience of the Absolute". Ricky was increasingly drawn towards the Beatnik drug culture. I knew it was not right, and said so, and I watched with sadness as he pursued a fascination that would result in opium addiction (*see* p.156). He had taken the path of Thomas De Quincey, who first experienced opium while an undergraduate at Worcester College in 1804 and later wrote *Confessions of an English Opium-Eater*.

Self-remaking: typing, CND
My parents came up before my 21st birthday, and stayed at the Mitre. We had dinner in the Randolph dining-room and they came and looked at my room on staircase 5. I spoke of wanting to become a writer. With some birthday money I bought a portable typewriter and set about teaching myself to type. Stuart Holroyd had told me that it was important to take a typing course, and I booked myself into a local typing school and was taught touch-typing to music. Sometimes, late at night, I encountered Ricky in the basement washroom at the bottom of my staircase. Stoned, he would say with glassy eyes, "It's all futile anyway, so why bother to write anything? Give up and take weed like me." He had retired into a drug-dream.

I was questioning my values and assumptions. We were above all a questioning, thoughtful generation. We looked behind the received social truths and sought to know the meaning of life. We were a seeking generation, a generation of seekers. Having written in favour of the nuclear deterrent for Biggs-Davison's magazine and having voted against unilateral nuclear disarmament a year earlier, I questioned my assumptions and I reluctantly allowed myself to become college CND (Campaign for Nuclear Disarmament) representative, justifying my outlook on the grounds that I was remaking myself and should eliminate all traces of the Young Conservatives to be an Angry Existentialist.

H.J. Blackham
One sunny evening H.J. Blackham, author of *Six Existentialist Thinkers* (which I had read several times), visited the college and gave an open-air talk in the Provost's packed courtyard. I can see him standing and addressing us from a lectern on Kierkegaard, Heidegger, Jaspers, Marcel, Sartre and Camus. I went and had a talk with him afterwards, very much the resident college Existentialist.

F.R. Leavis
Soon afterwards I heard F.R. Leavis in a crowded hall. He arrived late, looking like a tramp, wearing an army shoulder-bag which he dumped on the stage and rummaged in for his notes. Then he stood at the lectern and spoke with a rapid, rambling delivery. I remember he praised D.H. Lawrence's letters, which he said, "were dashed off in great haste". I was not impressed and made no attempt to speak to him at the end.

Visit to Cliveden, Lord Astor
My call to Reality put me in unexpected situations. I still looked in at the Randolph and had got to know some of the girls there and the actor who played the intense piper in the Polish film *Kanal*, Vladek Sheybal.

One night John Hamblett announced there that he had been invited to a party at Cliveden, Lord Astor's house, and asked if I would go with him on the back of his scooter to make sure he did not fall asleep during the return journey. Just after dusk we drove through the great wrought-iron gates and were soon sipping champagne on the raised terrace among a couple of hundred 'beautiful young people'.

Cliveden was where the Profumo Affair would take place. There was swimming in the swimming-pool where a year later (on 9 July 1961 according to Ivanov's memoirs, *The Naked Spy*, and according to Christine Keeler's own later memoirs, *The Truth at Last*)[3] Profumo encountered a naked Christine Keeler. About 5 in the morning, after dawn, I talked with Bill Astor as he came to refill my glass. In due course I would get to know Lady Astor, who had experienced the Light before the Profumo Affair burst upon public attention in 1962/3, and I wonder if being taken to her world was helpful to my eventual path. (*See My Double Life 2: A Rainbow over the Hills.*)

Self-remaking: retiring from cricket, last game
My remaking of myself ended my playing of cricket. That summer I had

played four times for the college at cricket and made a good score each time. I increasingly felt that playing cricket had wasted a day. My fourth innings took place shortly after I attended the chaplain's sherry party. I made 50, hitting the ball hard and middling it with a certainty I never had when sober.

I went back to Chigwell School to see my brother Robert collect a prize at Speech Day on 25 June 1960, and walked down to the 1st XI pitch to watch the School – captained by my brother – play the Headmaster's XI. The Headmaster's XI were one short and Robert asked me to play. Flannels were found, and, batting at no. 3 I was aware that I was making the numbers up and should not be at the crease too long. I hit everything I could hard and high, not caring if I were out, and I just could not get out. Fielding at mid-off, my brother urged me to give up my wicket as I was stopping the School from winning. I tried to oblige, but my high hits kept missing the fielders and I ended on 62 not out, and the match was drawn. As I returned to the pavilion to the applause of several of my former teachers I thought that if I were to stop playing cricket I should go out on a high point. I never donned flannels again. I had played my last match.

I had derived benefit from Ricks's acute intelligence and had ransacked poets and literary authors for their approaches to Reality, but ever drawing nearer was the pressing need to work out a way of earning money from a BA in English Language and Literature while carrying forward the literary life I saw ahead.

Intelligence: raising money
Now my thoughts turned to a form of intelligence that differed from the one I had encountered with Ricks. It loomed as I saved to spend five weeks in Greece during the summer vacation.

Raising money: debt-collecting, Soho Fair – Bernard Kops, John Osborne
I had initially raised money for the trip by working part-time for a small debt-collecting agency which was run by a Worcester College 'scout'. He asked me if I would join him for a couple of weeks at the beginning of the vacation. He was thin, lean and lanky, and had been a notorious jewel-thief. He had been in prison and escaped twice through impossibly narrow openings, and was nicknamed 'Rubberbones'. After term ended he rode about on a motor bike collecting debts. I sat behind him on the pillion and rang doorbells and tried to collect debts from impecunious and elderly dons who reluctantly shuffled from their manuscripts to wheedle articulate excuses at the front door. I made enough commission from what I collected to fund the basic costs of my trip.

I supplemented this money by selling programmes at the Soho Fair. I had heard about this from Herbie Butterfield, one of the Randolph Set. I contacted the organiser and reported to a house in Noel Street on 9 July. I paid £1 for 20 programmes, stood on various Soho street corners selling them, and pocketed 10s. when they had all gone. I then bought another 20 and did the same again, and so on for a week. Several of the Randolph Set were doing this, and we met up in the Helvetia or one of the other Soho pubs at regular intervals to compare notes. I remember the dramatist Bernard Kops, and on another day the dramatist John Osborne, walking by.

The writer as spy: Marlowe, Defoe, Maugham, Greene; letter to Major Goulding
I had pondered other ingenious ways of making money. I was aware that the family business was in the hands of my cousins and was not available to me, and that I would soon have to earn my own living. I had been interested in the British Empire and was aware that the generation before mine had been able to go out to India and experience the subcontinent. Biggs-Davison had told me that he had served in the Indian Civil Service. His posting was at the end of the British Raj, which provided a route for young men to go out and live in the Indian Empire. Following India's independence that course was not open to me. I did not want to become a colonial administrator and spend my life in one of the colonies in Africa or on one of the colonial islands. I wondered how I could work abroad for a while and see a bit of the world.

My reading within and outside my course had brought to my attention a tradition of writers who worked in intelligence. Christopher Marlowe was thought to have worked for the Government[4] under Sir Thomas Walsingham (and his deputy Sir Thomas Heneage, who had owned Copped Hall near Loughton) and to have put then hitherto unpublished intelligence about the Ottoman activity in Malta in *The Jew of Malta* (1589 or 1590). According to the coroner's report of the inquest[5] on his death, he was stabbed by a Government agent, Frizer, in the company of Skeres and Poley, two more Walsingham agents.

The Rainbow portrait of Elizabeth I (c.1602) shows her in an orange cloak decorated with eyes, ears and mouths. It was a warning that she could see and hear everything through her intelligence agents, and that all plotters would be found out. Marlowe was one of her eyes, ears and mouths. (*See* p.xx.)

Daniel Defoe had been a secret agent in Edinburgh in 1706 and had intrigued the Anglo-Scottish union of 1707.[6] Somerset Maugham began working for the Secret Intelligence Service in 1915 and was sent by them on a special mission to Russia in June 1917 to keep the provisional government in power and Russia in the war.[7] He was supposed to counter German pacifist propaganda, but the Bolshevik Revolution torpedoed his work two-and-a-half months later. T.E. Lawrence[8] (my hero) was an intelligence agent who led the Arab revolt against the Ottoman Empire and was instrumental in sweeping the Ottomans away. A.A. Milne had worked for MI7b, writing propaganda as one of 20 of the best British authors during the First World War.[9] And Graham Greene had been recruited into MI6 by his sister Elisabeth, who worked for the organisation.[10] He had been posted to Sierra Leone during the Second World War, and Kim Philby (at that time a Soviet agent) had been his controller.[11] Possibly Kipling[12] and also John Buchan (first in the Intelligence Corps and then as Director of Intelligence under Lloyd George)[13] had worked in operational intelligence. Arthur Ransome,[14] Compton Mackenzie,[15] Malcolm Muggeridge[16] and A.J. Ayer[17] had also worked in intelligence. I did not know it then but Wordsworth may also have undertaken spy missions for the newly-formed British Secret Service in Germany and in England during the 1790s and was in the Duke of Portland's secret book of payments next to the chief British intelligence agent in Hamburg (Crawfurd) as receiving £92.12s on 13 June 1799.[18] And Byron, who fought the Ottoman Empire in Western Greece in 1824, may not have used his own money when refitting the Greek fleet and paying the anti-Ottoman freedom-fighting Souliotes as commander-in-chief of the Greek army.[19] Like Lawrence, he may have been fighting the Ottoman Empire with British-intelligence funding.

I wondered if I could do something similar by exploiting the international situation. In 1960 the Cold War was at its height. The main issue was a possible thawing of relations between the US and Soviet Russia. There had been moves towards peaceful co-existence, Khrushchev's policy, which was in conflict with Mao's Chinese belligerence towards Western capitalism and had caused the Sino-Soviet split. However, peaceful co-existence had proved elusive, and Khrushchev had used the Soviet shooting-down of an American U-2 high-altitude reconnaissance plane to refuse to attend a summit conference in Paris and to walk out of the Ten-Nation Disarmament Committee in Geneva. I was in favour of disarmament talks but I was very much on the side of the West and against Soviet Russia's obstructiveness. I was on the side of President Eisenhower and of Churchill's British successors and at heart favoured the nuclear deterrent and the British Empire, and supported Suez. I had been surrounded by left-wingers at Oxford and somehow I had allowed myself to be CND representative of my college, which I privately regretted. Somehow I had a CND persona round the real me, and I only believed in the part of CND that urged disarmament talks.

Within Greece, where I was heading, the main issue concerned Enosis. EOKA's war for the self-determination of Cyprus (which had blown up Bunny Gaymer of Chigwell over Northumberland by planting a bomb on his plane in Cyprus in 1956) was now over and Cyprus had been liberated from British colonial rule. Cyprus had achieved independence in 1959. However, Enosis, union with Greece, had not been achieved. The leader of EOKA-Enosis, Col. Grivas, had reluctantly accepted independence and had returned to Greece. But he still wanted union with Greece. (In 1964 he would return to Cyprus and form EOKA–B in opposition to Makarios, who was content with independence and did not support union with Greece.) I could locate Col. Grivas in the interests of maintaining stability in the Mediterranean at this point in the Cold War. He was then the most hated figure within the British Establishment as the man responsible for killing 371 British soldiers between 1956 and 1959.

I wondered if I could earn some money in August out of the international situation, and then make a career by following in the footsteps of Marlowe, Defoe, Maugham, and Greene. I wondered if I could quest for Reality in foreign cultures while working in intelligence as a freelance. (I knew that a 'free lance' was originally a medieval mercenary whose lance was free and hired out for specific missions rather than pledged to the continuous service of one employer.) If I worked in intelligence for a while my period of service would come to be regarded like war service. It was something writers did along their path.

The idea deepened all through the Soho Fair, and shortly before leaving for Greece, on the morning of 14 July 1960, while still at Journey's End, in a 'free act' – breaking away from past habits and choosing my future anew, remaking myself by my actions – I rang the War Office in London and was put through to a Major Goulding. I explained my thinking and said I was going to Greece. I told him I would find Grivas. It was an impossible objective, but I was full of the confidence of youth. It was like telling his modern equivalent that I was going to find Osama bin Laden. He asked me to write in.

So immediately after the call I typed a letter on my portable Olivetti typewriter:

Dear Major Goulding, I write to follow up my telephone call this morning seeking information concerning future employment in one of the civilian branches of Intelligence.

I explained my background, and then said:

As regards the future, I am afraid I can only be rather vague. My French is far from fluent, and I only know enough of other modern languages to satisfy my basic needs. If possible, however, I should like to be fairly freelance, and to travel abroad. I would like to know whether one of the Intelligence branches could make use of me this time next year. I would also like to know what scope they could offer me.

I said I was about to leave for Greece and gave my postal address as Hotel Byron, Aiolou Street, Athens.[20] Looking back, I reflect that I would never have written that fateful letter if I had not jumped from Law to English Language and Literature.

In Greece: awareness of British Council, my encounter with Col. Grivas
I heard no more before I left for Greece. I had met an English lady school-teacher, Mary Hedges, who had finished a year's course at Oxford and was going to teach in Ankara through the British Council. I had arranged to travel out with her and leave her in Greece. I took a boat to Belgium and hitched to Amsterdam, where Mary was staying with friends, and we travelled by train via Yugoslavia. We went to Athens and saw the Acropolis in a fierce heat and then got straight out to the Greek islands where I planned to work out how I could locate Grivas.

We arrived in Spetsai (or Spetses) and were invited to spend five days on a yacht in the harbour by a Greek local. Every morning we went ashore, and every day the '*krik-krak*' (fast motor launch with a low back) sped across to the island of Spetsopoula, where the billionaire Stavros Niarchos lived. Thinking that Niarchos might know where Grivas was, I sent a message via the pilot asking if we could visit Spetsopoula. I can see the '*krik-krak*' returning and the pilot leaping out yelling to me "Niarchos, Niarchos" and waving a letter – which merely regretted that he would be unable to receive us as he had only recently arrived.

We went on to Porto Cheli, a tiny place, and while swimming met a rich Athenian couple who had a summer residence on the hill. In the evenings we all ate in the only seaside café, which served good yoghurt and a carafe of retsina.

One evening at dusk a dozen Greek fishermen sitting at a long table in the waterside café all stood up and formed themselves in an unsteady line. A man with a domed head and parchment-white face arrived in fisherman's clothes (a dark polo-neck sweater and dark trousers) and paraded up and down the line, inspecting them. A waiter in a white jacket was hovering near me. I raised my eyebrows to him and indicated the man conducting the inspection.

"Grivas," he whispered to me, "Colonel Grivas."

It was indeed the Greek leader of EOKA who had lived underground in Cyprus while fighting the British there and supervising the killing of 371 British soldiers, and successfully bringing self-determination to Cyprus: the first elections of the new Cyprus had taken place in July.

I could hardly believe my luck. I had been wondering how to contact him and now he had walked into the waterside café where I was eating. It seemed an amazing coincidence. He could have been anywhere in the whole of Greece and the Greek islands and within just over a week he had placed himself within feet of me. I have since wondered whether he knew of my interest in him (via information leaked to him by associates of Major Goulding), and whether he had arrived to take a look at me. A couple of years before, at the height of EOKA's activities in Cyprus, I could have been a target, a victim of an EOKA assassination. He was a professional guerilla who had personally killed many British soldiers, and even then he could have shot me in the café in cold blood.

After the inspection Grivas sat at the long table with the fishermen. His chair was not far from mine. I sent a message over to him via the waiter: "Can I please interview you for a British newspaper?"

He turned and fixed on me his terrorist's gaze. The answer came back, "He say no, he don't like Macmillan [then the British Prime Minister]."

I sent a return message saying: "I'm not part of the British Government, I will interview you sympathetically about Enosis, Greek rule in Cyprus, which you still want to achieve."

This was too much for Grivas. Suddenly he stood up and everyone else round the table jumped to their feet and lined up again, and after another brief inspection he headed for the door that led to the road outside that ran alongside a flat, unfenced farmer's field.

I stood up and followed him out onto the road. There was no trace of him. It was twilight, and he had simply vanished without trace. He had a reputation for being a Pimpernel. I wondered if he was lying spread-eagled in the shallow ditch of the nearby field.

I may not have been able to interview Grivas, but I flushed him out of the café in Porto Cheli and the dozens of dead British servicemen would be pleased about that. And I would have something to report to Major Goulding. Soon afterwards I left Mary in the care of the Greek family, waved goodbye, wishing her well in Ankara, and headed off on my own to Athens.

Return journey: Rupert Brooke
The next part of the holiday was a disaster. At Oxford I had met a neurotic heiress who was on the fringe of the Randolph Set, Jill (her abbreviation of Gillian) Bradbury. Her health was poor, and she was outside Oxford for part of each term and often in the company of her young mother when she returned. She had invited me to stay at her home, and in June I had spent a few days at Ludham Hall, Braintree, and had walked through the palatial rooms, climbed the tower, trudged across the estate to the Blackwater and collected eggs from the hens. She was offering a temptingly comfortable set-up in Essex if I could bring myself to co-exist with her. It was as if

Providence were offering me an alternative to Major Goulding and questing abroad. She wanted me to stay on but I felt my time was not my own and left. After that she insisted on flying out to Athens and travelling back with me.

I met her plane but by now I had almost run out of money and she wanted everything 5-star. We went to Euboea, to which I felt drawn because of the silver drachma I had bought in Seaby's some years back. In Chalcis Jill booked in at the most expensive hotel while I slept on the beach. We travelled around as best we could, but she complained that Greece was ugly and that I was content to eat in cheap places (as opposed to the very expensive places she wanted to eat in).

From Chalcis we took a boat to Skyros to see the tomb of the English poet Rupert Brooke. It is in an olive grove on a hill, and in the course of climbing up to it I encountered a grave that had collapsed inwards. I saw the skeleton lying on its back, looking at the blue sky, surrounded by pines and whirring cicadas in the heat. I pondered on Reality and sensed there was wisdom in my insight. I wrote a few poems, feeling a common bond with Brooke.

We took a boat to the mainland and hitchhiked, and caught a bus into Yugoslavia. Jill slept in her sleeping-bag under the stars as I did, but she could not sleep and talked all night, keeping me awake, and I just wanted to escape. (She was like the neurotic woman – Eliot's first wife – in 'The Waste Land', who said, "My nerves are bad tonight.... /Speak to me.... Speak."). I had now more or less run out of money. She had hundreds of pounds of travellers' cheques but would not cash any to lend to me. In Skopje I changed my last £10 into Yugoslav currency and had just enough to buy a bus ticket to Dubrovnik and a boat ticket to Rijeka in Croatia, after which my return train ticket could be used.

On the boat she behaved unreasonably, sitting in a German's bagged deck-chair and complaining when she was shouted at. We passed along the beautiful wooded Dalmatian coastline, but I was too concerned to avoid Jill and various irate passengers to relax and enjoy it. To my great relief she returned by plane from Venice and I took the train.

Nothing would have induced me to settle with her in Ludham Hall. I returned to England still bent on devising a way of making money rather than marrying into it. My encounter with Col. Grivas (who had actually just been made General Grivas) had strengthened my feeling that I could make a living out of international relations.

Goulding's reply

I found a letter from Major Goulding waiting for me. It was written from the War Office and dated 5 August 1960. Across the top was typed: "From: Major G.S. Goulding Int. Corps. (MI.1 Co-ord)." The letter said:

Dear Hagger, Thank you for your letter dated 14 July 1960 asking for information about the branches of intelligence work open for civilian recruitment. I am to say that in the interests of national security no information can be given on this subject but that your name has been noted in our records and we shall get in touch with you should your services be required at any time in the future. I am, sir, your obedient servant.

The letter was signed "Goulding" and underneath was his rank: "Major."[21]

Sherry with the Provost – Sir John Masterman, The Double-Cross System
I put this letter out of my mind and plunged into Victorian novelists and poets for a collection. I went for solitary walks in the Forest. The prospect of finding a job in a year's time left me faintly depressed, and I returned to Oxford in inner turmoil.

We were out of college for our third year, and I had found digs in a first-floor room a bus ride down Walton Street. It was in a tiny terraced house and I was in close proximity to the landlady and her husband, a most uncongenial couple who went to bed at 10 and turned all the lights out, and complained next morning if I had come in later and crept up the stairs in the dark. I stood it for a fortnight, during which Jill Bradbury visited me. We went to a pub round the corner, The Jericho, and the novelist-don Iris Murdoch, who had been grouped with the Angry Young Men, looked in, spotted Jill (whom she knew) and came over for a chat.

It became clear that I was expected to be back by 10 every night and, reacting to a card in a newsagent's window, I found a room at 57 Southmoor Road, a house with an absentee landlord. I had the first-floor room at the back, overlooking a garden and, beyond a canal, Port Meadow.

The absentee landlord appeared once a week to collect rent, which was £2.10s. My parents visited soon after I moved in, and my father was shocked. He said, "It's no better than a condemned house." I lived next door to two secretaries, and to my room undergraduettes I knew came for tea, including Jill Bradbury, who picked up my Tutankhamen figurine from the mantelpiece and dropped it, chipping a piece off its foot. Here came John Ezard, now out of hospital. We went for a walk in Port Meadow, along the tow-path by the brimming river towards Binsey Green. We passed a number of swans, and the river looked high and arctic. Beyond it were flat fields and the distant spires of Oxford.

I had almost forgotten about Major Goulding's letter when in early November I went to my pigeon-hole, opened an envelope and found a card from the Provost inviting me for sherry the following Sunday morning. (I believe it was 6 November 1960.) I was surprised but assumed that there would be between twenty and thirty undergraduates present and that he was probably holding a number of such gatherings to include all under-graduates.

The Provost, Sir John Masterman, was a remote figure. I saw him each evening at dinner in the hall. We all stood while he led in his dons, who walked behind him in single file and took their places on top table. I had made contact with him at 'handshakings' at the end of each term when we queued outside a door and entered one by one and sat to hear our tutor's report on our progress. Masterman would turn to me and say, "That's very good, Mr Hagger," and extend a hand which I would shake and then depart without a word. But I never saw him wandering in the cloisters or strolling in the gardens. There was a 'Provost's Garden' which was fenced off and separate.

I duly went to the front door of the Provost's Lodging at the end of the terrace. Masterman opened the door and admitted me to a large room. I was surprised to find that I was the only guest. Masterman poured me a sherry and invited me to sit in a large high-backed chair against the wall just inside the door while he sat some distance away, facing me.

I did not know at the time that he had been educated at the Royal Naval Colleges of Osborne and Dartmouth and at Worcester College before the First World War, or that he had spent four years as a prisoner-of-war in Germany. I did not know that he had been tutor of Modern History at Christ Church, or that he had been mentor to his pupil Sir Dick White, head of MI5 and then of MI6. I did not know that during the Second World War Masterman had been Chairman of the Twenty Committee which turned captured German agents into double agents and sent them back into Germany with misinformation about the location of the coming allied invasion of France on D-Day and about the range of the V-1 and V-2 rockets (causing many to fall short of London). 'Twenty' was a pun on XX, 'double cross'. I did not know that he had written a report on this work, *The Double-Cross System*, in July–September 1945 and that he was at the time of our chat asking MI5, who devised the system, for permission to publish it. (In 1961 the Director-General of MI5, Roger Hollis, who had read English at Worcester College and was suspected of being a Soviet agent, would refuse, and when the book came out in the US in 1970 Masterman would be threatened with legal action until it was finally published in the UK in 1972.) (*See* p.xxxi.)

Masterman said that he had been told by a "friend" that I might be inter-ested in Government service. He asked me to share my thought processes. I said I wanted to be involved in the Cold War and spend time overseas. I told him how I had encountered Col. Grivas in Greece. He was extremely inter-ested in this encounter: I had told Major Goulding I would find him, and I had found him. I had shown what I was capable of doing. He talked about the way of life of someone working in intelligence, and the difficulties of maintaining secrecy. "It's very difficult to advise you as to what you should do," he said. "Someone who sat in the very chair you're sitting in and agonised about his future is now Chief of MI6." (He was referring to his protégé Sir Dick White.) He said he would report the conversation we had just had and that I would hear something soon. I finished my sherry and left.

57 Southmoor Road: Caroline Nixon
I was still not sure if I wanted to work in Government service. I had recurrent dreams of being executed as a soldier at night during the First World War. When I woke I attributed these dreams to my letter to the War Office rather than to an earlier life.

I now felt I should be preparing to become a writer. I was reading Victorian novels – often a novel by Dickens or Thackeray each day – and I longed to read Hardy, Yeats and Lawrence, all of whom wrote after 1860 and were outside my course. I felt I had to start writing to get into the habit, and I had an urge to start a play. It began as a poetic drama and the more I wrote the more realistic it became.

The two secretaries next door, whose room was three times the size of mine, encouraged me to look in on them for coffee, and there I met the President of the Oxford Union for Michaelmas 1959, Joe Trattner, a balding, big, bluff American who always wore an overcoat and scarf. I walked with him to The Jericho, a pub with sawdust on the floor, and he told me how when President he had dealt with a protest against Prime Minister Macmillan when Macmillan came to the Union and how he handled the Union officers such as the well-connected Peter Jay (who later became Economics Editor of *The Times* and Ambassador to the US) and Paul Foot (the son of Lord Caradon and later an investigative journalist).

One of the secretaries sometimes felt depressed and would go and sit by the canal. I sometimes heard her through my open window crying quietly in the twilight by the canal, and I wondered what the mind that was doing the crying was enduring. One evening I looked in for coffee next door and found her by herself, wearing black. Caroline Nixon was a very young, beautiful blonde who did not look unlike Marilyn Monroe, and I began a relationship with her which lasted the rest of my time at Oxford. She was full of feeling. When she was happy she brimmed with confidence, and when she was not happy she was withdrawn and vulnerable. Sometimes we went for a walk across the railway bridge into Port Meadow and looked at the wild horses and walked to the bridge over the river and crossed over to the tow-path. We returned home just before dark and I would toast sliced bread against my gas fire.

Letter from Admiral Sir Charles Woodhouse, meeting in Carlton Gardens
I was soon thinking again about intelligence. Masterman had said he would report our conversation, and towards the end of November I received a letter headed: "Personal and Confidential, From Admiral Sir Charles Woodhouse." The address was Co-ordination Staff, Foreign Office, Carlton Gardens, London SW1, and the date was 21 November. It said:

> Dear Sir, Your name has come to me indirectly [i.e. from Masterman] with the suggestion that you may be interested in Government service involving periods of duty overseas. If this is so, I should be grateful if you would complete the attached record form and return it to me. I should also like to have a talk with you in this connection and suggest you call upon me at the above address on Thursday December 1st at 11.15 a.m. I would emphasise, however, that at this stage our talk must be regarded as being of a purely exploratory nature, and that it does not commit either side.

I had to let him know that the date and time were convenient, and I was told that a second-class return railway fare would be refunded if I had to make the journey "specially for this purpose".[22]

I duly took the train to London on 1 December and found Carlton Gardens between Pall Mall and Carlton House Terrace and entered a large Belgravian house with a magnificent crested fireplace in the entrance hall. Two houses seemed to have been knocked into one, and I was told that Lord Palmerston had lived there and that it had been the headquarters of Gen. de Gaulle's Free French movement from 18 June 1940. I was shown up to a small room on the first floor, where the Admiral came to the door, a courteous man of 67 wearing an elegant suit.

I did not then know that Admiral Sir Charles Woodhouse had joined the Navy in 1906 and had been a gunner in the First World War, that he had been Assistant Director of Naval Equipment at the Admiralty in 1935 and that as Captain Woodhouse he had commanded *HMS Ajax* in the Battle of the River Plate off Argentina and Uruguay in December 1939. I did not know he had attacked the German pocket battleship (i.e. a warship armoured and equipped like, but smaller than, a battleship) *Admiral Graf Spee* and shadowed it to Montevideo, where its German captain scuttled it and committed suicide. In the 1956 film *The Battle of the River Plate* (which starred John Gregson, Anthony Quayle and Peter Finch) he had been played by Ian Hunter. I did not know he had then commanded *HMS Howe* and that in 1944 he was Churchill's Director of Naval Ordnance at the Admiralty. He had retired in 1950 and was now working part-time within his retirement.

The Admiral talked in a friendly, avuncular way about what it would be like to work in Government service. I remember he said, "You may be low-down in a British Embassy in some country. To the outside world you'll seem quite nondescript, but actually you'll be doing better than those who are looking down on you. You'll have more in your bank account." He also said, "You may interview someone as you tried to interview Colonel Grivas, and write a report. But you'll keep some things back and put them through to the branch of intelligence you are with." My attempt to interview Grivas had been seriously noted. He also said I would have to appear before the Civil Service Selection Board the following March – in other words, take an exam in open competition, answer written papers – and that he would like to have access to the Civil Service's report. He asked if I would sign a written authority which he placed before me for him to do this and I signed there and then. (*See* p.128.)

He was quietly spoken and friendly. He said, "I'd like you to choose a couple of friends and tell them about this talk and ask them what they think, ask their advice, have a discussion with them. Don't do it in a pub, for no pub is secure, people sit and eavesdrop. Every pub in the country has someone in it all the time who will report back to us. Choose somewhere where you can't be overheard. I'd like to know the names of the friends you are proposing to approach." I thought that to tell one's two closest friends was a strange way to keep a secret, but I see now that this was the beginning of a vetting, that the System would open a window on me through them: without either of them realising it they could discuss me with strangers who approached them in pubs. I named Ricky Herbert and John Ezard. He said that I would be contacted about the Civil Service exam and that he and I would be in touch again after I had taken the exam papers.

I came away still unsure if I wanted to work for the Government. I did not like the idea of working in a British Embassy abroad. It sounded a full-time job and would leave me little time to do what I should be doing: questing for Reality through my research and writing. I had been clear at the outset in asking for freelance work, and I was now being asked to think about full-time work.

Discussions with Ricky Herbert and John Ezard

I returned to Oxford and sounded Ricky out that evening. I said I had something to tell him which he should promise to keep to himself. He listened intently and said at the end: "The truth is, Nick, you can start off thinking you can control them but then discover that they control you. It's like Goethe's Faust. He believes *he* can control Mephistopheles but in the end Mephistopheles controls *him*. You need to be careful that you don't suffer Faust's fate." Looking back, I believe this was very sound advice, but being young I thought I could circumvent this danger.

It took me longer to sound out John Ezard. I said I wanted to research in foreign cultures for future books and that I might have been offered a way of doing this. He listened more sceptically and said, "Will they get in the way of your research? Will you find you've no time to research because you're too busy working for them?" I pointed out that I needed to work and that I was looking for a job that could combine research with the need to earn a living, and that the job I might be offered could enable me to discover new things which I could put into my own work, as did Marlowe and T.E. Lawrence.

Looking back, I realise that I had been seen by two very prominent members of the Secret British Establishment: the man who ran the campaign to misinform Hitler about D-Day, and the hero of a famous 1939 naval battle. I realise now that I was seen by men of such high stature – possibly because of my association with Worcester College which was linked to Masterman and Hollis – that it could only mean that the Secret Establishment's interest in me was considerable. However, at the time I did not know what the two men had achieved and so I did not have this feeling and I had private doubts about taking the discussions any further.

Wisdom: decision to lecture abroad
Back in Essex for the Christmas vacation I spent a week working for the Post Office. I delivered Christmas parcels from a large removal lorry with a tail held by chains. On my free days I went up to the British Museum and worked in the Reading-Room as, since its opening in 1857, had Dickens, Marx, Shaw, Orwell – and Colin Wilson. At lunch-time I sat on the front step between the Graeco-Roman-style columns, and at closing time I always stopped and looked at the autographed manuscripts of writers on my way out to the steps.

I knew I had to start writing something, and I drafted the outline of a play, which had the provisional title *The Molten Owl's Song*.

Colin Wilson invites me to stay in Cornwall
One night in the new year (on 5 January 1961) I returned home late from a day in the British Museum and discovered that I had left my front-door key behind. Journey's End was in darkness. I crept round to the back and found a ladder that just reached to my brother Robert's window-ledge. I climbed and tapped on his small window. He sat up in bed, opened the window outwards and said, "Colin Wilson rang. He wants you to go down to Cornwall tomorrow to write an article. He will pay your fares." I climbed in through the window.

The next day I chatted to Colin Wilson on the phone. That afternoon I caught a train from Paddington to St Austell and rang him from a red phone kiosk near the station. I waited for his car. He drove me back to Tetherdown. Once again I sat on the large sofa and, holding goblets of red wine, we discussed the article. Then I walked to the chalet in his garden and slept in a bed in one of the two rooms.

We wrote the article on the first day. *The Sunday Dispatch* were paying £100 for an article on drug-taking at Oxford, and I provided some vivid details from what I had seen. The article had to be rewritten and eventually caused a storm of controversy. Questions were asked about it in the House of Lords.[23]

I spent the weekend with him. We settled into a rhythm. I camped on the sofa while Colin sat in his chair by the permanent log fire with his electric typewriter on an arm which he pulled across or pushed aside. He inundated me with chapters to read and extracts of his work. On one occasion the baker came to the door and he showed the baker how far he had got. The baker stared at the typescript thrust under his nose, gave an appreciative grunt and then returned to selling the loaves in the basket he had brought to the door. In those days Colin Wilson was lean, vigorous and mentally energetic, and virtually every sentence he spoke contained another writer's name. He was the charismatic writer I had heard in the Fleet Street coffee-house. I told him about my encounters with Sartre and Hemingway, and with the Metaphysical and Romantic poets, and he was very definite as to how one should live as an Existentialist. He described his early struggle to read books while doing odd jobs – he would have Shaw open while wheeling barrow loads of cement and read a page between wheeling loads – and told me about Continental writers such as Wedekind and Durenmatt, who were on the fringe of my consciousness. That afternoon we shopped at a new super-market, and I was astonished that the heaped-up trolley I pushed came to about £120 at the check-out, a dozen times the weekly wage in those days. He said it was on his overdraft, but I was still immensely impressed.

Those were exciting days. It is impossible to communicate the sense of intellectual excitement that being in Colin Wilson's company generated at that time, when the tiniest everyday event was related to an overall Existentialist philosophy, and knowledge was related to living in a way that no Oxford tutor related it. And there was a directness and openness about his conversation which cut across all taboos and seemed liberating. "I sit here and work," he said, "and Joy brings everything. Just call 'Pepper' or 'Salt' or 'Sex' and it will appear."

At night I slept in the chalet. The window looked across the cliffs to the sea, and each morning I woke early and gulped in the fresh air. I walked down to Gorran Haven and had coffee and bought a paper because Colin did not surface until getting on for 11.

Decision on Gorran harbour wall to spend ten years abroad as itinerant lecturer
On the Sunday I stood on the wall of Gorran Haven harbour and looked at the sea and, wondering what I would do in a few months' time, felt an exile like the Old English Wanderer and Seafarer. In one of my discussions with Colin Wilson we had touched on writers who had gone abroad and lectured to overseas students such as Robert Graves and John Heath-Stubbs (in Alexandria), and William Empson and Edmund Blunden (in Japan). A host of writers had lived as expatriates at universities in exotic places, and the British Council had acted as an agency and set up contract appointments at universities in foreign countries for Lawrence Durrell (whose *Alexandria Quartet* was much discussed at that time) and for Anthony Burgess (who had written *The Malayan Trilogy*). In the early 1960s the British had not withdrawn east of Suez, and maintained a world-wide operation for overseas lecturers on a far grander scale than happens today. To teach in an exciting place would be like crossing the frontier of Western civilization and teaching the "barbarians" rather than doing battle with them. It would be like leaving Rome for the extreme conditions of barbarian life. Mary had written urging me to teach in Ankara for a year, and the idea merged with my ruminations on lecturing abroad.

Suddenly, standing on the harbour wall at Gorran Haven, I made an existential decision. I knew I had to live abroad. I did not know where. I had to get away from England and work out my own 'existence philosophy' through fresh and strange impressions. I had to live *outside* my own civilization and discover myself as a writer, find out what kind of writer I was to be. I would become an outsider and quest for Reality in unfamiliar surroundings. The prospect of living alone in an unknown place filled me with a certain dread, but one of my favourite Old-English lines was from *Beowulf*: "*wyrd oft nereth unfaegne eorl thonne his ellen deah*", "Fate often preserves the undoomed warrior when his courage is strong". I prided myself on being undoomed and on having courage. I was sure I would survive and that my quest would be successful.

When I returned to Tetherdown Colin took me to The Rising Sun, Portmellon, where there was a water-splash as the tide sometimes covered the road. I told Colin Wilson, my role model as a writer, the author of *The Outsider* and *Religion and the Rebel*, of my resolve. I said: "I shall become a wanderer, an exile, for ten years, an itinerant lecturer, and search among foreign cultures and religions." I meant that I would search for Reality abroad. This turned out to be a prophetic statement, and The Rising Sun prophetically suggested Japan. Colin nodded. (In fact, he followed suit. In spring 1961 he himself made arrangements to do a lecture tour in the US the following September and in 1966 became writer-in-residence in New York.)[24]

My weekend with Colin Wilson had shown me the writer's way of life just as my week with Mark Liell had shown me the solicitor's way of life. Standing on the harbour wall at Gorran Haven I had glimpsed my future, and in my own mind had taken a fork in my path which led away from the Admiral's path.

Brains Trust at Oaklands School

Having been confronted with a possible future as a lecturer abroad, I was again shown Oaklands School. I had been invited to take part in a Brains Trust of young people who were ex-pupils there on 9 January.

An arrangement to catch the right train from Cornwall had been made, but somehow we all overslept. Colin Wilson drove me at breakneck speed to St Austell, and we arrived to see the London train pulling out of the station. Without hesitation, and with a promptness typical of the excellent host that he was, he set off for Plymouth to race the train. "I don't like to be beaten," he said. He drove incredibly fast, but when we reached Plymouth, once again the train had just gone. There was nothing I could do except wait for the next train. I said goodbye to Colin, who went off to buy books in Plymouth, and settled down to wait.

By the time I arrived at Oaklands School, Loughton, the Brains Trust was in progress. I took my place at the speaker's table, late, explaining to the audience (which included my mother) that I had been delayed in Cornwall. Members of the audience were asking questions, which the panel answered.

My mother asked, "What is the ideal age to get married?"

I replied without hesitation: "About thirty. Because by then you'll have done what you want to do." Thirty might be the ideal age to get married, but as we shall see within nine months I would negate this ideal. For more than an hour I sat in the Oaklands hall at a table below the stage and, as during the dusk when a mist rose over the Oaklands fields and the day I told Colin Wilson I would spend ten years abroad, was shown a future vocation that was waiting for me, for which I had to prepare myself – although at the time I did not know it.

The wisdom of the East: visit to British Council to learn about contract appointments

Back at Oxford I knew I wanted to become a writer like Colin Wilson and that I should get into the habit of writing. While completing my course I worked on my play and wrote some of the poems of *A Well of Truth*, including 'Ode to a Prospect from a Window Frame' that includes the phrase "a well of Truth"; the prospect being of Port Meadow, Oxford and the window frame being the one in my first-floor room at the back of 57 Southmoor Road.

For some months I had developed an increasing interest in the wisdom of the East. Ricky had always been interested in Buddhist and Hindu thought, and Kingsley's interest in Eastern thinking had grown. We had all discussed the *Bhagavad-Gita,* and I had studied the *mandalas* of Tibet – sacred art showing a circle – after reading about them in Jung. I knew as early as March that I had to go to Japan. To that end I contacted the British Council, knowing it acted as an agency and set up contract appointments at universities in foreign countries, and was invited for an exploratory interview on Saturday 11 March.

After I accepted, the Provost, Sir John Masterman, invited me to a ten-minute meeting (from 9.40 to 9.50) on that same morning. Knowing it would be a short meeting, I looked in on him on my way to the station. He wished me well for the coming Civil Service exam during the Easter vacation. (The exam included an oral test in a foreign language, and I had done this – a French dictation – at Queen's College, Oxford on 2 March, as he knew.) I told him I was thinking of lecturing abroad in a British-Council-sponsored post, and was interested in Japan.

I left Masterman and went straight on down to London with Caroline by train and at 12 o'clock introduced myself to the British Council and had an exploratory chat at its headquarters at 65 Davies Street while Caroline shopped in Bond Street. My interest in going to Japan was noted. That night we stayed at Gresham Hotel at 36/38 Bloomsbury Street, a small hotel I had noticed as I walked to and from the British Museum.[25]

I spent the Easter vacation in Essex. I had finished my play and the Meadow Players were interested in performing it at Oxford but wanted me to rewrite Act One. I had to revise for the summer's exams and I reluctantly pushed the play to one side. I had finished the English course, and had written essays for Ricks on Blake and Yeats outside the course – Michael Horovitz lent me his typed postgraduate essay on Blake – and I now had the drudgery of revising Old and Middle English so that I could translate passages into modern English. Snippets of poems came of their own accord, often at inconvenient times.

Retreat from intelligence
The Civil Service method II exam took place on 10 and 11 April at 6 Burlington Gardens, London W1, near Piccadilly Circus. The Admiral had told me I would need two referees and my father had written to me on 27 November 1960[26] to say that his boss, the Clerk of the Council J.W. Faulkner, and the solicitor Mark Liell would oblige. But now that I was thinking of lecturing abroad I was no longer keen on Government service. The Civil Service Commission's booklet stated on p.11[27] that method II was an entry to the Senior Branch of the Foreign Service, and I was not sure that I wanted

to join the Foreign Service, whose world was as different from the world of Colin Wilson as being a Young Conservative was from being an Angry Young Man. I had moved away from siding with the West against Russia towards supporting internationalism based on the British Empire and the Commonwealth, and deep down I was already thinking I should decide to lecture abroad with the British Council and begin a search among foreign cultures and religions.

Civil Service exam, insistence on being independent of System
I sat the four papers of the written examination. They were spread over two days: an Essay paper, an English paper and two General papers, one of which required me to discuss the logical force of several arguments.[28] I enjoyed answering the literary questions but not the unpalatable, turgid questions about "expenditure on public roads in Great Britain" and charts of vehicle licences.

In addition to the written examination there was a series of "tests and interviews at the Civil Service Selection Board".[29] I had to sit in a group of would-be ambassadors and discuss the *nouveau roman* and Nathalie Sarraute, among other topics. Having debunked the *nouveau roman* with Colin Wilson I could hardly contain myself at the bland, dinner-table, passionless approach of others in the group who were not concerned with the merits of the works but only concerned to name-drop. Colin Wilson would not have stood for this. The Angry Young Man and the Young Conservative in me had co-existed uneasily, but the Existentialist writer in me could not co-exist with these smooth diplomats. There and then I decided the Foreign Office was not the place for me.

I was then interviewed on my own by a suited civil servant. I explained that I wanted to be a writer and to work freelance, and said I could see myself lecturing to overseas students in the tradition of Graves, Heath-Stubbs, Empson, Blunden, Durrell and Burgess. During the hour-long interview I retreated from full-time work in the Foreign Service to the position I had set out to Major Goulding. I emphasised that I wished to be independent of the System, and to have as much leisure as possible.

The Admiral again
Back in Oxford I wrote to the Admiral on 25 April to tell him that I was in touch with the British Council and looking to lecture abroad. He replied from an address in Carlton Gardens, dated 1 May 1961 and marked "Personal and Confidential":

> Dear Hagger, Thank you for your letter of 25th April. You will remember that at the talk we had here last December I told you that candidates for

this Department had to appear before the Civil Service Selection Board, and you gave me written authority to have access to the report made on you by that Board in the open competition. I very much regret that the decision which has now been made is that this Department has no vacancy suitable to your qualifications. I should however be glad if you would tell me in due course what employment you decide to take up, and if at any time in the future you would like a further talk you have only to write to me to ask for an appointment.

I felt relieved. I had escaped full-time employment in the Foreign Service and could now choose to go abroad on my own terms.

Alasdair Clayre and Stephen Medcalf
But I was still discontented. I had had enough of work I did not want to do and I wanted to concentrate on what I did want to do.

When I returned to Oxford for the summer I said as much to two associates: the All Souls don Alasdair Clayre, a *protégé* of Isaiah Berlin, who had asked me to interview Lord David Cecil for a magazine, which I did (and can remember his saying that Hemingway was "a poor man's Conrad"); and Stephen Medcalf, a research student who had been at Chigwell and accompanied me to Marathon – he was three years older than me – and who later became an eccentric don at Sussex University. Both came to tea from time to time and firmed up my intention to become a lecturer. I recall telling Alasdair that my problem was to find a lecturing job that would allow me to write.

Alain Robbe-Grillet
Alasdair and I went to hear Alain Robbe-Grillet, a French avant-gardist, *nouveau-roman* novelist and writer of the screenplay of the film *L'année dernière à Marienbad* who described objective art in great detail. Reminded of the discussion about Nathalie Sarraute at the Selection Board interview, I debunked his objective art as Alasdair and I walked back. I knew that Reality was not found by describing realistic objects. (I was shocked to read many years later that Alasdair had killed himself by jumping in front of a train in January 1984, on the morning his book on China was published.)

I was visited by Naseem Khan (who became a journalist, worked for Arts Council England and founded a small charity); Geraldine James (who began work at the Royal Shakespeare Theatre, Stratford in July); and Jill Bradbury, who kept inviting me back to Ludham Hall and when I declined persuaded Ricky to stay for ten days instead. (He later described being turned into her slave.) My conversations with all three, and with Caroline, reinforced my intention to lecture abroad.

Colin Morris

I was also visited by Colin Morris, the author of *Reluctant Heroes* and a writer of scripts for *Z Cars*, whose research assistant had written saying that Colin Wilson had given him my name.[30] He had tea in my room on 5 June, a portly man who sat on a high-backed chair in the middle of my bedsit and filled the space while I sat on my bed. He wanted local colour and invited me to attend an interview at the BBC with a view to presenting a programme on books. I went but found the two before me in the queue had brought show-reels, and it was clear that the BBC were looking for film-based editors rather than presenters. So I regarded the BBC as a turning off my path which led into thickets.

Offered British-Council-sponsored lectureship at University of Baghdad

I was still bent on going to Japan with the British Council. I had had a discussion with Ricky in the Randolph on 30 May in which he asserted that there were no accidents and that there was "no self". I declared, "I am going to go to the other side of the world and return with the wisdom of the East." I meant that I would return having discovered Reality.

However, it soon became apparent that it would be hard to go to Japan immediately as there were no vacancies there for September. The British Council advised me to consider going elsewhere for a year. It must have been just after the gruelling and long drawn-out Final examinations (during which I had a tummy bug) that I went down to London one late afternoon and ran into Herbie Butterfield (one of the Randolph Set who had put me in touch with the Soho Fair) in a crowded London street. Unusually for him he was in a dark suit. He was also reading English. He had an engaging blink and I had been to the house where he was living with his girlfriend and sat in a room with floor-to-ceiling shelves crammed with books.

He told me he had just been interviewed by the British Council for a job at the University of Baghdad, that he had got it but had decided while walking away that he was not going to go as he was going to marry his girlfriend. "You can go in my place if you like," he said.

Baghdad was then known as a dangerous place. The ruler was the revolutionary Brigadier-General Abdul Kareem Kaseem, who had opposed the British by demanding the return of Kuwait. But Baghdad was also a very romantic and historical place. I needed to learn about the time of the Caliphate and Ali Baba, and if I could not explore the wisdom of the Far East, then the wisdom of the Middle East was a good substitute and would make an excellent start for my quest for Reality.

The job he was offering me was the sort of job of which I had dreamt. Now it might be becoming a reality I was terrified at the thought of becoming a lecturer and exposing my nervousness to public gaze, but if being a lecturer gave me some time to begin my quest in the Middle East and Islam, then I would force myself to do what I dreaded – I would existentially choose to act against my own nature. There and then I turned and walked to the British Council's headquarters at 65 Davies Street and registered my interest in going to Baghdad. I had a preliminary interview at the British Council on 23 June.

Being already on the British Council's books, I was interviewed again very soon afterwards (on 26 June) by Arthur Plowman, the Head of Department in the Faculty of Letters at the University of Baghdad. He was an elderly man with a face like a skull and dreamy eyes and a lifetime's service in the British Empire, and I intuitively sensed that he had accepted me. At the beginning of July I was asked to have a medical. Soon afterwards I heard that I would be going to Iraq at the end of September.

Would I have opted to apply to go to Iraq if Herbie Butterfield had not offered me the chance to take his place? Probably not. Was it luck – sheer chance – or was it Providential, that meeting with Herbie? If I had stopped walking and looked in a shop-window for even ten seconds, our paths would not have crossed. Was our intersection a coincidence and no more? Or was Ricky right to assert that there are "no accidents", that everything that happens is by Providential design? I felt elated, for all that year I had wanted to escape England, and the escape had just happened. And it had come to me just as Col. Grivas had come to me. Had I attracted my escape in accordance with an obscure law I did not understand?

Be all this as it may, I was sure I had answered a call to begin a quest for Reality in a Biblical land. My path through the dark wood had been tangled and thorny, and I still had a long way to go before I was out of the wood. Looking back, I see that my path was full of obstacles and bogs, which I had circumvented by my choices. Ahead was a dark time and I am glad that this was concealed from me as I followed my path through undergrowth, unaware of where it would lead.

CHAPTER 3

The Journey: Awakening

"I did it all for myself, without any aid or guidance, and so I did not know
where I was going. I was travelling down a completely unknown road,
without the slightest idea of what was at the end."

Nicholas Hagger
Diaries, Awakening to the Light, 24 October 1966

I had always intuitively known that I had to make a journey overseas to
confront Reality. I was not sure where it would take me or what form the
confrontation would take, but I knew I had to find a path through the
deepest valleys and bogs of my dark wood, and that if I sometimes felt lost
on the way I would end my journey on the right path to emerge from its
impenetrability. Deep down I knew I had to undergo some sort of
awakening and transformation that would bring to birth a new centre and
sensibility which would turn me into the kind of writer I knew I had to be.
Although I did not know I was already on a universal Mystic Way I was clear
that I would encounter new experiences, and that over a period of time, a
decade – the "ten years" I had forecast to Colin Wilson – there would be a
change in me that would complete my remaking of myself, open me to my
imagination and inspiring Muse and prepare me to write about the unity of
the universe.

It was something I had to do if I were to locate, and eventually convey,
the knowledge and wisdom of my Shadow.

Episode 6:

Marriage and Dictatorship

Years: 1961–1962
Locations: London; Loughton; Midhurst; West Dulwich; Baghdad; Babylon;
Basra; Amman; Damascus; Beirut
Works: *A Well of Truth*; *Juben*, synthesis
Initiative: lecturer in Iraq

"I would make a pilgrimage to the Deserts of Arabia to find the man who could make [me] understand how the *one can be many.*"

Coleridge, *The Notebooks of Samuel Taylor Coleridge*, vol. I, 1561

In my next episode there was a conflict between the domesticity of my marriage and the dangerous dictatorship in Iraq.

Marriage and leaving for Iraq
Announcement of marriage to Caroline

Now I knew I was going to Iraq, the question became: what would I do about Caroline? I had a discussion with her, and she said she felt deeply about me and wanted to join me in Baghdad and find a job there. But as soon as she tried there were obstacles: visa complications, objections from her parents – she was 19 – and lack of work. It rapidly became clear that the only way she could accompany me and live with me in a Muslim country at that time would be as my wife. Back in Loughton I thought about the next step very carefully. I wandered through Epping Forest, examining my feelings for her, and I reckoned that I had a stark existential choice: either marry and live with her for the few years ahead that I could foresee, or say goodbye now. Mary returned from Ankara looking glamorous and sunburnt, and said when I met her, "You don't need to marry her."

I had to attend a two-week training course (from 31 July to 11 August) put on in London by the British Council for language teachers going abroad. A large lecture-room was full of us, and I encountered Naseem Khan on her way to Finland. A much-moustached, silver-haired F.C. Billows introduced the direct method of teaching language by speaking at us in Turkish. (In mid-afternoon that day I went out to an adjoining room and found him fast asleep on his back on the carpeted floor.) While listening to speakers I had plenty of time to work out what I should do about Caroline.

As soon as the course was over, on Saturday 12 August, eating my words in the Oaklands hall that the ideal age to marry would be 30, recognising that I now had to act against my better judgement and base my decision on pragmatic realism rather than a lofty ideal, I visited Caroline at her parents' home in West Dulwich and in the garden, on the side lawn near a swing-seat, on a sunny day, asked her to marry me. I was 21.

There were introductions to each other's families and many organisational arrangements. My parents had wanted me to become a solicitor and marry an ex-Oaklander and go into politics. They blamed John Ezard and Colin Wilson for my not becoming a solicitor. They had adjusted to my going abroad and to not seeing me for nine months, and now they had to adjust to my wife's not being an ex-Oaklander. If they were disappointed they did not show it. My younger brother Rob was now training to be the solicitor I was supposed to have become, and perhaps they transferred their dream for a son to be a solicitor to him.

We began organising the wedding. Caroline's parents lived in a large house owned by Dulwich College Estate in Alleyn Park, West Dulwich (since pulled down). Her father, Group-Captain Leslie Nixon, had retired from the RAF. He had started in the army in the Artist Rifles in the Royal Sussex Regiment in 1914. He had joined the Royal Flying Corps (then a branch of the army) as a lieutenant, had been shot down and had been interned in Holzminden prisoner-of-war camp during the First World War.[1] On his release he had been seconded to the British Indian Army: the 14th Murray's Jat Lancers in Kashmir. He told me he had been an eyewitness of Gen. Dyer's massacre at Amritsar in 1919 when (he claimed) Dyer panicked before a mob of 25,000 armed with billhooks and swords and ordered his 50 armed troops to fire on the crowd for ten minutes, killing 379 and wounding 1,200. He had then joined the Royal Air Force and had fought among 'the Few' during the Second World War. The reception would be at Alleyn Park.

Conference at Dunford College, Midhurst

From 22 to 27 August I attended a training conference arranged by 'Oversea Service' for the British Council. (Oversea Service was supported by the YMCA, the Colonial Office and the Imperial Institute,[2] and it had been holding training conferences since 1954.) It was held at Dunford College, Midhurst, Sussex.[3] The house was the birthplace of Richard Cobden, the reformer who was behind the repeal of the Corn Laws in 1846 and who stood for free trade. Over twenty of us were lectured by various unhyphenated-double-barrelled ex-colonials and ex-imperialists on what we might expect in the countries we were about to live in. The main event of each day took place on the croquet lawn in the evening where a permanently dazed-looking, dark-haired comedian among us, Logan-Reid (with whom I shared a room), put his foot on his ball and ruthlessly hit any ball near his into a ditch.

Wedding

The next two weeks were hectic. Caroline and I had TAB and cholera inoculations, visited the *padré* who would be marrying us (a friend of the Group-Captain's), hired morning dress, attended the rehearsal, planned the honeymoon, invited the wedding guests and shopped and packed to live for at least nine months in the desert heat of Iraq.

I married Caroline on 16 September 1961 at St Clement Danes, which stands outside the Law Courts in the Strand (where I had often walked as an articled clerk), the church whose bells say "Oranges and lemons". It was the central church of the RAF, a recent rebuilding as the previous Wren church (itself a rebuilding of a church founded by the Danes in the 9th century and of another rebuilding by William the Conqueror) had been almost destroyed by the *Blitz* in May 1941. A couple of 'the Few' attended. At the reception in West Dulwich the Group-Captain said he was sorry we were going to "an enemy country". We honeymooned in and around Arundel and visited villages such as Pulborough, going no farther as we had to leave for Iraq on 30 September.

The University of Baghdad had supplied air tickets and the British Council a clothing allowance of £100 to buy tropical clothing, but otherwise I had no money. I had lived off my grant, which had now stopped, and my father gave me £180 in national savings certificates, which he had saved for me from the time I was a boy. I cashed these and the

Nicholas and Caroline leaving St Clement Danes

balance in my Post Office book and left for Baghdad with £8 in the world, and a few wedding presents. Our baggage was limited, and we were prepared to live out of the contents of three suitcases for getting on for a year. I was desperate for my first salary payment.

Dictatorship in Iraq

We flew to Baghdad by Iraqi Airlines on 30 September 1961. It was my first flight, and I had my first contact with happy-go-lucky Arabs when the pilot invited me into the cockpit high above clouds and cheerfully allowed me to take the control column and steer the plane. In the course of doing this I tilted the plane down and up, and when I returned to my seat nearly everyone was bent over a paper bag, so bad was the turbulence I had caused.

Baghdad

At Baghdad airport we were met by the Representative of the British Council, A. Ross-Thomas, a sandy-haired, balding man whose paintings of Iraqi landscapes hung over mantelpieces all round Baghdad. The airport was full of noise. A crowd of Arabs had just cut the throat of a sheep to celebrate an arrival and were dipping their hands in the blood and putting handprints on a nearby wall to ward off the Evil Eye. A radio played whirly-twirly Arab music. We were driven to the Hotel Sindibad in Rashid Street, where dinner was routinely served at 10 p.m.

I was elated to be in Baghdad. I knew it had been founded in c.762 when the caliph al-Mansur moved the capital of the Abbasid Caliphate from Damascus to Baghdad. I knew it had become the Islamic world's centre of learning and commerce. In its House of Wisdom (a library and translation institute founded by caliph Harun al-Rashid) translations were made of Greek, Middle-Persian and Syriac works, and Greek and Indian science were introduced. I knew that Baghdad had become the largest city in the world with more than a million inhabitants between 762 and 930. I knew that Baghdad, and the House of Wisdom with it, had been destroyed by the Mongol invasion of 1258, after which the city had gone into decline. It was 1381 in the Islamic dating system and many scenes recalled the Middle Ages.

In 1917, after the collapse of the Ottoman Empire, the British had occupied Iraq and established a colonial government. The Arab and Kurdish peoples had resisted, and in 1920, on the orders of Winston Churchill, Colonial Secretary, the revolt was put down, some said with tear-gas shells. Churchill then dreamed of creating a new nation, Iraq, that would bring peace to the warring Sunnis, Shiites and Kurds, and one of the roles of lecturers in English was to continue the reconciliation of these peoples. (We did not know that there would be a Sunni-Shiite civil war throughout the Middle East over 50 years later.)

The next morning I reported to the University, having driven in a taxi through hot, messy, sprawling, dusty, noisy streets that were full of soldiers and passed desert sand, palms, barefooted Arabs, sheep and goats. I warmed to Baghdad, city of Arabian nights where so much history had happened. I was saluted by officials and by the staff *farrash* (servant) and said "*Salaam a lecum*" to each. I negotiated an advance on my first month's salary. I discovered that my monthly salary was at the level my father's had reached after 40 years.

Back at the Hotel Sindibad we reviewed options presented to me by the University and British Council as to where we might live. In a heat of 120 degrees we visited the first option, an unfurnished *mustamal* (villa), an empty building just off Rashid Street with thick stone walls and floors. But the rent was £400 for a full year, excluding servant, food, fridge and furniture, and with capital of £8 and a salary of £112 a month I could not see how we could afford to pay twelve months' rent when we would only be in Baghdad for the nine months of my contract. The same applied to all the other options except the last: the YWCA by the airport.

Consequently we moved into the virtually empty, spacious and well-furnished YWCA, which was run by a Lebanese woman, Sophie Moubarak, who had been mentioned at the Oversea Service conference. We took the large double front room with a side view over the rural perimeter of Baghdad airport and were guarded by a watchman (Hachim) and looked after by a one-eyed servant (Yelda) who cooked our meals. We had the use of the enormous sitting-room downstairs, where slim newt-like lizards lived on the mosquito-netting in the windows and licked any flies that came too near, darting out a tongue and pulling them in their mouths before you could blink. Up one end there was a table-tennis table, near where we ate, and off it there was a library with hundreds of books. The board and lodging for the two of us was around £36 a month.

Almost immediately Caroline was offered a job at the kindergarten of the Mansur School next door, from 8.30 to 12.30. We settled into a routine of rising early, at 6 a.m., working until lunch-time, having a siesta from 2 to 4, and going to bed around 11.

To go to work I caught an antiquated bus to Rashid Street and then joined a group taxi from the main square, Bab Sherge, which I shared with sheep, goats and women wearing black *abayas*. I collected an advance on my salary and met my students, all of whom seemed older than me, in the college cafeteria, where they insisted on a group photograph. They announced, "We are very pleased to know you, we will now have a party." They took me to Ctesiphon, the Persian Sasanian winter capital, for a picnic. We sat under the famous arch of the ruined Palace of the Sasanian king Shapur I.

Nicholas with students in college cafeteria, Baghdad, October 1961

Sandfly fever, Dr Shubber
The YWCA was out in the sand desert. There was no air-conditioning, and it was so hot at night that we had to sleep with the windows open. Minute sandflies crawled through the fine mesh of the mosquito-netting and I was bitten all over, and was soon delirious with a temperature that fluctuated upwards from 104°F. I could not go to work for a few days. I was in bed with a high fever and malarial-type sweats and shivering, and could not keep

gibberish out of my head. I kept seeing confused and hideous pictures. Bites from the sandfly of the genus *Phlebotomus* transmit the viral disease leishmaniasis that can cause encephalitis (or inflammation and swelling of the brain).

My aunt Argie had written to an Iraqi doctor, Dr Shubber, whose wife had been a nurse at the London Hospital. I first met him when he visited me, having been sent for by Caroline (who had no sandfly bites).

"How are you?" he asked at my bedside.

"I've got a temperature of 107," I replied in a lucid moment.

"You can't, you would be dead," he said, taking my temperature. Then he said, "Oh," for it was indeed 107. He later told me that I could have died that day.

Life at the College of Education, University of Baghdad

When I recovered, through Caroline I was offered a daily lift to work in the minibus of the school next door. We were woken by the *muezzin*'s first call from a nearby mosque at 5.30 a.m. Akbar arrived with an empty minibus at 6.45 a.m. We drove from Mansur (or Mansour) under wonderful dawn skies through some of the 15 million palm trees alongside the misty, shimmering Tigris. In the early morning, sun-shafts burst through every gap in the palm leaves and spotlit the sand beneath them. We drove across the bridge to Waziriyah, and periodically Akbar would spot a friend and slow down and shout through the window, "*Schlon saher, schlon ek?*" ("How are you?") A jocular rhyming reply was, "*Nejleh gaher.*" ("I have a filthy cough and a horrid cold.") Akbar dropped me outside the College of Education and then began his school run, collecting children from their homes to take them to school.

My first lecture was at 8. Lectures were informal and chatty and book-related, and took place in antiquated dark classrooms with a raised *mullah*'s dais. I taught English Language (composition and dictation) and found explaining grammatical rules (such as using 'some' in statements, 'any' in questions or negatives) tightened my own use of language. Looking back, I see that explaining English grammar to overseas students was a good training for my future writing. I also taught English Literature: poetry, which meant specific poems by Wordsworth, Keats, Coleridge, Tennyson, Browning, Arnold and Fitzgerald; and prose, meaning novels by Dickens and Trollope, including *Great Expectations*, which 3B loved, chanting the name Pumblechook in entranced wonder. Most of the students were a little younger than I was though some were much older. They were quite lively. Whatever I tried to teach them, they had a lot to say.

Locusts

When I had free time between lectures – I only lectured 12 hours a week at the College of Education and was asked to do a few additional lectures at a nearby Institute – and wanted to escape the long staff room where Arthur Plowman sat and we all had tables round the walls, I went to the nearby resource centre, the Centre for English Studies, and worked in the small garden where I had a table and chair. Sometimes the bushes were full of locusts, and I often prepared lectures and marked books with a dozen locusts over four inches long crawling round my writing hand and many more crawling on my back.

Smallpox Alley and scorpion

I returned home at 1 p.m., travelling to Bab Sherge on a bus or in a group taxi. We passed mosques with golden domes and blue-and-yellow minarets. I then walked along "Smallpox Alley" (I called it), a narrow medieval Ottoman-Turkish street with an open sewer down the middle and, braving the line of begging *abaya*-ed women near the bus-stop, took the 20 bus to the YWCA. There Caroline would be waiting for me. One-eyed Yelda, a Christian Chaldean who spoke Aramaic, the language of Christ, had lunch waiting for us. Lunch generally consisted of egg-plant.

Once he stopped me treading on a scorpion in the middle of the marble kitchen floor. He surrounded the scorpion with paper and set it alight, and we watched the scorpion, within a circle of fire, bring its tail over its head and sting itself to death.

After lunch we had our siesta under the ceiling fan, which looked like an aeroplane propeller. We wound towels round our middles to avoid catching a chill. After our sleep we rose. Sometimes I sat and worked or wrote until dinner, sometimes we went out – sometimes to Dr Shubber's house for dinner with his family. When we stayed in I worked at my desk in the corner of the room, sometimes with a bottle of local white wine (which often had dead flies floating in the top), until Caroline persuaded me to abandon my work. In those Baghdad evenings we were very happy.

Gen. Kaseem at the Turkish Embassy

We were invited to celebrate the 38th anniversary of the Turkish Republic at the Turkish Embassy on 28 October. We were drinking long whisky-and-sodas and shelling and munching pistachio nuts (*"fistak"*) in the grounds at the back when soldiers suddenly began jumping up and down on the settees which stood in the open air, as part of a security check. Then Gen. Kaseem, the despot responsible for the revolution in 1958 and for murdering the Royal family, made his entrance in military uniform and walked among us, surrounded by his guards.

Suddenly a band struck up the anthem, and I saw people running in different directions. Kaseem, bare-headed, saluted throughout the anthem about a yard from me while I stood to attention. For a minute we stood side by side, he looking at me out of the corner of his eyes, and when the anthem was finished he moved away. Ross-Thomas, the Representative of the British Council, approached and said, "I say, you're brave. Didn't you realise he's a target at the salute? There might be snipers on the rooftops beyond those palms. When Kaseem takes the salute you get as far away from him as you can."

Life in Baghdad: Caroline's modelling, Sabih Shukri, Major Carson
Being out in the desert, we always had scenes beneath our window that could have come from the *Bible*. There was a *sarifa* (mud-hut) settlement near us, and there were always sheep, goats and camels, including one-humped dromedaries, and fodder-laden donkeys being driven along the sandy tracks by shepherds in long robes or bare-footed boys in striped night-shirts (*jellabas*). There were parrots and other vivid birds, one of which Yelda called a "*baba ra*".

One day I heard a shriek from Caroline and rushed downstairs and found Yelda standing over a small whimpering puppy with a knife.

"Yelda's cut its ears off," she sobbed.

"Sir," he said, puzzled, still holding the ears, "we always do this or bugs get into ears and kill it. This help the dog."

In the evenings groups of pye-dogs prowled below our windows. Once when it was very hot we risked the sandflies to sleep on the flat roof. We wheeled our beds out and lay and watched the crescent moon on its back over rows of silent palms that ringed the airport, and marvelled at incredibly bright stars.

At the weekends we took a taxi to the *suk* (market) – the taxi-driver always asked for "*rubba dinar*" (a quarter of a dinar or 250 fils) – and we looked at the carpet-sellers and revelled in the intimate atmosphere in which artefacts of beauty were bargained for over small cups of "*chai*" (tea).

In early November the rains came. Baghdad had always been full of hazards. Manhole covers suddenly went missing at bus-stops, so if we were not careful we could fall fifty feet down into the open sewers while getting off a bus. Now the electrical system was alive, and it was safer to ring door-bells with a pencil in case we got a shock. All the roads turned thick with mud, and Arabs hitched up their nightshirts and tip-toed through the streets, while the boys gleefully welcomed the coming of water after the baking summer as we welcome snow, and joyfully rolled in the puddles. The *sarifa* (mud-hut) families were amazingly welcoming, and one morning I was invited in to take tea with twenty mud-hut dwellers, and learned that their weekly income was 4/2d: two bottles of *leben* (yoghurt) sent to market.

We saw quite a bit of Dr Shubber. Caroline had appendicitis and Dr Shubber operated on her on 9 November and waived his fee. She had a private room in the hospital, and when I went to visit her I passed through wards where families of a dozen or more squatted round the beds, brewing tea from small stoves on the floor.

A young blonde woman in Baghdad causes a perpetual sensation. The assistant in the marketing board of the Dutch Embassy, Coen (short for Coenraad) Stork (later Dutch Ambassador in Cuba and Romania), had met us at the Turkish Embassy and invited us (on 19 November) to a cocktail party at his book-lined home. Many British Embassy personnel and their wives were present, including the British Ambassador, Sir Roger Allen, who the next day sent me his card in an envelope. I was probably supposed to visit him, but I had rejected the Foreign Service and did not.

Coen Stork asked Caroline to model some clothes at the first (two-floor) department store in Baghdad, Orosdi-Back, in Rashid Street. (The fashion show presented Dutch and Belgian clothes to Iraqis.) I discovered what marriage was like when she returned from her first modelling rehearsal to say that she had been offered a lovely three-piece suit (which she had with her) at the bargain price of £65. In vain I protested that we had to pay £36 rent and £30 towards the advance of my first month's salary, and had to live off the rest of the £112 for a month. She pleaded, and said her salary would buy our food. The suit became an issue, and, aware that I had uprooted her from her own country, I gave in, knowing it was economic madness.

After the live event the owner of Orosdi-Back held a party for the models (on 23 November), and we were taken on to dinner by the managing director of the store, Sabih Shukri. (He had been sent to London as junior clerk of an Iraqi bank when he was 16 and would become founder, managing director and chief executive of Allied Arab Bank in the City of London.)[4] A few days later he took us to eat *mazgouf* (carp) by the Tigris.

Through her modelling and the parties we had attended Caroline had come to the attention of the British Embassy and was asked to work in the Embassy Commercial Office, which was hidden above a bank. She left the school next door and was given a lift into work by Major Carson, the Embassy's Military Attaché. This arrangement came without any instigation on our part, and I wondered if the Admiral's organisation was keeping an eye on me through the daily chats Caroline had with him in the car to and from work. During these car journeys they observed the new equipment of which the "brave Iraqi army" had taken delivery.

On one occasion they found a new Russian truck of unknown use. It was parked near the YWCA, and via Caroline I was asked to take a look at it. I walked all round it. It was covered in a large tarpaulin, which I tried to lift, and was nearly arrested by the army when several soldiers suddenly appeared. We had a good view of the road from the YWCA, and, the Military Attaché having requested it, we took to counting the tanks that went by each morning, which Caroline relayed to the Military Attaché on their way to work. Troops seemed to exercise on the waste ground near our window, and we often saw platoons marching by, all out of step.

We were invited to have dinner with Dr Shubber and his family a couple of times, and we had our Christmas lunch with the Shubbers. They gave me a plate decorated with a bearded, winged bull.

Basra: Shatt al-Arab

At the start of the mid-year break, on 18 January 1962, we flew to Basra. In the air above Ur, sitting with my eyes closed, I received the words 'Life Cycle' and scribbled down headings for a work on a whole life and its cycle. I have this work in mind now. The principle of a life cycle passed into an embryonic version of my vision of civilizations – the life cycle of civilizations – which eventually became *The Fire and the Stones*.

From Basra we took a boat up the Shatt al-Arab towards Abadan. As we progressed up the brown river we passed through idyllic scenery: peasants burning peat among 'jungle' palms on the banks on either side, signs of peace and tranquillity. For several hours we were transported into a pre-industrial age, and the visit left a lasting impression.

Gourna: Tree of Knowledge

The day after our return to Baghdad Sabih drove us to a lake beyond the Euphrates in very fertile ground. We visited Gourna (or Qurna), where the Tigris and Euphrates meet, the site of Paradise. Dug-out boats were drawn up on the shore, and we saw the split trunk and leaves of what local tradition claims to be the Tree of Knowledge, known as the 'Tree of Adam and Eve', which was said to have been planted by Noah after the Flood on the exact spot where the Tree of the Knowledge of Good and Evil that bore forbidden fruit stood in the middle of the Garden of Eden according to *Genesis* 2.3. Abraham was supposed to have prayed beneath its branches. Nearby we saw a tomb with a small dome, the tomb of the prophet Ezra (457–432BC). It was claimed by both Christians and Muslims.

Bethlehem and Bethany

On 22 January we took a group taxi across the desert via Rutba to Bethlehem. From there we travelled to Jericho, the Dead Sea – we walked to the caves where the Dead Sea Scrolls were found at Qumran and saw some jars being carried out – and to Bethany, where we saw Lazarus's tomb. There Jesus is supposed to have raised Lazarus from the dead, standing three rock-steps down in an ante-chamber before the inner burial chamber where Lazarus lay. We also saw the site of Martha's and Mary's house, and the River Jordan.

Jerusalem

We went on to Jerusalem. We visited the Mount of Olives where Jesus lived; Gethsemane, the grotto where Jesus was arrested; Calvary, where a church has been built over the original rock; and the Garden Tomb near Damascus Gate (as opposed to the cave in the Church of the Holy Sepulchre). In the Via Dolorosa I bought a silver Russian-Orthodox cross. We went on to Amman, Damascus and then Beirut. Throughout these travels I had Camus' *L'homme revolté* on my knees.

We returned to Baghdad by desert bus, bumping over the red-brown sand and stones with no track and only a compass as guide. We had to wait eight hours at the Iraqi border throughout an extremely cold night because the chief of police was asleep and could not stamp our passports.

Back in Baghdad I pondered on Christianity and felt that nothing divine happened in the Garden Tomb. However, I had a profound sense that I had visited these places for a reason that would be revealed in the future. In fact, I drew on memories of these places in several of my future books.

Plane crash

Soon after our return, from the side window of our room we saw a plane crash on the runway next to the YWCA. It could not lower its undercarriage and had to land without wheels. It circled several times, using up fuel while word spread and crowds gathered all round the perimeter fence. Eventually the plane came in low, skidded, slewed sideways amid a cloud of red dust and came to a standstill. All round the airport Arabs climbed over the fence and rushed towards the aircraft, cheering and ululating with joy, and I felt a bond with the invisible human beings whose lives had been at risk, and was thankful that they were safe.

Synthesis: early Universalism

I had been reflecting on the new impressions and sensations of the Middle East for more than three months and, mindful that wisdom includes the practical application of experience and knowledge, abruptly began to synthesise all the knowledge I had acquired in all subjects, including the sciences and philosophy. This was an early form of Universalism. Working in a corner of our room in the YWCA, I felt wonderfully alive. I had seen much that was visually interesting and many vivid things – the streets were full of different ethnic groups such as Lurs carrying furniture on their backs, or peacock-worshipping Yezzidis – but I had not met any Sufis and the

Islamic culture I had experienced seemed decayed. I was aware that my vivid social and political impressions were in some way an obstacle to the long-term philosophical Reality I should be finding. Reading Camus and synthesising my knowledge in all disciplines were a way of understanding my experience. During the long Baghdad evenings my marriage – our marital home – was where I tried to understand my experience, including the dictatorship in Iraq.

I found the Arabs lacked depth and were more decayed than Westerners. My synthesis was an approach to Reality, a practical attempt to digest the wisdom of the Middle East and bring wisdom to birth in my own soul. I was glad I had come to look at Iraq, and I would draw on my memories in *Armageddon*, but I did not intend to remain in Baghdad like Ross-Thomas and become an expert on the differing customs of each region. I knew I had to move on, and I handed my resignation to Arthur Plowman, to take effect from July.

Sabih had said we could exercise his grey stallion, which was stabled on the edge of the desert. For a couple of weeks in February Caroline rode almost daily in the desert, and on a Friday (the Muslim day of rest) I borrowed another stallion from the same stable and we rode bare-backed into the desert side by side.

Dictatorship: University and Secret Police
The bizarre outer distractions of Baghdad were very soon in evidence at the start of the new term in February. Almost immediately it was Ramadan, the Muslim month of fasting.

Unrest at the University of Baghdad: 3B
I had a notorious class, 3B, who had followed an elderly, lady lecturer home and threatened to beat her up unless they all passed the coming examination. They had rioted when I caught two of them blatantly cheating during my examination: they had risen up like a pack of cards when I confiscated the papers of the two cheats, and they fell all round me as I stood my ground until reinforcements arrived, led by Arthur Plowman.

In the long staff room the English lecturers sat at one end and the Russian lecturers at the other end. Arthur Plowman, from the English end, ranted at the staff and said that all 3B should fail. Three of us failed 15 of them. He then changed his mind and gently said they should all pass.

One of the 15 was a young lady, Semira, who wore an *abaya* to college but sang in a Baghdad nightclub every evening. Her passably-accurate English compositions were about the men she went home with. At the next staff meeting in the long staff room Arthur realised he had directed that Semira should pass. He asked me for her script, snatched it from my hand and wrote "Failed" across the top. We all protested that Semira was good enough to pass.

Somehow the students got wind of what was going on in the staff room. Word spread that the University was making it harder for them to pass, and so they went on strike. I had a few welcome days' holiday, and eventually lectures resumed. No one knew whether Semira had passed or failed.

Freedom of speech

We had all been told that there was a spy of Gen. Kaseem's in every class. I was soon in trouble for uttering the word "king" in a lecture. I had to teach Tennyson's 'Ulysses', which begins "It little profits that an idle king". Any mention of any king had been banned by the revolutionary government of "the honest and faithful Leader Brigadier-General Abdul Karim Kaseem" (the words with which the *Iraqi Times* began every front-page story). The member of 3B who we all knew was Kaseem's spy complained about my use of the word "king".

I told the class, "I don't care what dictators there are out there, there is freedom of speech in my class. Outside this classroom there is no freedom of speech, but within it there is." To illustrate the freedom within my class I gave them a short introduction to Existentialism.

A group of 40-year-old students waited for me as I left a couple of days later and told me, "We discuss you every evening in the hostel, and we say we must talk with Mr Hagger on the subject of Existentialism."

Babylon

I relocated my reason for being in Iraq when (on 23 February) one of my colleagues, a small, grey-haired lecturer called Gordon Groos (a Dutch name) drove us to Babylon. On the way we saw some storks on top of an old *caravanserai* (an inn with a central courtyard for camel caravans). They had just arrived from Africa and they were also perching on telegraph poles and minarets. We stopped and climbed onto the roof of the *caravanserai*. I had been reading the *Rubaiyat of Omar Khayyam* in the 1859 edition of Edward Fitzgerald's translation with 3B, and I quoted from the roof, thinking of Kaseem as the Sultan:

Think, in this batter'd *Caravanserai*
Whose doorways are alternate Night and Day,
How Sultan after Sultan with his pomp
Abode his Hour or two and went his way.

I loved Omar Khayyam, who perfectly evoked my feelings about Baghad.

Babylon consisted of low sand-coloured walls, some with bulls and griffons on them. The palm-lined Euphrates was nearby. We had the site to ourselves except for a couple of security guards. We wandered round and I picked up some slabs with cuneiform on them, and Nebuchadrezzar's (or Nebuchadnezzar's) stamp which meant that they could be dated to the 6th century BC. I was arrested by the security guards and was made to surrender them as "Government property". We went on to Nimrod, the *ziggurat* (or high place) which was the original site of the Tower of Babel. I found more slabs there, and poked in the unexcavated town nearby and found a coin. As in the case of my visit to Jerusalem and the other ancient places in the Middle East, I sensed that I had come to Iraq to absorb past civilizations for a project that lay ahead in the future. I felt that I was working towards my destiny.

Kaseem, "immortal" tyrant
On my way back from the University I often passed the Ministry of Defence. It had railings around it and on high, on a small pillar behind the railings, was a bullet-ridden car in which "the honest and faithful Leader" (*zahim*) had survived one of the 28 assassination attempts against him since he took power three years previously. One of the attempts took place in Rashid Street and one of the assassins was the young Saddam Hussein. Kaseem had crawled from the bullet-ridden car screaming, "I am immortal," and in speeches afterwards he ranted, "They can shoot me from the right and they can shoot me from the left, but they will never kill me, I am immortal." The postage stamps floridly hailed him as "the Great and Glorious, Honest and Faithful, Bright and Shining Leader whose Immortal Revolution of July 14 1958 shall outlive history, who has given freedom to all Iraqis and who shall be ranked as a prophet". The Leader's picture was in every street and in every shop. He had become a tyrant.

The poor
The poor had not benefited from the Revolution. They were everywhere. They leered and squinted, suffering from trachoma (an eye disease). They had scars and boils and faces pocked with smallpox. They blew their noses into the gutter and hitched up their robes and squatted to defecate in full view of everybody. They lived a basic and somewhat ugly existence, and the brave army did nothing for them except cane-beat or rifle-butt them into line when the Leader drove past.

In Iraq I sympathised greatly with the poor. Every day I passed lines of women in *abaya*s who held their hands out, pleaded with trachomatous eyes and implored from pocked faces, "*Filous,*" and I often put 10 *fils* in each hand. I was on the side of the poor and downtrodden and against the system that oppressed them, over which Kaseem presided as a figurehead. But I sensed that they were all victims of a particular stage the Arab civilization had reached, and I was not on the side of Communism at all. If anything, I accepted their plight with the same resignation that Dr Shubber accepted it, and tried to ameliorate it.

Students: fight on campus, death of a student and my alibi for a girl student
The military dictatorship orchestrated tension over Kuwait, and I was watchful as I walked between buses in Bab Sherge in case I was attacked. It was wary of the Kurds, who were 500 miles away, and very wary of the students and of any freedom of expression they might direct at the regime. At the end of Ramadan, after the *Eid* (the feast after a month's fasting from sunrise to sunset), there was a crack-down on the students.

Earlier in the month I had found myself in the middle of a fight between Communist and Nationalist students on the University campus. About thirty students, including some from 3B, scythed and kicked each other. I shouted "Stop this," and they all ran off. Then the army arrived with Sten guns, and I made myself scarce so that I would not have to denounce any of the students I had seen.

Now there was another skirmish between the Communists and the Nationalists, and a boy was knifed through the heart and killed outside the Dean's door on a Sunday (a normal working day, Friday being the Muslim day of rest), and eight others were taken to hospital and placed on the danger list.

One of my best students, a fair-haired girl called Kawther, approached me in some distress and told me, "They are saying I killed the student. Please say I was in your class."

I looked at my register for that Sunday. She had been absent. "Did you kill him?" I asked.

"No," she said.

I did not know whether to believe her but I gave her the alibi she wanted. Soon after there was a demonstration on the campus. Students called "*Ya-yescot*" ("hip hip-boo") and fled when the army arrived, and were chased by portly army men.

Chief of Secret Police becomes Dean of College and purges students
One day I arrived at the college to see a long queue of students. They were waiting ouside the gates to approach a table at which (I found out) sat the Chief of Secret Police, Yusef Abood.

Near him was a large Black Maria with open doors. Each student went either left into the college; or right into the Black Maria, and thence to prison. One of the students told me, "The college has been closed. Every student must re-register, and perhaps must go to prison. The old Dean has gone to prison. Our new Dean is the Chief of Secret Police."

College resumed the next day. I soon discovered that half of 3B were missing. When I called the register from the *mullah*'s platform there was a silence after every other name I called. One of the more reliable students said, "They're in prison, sir."

Students in prison in zoo cages

I resolved to visit the missing students. I obtained directions to the prison from the college Administration and took a taxi to the prison gates. It was a baking day. The prison was ringed with a timber-framed barbed-wire fence and gates. A soldier in uniform let me in, and I wandered across the sand to a number of waist-high zoo cages with vertical bars. I bent and peered within each. Each was enclosed on three sides and open on the fourth, barred side. The first three contained strangers.

The fourth contained many of 3B. Several students were sitting on the sand, their knees drawn up under their chins, holding the bars in their fists. "Sir," several greeted me, "God save you, sir. Thank you for coming, sir. *Kefalek*, how are you, are you fine?" One of them said, "I'm sorry my homework will not be in but as you can see there are no facilities for writing in this prison."

I was greatly touched by the evident affection 3B had for me, even though I had stood up to them for cheating and had failed 15 of them. Soon afterwards they were all back in my class.

President of University proposed for execution
The new Dean, the Chief of Secret Police, Yusef Abood, called a meeting requesting "support for new disciplinary measures on knifing students". About a hundred people sat in a long room that had the atmosphere of a court. The new Dean presided over the meeting. He was prosecuting counsel. A simian man who shelled nuts as he gabbled in Arabic, he spoke at length beside a whirring fan.

An interpreter sat next to me and summarised briefly in English for us British lecturers. The new Dean exonerated the students and blamed the lecturers "for not disciplining students who knife students". He looked at me as he said this. Then he said strongly: "I ask you to vote that a committee be established to hang the old Dean of the College and the President of the University for inefficiency and crimes against the people." And he began to trump up more detailed accusations.

Arthur Plowman sat next to me, a look of horror on his face. He looked shell-shocked, totally paralysed. He was exercising no leadership of his Department.

I leaned forward and whispered to him, "We all need to walk out together."

Plowman pulled himself together and said, "Yes, we walk out. No one must stay."

The entire English Department stood and walked out, most of us not understanding what was being said.

My Secret Police file

During April I travelled back from the University with an immaculately dressed student of mine who was twice my age, Yaseen Salman. He wore Western clothes and a red *fez*. We sat in the bus together and talked.

One day he said, "Sir, can I please pass the examination. I live in a *sarifa* (mud-hut), I have four wives and sixteen children, and if I fail I must repay three years' grant of over £600, and my family will not eat. I know my English is very poor, but you are a kind man. Please to remember my wives and children when you mark my paper." And as I made sympathetic and (at the same time) neutral, noises he added, "Oh, I do part-time work in the Ministry of Defence. I know the Secret Police are watching you. I have seen your file. If you will help me I will help you. I will tell you about the Secret Police information on you."

I wanted to know more about the Secret Police. One day when we were out the army had arrived and according to Yelda had gone to our downstairs phone, unscrewed the mouthpiece and put in a steel band. He told me on our return. I went to the phone, unscrewed the mouthpiece and removed the steel band. Soon afterwards two soldiers had arrived. I let them in and they blatantly went to the telephone, unscrewed the mouth-piece and reinserted the steel band which lay beside it. They told me forcibly in Arabic that I must not touch the mouthpiece. Our calls were being blatantly recorded.

Being honest and valuing Western standards I did not compromise my judgement. I reserved my right to bring an open mind to his exam paper. He nevertheless went ahead with his side of the bargain, and each day we travelled together he had new information to give me about the difficulties I was in with the Secret Police.

The case against me was very simple. I had been observed talking with Communists, and I had given Kawther of 3B, a well-known Communist agitator, an alibi. Kawther was deemed to have knifed the dead student outside the old Dean's door. Convicting Kawther would expedite the conviction and hanging of the old Dean. I had hindered this process. There were deliberations that I might be arrested. Yaseen promised to tell me if a decision was taken to arrest me.

Exit visa: leaving Iraqi dictatorship

I could not wait to leave Iraq now. The heat had returned. At the YWCA I spent time during the afternoon heat reading in the cool of the library. There were many novels by Graham Greene, and I read them all under a ceiling fan which rotated like a propeller blade. I carried forward plans to buy a cheap cottage in Cornwall – my father had found a place in Falmouth and another at Coverack – and I worked on where I would teach next. The British Council had written that in view of my work in Baghdad the interview for my next job would be a formality, and they wondered if I would go to Bangkok or Laos, which was close to North Vietnam, as there was still no vacancy in Japan. In May it was confirmed that Caroline was pregnant and that the baby would be due in December, and I resolved to spend the next year in England so that the birth could be supervised by an English midwife.

To leave Iraq in Kaseem's day meant visiting every Ministry and getting a clearance stamp from each. Only when there were a dozen stamps would an exit visa be granted. To leave by 6 June (my scheduled day of departure) required Ministry-visiting to begin in mid-May. I made long visits to several Ministries, the worst of which was the Ministry of Electricity, which had no record of the YWCA electricity and therefore could not give me a clearance stamp.

I was making so little progress by the end of May that we despaired of getting out before July. Then Yaseen told me, "The Secret Police are delaying your exit. They are creating difficulties for you because of Kawther. I will write something on your file that will help you. But you should telephone the Dean, Dr Yusef Abood."

If the Secret Police were delaying my departure, it sounded good advice to go to the Chief of the Secret Police but he blamed me for delaying the hanging of the old Dean by giving Kawther an alibi. Abood might delay my exit even more.

I did as Yaseen advised. I gave him time to write on my file and then rang Abood at the college, not at the headquarters of the Secret Police. (The Chief of the Secret Police had in effect moved his headquarters to the college, and the Secret Police were now technically my employer.) I explained that I was leaving and was meeting resistance at the Ministries.

Abood said, "Hold on," and there was a long delay while he presumably made a phone call to the branch of the Secret Police that held my file. Then he said, "Let's get things shifting, then." And suddenly clearance stamps were produced in minutes. I made more progress in the next two days than I had in the previous two weeks.

The end-of-year gathering took place in the open air after dark under floodlights. Seemingly unaware that the college was now a branch of the Secret Police, Arthur Plowman spoke very emotionally before hundreds of students. The elderly lady teacher who had been threatened by 3B was leaving after many years at the college and Plowman ended his eulogy, his voice breaking, "Well done, thou good and faithful servant." He was in tears.

The last time I left the University I travelled to Bab Sherge with Yaseen. He wore his usual red *fez*. The examinations were now over. I had marked his paper. He had easily passed on merit. I suffered no crisis of conscience. I told Yaseen that he had passed.

"God save you, Mr Hagger," he said, "my wives and children will say 'God save you'. We will drink tea to you in our *sarifa* (mud-hut) tonight. My four wives will be very grateful to you."

I had been partly implementing Churchill's dream of reconciling the Sunnis, Shiites and Kurds into one Iraqi nation, and, looking back, I feel that by and large within my lecture room I succeeded as I had harmonious classes of students. There were exceptions, such as the killing outside the Dean's door. Now, more than 50 years later, that reconciliation has fallen apart. The Shiites rule and there are almost daily car bombs in Baghdad which kill a thousand Iraqis a month in a latent civil war.

I left Iraq by air on 4 June. The Iraqi Airlines plane took off from the runway nearest the YWCA. The plane banked, and beyond the wing I could see the YWCA beneath me, in a wasteland of sand surrounded by thousands of palms. I could see Yelda, our servant, sweeping the flat roof.

I looked back on the nine months I had been there. They had been picaresque and full of incident, and half 3B would end up as butchers in some future tyrant's security machine. I had visited many ancient places, which my journey had meant me to do, and had absorbed the wisdom of the Middle East. I had disciplined myself to sitting at a desk in great extremes of temperature and attempting to write. I did not know it but I would draw on my impressions of Iraq in *Armageddon*. There had been some purgation in the harsh desert conditions.

But I had somehow remained stuck in the outer world of Kaseem's sycophantic dictatorship. I was under the dictatorship of my ego. I knew I needed a development within that had not yet taken place. I was sure my marriage would bring this development to birth, and that I was right to escape Iraq as its surface variety was an obstacle to this development.

Episode 7:

Vitalism and Mechanism

Years: 1962–1963
Locations: London; West Dulwich; Loughton
Works: *Mandalas*; *A Well of Truth*; 'The Riddle of the Great Pyramid';
Juben: Confessions of a Rationalist

""Wisdom and Spirit of the Universe!
Thou Soul that art the eternity of thought!
And giv'st to forms and images a breath
And everlasting motion!"
        Wordsworth, 'Influence of Natural Objects', and *The Prelude*, bk i, 401

In the coming months I would be torn between two beliefs: that the soul is immortal, which I had absorbed through my reading of literature on my path to Reality; and that mind is mechanistic brain function and perishable, an alien, scientific view that had invaded me during my synthesis of knowledge in Baghdad. My intuitive quest for wisdom was challenged by this mechanistic view that would have been alien to Romantic poets, and this episode obstructed my path like a dense thicket.

Mechanism: brain and birth
We returned to England with enough to live on for a year. We were met by Caroline's father, who drove us back to West Dulwich. We lived in an upstairs room in that large house which was due for demolition in a year and a half's time. It was a relief to be out of the Baghdad heat and away from its politics.

For the first month we savoured being back in England, and my grandmother paid for us to take a short holiday in Jersey. We flew to St Helier and stayed in a hotel on a cliff near Gorey. I sat on the beach below with my heavily pregnant wife, reading Conrad's *Under Western Eyes*. We toured the island, enjoying the green of Jersey after the yellow desert and appreciating the simple orderliness of the people after the raucous Arabs. In September at my father's request I gave a talk about my experiences in Iraq at the end of a Rotary-Club lunch at The Bald Faced Stag, Buckhurst Hill.

London: brain and soul, research into brain function – the physiological basis of thinking, mechanistic view of mind

With a lump sum in the bank, I could prepare myself to be a writer. In Iraq I had become interested in the conflict between brain mechanism and vital inner growth. On the one hand was the doctrine that all natural phenomena including life can be explained by physics and chemistry, which I encountered in the many non-fiction paperbacks I had acquired. On the other hand was the doctrine I had absorbed from European and Eastern literature, that life originates in a vital principle that is distinct from chemical and other physical forces, and perhaps includes souls. I reread Grey Walter's *The Living Brain* (one of the paperbacks) and thought about the materialist view that mind is brain function and can be explained mechanically by physics and chemistry. I also read Jung's focus on *mandalas*, sacred Tibetan wall-hangings with a circular design that Jung held to be a symbol of a psychological centre beyond the personality or ego. *Mandalas*, Jung reckoned, were symbols of self-unity and completeness, symbols of a deeper level of the self, the soul.

The contrast between the mechanistic view of the brain and the Tibetan view of the soul was an objectivisation of a conflict within my own inner life, and I found external images for it. I visited the Upjohn brain in London, a vast octopus of jumping lights which simulated the physiological basis of thinking. (Maurice Edelman provided a more subtle visual aid: his Darwin III and IV perceptual machines, computers in which groups of neurons form perceptions.) I also bought a book on Tibetan *mandalas* at a small bookshop near the British Museum and went into the wisdom of India, China and Japan.

Out of the tussle came a dialectic between a mechanist and a believer in the soul which I wrote as a Dostoevskian novel throughout the autumn. I was divided between believing that death was the end for the mind and believing with the poets that there is a soul which survives death, and the novel, *Mandalas*, worked out this self-division. I carried forward my theme by writing a short screenplay, *Tristy*, about an energetic, vital young man who had a sense of purpose.

My antipathy for Christianity – even though my two brothers and sister now sang in the choir at St Mary's, Loughton – led me to side with the materialistic view: I absorbed the view of science and thought Christians who believed in the soul had not understood that all mind could be reduced to electrical activity in the brain. We lived through the Cuban crisis on Saturday 27 October, expecting the outbreak of nuclear war any moment in West Dulwich and during a visit to the Charing Cross Road, and, our minds attuned to Moscow and the prospect of sudden annihilation, I lived on the verge of extinction and pondered the view of science: we could be exterminated at any time, death was the end and life had no meaning.

But deep down I knew the mechanistic view of science should be questioned. I took note of all growing things. In the afternoons I went for a walk, often to Dulwich Park, where there were ducks and squirrels, or dug weeds in the vegetable garden at the house, and in the evenings I sometimes walked down to the pub at the end of the road, the Alleyn's Head, and drank with some of the teachers from Dulwich College and discussed what they were teaching. Otherwise I researched and wrote in a room near the railway line, wrestling with my inner conflict, while rats scratched under the floorboards and periodically an electric train rushed past, drowning all sound.

Birth of daughter, Nadia
My wife's pregnancy advanced and one evening in December she gave birth at home. She had not wanted to have the child in hospital, and the midwife arrived soon after the contractions began. I was excluded from the birth but listened through the door: "One more push."

Our doctor came. He found me and announced that I had a daughter. It was a cold, icy night, and, having spent time with my wife and daughter, I walked with him to the Alleyn's Head afterwards and bought him a pint of beer. We talked about the mystery of a new life and a new person, a new growth, and I could not see my daughter in mechanistic terms.

The winter of early 1963 was extremely cold. Snow had fallen on Boxing Day – it began as my father made a speech at a family party at Journey's End – and lay on the ground until March. The effect was arctic. There were wonderful snowscapes. My wife and I cared for little Nadia. As I watched the new baby the conflict within myself shifted. I could not believe in the mechanism and materialism that had seemed so plausible in the autumn. I moved back towards a view of humans as comprising feelings and a soul. My own inner growth undermined the dialectic of my writing, in which science confronted religion, and it increasingly looked like a skin a snake had shed.

All works of art are models of reality. Authors, painters and composers say, "Life has patterns like this." I had embarked on a view of reality I had outgrown. Equally, all works of art mirror the extent of their creator's inner growth. By the spring I had moved beyond the inner state I had known in the autumn. I had started to grow in the deep snow of early 1963 and would not be satisfied with any art I produced until my growth was complete. I had set myself the long-term task of becoming a serious writer about the meaning of life and our Age in the tradition of T.S. Eliot. I was clear that I should remake myself into a writer of high seriousness and that I should not become an entertainer who sold books to make a living. I did not know that I would continue to grow, and outgrow my own work, for the next 25 years.

Death of Kaseem

In February there was a revolution in Iraq and Kaseem was overthrown. Brigadier Arif, a former school friend of Kaseem's and participant in the 1958 Revolution, personally led the assault on the Ministry of Defence, where Kaseem defended himself with a pistol to the end. According to information I was later given he fought to the last round and came out at the salute and said to Arif, "I spared your life, now you spare mine." He was arrested by Arif, driven to a television station and, together with a hated judge and another man, shot during a live broadcast. An Arab then cut off his head and swung it to and fro in front of the television camera for all to see. The television then played Mickey-Mouse cartoons.

So ended the life of a tyrant who had butchered the Royal family and dragged their bodies through the streets behind a lorry in 1958. He had died as he had lived, by the gun, and he was not after all immortal. I recall standing a yard from him as he saluted at the Turkish Embassy and watched me out of the corner of his eyes. I imagined his head being cut off and wondered again about the mechanist's bleak, nihilistic view of a life. Did the tyrant have an immortal soul?

Yusef Abood, the new Dean and Chief of Secret Police, was put in prison, and Arthur Plowman and a number of the foreign lecturers were ordered to leave. Now my decision to leave Iraq when I did seemed a good one.

Vitalism: gardening and father

Father's brain haemorrhage

In April my father had a brain haemorrhage while pruning the roses in the front garden at Journey's End. He was taken to Whipps Cross Hospital, and was put on the danger list. Two days later I visited him. He gave me a limp handshake and seemed in an emotionless dream. He did not understand what I said. The next day he had four fits with convulsions. In early May he had two heart attacks, and a week later a third one, and then a fourth.

I visited him. He told me he had felt a crippling pain as the clot moved from his leg to his heart, and that he had struggled for breath. I related to him through my feelings and saw him as a soul trapped in a decaying body. I moved further away from mechanism during his illness.

George MacBeth and B.S. Johnson

I consciously nourished my soul at poetry readings given by the Dulwich Group of Poets. They were held at The Crown and Greyhound. I bought a beer and then sat upstairs in the long room where readings were held. I can remember hearing the dandified George MacBeth and Edwin Brock. Howard Sergeant sometimes chaired meetings.

I remember talking with the experimental novelist B.S. Johnson, a conversation which carried on while we had a pee during which he said: "I am concerned to push the technical experiments in the novel to their upmost." (He was in the tradition of Sterne's *Tristram Shandy* and Joyce, and in 1969 he brought out a novel, *The Unfortunates*, whose pages came loose in a box without binding so that readers could change the order of pages as they felt fit. Johnson committed suicide in November 1973, depressed at his lack of commercial success, which to me highlighted the dead-end of technique-first writing. He has subsequently had a cult following.)

I apply to British Council for a lectureship in Japan
Deep down I knew that I had to get away from the sceptical mechanistic West and go to Japan to absorb the wisdom of the East and strengthen my view of the soul. At the end of May I contacted the British Council and applied for any job that might be coming up in Japan. I was told that a post should become available in July, and that I would be a strong candidate.

Work in Dulwich Park as gardener, and vitalism
Meanwhile, I was waiting to go to Japan, and no office would give me indoor work for a few months. Desperate for money – down to my last £8 – and wanting to study growing things and move away from mechanism, I made contact with the administrators of Dulwich Park where I had often walked. I accepted their offer of a temporary job as an LCC (London County Council) gardener on 5 shillings an hour. On the first day I hoed sorrel and ground elder round the famous Dulwich rhododendrons with an ex-naval rating, John Armstrong. Surrounded by shrubs and plants, my soul throbbed with vitalism and rejected mechanism.

It was a hot summer and I worked from 8 until 5. Sometimes Caroline brought Nadia down in the pram to see me in the afternoon. It was hard, back-breaking work, but no more than many writers had had to do, including Colin Wilson. Sometimes I had to dig a long trench with a fork in a great heat, but the discipline did me good. It was mindless work – I sometimes wondered if I was committing "mind-suicide" like T.E. Lawrence who had entered the RAF under an assumed name – and looking back I can see that I was purging myself, beginning a purgation of my lower ego and its senses as part of my remaking of myself.

Ricky visited me and told me that Graham Wallis, the outsider who had lived in Worcester College, had died. (In due course I wrote a very short story, 'A Barbiturate for a Bad Liver', about his death.) Ricky said that although he was teaching English as a foreign language in London he wanted to try opium, which I saw as a surrender to his lower ego and its senses and opposed. (*See* p.109.) My disciplined regime was like being in a monastery and tilling fields all day. In the evenings, worn out, I began

Confessions of a Rationalist,[1] which represented the current stage of my inner growth, a move against the rational, social ego. (For this I read Constant's *Adolphe* and Crébillon fils' *The Wayward Head and Heart*.) I also wrote a long short story, 'The Riddle of the Great Pyramid',[2] which was about the apparent purposelessness of the toil that built the Great Pyramid. Indirectly I was comparing my own back-breaking efforts with those of the slaves who built the Great Pyramid.

While I toiled in the summer heat of June, I observed the life cycle of rhododendrons, which revert to type, and of azaleas. I learned about their habits and those of begonias, bellis daisies and polyanthus. I studied the activities of seeds, of germinations and sprouting, and moved further away from mechanism. Voltaire's Candide discovered that the secret of happiness was to "cultivate one's garden", a practical philosophy that ignored specu-lation, and, surrounded by growth, I found my time in Dulwich Park a very rewarding time of inner growth. I did not then know that one day I would have to oversee gardeners at schools and a historic house, and that for more than 50 years I would be drawing on knowledge I acquired as a park gardener that June.

Gardener in three schools

At the end of June I was moved out of the Park to three local schools. Working from a shed in the grounds of one of the schools I cut the grass together with an illiterate rascal called Gordon who pretended to read a newspaper every tea-break, sometimes holding it upside down. He was paranoid about our Superintendent, Mr Marshall, who he thought was constantly spying on us, and repeatedly urged me to cut short our tea-break in case anyone was watching. From my folding chair in front of our shed I surveyed school life at Rosedale School, at Langbourne Junior off Bowen Drive and especially at Kingsdale School, which we tended in rotation. I watched the pupils race around in their playground at lunch-time.

I was outside the school activities, an outsider, and felt at peace. I did not know that one day I would own three private schools, and looking back I cannot help feeling that Providence was giving me a nudge by showing me the activities of three schools from the gardeners' shed.

Offered lectureship in Japan

In the middle of July I was told that the post *had* become vacant in Japan. I was interviewed by the British Council, and at the end of July I had a second interview at which a Japanese, Dr Shumoto, asked me a number of questions. During the wait to hear from Japan my father had another stroke, which left him unconscious for five hours. I visited him the next day in Whipps Cross Hospital. He was dazed.

In the second week of September I learned that I would be lecturing at Tokyo University of Education and Keio University, Tokyo, two universities who would share me from November. I was overjoyed, but had some misgivings at the prospect of leaving England when my father was ill. Caroline was resigned. Nadia was now nearly one and was healthy, and we would be earning some proper money.

Work in library
The day I heard about Japan I changed jobs. It had begun to get chilly outside, and Gordon was becoming more difficult to work with – everything I said was relayed to Mr Marshall in an attempt to ingratiate himself – and so I took a job in the Kingswood library, processing books and stamping dates. I was being shown books as finished products and invited to consider how my own work could find a place on these shelves. Looking back, I again cannot help feeling that Providence was giving me a nudge.

Father's third stroke, death and funeral
A week after I started at the library my father had a third stroke and was unconscious from 8 a.m. to 4 p.m. He was too ill to be moved to hospital. He lingered on at Journey's End for another month, occupying the room on the half-landing to the left of the first flight of stairs – the room into which I climbed late at night after learning that Colin Wilson had asked me to go to Cornwall. His breathing became more and more laboured. Every fifth breath was difficult.

I visited him on 8 October and he insisted we drank Guinness from our silver tankards. He half-sat up in bed, propped up by pillows. I poured his bottle into his tankard and handed it to him. He took one sip, went into a choking convulsion and wept, "This is the end." I tried to reassure him, but he insisted, "No, this is the end." Downstairs the television tube failed and the picture shrank to the size of a postage stamp. Two days later he slipped into a coma and five days later he died.

As soon as I heard of his death from my mother I went to Journey's End. I found the family drinking port, relieved. I went up to my father's room on the half-landing and stood by the bed on which he lay covered by a sheet. My mother came into the room and said, "There's nothing terrible in death." She pulled back the sheet and left me alone with him.

I gazed a long time at his still face and closed eyes that had, with the best intentions, opposed my destiny, and I thought of his heroic struggle and suffering. He had had polio at 14, and had seen six of his ten children die in infancy. Within the last seven months he had endured 2 brain haemorrhages, 4 convulsive fits, 4 heart attacks and 4 strokes. He had been a stoic of massive proportions, and I was glad I had made my peace with him over the final ritual Guinness. I was filled with a sense of the ultimate futility of his long struggle, but in spite of my nihilism and despair I had a strong feeling, or conviction, that mechanism was wrong, that there is a soul and that his soul had fled to another world.

The funeral took place three days later in St Mary's church, Loughton. The coffin was carried in and placed on a trestle-table-like bier at the front. The church was full, and I saw Thompson, the Chigwell Head, standing at the back. I shook hands with many of the congregation after the service, and then we drove through the Forest in Austin Princesses to Parndon Wood Crematorium. We passed men who stood to attention and crossed themselves or took off their hats. Later, watching smoke rise from the chimney, I was sure that the soul is not mere mechanistic brain function.

W.B. Emery and the Great Pyramid
The library touched on my literary work. The librarian, who was called Fowler, had a beard. One day he said of my impending visit to Japan, "You're a thinker *and* a man of action. If you're going to be a poet you will write about eternity." Looking back, I now recognise the aptness and acuity of his comment.

Another day a man with dark hair and spectacles came into the library and Fowler introduced me. He was W.B. Emery, the Egyptologist. He had spent his life excavating in the Nile Valley at Amarna, Luxor, Thebes and Saqqara, and was now a Professor of Egyptology. Later I encountered him walking in Alleyn Road. Knowing he had published *Great Tombs of the First Dynasty* in three volumes, I stopped him and told him about my long short story, 'The Riddle of the Great Pyramid'. I asked him what he thought the riddle was, and was pleased he did not know. His frank admission confirmed to me that there was a riddle.

Looking back, I see the encounter as significant. I detected another nudge from Providence for I had been put in touch with someone I needed to check the theme of my story. (When I researched the Egyptian bull-cult in 1981 I found that Emery had discovered a Sarapeum-like labyrinth among the 1st-dynasty tombs, and had thus provided the first evidence for the bull-cult.)

Getting off to Japan: flat
We had to vacate the Dulwich house in the course of November. It had to be demolished so smaller houses could be built on the land. I stopped working at the library, and we moved to Journey's End. I bought a maisonette in Loughton (9 Crescent View) on mortgage for £2,750 as an investment I could begin to pay off, and prepared to let it while I was away. I was given a clothing allowance of £100 by the British Council, which I spent on tropical

clothes, but otherwise I had just £5 to my name. I had mixed feelings about starting a new job in Tokyo when my father had just died, but my younger brother Rob was living at Journey's End and would keep an eye on my mother.

Visit to Dick Paul in Palmerston's lounge, Carlton Gardens
It was my intention to visit China while I was in Japan. With this long-term aim in view I had written to Admiral Sir Charles Woodhouse on 14 October to report that I would shortly be leaving for Japan. He replied from his home address in Warlingham, Surrey the next day:

> Dear Mr Hagger, Thank you for your letter of 14th October. As I am no longer at the place where I saw you in May 1961, I have passed your letter on to the appropriate quarter, and I have no doubt you will be hearing from them shortly.[3]

On 18 October I had received a letter from Co-ordination Staff, Foreign Office, in Carlton Gardens:

> Dear Mr Hagger, Your letter of 14th October has been passed to me. I should be very pleased to see you at the above address and suggest you come here at 3.15 p.m. on Wednesday, 6th November. I shall assume that this is convenient for you unless I hear to the contrary.[4]

It was signed R.L. Paul.

I had duly gone to see him on 6th November, and I remember Dick Paul as a grey-haired man with a very red face, tall and big-shouldered in a dark suit, greeting me in front of a magnificent fireplace with a striking crest. He said we were in "Palmerston's lounge" and spoke of how de Gaulle had planned the French Resistance from before this fireplace during the war. (I gathered that the wall had been knocked through between two adjacent buildings.) We talked about my forthcoming journey to Japan and my intention to go to China, where Chairman Mao was as intimidating as Hitler, and he urged me to take any opportunity I could to see inside China.

Experience of the One by Strawberry Hill pond – vitalism and soul triumph over mechanism
The day before I left England[5] I visited Epping Forest. I walked up Robin Hood Lane to the Strawberry Hill pond. I stood by the fallen tree and gazed for a long time at the island. I was still bruised from my father's death.

Suddenly I became immensely aware of trees, mallards, water-boatmen, everything, and it was inconceivable that the whole scheme should be to no end. Everything had purpose. I intuitively sensed a principle in the universe which could not be reduced to science, a vital principle I thought of as 'the Life-Intelligence'. It had a purpose which could be deduced from its forms, of which we are one, and from the plan, but the purpose was removed from our understanding, so we would never know its ends. My soul was filled with a vitalist Reality that pervaded the universe and could not be understood mechanistically.

That experience by the Strawberry Hill pond ranked with the experience by the Worcester College lake. Both were mystical experiences, glimpses of a Reality beyond that of our everyday consciousness.

My inner conflict between mechanistic brain and vitalist soul had been resolved. I had stayed in England 17 months between returning from Iraq and leaving for Japan. In that time my daughter had been born and spent her first year in the mild British climate and under the supervision of the British Welfare State, and I had been on hand during my father's long-drawn-out death.

It was right that I should have been in England for this time, but my journey called me to seek the wisdom of the East for which I had yearned. I knew I would now make progress in the remaking of myself and in discovering the wisdom of the East.

Episode 8:

The Absolute and Scepticism

Years: 1963–1966
Locations: Tokyo; Nobe; Kitakamura; Nikko; Mt Fuji; Hiroshima; Kyoto; Nara; Gora
Works: *A Stone Torch-Basket* (including 'The Expatriate');
The Early Education and Making of a Mystic; 'The Silence'
Initiatives: Visiting Foreign Professor in Japan; speechwriter to Governor of the Bank of Japan; tutor to Prince Hitachi; discovers the wisdom of the East; awakening to metaphysical Light; First Mystic Life

"The struggle of the self to disentangle itself from illusion and attain the Absolute is a life-struggle."

Evelyn Underhill, *Mysticism* (1911), p.229

I was now torn between the Absolute (a metaphysical concept) and scepticism (which assailed me like a succession of brambles I had to sidestep as I progressed along my path). I encountered my First Mystic Life and opened to new inner experiences and images as my Muse poured new energy and inspiration into my soul. This episode in Japan began my transformation.

The Absolute in Japan

Arrival in Japan

We flew to Japan first class. It was a long flight. When we arrived in Tokyo I stepped out of the plane, crumpled and travel-worn, holding my eleven-month-old daughter in a blue blanket and clutching a blue teddy bear, and was puzzled to see a line of four Japanese in tails near a huge limousine. Then I realised they were greeting me. They were all august Professors. As one of them shook my hand my daughter was sick on his sleeve. One of the Professors scraped and fawned, "Your appearance will, I am sure, be acceptable to the students, Professor Hagger."

Discovery that I am a Visiting Foreign Professor – first since William Empson

It now dawned on me that I was a full Professor, "a Visiting Foreign Professor". We were driven through the darkness, through the concrete sprawl and slag-heap that was Tokyo to the International House, which had a large Japanese garden. We were shown to a room and told there was no urgency to prepare anything. We fell asleep very quickly. Next day after breakfast the limousine returned and I made visits to my two main universities, which were ferroconcrete, glassy modern buildings in different parts of Tokyo.

Nicholas's daughter Nadia in the garden of his bungalow, Tokyo

The following day we were driven to a furnished wooden bungalow at 108 Kohinata Suido-cho, Bunkyo-ku. It had a front garden with small palms and a small back garden with a veranda and a head-high wall over which we had a good view of Tokyo. There were clusters of bamboo and all the windows had mosquito-nets. It had a tiny maid's room off the kitchen. There was barely room for a maid to lie full length on the *tatami* matting. The kitchen was infested with cockroaches which scuttled in and behind the cutlery drawer. It had a television.

The bathroom had a deep and spacious erotic bath. It had a ledge halfway up for sitting on, and there was room for two to bath up to their necks in hot water. Here, I understood, my predecessor used to hold his classes at the end of his life. "His scholarship," I was told, "was not – er – to be esteemed."

Tokyo University of Education, teaching in Empson's room

My main university, Tokyo University of Education, was where the poet and Neoclassical critic William Empson had taught in 1931, as a Professor. I was told that Empson's university, Tokyo Bunrika Daigaku (Tokyo University of Literature and Science)[1] had been renamed Tokyo Kyoiku Daigaku (Tokyo University of Education, which went back to 1872), and that a particular room I would be teaching in was a room where Empson had taught. He had been sent home in 1934 for riding home naked in a taxi after a swim and (I was told) drunkenly fumbling the taxi-driver. It was only when I had met the students in some of the gloomy, dingy classrooms there and had talked to the staff and walked with some of the younger lecturers, who earned little more than £30 a month, that I was told by my assistant, the bespectacled Mr Kuahara, "You are the first Visiting Foreign Professor since William Empson."[2]

I was pleased to be a successor to Professor Empson, Christopher Ricks's mentor, as I was firmly in the tradition of poets who had lectured overseas that I had outlined to Colin Wilson.

James Kirkup

I heard how I came to be appointed. The post had been advertised and the poet James Kirkup (who had left England in 1956 to teach abroad) had applied from Kuala Lumpur along with four others. I had read Kirkup's book about his time at Sendai immediately before leaving England. The university had decided on Kirkup but no one would take on the responsibility of rejecting the other four applicants and so the British Council had been consulted, the intention being that *they* would appoint Kirkup. The British Council and Kirkup had quarrelled and, understanding "professor" as "lecturer", the British Council had advertised the post as such and had found me. The Japanese had followed the British Council and initially downgraded the position to lecturer but upgraded it back to "Visiting Foreign Professor" from 1 April 1964.[3] Meanwhile, they had concluded that I was better than Kirkup. Hence the welcoming party at the airport. With hindsight, I believe they wanted someone who was too young to remember what the Japanese had done during the war. Now, at 24, I had what Nietzsche and Rupert Brooke both had at a similar youthful age, a Chair. In a matter of 10 weeks I had gone from park labourer to successor to William Empson, the rational poet admired by the Movement poets, and replacement for the poet James Kirkup.

E.W.F. Tomlin, Representative of the British Council in Japan, friend of Eliot
At least ten days went by before I gave my first lecture. During this time we moved into the bungalow and were invited to lunch by the British Council Representative, E.W.F. Tomlin, technically my boss. He was author of *The Western Philosophers* and *The Eastern Philosophers*, both of which I had bought at Oxford and had on my shelves for several years.

Tomlin was that rarity in those days, a metaphysical philosopher. Although he represented Britain along with A.J. Ayer at philosophy conferences, he had written *The Approach to Metaphysics*. He had been influenced by his long friendship with T.S. Eliot – his last book would be entitled *T.S. Eliot, A Friendship* and would describe more than 100 letters he received from Eliot.[4] I did not know that he had been invited to dinner at Eliot's home as recently as 4 September 1963.[5] Nor did I know of his "profound disillusionment with the direction my organisation [the British Council] was taking".[6] His conversation was always against logical positivism and linguistic analysis.

He was then a dome-headed 50 and looked disconcertingly like Profumo. He lived alone with his maid and was always formally dressed, proper and correct. He sat at the end of a long, wide dining-table and we talked about Kierkegaard. He spoke up for metaphysics across the dinner-table and placed the soul in a social context. Things I had not been able to say in sceptical England were spoken of openly and with approval.

Tokyo University of Education and Keio University
I walked to Tokyo University of Education every Monday and Friday morning. I passed through a residential area under a pall of black smoke from a distant chimney and after 12 minutes came out by Myogadani station. I had different groups of students. They ranged from a group of PhD students to students with hesitant English, and I taught English Language and Literature, emphasising the 20th century. The students very quickly took to me as I was of their own age, and soon my lectures were very well attended.

Every Tuesday I went to Keio University on the subway (as the tube is called in Tokyo) and took two classes, from 1 p.m. to 3 for 180 and, after green tea, from 3.15 to 5.15 for 160. There was no microphone, and none was needed. The students all did exactly as I wanted. When I said, "Take up your pens," 180 hands immediately reached out, and when I said, "Write," 180 heads would go down, the boys wearing identical black students' uniforms.

Their movements were synchronised as though they were all under one group identity. At Keio I taught classes in modern English Literature, emphasising poetry.

Modern and traditional Japan

Travelling around Tokyo I soon had conflicting experience of modern and traditional Japan. The streets and subway were always crowded. There were always queues of fuming cars and taxis, and I had to fight my way through walls of people. I was far taller than the Japanese, and, even more than in Iraq, I felt different. There were not many Westerners about. The traditional Japanese streets with open rice-paper doors and paper lanterns were charming and inviting, but wherever any foreigner (*gaijin*) went there was hesitant alertness and suppressed tension and a desire to giggle. Modern Tokyo was garish and gaudy, vulgar and in bad taste – the Ginza was a riot of tasteless neon and much of the architecture was undistinguished ferro-concrete – but traditional Japan still had the old *samurai* values and could be found in *Noh*, *kabuki*, *ikebana* (flower-arranging), the *haiku*, Zen and its many wooden houses. The modern Japanese wore a suit but his mind was still traditional and he was ruled by an old feudal code of loyalty, by *on* (oblig-ation) and *giri* (honour). He did his utmost to avoid incurring obligations (for example, by bringing a present every time he visited a home) and his good name and preservation of face were of vital importance.

The modern Japan repelled me, the traditional Japan attracted me to its aesthetic values. I realised that there is a sensitivity in the Japanese spirit that is quick to appreciate beauty, and I warmed to the annual spring appre-ciation of cherry blossom and the annual autumn sadness (*mono-aware*). I was quick to understand the Japanese and how they thought, and knew (as many foreigners did not) how to avoid making demands that would make them anxious, ill at ease and resentful.

Brian Buchanan's house in Nobe

There were two other English lecturers at Tokyo University of Education: Dr Blyth, an expert and author of books on Zen Buddhism, who was ill – with whom I shook hands once in a corridor after he locked the door of his room; and Brian Buchanan, a balding, bespectacled elderly Scot who wore a brown suit and shared a room with me. He had been in Japan for many years. He had lived in Ireland. Mrs. Patrick Campbell had been his godmother, and he had known Maud Gonne who Yeats admired, and Synge. He had met many writers and political activists in Dublin: he had been dandled on Shaw's knee and he had met MacBride, who was shot by the British after the Easter-1916 uprising. He had witnessed some extraor-dinary events in his youth. He told me that he had been a guide in the Papal apartments, which I (mistakenly) understood to be in Avignon rather than Rome, and that the walls of Alexander VI's bedroom, which were not on public view, contained murals of naked ladies and nightingales. He had had many adventures, some of which would pass into my short stories, those narrated by Brewer.

Buchanan had a house at Nobe, a fishing village by the Pacific, and we soon left Tokyo and spent a weekend with him. The village consisted of thirty thatched houses by a long and completely deserted sandy beach. It was surrounded by horseshoe valleys where local peasants planted rice in paddy-fields. At night the air was filled with the sawing of cicadas and the croaking of frogs. We sat on the *tatami* matting with the rice-paper doors open, looking at the moon while exotic flying beetles flew in, attracted by our light, and crashed to the floor. We drank *saké* (rice-wine) and talked literature and history until it was time to totter for a last stroll by the dark moonlit water before returning to our *futon*s, the fold-out bedding that lies on a Japanese matting floor.

Buchanan nicknamed me "Shelley" because he said I facially resembled the Romantic poet who was his specialist subject.

Poems: 'The Expatriate', 'The Seventeenth-Century Pilgrim'
Back in Tokyo I found myself increasingly drawn to poetry and slowly realised I was a poet rather than a novelist, a perception I "forgot" from time to time and had to relearn. We used to walk to the Japanese gardens at Chinzanso. From the bungalow we walked down a steep bouldered incline that reminded me of Cyclopean Mycenae, to Edogawa bridge. In the gardens I particularly liked the stone lanterns which held a light that shone in the evenings, suggesting the Buddha's enlightenment, and fireflies were released from time to time. In those early days I wrote 'The Expatriate', a poem about an expatriate in such a garden – I also drew on the International House garden – and a sonnet, 'The Seventeenth-Century Pilgrim'. These were the first poems in *A Stone Torch-Basket*.

I was asked to write an article on contemporary English literature for the Japanese magazine *The Rising Generation* (*Eigo Seinin*). In the coming weeks I wrote 'The Contemporary Literary Scene in England: The Missing Dimension', which eventually appeared in the July 1964 issue. I distinguished the many writers who had a social and secular vision (such as the Angry Young Men) from the few who had a metaphysical perspective (such as Eliot). From the outset in December 1963 I was aware of the conflict between sceptical and metaphysical writers that I would later reflect in *A New Philosophy of Literature*.[7]

Thomas Fitzsimmons

In early December I discovered that an American poet, Tom Fitzsimmons, also taught at Tokyo University of Education. His time in Japan was drawing to an end. He was unwell, a large grey-haired man of 37 who had blown out from pemphigus, which he described to me in the staff room as "an allergy against yourself" and which required cortisone treatment. He was a brooding spirit of raw brilliance who was sceptical about the immortality of the soul. I took to meeting him in Tokyo and we spent several evenings drinking and discussing literature. (He was based at Oakland University, Michigan and would write or translate 60 books, many of which were in short-lined verse.)

Meeting with Junzaburo Nishiwaki

At Keio I tried to come across with friendly vigour. The students liked my lack of formality. The Professor in charge of me there said approvingly, "You have boiled up the students." There was an abstract statue in the grounds called 'Nothing' – it had a hole in it which symbolised eternity, and Stephen Spender had liked it on a visit – and after I had referred to this in a lecture several of the students asked to meet me in a nearby restaurant "for a metaphysical discussion", which was "chaired" by Shinsuke Ando, the young don who looked after me.

Just before Christmas Ando took me to meet Keio's Professor Emeritus and Japan's most famous poet, Junzaburo Nishiwaki, author of 'January in Kyoto' which came out a year after Eliot's 'The Waste Land' and had a similar effect on Japanese poetry. It could be said that Nishiwaki was then the T.S. Eliot of Japan. I arrived at his home soon after 3 p.m. for what should have been a half-hour's visit. Very soon whisky was produced, and I said that I had come to Japan to discover the wisdom of the East, and wondered if it could be found in his work.

The silky-haired bespectacled septuagenarian began speaking of the Nobel Prize, saying that if he were given it he would accept it for Japan's sake. He then startled me by saying: "I want to kiss hands with Mr Hagger and toast his figure, his face, his hair, his knowledge and his mind. He is the greatest Englishman, a real scholar. I am seldom wrong in my intuition, but one day he will be the greatest man in England – and not only in England, all of Europe. One day he will get the Nobel Prize. But never forget. Make the public come to you on your terms. Impose your will on the public. As Wordsworth said, teach the public the taste by which you are relished."

Ando had begun to interject, "As Professor Nishiwaki is unexpectedly drunk..." Then he said, "Professor Nishiwaki is not a sycophant." I did not leave until 11.30 p.m.[8]

Looking back, I see Nishiwaki's "intuition" as a call to a journey that would result in a distinctive body of metaphysical work in the footsteps of Goethe and Eliot.

Diaries

As part of my new determination I made a daily entry in a desk diary. I had kept a sporadic journal from my first day at Oxford. In 1963 I had begun to make regular short entries in my desk diary, and I now began to write fuller entries. Throughout my time in Japan I wrote a page a day in a red Collins Royal 52 diary, and I have written daily entries since, although not at such full length.

Earthquake

On Christmas Eve we had our first earthquake. For ten seconds the floor shook, the walls creaked, the windows rattled and the glass in the bookcase rang out. It got worse and just when I thought the ceiling was coming down and stood up instinctively as if to hold it up the rattling stopped. There were regular earthquakes during my time in Japan.

Tomlin and the Absolute: metaphysical philosopher

On Christmas Day, leaving our daughter with our maid Emiko (who had been maid to our predecessor who had held classes in the erotic bath), we attended a lunch party for all the British lecturers in Japan at Tomlin's house. Tomlin had gone to some pains to recreate an English Christmas, and there were paper hats and mottoes. There was a mishap with the Christmas pudding and Tomlin told us his kitchen staff were not lighting the brandy.

We visited Nobe and walked by the booming sea. On New Year's Day we were invited to lunch by Professor Narita (one of the Tokyo University of Education professors who knew Empson) and were served a 25-course meal (which, I have to say, made me sick).

Early in the new year I invited Tomlin for dinner on his own. I served him *sashimi* (raw fish) with horseradish. We discussed the history of science, brain physiology and the Absolute: the one Reality, "that which can exist without being related to anything else" (*Concise Oxford Dictionary*). He was a great defender of the Absolute, and he attacked Humanism and Existentialism. He took Eliot's position on Christianity, and I thought it detracted from his metaphysical philosophy to mix the Absolute with such doctrinal issues as the Virgin birth and the Resurrection. At one point I remember him blinking and saying gravely, at his most formal, holding chopsticks, "Oh, er, an enormous lump of horseradish has just come down through my nose."

The next day I was in turmoil. Tomlin had insisted that the purpose of life is to attain the Absolute, that "not having a metaphysic is committing mental suicide". I pondered oneness and unity – Reality – and I was aware of the limitations of scientific materialism and mechanism. I wrote down a quotation from Whitehead: "Scientists who spend their life with the purpose of proving that it is purposeless constitute an interesting subject of study." I pondered eternity and wrote down as many quotations as I could find on eternity. My diary entries contrasted the sceptical reality and metaphysical Reality.

In the first months of 1964 I was torn between the influences of metaphysical Tomlin and anti-Absolute Fitzsimmons, who affirmed the physical basis of everything. I planned to rewrite my novel as the conflict between a pro-metaphysical priest and a mechanistic scientist. I was on the side of the priest, on the side of growth; against Christianity.

Scepticism of Westerners

Suddenly I was surrounded by sceptical influences. A sceptic doubts accepted opinions on all religions. One of the Oxford Randolph Set, Adrian Hohler, turned up two roads away from me. He was with the British Embassy learning Japanese for two and a half years. He came to dinner and when I told him about Tomlin, said, "Tomlin's theories are more preposterous than mechanism."

With Anthony Powell

Then during hotter weather in April, when I had a troublesome ear infection, the English novelist Anthony Powell visited Japan. I had a short chat with him at the Japan-British Society. He was stockier than I had expected and spoke with an Oxford accent. His perspective was purely social. He told me, "Novelists fall into two types: those who produce and reduce, and those who produce and add." He belonged to the second type, he said, and his day's work was expanding 30 words into 90 and then into 300.

With Edmund Blunden

Just over a week later I met Edmund Blunden, the Great-War poet of 'Report on Experience', which begins "I have been young and now am not too old". Buchanan (who had known him for many years) held a small lunch in a Japanese restaurant for him, his ward and me. I sat cross-legged on the *tatami* matting next to Blunden, a hook-nosed, beady-eyed, quietly-spoken, modest man whose hair stood on end. He had been badly gassed in the First World War, and had several asthmatic attacks during the lunch. During one of these I clapped him on his back several times as he gasped for breath. At one stage I thought he was going to die. His reality was social (the Great War) and rural. We discussed different poets – among them Shelley – and

Epping Forest, including The Owl, a pub near High Beach. We arranged to meet there when we were both back in England.

(A date was fixed in 1966, 18 August, but he cancelled it at the last minute as he was unwell.[9] It was as well that the meeting never took place for on the day we had fixed, at lunch-time, a double police murderer called Harry Roberts, who was on the run and living rough in the Forest, burst into The Owl and robbed all the drinkers of their wallets, watches and jewellery at knife point.)

Work at the Bank of Japan

I had now taken up a lectureship at Tokyo University. On Wednesday afternoons I went and lectured on English poetry to a group of between thirty and forty Japanese students. On Thursdays, at Tomlin's request, I now went to the Bank of Japan for three hours and had conversation classes with the Vice-Governor, Tadashi Sasaki, and an Executive Director, and corrected the English of the Governor's turgidly written letters and speeches with one of his assistants. Nadia soon got used to my comings and goings. "Daddy *yoi-yoi*?" she would ask. I was not sure if she was speaking Japanese. '*Yoi-yoi*' in her understanding meant going to work.

Tom Fitzsimmons and self-unification

Fitzsimmons was an antidote to these work sessions. He continued to be a sceptical influence. After the 5-May holiday for *koi-nobori*, when carp streamers flew from flagpoles, I met him and we discussed a film we wanted to make. It was to be on the self-creation and self-unification of a dying man who sees all his opposites reconciled. In 1975 I wrote a long poem 'The Labyrinth' on the idea of the reconciliation of opposites, which also lies behind this present work. I am sure our discussions shaped my impending poetic development, and the theme of self-unification now became central to my thinking. (In 1999 Fitzsimmons applied the idea of self-unification in *Iron Harp*,[10] which drew on his war memories as an under-age merchant seaman after Pearl Harbour and memories of Japan, the Mediterranean and New Mexico.)

Kamakura

I was transforming myself. I sensed that I was beginning to live more deeply. My remaking of myself was working, I was cleansing my consciousness. I was more open to the Buddhist enlightenment, images of which abounded in Japan. One of the largest was in Kamakura. We visited it at the end of May: the 13th-century bronze *Dai-butsu* or Big Buddha, sitting serene and aloof in a grove, in the vision of metaphysical enlightenment. I pondered the Buddha's consciousness.

I became poetically alive and wrote 'The Oceanographer at Night' about escaping a sense of drift. I thought deeply about the decline of Western civilization in relation to its spiritual vacuum and discussed this with a lecturer at Tokyo University, Tony Rayner.[11]

Nobe: horseshoe valleys
Adrian Hohler had shared a large wooden house at Nobe with an Embassy colleague, who was pulling out, and he asked us to step in and pay half the rent. We went down to view the house, and as we slid open paper doors gigantic spiders fell on to the *tatami* matting.

We stayed down in Nobe the next weekend. The sweltering night was full of jungle sounds – croaking frogs, whooping birds, hooting owls and of course cicadas – and I walked in the horseshoe valleys among brightly-coloured spiders and brilliant butterflies and soaring shrikes. A red, black and yellow mountain adder slid out of a hedge and confronted me. I found the confrontation exciting and during subsequent visits I used to go out with a forked stick and sometimes encountered four or five snakes of differing colours, which I pinned briefly with my fork and then released. I walked to a *Shinto* temple under a huge hill and gazed at the boat that represented eternity (and bore the names of 15 Russo-Japanese war dead).

The Absolute: First Mystic Life
I wanted to experience Zen Buddhism. In June Fitzsimmons left to return to Michigan, and I attended the farewell party for him held by Tokyo University of Education in a *Ginza* restaurant. Fitzsimmons spoke of the Zen archery he had been doing, and I asked for further details.

Seeing my interest in Zen, Professor Yukio Irie, the professor in charge of me, promised to introduce me to a colleague and phonetic namesake, Professor Haga, who had written a best-selling book on Zen that made him a Japanese authority. Irie knew that I had briefly met my colleague Dr R.H. Blyth in a corridor at the university – he had smiled warmly and rather puckishly though suffering from the illness that would kill him in October, and shook my hand after locking the door of his room – and now I was duly introduced to Haga.

On 13 June I wrote a poem, 'Twilight', about a prophet meditating on the future, "squatting in twilight" before a fire in a "flickering cathedral square". I discussed this poem on 9 July, and it appeared in *The Rising Generation* in September.[12]

To Zen with Haga: in Ichikawa City meditation centre, timeless Being
In mid-July I experienced Zen. I met Haga and Mr Kuniyoshi Munekata, one of my graduate students at the University, and we took the train to

Ichikawa City and made our way to a meditation centre (*dojo*), a large room with polished boards and open sides near an overgrown garden with washing on a line. Haga smoked a cigarette and fanned himself during the introduction.

There were several rows of shaven seekers, and we meditated cross-legged in the lotus position, which I found acutely uncomfortable. There was group chanting and a bell rang, and then there was a long silence in which I was instructed to count my breaths up to a hundred.

I found this counting unhelpful. I knew of course that Zen was anti-rational and I wanted to know what enlightenment (*satori*) involved. No one told me what the Buddha saw and what I might see while meditating behind half-closed eyes. I was merely instructed to sit and count my breaths. The onus was on me to find my way from there.

In case any of us lost our attentive consciousness or, worse still, nodded off, a hefty man in a *yukata* (cotton summer *kimono* for men) lurked among our cross-legged rows with a wide stick, which he brought down on the back of any meditator he adjudged needed waking up. Having spotted inatten-tiveness or bodily distraction, he bowed, whacked the insufficiently-aware seeker on his back so there was a loud crack, and then bowed again in respect for his soul, his Buddha-nature. (During the eating of rice with chopsticks from a bowl held in one hand, anyone who spilt a grain of rice was also beaten because rice also has Buddha-nature.)

There was a lecture. The Master sat in a prominent position and we sat in rows. Speaking in Japanese, the Master set us a *koan* ('parable', 'puzzle'). It was translated for me in whispers by Haga and my graduate student, who sat on either side of me. A man was hanging on to the top of a tree with his teeth, and his Master came by underneath and asked him, "What is the truth of the teachings of Zen?" The man must reply because it is impolite not to reply to your Master. We were instructed to reflect on the puzzle, and if we had not found the answer by the time we went to bed then, he said, we should sit up and meditate instead of going to sleep, and we should die in bed if necessary.

There was one more meditation, while a flying beetle and a huge moth zoomed and flitted around our heads. Then we slept in *futons* on the *tatami* matting floor of an adjoining room. We were awoken early the next morning for another meditation, in the course of which, one by one, the seekers had to go to the Master, who was in a separate room, and give their answer to the *koan*.

It was all very orderly. While we meditated, a seeker rose and glided silently into the Master's room. There was a murmur of an answer, and then, crack! He returned beaten, resumed his cross-legged lotus position and the next seeker took his place. Again there was a murmur and a crack. Without exception everyone was beaten.

Haga whispered, "Would you like to go up?"

The hefty man was near me, holding his stick like a *samurai* sword. I shook my head.

On the train on the way home Haga asked me why I thought they had all been beaten.

I said: "They made the mistake of speaking. The answer the Master wanted to hear was a silence. As the *Tao te ching* says, 'He who knows does not speak and he who speaks does not know.'"

Haga, the Zen expert, said: "You are right. You have understood. Zen takes you beyond language to a place of silence where you can know *satori* or enlightenment."

I had reached the beginning of my First Mystic Life.

Koganji temple: beginning of First Mystic Life (20 July 1964–18 October 1965)
I wanted to experience *satori*. Ten days later I went to Koganji temple, near Sugamo in Tokyo, with the graduate student Mr Munekata. We passed tombs and a statue of the Buddha. The Master was bald and bespectacled, and wore a *yukata*. We meditated in great heat among rows of silent cross-legged Japanese and then slept.

We meditated again just before dawn with the rice-paper doors open to the night and whirring cicadas. The meditation lasted an hour and a half, and through my half-closed eyes, sitting like a Buddha, I now and again glimpsed the progress of the dawn in the polished floor. I went very deep and got below the level of time, differences and becoming to a timeless being in myself which could have existed forever.

I did not want the meditation to end, and afterwards felt very peaceful and inwardly whole. I saw how the Buddha might have reached a state in which his bodily aura was enlightened from within. My experience in the Zen temple began my First Mystic Life (*see* Appendix 1, p.489).

Course in Hakone, and shrines
Back in Tokyo it was stiflingly hot. The universities were on vacation, and in July and August we made more visits to Nobe. The sun was fierce and there were brilliant butterflies and dragonflies, hawks and snakes in the paddy-fields, and I bathed in a wooden 'barrel' with water bubbling at 110°F. I gave a course in Hakone, outside Tokyo in the mountains, and bathed in sulphur.

A few days later I took my family to Nikko. We saw the Toshogu shrine, the Kegon Fall, Lake Chizuka and the nearby pine forest. At the beginning of September I visited the Shinto shrine at Karuizawa with Ando. All through the hot summer I suffered from minor physical ailments caused by the change in climate and diet: tropical ear, pyorrhoea in my gums, tooth decay, sunburn and corns.

In September the Olympic Games took place in Tokyo, and the Olympic Park became a new shrine. We watched the events on television. Planes flew overhead and described the Olympic rings in the sky, and many foreigners descended on Japan.

Metaphysical theme

Back at the universities I was teaching books with a metaphysical theme I felt passionate about. At Keio Ando had wanted me to include European literature, and when I suggested teaching it within the context of Colin Wilson's *The Outsider*, to my surprise he enthusiastically agreed. I ordered 160 hardback copies, which were brought into my lecture hall in boxes and distributed. (Years later Colin Wilson told me, "Someone ordered vast quantities of the hardback of *The Outsider* in Japan." I was able to own up.)

At Tokyo University I read Eliot's *Four Quartets*. For a few weeks I wrote bits of a prose trilogy that explored a metaphysical theme. I was still torn between the religious vision of Eliot, Hulme and the Buddha on the one hand, and the healthy sceptical vision of Kazantzakis's *Zorba the Greek* on the other hand.

Climbing Mount Fuji: clean senses

Almost involuntarily I was undergoing an inner purification or purgation. I had begun to smoke intermittently before Oxford, prompted by the excruciating boredom of the solicitor's office, and had carried on in varying degrees for seven years. After a visit to the Tokyo doctor, Dr Morton, about my internal wheezing I now resolved to give up. For five days I fought the craving for nicotine by will-power, sweating out my self-denial. Then I climbed Mount Fuji in the company of Adrian and Tony. We took a bus to the fifth stage and then climbed towards the crater within a thousand feet of the top – to a height of 9,000 feet – before we had to stop and return to catch the last bus back.

The clear mountain air among the snowy crags cleansed my senses, and when the sun slid behind the crater and there was a sudden chill we encountered a bald Mexican singing. He craned back his head and held up a sow's bladder from which a jet of *saké* poured a yard long into his throat, and in that moment I felt that existence was essentially good. When I reached the bottom of the mountain my craving had gone.

In Hiroshima: nun

I had been invited to give a lecture in Hiroshima. The day after the British Council held a reception for the London Symphony Orchestra, during which I met Sir Arthur Bliss (who had white hair and a white moustache and shook my hand unintroduced and gazed at me with his blue eyes, a meeting which certainly coloured my later poem 'The Conductor'), I made an overnight journey on the sleeper train. I spent a wretched night on a bunk above a steel ladder – there was no seat beneath – being jogged and jolted under a bright central light that would not turn off, and I arrived without sleep or breakfast to address 300 girl students on Eliot in a vast hall.

I was greeted by a most beautiful American nun, Sister Frances. She would have been stunning in any worldly situation, and the contrast between her looks and her wimple and habit was acute. She chatted to me both before and after my one-and-a-half-hour lecture, and the spiritual simplicity, purity and beauty in her face and eyes found their way into 'The Silence'.

After the lecture I went to the Peace Memorial Park and gazed at the tangled iron of the dome of the pre-1945 Industrial Exposition Hall, which had been twisted and ruined by the A-bomb. I reflected on the horror of the 20th century and the inhumanity of war, and on the strange necessity of this atomic destruction which had ended a war that seemed unendable as the Japanese would not have surrendered without a command from their Emperor, and I saw the dropping of the A-bomb as fitting into a complex pattern. My view was similar to that of Arjuna, who came to accept war after his troubled discussions with Krishna in the *Bhagavad-gita*.

World history: Toynbee
I was becoming increasingly sure that I could relate the concerns of our Age to a historical pattern, and towards the end of November I bought all 10 paperback volumes of Toynbee's *A Study of History* at Kinokuniya bookstore in Tokyo. I took in Toynbee's view of the different world civilizations that made up the Free World and included Western civilization (an amalgam of the European and North-American civilizations). So began my long study of the rise and fall of civilizations in Gibbon, Spengler and Toynbee, which would result in *The Fire and the Stones*.

The next day, stirring to my historical theme, I wrote a poem 'And Scholars Will Ask', and a week later a companion poem, *'Odi et Amo'*.

The One in Nobe
I was teaching Modernism in literature, and down in Nobe I pondered the conflict between rural and city values. I revelled in the bamboo under a blue sky, at gentians and corn violets in the horseshoe valleys and at the circling shrikes above. Later I stood on the deserted Pacific beach in a great wind which flapped my trousers like sails and tore through my hair as the sea flooded in, and my *Diaries* record: "I felt at one with everything."[13] I felt a new joy at being alive. Picture 25

I knew that I had been undergoing "a development that is obscure, even to myself in its extent".[14] I wrote that I was going through a "momentous time", a "spiritual conflict" in which I acknowledged a new "spiritual or self-realisational depth" in myself. On 30 December I recorded that there had been an "increase in spiritual penetration" and a "heightened awareness of social trends".[15]

Nicholas at Nobe, Japan, holding a whelk shell mentioned in 'The Silence', November 1964

Scepticism and metaphysics

Into my new metaphysical outlook and transformation stepped a new sceptical influence: Frank Tuohy, who arrived in Tokyo in December.

Arrival of Frank Tuohy

He was Professor at Waseda University, the main rival private university to Keio, but we had more in common than that as he was the 44-year-old author of *The Ice Saints* and a master of the short-story form. I first met him at the British Council's scholarship interviews, which we both supervised, a portly, jowly man in a suit and waistcoat. I found him prosaic and abrupt, not realising that shyness made him put on an aggressive monosyllabic mask as a defence.

Sensing that Tuohy might fill Fitzsimmons' shoes, I invited him to Nobe just before Christmas. We travelled on a packed train. We were dressed informally now. We had to stand, and there was a sensitivity, a gentleness about him which was altogether different from the front he had put on at the British Council. We walked in the sun and drank a large bottle of whisky and talked about writing, and he began sharing his observations which, although I pulled against them because they were unmetaphysical and sceptical, made me reconsider my own artistic attitudes and therefore stimulated a development in my own art, particularly in my poetry. The next morning we walked to the Shinto shrine that had Russo-Japanese etchings, and talked about novelists and poets, life, social attitudes and writing techniques.

Tuohy and Wittgenstein

Tuohy told me that he had gone for walks with Wittgenstein and that he was the only living witness to Wittgenstein's last period. He reflected Wittgenstein's view that man is a social being and that all philosophical problems are a question of language. Tuohy was a Wittgensteinian. Nowadays Wittgenstein is regarded as being as significant as Socrates or Spinoza. However, I had always questioned the primacy Wittgenstein gave

176

to language. Reality is not to be found in language, and humans contact Reality in their more solitary moments. Reality is not exclusively social.

I questioned the Wittgensteinian primacy Tuohy gave to language, and there was thus a constant tussle between Tuohy and me. The tension could be located in my keeping quiet about the two fundamental assumptions Tuohy made in his conversation, that reality is social and that all philosophical problems evaporate when you focus on the language in which they are expressed. Sometimes I could not keep quiet and then I was in open conflict with Tuohy, who was often waiting for the conflict to appear.

At Christmas Tomlin had a Christmas party with turkey, crackers, carols and folk-music. Caroline and I shared a taxi with Tuohy both ways. In the taxi he was scathing about Tomlin's traditional Christmas. Tuohy was left-wing and critical of tradition. At the party a conflict clearly developed between metaphysical Tomlin and sceptical Tuohy, who both embodied different polarities of my inner experience.

In Kyoto and Nara: the Absolute of the Zen Stone Garden

In early January I went to Kyoto and Nara, Japan's cultural centre, on my own. I took the bullet train and sped over a sleeping city at dawn and watched the sun rise behind misty mountains and shine on curly-tiled roofs.

That first day in Kyoto I visited the Ryoanji Stone Garden – a 15th-century Zen garden with raked stones and rocks that had a deep and almost impenetrable meaning – but I did not comment on it in my *Diaries*. It was merely mentioned among golden and silver pavilions and castles.

I spent the night in a *ryokkan* (inn) and next morning went to Nara and visited the Tempyo shrines in the park or forest. Death-stones lined the steps up to the shrines. It was freezing, and sitting in an open-air restaurant I wrote a poem about how all culture is dominated by death: 'Winter in Nara (An Investigation of the Relation between Culture and Death, Civilization and Eternity)'.

Poetry: The Early Education and Making of a Mystic, 'The Silence'

I was choosing myself as a poet, responding to an inner whispering of vividness and limpidness. I was independent of Tomlin's philosophy and Tuohy's fiction. Towards the end of January we visited Nobe, and the sea jumped with diamond explosions in the sun. As I walked I was aware of a "fire in my head".[16] I was reading Pound's *The Cantos* and reflecting on the pattern in my own life and how this might be caught in a series of states of mind.

On 26 January I had the idea of writing a series of a hundred poems that revealed a pattern. Two days later I began writing an early draft of these. Some passed into *The Early Education and Making of a Mystic*. Some passed into what was to become 'The Silence', a long poem in the tradition of Wordsworth's *The Prelude*: "a group of autobiographical poems relating experiences that are apparently arbitrary by association and creating a pattern out of my life so that when seen in terms of each other the experiences assume depth."[17] I am now amazed that out of such unpromising and hesitant beginnings emerged a work that dominated the rest of the year, and longer, and which I still regard as my masterpiece, even though it was a Modernist sequence of images. It conveyed the tussle of my coming centreshift from my ego (my "Reflection") to my deeper wisdom and future self (my "Shadow") and provided a convenient daily structure for my coming transformation. Two days later I recorded that I must be prepared to choose myself as a poet.

Looking back I can see that this development had a certain amount to do with my relationship with Tuohy. At the end of January, for example, I had tea with him, and I see from my 1965 *Diaries* that we discussed resonance, what makes a poetic line poetic, the relationship between the familiar and the strange, and other poetic subjects. On the other hand, I was already groping towards being a poet before Tuohy arrived, and he may merely have accelerated a pre-existing process within me.

Death of grandmother

I went to see a *Noh* play. Bandy-legged musicians beat drums and whooped. I pondered its theme, "Life is but a dream." It left me brooding, for my grandmother – at whose house in East Grinstead I had spent part of the war – had died in Loughton after a fall at the age of 90. Had her life of ninety years only been a dream? If so, what had been its reality?

She had walked with me to her gate before I left for Tokyo, saying, "I'll walk with you to say goodbye to you for the last time." I had protested that she would see me return, but she knew: "No, I'm saying goodbye for the last time." I was sad that I had not been able to visit her in the last days of her life. I wrote my poetry with a heavy heart, aware of the dying-away of the man of ideas and the birth of the poet within myself.

Freeman, 'The Silence' and Modernism

On 25 April I "got the name 'Freeman'"[18] for the hero of 'The Silence'. The name floated in from the beyond and had a similar feel to 'Everyman'. It was a fine day, and I went on to Nobe (where Tony Rayner had taken over Adrian's half-share of the rent) and revelled in the croaking frogs. During my next visit on 2 May I poked among the rock pools, watched a starfish and observed a sea-slug spinning a yellow thread of eggs. I went up into the paddy-fields and found some wild orchids and observed newts with scarlet bellies swimming between the irrigated newly-planted rice.

It grew hot. I continued my researches into Modernism, and read Pound's 'Hugh Selwyn Mauberley' on the train to Nobe. It made a great impression on me. For my class on European literature I re-read Camus, Kafka, Hesse and T.E. Lawrence. I was now drawing on many of the Continental literary works I had read during my Oxford years. All the reading I had done outside my subject was now vindicated. I based some lectures on Frank Kermode's *Romantic Image*.

Chinese atomic bomb: Leon Stover
For several days I had to walk to work through radioactive rain: the Chinese had exploded an atomic bomb, and the fall-out came down over Tokyo as rain which was 120 times as radioactive as normal rain according to local American radio. Only an umbrella shielded my head from this hot rain.

During the fall-out Tuohy held a dinner on a sweltering night for Leon Stover, an American anthropologist who would set out his view that Stonehenge was a parliament.[19] (A letter I wrote Stover and his reply are in the Appendix of *The Light of Civilization*.)

I become tutor to Prince Hitachi: world history
The oppressive heat in Tokyo made us appreciate the relative cool of Nobe. That summer I went snake-hunting with a forked stick and caught a snake that puffed itself up and changed colour into a brilliant red pattern. I found a centipede five inches long with legs like rose-thorns crawling in the dust by our front steps, and a local told me it was deadly.

While I wrote my poetry and did my research that hot summer I found I had become a member of the Imperial Household. I had been told that I had been appointed tutor to a member of the Imperial family. At first it seemed I would be tutor to the Crown Prince (the present Emperor) but then it turned out that I would be tutor to his younger brother, Prince Hitachi.[20] On 1 July an Imperial chauffeur-driven car collected me and drove me to his small palace. Chamberlains lurked in doorways as I was shown into a ground-floor room. His Imperial Highness was then a grave, quiet, bespectacled, uncertain man of around 28 with immaculately smarmed-down hair. A Japanese who was also teaching him acted as go-between that first visit, but a week later I had a class with the Prince on my own, and met his beautiful wife, Princess Haneko.

Soon I was going three afternoons a week for between two or three hours each afternoon. Officially I taught him English, but it soon transpired that he did not know what to discuss with foreign Ambassadors during the many evening dinners he had to attend. He did not know what to discuss with the Egyptian Ambassador and when I mentioned the Sphinx and the Pyramids he looked blank. It was agreed that I should do a course on world history, starting in 3000BC and coming down to the present.

I bought two copies of Stewart Easton's *A Brief History of the Western World*, which defined Western civilization as the creation of the successors of the Greeks and Romans in the 5th century and covered its spread throughout the world. It therefore covered phases of history in the East on which the West had made an impact. It regarded Russia, Europe and America as belonging to a single civilization whose component parts could be distinguished. I came to disregard this view as I came to believe that there are many different civilizations, but the book served its purpose by drawing together all the empires and events. We worked through it for a couple of years, taking a few pages each class, and the Prince's knowledge of world history improved dramatically. This was the ground I later covered in my Grand Unified Theory of world history, *The Fire and the Stones*, and my historical work with the Prince was a preparation for that work.

We now fell into a pattern. Each time we had our class in the teaching-room (up the palace stairs and first right on the first floor), the door would open and a chamberlain would come in with ten books on a silver tray and say, "Please write ten questions for the Romanian [or whatever] Ambassador." Then and there I would devise ten questions from my reading of contemporary history and current affairs. Some of the questions must have shocked. Soon, through His Highness, I was asking the Soviet Ambassador about the disputed territory of Wallachia (which was then in Romania but occupied by Russia from 1768 to 1854) and the British Ambassadress about her bugbear John Osborne. In due course we read an English poem each session, often one by Keats or Shelley. The Prince read aloud in a stirring voice and then sat back, unwilling to look any deeper into the poem's meaning.

The Prince was very formal. There was a television programme two evenings a week about the doings of the Imperial family, which I had watched regularly, and at first I found his behaviour towards me was little different from the formal behaviour he displayed on film. But little by little he opened up.

Once he told me about his terror when the Americans entered Tokyo at the end of the Second World War. About eight years old, he was hidden under a bed and from under the bedspread he saw army boots reach the top of the stairs and approach. He expected to be bayoneted but a khaki arm reached underneath the bed and yanked him out.

He had been very sheltered. He had never heard of income tax and when I explained to him how it worked he said, "You work and then pay some of what you earn to the Government? It is not fair."

I said, "We non-Royals live under an unfair system."

There seemed to be little freedom of speech in the palace, but as in my classes in Iraq there was full freedom of speech in my classes with him, and I said exactly what I thought; presenting it in a slightly deferential way, referring to him as "Your Highness".

Bank of Japan and loan

University classes had ended for three months, but my classes with the Prince and with the Bank of Japan continued throughout the sweltering heat. I liked the Vice-Governor of the Bank of Japan, Tadashi Sasaki, a corpulent, smiling man in his late fifties with immaculately groomed hair. I read Anthony Sampson's *Anatomy of Britain* with him.

One afternoon I found him standing at the telephone. He gestured to me to sit down and put one hand over the mouthpiece and said, smiling: "It is Lord Cromer, Governor of the Bank of England. The Bank of England want a loan from the Bank of Japan because of the British Government's financial crisis. Shall I give it?"

I nodded and said, "Yes, please."

He nodded and returned to his conversation and the loan was granted.

At Zen Engakuji temple in Kitakamakura with Tuohy – centipede

I had regularly dined with Tuohy, usually at our house but sometimes at his. At the end of July Tuohy and I spent a night at a Zen Buddhist temple in Kitakamakura: Engakuji. We had to walk from the station, and on the way we stopped at Tokeiji temple to visit the tombs of my late colleague R.H. Blyth and Daisetsu Suzuki, then the best-known interpreter of Zen to the West.

I had been hoping that Master Asahina would meet us, but instead we found a young shaven Zen priest who promptly forbad us to wear socks. He knew that mosquitoes bit the feet of foreigners while they sat still in the lotus position, and told us: "You must achieve *satori* [enlightenment] in spite of the mosquitoes. You must overcome the mosquitoes, pass beyond them, be one with them."[21] He told a story about an old Master who sat under banana-trees meditating amid mosquitoes for two days. He was bitten all over and was found lying unconscious in a pool of blood – but he had achieved *satori*.

Soon afterwards we meditated in silence among whining mosquitoes. We were the only two foreigners among rows of Japanese, and as usual there was chanting and the spells of silence were haunted by a huge man with a vicious-looking stick, whose role was to beat anyone who looked unawake or showed any sign of being distracted.

Tuohy meditated immediately on my right, and, sensing shifting limbs from his massive bulk, I came out of my inner trance and peeped through half-closed eyes. A centipede like the deadly one I had seen at Nobe, with fat red legs, was crawling slowly towards us. Tuohy had seen it, and his breathing became noisier. The man with the stick approached and prodded him in the back. Tuohy collapsed in a terrified heap on the floor, causing a disturbance, but quickly pulled himself upright when the man with the stick prowled round to his front, detecting an opportunity to administer a beating. Together we sat totally still, transfixed as we watched the centipede crawl towards our knees. Just when it seemed it would touch one of my knees below my bare upturned feet it veered off to my left, but I could not relax and return to the inner vision now that my survival instincts had been aroused.

We were told to sleep in a nearby room on *tatami* matting, and that we would be sweeping the temple grounds at dawn. Sleep was impossible. Tuohy and I tossed and turned, imagining centipedes lurking in the corners of the room along with the usual cockroaches. Tuohy, always one to dwell on the awfulness of situations in his writing, groaned aloud, "Three hours more of this and then labouring? Oh God."[22]

We did not sleep a wink and before dawn we marched round the temple and its garden in a long line, and then Tuohy and I were set to sweep the path near the latrines, which stank. Tuohy muttered as he went through the motions and made half-hearted sweeping movements. I pointed out that what we were doing was symbolic of inner purification: "We are cleansing the path to the foulness in our soul, we are working on the cleansing of ourselves." To which Tuohy retorted, "I'd rather be me, unclean, than have to do this."

Soon afterwards we meditated again, and almost immediately I went very deep, and soon the only reality was a profound silence, across which unreal sounds intruded. Our lungs moved and cicadas scraped, and I knew among the dawn shadows that all was a unity. I had left the outer world of existence, with its emphasis on different phenomena, and had reached an awareness of Being in which all differences were really not different, like the pebbles in the Ryoanji Stone Garden.

At Gora: creative will
Caroline and I spent much of the summer in Nobe. One weekend there was a great wind that flapped my black shirt and sand trousers and there were white-crested waves. Another weekend it was very wet and we drank in Nobe with Buchanan and Blunden's ward, Alec Hardy.

Down in Nobe I read a lot of psychology. I contrasted Freud, who saw the artist as a neurotic, with Rank, who emphasised the creative will of the artist, and Jung, who also emphasised creativity. Among the cicadas and flying beetles of those hot Nobe evenings I confronted and rejected Freud.

In early August I went to address a conference in Gora and stayed among the sulphur-springs there. That hot evening I sat outside reading Ira Progoff's *The Death and Rebirth of Psychology*, and warmed to Rank's rejection of Freud. I wrote the first draft of a passage which includes the line "I cannot live by Freud", which is now in 'The Silence'.

Dinner with the Prince and Princess: Imperial ancestors in nesting-boxes, Shinto kami

When I returned to Tokyo I was invited to dinner with the Prince and Princess at the palace. The three of us went for a walk in the grounds, going out through billowing lace curtains. We headed past a lotus pool towards a pine wood, and, ducking under pine boughs and admiring a blue-tailed magpie while a chamberlain followed us with a camera, to make conversation I pointed out some nesting-boxes high up in the pine trees and asked, "Are those nesting-boxes for birds?"

"No," the Prince replied. "They are my ancestors."[23]

It is a shamanistic Shinto belief that the souls of Imperial ancestors became *kami* (divine spirits) on their death and dwelt in trees, and consequently the living erect nesting-boxes as homes for them.

We went back indoors and dinner was served in a small room. Four ladies-in-waiting stood in kimonos along one wall, listening to everything we said. I conversed in English with the Prince and Princess, and found the Princess full of vitality. She often seemed to

Nicholas and Prince and Princess Hitachi in their palace grounds, Tokyo, on 5 August 1965

forget her position and spoke jokingly in excellent English, and then remembered to defer to the Prince, who, being anyway rather monosyllabic, sometimes looked left out of the conversation. I kept trying to bring him in.

Trine and the infinite

The next day I pondered Shinto *kami* on the train to Nobe. Buchanan came to have a drink. He brought Penson, who had lived in Japan for over 40 years. Penson mentioned the most important book in his life, Ralph Waldo Trine's *In Tune with the Infinite*, which, he said, his father always kept by his bedside. He found his copy in a jumble sale in the 1930s and it had been by his bedside for over 30 years. This anecdote set me thinking about the infinite. In 1966 I discovered that my grandmother had left me her copy of the same book. On the flyleaf she had written 'E.G. Broadley, June 1924' – a year before her husband was diagnosed with cancer.

Second visit to Kyoto and Nara, with Bank of Japan: Stone Garden again
On 10 August, still thinking about the infinite, I went to Kyoto as a guest of the Bank of Japan. Caroline and I took the afternoon New Tokaido train on a sweltering day and were met in an air-conditioned car and driven to an air-conditioned room in an inn. Next morning we visited Nara and saw the Todaiji Big Buddha. After lunch at the Kyoto Hotel we visited the thousand

Ryoanji Stone Garden, Kyoto, Japan

statues at Sanjusangendo temple, which I brought into 'The Silence' as Freeman's "thousand selves".

The next morning I made my second visit to the Ryoanji Stone Garden, a picture of which adorns the back cover of my *Selected Poems*. I saw the simple pebbles and rocks as revealing that all existence is one underlying unity (being), and that the border or frame round it is quite arbitrary as it is infinite and boundless: the Absolute.

Tribute to Eliot
Soon after this I underwent another development involving a centre-shift. T.S. Eliot had died in January 1965. In his last book, *T.S. Eliot, A Friendship*, Tomlin recorded that I visited him after hearing of Eliot's death.[24]

Tomlin had told me that he had been invited to dinner by Eliot on 4 September 1963,[25] and he had said that he was making an arrangement for me to visit Eliot when I returned to London. This intention was overtaken by Eliot's death. Tomlin had asked a few British and Japanese Professors, including Tuohy and me, to write 5,000-word essays on Eliot. I had begun my article at Nobe, and had been thinking deeply about Modernism. I had written an article, 'Reflections on T.S. Eliot's Poetry', which appeared in *The Rising Generation* in May 1965.[26]

The Absolute: centre-shift
I had already begun the centre-shift from my ego to my deeper self or universal being. On 15 August I noted in my *Diaries*, "I have been undergoing some kind of a centre-shift.... I can feel the irrational all round my reason; it is a fact, something I can be aware of half a dozen times a day."[27] Ten days later I was still hunting for a poetic image of the relationship between reason and the irrational. (I eventually found it in the concept of a marriage of a man and a woman, the new centre being a child like Nadia, *see*

p.187.) I was pondering the infinite and the irrational, and in early September I lunched with Tuohy and discussed the image and symbol, while still writing my essay.

Inner images
A further development began on 11 September 1965. I had worked on my essay all day and could not sleep. I closed my eyes and a succession of images rose: scrivenings in a foreign language – Arabic or Hebrew – in yellow and blue; a puddle and an orb of fire within it; corn stalks with many ears of corn; a whirlpool. Then it seemed I was going down a well, and saw the orb of the sky getting smaller as I descended.[28] These images should be regarded as visions, a 'vision' being "something which is apparently seen otherwise than by ordinary sight; especially an appearance of a prophetic or mystical character, or having the nature of a revelation, supernaturally presented to the mind in sleep" (*Shorter Oxford English Dictionary*). Two days later on 13 September, I had more images (or visions) behind closed eyes, also late at night. A series of gold heads went slowly by as if on a conveyor belt: some Egyptian, some Negroid, some Babylonian. Then there were exquisite diamonds in green and mauve which lasted 30 seconds.[29]

When I got off to sleep I dreamt I was on the second floor of a Turkish Byzantine café. There was an earthquake and I rushed down the stairs and out into the courtyard through falling masonry to find everything in ruins, all foundations crumbled. Then I was in a morgue among many corpses, which suddenly sat up and came to life, jingling their bones.[30] When I awoke I thought I had dreamt about a centre-shift. I thought I had opened to my imagination and the bubbling-up from the spring of my inspiring Muse which could even occur in sleep.

I did not finish my essay until the end of September, and had then written almost no poetry for six weeks. The essay, a defence of Eliot's method in 'The Waste Land', 'In Defence of the Sequence of Images', was a vindication of the method I was groping for in 'The Silence': abbreviated narrative in an emotionally-linked sequence of images. Although I was tired from the heat and the effort of the reading and research, I felt I had justified my poetic method. Now I had time to walk to the Cathedral and gaze at the symbols which trap the eternal.

I also had time to meet the minor British Royals Princess Alexandra and Angus Ogilvy at a reception on 22 September 1965 at which Prime Minister Sato appeared, bowing wide-eyed round a semi-cirle of invited guests in a large room with an ice-lion in the centre.[31] He greeted me individually, bowing low and peeping up at me. I knew he went to a Zen temple and meditated when Japan's economic figures were lower than expected, and I wondered if he had been through a centre-shift before he became Prime

Minister.

Nishiwaki and the Absolute: the wisdom of the East as +A + −A = 0
On 5 October after I gave 165 students at Keio their grades Ando took me to a small nearby café with sawdust on the floor. Junzaburo Nishiwaki came in and joined our table. We discussed Eliot and he told me, "Not logic – witty combinations."

I asked him to convey the wisdom of the East as succinctly as he could, and he told me that the Absolute could be expressed as an algebraic formula, a "witty combination". In front of me I had a copy of *Encounter* which my grandmother had sent me, and a business-reply card had fallen out on the table. He picked up the reply-card and said: "The Absolute is where there is no difference." He wrote on the card: "+A + −A = 0." Under +A he wrote "to be" and above the nought he wrote "great nothing". (*See* p.xxvi.) Across the top of the card he wrote "algebraic thinking".[32]

Card on which Junzaburo Nishiwaki wrote +A + −A = 0 on 5 October 1965

His few words resonated in my soul. They came as a revelation. In a flash I saw the unity within all opposites. It was as though an earthquake had taken place within my being. I grasped that the wisdom of the East set out a progression, via a reconciliation of opposites, to perceiving the unity of the universe. Like Jason I had been on a quest for the golden fleece, *truth*, and I had now found it.

I went home and pored over the reply-card (which now hangs on my study wall). I was still sleeping very badly, and on 6 October, still awake at dawn, I thought I understood the Absolute in terms of the Stone Garden: at the underlying level of unity there is no difference between the particular forms of existence, and the Absolute manifests itself through unity.

More images, Tuohy invites me to China
My development reached a climax in mid-October. On 8 October I went to a Tutankhamen exhibition, and saw the gold mask which had arrived in Japan from Egypt. It eerily corresponded to one of the Egyptian gold heads I had seen on 13 September. The next day we went to Nobe. The trees were full of autumnal tints, the sky was blue, the rice had been harvested from the paddy-fields, which were full of stumps, and dry rice hung like straw from poles. The sea had a typhoon swell. Back in Tokyo, on 10 October I wrote the

passage about the Stone Garden in 'The Silence'.

Later that same evening I went for a drink with Tuohy. To my aston-ishment he invited me to go to China with him the following spring, to write some articles for *AP*.[33] Dick Paul had urged me to take any oppor-tunity that came my way to go to China, and now, without my having to make any sort of effort to create such an opportunity, the opportunity had presented itself. I was reminded of how I had sought for Col. Grivas and he had come to me, and again wondered if Tuohy's invitation was coincidental, obscurely contrived or Providential.

Later that night I dreamt Tuohy told me, "Your energy is outgoing in one direction like a stream or unimpeded shoot."[34]

In the late evening of 11 October I went to the bathroom from our dark bedroom and, turning on the light, was flooded with golden light behind my closed eyes. The pattern was of rings, each linked together into a golden net.[35]

Prince and Princess Hitachi leave for State visit to the UK
The next few days I worked very intensely on sections of 'The Silence'. I fulfilled my teaching commitments and attended a farewell reception at the palace in the presence of Prince and Princess Hitachi. They were making a State visit to Britain at the expense of the British Government. I had been involved in planning this visit and had given advice on how to address the various people the Prince might expect to meet.

Now forty formally-dressed very old Japanese men lined the wall and the Prince went round bowing. He shook hands with me, the only foreigner, while the Princess walked behind, carrying a nosegay. Then there was a collective chant of "*Banzai*" ("Victory").

Tao
On 16 October I spent the morning again searching for an image for my centre, and found it in the image of a child between a husband and wife (Nadia's role in my marriage, *see* pp.184–185). I wrote the "poet of the self" passage. On Sunday 17 October I was so tired in the afternoon that I slept.

I seemed to sink down within myself, and when I awoke at 4.30 p.m. and went to my study and looked out of the bungalow window I seemed to be a floor below my thoughts. I sat down and thought about the centre of my self in relation to the cosmos. My *Diaries* record: "I understood *Tao*, that just as my self-centre unites me, so *Tao* could unite life and death and all cosmic opposites and pluralities, so that all men are brothers."[36]

Light, satori: *round white Light in soul, end of First Mystic Life*
The next morning, Monday 18 October, something extraordinary happened

to me. I stayed at home, and my *Diaries* record: "All morning I have been filled with a round white light: I cannot see it, except occasionally when I glimpse it and am dazzled, but I know it is there. It is like a white sun. This is, I suppose, what Christians refer to as the soul – the centre of the self. And the mystical experience is given meaning by the relation between the centre and the sun, so that everything is one."[37] I observed that it was not the universe that had changed, but my self and my perception of it "so that it now seems more harmonious".

I did not know it at the time but my experience on 18 October ended my First Mystic Life. Looking back I can see that these brief gleams in 1965 represented my first illuminative life, a first glimpse of *satori* (enlightenment) following a shift from my rational, social ego, a new centre within my self, my soul. I had no doubt that the development was a consequence of my long process of self-discovery that lay behind my writing of 'The Silence', and that I had glimpsed Light within my soul.

On 31 October I connected the experience with a passage I found on "luminous phenomena, photisms" in William James's *The Varieties of Religious Experience*, in which James quotes Charles Finney's *Memoirs* (1876): "A light perfectly ineffable shone in my soul.... This light seemed like the brightness of the sun in every direction. It was too intense for the eyes.... I think I knew something then, by actual experience, of that light that prostrated Paul on the way to Damascus." This quotation is in a chapter on "conversion" and James shows that conversion cures and unifies the sick soul and divided self.

The Absolute and scepticism

It is in the nature of the Mystic Way that nothing is simple, that as soon as progress is made there is immediate regress. I suspect that the Light I glimpsed in my soul was too dazzling for me to see again without damage to my self, that I had to transmute my self within like an alchemist to be able to withstand the divine vision. I sensed this at the time, for I recorded in my *Diaries* on 18 October that this white sun might explode with energy, causing me to go completely insane.

Metaphysical vision versus social perspective

Anyhow, almost immediately I backtracked, not wanting to believe that this sun was eternal, wanting to be one with my fellow men who had not seen this Light. I swung back from the metaphysical vision of *The Secret of the Golden Flower* to a materialistic, humanist view of suffering humanity, safe in the view of darkness after exposing my being to the Absolute.

Baroque pearls, Baroque art
Two days after the experience, on 20 October, Tuohy, Caroline and I visited a Jewish trader in Tokyo and I bought two strings of baroque pearls. Baroque pearls are misshapen pearls, and they found their way into the dedication of 'The Silence', the pearls symbolising images. I was groping towards a new Baroque principle in art, and had received the lines:

I heard a cry from the old Professor's darkened room,
'The Age of Analysis is dead!'
Books lined with dust, a buzzing fly....
                            While, naked on the petalled lawn,
A new Baroque age is born.

Bankruptcy of Tuohy's scepticism
I read Nietzsche, Rilke, Camus and Dostoevsky for my teaching and continued 'The Silence' and felt anew that "life just is and that all the meanings are rational impositions".[38] I was pulling away from Tuohy, who had asked me to explain the Japanese code of behaviour to Peter Jenkins, the *Guardian* columnist who had visited Japan and spoken with Tuohy. I explained *on* and *giri* to him at some length.

Soon afterwards, on 12 November, Tuohy came to dinner. He was very bleak and insisted that Nietzsche, Blake, Rilke and Dostoevsky had "nothing important to say". He was clearly undergoing a crisis in his writing career as he had written what he described as "a nihilistic letter" to his agent that afternoon. He had drunk too much, and at the end of the dinner he fell on the floor and crawled on his hands and knees. He said his writing was "all cod" (i.e. a hoax) and that "security and a warm fire are the most important things".

I now distinguished a "social-rationalist" tradition of writers that included Kingsley Amis, Larkin and Tuohy, and an "individualist" tradition in which the writer develops and discovers his soul, which included William James, Rilke, Eliot, Colin Wilson and me. I had now come down on the side of the irrational against reason, but I was still determined to include the social, rational world. I was emotionally on the side of those who saw an invisible Reality behind the world – the poets Blake, Watkins, Barker and Gascoyne – but I refused to accept that the phenomenal world was as unreal as *Noh* drama and Buddhism maintained. I applied this thinking to my next long poem, the idea for which I stated on 3 December. It was to become 'Old Man in a Circle'.

Social perspective
My renewed outer, social perspective expressed itself in 'The Silence' as

renewed attention to the decaying social background of European civilization. I related this to Toynbee and the *Old Testament* prophets. I now began editing my poems together, like a film editor, to make one continuous narrative, to reflect my increasingly unitive view. I thought about European decay over Christmas.

Dinner with Prince and Princess Hitachi

The Prince and Princess invited us to dinner, a six-course meal by candle-light on a long wooden table with four kimonoed ladies-in-waiting lurking in the shadows by a screen, and while Caroline chatted fluently to the Princess I exhausted all the safe, acceptable subjects (such as riding and dogs) with the Prince.

On Boxing Day Tuohy came to dinner and we discussed the decay of Britain at great length, a social theme. Being Labour, Tuohy placed greater importance on the welfare of human beings than on the health of the civilization.

I reconcile metaphysical vision ("vertical vision") and social perspective

I was reconciling my metaphysical vision with a new social perspective. In January I slept badly, torn between the two. In 'The Silence' I was showing a healthy man opposing a sick society whose religion is dead and rediscovering spiritual vitality. We sometimes took our daughter to the Cathedral and on the way home my daughter played hide-and-seek with the full moon: "Bo, I see you moon." I saw the moon as my inner sun.

In Nobe I read Blake and Vernon Watkins and wondered if the phenomenal concealed the real as they maintained, or whether the phenomenal alone exists as Nietzsche and Rilke maintained. At night, after drinking *saké* and walking under brilliant stars, I lay awake in silence, unable to sleep, and imagined myself dying and then dead and being nothing, and felt a cold terror under the stars. I was sure there was nothing real – no spiritual reality – behind the phenomenal. Later I wrote in my *Diaries* of "the vertical vision".[39] I contrasted vertical growth with horizontal ease and Establishment decay. In 'The Silence' I expressed the vertical vision as a shoot breaking a crown.

It was the conflict between my metaphysical inner sun and social scepticism that had brought about the centre-shift within myself. Looking back, I see that this layer of experience formed a base for my growing Universalist combination, and union, of metaphysical and social perspectives. Nishiwaki had written out the wisdom of the East: $+A + -A = 0$. Metaphysics + social reality = the Universalist whole view of the universe. I had been groping towards Universalism in 'The Silence' and I can now see that I made an early Universalist statement in that work.

My First Mystic Life had now ended, weakened by my new social perspective and by my impending visit to China.

Episode 9:

Civilizations and Communism

Years: 1966–1967
Locations: Tokyo; Nobe; Hong Kong; Kowloon; Canton; Hangchow; Shanghai; Nanking; Peking; Nakhodka; Khabarovsk; Moscow; London; Loughton; West Dulwich; Bognor; Edinburgh; Belfast; Dublin; Gort; Sligo; South-East Asia; India and other world civilizations
Works: 'The Silence'; *The Wings and the Sword* (including 'Archangel', 'Blighty', 'An Inner Home', 'The Conductor', 'An Epistle to an Admirer of Oliver Cromwell', 'Epistle to His Imperial Highness, on his Birthday' and 'The Rubbish Dump at Nobe, Japan'); 'Old Man in a Circle'; *A Spade Fresh with Mud* (including 'A Spade Fresh with Mud', 'Limey'); *The Noddies*
Initiative: discovery of Chinese Cultural Revolution

"In our time, the writing and publication of universal histories is an important public service ."
Arnold Toynbee, Foreword to the English edition of
the *Larousse Histoire Universelle*

My First Mystic Life had come to an end in October 1965 and though I was still reflecting it in 'The Silence' which drew on its more intense experiences until June 1966, I was now thrust into the outer world of social reality.

The next episode confronted me with the main ideological conflict of our time. I now engaged with the values and tenets of Western civilization and of the world civilizations of the Free World, and with the values and tenets of Communism, which was still threatening to sweep the world and triumph in the Cold War.

Communism: China and discovering the Cultural Revolution

I prepared for the visit Tuohy and I were to make to China, which would plunge me into this conflict. No one travelled to China at that time – Mao had sealed his country off from the West – and obtaining Japanese exit and re-entry visas proved a problem.

Leaving for China

I rang Emé Yamashita, a former private secretary to Prime Minister Sato who was now Chief of Trade Policy in charge of handling the China problem[1] and who had come to Buchanan's Christmas parties. He referred me to an official in the Foreign Ministry, the Chief of Passports Section. Tuohy and I visited him. We took a bottle of whisky with us to give him an obligation (*on*) and placed our bribe on his desk. It remained there for a few minutes while he talked, and then he transferred it to the floor. We were given our exit and re-entry visas.

Throughout February I read forty books on China, having ransacked the few available libraries in Tokyo. We were to write a number of newspaper articles: two for *The Sunday Telegraph*, two for *The New York Times*, eight for *AP* and one for *Newsweek*. I codified my reading in a pocketbook which I could carry around with me, and in a month I became an authority on Communist China.

Aware that I was going to a dangerous country, I took the precaution of again contacting Yamashita, who was in charge of the Japanese commercial effort in China. He gave me a letter of introduction[2] to a Mr Soma in Peking, who would make representations on my behalf if I were detained.

Before I left for China Buchanan, my colleague, rang me and begged me not to go as "you may not get out". I reassured him, but after some reflection I took the additional precaution of writing to Dick Paul to make him aware that I was travelling to China as he had requested and that I hoped to get out without being incarcerated.

With Tuohy in Hong Kong: plane crash

I had had a premonition about the plane I would catch to Hong Kong, and on 13 February recorded in my *Diaries*: "Put my papers in order in case of the unlikely event of my being killed in an air-crash in China."[3] I flew to Hong Kong on 3 March in a Canadian Pacific DC8. It was a terrible flight. There was a lot of air turbulence and we went through a storm. The plane was only half full, and at one point the Captain came and stood by the seat in front of me, a slightly hook-nosed, balding man in a white shirt with epaulettes and a navy tie. He chatted to two air-hostesses who were standing in the central aisle. They were Asian, one Chinese and one Japanese.

I met Tuohy and we spent two nights in Kowloon. We took the ferry across to Hong Kong, where we encountered Princess Margaret, who was making a royal visit.

The following day as we stood on a Kowloon station platform to catch a train to China, Tuohy handed me a newspaper without comment. I glanced at the front page. The headlines reported that a Canadian Pacific plane had crashed at Tokyo airport, killing between 60 and 70 people including the crew and the two air-hostesses. The plane I had flown on had turned round and returned to Tokyo. The hook-nosed captain and the Chinese and Japanese air-hostesses were pictured on the front page.

I stood quietly, full of sorrow and awed by my precognition. I had sensed that something would happen to my plane, and seeing the three of them standing together and chatting within 24 hours of their death, waiting for their extinction, condemned without realising it, I felt at one with my fellow human beings. Were we not all standing before a wall, every moment of our lives, and unaware that execution was imminent?

Canton

The train took Tuohy and me through paddy-fields and blue hills to Canton. We were met by a guide, who was surprised we were not Japanese, and driven in an old Humber Hawk to our hotel through streets crowded with blue-clad pedestrians and cyclists – there were very few cars – and past posters of American soldiers being strangled by Chinese.

Canton was a hot, southern town. Everyone was on the streets, in the open air. We jostled through crowds to a primitive department store. In the evening we visited the Communist opera, *The East is Red*, which recounted the Liberation, the fall of capitalists and the victory of the proletariat who rushed about the stage waving red flags and were greeted with thunderous applause. Any mention of Chairman Mao was applauded, and I slowly began to grasp that the Chinese around me had been conditioned to behave in accordance with a political myth.

This realisation was confirmed the next day when we visited a People's Commune towards Fushan and toured the small primitive whitewashed farm outhouses of the peasants. Everywhere we went we were applauded. There was a deceptive spontaneity in the happy faces. We walked on the foreigners' island near the Pearl River and the next day we visited a teacher training college (which was later the Red Guards' centre for South China) and we were mobbed by students with joyous faces. It was exhilarating to be with such joyous happiness, but deep down I knew it resembled the propaganda joy in *The East is Red*.

China had not thrown up a new joyous man like the being in Blake's 'Glad Day', but a conditioned reflex, a new man who had lost his freedom and was compulsorily joyful. We visited *sampan*s on the Pearl River and went to a boat primary school to see how happy the Pioneer children were, and the guide asked, "Have you any criticism?" and spoke of the benefits of self-criticism. Tuohy and I sensed that self-criticism had contributed to the reconditioning of the Chinese people.

Hangchow
We flew to Hangchow, which had a quiet, majestic beauty and serenity. There was a stillness after the bustle of Canton, a great lake and distant mountains.

We visited a middle school and listened to a lesson in which the pupils were taught that British working conditions have not changed since Dickens' time and that in America blacks are whipped for smoking in the street. I tackled our guide Mr Wi about the untruth of these assertions, and said that education should be free from propaganda. Mr Wi (who, because he had a babyish face, Tuohy nicknamed "Missed-a-wee") disputed what I said.

After lunch by the lake we visited a tea commune where joyous four-year-olds performed a tea dance and then came to us to shake hands and ask, *"Susu nin ha?"* ("How are you uncle?"). The children were tiny but they had been conditioned to be spontaneous with perfect manners.

Shanghai: former landlord in pigsty, match king under house arrest
We took a freezing train to Shanghai, and again we received a joyous welcome from more children and from the workers in a workers' community and in tool and thresher factories.

We visited the Ma Lo commune and the peasants proudly showed us the former landlord's house, which they now occupied. They took us to the former pigsty, and a man in a padded blue boiler suit sat up from the straw. They brought him out. The peasants gathered round him in a wide circle, and our guide explained: "He is the former landlord. You see, we have kept him alive." The landlord stood impassively, his hands limply by his sides, while the peasants all grinned joyously, and in that moment I felt very sorry for the former landlord who was being treated like a leper, a social pariah. Impulsively (and probably dangerously) I strode into the centre of the large circle, shook his hand and gazed sympathetically into his submissive eyes. I indicated my respect for him as a human being in contrast to their contempt for him as expendable and remouldable material.

In the car afterwards I quoted Mao's famous saying in support of free speech, "Let a hundred flowers bloom and a hundred schools of thought contend." Our guide, who was sitting in the front next to the driver, turned round and corrected me: "No, let a hundred flowers bloom through weeding out the past." Our guide wanted me to know that the peasants had weeded the former landlord out and were now blooming.

Next morning we were taken to meet Mr Liu, the son of the former match king of Shanghai. His fortune, some £140 million, had been impounded by the State but he was allowed to enjoy the benefit of some of the interest it accrued while he was confined under house arrest. He had been at

Cambridge and greeted us in perfect English, a man in his fifties looking immaculate in a suit. He served us tea, coffee, biscuits and iced cake, and in the course of being grateful to Chairman Mao for being allowed to live as he did, he said: "I have had to unlearn my capitalist ways, I have been remoulded. These Americans call it brainwashing, which is the process of seeing things in their right perspective. It takes a long time and patience."

He had cleverly told us what had happened to him despite the presence of our guide and Party minder. He spoke like a Westerner, but then, almost in mid-sentence the reconditioned, remoulded mechanism took over and, like a gramophone record repeating, he cut in: "Thanks to Chairman Mao I have my life, my interest and a chance to understand Communism. Thanks to Chairman Mao I can take part in the new China from this house." I was nauseated at the way Mr Liu had been treated as material to be remoulded.

We returned to our hotel at 12. I went to my locked luggage and discovered that it had been torn and opened during our visit to Mr Liu. The letter of introduction written by Emé Yamashita to Mr Soma had been opened, read and returned to a different place in my luggage. On the way back the guide had questioned Tuohy about photographs he had taken of junks and nuclear shelters. Now *we* were being treated as material.

We went on to visit the children's district palace and watched tiny children follow an assault course based on the Long March which had swept Mao to power. They queued to knock down a life-size cardboard cut-out of President Johnson, and three-year-olds sang us 'Embroidering the Portrait of Chairman Mao'. I knew the Party propagandists had put the smiles on their innocent faces just as they had conditioned 800 young Pioneers in blue shirts and red scarves to smile and applaud us.

All the Chinese who smiled at us smiled with conditioned gratitude. However, bearing in mind that millions of Chinese had been starving in the 1940s, could I really say that well-fed remoulded minds were less good than unremoulded starving children? I told Tuohy that it was the dilemma – and solution – of Dostoevsky's Grand Inquisitor who fed the poor and gave them happiness in place of their freedom, which had included hunger and unhappiness.

The next day in Shanghai we began to realise that there was a new movement to suppress criticism. At Futan University we were told that intellectuals who despise labour had been influenced by capitalists, landlords and bourgeois teachers, and so all intellectuals must be encouraged to love labour by working in the countryside. The final Communist vision was of a breaking-down of barriers between peasants, workers and intellectuals, between country and town, and between manual and mental labour. No one said that the Cultural Revolution – a new remoulding – had begun, but we had indirectly been told of its beginning.

Nanking

We went to Nanking by train. In Nanking our guide was hostile and suspicious, probably having been sent a report of what was found in my luggage. He was watchfully silent as we visited a department store, Nanking University and the Ming tombs. Yet again we were applauded by 400 children, and I saw that the intellectuals were being suffocated so that the Party could be sure of the children in the future. I saw that China was a society conditioned to guarantee the survival of the Communist Party.

Peking. Visit to Peking University, my discovery of the Cultural Revolution in March 1966

We made the long train journey to Peking (as Beijing was then known), where we were met by our guide Mr Tsu (pronounced Chou) and driven to the Hsin Chiao Hotel. Peking in March was a place of brown mud and dust. We visited the Great Wall. The people were more dour in the north, more grim and less joyous.

The next day we visited Peking University, expecting to see thousands of students. But the huge campus was virtually deserted, as were its curly-tiled buildings and carved stone bridges. We were taken to see a 2nd-year class. Ten students read slogans about Chairman Mao from the blackboard. I asked to see a 3rd- or 4th-year class. I was told by a Professor, "They are in the countryside." I probed and was told by a clearly frightened Professor Chao in the US house: "They went in August and will be back some time soon. It's socialist re-education."

Over lunch Tuohy and I discussed the situation and agreed that the 3rd and 4th years were being punitively remoulded in Sinkiang.

After lunch we visited a students' dormitory. A 5th-year student acted as spokesman for the dozen students there. He said: "The 3rd and 4th years are sent individually to Sinkiang, and live, eat and work with the peasants, who supervise them. They have no books. History and philosophy are being remoulded to get rid of bourgeois ideology, and have been moved permanently to the countryside."

Outside the dormitory I stopped a student and asked, "Why aren't you in Sinkiang?"

He replied, "Because I've got a medical certificate." (*See* pp.509, 513.)

"In other words," I said, "attendance in the countryside is compulsory unless there is a reason for exemption?"

Mr Tsu tried to intervene and hustle me away. But I insisted, and the student furtively agreed.

I realised instantly that I had unearthed evidence of a new movement that compelled students to go into the countryside. I did not realise until later that I had discovered the first evidence of what would come to be known as the Cultural Revolution.

As soon as Tuohy and I were able to confer we agreed that we had uncovered a purge.[4]

I resolved to find evidence for this purge. That evening Mr Tsu took us to a film about the creation of a commune. Afterwards I told Mr Tsu that I wished to return to Peking University for a discussion with the Vice-President (who was running the University): "I am not satisfied with the explanation we have received. There were no students. I want to hear where the students are."

Mr Tsu said we could not return to Peking University and tried to convince us that we had misunderstood the 5th-year student. All next day, which was icy, I kept up my demands while we visited the Forbidden City and a prison, where counter-revolutionaries impassively made gloves.

In the evening Tuohy declined to accompany me to a play about a Viet-Cong hero who was executed by Americans with a joyous expression on his face. I had Mr Tsu to myself, and I persevered. In the interval I told him how my students were imprisoned in Baghdad. He suddenly relented and said, "I will arrange for you to see the Vice-President at Peking University."

Lunch at British Legation

The following morning I woke to a dust-storm. There was a red peppery dust on our window-sills. We visited the Temple of Heaven. Tuohy announced that we were to lunch at the British Legation (an invitation I believe, on reflection, he intrigued the previous evening while I was at the play). We were received by Donald (later Sir Donald) Hopson, the Chargé d'affaires, in an old-style Peking house that, I wrote that evening, looked "like a fire station".[5] (The reference to fire was a premonition, perhaps prophetic, as the office was set on fire by Red Guards on 22 August 1967.) He introduced himself as "Donald".[6]

We lunched inside the Legation at a long table. I cannot recall how we managed to give Mr Tsu the slip, but he was not present. I gave a full account of my encounter with the 5th-year student and we discussed our suspicions about the coming purge. Donald Hopson was extremely interested and said that my persistent approach was exactly what was needed in the current situation. Donald urged us to continue to press for a meeting with the Vice-President.

Interrogating the Vice-President of Peking University

The next day, 19 March 1966, Mr Tsu took us to meet Professor Wang, the Vice-President at Peking University, and other nameless young Communist observers. Mr Tsu said, "No notes to be taken. No photographs."

I asked the questions and under their noses I took a complete transcript of the hour-long interview (*see* Appendix 4, pp.509–514),[7] in which it was made clear that students in the countryside were following a Party line, not a University line, and that their courses had been interrupted. In addition to Sinkiang some students were in Szechwan and some in Hopei.

Tuohy had a camera strapped round his neck. His camera was near his hands, and from time to time he gave an elaborate cough, moved up his right hand to cover his mouth and furtively clicked his camera with his left hand. This way he took several pictures, one of which was good enough to use in our articles.

The students were clearly being indoctrinated, remoulded and purged. This was in fact the first hard evidence the West had of the coming Cultural Revolution, which broke in August.

Mao's lies
Throughout the rest of the day I skirmished with Mr Tsu. We had heard in a classroom that the British concessions were seized by Mao in 1949. I said they were given back voluntarily in 1945. Mr Tsu said that the Chinese history books clearly stated that Mao had seized them in 1949, and that Mao had personally approved the history books.

I said, to his evident irritation, that in that case Mao had lied. "You cannot trust Mao's history books," I told him.

In the afternoon we visited the Garden of Delight in Harmony, which had a green lake "like a meditating mind on which the world is an unreal reflection".[8] In the evening we ate Peking duck in an old Peking street. I told Mr Tsu how the Party ruled in Orwell's *Nineteen eighty-four*.

I asked him: "If the Party told you that Chairman Mao has been wrong, would you believe it?"

He answered: "Impossible." (Meaning that it was impossible for the Party to say that Mao was wrong.)

"Would you betray your father to Chairman Mao?" I asked.

"Of course," Mr Tsu said. "My father merely begat me, whereas Chairman Mao saved me."

Communism and the West
In my skirmishes with Mr Tsu I had been on the side of: Western freedom of thought; the right to vote out a country's leaders; the truth of history; and the individual's perception of truth. I was against: Communist materialism; and Party propaganda and remoulding. Western Christendom was better than that.

The next day we went to the Peking children's palace, which was in part of the old Imperial Palace. Children and Pioneers joyously fired machine-guns at cardboard GIs and waved flags, and I felt like Christ looking with great sadness at their miserable remoulding. Children should not be regarded as material to be remoulded for the benefit of the regime.

After lunch we went to a church we had located.[9] The main doors were barred. Old men sat or camped outside. One small door was open and we went in. An old woman knelt in prayer, and there were 14 framed pictures of the suffering servant. Again I identified with Christ.

Later we visited two museums, one covering the period from the beginnings of man to 1926, and the second one covering from 1926 to 1966. At this second museum rows of Red-Army men in uniform sat on the floor, being indoctrinated.

We walked in People's Square. I pondered the shallow, rootless, happy, conditioned, unfree world of the Chinese, who comprised a quarter of the world's population, and I reaffirmed the individual against the collective: Christ's values.

It was time to leave China. From Peking we flew back to Hangchow, and then back to hotter Canton. From there we took the train back to Hong Kong. At Kowloon station fifteen porters dived for our luggage and expected tips. I was back in freedom and sanity, but Hong Kong seemed a materialistic, trivial place beside the weighty thoughts China had inspired. We flew on to Tokyo, and improbably Caroline and Nadia were at Tokyo airport to meet me. There was much to digest, and I had many newspaper articles to write.

Communist phase of Chinese civilization

China had changed me. I had rejected materialistic Communism and had experienced the underlying power of the Chinese civilization beneath its Communist phase. I now thought deeply about the decaying social structure of the European civilization, which was as wanting as China's, and sensed that it was in a process of transition. I opposed the remoulding and reconditioning of a quarter of the world's population, and had a yardstick I now applied to Western civilization, which was an amalgam of the North-American and European civilizations.

I help Tuohy with 14 newspaper articles

I returned from China with a universal law: that the more society suffers from unreal living (which I equated with social ego), the more it is in decay. As I worked on the newspaper articles I mulled over a complementary law: that vitality poured into institutions from the central self (the product of spiritual striving) arrests, indeed reverses, decay.

I spent several days sitting with Tuohy, pooling ideas and writing down his dictation of drafts for our articles. He frequently digressed to talk about style, and told me, for example, how sentences connect and how form is physiological. He banned all adverbs and relative pronouns. I found much of this advice very helpful. Working with Tuohy I felt as Pound must have felt working for Yeats, or Beckett for Joyce. Learning the art of good writing is to some extent an oral tradition, and an apprentice bard has to attach himself to a Homer and learn the technical tricks. Tuohy was the only Homer available in Japan. He was moody while we worked together, and told me that for him writing was like sitting on his pot as a child.

Cultural Revolution disbelieved

We left all reference to our discovery of the new purge (i.e. of the Cultural Revolution) out of the articles and sent a cable to *Newsweek* in New York offering them the world scoop on the Peking-University purge for $2,000. *Newsweek* replied rejecting this opportunity and asking for the article we had agreed to write.

During the following weeks we offered our scoop to various "experts". Edward Crankshaw wrote back saying flatly that he did not believe our story, that if it were true there would be a purge as significant as Stalin's purges in the USSR of the 1930s.

In August 1966 the Cultural Revolution broke as a news story and our scoop ended up as a retrospective account in *Encounter* of December 1966. My share of what we were paid was £50. Ever since when told that a particular writer is a "China expert" I have not been impressed.

Our articles duly appeared in *The New York Times*, *The Sunday Telegraph*, in *AP* and of course in *Newsweek*. The China trip paid for itself and there was a small profit.

SIS: lunch with Keith Priest

I had found a letter from Dick Paul on my return. It was dated the day I had left for China, 3 March:

> Dear Mr Hagger, Thank you for your letter. It was pleasant to hear from you again. Do let me know when you are in London during the summer and come along for a chat if you can spare the time.

Soon afterwards I received a letter from Keith Priest of the British Embassy, Tokyo, dated 24 March:

> Dear Mr Hagger, When I was recently in London I met Dick Paul, who told me that he has been in touch with you and that you were visiting mainland China between 5 and 21 March, together with Frank Tuouy (*sic*). Paul suggested that, since I was shortly returning to Tokyo for my second tour, it might be a good idea if we met, for, as you will no doubt

realise, we in this Embassy are most interested in the impressions of China gained by travellers like yourself. Would you be free for lunch one day?

He wrote again on 28 March after I had rung him:

It occurred to me immediately afterwards that I must have appeared very rude in that I did not suggest that your wife came to lunch as well. This is of course what I had originally intended, and I do hope that she will be able to come.

We lunched with him the next day. He was a large man with soft eyes. At the outset he asked me to say nothing to Tuohy about our meeting. He said that I had scooped the entire Secret Intelligence Service over "Peita" (Peking University), so when would I go again? He asked a lot of questions: how much did I earn, how much was I getting from *Newsweek*? During the lunch he insistently asked, "When could you go again? Could you go before December?"

He visited me at our bungalow the next day and stayed for an awkward quarter of an hour while we all made small talk.[10] He fell down the step outside the front door when leaving and just managed to avoid falling into a nearby rose-bush.

Selecting interpreters at Ministry of International Trade and Industry
Yamashita, the Chief of Trade Policy, now asked me to spend an afternoon a week at the Ministry of International Trade and Industry (MITI). He had covered me while I was in China and I had to reciprocate. I had to interview 50 officials of the Ministry of International Trade and Industry for an hour each in a rolling programme that would be spread over the coming year. I had to examine their English and choose the best six, who would become multilateral conference interpreters.

My interviewees were extremely articulate and during our conversations I was in effect interviewed by 50 MITI officials, some of whom questioned me closely about my visit to China.

Revising 'The Silence'
Soon I was able to get back to 'The Silence', which I edited, revised and typed up. The title came to me on 28 April. The combination of China, three weeks of Tuohy's scepticism and reviewing my poem had turned me away from metaphysical Reality. I wanted to express the decay of European civilization. I made sure this was in my poem. When finished the poem was nearly 1,450 lines long.

I showed it to Tuohy. He praised much of the technical side but wanted it to be social-rationalist discourse rather than image and to obey the linguistic principles of Wittgenstein. He proposed that there should be marginal glosses in the manner of Coleridge's 'The Ancient Mariner', and I implemented his proposal. But he applied Movement criteria to the poem, and was sceptical about the metaphysical theme. So I eventually showed the poem to Tomlin, who, as a friend of Eliot, immediately understood my post-Modernist aims and outlook. "Mr F.T." of the dedication began as Frank Tuohy and turned into Frederick Tomlin, reflecting the tension between the two polarities in my being.

In May and June I pondered how stillness took me into the silence of eternity and the Zen Reality. I felt that inner vitality and growth can be found in a healthy culture. I had left the decayed West and had come to the healthy East to find this drive in myself, which in 'The Silence' I called a drive to my Shadow. I had had to leave the West and go on a journey to discover this vitality within myself in the East.

Communist Soviet Union and Western civilization

Return to England via Russia

In Britain the Labour Party had won a General Election, and I wanted to return to experience the new post-imperial atmosphere and decay within the European civilization. I had arranged for all three of us to return home in June for a visit of ten weeks. We would travel the cheapest route on money largely advanced by the Bank of Japan.

The day before I left I wondered if history has a pattern. I wrote in my *Diaries*: "I would like to believe in Britain's freedom to emerge...but deep down feel there is a decline ahead, a decline into a USE (United States of Europe)."[11] (The USE as I conceived it then was identical to the EU.)

We travelled from Tokyo to Nakhodka on a Russian boat. It was festooned with coloured streamers as we left. We ploughed through sun and then mist while Russians played chess on the back deck and in the evenings did Cossack dancing, sitting on their haunches and shooting out each leg in turn and raising their arms and whirling in thrilling abandon. We passed Hokkaido and on the third day arrived in Nakhodka, a trafficless town whence we took a seemingly pre-1917 train to Khabarovsk. After a glimpse of a snowless Siberia we flew in a deafening turbo-prop Aeroflot plane that throbbed and rattled like a wartime bomber.

Moscow

Nine hours later we were in Moscow and drove to the Hotel Minsk in Gorky Street, which had an open, doorless lift.

We now began to get to know Russian life. Everything suddenly became a battle. Catching the waiter's eye, obtaining Nadia's bedding, buying Appleade, booking an Intourist tour – all took hours. Nevertheless I managed to get us on a tour of the Kremlin for noon the next day.

On 9 June 1966 we walked round the Archangel Cathedral. It was the height of the Cold War and, looking at the murals of Grand Dukes on pillars, I suddenly had a vision of world leaders near a Leaders' Hall, a world government.[12] I had had a glimpse of a coming World State. I foresaw the end of the Cold War and the reunification of Europe.

As I looked at the early 16th-century icons and murals of Grand Dukes I glimpsed a new poetic form, a poem on Communism in pictures which would combine my impressions of China and of the USSR and foretell the end of the Cold War. I began this poem immediately. It became 'Archangel'.

We went on to Red Square and visited Lenin's tomb. Lenin was lying in state in a dinner-jacket within a glass coffin. I saw Lenin's pale face under a brilliant light.

Berlin

That evening we caught a train to Brest, Warsaw and Berlin, which we approached through the dark ruins and dimly-lit streets of the eastern side. Suddenly we encountered the blaze of West Berlin. I wrote the first 150 lines of 'Archangel' on the train, and two days later we had crossed Flanders and arrived in London at Victoria Station.

Loughton

We were met by Caroline's parents, who drove us to 55 High Beech Road, Loughton, a house my brother Robert had bought, which we were renting so as not to disturb the tenants in our flat. I arrived a practising poet who had something to say: my vision of Reality within the decaying European, Byzantine-Russian and Chinese civilizations.

In Loughton I caught up with my family, including my widowed mother, and gloried in English things: in red pillar-boxes, the whine of a milk float and white-flannelled cricketers on Loughton cricket field. After China and Russia and the Communist threat of imprisonment and execution this was a quaint, stable, secure, little life.

I walked in the Forest to the two ponds of Earl's Path and gazed at the pale water lilies, the golden water irises and the sodden leaves under the beeches. I re-entered the little life of shopping, doctors' surgeries and television news. No one wanted to know too much about the Far East, and I was content to renew my roots in the West.

SIS again: meetings with Dick Paul and Dennis Stone, and sale of China photos

I was acutely conscious that I had Britain for ten weeks and would then be separated from her again. I was an Outsider, but I drank in every impression, gazed at every detail in the buildings as I had done in Iraq, saw everything my family took for granted with fresh eyes.

Through Keith Priest an arrangement had been made for me to see Dick Paul in Carlton Gardens. I again shook hands with the red-faced, grey-haired, black-suited Dick Paul in "Palmerston's lounge". He spoke admiringly of my interrogation at Peking University.

He passed me on to Denis Stone, who offered to help me find out more. He arranged to have lunch with me the following week, and on the way home I stopped at every statue, looked at the crowns on the lampposts and gazed admiringly at churches and cathedrals.[13] I marvelled at the sumptuous wealth of Britain's cultural heritage and compared it with the bare cathedral in Tokyo.

On 22 June I lunched with Denis Stone in the Fontainebleau, Northumberland Avenue. He questioned me in great detail about China. After lunch we walked across Trafalgar Square and down the Mall and into St James's Park, and I saw Big Ben peep over trees and, turning, Nelson raise his arm. We crossed the Mall and Denis Stone left me near the Crimean war memorial[14] in Waterloo Place.

I went on to Carlton Gardens and met Kathleen Draycott of the Foreign Office, who wanted to see a selection of China pictures I had looked out, with a view to buying some of them. She was flustered, in the process of moving to Millbank, but she asked to borrow my photos and said she would make her choice and return the rest.

She wrote on 29 July saying that the Foreign Office wanted to buy 17 photos for 25 guineas. I received a cheque from the British Embassy, Tokyo on 20 September.

Revisiting British past
I drove out into the Essex villages and marvelled at the steeples that dominated the flat countryside, gazed at the green leaves, greedy for each English detail. I retraced my childhood, I discussed situations I remembered with my mother and went back to Chigwell School for Speech Day. I reconnected myself to my British past but I was also eager to establish the UK's role in world history, and its future. Half of me was reflecting on world history.

I had quickly made an upstairs room at the back of my brother's house into a study, and I spent whole mornings writing 'Archangel', my poem on Communism, the first poem in *The Wings and the Sword*. Some evenings we dined with my mother in the nursery at Journey's End, and some evenings I went out with my younger brother Jonathan to The Holly Bush or The Royal Standard, or further afield to The Owl. I visited Waltham Abbey. I regarded myself as the chronicler of Britain's decay, and I broke off from 'Archangel' to start 'Blighty', in which Britannia is seen as a decaying whore.

In July I met John Ezard, who was working for *The Oxford Mail*. He had predicted that I would move away from the West and towards the East, and that on my return we would be out of shouting distance. We talked across the distance between us. He said he was no longer interested in ideas, theories or the universe, whereas I looked for a life beyond bourgeois 'normality'. I had tea with my former Oaklands teacher Mabel Reid, who had just retired and was living in Elm Cottage near the school.

I lunched with my Aunt Lucy, who in the late 1920s had stolen my mother's fortune, and I disturbed her enough with my forecast of decline and decay to give her a sleepless night worrying about her business and a crash in shares. (I brought her into 'The Silence' as Mrs Hall.) I went to Dulwich. Caroline's parents had moved from their demolished house to 177 South Croxted Road, and I strolled in the Park, gazing at the ducks, widgeon and quails on the small lake and feeling for the Park labourers.

First of 1,000 stories: 'Limey'
I visited the library where I had worked briefly before leaving for Japan. The librarian I was under, Fowler, had moved elsewhere, and I found myself chatting to the warden. He told me a story about his life in Canada, and that night I had the idea of writing 100 stories, prose-poems that would focus on intense experiences that shaped people's lives.

On 15 July I wrote 'Limey', which was based on the warden's story. This was the first of 1,000 stories in my prose-poem style. Each evening I now went to The Standard for a nightcap and I took my writing with me and did my corrections, sitting in the corner, just as Sartre had done in the Café Bonaparte in Paris.

Poetry: 'Archangel' on Communism
Communism had set me thinking about revolution generally. I went to London and visited the Banqueting House, and saw the window through which Charles I stepped to his execution on a platform outside. I resolved to write a poem on Cromwell, which I began to draft. Another day I went to the Tower, and on another day I visited the Rhymers' Club cellar in Cheshire Cheese, meeting-place of the poets of the 1890s. I deliberated on spiritual reform, which I felt was a better way than political revolution. I was still writing 'Archangel'. My haloed Archangel Michael in the Russian icon I had seen embodied the Russian Byzantine tradition and prophetically looked forward to a time when Communism had collapsed and there was a world government that acknowledged spiritual reform.

I finished the poem on 23 July. After writing the last line I went for two glorious walks in brilliant sunshine, one of them to the Stubbles and the Witches' Copse. Two days later I walked to the Iron-Age hill-fort, Loughton Camp, and saw the pollarded trees as brain nerves. In my mind I stood for a tradition of Protestant Reformism or Puritanism, for reforming doctrine into the experience of 'The Silence' and eternity out of which a world government representing all civilizations might grow.

East Grinstead and Bognor

We revisited the places of my Sussex childhood. We spent a week in Bognor with my mother, younger brother and sister. On the way down we travelled through East Grinstead, where I had lived during the war, and visited the 13th-century Hill Place and the artist Gwen Broad, who had written to me on the day of my christening. She was slightly scrawny and severe-looking, with red-rimmed, devout eyes. We visited Broadley Brothers (the East-Grinstead branch of the family business) and I returned to St Anton, my grandmother's house in East Grinstead. I found the arbour over the winding path, and beyond it the toolshed where Percy had worked the grinding wheel to sharpen knives. I visited Beecholme. To my dismay the pine tree had been cut down. I went on to Daledene, my grandfather's last house where a wall had recently been built along the front.

As soon as we arrived at the Marlborough Hotel, Bognor, we gathered in the television room and watched the World Cup soccer final, England v West Germany, and cheered when Geoff Hurst scored the only hat-trick a British player achieved in a World Cup final in the 20th century. He would become an Oaklands parent and years later would open two fêtes for me.

At Bognor I spent much of each day reading on the beach about Cromwell. In the evenings we drove out to surrounding villages, including Felpham, where I saw Blake's house. We went to Chichester.

One day we were visited by my Aunt Lucy, George II's widow, and her son Tom II, his wife and three young children. We received them at the Marlborough Hotel. It was cold and windy and we went down to Bognor beach and sat in the shelter of a beach hut. Lucy sat on a stump and I asked her questions about how she and her husband George II acquired the family business some time after 1926. With my mother listening in appalled and fascinated silence, she told me that George II had bought my grandmother out between 1931 and 1952 with payments of £250 a year, and that a bank manager had advised George to invest the payments in 100% War Loan. She said that when War Loan slumped to 80% George advised my grandmother to sell, but she did not act on his advice and lost most of her savings, whereas if she had reinvested them in a building society, she would have been all right. Looking back, I can see that I was trying to get to the bottom of what happened in 1931 (*see* p.10). Her son Tom returned from playing with the children, including Nadia, on the beach and prowled to and fro, aghast at what she was saying and trying to change the subject. He eventually said, "Mother, that's quite enough." My mother led us all to have tea in a nearby outside café.[15]

In Scotland and Ireland
I wanted to get the feel of the UK as a whole for 'Blighty' and 'Old Man in a Circle', and to connect myself to literary places that might come into my lectures. Alone I made a quick tour of Scotland and Ireland.

I flew to Edinburgh and walked among the black-grey buildings and crumbling closes along Royal Mile. I visited Holyrood Castle. I considered how Lord Darnley (James I's father) was apparently murdered on the instructions of the Earl of Bothwell, who then married Mary Queen of Scots (James I's mother), and the parallel with Hamlet's father being murdered by Claudius, who then married Gertrude. James I had married the 14-year-old Anne of Denmark, and I wondered about the play's setting at Elsinore in Denmark. I pondered how the setting and theme of *Hamlet* seemed to echo the life of James I. I then visited Knox's House.

I took the train to Glasgow and flew to Belfast. I toured the drab terraces and gaudy 1890s pubs.

The next day I went to Dublin and toured the city in a taxi driven by one of the 1916 rebels. He took me inside Kilmainham prison and showed me the yard where the Easter-1916 martyrs were shot by the British. I visited all the places connected with Joyce's *Ulysses*.

The next day I took a train to Gort and visited Coole Park, where Yeats's friend Lady Gregory lived. I thought of the many-sided Major Robert Gregory who died young, like my Uncle Tom. I went on to Sligo and visited Yeats's grave in Drumcliff churchyard under Ben Bulben.

I returned by air. The next day, still in a mindset of locating poems in places, I sped up to Huntingdonshire, visited Cromwell's house in Ely and went on to Little Gidding, made famous in Eliot's *Four Quartets*, and Ferrar's tomb. I thought about rooting my own poems in places, as I was later to do.

Essex places
During the last week of my holiday I felt like an extrovert tourist. I had lost contact with the silence, I was living an outer life rather than the inner life I had found in Japan. I went to church at St Mary's, Loughton. My brother Robert was a churchwarden. He handed me two books. There were two hymns by George Herbert, but I found the service a communal drama that ignored the silence. I was aware of the increasing urbanisation of once-rural Loughton and looked in vain for its rootedness in Western civilization.

I had been preparing for a development in my view of world civilizations which had not yet happened. I had been in a kind of no man's land. Deep down I knew I had to return to Japan and get back to world history with the Prince. Meanwhile people appeared.

Jill Bradbury rang several times and on 14 August was dropped off by her boyfriend so she could see us for a couple of hours. Caroline and I drove her to Lippitt's Hill, where the poet John Clare was a mental patient, and the three of us walked in the Forest near High Beach. Jill had grown her hair well down over her shoulders, and she wore trousers and walked across the leaves in bare feet. She talked about her past, saying she had lost herself at Oxford and that her world "shattered in 1961" (the year I married). She said, "I come and listen to you because you think as I do." She came back and had tea with us, and then her boyfriend collected her.

She committed suicide in September. I did not find out until early 1971.

Ricky Herbert and John Ezard

Two days later I met Ricky at Notting Hill Gate. He had a limp, having been knocked down by a bolting horse. He told me Jill had been in a mental hospital in Northampton in 1964, the sister mental hospital to Lippitt's Hill. He asked, "How is your inner life going?"

I told him about the silence and white light, and he became very excited and spoke of the death of the ego.

I said, "The Oxford nihilism was a prelude to inner unity."

He agreed.

I said, "Unreal living is a prelude to real living."

Again he agreed.

We moved to Chelsea and drank four and a half pints and discussed the new Reformation. By the time I reached home I had renewed contact with my inner spring.

Three days later I met John Ezard in The Royal Standard at lunch-time and told him about my meeting with Ricky. He reiterated: "Ricky must have developed the same way as you. I have abandoned all ideas and no longer need to interpret experiences. We have no common language." He added, "You are living at a deeper level than when you left England." The Group-Captain (Caroline's father) said the same that evening. My centre-shift had not gone unnoticed.

Leaving England

My last day in England I felt a great sadness. I went up to the Forest to say goodbye. It was very peaceful. In the garden of Journey's End, under the nursery window, Nadia blew a string of soapy bubbles through a wire ring, and, watching them float and explode, I thought it was an image for our ephemeral universe. I went to The Owl and later had a final drink with my brother Jonathan in The Standard. Caroline was tearful when I got home. She wanted to stay in England and not return to exile. I felt the same.

Next morning, on the train at Liverpool Street I felt tears coming as I leaned out of the window to say goodbye to the family members seeing us off. I was not sure whether my feeling was for my family, for the Forest or England, or all three, but I knew it was attributable to an impending separation from something.

I now felt I belonged to England. Being an exile had taught me to value her and love her. Britain was decayed, but I had rediscovered my roots in the past. And, crossing the Channel, I felt a nomad. I was insecure, and for the next 24 hours both Caroline and I had wet eyes several times.

My feelings had purified and intensified. My purgation was continuing almost unnoticed. I was living through my new centre. Deep down I was resolved to get to grips with world history.

Return to Japan via Moscow

We returned to Japan the same way that we had come, via Moscow, where we stayed in the fortress-like Hotel Ukraina. The next day I visited Semyonovsky Square, where Dostoevsky awaited execution, and the Dostoevsky Museum, which had a picture of Stariez Amvrosec (thought to be the original for Father Zossima in *The Brothers Karamazov*). In the afternoon I went to the Revolution Museum and unsuccessfully tried to see their portrait of Kalyaeev, one of Camus' "*Justes*" who assassinated a Grand Duke and then asked for death.

Khabarovsk: 'A Spade Fresh with Mud'

We flew back to Khabarovsk. We had to wait for our train, and after lunch at the airport restaurant (during which I fell into conversation with a Baptist missionary) we boarded a coach that was laid on to kill time and toured Khabarovsk. The coach pulled off the road into a cemetery and out of the window I saw the funeral described in my short story 'A Spade Fresh with Mud'.[16]

We took the train to Nakhodka and the boat to Japan. During the voyage it grew hotter. I worked on Cromwell and pondered opening a school for self-realisation, but correctly identified this course as an escape from art.

Civilizations: world history and poetry

Back in Japan for one more year, I resumed my former way of life. I continued to read world history with the Prince. I revised a couple of poems, 'The Oceanographer' and 'Twilight', and made some revisions to 'The Silence'. I immediately sensed the oneness of the earth and the universe, from which selfhood separates, and thought again of the death of the ego, the Buddhist dying-away from self, which I had partially undergone.

I found Tuohy more social-rationalist than ever. He was unable to write, having writers' block, and was full of negative remarks about writers he knew I admired. The oneness of world history fitted in with the oneness of the earth and the universe. I went down to Nobe with the family and Buchanan and talked about the decay of Britain and the role of the UK in world history against booming Pacific rollers and tinkling autumn crickets.

Jean-Paul Sartre and Simone de Beauvoir

The two French Existentialists Sartre and Simone de Beauvoir came to Japan. Because they were anti-Gaullist the French Embassy held no public reception for them. They spoke at Keio University. I had lectured on M. Roquentin's response to the Negro singer in *La Nausée*, and I sat in a hall among 2,000 Japanese while de Beauvoir harangued us on feminism for an hour in French.

Then Sartre, dressed in a navy suit and looking more thin, tall and respectable than the man I met in 1959, took over. He sat sideways on before the microphones and spoke barely audibly about how being an intellectual meant opposing the Americans in Vietnam and the French in Algeria, and on how women and intellectuals are the victims of the structure of their society.

There was nothing about *La Nausée* and nothing about the philosophy of Existentialism, the two subjects I wanted to hear. I was mortified that my erstwhile hero, Sartre, should now stand for a corrupted philosophy of Existentialism that saw free choice as supporting Communism and opposing the West. I was firmly on the side of the Free World and a benevolent world government that could bring peace to all humankind through the unification of all the civilizations of world history.

Jon Halliday

I opposed Communism when Jon Halliday, who had been in the Oxford Randolph Set, came to dinner during a visit to Japan. He was staying with Adrian. He told me that he was teaching at Reading University and was still a Marxist. He wore rimless glasses and embodied Sartre's view that an intellectual opposes the Americans.

We discussed China. I showed him the articles Tuohy and I had written on China, and he buried himself in them for a long time. He did not want to hear any criticism of Mao, and when I pointed out that Communists under him may have killed 20 million he said that was a mere "culture pattern".[17]

Years later he married Jung Chang and helped her write *Mao: The Unknown Story*, which claimed that Mao was responsible for killing not 20 million but 70 million Chinese.

History as world civilizations: study of civilizations, 'The Decline of the West' – course for postgraduates on the decline of the West in Gibbon, Spengler and Toynbee

From my reading of world history with the Prince I was now convinced that world history is the history of many different civilizations, and I increasingly reinforced this view by dipping into the ten volumes of Toynbee's *A Study of History* I had bought in November 1964.

I was sure that the Chinese and Russian civilizations had passed through many stages, and that Communism was but a phase in their quite separate civilizations. The European civilization was older than the North-American civilization, which were loosely grouped together under the term 'Western civilization', and there were other living civilizations, such as the South-East Asian and Indian civilizations, which I planned to visit on my way home from Japan. My view of world history as separate civilizations was in conflict with Marxists' view of Communism.

This conviction found its way into my class of postgraduate students, who evidently reported back. It must have been about this time that Professor Irie, who was in charge of me, asked me if I would teach a course on the decline of the West to the postgraduates.

I said, "What if I think that the West is not declining?"

He said, "Oh, but we would still like a course of lectures entitled 'The Decline of the West'."

I promised I would begin this in the second semester in the following February, and began assembling material on Gibbon, Spengler and Toynbee for this course.

Tomlin was unaware that I was preparing for this course. Arnold Toynbee visited Japan shortly afterwards, and Tomlin visited him in his Yokahama hotel on 9 November 1966.[18] I did not know about Toynbee's visit until after he had left Japan. Toynbee was 78 and (Tomlin told me) somewhat deaf but looking back, I cannot help feeling that something that was meant to happen did not happen.

With Keith Priest on the liberation of China

Caroline and I had visited Keith Priest on 19 September. Keith met us outside his house and Melissa (still a fetching blonde of about 40 with a trim figure) had a log fire blazing. She said, "I am cold. I don't want to put my winter clothes on."

The Cultural Revolution had now burst upon the attention of the world, to the astonishment of China 'experts' such as Edward Crankshaw, and we talked about Peking University and the Red Guards and agreed that my findings had been proved right. Melissa became slightly drunk and said to Keith, "Poppet, if you want me to wear a mini-skirt like this...", giving everyone a demonstration and an eyeful.[19] When we left she hung on to my arm in the garden. I saw them again at Tomlin's cocktail party on 3 October, when Priest was not too anxious to speak, aware that any conversation he had with me would be under Tomlin's gaze.

I had been taking a close look at the present phase of the Chinese civilization. From my studies with the Prince I had worked out that the next phase of Chinese history would involve a slackening or weakening of Communism, a Thermidorian Reaction as after the French Revolution or a Restoration as after Cromwell's Revolution. The Great Leap Forward of 1958–1961 had been a disaster and had resulted in between 18 and 42 million deaths by starvation due to famine. Mao's authority had been questioned – hence his purge of his opponents through the Cultural Revolution. Since history was moving China in a restorative direction, a process the Cultural Revolution was attempting to arrest, I had come to believe that the restorative process should be accelerated to dislodge the tyrant responsible for at least 20 million deaths of his opponents. China should be 'nudged' from within, history should be given a nudge forwards. I believed it was possible to influence the direction of the Chinese civilization.

Yes, China had a fifth of the world's population and could only maintain its stability and harmony if it were ruled by an autocrat. That had been the case ever since Emperor Shi Huang-ti, or Qin Shi-huang, Emperor of the State of Qin (pronounced 'Chin') from 246 to 221BC and of a unified China from 221 until his death in 210BC. He had built the first Great Wall by connecting existing defensive walls into a single system fortified by watch-towers. (It would soon be discovered, in 1974, that his city-sized mausoleum was guarded by a life-sized terracotta army of over 8,000 soldiers, 130 chariots and 670 horses.) But under another autocrat China could quietly decommunise. The restoration of Chiang Kai-shek was the solution, a reverse of the ousting of Chiang trumpeted in the opera *The East is Red*. China should be nudged into its next phase, and with nuclear weapons no longer in the hands of extremists the world would be a safer place.

I put all this to Keith Priest when I visited Keith and Melissa on 31 October. Melissa tactfully went out "to write a letter" to leave Keith and me alone, and I put it to him that China's fourth nuclear test would threaten peace in Asia and that Mao should be overthrown from within to improve the lot of all Chinese and of humankind. There should be a liberator who, with the help of Western intelligence agents, would contact disaffected army officers, and after the overthrow – a 'nudging' forward of the historical process that was already taking place – Chiang Kai-shek would be reinstalled to take control of China's nuclear weapons. It needed an existential decision, 'a free choice', by someone behind the scenes to say, "We are going to do this." Keith listened with great interest.

When I had finished he called Melissa in and summarised what I had said in neutral terms. She said to me, "He's really with you," and to Keith, "Don't be so wet and dispiriting."

Keith said, "This is visionary."

Though I had no relationship with Keith's organisation or status within it apart from my social meetings with him, he promised to write a memorandum "to the very centre in London".[20]

Poems and unity: 'An Epistle to an Admirer of Oliver Cromwell', 'An Inner Home', 'The Conductor'

While I was assembling my course on the decline of the West I was discussing evolution and philosophy with the postgraduates. We read Whitehead and phenomenology. My reading was a preparation for *The New Philosophy of Universalism*, my challenge to modern philosophy. I believe my thinking about the universe and consciousness at this time came out of a new inner purpose.

I had completed the self-discovery reflected in 'The Silence' and was living from a new centre which reflected the unity of the universe and consciousness as in Wordsworth's view of the universe. To place Puritan Revolution – which was evident in the Russian and Chinese Revolutions – within the context of the unified universe, I began my longish poem on Cromwell, 'An Epistle to an Admirer of Oliver Cromwell' (a 'Moral letter after Horace'). I expressed my sense of inner growth in 'An Inner Home', which drew on my recent visit to Waltham Abbey and set my growth against the enduring Epping Forest.

I had been down a way of action and since coming to Japan had embarked on a way of contemplation, and was now concerned to combine the two in a self-unification. I wrote 'The Conductor', which presented an image for uniting the way of action and the way of contemplation. In England I had attended a promenade concert at the Royal Albert Hall. Sir Malcolm Sargent was conducting, and the idea for 'The Conductor' had come to me.[21]

I read about 'The Way of Contemplation' in Evelyn Underhill's *Mysticism*, and of "a gradual handing over of the reins from the surface intelligence to the deeper mind" until "individual activity is sunk in the great life of All". That was exactly what had happened to me while I was writing 'The Silence'.[22]

I recorded in my *Diaries* on 24 October, "The main thing about that poem ['The Silence'] was that I did it all for myself, without any aid or guidance, and so I did not know where I was going. I was travelling down a completely unknown road without the slightest idea of what was at the end."[23]

Fortune told from the I Ching

I had come to see the unity of the universe as 'the All' (an Eastern concept), my understanding of which was extended by discussions on the 'Will of Heaven' I had at the end of October and in early November with one of my pupils at the Bank of Japan, an Executive Director, Mr Fukuchi. He explained that Zoroastrianism had left an impact on China in *yin* and *yang*, which are united within the *Tao* whereas Ahriman and Ahura Mazda had no equivalent unity in ancient Persia.

He told me that the first mention of *yin* and *yang* was in the *I Ching*, c.1143/2BC, on whose 64 hexagrams he was an authority. Originally, he said, a hexagram was arrived at by heating a tortoiseshell until it cracked, but now it was done through laying 50 bamboo sticks on a table. His hobby was to use the sticks, and next week he brought them to our class and told my fortune. He placed one stick on the table (to signify God) and held the remaining 49 over his head, and then divided them into two (heaven and earth) and went on subdividing each group until he was left with hexagram 46, *Shang*, whose variation is hexagram 32, *Hang*. '*Shang*' means 'earth-wind' (bottom and top) and 'ascent, advancing upwards blindly', 'great progress and success'. Mr Fukuchi said: "That is the Will of Heaven for you. This must be one of the best hexagrams in the *I Ching*." [24]

As part of my ascent or "advancing upwards blindly" to a union between action and contemplation I began writing the 100 stories or prose-poems I had glimpsed in England. I contemplated images of action within the human All. Throughout November or December I wrote one or two stories a day.

The Prince's birthday

I had been invited to a reception for Prince Hitachi's birthday. On 23 November I conceived the idea for 'Epistle to His Imperial Highness, on his Birthday'. I wrote in my *Diaries*: "I could not think of a suitable subject until in the end I hit on the idea of criticising the Prince, while seeming to praise him, by contrasting the unimportance of his birthday with the plight of less fortunate people in Asia.... Out of this grew, in this one day... the very rough draft of a poem about Japan; the theme being that Japan has risen from the ashes of the war and is poised for economic empire through the Asian Development Bank." [25] I had been discussing the Asian Development Bank with Vice-Governor Sasaki of the Bank of Japan, who had attended its Inaugural Meeting. He expressed the view that Japan had dominated it too much. [26]

I duly attended the reception and learned that Princess Haneko had seen me walking, deep in composition (and contemplation) wearing old clothes near Edogawa *bashi* (bridge), news of which had been discussed at the Imperial dinner-table that night.

'Epistle to His Imperial Highness, on his Birthday', 'Old Man in a Circle'
I wrote the 'Epistle to His Imperial Highness, on his Birthday' during December, and tilted back towards poetry. Writing prose as opposed to poetry made me feel I was living less deeply. On 7 December I wrote in my *Diaries*: "I feel I am losing touch with my inner life.... As long as I am writing stories about other people, this trend will continue: action at the expense of contemplation. I live more deeply in poetry than I do in prose. In prose I am perceptive, in poetry I am all-intuitive."[27] Just before Christmas I started my next long poem, which became 'Old Man in a Circle'.

Eastern civilizations: I write speech for the Governor of the Bank of Japan to open the Asian Development Bank
It was now clear that Japan was poised for economic empire through the Asian Development Bank. I could see that Japan should work selflessly for a united Asia, a union that could take its place in a coming world government, and through writing the 'Epistle to His Imperial Highness, on his Birthday' I believed that the Prince might have a role in helping to unite the opposites in Asia.[28] It therefore seemed almost Providential that Governor Usami of the Bank of Japan had asked me to write a speech for him to declaim at the Opening Ceremony of the Asian Development Bank in Manila on 19 December. I spent five hours at the Bank of Japan on 8 December writing the speech, in which I described the Asian Development Bank as "the first Pan-Asian Parliament".

I also had to correct a speech that underlings had drafted for a dinner President Marcos of the Philippines was giving. The draft was terrible. It included the following sentence: "I should like to thank you, Mr President, for the conveniences you have given the ADB." I asked the Bank of Japan's secretary, Mr Ichiki, "Has President Marcos paid for any lavatories?" Ichiki looked shocked. I explained the meaning of 'public conveniences' and was given a completely free hand to rewrite the speech as I thought fit. I put in the idea of 'Epistle to His Imperial Highness, on his Birthday', that Japan should pour aid to the less fortunate in Asia.

I also wrote the statement Usami was giving at the airport. Usami was representing the Japanese Government, and I learned that Japan intended to give the ADB more financial assistance.[29]

The Prince and I are go-betweens for Prime Minister Sato and Fred Emery of The Times
I was still poring over civilizations and world history. I had been pondering the development of the Japanese civilization. *The Times* correspondent in Tokyo, Fred Emery, had written an article saying that the Japanese economy was faltering: the Prime Minister, Sato, was unpopular as a result of a "black

mist of corruption" and Japanese shipping was in decline. At the reception for the minor British royals Princess Alexandra and Angus Ogilvy on 22 September when several hundred British and Japanese businessmen formed a semi-circle Prime Minister Sato had bowed to me, looking up with wide-open eyes, and he had stared at me, perhaps knowing that I was Prince Hitachi's tutor. I knew Emery. He had invited us to a couple of his parties at home and he and I had spent part of one hot Tokyo evening discussing Bancroft's School where he had been, a neighbour of my own Chigwell School.

The day after the article, on 14 December, the Prince rang me about 9.30 p.m., hummed and hahed and eventually expressed the Japanese Government's displeasure at the article, would I communicate this to Emery? I rang Fred Emery, who immediately said, "What a splendid response." I then rang the Prince saying I would bring *The Times* article with me to the next class and that we would go through it.[30]

Later I reflected that the Japanese Prime Minister had protested to *The Times* by getting the Prince to use me as a go-between. I felt I was becoming an insider. I was working on charting the progress of the Japanese civilization, and was being used to advance the self-interest of the Japanese administration. I knew I would soon be deciding to return to England.

Offered Chair for life, I decide to leave Japan in October
In January I announced that we would be leaving Japan on 18 October. The decision caused me some soul-searching because Professor Narita had invited me to stay on with a Chair "for life". However, I had not gone to Japan to live there until the end of my life. I had gone to discover the wisdom of the East. I was a Westerner, not a Japanese. Besides, Nadia's convent school was to close in July, and there was not another satisfactory school in Tokyo. It made sense for us to return to the flat in Loughton and for Nadia to attend Oaklands School.

I made my announcement to Professor Irie at my main university. Two days later he said: "We shall be sorry to see you go. We want your successor to be exactly the same as yourself. We want someone like yourself in every respect."

It may have been connected with my decision to resign, although it may also have been connected with the concern Sister St John had shown for Nadia's well-being at her school earlier in the day, which had moved me; but a few days later, sitting in my study at home, for two hours I felt a great sorrow from the bottom of my being, somewhere between my stomach and my throat (possibly in my heart), and at the same time I felt a deep love for everything from my new centre, for the All.

I wrote in my *Diaries*:

I am existing in the depths of my being, I am pure feeling and the feeling is love.... I am alive in my depths... and I feel as if I am going to burst into tears because everything is good. My wife is clattering knives. That is good. Everything is good: the rattling window, the chord on the piano, the condensation on my window. I have seen to the very bottom of my being, and there is no abyss. Just a profound sadness and great exultation.... Everything is good because my feeling is pure.[31]

I now redoubled my literary work. For the first six months of 1967 I had continued to write a story – sometimes two – each day and I intermittently worked on my poem on Europe, 'Old Man in a Circle'. My *Diaries* were filled with observations about the decline of Western civilization and the future of Britain.

Lunch for contributors to book on T.S. Eliot
Meanwhile, the book on Eliot to which I had contributed, *T.S. Eliot: A Tribute from Japan*, was launched at Sophia House on 11 January 1967. The British Ambassador, Sir Francis Rundall, was present and met us contributors, who included Tomlin, Tuohy, Professor Nishiwaki and Kenichi Yoshida. (Two Jesuit priests, Father Peter Milward and Father William Johnston, were also contributors and present.) In his speech the Ambassador spoke of originality and looked at me, and later came by with a twinkle in his eye, clearly wanting to talk.[32]

Study of civilizations: my fourth way
I began my course on the decline of the West. I set my postgraduate students to read about 200 pages for each two-hour Monday-morning class. We discussed the pages in class. We looked critically at Gibbon's *The History of the Decline and Fall of the Roman Empire*; Spengler's *The Decline of the West*; and the phases of the growth, breakdown, disintegration and decay of civilizations in Toynbee's *A Study of History*.

While having these intensive discussions I saw a fourth way of accounting for the rise and fall of civilizations, which would eventually emerge in *The Fire and the Stones* (revised and brought up to date as *The Light of Civilization* and *The Rise and Fall of Civilizations*). My reading of history in 1966–1967 would bear fruit in a number of works more than 25 years later.

With Priest on liberation of China again
I had still been focusing on China. I had rung Keith Priest on 19 December after the Prince's phone call on behalf of Prime Minister Sato, and he had invited me to an At Home on Boxing Day. He had mentioned China and said in response to my urging on 31 October that China should be liberated,

"London are very interested in you, you know."[33] I decided not to go to the At Home.

We had gone down to Nobe for the New Year and spent a day huddling over an oil stove as the fall-out from Mao's fifth atomic explosion (detonated on 28 December) came down as rain. I had met Priest again on 9 January and told him that Mao could be out within a year. I said that the Vice-Governor of the Bank of Japan had told me that, according to his Bank's intelligence, Chiang Kai-shek was reported to be ready to return if general chaos ensued as a result of the Cultural Revolution. I had seen Chiang's return as the way forward.

I visited Keith and Melissa Priest again on 25 January and presented a plan to liberate China from Maoism. It was based on hard intelligence I had heard from the Vice-Governor at the Bank of Japan, that the Soviet Union were ready to enter China to carve off Dairen. The Soviet plan could be linked to the activities of disaffected Chinese army officers.

I saw Keith and Melissa again at Tomlin's farewell for his no. 2 on 9 March. Keith asked me if I thought the "Red-Guard movement" was slowing down. He invited me to lunch the next day. Melissa said she would be elsewhere and when I said I was sorry she said, "Oh, you man, you," and hung on my arm.

The next day Keith and I discussed China over soup, steak, apple-pie and cheese prepared by Melissa and cooked by her maid.

Tuohy leaves Japan
Tuohy's term in Tokyo had now come to an end. He gave a couple of talks – one entitled 'Desirable English and Available English' – at the annual British Council conference. His delivery had an almost Johnsonian authority and one lecturer later remarked privately to me, "Blunt but true." This phrase summed up Tuohy's talent. I saw Tuohy a couple of times after that, and in mid-March he came to a last dinner.

Next morning we visited him just before he left Tokyo to return to England. He was in a suit and waistcoat, and his hair was brushed very neatly. He looked immensely sad and spent a long time saying goodbye at the window of our taxi as we left. He stood limply and his eyes were slightly red. Then he turned messily and walked back up his path. He had been sceptical but he had taught me a lot.

I visited Keith Priest on 4 April. He said (dusting his spectacles and looking at the ceiling), "I saw Buchanan the other day. He didn't see me, of course." And: "I've never shaken hands with Tuohy. I've often seen him but I've turned away."

I asked, "Any special reason?"

He said: "No. He was in Poland, wasn't he?" And: "What nationality is

Wittgenstein?"

He was suggesting that Tuohy, and his mentor Wittgenstein, were politically unreliable. This took me aback and I was shocked. Writers and philosophers were universal and viewing them in terms of their nationality, even though the Cold War was at its height, somehow degraded them.

Tokyo was not the same after Tuohy had gone. There had been a heavy fall of snow, which hung on the fruit trees like blossom, and there was a slow thaw. I took my family down to Nobe. Once it was wet and there were drops of rain under every bud, and the plum blossom was out. Another time the paddies were full of croaking and some frogs sounded like castanets. The next morning I slid open the window and lay in my *futon* and watched birds flit in the glorious air.

Tuohy's departure had set me thinking about my future. I pondered my next post. The British Council had offered me a job in Libya, which appealed because of its Mediterranean location and proximity to Egypt, but they then informed me that the post had been filled, and I was reconciled to spending a year in England.

I was full of world civilizations for my postgraduates' class, but I was also thinking about England. I wrote a play between 6 and 23 May, *The Noddies*, about my experience as a park labourer in Dulwich Park.

I was incensed at de Gaulle's rejection of Britain's application to join the European Economic Community for I saw the UK's world role in relation to a coming European Union. In June we listened to American radio for news of Israel's progress in the seven-day war.

Dinner with Kenneth Rexroth
Although I followed world events I continued to be a practising poet. My Californian colleague at Tokyo University of Education, Ruth Witt-Diamant, invited us to meet Kenneth Rexroth, the American poet, who visited Japan towards the end of May. He was an elderly, grey-haired slightly dandified man with a ribbon bow-tie who had organised a reading of the San Francisco poets in 1955 out of which the 'Beat Generation' was born.[34] He had little to say about poetry. He came across as slightly paranoiac. He was suspicious of Spender because of his links with the CIA (which had funded the magazine he edited, *Encounter*).

I remember he said to Caroline: "You remind me of an Austrian tart I once knew. That's intended as a compliment, she was the most beautiful woman I've seen." (Tuohy had once said something similar of Caroline: "She has real beauty and elegance, she's the most beautiful woman I've met.")

Ball lightning
The summer was stiflingly hot. At the end of July there was a vicious storm after dark. The lightning was like lights being turned on and off almost continuously. It turned to bolts which echoed down and fell all round our bungalow. At least six just missed us. I went to the French windows and looked up and saw a jagged fork leaping down straight at me. Instinctively I turned and gathered Nadia into my arms, still watching the descending fork over my shoulder. It cut away at the last minute and struck some scaffolding just beyond our garden wall, about ten yards from where I stood, and there was a round ghostly glow, like a ball. I believe it was the little-understood 'ball lightning'. Immediately afterwards another bolt knocked down the concrete post of a clothes-line next door and burnt all the washing. Then there was an awesome quiet and suddenly the cicadas began singing and all was cool. Everything was back to normal.

Poems: 'The Rubbish Dump at Nobe, Japan', 'The Sea is like an Eiderdown'
We escaped to Nobe whenever we could. On 17 July, in Nobe, I had had the idea for my poem 'The Rubbish Dump at Nobe, Japan: An Investigation of Nature and History, Pattern and Meaning', that became 'Fire-Void'. A fortnight earlier I had been teaching Spengler's *Decline of the West*, and the poem grew out of my historical thinking.

One day in August I awoke to a brilliant dawn. The sea was a succession of rolling waves that crashed and foamed in. We went down to the beach and, lying on a rug, I composed a poem, 'The Sea is like an Eiderdown' in my head.

Nearly drowned in small tsunami
Caroline and I took Nadia in for a swim with her rubber ring. We were just out of our depth when I turned and saw an enormous roller coming in. It was about four feet above the surface of the sea. I grabbed Nadia as it crashed down on us. My bloodstone ring on the little finger of my left hand was torn off and lost. The roller carried on up the sand and shingle, over the top of the beach and into scrub.

An earthquake had set off a small *tsunami*. As we waded quickly for the shore another huge roller appeared about a hundred yards out, again about four feet above the surface of the sea. It was racing in, and, unable to flee it, holding Nadia by her arm, I turned and faced it. It crashed down on us and we were buried in boiling foam. The water receded and I saw another wave just as large bearing down on us. I held Nadia high above my head as I waded for the shore and took a deep breath. The full force of the wave hit my back and knocked me onto my side. But I managed to hold on to Nadia and stood up, and Caroline and I waded hard for the beach.

The three tidal waves had swept over the top of the beach and quite a distance inland, and we were extremely lucky not to have drowned.

Farewell gatherings

In September I prepared to leave Japan. There was a round of visits to the tax office, I had a wisdom tooth extracted and Nadia had her tonsils removed. There were farewell gatherings.

The Bank of Japan's gathering was in a *sushi* bar called the Edinburgh. I was served large wriggling prawns out of a tank. I had to gulp them down, heads and all. The Keio gathering was in a restaurant in Kyobashi, which had a *saké* vat. We could taste the wood in the *saké*. We were served a live sole that squinted dolefully through its two eyes while we picked the flesh from its back with chopsticks. Then it gulped a couple of breaths, wriggled its bare spine and fins, flipped its tail and, with a reproachful, hurt squint, died. Tokyo University of Education held a dinner at the Mikasa Khaikan, and Tomlin had us for a brief drink at the Sanbancho Hotel.

The Prince and Princess had us to dinner at which we were served roast beef. The Prince presented me with a dark blue urn on which there was a gold chrysanthemum crest, the imperial seal of Japan. A chamberlain explained before I left that it was an urn for my ashes, that in the Shinto religion an emperor has the power to bestow eternal life and Emperor Hirohito had bestowed eternal life on me for teaching his son. The Prince also gave me a tie-pin on a chain with an emerald on the pin. At the end of the evening the Prince said sadly, "I shall remember you until I die."

I made a last visit to the Prince's palace. On my way there the air-conditioned car slowed and Princess Haneko was alongside my window, walking with a shopping-bag. At the dinner she had bemoaned that she was not free to do things she would like to do, such as go shopping, and I had told her, "You should just go. Slip out of the palace. People will not expect you to be shopping on your own and therefore they won't recognise you."

"You see, Professor Hagger," she said, "I have been shopping as you suggested."

"Good," I said approvingly.

During the last six months we had only seen the Priests twice. On 8 June we saw them at the British Embassy's reception for the Queen's birthday and farewell to the British Ambassador, Sir Francis Rundall. Melissa gave a heated account of her recent visit to her daughters in Britain, saying England was "terrible, foul, horrible" so loudly within the earshot of some fifty guests that Tomlin came across to enquire what was so horrible. She said, "England."

Being Representative of the British Council whose job it was to present Britain in the best possible light, Tomlin was visibly shocked. Her husband's work in the British Embassy was supposed to advance the cause of England, and she had talked England down in front of several Japanese. Kenichi Yoshida was standing near us, and when I asked if he was a Japanese spy she said, "Yes." I now reckon that her denigration of Britain was for his benefit: brilliant cover to put Japanese intelligence off the scent.

We also saw them at another Embassy party on 26 June when she asked me to help her with an idea for a novel she wanted to write, which would be called *Two Tunnels to Zushi*. She told me she could never write it because there would be too much sex in it and it would cause a problem in her marriage.

On 25 September Keith and Melissa invited us to dinner. We discussed China, and, referring to my call for the liberation of China, Keith lamented the cautious nature of "officialdom", which was inherently uninterventionist. There was a good deal of banter. Melissa brought the drinks and said, "I can do martinis, I'm a double-o-seven girl."

I said that I had read in Wynne's memoirs that Penkovsky had kept the secret-service girls busy. "Does that go on?"

Melissa said, "That's what I do all the time."

Keith said, "So that's what you do in London."

Melissa said, "But I'm discreet, I keep it quiet."

Keith said, "Oh, that's all right, then."

Over dinner the conversation turned to dreams of changing the world, and Melissa said, "I've seen so many men who've been hurt by having dreams and ideals, and they've never happened." She asked me what my dream was. "Is it revolution in China? Would you like to work on it more full time?"

I half-wondered if she had been asked to suggest that I joined the SIS full-time. I said, "I want to live outside the System on a £15-per-week job and write." I was firmly sticking to the line I had taken at my interview with the Civil Service.

Keith and Melissa had been a channel to an organisation that was remote, and I did not expect to see them again.

Kamikaze

As one of my last acts in Japan, I went to the Hong Kong and Shanghai bank to collect a currency licence. This would allow me to send my bank funds back to the UK.

The cashier asked me, "Have you seen everything you wanted to during your stay in Japan?"

I said, "Yes, but I haven't met a *kamikaze*."

To my surprise he said, "Please come and have tea with me now."

He took me to a small room nearby, ordered tea and told me, "I was a *kamikaze."*

He told me about a raid which 378 Japanese pilots made on Okinawa on 31 March 1945. They were supposed to fly low over US ships three times and crash the third time, but there was low cloud. He had not crashed his plane. He had flown around in shame and lost face, and had met up with two other pilots' planes. Talking over their radios the three pilots agreed that they should return home despite their shame. They were the only pilots to return alive.

To their astonishment they were greeted as heroes. There is now a national monument to them, which he visited every 31 March.

Leaving Japan

The same day I took Caroline to the airport and put her and Nadia on a plane for London. Buchanan and Professor Irie came to say goodbye. After they had gone I returned to spend a night in International House where four years earlier I had had the idea for 'The Expatriate'.

I left Japan the next day. I reflected that my four years had put me in touch with a new centre within my self. I had operated at different times as a poet, historian and philosopher, and sensed that I had much more work ahead, a life-long task, in these three disciplines. I had taught at three universities, had written international speeches for the Governor of the Bank of Japan, had taught the Prince world history and had interviewed fifty officials within the Ministry of International Trade and Industry. I had had a very privileged view of the workings of the Japanese civilization, and had discovered a new movement, the Cultural Revolution, within the Chinese civilization. I had opposed Communism by standing up to the tyrant Mao, who had been responsible for at least 20 million deaths of his opponents, and by attempting to 'nudge' China into its next historical phase. In doing so I had sided with the European civilization.

But perhaps most important of all, I had learned that world history was the sum of all the sequences of events within a number of different world civilizations, some of which I was about to tour.

Civilizations: South-East Asian and Indian civilizations

I spent three weeks returning home on my own through the Far East. My main university paid my first-class air fare in cash, and I flew second class and was able to stop off at 14 different cities, the hotel bills being covered by the difference between the first- and second-class fares. The tour, the full details of which are in my *Diaries*, provided an excellent review of civilizations and helped shape the historical view that eventually became *The Fire and the Stones*.

Tour of the Far East: Manila, Hong Kong, Macao, Singapore
My first stop was in Manila, where I absorbed the Spanish colonial background and visited places connected with the Japanese occupation and US liberation. I walked in Quiapo square and watched a Filipino being tied to a cross with ropes while lying on his back, to express his religious devotion. In the evenings I sensed the danger and decay of the place.

Next I widened my knowledge of Chinese influence. I flew to Hong Kong. I found a crowd near a "Danger" sign near the Peninsula Hotel. I joined them and was told there was a bomb in a red can, which I could see in the middle of the road 50 yards away. The bomb-disposal squad packed sandbags round it and shot it up with a pistol. There was a report like a thunderflash. Round the corner there was another bomb. I saw the bright yellow blast.

I went to Macao by hydrofoil and walked on the Portuguese waterfront and noted Maoist slogans and dress. I returned to Hong Kong past distant Chinese mountains in a causeway of setting sunlight. The next day I visited all the historical sites.

Then I flew on to Singapore, which was humid, visited the sites and went to Jahore across the causeway the Japanese used for their invasion during the Second World War. On the way back I passed some fire-walkers: yogis in yellow stood with bare, ash-marked feet near a fire that was already ashes.

Vietnam: Saigon, visit to Bien Hoa
Next I looked at the South-East Asian civilization in Indo-China. I flew to Saigon. The Vietnam war was being fought and our plane was shelled as we came in. We had to climb steeply and our bodies were exposed to the pressure of many Gs. We approached the airport from a different direction, almost nosediving onto the runway.

Saigon was a wartime city with girls camped in the corridors of the Des Nations hotel, and there were currency dealers everywhere. I had a drink on the veranda of the Continental (where Graham Greene sat while visiting South Vietnam for *The Quiet American*). That night from my hotel roof I saw the distant flash of a bomb across the river and flares, and heard the distant thump of guns.

The next day, acting from an inner compulsion to seek out danger, I went to Bien Hoa in an American army bus with anti-grenade mesh over the windows. I just got in, wearing mufti, and travelled with several uniformed GIs. We drove along an insecure road that was frequently mined and ambushed by the Viet Cong, over the river and through palms and swamp land, past rural villages of corrugated hovels and melon-stalls. Eventually we came to Bien Hoa air base, several large compounds enclosed in barbed wire and sandbags, where there were dozens of transport planes. I looked, aware that the base would be significant in the future. (The base would be attacked by the Viet Cong during the Tet Offensive of 1968 and would be stormed and captured by them on 25 April 1975 during the decisive battle of the war.)

I returned on the army bus to Cholon, the Chinese suburb of Saigon. I got off the bus intending to wander in Chinatown. But a storm loomed. There was thunder, and a GI waved me into the Cholon base without checking my security. I found myself sheltering from the rain with uniformed GIs, who invited me to take a beer from a very tall fridge. Then a wall-mounted phone rang. "Answer it," a GI called. I duly did. An American voice said, "General —— here, have you got the address of the Annapolis Trenching Billet? It's on the board in front of you." I looked at the board and gave the General the address and hung up. Then a guard whistled and said, "Your bus is here." I ran out through the rain and got on another bus, which took me into Central Saigon.

My foray into the countryside round Saigon had convinced me that the Americans had an almost impossible task in winning the war. Each base was permanently under siege, and the Americans were so lax about security that sympathisers with the Viet Cong could easily infiltrate them, just as I had done.

Cambodia: Angkor Wat, Phnom Penh, Prince Sihanouk
I flew on to Angkor via Phnom Penh and visited the stunning Khmer ruins in the jungle, which closed round them in the 13th century. I was driven through the jungle in a motorcab (a box hooked onto a motor bike). I looked at the Buddhist and Hindu statues, including several of a detached Siva. It was barely safe as the Khmer Rouge were in the jungle. (They had not yet overrun Cambodia.)

I flew back from Siem Reap to Phnom Penh, a pleasant French town on the rivers Sap and Mekong. Prince Sihanouk, the leader, arrived at the airport in a convoy, sitting beside the President of Mauretania. I was driven to Le Royal and then travelled round Phnom Penh by *cyclo-pousse* or *trishaw* (a three-wheeled pedalled vehicle), pedalled by a boy. Later that night he took me into an opium den. I was invited to smoke opium but declined.

Next morning he pedalled me again. We encountered a crowd waiting for Sihanouk. He parked his *trishaw* and joined the throng that lined the kerb. When Sihanouk passed in his limousine the boy jumped up and down, cheering loudly and clapping his hands over his head. Then he got back on his *trishaw* as though nothing had happened.

Earlier I had asked him, "Do you like the US better than the Viet Cong?"

He had said, "I no say, I too small. If I say, policeman handcuff me and take me to prison."

I have sometimes wondered how he fared under Pol Pot. Did he survive the killing fields by leaping up and down and cheering and clapping, the "small" man's way of surviving a tyranny?

Mr Van of Viet Cong Embassy in Phnom Penh
I had the idea of going to North Vietnam to write some newspaper articles, and the next morning I visited the Viet Cong Embassy in Phnom Penh. I was told to clear off by an old woman, and was manhandled and bundled out of the gate by an old man and a fearsome young tough. I kept ringing the bell at the gate and the old woman reappeared with a form which included the heading *"motif"*. I filled in the form in French and she took it back in.

Eventually she returned all smiles, and I was shown into the Embassy and a room with a glass case, a picture of Ho Chi Minh and a replica of Tran Van Dang, a Viet-Cong terrorist, at the sandbagged stake awaiting public execution in a Saigon marketplace in 1965. (Blindfolded and tied by his elbows he waved his hands and shouted, "Down with the Americans" before he was shot by South-Vietnamese soldiers.)

In came a mild Mr Van, a smiling man with a parting down the middle and a blue shirt. I asked to be taken behind Viet Cong lines with a view to writing an article in a Sunday newspaper. He wrote down my details, including the dates of my visit to China, and said he would refer them to HQ. On the way out the three chucker-outers saluted me. Nothing ever came of my approach.

Bangkok, Calcutta, Katmandu, Delhi – and Paradise
I left rural Cambodia and flew to industrial, built-up Bangkok. Early the next morning I visited the floating market in a boat, nosing through brown-green water past hovels on stilts and *sampans* (flat-bottomed skiffs) laden with fruit. I then visited the royal palace and marvelled at the images on the temples.

Then I flew on to the Indian civilization. I landed in Calcutta, and drove from the airport through paddy-fields and palms, passing bare-footed stragglers and squatters in the road.

That evening firecrackers celebrated the coming of the goddess as a sacred cow. I left my hotel and walked round town, stepping over and round the hopeless homeless lying on the streets. Some were limply propped against trees or lying on steps, making no attempt to cover their genitals.

My first impression of India in Calcutta was of pink and dirty stucco and balconies, honking horns and *rickshaws* (light two-wheeled hooded vehicles), and everywhere crowds of people, and many poor. I saw them at dawn as I drove to the airport, sleeping in the open air without bedding or cover; just sleeping where they happened to be as if self-preservation no longer mattered.

I flew on to Katmandu past Everest, which was bright white on a range against blue sky. I walked in the medieval Nepalese town's fresh mountain air among hens and sheep. A square tower on which was the enormous face of a curly-eyed Buddha looked down on me.

I was accosted by a Tibetan refugee, an anti-Maoist guerrilla seeking to raise funds to buy weapons to use against the Chinese. He took me off to a barn-like house. We climbed up wooden steps to the straw-covered first floor and sat on sacks of oats, and on the straw he unrolled *thanka*s (Tibetan silk paintings showing a Buddhist deity or scene). I bought one for $8. Soon afterwards I encountered an ex-Gurkha and for $30 bought a *thanka* of Yamantaka, conqueror of death (one of the fierce protective deities whose worship was introduced by Padmasambhava in the 8th century).

Later I went up to the first floor of another barn and for $21 bought a 400-year-old *mandala* (sacred art showing a circle). It was of a cosmic clock. That night once again there were fireworks for the goddess – the festival was a day later in Katmandu than in Calcutta – and I was told that the fireworks were to wake people up to the sacred cow.

I flew on to Delhi and visited the old Red Fort and the Mughal Palace, the design of which reflects the Muslim Paradise. I read the Persian couplet inscribed in the palace: "If there is a Paradise on earth, it is here, it is here, it is here." I thought about the role of the Mughal period within the Indian civilization.

Istanbul, Budapest, Vienna, Paris

My next stop was Istanbul, where I visited the Byzantine and Ottoman ruins, which I would later place in the Byzantine-Russian and Arab civilizations respectively. I visited the Sultan's palace and *hareem*, Hagia Sophia (the church Justinian built) and finally Mehmet's Topkapi palace.

After that I considered the Austro-Hungarian empire. I stopped at Budapest and visited both sides of the Danube, and then went to Vienna in pursuit of the Habsburgs. I visited the Kapuziner crypt which contains the Habsburgs' tombs, and the Summer and Winter palaces.

Finally I went to Paris and stayed in St-Germain-des-Prés among the Maoists and drank in Sartre's Café Bonaparte. I visited the British Council to see if there might be work teaching English as a foreign language in Paris.

Return to England with experience of civilizations

I landed at Heathrow, and found Caroline and Nadia waiting for me. As a result of my time away from the European civilization I had got to know the Arab, Japanese, Chinese, Byzantine-Russian, South-East Asian and Indian civilizations, and numerous empires within those civilizations. I had a clear concept of Western values and the Free World, and had rejected totalitarian values.

This had come about because I had been on a series of wanderings, a kind of Odyssey, through the political causes of our time. I had not left England in 1963 to study world history – I had sought to absorb the wisdom of the East, and had done so with considerable success – but I returned in 1967 with a better grounding in world civilizations than I could possibly have expected. I seemed to have acquired this knowledge by accident, but it shaped the historical view that eventually became *The Fire and the Stones* and as it was crucial to that work had I been led to it by Providence rather than by chance or accident?

I thought again that I had achieved an enormous amount during my four years in Japan. In the course of my journey I had become a poet and, having located a new centre in myself, I was stable and growing. I had worked hard and had been trained into adopting the Japanese work ethic. I was sure I would experience new growth through my improved knowledge of European society and world civilizations and was on course to achieve the wisdom of my 'Shadow'.

It seemed inconceivable that all this was about to be shattered by an upheaval that at the time would seem catastrophic. I did not know it would complete my rebuilding of myself and bring me face to face with Reality.

PART TWO

Path through a Dark Wood

"The woods are lovely, dark and deep
But I have promises to keep,
And miles to go before I sleep,
And miles to go before I sleep."
        Robert Frost,
        'Stopping by Woods on a Snowy Evening'

CHAPTER 4

Way of Loss: Dark Night of the Soul,
the Purgative Way

"There's a saying of Goethe's.... Beware of what you wish for in youth, because you will get it in middle life."

James Joyce, *Ulysses*, Scylla and Charybdis (episode 9), 1922

The next four years I lived in the outer world and progressively encountered difficulties in my everyday life, and desolation. Looking back, I can see that I entered a Dark Night of the Soul, a crisis that is more properly called a Dark Night of the Senses as it is a purification of the senses. My Purgative Way detached my senses from the life of my ego. Arguably this began as early as late 1965, after my first illumination and centre-shift, my First Mystic Life. I came to see it as a Way of Loss – a loss of my ego's attachments and a strengthening of the new centre I was now living through. Outwardly all that I had been attached to went wrong while I underwent a subterranean purification of my inner being.

Episode 10:

Establishment and Revolution

Years: 1967–1969
Locations: Loughton; London; Swanage; Tunis; Carthage; Sabratha; Leptis
Magna; Tripoli; Western Libya
Works: *The Eternicide*; *The Age of Cartoon*
Initiatives: proposes and works for pro-Western *coup* in Libya; articles on Libya
for *The Daily News*; recruited by SIS

"And the fifth angel sounded, and I saw a star fall from heaven unto the earth.... And there came out of the smoke locusts upon the earth."

Revelation 9.1, 3

My interest in world civilizations had led me to be interested in revolu-

231

tionary change: the forcible replacement of an old system by a new system. Vietnam had concentrated my mind. It was a time of revolutionary protest in Europe and Asia, and I was interested in the change that seemed to be coming to England.

In my next episode I was torn between assisting the Establishment and changing it. I sympathised with defending the West's international stance *and* with internationalist change and revolution against the West. I had had elements of both these stances within myself ever since I sympathised with the Young Conservatives and Angry Young Men at the same time. From within the London Establishment I followed the revolutionary movements in different parts of the world, including the Viet Cong in Vietnam, where I had just been.

Establishment: England
We lived in the maisonette I had bought, 9 Crescent View, Loughton. Crescent View is a terrace of brick flats with a sloping lawn. Our flat was two-bedroomed on the ground floor. Two very old ladies lived in two of the other three flats off our entrance.

Living in Loughton, teaching current affairs to Japanese in London
Nadia started at my old school, Oaklands, in nearby Albion Hill, just across the High Road. The Saturday after we moved in there were fireworks in the school field. Several hundred people attended and the parents served food in the hard tennis-court. I encountered Miss Lord, my old Headmistress, dragging a box of crisps behind her, and had a chat. In the afternoons I walked up Albion Hill past Oaklands and Mabel Reid's cottage to look at the cows in the field across Nursery Road. The following Friday we took Nadia in for tea with Mabel Reid and sympathised with her near-blindness. It was inconceivable that in 15 years' time I would buy Oaklands from Miss Lord and Miss Reid.

Twice a week I went to London to give English lessons to Japanese. I spent one day with the traders of JETRO (The Japanese External Trading Organisation), who were linked to the Ministry of Internal Trade and Industry. I had been introduced to them by Yamashita. They were in offices on the corner of Park Lane and Oxford Street. I spent another day with the bankers of the Bank of Japan near St Paul's. What I earned covered our weekly food but otherwise we were living off what I had saved in Japan. It now seems a very basic existence: we had no car, which meant walking everywhere (and keeping fit), and we had no central heating, which meant keeping warm with paraffin heaters.

Sometimes I walked in the Forest, scuffling through copper-beech leaves. We frequently visited my mother at Journey's End, and sometimes went to

Dulwich to see Caroline's parents. In the evenings I often met my younger brother Jonathan, who was training to be an accountant. He had been on audits when he had done nothing but tick, and it fell to me to encourage him to persevere with his ticking.

I met John Ezard a couple of times in The Standard. He was about to start with *The Guardian* in London. He told me: "I've got to the top of a profession I entered by accident. I went to the local *Gazette* office to apply for a post as library assistant, and was offered a job as local reporter, and have gone on from there." He still professed to be uninterested in philosophy or the meaning of life: "My attitude is Wittgensteinian and Cambridge."

At the end of November I met Tuohy in Soho, and drank with him at the Yorkminster. We lunched in an Italian restaurant round the corner.

In December it snowed heavily. I went for a walk in the Forest and the tree-trunks had snow on them. The hoof marks were frozen and the leaves were crunchy, and there was a golden sun. The ponds had ice and snow on them, the air was cold. I had ruddy cheeks and took great strides and revelled in the sounds my feet made, the smack, crunch and crack of my progress over the snow. I rejoiced as the frosty tiles of cottages showed through trees.

The snow lay on the ground over Christmas until mid-January. Then there was a thaw and, to her disappointment, Nadia's snowman dwindled. I took Nadia up to see the cows. The next weekend we all went for a walk with Mabel Reid, and Miss Lord, Nadia's Headmistress, drove by and stopped for a chat.

We attended a wine-and-cheese party at Oaklands when the Parents Association made presentations to both Miss Lord and Miss Reid to mark the School's 30th anniversary. We attended an Open Evening at Oaklands soon afterwards. I talked near the piano in the Assembly Hall and then looked round the School with a couple whose daughter was in Nadia's class. The husband criticised a wall display which said "I love little pussy, his coat is so warm".

"It's not 'pussy', it's 'cat'," he said. "It needs someone to come in and modernise Oaklands." It was unimaginable that one day I would be doing the modernising.

Nadia was very settled at school, full of who had fallen over and the doings of the other children. I was aware that we would soon have to go abroad again as our money was slowly running out. It grieved me to see her so settled and to know she would have to be uprooted. Caroline was equally unhappy about the prospect of going abroad again.

Confusion is an aspect of the onset of a Dark Night, and all round me there seemed to be confusion. Mrs. Smith, one of the old ladies in our block, kept hallucinating. She imagined a "busman" was sitting menacingly in her

233

room and repeatedly knocked on our door to ask our protection. On one occasion she fled the building. It was a struggle to concentrate on the novel I was trying to finish, *The Eternicide*. She died in March. Then Mrs. Gray, the other old lady in our block, took to wandering off at night and had to be brought back. Eventually she had a fall and was taken to hospital with a broken thigh. She died under the anaesthetic. I had dealings with the relatives of both Mrs. Smith and Mrs. Gray, who involved me in the practicalities of clearing their flats. There were practical problems involving my family in Journey's End, and I was sucked in to help sort them out. Caroline and I were drawn into other people's emotional turmoil. The clarity I had found in Japan was elusive.

Tuohy had invited us to stay in his cottage while he was away: Tumbler's Bottom, Kilmersdon, Somerset, a stone slate-coloured building on the edge of a meadow. We stayed a couple of days. We absorbed the Somerset village life and visited Bath and Weston-super-Mare. We returned home via Avebury and Silbury Hill, whose mound I recognised as a *ziggurat* built to the moon-goddess.

On our return Caroline raised the prospect of our living abroad again. She had accompanied me to Iraq and Japan, but she said she did not want to be cut off from England, and her family, again. I explained that one more posting would pay off the mortgage on our flat, and that we could then sell it in July 1970 and buy a house. I would look to start a new job in England in September 1970. Caroline was not happy at the thought of leaving England, and we argued about working abroad once more.[1]

Revolution: protest

1968 was a year of protest, largely because of increasing US involvement in the war in Vietnam. It was the year of student protests. Early in the year there were student protests in Spain, France and Germany.

17-March Grosvenor-Square demonstration against Vietnam war

On 17 March there was a big demonstration against the Vietnam war in the UK, in Grosvenor Square, London, where the new US Embassy had been built in 1960. The leading figure was Tariq Ali, an Oxford student who had organised the demonstration on behalf of the Vietnam Solidarity Campaign against the war in Vietnam. The actress Vanessa Redgrave, wearing a white headband, headed the march along with Tariq Ali. The demonstrators began to tear up a fence and hedge and throw stones, earth, firecrackers and smoke bombs. Mounted police rode at them. Eighty-six people were injured. Vanessa Redgrave was allowed to enter the US Embassy to deliver a protest, and later she spoke at the rally in Trafalgar Square.

Soviet invasion of Czechoslovakia, student revolution in France
Meanwhile in Czechoslovakia the Prague Spring had begun with the election of Dubček as First Secretary of the Communist Party of Czechoslovakia in January.

In May there was violent unrest against de Gaulle in France. It was revolutionary and anarchist. The leading figure was Daniel Cohn-Bendit, 'Dany le Rouge' ('Danny the Red'), who was active in both France and Germany. His expulsion from the University of Nanterre was cancelled as a result of the demonstrations. There were calls for the beginning of a revolution in the UK on the French model.

At 'Free-Greece' demonstration
I had been following these events with my Japanese pupils. The Japanese wanted to know whether the student protests against the Vietnam war would lead to a rebellion and revolution. In Greece the Government had been overthrown in April 1967 by a military *junta* led by a group of colonels. Two of the Japanese had asked me about a 'Free Greece' demonstration that was looming. I decided to look in on the demonstration so I could talk about it in coming one-to-one classes. I drove to Trafalgar Square.

There was a platform near the National Gallery, and a crowd round it, in which I stood. Below me there was a sea of faces surrounded by police. Officials read messages from representatives of the Labour Party, the unions and the Greek Patriotic Front. The star of *Never on Sunday*, Melina Mercouri, spoke, an impressive fusion of sensation, emotion and thought. Kingsley Amis was standing behind me, lifting Greek children so they could see over the heads of the crowd. Then there was a march on the Greek Embassy, up the Haymarket, up Regent Street, into Oxford Street.

I went with them. We marched twenty or thirty abreast, behind banners, silent. It was a brisk march, it felt like being in an army on the move, all following one idea. There were occasional calls: "*De-mo-kra-ti-a* in, in, in; fasceesm out, out, out." And: "Dya want democracy?" "Yeah." "Dya want freedom?" "Yeah." "Dya want dictatorship?" "Nah." "Dya want fascism?" "Nah." Outside the Greek Embassy there was booing, whistling and shouting, "Fascists." Then we were in Park Lane, queuing to cross the road and join a rally in Hyde Park, and there was a sense of anti-climax.

I caught a passing bus to return to my car. The end of the march had felt like an uprising, but the thousands who marched were powerless to do anything to change the rule of the colonels in Greece. I was pleased to have made contact with the new political consciousness that had stirred in Britain.[2]

Spring turned to summer. The pear blossom in the garden at Journey's End was like melting snow, everywhere leaves were tender and green.

Daisies lay like breadcrumbs on the grass, and in the Forest ponds wriggling tadpoles clustered round weed like thorns. I gave a lecture on Japan ('Understanding the Japanese') in a huge house overlooking Epping Forest. We went down and stayed with Tuohy in Somerset.

Prospect of lecturing in Libya

At the end of June the British Council wrote and offered me a lectureship in Tripoli, Libya, where I had nearly gone the previous year. I would have to appear before a board on 10 July. Our money was running out, and the prospect of Tripoli had reopened my ambition to go to Ghadames and write *The Lost Englishman*, a title I had had in mind for some time.[3]

I now had several discussions with Caroline, pointing out again that we would be able to save enough to pay off our mortgage. Caroline did not like Essex places or Essex people –[4] she found them cold and unhistorical, false and lacking in taste – but she was still reluctant to uproot Nadia and still wanted to stay within reach of her family. It was again evident that although she had accompanied me to the dangers of Iraq and the climatic extremes of Japan, she did not really want to go to Libya – or anywhere else outside the UK. In our discussions I felt ourselves being pulled apart by a decision that had to be taken on financial grounds, and I tried very hard to restore our former relationship.

I had finished my novel, *The Eternicide*. It needed more work doing to it, and I was now interested in the 1968 student revolution, and in the anarcho-syndicalism and Maoist revolutionary outlook that had swept Britain from France. I wrote a TV script, *The Busman*, about the hallucinations and death of our neighbour, Mrs. Smith. I was already planning my next novel, which became *The Age of Cartoon*. It was about revolution in Britain and the demand for justice. I was invited to a gathering at Holmhurst in Manor Road, Loughton, which became Beechwood in that novel.

Biggs-Davison was present and we discussed the student uprising and Maoism. During the buffet supper he invited me to the Commons: "Get in touch with me at the House. This isn't a conventional ending to a conversation. I mean it, next week."

Drink with Biggs-Davison at the Commons

Biggs-Davison's secretary told me he had suggested 11 July. At his instigation we had a drink on the House-of-Commons terrace the day after my interview for Libya, which seemed to go well. We discussed revolutionary change, the student revolution and publications such as *Black Dwarf* (which Tariq Ali was heavily involved in), which I had been reading. He told me, "I've been reading *Black Dwarf* too. I was talking to an ex-Chief of MI6 recently." I understood him to mean Sir Dick White, who ceased to be Chief of the SIS in 1968. "He says this student business is almost over."[5]

I told him I was fascinated by the student mentality that rejects the System, a variation on the Outsider theme. I presented the Maoist revolutionary's point of view from my knowledge of China and my approach to the Viet Cong in Phnom Penh.

Concern over Caroline's brother Richard's marriage

The day after my meeting with Biggs-Davison I heard that I was definitely going to Libya. I told Caroline that we would be having a car, that we would be paying off our mortgage and that we would take root in England in July 1970. That was the deal.

We had been to see Caroline's half-brother Richard Schorer-Nixon in Kimbolton, Huntingdonshire a couple of times. Richard had served with the British army in Palestine in the 1940s. After our first visit we had driven to Little Gidding as I had taught Eliot's poem 'Little Gidding' while teaching his *Four Quartets* in Japan. During our next visit I absorbed the British village life of Huntingdon, including the social structure round the local beagles. During that visit it became apparent that Richard and his wife were to separate, and Caroline's parents asked if I would talk to him.

We returned and stayed with Richard and his wife on 19 July. I had a long talk with him on his lawn. He told me his marriage was an empty "snail shell": "Snails die and leave their shells behind." The next day Richard drove me to the Bedford Regatta and among the crowds sitting on the embankment with feet dangling near the green river I saw the young girl who would become his second wife. I did my best to shore up, reinforce and restore his marriage, but the problems were too great and I returned to Dulwich to report that my mission had been unsuccessful.

My inability to change Richard's mind had an effect on Caroline. In a weird way she seemed to feel that if he could break with his wife over issues, then she could break with me over the issue of where we lived.

21-July Grosvenor-Square demonstration against Vietnam war

The next day I was due to attend another demonstration against the Vietnam war in London. Richard asked if he could come too and I met him near Trafalgar Square, which was three-quarters filled. We listened to the speakers. I was there purely as an observer, to have a look.

The march set off up the Haymarket. We marched behind a banner. There was chanting up Charing Cross Road and we turned left down Oxford Street. There were frequent stops. Many of the marchers held red books like those waved in the Chinese Cultural Revolution. In Duke Street everyone linked arms and jumped up and down, shouting, "Ho, ho, Ho Chi Minh" (the ruler of North Vietnam), and a group wearing Chinese clothes shouted out: "What shall we have for breakfast? Let's eat the American Ambassador for breakfast."

Grosvenor Square was enclosed by cordons of police and there were police horses. Suddenly the demonstrators at the front burst through the cordons into the gardens and fought with the police. The mounted police exercised crowd control, and headed the demonstrators back towards the march. We stopped and the demonstrators round us burst through a hedge and captured part of the garden. They broke off branches and threw them at the police. There were fist fights. We were told "Keep moving" by police using megaphones. As we moved out to Park Lane, scaffolding was torn down and boxes were set on fire near a petrol station.

The violence spilled over into Park Lane, and there was stone-throwing outside the Hilton Hotel. Now the mob ran amok, tearing up pillar-boxes, overturning cars and smashing Rolls-Royce windows. We were chased by the police. A bloodstained Egyptian near me yelled, "Fascists."

There were cries of "To the palace" and "Re-vol-ut-ion, re-vol-ut-ion".

For a while it seemed possible that the mob would rush down Constitution Hill, storm Buckingham Palace and overthrow the House of Windsor. But the march carried on down to Piccadilly. Demonstrators tore down a Union Jack and gathered in Piccadilly Circus.

Richard and I caught a bus to Marble Arch and found a Joe Lyons tea-house. We ordered lemon tea and apple strudel and cream, and later parted to return to our respective homes.[6]

Leaving to lecture at the University of Libya, Tripoli: multiplicity
I had devoted little thought to poetry, although I had written some lyrics and had thought about Old Norse saga. Now that I was about to leave England I thought hard about the poems that might be ahead of me. In early August I had the idea for a poetic epic, a vast work for which I made preliminary notes. In early September, while pondering 'The Silence' I came up with the idea of using the sonata as a poetic form in another poem. This idea was implemented in 'The Four Seasons' (1975). In early October I had the idea for a poem that would be based on Rodin's Gates of Hell. I implemented this idea in *The Gates of Hell* (1969–1972). I identified my art as a Baroque art.[7]

However, that summer I somehow lost my way. I became sidetracked from my path into my Japanese pupils. I took one of them to meet Len Murray (later Lord Murray), who was no. 2 at the TUC. I was diverted into the student revolution. I digressed into TV drama: the TV script about the death of Mrs. Smith, our neighbour, *The Busman*.

In September I twice drove round the villages of the Essex-Suffolk border and Constable country. I would have loved to have lived in one of these villages and not gone abroad. I walked in Epping Forest: across Warren Hill heath to Grimston's Oak, up to Peartree Plain, along Green Ride, through Long Hills and back across Fairmead Bottom. All the way the wind swooshed in the trees and tugged at the grasses on the heath. I took in the conkers and acorns, the hawthorn berries and black elderberries, and the hips and haws. I wrote in my *Diaries*: "I will never be able to tear myself away from this part of the world."[8] But like Masaccio's Adam I once again became an exile from Paradise.

I left for Libya having forgotten what I was looking for. I had lost the clear view of my direction that I had discovered in Japan. I found my relationships with my mother and solicitor brother had become strained. Caroline now doubted what we were doing.

It is typical of a Dark Night that what has before seemed clear now appears confused as all the ego's worldly attachments and desires break down. In the bathroom at Crescent View there were two mirrors, and as I stood between them, naked after a bath, I saw in one mirror: image behind image of myself receding ever further. I was lost in multiplicity.

Revolution and Libya
Drive through France and Tunisia: Carthage
We drove to Libya in the green Volkswagen Beetle 1200 I had bought. We crossed France, stopping at Versailles and Fontainebleau, and spent a night in Avignon. We visited the Palace of the Popes the next morning. I looked for, but could not find, the erotic paintings in Pope Alexander VI's bedroom which Buchanan had seen. We drove on to Marseilles and took a boat for Tunis. Lying awake on a bunk in the creaking, throbbing cabin I briefly glimpsed my true path: "I am the author of 'The Silence', and don't even think of that, for most of the time.... I am the author of 'The Silence', my life is a quest for the meaning of life."[9]

We slept in Tunis, a white town with blue shutters and Arabs wearing red skullcaps. Early next morning we drove to the ruins of Carthage, and I stood for a long time by green water lapping under an orange sun over distant black mountains and thought of Hannibal, Scipio and St Augustine. We drove through Tunisia, past a Roman amphitheatre and through a dust-storm to Libya.

Tripoli
Tripoli was a yellow Italian town spread across sand interspersed with palm trees, ugly modern buildings and petrol stations. It dozed alongside a silver sea. We spent our first night there in the depressing National Hotel, all marble floors and surly servants and greasy food. Next morning I visited the University of Libya and met my Head of Department, a severe-looking bespectacled UN-appointed New-Zealander; the grim Dean, who spoke no

English; and various University officials at the Faculty of Teacher Training.

I returned to Caroline and Nadia and we met up with one of the suited Arab property agents who had hung around the National bar. He drove us in his wide car to meet our future landlord, Mahmoud Ben Nagy, a young, handsome ex-army man from an old Turkish Ottoman family who encouraged us to call him 'Ben'.

The next day Ben took us to a flat in Collina Verde. It was down a sandy lane opposite the Ben Ashur mosque, and faced a greengrocer's. The flat was on the ground floor and had a raised bulging Turkish balcony with a gold-coloured rail that looked down on a small garden with an orange-tree and a grapevine, under which I parked the Volkswagen. Inside there were two bedrooms, and all the floors were marble.

Caroline in the garden near Ben Ashur mosque, Tripoli, 1969

We took it and there, a couple of days later, we unpacked the flat-packed Bulgarian furniture the University provided, and, without any assembly instructions whatsoever, somehow assembled it. The furniture was inade-quate and we had to buy many essen-tials to set up home in addition to paying import duty on the car. An advance on my salary was soon spent. Full details of this time can be found at the beginning of *The Libyan Revolution*.

As we had not got straight our landlord, Ben, invited us to a candlelit dinner which was served by his servant Ahmad in his vast villa in Giorgimpopoli. Ben spoke immaculate English and there we met his two brothers and learned that he had been no. 3 in the army with the rank of Colonel. His younger brother told me that he had resigned because his best friend had been assassinated in Benghazi on the orders of the army chief. Ben was rumoured to be next on the list as he had been in Egypt during Nasser's Revolution and in Iraq during Kaseem's Revolution, and was regarded as a dangerous potential revolutionary. Now he had his own property company.

Libya in November 1968 was a virtual colony of the West, and supplied the West with cheap oil. It was still ruled by King Idris and his pro-Western ministers, who sold plots of the country to oil-prospecting companies. It consisted of a few towns, mostly near the coast, and vast stretches of desert. There was a large Western community who manned the schools and univer-sities, hospitals and many companies.

We soon found our way around Tripoli, and drove down Sha'ra Adrian Pelt to Castle Square and the Old City, and ventured into its narrow arched streets and took in old men sitting in *barracans* (blankets descended from the Roman *toga*, one end thrown over a shoulder) and women peeping from white *farrashiyas*. It was 1389 in the Muslim calendar, and some parts of Tripoli had only just begun to move out of a mental Middle Ages. We drove back up Istiqlal Street to the King's Palace.

I soon settled into the teaching at the University of Libya. The Head of Department had individual interviews with us British lecturers and handed us out timetables. I met my classes and began to learn their names and test their levels. There was less literature than in Japan, and more language. I soon adapted to the new circumstances: North Africans, many from the desert, who wanted to teach and saw the West as a passport to getting on.

To Sabratha with Col. Ben Nagy
The next Sunday (3 November) Ben drove us to Sabratha, a Roman town by the sea that was not unlike Carthage. It was one of the three towns of *Tripolis* (the other two being Tripoli and Leptis Magna). On the way Ben gave us an account of Libyan history and described how the King opposed the Italians and won independence. I gazed at the Temple of Isis and Apuleius's basilica.

On the way home we talked about the future of Libya after the King. I asked if the Crown Prince would be strong enough to change Libya to the British system of free parties without the use of the army. Ben said that the army had no role in Libya because there would be no popular support.

We passed peasants who were scraping a living off the dry land. I talked about the poor, who, I said, should be liberated from their poverty by Libyan intellectuals such as him.

I was genuinely concerned about the Libyan poor, just as I had been concerned about the Iraqi poor. Libya was oil-rich, and the oil wealth had not reached the poor. Ben said that the King was responsible for not distributing Libya's oil wealth.

I saw that it would be in Britain's interests to have an additional supply of cheap, good-quality Libyan oil, and that a new deal might benefit Libya and be shared with the poor. I said, "King Idris is an old man now, he's nearly 80 and pro-West. He should hand over to a group of younger men who are pro-Western."

Ben said, "A *coup* would have to be planned very carefully, when both the King and the Crown Prince are in one of the two cities, Tripoli or Benghazi. Failure might lead to the secession of Cyrenaica, which would be bad for the country."[10]

As we drove back in a green sunset I realised that Ben had admitted that he had been considering starting a revolution.

The Daily News: *Chatter and Ansari*
Now I was in on his secret, further invitations followed and I met his circle. Two days later he invited us to his villa for *mafroum* (vegetables stuffed with mincemeat) and we met Shukri Ghanem, a young partly-Turkish oil executive who spoke faultless English and would become Libya's Prime Minister. He said, "Four teachers in your college are now in your Foreign Office."

The next night we were invited to a party Ben held. Ten single girls – teachers, nurses and UN secretaries – drank whisky with army and police colonels and a moustached, mournful newspaper magnate, Chatter. Shukri introduced me to him: "Nicholas is at the University. Perhaps he will write some articles for you." Chatter told me that he brought out *The Daily News*, an English-language paper. He said: "You might write some articles for it." But he said I would have to write under a pseudonym as I had a University contract.

I visited Chatter in his office near Castle Square. He sat tiredly at a desk, looking very mournful. He said almost immediately, "See Mr Ansari, our director, to discuss work."

Ansari was an Egyptian in his early forties with tinted glasses. He had been expecting me and said, "I suggest you write things on Libya for the Government."

I returned to Chatter who said he disagreed with what Ansari had suggested. He would rather I edited journalists' proofs.

I went back to Ansari, who said, "I disagree. That's too dead. You could summarise these two books."

I was being batted between Chatter and Ansari without any clear idea of what I would be doing, and I decided to let matters rest there for the time being.

I raised my bewilderment with Ben, who said: "You need to understand, Chatter is in partnership with the Minister of Information, who has nominated Ansari. So Ansari works for the Ministry of Information. He is a Government man. Chatter is not free to act without Ansari's approval."[11] He advised me not to sign anything and to work on a purely personal basis. Ben spoke authoritatively, like the leader of a revolution.

To Leptis Magna with Ben Nagy: talk of revolution to eliminate poverty and increase the flow of Libyan oil to the West
Soon afterwards, on 15 November, Ben took us in his large car past white beaches towards Leptis Magna, Libya's main Roman town. On the way I saw a scarlet-robed Bedouin standing on red-brown earth, a tiny figure against a vast sky, and was moved by the tininess of man against the vastness of Nature.[12] I had a pantheistic sense that the One was everywhere. I felt close

to Roman – and Mediterranean – man. I responded to the North-African universe Camus had described further along the coast in Algeria.

Leptis Magna has acres of Roman streets and white ruins by a deep blue sea. Standing on mosaics among fallen torsos and sun-god heads, I soaked in the Roman atmosphere. On the way back I warmed to the wide open spaces and was concerned at the poverty of the Bedouins and Arabs we passed.

As we drove towards a green-and-orange sunset I asked Ben, "Do you feel you have a duty to change the lives of peasants like that, the poor?"

He said, "Yes, I do."

With an eye still on using the export of Libyan oil to benefit the poor I said, "Unless something happens those peasants will always be like that, struggling through poverty. Their lives won't improve."

Ben said, "I agree I have a responsibility to act for all the people when the time is right. But if I choose the wrong time I may ruin it for others. I would rather be a peasant. An intellectual worries about society, about justice. If you're an intellectual you suffer, you suffer."[13]

His revolution was now an open secret. He drove us back to his villa and invited us to stay to dinner. Shukri turned up.

Tripoli: meeting with Libyan ministers and intellectuals, a pro-Western coup – Ben Nagy and Shukri Ghanem

By now my everyday life had acquired a pattern. I woke to cocks crowing and the loud call from the mosque at the end of our sandy lane. In the mornings I left the flat and drove along sandy tracks and pitted roads to the University. There were a dozen Western lecturers (mostly British) in our small staff room, and I taught classes in English Language or Literature to groups of about twenty Arabs, a mixture of the very rich and very poor.

I returned home for lunch. Nadia had been at school, and in the afternoon I walked with her and Caroline along the sandy, cactus-lined lanes. I taught Nadia to ride her bicycle, running along behind her and letting go. There was always a group of Arabs sitting outside one-eyed Mohammed's greengrocer's and our *ghaffir* (gardener-caretaker), Milud, snoozed through the afternoon siesta in the shade of our garden.

Sometimes we went for a picnic among pines near the blue sea down the Homs Road, sometimes with another British-Council or teacher's family. Sometimes we had an Arab dinner with Ben, sometimes we were visited by Shukri. As the weeks went by Caroline – who had not wanted to come to Libya – became more distant from me. Sometimes I lay awake at night, and listened to hooting owls.

Ramadan came. Ben and Shukri had to fast during daylight hours for a month and contemplate the revealing of the *Koran* to the Prophet

Mohammed. The two of them came on 27 November and drank tea. Shukri told me his father had helped create the Tripolitanian Republic in 1918, and was therefore against King Idris, who was based in Cyrenaica. He said that Ben's uncle had represented Tripolitania and opposed Idris in 1949. It came out that Ben was also the Prime Minister's landlord.

They came again on 6 December with some *baklava*. Shukri explained it was a Turkish dish and that he was a quarter Turkish. He explained that the Libyans asked the Ottoman Turks to rule them in the 16th century. He made out that the Turks and the Arabs were equals until T.E. Lawrence divided them by saying that the Turks were the masters of the Arabs. I defended T.E. Lawrence's view of the Ottoman Turks and his moves to overthrow their imperialistic empire.

During Ramadan Caroline had taken to disappearing on long shopping trips on her own in the afternoons, after I had returned from work with lectures to prepare for the next day, and she withdrew from me in the evenings into tense silences. She would not discuss her change of outlook. She did not want to be touched. Nadia, who was six, was very affectionate ("I want to marry you") but I was very much on my own and felt I had lost my way in the outer world.

The end of Ramadan on 19 December was signalled by a blast from the Castle cannon. There was chanting and excited howling on the mosque's loudspeaker. The Feast, the *Eid*, had come. Fasting was at an end. Shukri came to celebrate and told me a Christmas story.[14]

We went to the Independence Day parade on 24 December. We watched columns of soldiers and armoured cars approach the Crown Prince in Castle Square. The Libyan Air Force and American thunderjets from the Wheelus Air Base roared overhead in what looked like a dress rehearsal for the coming *coup*.

On Christmas Day we went to my Head of Department's house. All the Western lecturers gathered for games, and brandy was lit in a blue flame, from which we all took hot snap dragons: raisins. It was strange to celebrate Christmas with views of sand, palms and a deep-blue sky through the windows.

It was now clear that Ben was completely committed to having a revolution. He went to Casablanca from Christmas to the New Year. He came round with Shukri on 5 January, bringing champagne and chocolates, and we discussed the King. Shukri said, "I would like to be Prime Minister one day, I am inspired by justice." They came round again on 17 January. Ben came by himself on 7 February and said he was going to Cairo – "with the man I went to Casablanca with, to secure our exits".

There was talk of who his President would be. Ben said, "You'll be the first to know when it happens. We'll make you British Ambassador. For sure.

There won't be a British Ambassador unless it is you. You will also be in charge of dealing with Western companies wanting to buy plots of Libyan land to prospect for oil. Of course, you will be well remunerated for doing this. And the poor will benefit as we will make sure the money reaches them. All the Western oil companies will have to deal with you."

The way he presented it I would be presiding over business worth billions of dollars and would become rich in the process. I reflected that his plans for revolution now mirrored the revolutionary outlook of the hero in my novel, *The Age of Cartoon*, and there was harmony between my writing and this part of my outer life.

King Idris

Nothing much happened until mid-March. On 13 March I saw the King sitting in the back of his Rolls-Royce, an old man with a yellow beard, officially 79 the next day (although Ben insisted his true age was 87).

A few days later, after a blue storm over the Sahara, wind whirling and rain lashing, Ben invited us to dinner along with some single girls. I was at one end of the table and Shukri at the other.

There was a ferocious quarrel between Ben and Shukri as to who was to blame for the corruption of Libya. Ben said it was the King, "that stupid old man". He said, "He's done nothing for the ordinary Libyan people, the poor. I'd sooner have the Devil as King than Idris. The Tripolitanians only accepted the Sanusis during the lifetime of Idris. The Tripolitanians won't accept the Crown Prince."[15] Shukri said the Prime Minister (who was Ben's tenant) was to blame.

They shouted at each other across the table, striking increasingly dismissive and warlike postures. Then, eyes smouldering, Shukri stood up and strode out into the night.

I realised that the quarrel was really about whether there should be a *coup* against the King (Ben's view) or whether the King should merely dismiss the Prime Minister for not solving the problems of Libya's poor (Shukri's view).

Journalism: I write articles for The Daily News as 'the Barbary Gipsy'

At the beginning of April my financial state was parlous. We had had to borrow to furnish our flat adequately. The Italian store, Guido's, had given me credit, and each month I was only able to reduce what I owed by a little after settling Ben's rent and meeting living expenses. I needed some more income.

I decided to approach Shukri, who had introduced me to Chatter, and remind him that I had been taken on but that Chatter and Ansari had not been able to agree what I should be doing. I went to Shukri's office in the

Ministry of Economy and was shown up to his room by the Arab doorkeeper.

Shukri greeted me warmly. I said I was sorry he had had a disagreement with Ben. He smiled and said with great dignity, "I do not believe that the King is to blame for everything. I believe it is the Prime Minister's doing." I then came straight to the point. I asked him if he could fix me up with a job on Chatter's newspaper, *The Daily News*.

Shukri said I would have to work under a pseudonym and that I could get 50 or 60 Libyan pounds a month for perhaps two evenings' work a week. He duly spoke with Chatter.

And so it was that, walking past Ansari, I again sat in Chatter's office near Castle Square. Chatter said I could have the two centre pages in *The Daily News* to fill each Sunday. He wanted me to write articles on Libya that would appeal to the 60,000 Western expatriates in Libya. He said the pay would be 45 Libyan pounds a month, tax-free. I said that Shukri had suggested more, but he said he could not afford more.

I then sat with Ansari, who said I would be able to interview BOAC and the oil companies. I said I would start with an article on the Castle, which I could see out of the window.

He asked what my pseudonym would be. I had just written a poem titled 'Barbary Shores'. The Libyan coast was known in Ottoman times as the Barbary Coast. I reflected I was like Matthew Arnold's Scholar-Gipsy. I said, "I will be 'The Barbary Gipsy'."

And so for the next four months I wrote two pages in Tripoli's only English-language newspaper.[16] It came out weekly, on a Sunday, and I wrote the two centre pages about Libya. Each Friday, the Muslim day of rest, I set out with a camera and took photos of a Tripoli ruin or a Libyan tourist attraction such as Sabratha, Leptis Magna, Gourna or Suk Al-Jum'a (a camel market). I wrote the text each Saturday and delivered my copy to Ansari, who edited it. On Sunday the paper came out. I was told that King Idris was my earliest reader.

Expatriates sometimes asked me, "Have you read this week's Barbary Gipsy?"

"No," I'd say, and they would tell me what I had written. I concealed my smirk and feigned interest as if I were hearing it for the first time.

Ministers: the Minister for Petroleum
In early April Ben began hosting parties for a ring of Libyan ministers who wanted to bring about a pro-Western *coup*. I did not know that the King (who had no children) had told his ministers that he was getting too old to govern. He proposed to abdicate in favour of his nephew, the Crown Prince. However, the Crown Prince lacked charisma and Tripolitanians did not see

him as Idris's successor. A *coup* had formed round the Minister for Petroleum, who (it was made clear) would not be the President.

Ben gave several parties for the Minister for Petroleum, Khalifa Musa, a thickset, balding man with a husky voice and a fleck in one eye. He had been selling parcels of Libyan land to foreigners so that they could prospect for oil. Also present were the Minister of State for Prime Minister's Affairs, Beshir al-Muntasser, a rotund man with greased black hair who was related to the newly-independent Libya's first Prime Minister; and the Minister for Youth, a thin aquiline man with oiled hair and a moustache.

The parties began about 10.30 p.m. The ministers wore suits and drank whisky, and there were half a dozen Yugoslav nurses or secretaries. There was a good deal of banter and laughter. On one occasion the Governor of the Bank of Libya approached me, shaking coppers in a tin and saying drunkenly, "The Bank is bankrupt, please give generously." There was dancing to Western pop music that defied the Sanusi puritanism.

The parties ended about 2.30 a.m., usually when (as on 5 April) the Minister for Petroleum abandoned his previous restraint and pushed a Yugoslav girl into the fountain in Ben's garden. On one occasion he was pushed into the fountain himself, to general merriment.

On another occasion (on 10 April) he fell off a stool shaped like a horse's saddle onto the floor. He was too heavy to move. I know because, being the nearest to him when he fell, I stood over him, placed both hands under his fat shoulders and tried to lift him to a sitting position, without success. The Minister of State for Prime Minister's Affairs stood nearby, muttering, "He is quite all right, very bad chair. Khalifa, get up."

I felt I was losing myself in events that had ceased to be amusing. When I had first talked revolution with Ben, it was out of concern for the poor and to guarantee Western control of Libyan oil, not to line the pockets of these exploiters. From the outset I saw these parties for what they were. Next time I saw Ben I said prophetically: "Falling off a stool suggests 'there is something rotten in the state of Denmark'. If the King's administration is rotten, it will be overthrown, not from within but from without."

Ben looked sheepish and said, "No, no, that won't happen."

I wrote in my *Diaries* of "the Profumo-type follies of a newly independent, dying pre-populist state" and of "the Farouk extravaganza". And: "I join the damp orgies of the ruling class, but I sympathise with the poor."[17] Again, prophetically: "The follies and blatant luxuries of a dying order. A futile round of partying, utterly futile. And philistine. But like all excess, not unenjoyable. Farouk's Egypt all over again."[18] I was a fascinated observer of the decadent last rites of the ministers' too-publicly-run *coup*.

With Angus Wilson

In mid-April Angus Wilson, the British novelist, visited Tripoli. Ansari agreed that I should interview him for *The Daily News*. I rang him in his room at the Libya Palace Hotel and we met in the bar downstairs. He was a squat, ruddy-faced man with white hair who gushed impressions, and bickered with his secretary Tony. I did not know that he had been a code-breaker at Bletchley Park during the Second World War.[19]

He seemed to be very interested in my life and asked me many questions. He remarked: "This is a very philistine place. It's newly experienced wealth – from oil – like the Tudors, or else it's Puritanism, the tension here."[20] He was quite right. There was a tension between the ministers' follies and the Islamic puritanism of the veiled, peeping women and of some of my students, who hoped for a different kind of revolution, one that was alcohol-free.

The next day Angus Wilson gave a lecture at the University. He spoke without notes about the writer and society and how his novels began with the image of someone asking, 'How did I get like this?' He leapt from idea to idea with great fluency. I met him later and we walked to the waterfront so I could take his picture for the newspaper. He posed, leaning on the balustrade, crossing his legs.

We then walked along Adrian Pelt, discussing the novel. He said a writer should not have a distinctive, identifiable voice as he should not approach experience with a preconceived notion of it. I remarked that Tuohy had asserted that a writer should have a distinctive voice. He stopped and said: "You'd be well advised not to follow Tuohy's advice. He's very insecure, I know as he wrote me several letters. A writer should *not* have an identifiable voice. I can't read Greene because I know what it's going to be like, because of his individual, recognisable voice."[21] He told me that a writer is like a spy who operates under cover in the social world.

Like Sartre and Hemingway, Angus Wilson was public property and belonged to everybody, but for twenty minutes he had focused completely on me. When I left him I was glad I had ignored Tuohy's Wittgensteinian advice regarding 'The Silence'. I resolved to continue to be open to experience, to continue my quest to understand the universe without judging it in terms of preconceived pessimistic, social-rationalist ideas.

It was getting hot and we spent afternoons sunbathing on our roof, and once in a friend's garden, sitting under a mulberry tree near pomegranates in red-orange bloom. There were pink oleanders outside our bedroom window and the bougainvillaea was out in the Castle.

Chief of Police, Col. Ali Shilabi, gatecrashes a gathering of coup ministers

Ben disappeared to Tunis for three days. He visited me on his return and said he had been to Djerba, an island off Tunisia. He had *rendezvous*ed with someone important to his revolution.

Soon afterwards he held a large party. There were chiefs of police, immigration and customs present along with other second-ranking officials. There was a disturbance in Ben's front garden. Ben's servant Ahmad had discovered the current Chief of Police, Col. Ali Shilabi, spying on us through a window. He had climbed a high gate and dropped down into Ben's garden. There was disbelief among the ministers and police. Ben and several others ran out into the dark garden, and there was violent shouting.

I saw Shilabi. He was balding with a large dark moustache and wore an open-necked white shirt. Beshir said to me, "This is very bad, he is the Chief of Police. He is with Omar al-Shalhi." Omar al-Shalhi had been the King's chief adviser since 1964. The high gate was opened and Shilabi was manhandled and forcibly pushed out. Afterwards Ben said to me at the bar, "He wanted to find out who is here. He tried to breach our security. We will have to be more careful now."[22]

Ansari accused of being an Egyptian spy
So Omar al-Shalhi knew about the planned revolution now – and perhaps also the King. On 26 May it seemed that they might not be the only ones. I went into Chatter's office and Ansari beckoned to me. He said conspiratorially, "I have been accused of being an Egyptian spy. In a letter to the Prime Minister. No action is being taken because the letter was unsigned. But it may mean that I will be watched from now. I tell you, we must be careful. Let me know if you feel you are being watched."

He meant 'watched by the Libyan secret police', but I thought that if he *was* an Egyptian spy he might have heard about Ben's parties from Chatter, one of Ben's guests, and news of Ben's *coup* may have found its way to Egypt.

I was on my guard. I did not go to BOAC or the oil companies as he had directed, suspecting they were targets for Egyptian intelligence and that Ansari had tried to use me to obtain intelligence on British concerns for his Egyptian masters and their Soviet masters. During this part of the Cold War the KGB used Egyptian agents to gather information as proxies on its behalf.

Establishment: recruitment
Recruited to the SIS by Andrew Mackenzie
I had received a couple of letters from Buchanan in Japan. In the course of my reply I had told him about the goings-on among the ministers. I do not know whether there was any connection, but I now received a short letter from an Andrew Mackenzie of the British Embassy, referring to a meeting I

had had in London and asking me to meet him outside the Bank of North Africa on Friday 30 May (the Muslim day of rest) and bring the letter with me as he would ask for it back.

The timing of the letter was extraordinary. For we still owed Guido's more than £250, and I was wrestling with a choice: if both Caroline and I went to England during the summer vacation we would still be paying off Guido's in December. If I stayed and Caroline returned to England for a holiday the £100 not spent on my air ticket would pay off Guido's account sooner.

On Friday 30 May I loitered near the Bank of North Africa (a symbolic meeting place suggesting banknotes) in the late morning and was approached by a sprightly, lean, short man with a moustache and neatly-kept dark hair. He had a brisk, dapper walk. He immediately reminded me of the spy Greville Wynne. He asked, "Mr Hagger?" He said he had recognised me from a photograph.[23]

We walked towards the nearby Café del Poste, which had multi-coloured strips hanging in the doorway to keep out dust and flies. He said, "I am Head of Tripoli station in the SIS, the Secret Intelligence Service, MI6." Over coffee, speaking very quietly, he said, "I know you have penetrated a group of ministers who are planning a *coup*, and I would like you to work with me to give me a window on the development of their plans."

We began to get to know each other. He asked me in general terms about the University and my family life, and about my articles for *The Daily News* and said he was Scottish, although he had no Scottish accent. I found him very easy to talk to, and I liked him.

He then said we would go for a drive in his car, which was parked nearby. It was a large Fiat 650. I sat in the front passenger seat, and he said: "It is in the interests of our country that if there is going to be a revolution in Libya, then it should be a pro-Western revolution. I am asking you to serve your country, for patriotic reasons. You will be independent and will carry on doing what you would normally do, but you will share what you're doing with me in the national interest so we can keep Libya within the Western fold. You will continue doing your work at the University and your articles, and you will be doing secret work for me. You will be my eyes and ears." Then he said, "But I know you have a supermarket account to pay." He knew that I owed more than £250, and he said he would ask if this account could be settled with a payment 'after tax'. "Will you serve your country for patriotic reasons on the basis I have just described?"

He was asking me to serve my country. He was like the posters of Kitchener pointing and saying: "Your country needs *you*" at the beginning of the First World War. Many civilians had answered the call in 1914. I was in the position of my uncle Tom who volunteered though under age and was killed in 1918. I had his wings, and perhaps his genes.

I knew I had to answer my country's call, even though there was a risk to me and I had to consider my family, my wife and daughter. I had got to know several in the SIS since my fateful letter to Major Goulding, but I was curious to know more about the SIS, the real world of James Bond.

The Cold War was at its height and even though my perspective was one of world civilizations and internationalism, Soviet influence was everywhere. The view was around that the Cold War was in fact a Third World War between Communism and the West, which had begun in 1944 and was still continuing. Keeping Libya from becoming a Soviet satellite was an important policy goal, as he pointed out. I saw immediately that a connection with his organisation might help Ben's revolution to succeed – and the ministers' plan to make me British Ambassador.

I had instantly known what my answer would be while I listened and deliberated.

"Yes," I said, "I will."

"Good," he said. "We'll be working together." Then he wanted me to give him a summary of Ben's parties and the coming revolution.

I talked as he drove. I told him that Ben was going to insist that I was made British Ambassador, and that I was to have a role in selling Libya's oil to foreign companies, from which the poor would ultimately benefit. He listened without comment. Perhaps he knew it all already.

About an hour later he made an arrangement to meet me the following Tuesday. He dropped me off near my car and said, "Walk slowly from this corner." So began my training in how to operate within my new profession.

In T.E. Lawrence's footsteps

Ricky Herbert had warned me that Goethe's Faust believed *he* could control Mephistopheles whereas in the end Mephistopheles controlled him (*see* p.122). I was confident I would not suffer Faust's fate. Andrew had said that I would continue doing my work. I had not sold my soul to Mephistopheles. I would remain independent while carrying forward my ideals and answering my country's call.

I had written to Major Goulding in July 1960, impelled by my budding writer's Faustian curiosity and by my need to find a way of earning a living that would allow time for my quest. Now, nearly nine years later I had been approached by the Head of SIS's Tripoli station, who was interested in the revolution I had persuaded Ben to implement. I was now a British intelligence agent, following in the footsteps of T.E. Lawrence (whose initial cover had been his work as an archaeologist in ancient cities of the Near East). I was now a player in what Kipling, in *Kim* (1901), called "The Great Game", referring to the strategic rivalry between the British and Russian Empires. I

251

was an ear, eye and mouth on the orange cloak of State which sees and hears everything. Although I had long known that an approach would come from his sector of the Establishment, when it came it was unexpected and had taken me by surprise.

That afternoon I took my family down the Homs Road to a beach near sand dunes, and I was pleased at how close we all were. My restoration of my marriage seemed to have worked.

Episode 11:

Liberation and Tyranny

Year: 1969
Locations: Tripoli; Djerba; Loughton
Works: *The Age of Cartoon*; *Daily News* articles; *The Gates of Hell*
Initiative: eyewitness of Gaddafi's *coup*

"I said, 'I will watch how I behave, and not let my tongue lead me into sin; I will keep a muzzle on my mouth as long as the wicked man is near me.' I stayed dumb, silent, speechless."

Psalm 39.1–2, Jerusalem Bible

The next episode consisted of a conflict between rival revolutionary *coups*, one pro-Western that I was engaged in, which would liberate the poor from poverty, and the other anti-Western, which sought to impose a tyranny of which I would be a victim.

Liberation: pro-Western coup
Party for faction of pro-Western coup *at the Minister of Health's farm*
The day after my meeting with Andrew Mackenzie there was a party at the Minister of Health's farm. We met the Minister for Petroleum at the house of the Minister of State for Prime Minister's Affairs, Beshir al-Muntasser. Ben and his two brothers arrived with four Yugoslav girls.

Ben said to me in front of the two ministers, "I want you to come to Djerba with me. When do you finish at the University?"

I told him when classes stopped, and that I was thinking of returning to London for a holiday.

"We will be there for a few days," he said. "In early July, before you go to London. It will not cost you anything. I shall go off and leave you. I shall go fishing."

There was laughter. Beshir said to me, "Hidden meaning."

"I shall go to Sousse," Ben joked.

It was clear that he would be meeting someone in Djerba, and that he wanted to use us as cover.

"And," Ben added, "I am going to London on Friday to see my doctor."

The ministers laughed.

We all drove out to the Minister for Health's farm. The Minister for Health wore a red *fez*. He was lean and greying. We sat on his raised terrace near an illuminated fountain in the hot dark. We drank whisky, looking down on the tops of trees. Crickets fluted under a huge moon. In a cage nearby there were a peacock and a gazelle. The three ministers spoke about Ben in English and agreed with Khalifa, "If Ben had stayed in the army, he would be a General by now."

There was sporadic dancing to Western music and we ate juicy chops with our fingers. When the Minister for Petroleum pushed one of the two Yugoslav girls called Maeda into the illuminated fountain and was splashed in retaliation it was time to go home. Beshir asked if Caroline and I would stay with him at Al-Bayda.

As I went to the bathroom I passed the Minister of Health's bedroom. The door was ajar, and I saw a holster and revolver slung round the bedstead at the head of his double bed. Being a minister in an Arab country meant that you had to be prepared for an attack in the middle of the night. (A week later the Minister of Health was sacked.)

Meeting with Andrew Mackenzie: scenario of coup

I met Andrew Mackenzie on Tuesday 3 June. I walked up to Sha'ra Ben Ashur a little before 8 p.m. A soldier looked at me with some suspicion, so I stood in a bus queue. A bus came and everyone got on. I was left standing at the stop. The soldier moved towards me, so I walked off and Andrew Mackenzie slowed his wife's car alongside me and picked me up.

He drove me to his home, which was not far away. He explained he was not on speaking terms with his wife. He said, "She leaves me notes. 'Could you turn the gramophone down please?' She accuses me of scratching records." He offered me tonic water as he disapproved of too much alcohol (perhaps a reflection of Scottish puritanism). He said his seven-year-old son was backward and was in a low class for his age. He asked me to go through the events behind Ben's parties again.

At the end he asked rhetorically, "What is Ben up to? His 'doctor' must be Dr Omar Muntasser, Libyan Ambassador in London. It's a Muntasser conspiracy, with Nagy family aid. Hence the spate of parties, which are cover for the plotting. Dr Muntasser is disappointed. Bakush [a previous Libyan Prime Minister] didn't make him Foreign Secretary, and he got Beshir in instead. Beshir has invited you to dinner and to stay. Beshir is acting for Dr Muntasser. Ben wants to prevent a Biafran situation: the secession of Cyrenaica. The Muntassers are the only family that can hold the provinces together. Ben is running errands between Muntasser – he is going to London on Friday 6 June to see his 'doctor', meaning Dr Muntasser – and someone in Sousse, who he planned to see before."

We talked until 1.30 a.m. Then I slipped out of his front door and walked home along the dark, deserted sandy lanes, watching out for pye-dogs which roamed in packs.

Party at the King's farm

A couple of days later (on 5 June) there was another party. To my surprise, this was at the King's farm, in a wooden hunting lodge. There was a large ground-floor with basket seats hanging from the wooden ceiling, and an upstairs that filled half the first floor, access to which was up a central wooden staircase. There were some twenty or thirty guests, and the food was served by the King's personal servant.

The fact that the King's place was being used suggested to all that the King was looking with favour on Ben's enterprise. As Omar al-Shalhi was the King's adviser, it was possible that al-Shalhi knew about the plot and had joined forces with Ben. There must have been a *rapprochement* between the al-Shalhi family and the ministers supporting Ben's *coup* following the expulsion of Col. Ali Shilabi. It seemed as if two *coups* had made common cause.

There was the usual banter, and Ben said: "I am going to London tomorrow to see my doctor."

There was general laughter.

Beshir said to me (confirming Andrew Mackenzie's analysis), "Dr Omar Muntasser is the Libyan Ambassador to London. He is the son of the first Libyan Prime Minister, from 1951 to 1954 and again from 1964 to 1965. And he is my relative."

"Yes," Ben said. "You are returning to London for a holiday. You should interview him for your newspaper."

The Minister for Petroleum, Khalifa, and Beshir both said, "Yes, you should interview him." I felt the three of them had planned to ask me to interview Muntasser.

And so when I was next in the office of *The Daily News* I told Ansari that I was going to London in July and that I might interview the Libyan Ambassador there.

He quickly said (perhaps thinking of information he could supply to

Egyptian intelligence), "And you could interview the British Foreign Office as well. You could write an article on Libyan-British relations from both sides."[1]

Ben came round on 8 June, having "seen his doctor" in London, but was not eager to talk about their meeting.

Omar and Abdulaziz al-Shalhi

The next evening I met Andrew Mackenzie at 8 p.m. on "the waterfront" (Sha'ra Adrian Pelt). Andrew Mackenzie picked me up and drove me through the Tripoli streets as we discussed the implications of the party's being on the King's farm.

Andrew Mackenzie said there were two al-Shalhi brothers, Omar and Abdulaziz. They had been placed in positions of power after a Sanusi family feud in the 1950s in which their father, Ibrahim, the King's closest adviser, was assassinated by Muhi al-Din al-Sanusi in 1954. The King had thought of Ibrahim as his son and of Ibrahim's sons as his grandsons. Ibrahim's eldest

Tripoli waterfront

son, al-Busayri, had replaced him as chief adviser to the King, but he had been killed in a car accident in 1964. He was succeeded by the elder of his two brothers, Omar, who became chief adviser in 1968. His younger brother, Abdulaziz, was Head of the Committee to reorganise the army after the 1967 war, and would clearly be known to Ben, who had been an army colonel. Between them, the two surviving al-Shalhi brothers controlled the palace, the King's court and the positions in the army, and there was considerable evidence that Abdulaziz al-Shalhi planned to overthrow the monarchy.[2]

Andrew Mackenzie said, "If the ministries of Ben's *coup* have made common cause with the al-Shalhis, then Abdulaziz al-Shalhi is a very important figure in the coming *coup*. He will be the power behind Dr Omar Muntasser's *coup*. Muntasser will front the new regime as President, but the al-Shalhis will continue their present influence. The King has got too old to rule and is arranging for a pro-Western successor regime that will have more ability and teeth than the Crown Prince can provide."

At the end of our drive Andrew Mackenzie put me out on the waterfront and I walked back to my car.

Envelope

I met Andrew Mackenzie again on the waterfront at 10.45 on Wednesday 11 June. This time I picked him up and he instructed me on which roads to take. He handed me an envelope bulging with Libyan banknotes, which, he said, was 'after tax' and contained £300 to settle Guido's account and a payment to me of an additional £50 for the month of June. The envelope contained the equivalent of nearly eight times my monthly earnings from Chatter (£45 per month), a huge sum by the standards of 1969.

Andrew Mackenzie said he was very interested in Viktor, my Czech friend at the University. Following the Soviet invasion of Czechoslovakia in 1968 many Czechs wanted to defect and bring with them scientific (and in some cases nuclear) knowledge, but few had knowledge of the quality that, it was believed, he possessed. I had already urged him to join the Free Czechs, and Andrew Mackenzie hoped that he would turn against his Soviet masters.

I returned home quite late and (having been given permission to do so by Andrew Mackenzie) showed the contents of the envelope to Caroline, who was delighted and elated. At one stroke our debts, run up by having to set up home and pay car-import duty out of an advance of salary, had been paid off and we could now both return to London after giving Ben cover in Djerba. We were now in harmony and very close.

But I still had a pro-Western *coup* to deliver. I met Andrew Mackenzie on the waterfront on 18 June. I was being trained in different ways of setting up meetings, and this time I had to walk along the waterfront at 9 p.m., and if he did not pick me up, return at 10 p.m., and if he again did not pick me up, return at 11 p.m. Exams were in progress, and I should be at home marking. In fact, he picked me up at 9 p.m. and we focused on who Ben might be meeting on Djerba or in Sousse.

I met Andrew Mackenzie a week later on 25 June. This time there had to be a coded telephone call to arrange our car meeting. I had to ring him from a public phone and suggest a "stroll on the waterfront". From now on I had to identify myself over the telephone as 'Henry'. I was looking at a travel document as I "strolled", and I became so engrossed in it that I did not see him. He leaned out of his window and had to call to me. For this meeting he had asked me to type out my news and hand it over after five minutes of driving, during which he had his eyes on the rear mirror near the top of the windscreen to check we were not being followed. "The first rule," he said, "is not to get caught."

Meeting with Viktor

I had spoken to my Czech friend from the University, the mathematician Viktor, at Andrew Mackenzie's suggestion, and we now drove to pay him a visit in his flat further down my sandy lane. I had said that Andrew Mackenzie might be a useful contact and asked if I could bring him in for a drink.

When we arrived Viktor, a large man of about 50 with a furrowed brow, limply wandered off and returned with polish, which he sprayed on the table (as he had done for me on my first visit). As he wiped the table with a cloth he apologised for having no drink. His Czech wife was away, and he smoked as we talked and tossed his cigarette on the carpetless floor. His wife, he said, had cancelled her Party card following the Soviet invasion, and: "This will cause trouble for me in future." He said that his wife would be returning with their 11-year-old son and that he would have to find a school for him. This had proved problematic.

Afterwards Andrew Mackenzie said to me in his car, "He's tired. He has rather a weak face, he has allowed himself to go. He may not carry his plan through. But he is definitely recruitable. When I am ready I will recruit him, and he will recruit first a Czech and then a Russian. He has a child who has to be schooled, and he wants to start a popular movement against the US and the Russians, a movement to disengage the superpowers from Europe by popular agitation. I can help him with these things."

I agreed with everything Andrew had said. I was opposed to the Soviet invasion of Czechoslovakia in 1968 just as I had been opposed to the Soviet invasion of Hungary in 1956 and the Soviet occupation of various states during the Cold War. I was on the side of the European civilization and against the Byzantine-Russian civilization which occupied its eastern territories. I was on the side of freedom for Europe. My view was that if Viktor was willing to help Andrew Mackenzie and the UK, it would be a blow in the war to liberate the world from Soviet occupation and end the Cold War. I wanted humankind to be ruled by a benevolent world government, but I did not want part of humankind to be oppressed by a totalitarian dictatorship. Andrew had right on his side.

Visit to Djerba, and American couple: Ben Nagy meets Col. Saad eddin Bushwerib of Libyan army, who is to carry out coup
The next time, *he* "strolled" and *I* drove, and he got in and sat sideways-on in the front passenger seat and trained me in how to drive and look in the mirror and talk all at the same time – and how to accelerate away, overtaking cars in front, if given an order to do so.

I had told Andrew Mackenzie that Ben had once mentioned Saad eddin Bushwerib, an old army friend of his who lived in the block of flats behind ours and had a view into the windows at the back of our flat. Andrew Mackenzie thought that he might be the main army contact of Ben's. He suspected that Ben would meet him on Djerba or in Sousse to plan the military details of the coming *coup*, and he told me I was to watch Ben on Djerba like a hawk and not let him out of my sight so that I would not miss this crucial meeting.

My "strolling" meetings on the waterfront, triggered by coded messages and carried out with acute watchfulness, were by now almost instinctive. I looked forward to them. I found I was transported into a heightened awareness and observation, a higher consciousness. There was palpable danger in what I was doing. However I looked at it, I was spying on an attack on the Libyan State that I was part of and would benefit from (by controlling the sale of Libyan oil), and if I were caught I could be thrown into prison or even shot. On the face of it, shooting seemed unlikely as the King seemed to have acquiesced in handing over his power to the plotters, but he was surrounded by factions, as had been apparent during the arguing over the expulsion of the Chief of Police, Ali Shilabi. If Ben had not made common cause with the al-Shalhis, then Ali Shilabi or the al-Shalhis could have me arrested or shot for jeopardising their own influence and interests.

The sense of danger was like a powerful drug. It made my adrenaline flow, it was exciting, and for the time of our drive I lived with great intensity, full of purpose, unified within, instinctively watchful for any signs of danger. I carried this intense watchfulness with me to Djerba.

In early July after the end of term we took Nadia to stay with a friend of hers, and Ben drove Caroline and me to Djerba, an island off Tunisia. It was traditionally the island of Homer's 'lotus-eaters'. It had a local *suk* and low hotels along white beaches where modern fun-lovers and escapists 'ate' lotus.

We stayed at the Tanit Hotel, a complex of chalets by a beach. There was a nightclub by the sands. We spent some time there each evening, and Ben danced with single girls. We breakfasted by the pool, and we spent much of each day lying on the white hot beach and cooling down in the waves.

Ben began talking about a business venture involving hotels. I assumed this was a cover for the meeting he was waiting to have, and watched him carefully. However, the third afternoon he went missing while we were on the beach. One moment he was with us on the beach in shorts, and then I was suddenly aware that he was not around. Without letting us know, he had driven away.

He returned several hours later, saying he had driven to the Hotel Ulysses to consider buying part of a hotel as a business venture.

Over dinner I pressed him and he said sheepishly, "I can tell you, I met Saad eddin Bushwerib. He's an army commander. He lives in the block of flats behind yours in Tripoli." Ben seemed to have forgotten that during a visit he had pointed out his blind-covered windows.

We were away four days and returned to Tripoli on the fifth day (10 July).

Before I could report to Andrew Mackenzie we were swept off to have dinner with an American couple (on 11 July).

Just before we went to Djerba, after the party at the King's farm, we had been visited (on 2 July) by an American couple who we had briefly chatted to at a party given by a British oil employee and his wife way back in February: Kat (short for Kathleen) and Buddy. They turned up on our doorstep unannounced, saying, "Hello from February, can we come in?" Busy couples do not turn up five months after a brief introduction at a party. My first thought was instinctive. I wondered if someone in the CIA had encouraged them to call.

I let them in, and we all sat and chatted. Kat described herself as a "Louisiana belle". She was about 30 and had long black tumbling hair and dark brown eyes. She was of Spanish descent with a Spanish maiden name (Abreo). She was very much "a belle", and her husband was a 40-year-old Texan from Dallas who worked in computers for Amoseas oil company. They told us that they had triplets (three girls) and a younger son. They invited us to dinner on Friday 11 July, the day after we returned from shadowing Saad eddin Bushwerib on Djerba and before I could report to Andrew Mackenzie.

They picked us up in his wide Dodge car and we dined out as a four. Somehow they knew that I was writing the 'Barbary Gipsy' newspaper articles. Kat said she would like to write for *The Daily News* and asked to be put in touch with the editor. Her husband urged me to get out of teaching and writing into computers. (In 1967 I had visited the British Post Office's computer in London, which filled a room, and was now hearing at first hand – ten days before US computers put two men on the moon – that smaller computers were the future.) He offered to teach me two computer languages, PL/1 and Fortran, and make me an analyst-programmer on $1,000 a month. He said that if I went along with what he was proposing he would be able to find me a job. He promised to supply me with manuals so I could teach myself.

So it was that three days after my first meeting with Andrew Mackenzie and now one day after my return from monitoring Ben's meeting with Saad eddin Bushwerib, an American oilman from Dallas and his wife wanted to be our friends. I was to get his wife writing for *The Daily News* and he was to teach me a computer language and find me a job. I was being befriended by an almost complete stranger who was offering to provide free training so I could change my profession. It was a bizarre situation, but although I knew I would not be introducing Kat to Chatter I decided to play along with the situation as I would soon be dealing with Western oil companies and I had to start somewhere with oilmen. At no time did either of them ask me about the coming *coup*.

Did the American CIA know about the coming *coup*? Did they know my role in it? Did they know that I would be dealing with Western oil companies? Did they know of Andrew Mackenzie's approach to me? Although there was Anglo-American co-operation over intelligence in those days I did not believe that knowledge of agents' identities was shared. How much did the CIA know about the inner workings of Tripoli's SIS station from their own sources? Were they able to monitor Andrew Mackenzie's communications without his knowing? Did the CIA know I was the Barbary Gipsy and could they have arranged for someone to let this couple know, to give them a pretext or incentive to visit me? Was this seemingly-innocent, pleasant expatriate couple being manipulated by the CIA without their realising it? All these questions ran through my mind after they had gone, and I thought they were pertinent questions.

Three days later (on 13 July) I had a meeting on the waterfront with Andrew Mackenzie and sheepishly confessed that despite my best efforts not to let Ben out of my sight he had given me the slip while I was on the beach and had met Saad eddin Bushwerib. Andrew Mackenzie looked on the positive side: "At least we now know that he met Saad eddin Bushwerib."

I had another meeting with Andrew on 18 July, when, sitting under a street light in his car, he urged me (in a message that was disconcertingly similar to the Texan's): "Get out of teaching as quickly as possible. Otherwise you will become a nomadic lecturer, and we all know how they end up. Like your colleague Eric Brewer, who was at the University of Baghdad with you, I believe. He's got no money, he's got children to educate, he's hag-ridden by fears of losing his job, and so he's a hack, he does whatever the Libyans want him to do. For a bachelor it may be an agreeable existence, but for a married man, no, get out of it."

I sensed that he was speaking to a brief, that he was trying to pull me into working full-time within his organisation so that I would no longer be independent of the System. But I had to admit that there was truth in his words.

London. Meetings with Keith Priest and Melissa, and John Harrow
According to Andrew Mackenzie, Col. Ali Shilabi, the Chief of Police, had been pressing to meet Caroline and me, having seen us at Ben's house. I wanted Caroline to escape his clutches, so I returned her to England with Nadia on the first available flight. The next day Khalifa, the Minister for Petroleum, had a gathering at his house to watch Manchester United play against European opposition on television.

Afterwards I locked the flat, left my green Volkswagen under the grapevine, and spent a night (21 July) at the Libya Palace Hotel (where, watching television in the foyer with thirty cheering Arabs I saw the American Apollo-11 landing on the moon). The next day I took a taxi to the airport and flew to London.

I joined Caroline and Nadia at the Dulwich house where Caroline's parents now lived, 177 South Croxted Road. We visited Loughton the next day. I found it more urbanised and proletarianised.

A couple of days later we drove to Oxford and revisited old haunts: Port Meadow, Worcester College, the Star Bar of the Randolph, the Golden City Chinese restaurant. We went on to Stratford-upon-Avon and stayed at the Falcon near Shakespeare's New Place. We visited the church and Shottery, and then by arrangement met Buchanan at Alveston Manor. He wanted us to return to Japan, where he said "our stock" was very high. He was visiting Europe with a young Japanese student, whose presence inhibited conversation over dinner.

The next day we drove to Somerset and lunched with Tuohy at Kilmersdon. After lunch we sat in the clover field in front of Tumbler's Bottom, surrounded by borage and ox-eye daisies. We visited the church at Mells where Sassoon is buried. In the evening we had a long conversation about voice, further to Angus Wilson's comments, and agreed that writers fall into two camps: those that explore and include, who have no voice; and those who interpret in terms of their own vision and exclude – shut out – who have a voice. I wrote in my *Diaries*: "Not having a voice is a sign of exploration and truthful reporting about the universe."[3]

I had been asked to write articles about England for *The Daily News*. Back in West Dulwich I finished *The Age of Cartoon*, and researched and wrote my articles about the new London. I visited the new in-places like Le Kilt, the Round House, the Arts Lab, the Seed restaurant and Carnaby Street, and caught swinging London in terms of Merrie dandies. I went to a poetry reading at The Freemasons Arms, Belsize Park and I took Caroline to the Colony Room, an out-of-hours drinking club of which I was a member that opened in 1948 and was frequented by post-war writers: Dylan Thomas, Louis MacNeice and E.M. Forster. There I drank champagne with the artist Francis Bacon. Muriel Belcher, the legendary Portuguese-Jewish hostess of the Colony who sat on a stool near the door, said to me, "Caroline is very nice and you are very lucky to have such an attractive wife."

I had rung Keith Priest, and we visited him in Surrey on 2 August. Melissa had been to a wedding and had been drinking champagne. She sat on a low table, widening her eyes and laughing raucously. She said of Keith, "He's horrid to me these days." She refused to get coffee. I had told Keith about his organisation's approach to me, which he already knew about, and when Melissa said, "We quarrel incessantly in England," Keith said to me: "It's a pity you can't use your influence with the F.O. [Foreign Office] to get us posted abroad."

Somehow the roles had been reversed. In Japan, he had belonged to the organisation and was feeding me snippets of officialdom's interest in me, whereas now he was indirectly asking me to put in a good word for him to influence a new posting abroad. That was the first time it had occurred to me that I might now have that kind of influence. Melissa reinforced his appeal to me by sitting with Caroline and discussing how I should wear my hair and saying she would love to come and have a drink with us in The Crown and Greyhound in West Dulwich.

I had to interview the Foreign Office along with Dr Muntasser as Ansari had directed. I raised the possibility of an interview with the Foreign Secretary, Michael Stewart, with Keith, and he suggested I should contact a John Harrow.

On 5 August I rang John Harrow at the number Keith had given me. He was expecting my call and wanted to know what food I liked. He arranged to meet me at Veeraswamy's, an Indian restaurant in Swallow Street, just off Regent Street at 7 p.m.

John Harrow was tall, thin and clerical with serious eyes and an eyes-down smile. He was extremely pleasant and questioned me in some detail on Libya and the coming *coup*. He said, "You're doing an excellent job. Andrew Mackenzie can't go and speak to the ministers you are speaking to." As regards my interview, he said Michael Stewart was away on holiday and that an appointment with his Minister of State, Goronwy Roberts (later Lord Goronwy Roberts) was under consideration.

He also seemed to follow up on what Andrew Mackenzie had said, that I should leave teaching as soon as possible. He volunteered: "In the SIS, after 31" – I was then 30 – "you're First Secretary and probably get a Counsellor's pay. The job has a lot of responsibility. Detail is important. You're called in to help with other areas, but you don't trouble your boss more than necessary. Everyone is on Christian-name terms, including older people." He was suggesting that I should join the SIS in a year's time, when my work in Libya was finished.

He said he lived in the country, an hour on the train from Paddington, and returned home every Friday night. After dinner, knowing that I would catch a train, he walked with me from Piccadilly along the Mall to Victoria between 9.45 and 10.15, talking. We passed Buckingham Palace and had a nightcap in The Grosvenor Hotel.

Interview with Dr Muntasser, Libyan Ambassador to UK

I was now told to submit questions in writing to Goronwy Roberts. I received his replies by post and telephoned Dr Muntasser, who knew of me and said he was expecting my call. I went to his residence, 31 Phillimore

Gardens, on 18 August.

He greeted me warmly in very correct English with an Oxford accent. He was a very tall, erect, charismatic man in his early forties and had a dignified, open face and smarmed-down neat hair. He had an authority about his bearing that suggested he would make a natural President. We sat in a luxuriously furnished room with a high ceiling. He was very co-operative and helpful. He understood that I had already put the same questions I was asking him to Goronwy Roberts and had received his replies, and that my article would appear in Libya as a view of Libyan-British relations from both the Libyan and British sides. During my interview Muntasser sometimes asked what "the British Minister of State" had said. I read the relevant passage out. We got on very well.

At the end he said, "I would like to invite you and your wife to have a drink with me and my wife on Friday evening."

I returned with Caroline on Friday 22 August, and we talked generally. He avoided any mention of the coming *coup*. But at the end he escorted us to the front door and shook my hand and said, looking into my eyes, "I will be seeing you very soon in Tripoli." He gave me a very significant look.

I said, "I hope everything goes well." He understood what I meant, and nodded.[4]

I sensed that the *coup* was imminent, and was excited. Nevertheless, I was depressed to be leaving England. I had warmed to the peace and tumbling horse chestnuts of Dulwich, and we had a final walk in Epping Forest. We visited the two ponds on Strawberry Hill and Blackweir pond on Baldwin's Hill, and I gazed at the grating over its overflow. We found the Lost Pond which Epstein visited every day.

Caroline also wanted to stay. Our relationship had been stable except for one night when we walked home from seeing a film in London and she discussed our marriage. We stopped near the plague graveyard and talked until nearly midnight. She said she had not had a permanent home when she was a child because her father was moving about within the RAF, and she wanted a permanent home now. But she was reconciled to returning to Libya, and pleased that our mortgage on the Loughton flat would be paid off within a few months.

Back to Tripoli: dinners with Beshir al-Muntasser, news that the pro-Western coup *has been set for 5 September*

We flew back to Tripoli on 28 August, and again I was excited at the imminence of the coming *coup*. To our surprise we were met at the airport by a smartly-dressed Libyan. He said, "Beshir al-Muntasser has sent a car for you." This was completely unexpected. Beshir's chauffeur drove Caroline, Nadia and me, and our luggage, to Beshir's house.

The Minister of State for Prime Minister's Affairs was waiting for me at the door. He greeted me very warmly, beaming in a suit in the August heat. He said, "You have just arrived in Tripoli, you will have no food. You will have dinner here with me." I thought how thoughtful he was.

Dinner was served by his servant. We ate at a small round table. He told me that my article on Libyan-British relations had appeared in *The Daily News* the previous Sunday, 24 August, with a photo of Dr Muntasser.[5] It had been translated into Arabic and was carried in all the Libyan Arabic papers, no doubt at the request of the Minister for Information. My article had set the stage for a pro-British *coup* by drawing attention to the closeness between Libya and Britain.

While Caroline put Nadia to bed in a spare bedroom Beshir asked me for every detail of my meeting with Muntasser. I told him from start to finish. I told him, "Omar said to me, 'I will be seeing you very soon in Tripoli.' He will be here very soon."

"Yes," Beshir said. "It will be very soon."

After dinner Beshir saw that we were tired from the flight and were ready to leave. He said within earshot of the chauffeur, who was holding the car door open for me, "Come to dinner again on Saturday 30 August. I will send my car."

Somehow Beshir had taken Ben's place. I did not see Ben. I spent a couple of days preparing for the new University year, which began on 1 September. Chatter had published all the articles I had sent him from England, and he was counting on me to provide two pages for the next article. There was no time to visit a new place in Libya so I wrote an article about France based on my journey to Libya the previous October. Andrew Mackenzie had not been in touch. I expected him to contact me very soon.

I went alone to Beshir's house on 30 August. During dinner at the same round table, again served by his servant, Beshir suddenly said, "September 5th it will happen."

I knew what he was referring to.

"That's next Friday," I said.

"Yes. The King is in Turkey, having medical treatment. He is at a spa at Bursa having a leg ailment treated. Before he left, on August the fourth, he signed an instrument of abdication to take effect from September the second. He will abdicate in favour of Crown Prince on September the second. It will not be against King but Crown Prince, for Tripolitania. Saad eddin Bushwerib will carry it out."

"And Ben."

"Yes. You will know when it has happened because Ben's music will be played on radio at 11 o'clock. I have it on tape here, listen." He stood up from the table and went to a sideboard and switched on a tape recorder. I heard jazzed-up orchestral music. The piece went with a swing.

"When you hear this music you will know that it has been successful."

He then changed the subject and avoided any further mention of the coming *coup*.[6]

I had thought of the *coup* as 'Ben's *coup*', but in truth it had become the 'Muntasser *coup*'. It had now taken on a corporate identity for it had involved a commercial network. It was an alliance, I thought, of the King's chief advisers Omar and Abdulaziz al-Shalhi and of pro-Western ministers, army and police colonels who had met on Ben's premises to chart a way forward after the anticipated abdication of King Idris. Dr Muntasser would be President to preserve the old Tripolitania (West Libya) and rescue it from the coming federal rule of the Crown Prince that was expected to favour Cyrenaica. Muntasser would unite Tripolitania and Cyrenaica. The military *coup* would be carried out by Saad eddin Bushwerib and Ben, and would transfer power to the pro-Western clique, apparently with the King's blessing (judging from our visit to the King's farm). And I would be British Ambassador and sell plots of desert to oil prospectors. I would be their link with the West. 'Ben's *coup*', or Muntasser's *coup*, no longer referred to the activities of a particular individual but to a particular pro-Western emphasis of a commercial pattern which was intended to bring prosperity to post-abdication Libya.

The next day, a Sunday, I made preparations for my first day back at the University after the summer break. I was in possession of the date of the 'Muntasser *coup*': 5 September. I planned to ring Andrew Mackenzie on Monday 1 September to communicate this. I was waiting impatiently for Friday.

There was a deceptive ordinariness, an illusion of normality, in the last days of the Libyan *ancient regime*, and I was sure that the last days of the old regime in 1649 England, 1789 France and 1917 Russia would have felt no different. I was in the last days of a dying order and on the brink of a momentous change.

Tyranny: anti-Western 1-September coup

I am an eyewitness of Gaddafi's coup of 1 September 1969; Viktor

On the morning of 1 September 1969 I was awoken at 5 a.m. by what sounded like shots. Dogs barked and then there was silence. I thought they could not be shots and went back to sleep. There were more shots at 6.30. Again there was a silence. I thought they might be firecrackers to celebrate a strike against Israel.

It was my first day back at the University, and I set off for work in our green Volkswagen. The streets were deserted. Every shop and roadside stall was closed and there were no traffic policemen. Sure that there was a strike against Israel, I carried on. It was now clear that my car was the only vehicle on the roads. I reached the University gates but they were closed, indeed padlocked.

Puzzled, I looked at my pocket diary to check that I had returned to the University on the right day. I had. Then, farther up the road, there was a shot. An African-looking solder wearing plimsolls slowly raised a rifle and fired into the air. There was another shot.

Now I realised that a *coup* was in progress. Perhaps Ben had struck early without letting me know. I turned the car and headed back home.

The military action had come up behind me as I drove in to work, and now I had to go back through it. On every deserted street corner there were single soldiers in plimsolls firing single shots into the air, then slowly lowering their rifles and reloading. They were firing live rounds. I could tell as I could hear them echoing. My car was still the only civilian vehicle on the streets. I sat well down in my seat, and, holding my breath, drove past each soldier I encountered. Each soldier looked at me but did not shoot.

I was not frightened. I thought they might be Ben's troops and that they might be well-disposed to me. I felt no different from how I had felt when I left the Field Day in Pembrokeshire and headed for the cliffs. Ahead I saw an advancing armoured car and turned left. Now I was heading towards a distant sand-coloured tank. I turned right. I passed two more soldiers and jumped traffic-lights. Another armoured car was heading towards me and I turned right and then left back on to the road I had been on. I passed several more armed soldiers before I reached our flat in Collina Verde.

A British lady carrying an empty shopping-bag and hurrying home encountered me as I got out of my car. She said, "There's been a *coup*. My husband was turned away at bayonet point. It's army, the police are resisting." I thought Ben might be trying to arrest the Chief of Police, Ali Shilabi.

I entered our flat and told Caroline that Nadia would not be going to school that day. I explained there was a *coup* in progress. We decided that the safest place was our hall as there were no windows and we would be safe from stray bullets or ricochets. Caroline, Nadia and I sat there for a couple of hours, during which there were many shots in twos and threes like firecrackers interspersed with distant gunfire. There seemed to be a battle for the telecommunications centre down the road.

We had no television in Libya, like most other expatriates, and we listened to the radio. The local radio station was playing Western music. Suddenly a voice said in stirring English, "Citizens, you have waited a long time for this Liberation." There was more music and about 11 the music Beshir had played me came on. It was surely his signal that 'Ben's revolution' had been successful. Muntasser was the new leader, and Ben was the power behind the scenes.

I found the BBC World Service news. There was a dramatic statement: "There has been a *coup d'état* in Libya and forces say that the new leader is Colonel Saad eddin Bushwerib, an army officer."[7] The man Ben met on or near Djerba had seized power.

I felt elated. I had fed Ben the idea to help the poor and corner Libyan oil, and he had seen it through. I could not understand why he had brought the date forward, but ten months' plotting seemed to have succeeded. I could now look forward to occupying the British Embassy as Ambassador and would soon be in control of Libya's oil. I would soon be a multi-millionaire out of oil deals.

For two days there was curfew, with shooting outside, sometimes every few seconds, sometimes every few minutes. We stayed indoors and saw nobody. We were not on the phone. (Very few were on the phone in Libya in those days.) We listened to the radio. The BBC repeated that the *coup* had been conducted by Saad eddin Bushwerib and that it had been bloodless. But on the second day the BBC announced that Omar al-Shalhi, the King's Chief Adviser, had visited the British Foreign Secretary in London. He had asked the British to send troops to reinstate the King by flying him to the British base in Benghazi.

I frowned when I heard this. Omar al-Shalhi was supposed to be a supporter of 'Ben's *coup*'. Why did he want the King back? He could only disapprove of the *coup*.

The next day the gloomy Czech Communist, Viktor, who lived farther down my sandy lane, knocked on our door with bread. He said, "Today there is supposed to be a lifting of curfew between 11 and 2, but you have to have travel documents. I was stopped by two soldiers and could not produce any documents, but they let me return home. I met a student who told me, 'The regime are angry. There has been shouting over the radio. There may be a split in the Revolutionary Command Council with conflicting orders being given to soldiers.'"

Viktor said, "It has been announced that anyone who breaks curfew or is found to have a gun will be shot."

Nadia overheard me telling Caroline this last fact. On her own initiative she found her toy revolver and hid it in one of her Wellington boots.

The next day the BBC announced the lifting of curfew at 11 to allow people to buy food. We all drove to Guido's store. It was surrounded by groups of armed soldiers. The store was packed with Westerners and six armed men shouted, "No beer, no whisky, no wine, no alcohol." Guido, a wrinkled Italian with grey hair and an open-necked shirt, said, "You heard the army, no alcohol." He looked at me, made sure his back was to the soldiers and rolled his eyes. I said to Caroline, "That's unlike Ben and the ministers."

We returned via Castle Square. There was a demonstration. A large crowd was shouting beneath a lorry, on the back of which was mounted a gallows. A dummy was hanging by its neck. It had a large cross on its front and a placard round its neck, saying in English "Shalhi". It was presumably Omar but perhaps also Abdulaziz al-Shalhi.

I said to Caroline, "Ben would not have sanctioned this. The Shalhis supported Ben's *coup*. The *coup* can't be Ben's. This *coup* has been carried out by people who see Omar al-Shalhi as a corrupt exploiter of the monarchy. Omar called for the King to be reinstated because this is an anti-Shalhi, anti-Ben *coup*. Or could Ben have fallen out with the Shalhis? Could this be Ben's *coup* after all?"

We returned home and curfew resumed. At 5 p.m. the greengrocer's opposite seemed to be open. I walked to our gates, checked that no soldiers were in sight and crossed the narrow sandy lane, technically breaking curfew by leaving my garden.

One-eyed Mohammed came out. He wore his customary white skullcap. He said, "This very bad. King very good man. This Saad eddin Bushwerib and Ben Nagy. Ben Nagy will be no. 2." So perhaps it *was* Ben's *coup* after all?

An hour later the BBC World Service news reported that all the old regime's ministers were under arrest. Beshir, the Minister of State for Prime Minister's Affairs, was quoted as saying, "We did our best but the problems were too great." I knew Ben would not have locked Beshir up. It was now clear that it was not Ben's *coup*.

It now sank in that we were now living under the tyranny of a tyrant, an absolute ruler who (like the tyrants of early Greek history) had seized power without a legal right.

Shortly afterwards a friend of Ben's came to our door, furtively and in haste. He said, "I have a message for you. Ben and his brothers have disappeared. They are being hunted by the army. The country has been sealed off. If the army come here you know nothing." He left immediately.

There was no message from Andrew Mackenzie – I rang him from a phone box each time curfew was lifted but there was no answer – or from the British Council or the University.

Ansari says my article on Libyan-British relations triggered the 1-September coup
The next day when curfew was lifted I drove through the heat to the newspaper office. Ansari greeted me at the door. He said, "This Revolution was planned in Egypt. The Minister of Information is under arrest. We are waiting to be arrested." He added, "Your article on Libyan-British relations triggered this Revolution."

"Are you sure?"

"For sure. It has been said. The leader of the Revolutionary Command Council read your article in Arabic and had the Revolution on 1 September to stop a new closeness between Libya and Britain."

There was no time to get him to elaborate as Chatter wanted to see me. I wondered if Ansari, who was allegedly an Egyptian spy, had sent my pro-British article to Egypt and whether he had heard that I had triggered the *coup* from an Egyptian source.

Two last articles for The Daily News, *blocking intervention*
Chatter was sitting at his desk in an open-necked white shirt. He said, "I'm expecting the army to come and close us down. Get out on the streets now and write your impressions of the Revolution. Praise the Revolution as much as you can. Say the British must not intervene. We need you to say this to survive. I want to print your article before the army arrive."

I left the office and walked among hundreds of chanting, shouting demonstrators to Castle Square. I seemed to be the only Westerner on the streets. I did not feel frightened, but I did encounter glares and looks of hatred. There were banners and tanks decorated with palm fronds. Lorries were driving slowly around with thirty or forty young men and children standing in the back. They waved palm fronds and beat tom-tom-like on the metal sides.

I thought of Tolstoy's question in *War and Peace*, "What is the force that moves nations, Napoleon or the common soldier?" I drove home as curfew ended. I wrote a description of what I had seen.[8]

I did not know the name of the leader of the Revolution. The BBC had reported that Saad eddin Bushwerib was now Chief of Staff, and that in an interview given to a Cairo newspaper he had denied being the leader. According to Cairo Radio the new leader had given a three-hour interview to Mohammed Hassanein Heikal, Editor-in-Chief of *Al-Ahram*, in Benghazi. This seemed to confirm Ansari's view that the Revolution had an Egyptian origin and that as the Soviet Union controlled Egypt the KGB may have been involved. The BBC announced that the new leader had had the idea for the Revolution in 1956, the year of Suez, and had been inspired by Nasser.

I drove in to Chatter during the lifting of curfew the next day and handed in my article. It appeared on Sunday 7 September: 'Libyans Show Solidarity with the Revolutionary Command Council.'

Chatter asked me to write one more article about revolutions. In the long evenings after curfew, which was now from 7 p.m. to 7 a.m., I reflected on the stages of revolutions: prohibition; puritanism; extremism; reign of terror; dictatorship; and the Thermidorian reaction. In my article I tried to identify how the English, American, French and Russian old regimes had created a pre-revolutionary situation in their countries. The article was titled 'Old Regimes'.[9] This thinking resurfaced in *The Fire and the Stones* and in *The Secret History of the West*.

Each day we listened to the BBC World Service news to hear if the British had intervened. But the Libyan-British treaty provided for assistance if there was external aggression or interference. The Libyan Revolution was an internal *coup* even if it had been planned in Egypt and involved the Soviet Union. The British expatriates feared that if there was a British invasion there would be a bloodbath as Libyans would retaliate against the British. To our relief the British did not intervene.

My mother wrote saying that Biggs-Davison had mentioned me in Parliament as a constituent caught in the Revolution. She enclosed a letter from him asking whether I thought the British should have restored King Idris. I was still trying to establish who had had the *coup*. I did not want Idris back, I wanted the Muntasser *coup*, but the opportunity for this had passed and the safety of British expatriates was a major consideration of paramount importance.

Hostages
On Wednesday 10 September the University reopened. I met my New-Zealand UN-sponsored Head of Department. He said that banks would not be open until 20 September, and he lent us lecturers some money to tide us over. We lecturers sat in our Departmental Staff Room and did preparation until the students returned. We all felt that Tripoli was now an open prison. We were inmates, unable to leave as the borders were sealed. We were in effect hostages.

Circumventing prohibition
Guido, who was reported to be no. 2 in Tripoli's Mafia, now began selling foreigners black-market Bavarian black beer. When I next went into his store, with two soldiers standing at one end Guido said to me, "I have your vegetables and potatoes in a box." He indicated the soldiers with his eyes.

I had not ordered a box but I paid 2½ Libyan pounds and carried it to my car past the soldiers. There were 24 beers packed under vegetables and potatoes. I passed on many of the bottles to the foreign community.

Viktor, who had brought me bread, collected some of the beer. He said with typical gloom and Johnsonian authority, "Revolutions are uniformly distributed poverty. In Russia the workers pretend to work and the State pretends to pay. This one will be no different."

It was now very hot, probably 115°F in Tripoli, and we tried to keep cool. The flat had no air-conditioning, just one ceiling fan resembling an aircraft propeller, which circulated hot air.

The Daily News *closed, I am set up by Ansari and taken to radio station*
About 15 September everything grew worse. The Libyan press was closed
down. All staff of *The Daily News* were sacked by order of the new Prime
Minister.

Ansari told me when I went into the office. He sat limply at his desk
awaiting arrest. He said, "The Editor was arrested this morning. The army
were searching through this office. You know, there was corruption. The
Editor's machinery belonged to the Ministry of Information. You can be re-
recruited if things improve. The Revolutionary Command Council have
proclaimed three slogans, 'Freedom, unity and socialism.' Press freedom
means closing down the press." Having sounded critical of Chatter and the
Minister of Information and on the side of the Egyptian-inspired
Revolution, he suddenly sounded critical of the Libyan implementation of
the Egyptian-inspired Revolution. He went on, "Chatter has thousands of
pounds worth of machinery that is owned by the Minister of Information.
The Minister of Information paid our salaries. *The Daily News* never made a
penny. There is corruption to be rooted out. There may be hangings. The old
order must be wiped out. There can be no pity under socialism."

Then he said, "You can write a pamphlet on socialism for the
Revolutionary Command Council. This may involve an interview with the
new leader."

"Hmm," I said, non-committally. If Ansari was an Egyptian spy, he
would want me to interview the new leader. And if it was true that the new
leader had read my article and ordered the *coup* to block our pro-Western
coup, then he would be the last person I should be interviewing.

"You know," he said, "we should both go to the Revolutionary
Command Council's Censor, a Major, to clear up our situation. If we go and
talk with him there may be a positive outcome. Otherwise we may be
arrested."

I did not trust Ansari. It was a pro-Egyptian *coup* with Soviet support, an
anti-Western blow in the Cold War, and an Egyptian was insisting that I
went to meet the RCC's Censor to discuss the article that triggered the *coup*.

Ansari stood up, his eyes inscrutable behind his tinted spectacles, and
said, "We should go now. I will drive you."

I declined. I said, "I'm not going to go and see the Revolutionary
Command Council. If they want me they will have to find me." And I went
home.

It was now reported by the BBC that the leader of the Revolution was
Muammar al-Gaffadi (*sic*). He was reported to have been elevated to the
rank of Colonel for his work in carrying out the Revolution. He was
reported to have appeared on television and said, "I would like to say that
some journalists will be imprisoned, some will be punished and some will

be executed." I knew Ansari would say that Gaddafi was thinking of me.

A couple of afternoons later there was a knock on my front door. I opened the door. A Libyan in plain clothes and an army soldier beckoned me to accompany them. I could not refuse, I had no choice. Reassuring Caroline (who was just behind me), I went with them. They escorted me to a large Jeep outside my garden. To my surprise I saw Ansari sitting on the back seat. I sat beside him.

"It is best this way," he said.

I realised he had set up the arrival of the Jeep.

We were driven to a radio station that was surrounded by armoured cars. We got out. The army man and plain-clothes man led Ansari and me into a chaotic ground-floor corridor where uniformed men rushed about amid much shouting. I was taken into a large room. An immaculately-groomed man in army uniform sat at a desk in the middle of the room, with his back to the door.

Ansari said, "He is the military Censor. He is a Major."

Censor: now followed by fawn Volkswagen
With a wave of his right hand the Censor invited me to sit on the chair in front of his desk. To my horror there was a pile of my newspaper articles on his desk. Each two-page spread had been removed from the rest of its newspaper, and the pile was a couple of inches high. On top was my article on Libyan-British relations and I could see Dr Muntasser's picture.

I realised that the Censor would not have had this pile unless someone had given it to him. I realised that Ansari had supplied the Censor with my articles.

I now realised that Ansari was no longer in the room. He had left with the plain-clothes man. I was alone with my army guard and the Censor. I realised that Ansari had been asked to bring me to the Censor and provide evidence against me. My visit had been clearly planned and did not seem impulsive on Ansari's part. I wondered if those who planned the *coup* in Egypt had instructed Ansari to hand me over to the Revolutionary Command Council. The guard stood by my side.

The Major said in English: "I am the military Censor and I know about your activities. You are the Barbary Gipsy." He said sternly, "I know all about you. You are against this Revolution. I know you visited Muntasser. He has been escorted back to Tripoli under guard. You wrote these articles in breach of your University contract. You committed a crime against the people of Libya. Do you admit that you wrote these?"

Sitting by my guard I said, "I do." I could hear shouting in the corridor outside the door, and I half-expected to be led out and shot.

"You supported the King," the Censor continued, facing me across his desk.

I said, "I didn't. The King was our earliest reader, and in my article 'The Old British Consulate and the Baker'[10] I criticised the working conditions of bakers under the King's regime. I described them as waist-deep in a pit sunk in a shop. I opposed the King. I was on the side of the Revolution."

The Censor asked me to find the article and show him. I rummaged through his pile and extracted the two-page spread and read the paragraph I indicated.

He deliberated, then looked at me and said: "You are right. This article criticises the King. We are not happy about your activities and your visit to Muntasser. If you write one more word or do any work other than your University work you will be arrested. And I warn you, you will be watched by our Security from now on. We will know what you are doing."

He nodded to my guard. Was I now to be shot?

I was taken out into the corridor. There was no sign of Ansari. I was led through milling Arabs who were still shouting, between armoured cars to the gates. Still alive, I was put in a fawn Volkswagen and driven back to my flat by a driver who spoke no English. A few days later I heard that the military Censor was dismissed for being found in bed with a Western woman.

Caroline greeted my return with undisguised relief. She had been greatly worried for herself and Nadia, and the episode affected her sense of security in Libya. Two men now sat outside our flat in a fawn Volkswagen. Whenever I left, their Volkswagen followed my car. They travelled to the University with me and waited in the car park near the entrance to my building. When the banks reopened and I drove to the bank their car followed mine and they came into the bank with me and stood a yard away from me. One (who wore a *fez*) was older than the other, who smiled a lot. They were pleasant enough. I smiled and said "Hello" to them and they smiled and said "Hello" back, and when I went to the cashier's window they loitered discreetly about a yard away from my elbow. I was in effect under house arrest and only allowed out with my two minders.

The fawn Volkswagen preyed on Caroline's mind. She would look out of the window and see it sitting by our gate, and it worried her more than it worried me.

Egyptian origin of Gaddafi's coup: how Gaddafi's coup happened
It now came out that the new leader was Muammar al-Gaddafi, a Berber tribesman who had been born in the desert south of Sirte during the Second World War. He grew up in Sebha, where the 12 Free Officers were all at school together when Nasser nationalised the Suez Canal in 1956 and the British, French and Israelis invaded Egypt. He had supported Nasser's

seizure of the Suez Canal.

In the long hot evenings under curfew I pieced together the sequence of events involving the two *coups*. Muntasser's *coup* – 'Ben's *coup*' – had been too public. The ministers' parties had been penetrated. The Chief of Police, Col. Ali Shilabi, had reported what he saw and was keen to interview both Caroline and me – hence I had sent Caroline back to London early. Any one of the Yugoslav girls present at the Minister of Health's farm could have informed the KGB about Ben's parties for ministers, and the KGB could have passed the information through to Egypt. Ben's cook, Ahmad, was an Egyptian, and the Egyptian Ansari could have learned of the parties and the 5-September date from Chatter.

King was to abdicate on 2 September

In 1969–1970 Egypt had 17,000 Soviet advisers and a strong KGB presence. The KGB-supported Egyptian intelligence learned that there was a plan for King Idris to abdicate in favour of the Crown Prince on 2 September and that the abdication would be followed by the 5-September Muntasser *coup*. The King could then make out that he had handed power to the Crown Prince and that Muntasser's *coup* of 5 September was nothing to do with him. The KGB-backed Egyptian intelligence passed this on to Gaddafi. The Free Officers had links with Cairo as did Gaddafi, who had visited Egypt in 1968 on his way back from being trained at Sandhurst. Gaddafi may already have learned of the 5-September *coup* from a Libyan source such as Shilabi.

Gaddafi read my article on Libyan-British relations

Gaddafi knew the inner details of the 5-September *coup*: the playing of the music and Bushwerib's involvement on the morning of the *coup*. I was later informed by Andrew Mackenzie that the SIS believed that Gaddafi had personally read my article on Libyan-British relations in the Arabic translation, as Ansari had said. Gaddafi had seen the picture of Muntasser in the article and regarded the article as a prelude to the coming Muntasser *coup*. He was appalled at the prospect of extensive British support for a Muntasser-led Libya. He had discussed my article with his fellow-Libyan army officers who had links with Cairo and would soon form the Revolutionary Command Council. The timing of my article suggested to him that the Shalhi-backed pro-British Muntasser would replace the Crown Prince as successor to the King soon after 2 September when the King abdicated. It became urgent to block any Shalhi-backed successor, and Egyptian intelligence seems to have urged Gaddafi to strike on 1 September *before* the Crown Prince took over from the King rather than *after*.

How the coup *was organised*

A recent study[11] has pieced together what happened with reference to all the published sources. In 1956 Gaddafi formed a group within his secondary school in Sebha which met under a palm tree near Sebha Fortress. Gaddafi was forced to leave Sebha after a speech in 1961 condemning the presence of British and American bases in Libya. He went to Misurata to complete his schooling. In 1964 he enrolled at the Military Academy in Benghazi. The group had been meeting more seriously since 1963. It was renamed after Nasser's Free Unionist Officers Movement, and their revolutionary committee was named the Revolutionary Command Council. They met on public holidays and slept in the open. They amassed live ammunition. They collectively bought a sky-blue Volkswagen Beetle identical (except in colour) to my green one, which Gaddafi drove around. The *coup* was planned for 1969. By then they had cells in military camps across Libya. Gaddafi at first timetabled the *coup* for 12 March 1969 but on that date there was a concert featuring the Egyptian singer Oum Kalthoum, which would be attended by royal and military figures. It would be difficult to arrest these figures without causing mass bloodshed. A new date was set for 24 March, but the army got wind of the plan and removed King Idris to Tobruk where he would be under British protection.

For the Revolution to succeed the King and Crown Prince should ideally be in Tripoli. A new date was set for early September because some of the Free Unionist officers were to be sent to Britain for training at the beginning of September. Meanwhile King Idris went to Turkey for medical treatment and would be out of the country. September 1 was fixed on when they learned that the King would abdicate on 2 September and when my article and interview with Dr Muntasser appeared in Arabic in the Libyan press, suggesting that a Muntasser *coup* was imminent. (They had learned that the Muntasser *coup* was set for 5 September.) At the end of August Gaddafi travelled around Libya alerting his supporters. Zero hour was 2.30 a.m. on 1 September.

Opinions differ as to whether Gaddafi was in Benghazi or Tripoli at this time. According to one view he personally took over the radio station in Benghazi and broadcast news of the *coup* from there; and Khweildi al-Humaidi took the military headquarters in Tripoli and Tripoli's radio station. However, Gaddafi was deceptive. The extremely well-informed commander of the US Wheelus Air Base near Tripoli, Col. Daniel James (*see* p.286) believed[12] that Gaddafi and a handful of fellow officers, armed with a few revolvers and 48 rounds of ammunition, took the military headquarters in Tripoli and Tripoli's radio station. They were fired on, having been mistaken for Israelis. Once it was established that a *coup* was in process there was no major resistance because the officers on duty sympathised with the aims of the revolutionaries. The armoured cars and tank I encountered driving back from the University may have left barracks to subdue Tripoli *after* the storming of Tripoli's military headquarters and radio station.[13]

Gaddafi's supporters now occupied the Royal Palace. The Crown Prince was taken prisoner. His first words were, "Are you from al-Shalhi's group?"[14] (The Crown Prince seems to have known of the 5-September *coup*.) The King, told of the *coup* in Turkey, is reported to have said that it was an event "of no importance",[15] because he thought the *coup* was the one Abdulaziz al-Shalhi was associated with, the Muntasser *coup* of the group who had met at his farm.

Gaddafi mimicked the 5-September pro-Western coup

Knowing that twelve 27-year-old captains, junior captains and lieutenants would be seen as too young to run Libya, the organisers of the 1-September *coup* devised a strategy to get it accepted by the West. Gaddafi very cleverly left the structural details of the 5-September *coup* in place. By playing Beshir's music on the local radio and releasing Saad eddin Bushwerib's name to the BBC World Service, Gaddafi had cunningly led the Western media to believe the *coup* had been conducted by Saad eddin Bushwerib a few days early. He reckoned that the West would know in advance about the 5-September *coup*, and his deception persuaded the West to believe that the pro-Western *coup* they were expecting had happened. If they had known the truth, the US and British might have crushed the 1-September *coup* within its first week by invoking the 1953 twenty-year Libyan-British treaty of friendship and alliance and sending in troops.

Egypt behind Gaddafi's coup

Col. Nasser, the Egyptian leader, gave the impression of anticipating a *coup* by Abdulaziz al-Shalhi, the Muntasser *coup*.[16] Allegedly Nasser sent Mohammed Hassanein Heikal to visit Libya to find out who was behind the *coup*, and when Heikal left his plane at Benghazi he asked, "Where is Abdulaziz?"[17] Heikal gave the impression that Egyptian intelligence knew about the Shalhi-backed Muntasser *coup*. In fact, both Nasser and Heikal may well have known that the *coup* was Gaddafi's as Ansari had told me, "This Revolution was planned in Egypt." And as there were 17,000 Soviet military advisers in Egypt at that time and the KGB were in Cairo supporting Nasser, it could be that it was ultimately a Soviet-backed *coup*. It is likely that it suited Egypt, Nasser and Heikal to pretend to be mystified as to whose *coup* it was so they could conceal the Egyptian role in carrying out the *coup*. Under the cloak of mystification Heikal was briefing the new Libyan leader on behalf of Egyptian intelligence as much as interviewing him.

According to Heikal Gaddafi offered Libya to Egypt during this meeting. He gave Heikal a message to his hero Nasser, offering formal Egyptian rule in Libya: "Tell President Nasser we made this Revolution for him. He can take everything of ours and add it to the rest of the Arab world's resources to be used for the battle [against Israel, and for Arab unity]."[18] Gaddafi's offer of Libya to Egypt is further evidence for the Egyptian – and Nasser's – role in planning the 1-September *coup*.

Nasser declined Gaddafi's offer. He knew that if he and his 17,000 Soviet advisers formally took over in Libya, he would be opposed by the US, Britain and Israel. Furthermore, he was buying a new Soviet rocket system of SAM-3s and was on a war-footing with Israel, and it was too expensive a time to be pouring troops and money into Libya.

Bushwerib now Libyan Ambassador to Egypt

There was a further mystery regarding Saad eddin Bushwerib's role. On 1 September Bushwerib was in Italy, waiting to fly to Tripoli. A representative of the Libyan Embassy found him drinking coffee in a café in Rome and told him he was the new leader. He was not arrested but made Chief of Staff. Bushwerib clearly threw in his lot with Gaddafi on his return to Tripoli. It was useful to Gaddafi to have a senior military figure as Chief of Staff, and as Bushwerib was fronting the 5-September *coup*, having him as Chief of Staff protected Gaddafi from soldiers loyal to Bushwerib who might want to mount a new *coup*. Did Bushwerib betray the 5-September *coup*? Within two or three months he was made Libyan Ambassador to Egypt. Was he rewarded for revealing Ben's meeting with him under cover of a holiday with Caroline and me on or near Djerba to Egyptian intelligence?

There were conflicting stories about Dr Muntasser. According to one story he was kidnapped by Libyans in London and taken back to Tripoli in handcuffs. The Censor had told me as much. According to a press story he reported to the British and Commonwealth Office in London that he was being recalled to Libya for consultations, and arrived in Tripoli on 10 October. No more was heard of him for some years.

Gaddafi's perspective

I saw how useful I had been to the 5-September *coup* organisers. I had presented Libya in the Western media (*The Daily News*), and I had acted as go-between with Muntasser. My article on Libyan-British relations had gone out in Arabic across Libya and had suggested that the relations between Britain and Libya were close.

I also saw how what I had done might appear to the 1-September *coup* leaders, including Gaddafi. I had been seen at one of Ben's parties by Col.

Ali Shilabi, who wanted to interview Caroline and me. I was a link between the British Government (through Goronwy Roberts) and the 5-September *coup* leaders. I do not know if they knew of my link with Andrew Mackenzie, but I must have come across to the 1-September *coup* leaders as being very involved in the 5-September *coup*.

The pro-Western 5-September *coup* which the British Establishment had monitored was supposed to be philanthropic and liberate the poor from poverty. Almost all those involved with Muntasser's *coup* were in prison, including Beshir, and no one knew what Gaddafi's tyranny would inflict next. Would the poor benefit or be oppressed? I reckoned I had been lucky to get off so lightly. My position was vulnerable and Caroline was deeply worried.

Episode 12:

Purgation and Separation

Years: 1969–1970
Locations: Tripoli; Cairo; Luxor; Alexandria; El Alamein; Ghadames; Malta
Works: *The Gates of Hell*
Initiatives: finds SAM-3 missiles at El Alamein; organises Viktor's defection

"Do you not see how necessary a World of Pains and troubles is to school an Intelligence and make it a Soul?"
John Keats, letter to George and Georgiana Keats, 3 May 1819

The nightmare social conditions of living under a terrorist State in Tripoli and under prohibition imposed a general abstemiousness on all and accelerated the process of detaching my soul from the craving of my senses. However, the alarming events outside our front door had a corrosive, destructive effect on my marriage and exacerbated my Dark Night. In my next episode there was a conflict between my ongoing purgation and the anguish of my separation, and I became even more lost in the dark wood and could not find the right path.

Purgation: puritanical Revolutions's prohibition and terror, and Western defiance
Terror made us wary of going out during the day, and curfew kept us off the

streets at night. There was no television, no phone, no alcohol and little radio. We were thrown back on ourselves. The Libyan Revolution was puritanical and we began to live as puritans: I was forced to detach myself from any craving for alcohol I had. My Dark Night began to purge my soul by detaching it from my senses. Caroline and I had no disagreements but deep down she did not want to be in Tripoli and remained aloof.

Puritanical Revolution's anti-Western measures: Western lettering removed
The University at last reopened. The Vice-Dean had been arrested, and students were back part-time. They had been urged to defend the Revolution, and had been armed.

My Head of Department told me that my teaching group had expanded. My first lecture was in a long room. I entered and saw 120 students sitting at desks wearing military uniform with loaded rifles lying in the aisles or propped against their chairs. They were going on to a military parade after lectures. I was not sure if they had been issued with live ammunition. Standing before them and discussing a story by Hemingway about gentleness ('Cat in the Rain'), I hoped that they would not form themselves into a 120-strong firing-squad.

Now anti-Western measures were announced. It was announced that from the end of September all Western lettering would be banned. Western street names on road signs had to be scrubbed out or painted over. I had to paint out the Western numbers on my car's number-plates. The message was clear: Libya was now outside Western civilization, across the frontier, in Roman terms among the 'barbarians'.

Each day the Revolutionary Command Council issued decrees on the theme of "Freedom, Unity, Socialism" (freedom from the West, unity with Arabs and socialist policies). The decrees were reinforced by images of terror and coercion. Drawings of hangings appeared on many walls. I had to take my driving-licence and identity card to Castle Square to get 'Kingdom of Libya' overstamped 'Libyan Arab Republic', and I was shouted at in Arabic by the soldier who did the stamping.

For three weeks I had lived like one of the Egyptian Desert Fathers in Scetis. I had a flat rather than a hut on my strip of desert, but with basic food, no alcohol, a fawn Volkswagen outside our gate, no recognisable English lettering anywhere and a tense and fearful wife who wanted to be left alone, I was as deprived of sensual comforts as they were and was plunged into involuntary purgation. Some afternoons I sunbathed on our flat roof for an hour. The silence of the long desert evenings under curfew was broken only by the occasional drone of an army lorry and a howling pye-dog. During these evenings I began writing poems for *The Gates of Hell.*

Ben Nagy resurfaces
One day Ben arrived at my door. He would not come in. He said he had been in London on 1 September. He boasted, "I returned to Tripoli and complained that I was a victim of corruption under the ex-regime which forced me to resign from the army. I left the airport a free man. But it would be unwise for me to visit you again. Or any Westerners now. I am still your landlord but you must pay your rent to my agent and you will not see me. That is best."

Suddenly everything changed. The fawn Volkswagen disappeared. Now expatriates defiantly asserted their right to carry on as before the puritanical *coup* and prohibition by sharing their drinks cabinets in 'back-to-normal' socialising.

American offers to turn me into a computer programmer
Almost immediately the American couple, Kat and Buddy, returned to our door and invited us to a very early supper at their huge villa in Giorgimpopoli, which would end in time for us to get home before the beginning of curfew. Kat, dark-haired, self-styled "Louisiana belle" and (she told me) former beauty queen, made brandy Alexanders which (being made of brandy, cream, ice and nutmeg) looked like chocolate ice-creams. We took them on to the roof and, overlooking the nearby insane asylum in the evening sun, their triplets playing happily, her husband, who (he told me) was from Dallas, again offered to turn me into a computer analyst-programmer like himself. I would have to do between 50 and 75 hours at two or three hours a day under him, take a two-week course in London, and then I could start a new job he could almost guarantee on $1,000 a month. There was some summer lightning on the horizon and Chopin billowed out of the window below, and Kat looked vivacious and was encouraging.

I visited him at work the next day and collected a couple of computer books and half-heartedly went through the motions of beginning to learn PL/1 and Fortran, two computer languages that were even more boring than the Law. US computers had just taken Apollo-11 to the surface of the moon, and with hindsight I can see that this Dallas American was a man of the future, working in early computer languages that a generation later would evolve into the world-wide web. Soon afterwards the two of them called on us and took us down to the beach near the Crown Prince's palace to see the Phoenician ruins, and Kat lay spread-eagled against the cliff in a red trouser suit, her black hair tumbling round her shoulders.

House guest
Into this situation came an English friend of Caroline's, Daphne, a well-spoken English divorcée now living on Malta with her parents. She had been

living in Tripoli and had come round several times in March after her American fiancé, who was in oil and also living in Tripoli, had broken off their engagement. She had brought furniture out to Tripoli to set up home after they were married, and she was suing him for breach of promise to recover the cost of transporting the furniture. She came back from Malta for the court case and, having written to Caroline to ask, stayed with us as our house guest.

I was uneasy about the morality of her claim and was uncomfortable at supporting her in a case involving breach of promise.

Recruitment of Viktor by Andrew Mackenzie, three names of members of the RCC
We took her to meet Viktor. His wife – the daughter of a wartime Czech Resistance leader, a General, a good credential for mounting resistance to the Soviet Union – had just joined him. She had shortish brown hair and a very alert face. She was warm and brought their son through to meet us, a pleasant, slightly nervous 11-year-old. He soon returned to his room, and Viktor said he wanted to get him into Tripoli College (the school expatriates wanted their children to attend). He wondered if Andrew could influence his admission as he was attached to the British Embassy.

Viktor and his wife plied us with cognac and whisky, which they had somehow acquired despite prohibition. Viktor giggled at an impending "battle of the imperialists" (the court battle between an English lady and an American man). We crept home after curfew, pursued by baying wolf-dogs.

I had not seen Andrew Mackenzie for nearly a month. At last he responded to my telephone calls and arranged to meet me on the water-front. I had begun to think that my usefulness to the SIS had come to an end as most of my old contacts were in prison and had been paraded on TV. He picked me up and told me that he had lived down the *coup*. He said that it is the *coups* we *don't* hear about that happen. He said that my priority was now to find out who was in the Revolutionary Command Council as the names of the 12 Free Officers were not known.

He also said that he wanted to recruit Viktor. He said Viktor would initially be a window on the Iron-Curtain community in Tripoli, but would eventually return behind the Iron Curtain and be an important spy for the West, like Penkovsky, who had informed the UK and the US about the Soviet missiles in Cuba. "I want you to prepare him so that I can pop the question." I again thought that an approach by Andrew might help Viktor in his future life and went along with the idea. I said that Viktor wanted to get his son into Tripoli College.

I had discussions with different students about the Revolution, and asked if they knew the names of members of the Revolutionary Command Council. None of them knew as the RCC guarded their anonymity. Then one of my students sought me out. He said, "I have heard you want to know the names of the Revolutionary Command Council. I know three names. Please look on me kindly in the next exams."

I said I could only reflect the standard of his papers. He still gave me the three names, reckoning that it would do him good during the marking.

I now took to visiting Viktor down my sandy lane. The first time I called on him I found him lying in bed listening to Wagner (the entrance of the gods into Valhalla) and reading calculus. We discussed how Communism should have a human face and he agreed that the British Labour Party was his ideal form of government. He said, "I would like to work in England." I told him I had a friend who might be able to help him move to England. I invited Viktor to my flat on 7 October, when I knew my family and Daphne were out for the evening.

Andrew arrived a quarter of an hour early and arranged the chairs so that he and Viktor could sit forward and look into each other's eyes. Viktor arrived. I introduced him to Andrew, served them coffee and, having made sure that they had got on well, by arrangement at 8.30 said I had to go out for half an hour. When I returned they were still there, sitting forward and in deep conversation.

Andrew left soon afterwards. At the door, out of Viktor's earshot, he whispered that he had "popped the question" and that Viktor had asked for time to think. Andrew said, "I've given him a month." He wanted me to make daily visits to Viktor to reel him in.

Viktor told me that Andrew might indeed be able to help him, but that there were difficulties involving his wife and son that had to be discussed. He stayed until 12.30 a.m., long after my family returned. He left and walked home down our sandy lane.

Court

We had taken Daphne to her court. The courtroom had turned out to be covered in dust-sheets, and so we took her to sunbathe by the Uaddan pool. She had to wait a week for her court to reopen, and as she was staying with us we took her out for drives. We went to the villa once occupied by Mohammed ben Othman, who led one of Libya's early governments after independence in 1951. We took her up to see Kat and Buddy, where a Spanish psychiatrist with a goatbeard, Manuel, was holding forth. He invited us all to a party at his house the next night. There we met another American and his wife, who was a half-Irish, half-German Jewess, Ursula. There was also an Irish oilman, Jim, who struck up a friendship with Daphne. Despite prohibition there was alcohol in all these houses, and the drinking was a Western defiance of the puritanical *coup*.

Daphne's court case was heard on 8 October. Her lawyer, a Palestinian called Akram, told me he always won as he bribed the judge in advance. He tried to persuade me to be a witness and perjure myself. He wanted me to say that I had heard her American fiancé say he would marry her. I refused. Both Akram and Daphne were put out that I would not help.

Then the court doorkeeper shouted names in Arabic, and the case began. It was conducted in Arabic. The American (a bald, burly fellow) stood and answered questions put to him in English. Daphne gave her evidence in English. She – or rather, Akram – won. Akram said that damages would be assessed as the value of a car and between £1,000 and £2,000.

After the verdict we repaired to the Café del Poste near the Bank of North Africa (where I had first Andrew Mackenzie) to celebrate Daphne's victory. There she announced that she had broken off with her American fiancé because he bored her, which made me feel very uneasy as the case had been based on her desire to marry the American. She then went out to dinner with her Irish admirer.

First glimpse of Gaddafi
The next day I took Daphne to BEA to book her ticket back to Malta. There was a crowd outside the Ministry of Foreign Affairs and I saw the new British Ambassador arrive to present his credentials. (If the 5-September *coup* had succeeded, that could have been *me* presenting my credentials.)

On the way back I saw a large crowd outside the same building and suddenly there was a roar and Gaddafi, the leader of the Revolution, appeared and waved, a young man with a straight back-and-sides haircut in a peaked cap and military uniform. The crowd waved their hands and chanted "Ga-dda-fi" and the enthusiasm was so great that he was unable to struggle through to his Land Rover.

With the British Ambassador, Donald Maitland, at the British Council
Soon the new British Ambassador, Donald Maitland, attended a gathering for all British lecturers and teachers at the British Council. He had previously been PPS to the British Foreign Secretary. I was the first Council lecturer he spoke to. He said knowingly that he had read my article on old regimes and that it was well-thought-out and well-written. I asked him how he had found Gaddafi at the Ministry of Foreign Affairs. He said, "Oh good, can you ask me that as soon as I've finished my speech? That will make a good first question."

In his speech he talked generally about the situation in Tripoli. I duly asked the question and he replied that the RCC were a group of nationalists who were now putting Libya first.

Expatriates' defiant hedonistic parties

Daphne stayed a few more days. She went boating with her Irish admirer, Jim, and brought him to dinner with us. We all visited Kat's and the next day Ursula gave a party where we drank Pimms and gin. We did not know that the Irishman, Jim, had had a long affair with Ursula. He now told her he wanted to marry Daphne. There were raised voices, and he stalked out of the party, slamming the door. Daphne had just opened a bottle of gin to add a little gin to the punch. Unseen, she emptied the entire contents of the bottle into the punch-bowl and ran after him while Ursula sat in the bathroom and snivelled.

The punch was passed round in a communal rebellion against the puritanical regime, its *coup* and its prohibition. No one knew how powerful it had become and I remember lying on a bed in the guest room trying to stop the room spinning. I woke to hear Kat whispering in my ear. Caroline got me onto my feet and we staggered home after curfew.

The next evening the Irishman, Jim, came round. Daphne spent her last evening with him and stayed out until 6.30 a.m., returning to say a brief goodbye.

Daphne had gone but her presence as our house guest, the visits we made with her to Kat, the Spanish psychiatrist Manuel and Ursula and Daphne's tipping of the bottle of gin into the punch had set a chain of events in motion.

Sequences (or chains) of events

This narrative consists of sequences (or chains) of events. To Whitehead, an event is "a nexus of actual occasions" at a given time and place.[1] Geoffrey Read, a Leibnizian philosopher I knew who refined Whitehead's ideas of process, saw time as a succession of events, and past events are not obliterated but added to by present events.[2] The past therefore always persists in the present and new events in a sequence or chain are added to previous events and co-exist with them. This is similar to my view that sequences of events within episodes are like the sequences of scales in a spruce cone (*see* p.xxvii).

Like superstrings in physics, events cluster together, one after another, in chains. In each episode of my life there were conflicting sequences (or chains) of events. The chains of a lifetime seem to be tangled, mixed up together like a bowl of spaghetti, or like the tent-shaped net of a computer spirograph representing an oilfield which I saw on Kat's husband's office wall when I collected my computer books. But in actuality the chains or sequences of events are compactly arranged in spirals round the memory like the spirals on a spruce cone.

New controller, Malcolm Hall: Viktor's anger
Meanwhile, Andrew had handed me over to Malcolm Hall of the British Embassy, his deputy. He wore horn-rimmed spectacles and looked slightly overweight. He was about 35 and had dark hair and a strangely unformed, almost babyish face. He was to monitor me while I reeled Viktor in. But he had not met Viktor and completely misunderstood his nature and his pride. At our first meeting, on 13 October, he told me to say that the help Viktor had asked for in getting his son into Tripoli College would only be forthcoming if he said Yes at the end of his month's thinking.

I argued that it was best to provide the help and then Viktor's Yes would follow as natural gratitude. But Malcolm Hall was adamant that I should do as he had instructed. At the next opportunity I conveyed what "Andrew" had said – I did not tell Viktor that the message had come from Andrew's deputy, who he had never met – and Viktor reacted with predictable anger. He muttered that making his recruitment a condition of help showed there was no difference between Andrew and the KGB. His anger spilled over to me. He said, "You are brainwashing me, I know." I now had Viktor angrily on my line as I tried to reel him in.

I watch Gaddafi call for expulsion of Western bases in Castle Square
On 16 October there was a rally in Castle Square. Wanting to hear the man who had stolen my *coup* and brought change to Libya that had affected my life, forcing me to make existential choices within the context of a puritanical Revolution I had not chosen, I attended.

A huge Nazi-style eagle spread its wings over the platform. It was similar to the eagle with spread wings in the ruins of Hitler's Chancellery. (Like the National Socialist Hitler who was anti-British, anti-American and anti-Jewish, the nationalist-socialist Gaddafi wanted to expel the British and American bases and obliterate Israel.) A great drape hung from the Castle. It showed Gaddafi trampling Shalhi, symbol of the corruption behind the monarchy (and also of the 5-September *coup*), underfoot. Hundreds of Arabs under banners chanted slogans led by a black-suited man on the platform. Arabs swarmed over stationary tanks and hung to ladders propped against palm trees. I seemed to be the only Westerner present. I was standing on the waterfront pavement, near the sea.

Then music blared out *"Allahu Akbar"*, and the crowd roared. Down steps came Gaddafi, capless, surrounded by joyous uniformed members of the RCC (whose names I was supposed to be obtaining). There was a confused pause. Then guns fired into the air. Soldiers fired live rounds that whistled over our heads. Rifles were cracking all round the square, a machine-gun was rat-tat-tatting, artillery thumped and boomed, ships blasted heavy guns and jets thundered overhead in a show of force by the new military regime.

Gaddafi started speaking haltingly. He was calling for the expulsion of American and British bases in Libya. Now there was a continuous hubbub. No one seemed to be listening and Arabs began to walk away. His policy of expulsion did not appear to be popular. I sensed it was time to leave.

On my way back up the waterfront I saw Malcolm Hall. He was standing in his dark suit, white shirt and tie in the middle of a crowd of Arabs, arms folded. He was the only other Westerner I had seen. I walked up to him and past him. No sign of recognition passed between us for the square was sure to be full of secret police.

More defiant parties
That evening Manuel, the Spanish psychiatrist, brought Ursula, the Irish-German Jewess, round to visit us. During the conversation he was very dismissive of art, claiming that the artist is a neurotic. A butterfly fluttered round the room and died on our dried flowers.

The next day Manuel and Ursula held a party and invited Kat and her husband, and us. We drank Canadian Club in defiance of the puritanical *coup*, and Manuel again belittled art: "It's not real. It's not important to society. It satisfies a need like drinking from a beer can or cooking." I wondered what I was doing in the same room as these people. They played the truth game, in which everyone asked everyone else a question about themselves. I was inwardly cross at being in this situation.

At Wheelus Air Base after Gaddafi's confrontation: CIA
The next day, Saturday 18 October, Kat and her husband invited Caroline and me to Wheelus Air Base. There was an American party there and the Wheelus Base commander was present, a giant African-American, Col. James. He wore a gold crown on a long chain round his neck, and I asked him why. He said, "I've had enough of this bloody Revolution, I'm pro-King."

I did not know that a few hours previously Gaddafi had arrived at the entrance to Wheelus and had ordered a column of Libyan half-tracks (military vehicles with wheels on the front and caterpillar tracks on the back) to enter. Col. James had gone to the entrance and lowered the barrier, blocking the half-tracks. He had confronted Gaddafi, who wore a holster and kept his hand on the gun inside it in a display of terror. Col. James had a .45 in his belt. He told Gaddafi, "Move your hand away from that gun." Gaddafi had complied and gone away, his attempt to shut down Wheelus Air Base almost single-handedly having failed.[3] (*See* p.275.)

An English diplomat who worked in the British Embassy, who Andrew had mentioned, was present and asked me how we came to be there. I said we had been invited. Later we had dinner with Kat and her husband, sitting at a table for four, and I observed him watching us. Ursula was also there with her husband, and she said to me, "I thought this was for intelligence people only." She was very active all evening, talking to everyone privately, collecting information from all the guests.

The next time I saw Malcolm Hall he praised me for obtaining the three names of the RCC and then said, "I understand you were at Wheelus with an American couple on Saturday. When I heard this I was worried that you might be working for the CIA. You shouldn't see them again. The Americans can only create difficulties for you."

I was not sure if he was saying that the "couple" were in the CIA. He might have been making a feeble joke. I did not take kindly to being ordered not to see people again. I bristled: the deal with Andrew Mackenzie had been that I would share what I already knew, not cut people out of my life without explanation.

Americans expelled for CIA links: Head of Tripoli CIA

On 23 October Manuel came round with "sad news". Ursula and her American husband had been accused of being CIA agents – perhaps as a result of their information-gathering at Wheelus – and had been given 48 hours to leave Libya.

That afternoon we went round to their house and found a room full of people drinking bourbon despite prohibition. The expelled couple were overtly keeping their spirits up but tears were not far away. I overheard Ursula's husband say, "Honey, we're not in the CIA any more." We left as a storm broke with forked lightning.

Two days later there was an all-day goodbye 'packing party' at their house. A dozen expatriates drank bourbon and rum punch. Ursula introduced me to "Cliff, the Head of the CIA in Tripoli", who was sitting on a sofa, bespectacled in an open-necked white shirt, holding a glass. He had thinning hair and looked in his early fifties.

Cliff bombarded me with questions about my activities at the University. He knew that I had been the Barbary Gipsy; and he knew that I was friendly with Viktor. I sensed that he knew about my role in the 5-September *coup*, but he did not refer to it.

He asked me several questions about Viktor as a Cold-War asset, which I answered as neutrally as possible. I did not want the CIA taking Viktor from me before his month's thinking had expired. Then he turned to Ursula and her husband and said, "I just wish we knew who is in the RCC." I found it hard to believe that he had no names whereas I had found three, and I probed his knowledge of the RCC. He genuinely did not seem to have any idea who was in the RCC.

He asked me, "How can the expulsion be reversed?"

I said, "By getting a member of the RCC to reverse it."

He said, "We don't know who's in the RCC. How do we get to the RCC?"

I was aware that he was inviting me to tell him my links with the RCC. I said, "The only way to reverse it is to go to the President at the University. He is related to one of the RCC."

The Head of the CIA made a note. Kat and her husband were in the room, and now Buddy sat on the sofa beside Cliff and talked with him at some length. Again I wondered if their physical proximity concealed a working relationship, but this was a social situation and I dismissed the idea. Again a storm rumbled, and we said goodbye to Ursula and her husband and walked home with the *muezzin* calling.

Expulsion reversed

Two days later Manuel invited us to another party at his house. Ursula and her husband were sitting in the corner.

"Am I dreaming?" I asked.

"You were right," her husband said. "The President *did* know someone in the RCC. Our expulsion has been cancelled."

There was general rejoicing and I now had a reputation for knowing what was going on inside the Libyan Revolution. The social invitations from Kat and Buddy multiplied, and I wondered if the Head of the CIA was egging them on.

Col. Gaddafi visits the University: "Some journalists will be executed"

Soon afterwards Col. Gaddafi came to the University on a very hot day. The front car park was filled with seated students. Gaddafi sat at a table in the open air, wearing an open-necked white shirt and no cap. Four uniformed men in red berets stood round him holding machine-guns. Gaddafi's eyes were constantly looking around. He looked to the left, straight ahead, then to the right, scanning for assassins or snipers, alert to possible danger. He spoke haltingly in Arabic. The student sitting next to me translated.

At one point Gaddafi stared at me – I was sitting about four rows from his table – and said menacingly: "I would like to say that some journalists will be executed for what they have written about the Libyan people." It was psychological terrorism, a deliberate attempt to spread fear.

Viktor questions defection: competition with CIA to recruit Viktor

I had seen Viktor regularly and he was still angry at the pressure Malcolm Hall had instructed me to exert. On 30 October I visited him. He asked what I thought of fighting taking place in the Lebanon, and I was surprised at how anti-American he was. (He had an Eastern-European view of the US.) He again asked me if Andrew could get his son into Tripoli College immediately. I had raised this issue again with Malcolm Hall, who had reiterated, "We can help after 7 November." In other words, after Viktor's month's thinking had expired and he said Yes. I explained to Viktor as tactfully as I could that "Andrew" had said the Embassy would be able to arrange his admission but it would take a little time. "Why?" Viktor asked defiantly. I explained that London had to be involved. (I could not think how else to explain the delay until 7 November without enraging him.)

Viktor immediately said, "Can Andrew not help a friend without London knowing? Can *you* not get him into Tripoli College?" Then, quite unreasonably (for he had requested me to ask Andrew, *see* pp.281–282), "Why did you tell Andrew? You are clearly not free to act on your own." Cold-War suspicion came to the fore. He said, "To tell Andrew was an unfriendly act. Human relations are important to me, and I had hoped to have a relationship with you and Andrew, but now I know it is not possible." He refused to believe in my good intentions. Malcolm Hall had been supplying me with alcohol to give him, and now he again said (this time of the alcohol), "I know you are brainwashing me. I know."

The situation had got out of hand. I would have got his son into Tripoli College and then counted on his gratitude to reciprocate. I had gone as far as I could with pressure and threats. I rang Andrew and asked if I could meet him.

We met on the waterfront and I explained that pressure was not working. He listened while I explained the mess Malcolm Hall had made of running Viktor, and then announced I would be dealing with him from now on, not Malcolm Hall. He also told me that the CIA had been after Viktor and were trying to snatch him from us. The Head of the CIA in Tripoli had indeed been trying to get information from me.

I was being targeted by the CIA and I thought I could keep one step ahead of what they were doing.

Separation: intensified Dark Night of the Senses

It is still painful to record the chain of events that led to the collapse of my marriage and which intensified my Dark Night. I want to skate over this part of my story but I must face it as the events were important to my development. I should probably have paid more attention when I told Caroline after Daphne's departure "You are very mature" and she said: "Detached, bored, not mature."

Extreme conditions

Caroline had accompanied me to the parties and CIA intrigues that filled October and had been triggered by the arrival of Daphne as our house guest. During these events my head had been full of intelligence matters. Hers had not. The conditions through which we had lived had been highly abnormal: prohibition, terror on the streets, fear of imminent arrest, concern for the safety of our daughter. I believe that if I had not met Andrew Mackenzie outside the Bank of North Africa we would not have attended any of the social events of October or met any of the Americans who appeared after that event or encountered the amoral hedonism that defied the puritanical regime.

Every day Caroline expected me to be arrested for working against the regime and taken away, as had happened when I was taken to the radio station. Now Gaddafi had threatened journalists with execution. Caroline, worried to distraction about the safety of our daughter, was exercising her judgement within extreme conditions, and I was too preoccupied with Andrew, Viktor and the RCC to grasp how desperate she was feeling within, and how much she wanted to get herself and our daughter out of Libya.

At the beginning of November Kat had a party in her Giorgimpopoli villa. There was a log fire, and her husband disappeared with Caroline. Kat found them on the roof together. Caroline shut herself in a room and cried while Kat and I talked on the front step. Other Americans stood behind us, and I sensed that I was being walled round. I thought Buddy might be questioning Caroline about Viktor, and I was so confident of being able to control the situation that I did not leave. We slept that night in a guest double bed – Nadia was staying with a friend – and I remember the blue sky over yellow battlements the next morning, and Kat in her "robe" brightly pouring coffee.

When we got home Caroline cried and said, "You're my only security, everything's crumbling, I ought to go, for your sake," and: "I regret these incidents that have spoiled our marriage. Why won't people leave me alone?" I still thought that the incident on the roof was CIA-inspired.

We drove to the Homs-Road beach and I said wryly: "Marriage is cohab-itation between two strangers who share common experience." The Mediterranean came in, wave upon long ribbony wave. We walked below the rocky sea-cliffs and I bent and picked up two green corroded Libyan coins near some sea lavender and said: "Like our marriage, us. We've gone green and corroded."

Caroline began crying behind her dark glasses and a pearly tear rolled down her chin. She said, "I've messed things up, I've messed up our marriage." But I still saw the situation in terms of the intelligence world rather than her beauty. Later she became blank and self-justificatory, and when our ginger cat messed on Nadia's bed she burst into tears and asked to be left alone.

Viktor's answer

Viktor's month was now up and on 6 November I went round to hear his answer. It was Yes, conditional on there being a probationary period until June.

He said he had doubts about the value of the work he could do: "It is the people that change history, not individuals like Sorge or the Rosenbergs." His view of the people as the force for change was Communist, and his reference to Sorge and the Rosenbergs hinted at the nuclear secrets he would bring with him (and possibly the risk of execution he faced). Then he became gloomy and said that people are solitary and lonely, that all the mass media we absorb are a waste of time, that our talk is all superficial and only silence is deep. Having written 'The Silence', I agreed. He had great integrity and insisted (unreasonably) regarding his son, "You should have asked me before you went to Andrew." I was conciliatory and tried to defuse his confrontational tone. He gave me a brown paper bag containing what looked like toadstools, saying they were mushrooms, and I wondered if the KGB were using him to poison me.

I rang Andrew and met him on the waterfront and told him Viktor's answer. He was overjoyed, and there was great rejoicing. Andrew repeated that the CIA had been after Viktor and wanted him to work with them, and that I had successfully fought off a strong American challenge. Andrew now withdrew the supply of alcohol to Viktor. We had solved his problem by helping him to defect, and there was now no need for alcohol to numb the pain caused by his problem. I had reeled him in by establishing a relationship with him despite Malcolm Hall's attempts at blackmail and threats.

I now wanted to escape the outer world of Viktor and Americans and return to poetry. I wrote in my *Diaries* on 8 November: "I must be a poet about my life. This is *Life Cycle*. The bits, of contrasted moods, that make up a seeking and exploring…. The aim of *Life Cycle* is to recapture experiences I have had and relate them to certain ages: a kind of *Prelude*. The significance and meaning of life reviewed." Had the events of the next month been different I might have started this work before Christmas. This project has been waiting for me for more than 50 years and will be my next work.

American couple

Intuitively I had half-sensed a disaster was coming, but I did not sever my connection with Kat and her husband, believing that Caroline was too dependent on me to leave me, not realising how desperately she wanted to escape Libya.

We should not have gone but Caroline and I spent an evening at Kat's, talking with her and her husband until 3 a.m. in front of the olive-wood log fire. The logs were green and steamed, we sipped vodkas and rums and enjoyed the warm atmosphere despite the cold Revolution and prohibition outside. Kat and I were getting closer. She had somehow turned to me and I remember saying that I was prepared to choose poverty and leisure against satiety and possessions, to keep the senses alive – not realising I was bringing my soul to birth amid hedonistic sensuality. I had already begun my self-stripping, a feature of the Dark Night. We stayed the night.

The next day Caroline and I were incredibly harmonious and close. Our marriage seemed to be perfect. A few days later the poinsettias were out round our balcony and I wrote of reacting to them with "instinctive holistic joy".

Kat went to Italy with another American wife, and Caroline and I went up to spend an evening with her husband and the triplets and there was a palpable peace in the room. When Kat returned we again went up and our families sat round the fire, drinking cognac.

On 17 November I had a letter from Buchanan in Japan, saying that my post would be vacant and that Professor Narita and Professor Irie would be happy for me to return as Visiting Foreign Professor. The same bungalow would be at our disposal. I showed the letter to Caroline and said I proposed to decline the offer because Libya was our last overseas posting and I would be living and working in London from the following summer.

Now the first foreign banks and hospitals were nationalised. The Revolutionary Command Council had opened the Crown Prince's palace to the public to expose the luxury in which the ex-regime lived. We went to see it with Kat and her husband. The internal walls were of fine silk and there was a view of the sea from many windows. It was to prevent the Crown Prince who lived there from ruling Libya that the 5-September *coup* had been planned. We also went to the palace where Mussolini stayed when he visited his troops in 1940. I did not understand it but intuitively I had a profound sense that my marriage was crumbling and that I had somehow abandoned myself to events.

Break-up of my marriage
The end came abruptly. On 4 December, as usual I put Nadia to bed, having looked at her writing, dodged her six-times table and read her a story. When I came out of her room Caroline was ironing her *kimono* on the ironing-board. I told her that Kat had asked to talk to me. (She had sent me a message, hand-delivered by a friend who was driving our way, asking me to go up and see her.)

Caroline stopped ironing and said, "I know what she wants to talk to you about." She said: "Buddy has asked me to marry him, and I've promised I will."

I was winded. I could not believe what I had heard. It was all arranged. He was going to buy a large house in London in Portman Square, just north of Oxford Street, and they would live there. She would have Nadia. They might eventually go to America. I began to argue but it was a *fait accompli*. She said she had fallen in love with Buddy and he with her, and that she would (understandably) rather live in England than in Libya.

I had to collect my thoughts. I left the flat and got into the car. Did ten years of marriage end like that, abruptly beside an ironing-board? I drove to Kat's and found her alone and told her. She did not seem to be surprised. Manuel had got wind of what was afoot and had said something to her. That was why she wanted to see me. She looked at me, her beauty-queen hair tumbling round her shoulders, and said, "Bring Caroline up here and we'll sort things out."

I cannot exaggerate the despair I felt as I returned home. I was bewildered. I had struggled to hold my marriage together for many months. Suddenly the will to fight on had gone out of me. It was as though the situation had passed beyond my control and was somehow out of reach. I had told her we would be living in London but I could not afford to buy a house in Portman Square. I could not compete with the American life-style that was being proposed. Yes, Caroline was very beautiful, but if she did not want to live with me then perhaps it would be best to let her go.

Overwhelmed by the situation I did not now see a CIA manoeuvre, I saw a genuine transfer of love. However I looked at it, there had recently been interference in our marriage from outside which I had thought I could control but which had proved uncontainable. Did I want to reverse the turn of events? Half of me said "No", and even, "Good riddance." But I could not bear the thought of being separated from Nadia.

Caroline had put a hot-water bottle in my bed and we lay in silence, back to back, each thinking about the future. It proved to be our last night together. We talked desultorily, but her mind seemed so clearly made up that there was little to say.

I was very clear that I was in this position because of my intelligence work. I was sure that was what had brought Buddy and Kat to our door. Bushwerib, Chatter, Viktor, the 5-September *coup*, the composition of the RCC – I was sure that Cliff or someone had used them to collect information from me. My *Diaries* simply record: "Break-up of my marriage. A bleak day." My Dark Night was upon me in earnest.

Upheavals; RCC dismiss Head of Department
I have said that the Dark Night of the Senses detaches the soul from the web of the lower senses, a process that leaves them in emptiness and darkness. The Mystic Way demands detachment from the ego's sensuality. Sometimes,

if the withdrawal of attachment is too slow in coming, life sweeps away the object of the attachment to allow self-stripping to accelerate, a paring-down, a remaking of oneself. In this sense, suffering can be a precious gift for it affords the possibility of a change, a transformation, that would not otherwise happen. And events that at the time seemed disastrous may later appear as a blessing.

The next day Caroline, Nadia and I went up to Kat's villa and the four of us had a meeting while the four children played outside. Kat's husband reaffirmed that he would be living with Caroline, who reaffirmed that she wished to end her marriage to me. Kat questioned her husband and I questioned Caroline. As the meeting developed I was filled with an overpowering brinkmanship, a feeling that to throw them together would bring her back, that to push her away would bring her to her senses. I became convinced that to push away was to keep. After an hour Kat stood up and said to me "Come on," and we left together.

We went back to my flat. Kat was amazingly strong and feeling that I was devastated held me and whispered to me, "You'll be a great writer one day after this suffering, it'll deepen you and your work." Instinctively I knew that I was like an oyster enduring a piece of grit which would irritate its sensitive inside into producing a pearl, but at the time the pearl seemed a long way away and the process unnecessary.

I was taking each day at a time, not thinking in terms of months or years. For the next nine days, which were a holiday for the Feast (the *Eid*), we lived in my flat. We had been thrown together in circumstances that were extremely abnormal: the streets outside had been made a nightmare by the RCC, and now my domestic life was a nightmare too. Kat cooked steaks, bought frozen from Guido's, and served them on paper serviettes in the American way and we ate by candlelight and drank Guido's white wine and reviewed our lives and our future need to grow. When I broached the CIA, shutters came down and she changed the subject. Though a couple of times she did ask if I would take her to meet Viktor, which I declined to do. We talked a lot, thrown together, as if that could compensate for our emotional misery.

Very early on Kat asked if we could both visit Manuel. I did not know that she had been pursued by Manuel – she was of Spanish descent and when together they sometimes spoke in Spanish – and that according to Ursula (who told me this later) Kat had said she used me as a decoy to make Manuel jealous.

We arrived at Manuel's to find him packing as he too had now been expelled by the RCC. I could not establish why. When I asked he just shrugged.

An air rifle stood in a corner. I picked it up and examined it.

"It is for sale," he said, "Five pounds."

It was a capital offence to possess a firearm under the Libyan Revolution, but, conscious I had nothing to defend my flat with if it was stormed by a mob, I bought it. "If the RCC find it," Manuel said matter-of-factly (and perhaps with some glee), pocketing the £5 note, "you will be shot." He handed me a small cardboard box with a lid containing ammunition.

He then had a private talk with Kat in the kitchen and suggested she went to Madrid immediately to live with him. She reported this after we had left his house. She did not say what her reply had been.

Twice after that Manuel came round, bringing valium, which he urged both of us to take. He insisted on seeing Kat alone and urged her to leave me. On his last visit he offered to leave his wife to live with her.

Kat now resolved to return to her children. She tied a leopard scarf round her throat and said, "I must go back." It was Nadia's birthday, and Nadia came. Kat cooked us all lunch and I gave Nadia a nurse's uniform. We took Nadia back to the Giorgimpopoli villa where Caroline was living, and had an unsatisfactory meeting with Kat's husband, who refused to give Kat any maintenance if she went to Madrid.

Kat returned to me for one last night, and the next day she moved back to her villa. Her husband moved out to stay with the Irishman, Jim. Caroline moved out with Nadia to the house of a colleague of mine and his wife, leaving me alone with the air rifle, which I picked up several times a day and cocked. I stopped short of loading it. Life is most intense when lived under the imminence of death.

The Feast was finished but there was a strike at the University. The New-Zealand Head of Department had been dismissed by the RCC – he too had been expelled – and classes were suspended, pending a new timetable. I was told that I was being considered as a candidate to succeed him, but I had far too much on my hands to think about a timetable.

I set off from the University to drive home in my green Volkswagen, and stopped to join the Homs Road. A large lorry with a cab twice the height of my car overtook me and double-parked, waiting for the Homs Road to clear. I looked up from my right-hand-drive seat and saw the driver, an Arab, looking down from his left-hand-drive cab. Quite deliberately, with a contemptuous expression in his eyes that said "Western imperialist" (or perhaps "opponent of Gaddafi") he pulled his lorry across my front, ramming my right wing, turned left into the Homs Road and drove off unscathed, having done structural damage that forced open my right-hand front door. I was jarred and shaken – I had been stationary – but otherwise unhurt. As if I had not enough on my plate already I had to drive home with a partially-open right front door, which, having wound the window down, I held in place with my right elbow.

My car was insured in England but with a high excess. It was impractical to enter into a lengthy postal negotiation from enclosed Libya with the insurance company about the hit-and-run driver who had damaged my wing and door. I could not afford to buy a new front wing and door yet and so I carried on driving the car as it was.

Andrew Mackenzie was meeting me in my car now as he was preparing to return to England and had sold his car. In our subsequent car meetings Andrew wore a leather right-hand glove and sat leaning towards me as if whispering in my left ear with his arm across the back of my driver's seat as if he had his arm round my right shoulder. He held the door to through the wound-down window while I drove. It was cold at that time of the year, and he wore an overcoat and scarf to protect himself against the freezing air that rushed through the open window of the moving car.

I visited Nadia and had unsatisfactory discussions with Caroline. In the evenings I went up to Kat's villa and had dinner with her in front of the hissing log fire. Then one day the Morality Police arrived at the Irishman's and asked questions. Fearing deportation, Kat's husband moved back to his own villa. He arrived while I was there. He was quarrelsome and menacing.

Suddenly Kat shrieked and crashed her hand down on a sideboard and shouted: "I'm emotionally in pieces, I want to go back to the States with my children, and then go to Madrid." She and her husband talked quietly in the bedroom and reached agreement that she should go with her children in four days' time and have her maintenance, provided she did not have any contact with me.

Christmas was approaching. I was totally alone in my emotional desert. Kat did not want to see me as she did not want to endanger her maintenance, and my colleague (who had been in the British Army's Intelligence Corps) did not want me to visit Caroline and Nadia as he said I might "unsettle" them.

I had told Andrew of the situation on 6 December. He listened intently and was clearly very shocked. I had asked him how Caroline and Nadia could obtain a visa to leave Libya for England when lecturers such as myself had been told that there would be no exit visas until they had completed their contracts. He said he would investigate and report back. He eventually said that there had to be an 'Evidence of Agreement', which would be signed by the two of us and the Vice Consul. There had to be a document that made it clear to the Libyan visa authorities that there had been a legal agreement for an alternative financial and residential provision for my dependents. Its wording had to convince the Libyans to issue an exit visa for them. On 16 December Caroline and I visited the British Embassy and (in my case, considering it a job that had to be done to get them out of Libya and back to London) we signed the Agreement before the Vice Consul.

Caroline was now preparing to leave. I was invited to go round and see Nadia on Christmas morning, and had the agonising task of explaining to her that she would be going home to England, and that I would be staying in Libya to complete my work. I told Caroline she could have the furniture in Crescent View so long as I had the photos. (I did not want material possessions but treasured the rootedness of memories.) I was taken aback when she said she had promised to give our hair-dryer to my colleague's wife when she left Tripoli. In those days it was almost impossible to buy a hair-dryer in Tripoli. I was on the verge of breaking down, and was unexpectedly invited to stay to Christmas lunch.

Christmas Day: Col. Nasser's visit to Tripoli, and SAM-3 missiles
Immediately lunch was over I drove to see Col. Nasser (to whom Gaddafi had offered Libya, *see* p.277) ride in a Jeep with Gen. Numeiri of Sudan and Gaddafi while hundreds of Arabs ran behind them chanting "Na-sser, Na-sser". The three men were driven through a succession of victory arches decked with foliage from Giorgimpopoli along the coast road to central Tripoli. (The custom of erecting victory arches had been left behind by the Romans, along with the *toga*, when they vacated Libya. The victory celebrated symbolically during this ride was Egypt's successful plotting and Libyan implementing of Gaddafi's *coup*.) Nasser stood in a suit waving, and, six feet away, I looked into the eyes of the man who had precipitated the Suez crisis I had followed so carefully.

The three leaders discussed Arab unity and on 27 December signed a tripartite agreement, known as the Tripoli Charter, to advance to unity. The plan was abandoned before it could be implemented. Egyptian intelligence had been involved in the 1-September *coup*. Nasser was visiting an Egyptian client state. He had taken delivery of a new SAM-3 missile system (three surface-to-air missiles on a mobile launcher) from the Soviet Union,[4] and it is likely that he offered a protective umbrella to the two other leaders. (*See* pp.277.)

My family leaves Libya
I saw Kat a couple of times more before she went to the States. Now she had her ticket and her maintenance she was relaxed again. I said goodbye to her with great sadness, and then I focused on Nadia. I took her to a beach, and when it was time for her to leave Libya I drove her to the airport while Caroline drove with Kat's husband. I waved goodbye to the plane near a pushed-aside boarding staircase which led nowhere. Then I drove back to my empty flat.

I sat alone at my desk and pondered how I had come to be in my present predicament. Had Caroline fallen deeply in love with Buddy or was she using him to escape the Libyan nightmare? Had the CIA split us up? Had the SIS split us up because they wanted to move me from being a university lecturer with a young family to a single, independent agent unhindered by a family, who would join them full-time in July? I was surely not important enough for a Western organisation to go to such lengths and act so inhumanely.

I would be a prisoner in Libya for the next six months. I was in a dark wood at night and I could not see my true path. My Dark Night had become very dark.

Defiance: Gaddafi's second visit to the University, my left shoulder knocks off his peaked cap

On 1 January 1970 Col. Gaddafi visited the University for a second time. Students, drawn up in ranks within platoons of classes, lined the road to greet his Jeep. Fascinated by a man whose actions had had effects on my life rather as Pierre in *War and Peace* was fascinated by Napoleon, I wanted to look into the eyes of the man who had stolen my *coup*, destabilised the streets and my marriage, threatened journalists with execution and driven with Nasser. I stood with my class and Viktor stood next to me, near his.

The Jeep stopped beside me. Four men in army uniform with red berets and machine-guns jumped out, and Col. Gaddafi climbed down. He had a short back-and-sides Sandhurst haircut and wore a peaked Hitler-style military cap with the crossed swords of the Libyan Revolution's emblem on the front.

There was a roar, and my students surged forward and surrounded Gaddafi and began kissing him. The four armed men in red berets lost control, and Gaddafi, his arms by his sides like a tailor's dummy, closed his eyes and winced each time he was kissed, screwing up his face. He was thrown against my left shoulder.

For a few timeless moments which I can still recall I had Gaddafi's head resting on my left shoulder, his eyes closed. Then he opened his eyes and looked into mine. I was shocked by how ordinary they were. There was nothing terrifying in the look he gave me. He was, if anything, rather frightened.

The rim of his round Hitler-like cap was above my left shoulder and I could see the brass badge with a wings-down eagle above two crossed swords within a wreath. I looked into the eyes of the man who had stolen my *coup*, who had struck on 1 September and prevented me from being made British Ambassador, and whose policies had contributed to the departure of my family. In those few unreal moments he did not seem a threat. He was three years younger than me. I felt free and in charge, as if I had somehow tamed my Napoleon. His Hitler cap was digging into my shoulder. As if making a statement about the Libyan Revolution – a free act of defiance to avenge what had happened to me as a result of the *coup* and to avenge his snatching of Libyan oil from the 5-September pro-Western *coup* – I shrugged at the jutting-out rim and his cap rolled off.

It fell into the road, and one of the soldiers in red berets bent and retrieved it from the dust before it was trampled on by students. The men in red berets took charge and forced my students back into their ranks. Gaddafi replaced his cap and led the way into the University.

Viktor had seen what had happened. He whispered to me, tee-heeing, "I saw you knock off the dictator's cap." We discussed the situation. "That was very strange," he said. "Gaddafi does not like being touched."

I led my students into the University hall and sat with them. Gaddafi appeared on the platform with the four men in red berets, sat at a table and took off his cap. He spoke into the microphone. From time to time there was opposition from the students, and at one point he was howled down.

Sitting in Gaddafi's audience I reflected that I had lived through the 1956 Suez Crisis and had seen its perpetrator, Col. Nasser, ride alongside Gaddafi a few days previously. Gaddafi had then been wearing his peaked dictator's cap and I had just sent it rolling in the dust.

No one then knew that in the years ahead Gaddafi would surround himself with young sex slaves – boys and girls – he raped and beat daily and with female body guards who were his playthings, that he would have a permanent apartment in the university where he could rape students he selected, bully the wives and daughters of his ministers and generals into submitting to him,[5] and that he would turn into a monstrous, latter-day Caligula, utterly depraved and evil in his ruthless demonstration of the power which, like Lucifer, he had grabbed through rebellion. He was cruel and perverted, but I had seen his ordinariness when I looked into his eyes, somehow I had seen through him.

Endings

I spent the mornings at work. From lunch-times on I spent great tracts of time alone in my flat, sunbathing, washing, ironing, cleaning and occasionally listening to the BBC Overseas Service news. There was a heaviness behind my lungs. I walked past Nadia's empty room and spent the evenings in, sweating out my misery as if it were an appalling cold.

I had made it clear that I would always want access to Nadia. Kat's husband came to collect Nadia's remaining toys, which he was taking to London. He said, "I feel I'm going to pieces. It's a bad situation, I mean, you wanting Nadia." I asked drily if it had never occurred to him that I might want to continue my relationship with Nadia. He did not seem to have considered the possibility, and had taken a very egocentric, partial view of the situation.

He went to London and had dinner with Caroline's parents. Then I received an envelope addressed in Caroline's handwriting. It contained an advertising leaflet she had picked up somewhere with a printed headline "Nothing is Happening". There was no written explanation but she was clearly sending me a message that all was not well.

Two weeks later, after his return from London, I went to the Giorgimpopoli villa. Standing by his front door I asked him what the plan was now.

After some evasion he said, "I don't think Caroline and I are going to make it. I want to be with my children."

I was immediately relieved. To push away *had* been to keep.

He said, "I haven't told her yet but I did tell her 'If anything happens to us, don't go back to you.'"

I was indignant. He was telling me that he was not going to continue with Caroline but was bent on continuing our separation. I wondered again whether an organisation had instructed him to split us up.

"When will you tell her?"

"I'm going back to London and I'll tell her then."

A woman approached, and stood by me at the front door. She was small and looked as if she was wearing a lawyer's wig. She called his name in an American accent. He said, "Excuse me," and had a few private words with her. She turned and walked back down the path.

He said to me, "That was Linda. I slept with her the night before I went to London."

In mid-January I received a letter from Kat saying she would be staying in the States. I knew he was attempting a reconciliation with her. She never did go to Madrid, and Manuel died a few years later on Menorca.

The February vacation was approaching. We lecturers were told that we could have an exit visa for the duration of the vacation. I wondered whether I should go to London, but even if I came to the conclusion that I wanted Caroline back, it would be pointless to go before Caroline had heard directly from him that the relationship was over as she would not believe me. We were later told that visas were not being granted to the UK, but *were* being granted to Egypt, so I went to Egypt.

Purgation: self-stripping in Egypt and Sahara
Visit to Egypt to meet Saad eddin Bushwerib

Andrew Mackenzie had suggested I should go, to meet Saad eddin Bushwerib. Ben had paid me a brief visit. He had not wanted to discuss the *coup*, but he had told me that Gaddafi was his "bootboy" when he was an army colonel. He told me that Col. Saad eddin Bushwerib had been made

300

the new Libyan Ambassador to Egypt. He would not be drawn into discussing the reason why. Perhaps Gaddafi wanted to make sure he was out of Libya and not about to mount a counter-*coup*. Or perhaps (as I had already suspected) Bushwerib had thrown in his lot with Egypt and Gaddafi before the 1-September *coup*.

I was supposed to go to the Libyan Embassy in Cairo and see Col. Saad eddin Bushwerib and find out. Andrew also asked me to find the location of the new Soviet SAM-3 missile system, which the Soviet Union had just sent to Egypt and which was believed to be somewhere in the vicinity of El Alamein.

Cairo

I flew into Cairo on 12 February 1970, the day 70 Egyptian civilians were killed in an air-raid on a factory in the outskirts at Abu Za'bal. Cairo was prepared for war. During the day distant guns thumped. At night there was blackout: all windows and car headlights were painted blue and there were no street lights. Cairo became a ghostly Hell. People loomed and faded in an eerie silence. Occasionally a searchlight swept the sky and an ack-ack gun opened up from a rooftop. There were sandbags on the Nile bridges.

I spent two days at the Horris hotel and then transferred to a small hotel overlooking the Nile, the Garden City House residential hotel. My room had a balcony. The other guests were a few elderly Europeans. I sat in the spring sun and watched the curved white sails of the boats drift like dorsal fins along the silver-green river and eaglets soar overhead, and observed the lorries carrying troops to Suez along the Corniche beside the Nile. At night I went down into the noisy streets and wandered among the shops and honking horns, taxi-drivers, guides and touts, and ate a solitary meal and drank Stella beer.

Gaddafi in the Libyan Embassy, Cairo with Bushwerib, now Libyan Ambassador to Egypt

I tried to visit the Libyan Embassy but I was told it was closed as Gaddafi had arrived and was staying in it. It would remain closed for the next few days. Inside, Saad eddin Bushwerib, the co-deviser of the 5-September *coup*, was meeting Gaddafi, the implementer of the 1-September *coup*, and I was a few yards away outside the front door. It is bizarre that three men who were so opposed to each other should have been so close together that morning. Nasser, the middle-man between the Soviet Union and Gaddafi, or Nasser's right-hand man, may also have been there, sharing details of the new Soviet SAM-3 missile system. And there may also have been a representative of the Soviet Union or the KGB.

Luxor and Karnak: ruins
I visited all the ruins: the Pyramids, Memphis and the necropolis at Saqqara. I flew down to Luxor. As I stepped off the plane's stairway onto the tarmac an Israeli Phantom nearly took off my head. It dived down from the sun, swooped, thundered twelve feet above me and roared up into the sky. I did not know if it was photographing the passengers or just asserting Israel's supremacy in the skies. I visited the City of the Dead and steeped myself in tombs and sarcophagi, funeral possessions, headless wicked souls and texts from *The Book of the Dead*. As the small motorboat chugged back across the Nile to Luxor it seemed I was crossing back to life.

Later, riding in a gharry along the Corniche by the Nile to the Temple of Amun at Karnak, watching the horse canter under the whip past a woman milking a goat, the fluttering papyrus at the cabman's feet which would be the horse's fodder and the scrawny old hag in black he stopped and spoke to, his wife, I renewed my contact with Nature and simple living and yearned for a permanent wife. Back in alienated Cairo I dined alone at the hotel and from my room watched the drifting silk-blue-and-orange river in the setting February sun, and knew I had to get away to Alexandria.

Alexandria: among Russians
A sad fat man in a *tarboosh* fell on me at Alexandria station and, with much puffing, waylaid me to a cheap hotel off Nebi Daniel, Hotel Leroy. I took a room overlooking the sweep of the bay. All the other guests were Russians, "sailors" who never left their rooms, some of the 17,000 Soviet military advisers then in Egypt. Zagloul Square was packed. I spent the evenings drinking in the gloomy emptiness of the blacked-out Cecil Hotel frequented by the characters of Durrell's *Alexandria Quartet*. Socialism and war-blackout had toned down the Mediterranean sensuality of pre-Second-World-War Alexandria.

I am arrested at SAM-3 missile site at El Alamein
I went to El Alamein on the desert bus on 19 February. I looked at the battle site, knowing I had a poetic epic (*Overlord*) ahead which would draw on this local terrain. I visited the El Alamein British Museum, and then wandered away across sand towards the bay to look for SAM-3 missiles. The villages of El Alamein and Sidi Abu Rasag were both prohibited areas.

After half a kilometre on the Alexandria side of the British Museum, in the vicinity of Sidi Abu Rasag, I saw what looked like a primitive military camp: a cluster of low outbuildings surrounded by barbed wire, a parked Jeep and a few men in military uniform. I thought a transporter loaded with SAM-3 missiles might be parked between the buildings, and continued walking as if to pass the barbed-wire compound.

The Jeep started up, left the compound and approached me. Three armed uniformed Egyptian soldiers were in the front. One said in broken English, "You must go with us into the camp and talk to the General."

I was driven into the barbed-wire compound, told to sit a chair on the sand and interrogated in the open air by an Egyptian who had three stars on his military tunic but said he was a captain, Capt. Taher Tomene. He asked me why I was there. I said I was a tourist interested in El Alamein. He said, "You know there is a Russian SAM-3 missile site here and you are looking for it." I was now sure there was a transporter, a mobile launcher, among the outbuildings. I denied this and explained that I was a "language teacher" in Libya who was exploring the battlefield of El Alamein.

He demanded that I should write out the names of the books I was using at the University, and their publishers, which I did. A couple of hours elapsed. At last he was satisfied that I really was teaching at the University of Libya, and I was released.

Over 40 years later I was informed by two Israeli academics that this was the earliest Western 'sighting' of the Soviet air-defence deployment in Egypt.[6]

I returned to Alexandria on the desert bus. On the way back I reflected that Egypt was on a war footing, with blackout at night, and the only way for Westerners to travel was through pre-booked tickets. I had pre-booked my seat on the desert bus (and in effect secured a permit to leave Alexandria) at the hotel's reception desk, and I was the only non-Russian guest. The hotel's reception may have been duty-bound to inform Egyptian intelligence, or the KGB, of my travel arrangement, and they could have alerted the soldiers in the barbed-wire compound, who could have been looking out for me when I walked over the brow of a sand-dune and headed towards the bay.

I also jotted in my pocketbook that "truth comes in layers, each day something new happens which adds significance to things past." (I was already groping towards my view, expressed in this work, that memory consists of layers of impressions superimposed on the self.)

I flew back to Tripoli on 23 February. I had a good idea of the Egyptian-Soviet presence on Libya's border, and had grasped that Egypt could only focus part of its attention on Libya as it was preoccupied by Israeli air raids.

Man in the desert

Gazing down at the desert through the aircraft window, I imagined a man standing with his feet on the sand, his head under the stars, and no civilization or materialist possessions to clutter him. This was the human condition: man at one with Nature, whereas city living shut out this relationship with Nature. I saw Western civilization as a distraction, a theme I was to develop in later poems. I saw that the way back to a real relationship with Nature was therefore a stripping of illusions, a turning-away from clutter and distraction, a paring-down, a Way of Loss; and that what would be left after this further purgation would be what was real.

That night I picked Andrew up at 10 p.m. He was walking on the stretch of the waterfront where I had walked with Angus Wilson, and I reported back about the SAM-3 site.

Into the Sahara desert, staying in Czech camps
There was still a week left of the vacation, and at my request (at Andrew's insistence) Viktor had arranged for me to go into the Sahara with the Czech Road Company, which had begun building a 310-km road from Nalut to Ghadames. I would be sleeping in the camps, and Andrew wanted me to gain a glimpse into Czech life following the Soviet invasion of Czechoslovakia. I had already arranged to leave Tripoli the next morning and go straight out into the Sahara desert.

We started at dawn. We travelled by lorry from the Company depot. Only a few kilometres of the road had been asphalted, and by noon we were past Nalut, heading into a great sea of sand along a bumpy track made by the lorries that supplied six camps. Here, in corrugated sheds in the middle of a stony waste lived the officially pro-Soviet Czech roadmakers and engineers for stretches of a year or more.

I stopped for lunch at camp 2 and spent the first night in camp 3, where Czechs sat in their primitive mess and slept in flimsy hardboard bedrooms, four in each room. I was given a wooden bed in a room with three Czechs. They were officially pro-Soviet, but I found them very human and not at all ideological. They told me that some had not welcomed the Soviet invasion. One of them said to me when we were alone: "We talk of work, women, going home, politics, how to get the Russians out of our Republic and whether there will be a Russian Revolution."

There was no lorry the next day, so after an austere breakfast I walked over the nearest sand-hill and stood utterly alone in a great buff sand-sea under a huge blue sky. Now *I* was the man in the desert I had imagined in the plane. The spring weather was not too hot and I spent the whole day wandering alone in the desert. I was amazed that it was alive. There were white and mauve flowers, small moths, flies, chirping birds and small slith-ering trails from scorpions and snakes. All round me was wide open space like the sea, and the air was incredibly clear. There was a deep silence save for the crunch of my footsteps. The desert was a living thing. Part of the desert was actually in flower, and all the while there was a great blinding mirror of a sun and my black shadow.

That night after supper I heard jackals whining. I went outside and glimpsed one. I followed it out into the desert until I could no longer hear the camp generator. Then I stopped and looked at the great frosty stars. They were like lights on a Christmas tree.

The next day there was a lorry. I set off at 8 with a land surveyor and a Tuareg, who asked me, "*La bass?*" (the Tuareg greeting, 'No problems?', 'Is anything the matter?'). We bumped into the Red Stony Desert under a vast sky and made camp 5 for lunch. I was still 40 kilometres from Ghadames, the underground town whose streets were dark tunnels, and no transport was scheduled to go there.

I spent the night in camp 5. I shared a room with a Czech engineer and the next morning set off to walk to Ghadames. The

Nicholas by a grave in the Sahara desert, February 1970

Czech engineer caught me up in a Jeep, and said, "I have a day off, I will drive you to Ghadames." It was just as well, for I would have got lost. There was not even a track, and we passed the grave of a Tuareg or Arab who had tried to walk: a body-length rectangle of stones in the sand.

In Ghadames: the Ain el Faras spring

Soon afterwards we broke an axle. We crawled slowly on and passed camp 6 and two hours later saw the oasis of Ghadames: a strip of palms beyond sand-hills the shape of grave-mounds. It took a long time to approach. We drove across the concrete runway which was the airfield, and passed the necropolis, hundreds of stone graves on a hill. Boys ran alongside us, and Tuareg in head-dress that showed one eye stared in curiosity. The Jeep stopped before the only hotel, a low white front near mud walls and palms.

And then I saw the spring, Ain el Faras. It was a square walled-in pool about thirty yards across. The water was beautifully clear and there were green underwater plants. Small white sulphur bubbles wobbled up. There were six worn, polished steps and the water sparkled and rippled sunlight. I tiptoed down and dipped in my hand. The water was warm.

The Ain el Faras spring, Ghadames

This spring was 4,500 years old, and the walls round it had been begun at the same time as the Great Pyramid. I sat and gazed at the water for ten minutes. Then I booked in at the small hotel (where I seemed to be the only guest), said goodbye to the Czech engineer (who returned to camp 5 to repair the broken axle) and spent the whole afternoon sitting by the spring.

Conduits from it crafted by the Romans carried water to the underground baths in the tomb-city where old men still wore *togas* and took them off to wash. The Tuareg left me alone, and I felt happy. I had recognised and found somewhere in myself that corresponded to the very ancient spring. I had found a timeless spring of creativity and forgiveness. Everyone was sinful and weak, and everyone was entitled to come to the divine spring, whose loving, mysterious bubbles had wobbled to the surface from unknowable depths every day from long before recorded history.

The next day I walked in the underground tunnels, peeping into underground homes and seeing men in *togas* living as their forefathers lived two thousand years ago. There were seven main underground streets, each named after a family. Three belonged to the Beni Ualid family and four to the Beni Uazid family. The Tuareg were outside the town and comprised two families, the Hoggar and the Orfogmas. Little had changed since the Roman time.

I went into the main square. A sermon was being recited on the mosque's loudspeaker. Then revolutionary music blared over the square's loudspeakers, and "*Allahu Akbar*". I was deep in the Sahara at one of the remotest limits of the Roman Empire but the Revolution had stamped its mark here. I bought some pieces of Saharan rock, Rose of the Desert, a crystalline rock that is only found near Ghadames and which is shaped into a rose by the desert wind.

By the time I took off from the concrete runway in a small plane and flew back to Tripoli I had stripped myself of the clutter of Western civilization and located a spring of love in my heart. I thought I wanted Caroline back.

Separation: Malta and reconciliation

Again I want to skate over the next stressful weeks in Tripoli: how Kat's husband rang Caroline, drunk and incoherent, and ended their relationship; how Caroline wrote saying she felt "shaky and rather frightened"; how I rang her from the Libya Palace Hotel and we had an achingly close conversation; how I wrote to her extending forgiveness; and how she wrote back asking for a year's separation "until I can prove to myself that I can be responsible and cope with my emotions and life generally".

In a second letter she wrote that she had met Daphne for lunch and that Daphne had invited her to Malta in April: "How do you feel about our meeting in Malta – if you can come over for a day or two? I agree that we should meet. I think we'd talk far better if we were both on foreign ground. I still feel the same about separating for a year."

I did not want a separation now, and although no exit visas were being granted to Libyan-Government employees like me, I managed to persuade the University to give me four days off "to attend an important meeting in London". It was like being an inmate of an open prison and being allowed out so long as I undertook to stick to the main condition, which was that I should return. In another letter Caroline reiterated the case for separation, saying she did not want to be "merely a pretty flower in your buttonhole". I sent her the money for her air ticket to Malta.

I had kept Andrew Mackenzie informed of these developments. I had met him on 2 March outside the pizza shop near what used to be the King's palace at 7.30. (He was munching a pizza in the street and as I approached, broke off a bit and offered it to me.) I had had a car meeting with him on 26 March at 8 p.m. I had now saved enough to buy a new wing and door for my car.

Gaddafi's third visit to the University

On 30 March, the day before Evacuation Day, Gaddafi came to the University again to address the visiting Arab ministers. I attended with Viktor.

Gaddafi arrived just after 5 p.m. looking tired. He seemed to have aged since his last visit, and walked stiffly. On the platform he spoke as if doped with drugs. He sat down with difficulty, propped his head on a hand and closed his eyes. When he left he was mobbed by students. He kept his arms by his side and several times grimaced with his eyes closed. He looked like a waxwork dummy being carried, inclining backwards, and I wondered if he had something wrong with his back or had been wounded and was in pain. I had a car meeting with Andrew Mackenzie that same evening at 8 p.m., and another one on 6 April.

Visit to Malta to discuss reconciliation

I left Tripoli on Saturday 11 April during celebrations for Evacuation Day, which marked the British withdrawal from the Tobruk and El Adm bases. The flight was delayed and I sat for four hours where I had watched Caroline leave, and thought: events gather round places like flotsam round a breakwater and on a beach. The sea comes in and washes debris away and then brings similar jetsam back to the same breakwater and beach. I had the feeling that there is a pattern beneath events that is as powerful as the tides. But the events themselves can never be washed away from the breakwaters of the memory. They cluster there in layers, though covered by the driftwood of succeeding events.

We wobbled over the brown crags of Malta and landed at Luqa, where Daphne and Caroline were waiting for me. Caroline was depressed, shaky and tearful. She wore dark glasses. Daphne drove us up to the north of the island, past stone walls and isolated castles, red poppies and yellow daisies, to a seaside village of modern flats in St Paul's Bay, and to the glassy Crystal Inn. Here I was to sleep. I would go round to Daphne's parents for meals.

In a small white room there, with a narrow bed and high window, Caroline and I met alone. I told her I had come to talk about the future, not the past, and that I wanted us to get back together. She told me, "We must separate", but did not give a reason. We had to break off to walk to Daphne's parents' for lunch, struggling against a great wind by a rough sea.

Interference

I need to skate over how a quarter of an hour after we returned she announced, "I don't want to talk again until 10 as Daphne and I are going out to dinner with two RAF men we met last night. I'll come to the Crystal Inn at 10."

I was taken aback. At her request I had managed to leave Libya despite restrictions on exit visas, and I had not expected that, under the circumstances, Daphne and her parents would sanction that an arrangement with two men Caroline had not known until the previous evening should have priority over dinner with me. It did not occur to me that an organisation might have put one of the RAF men up to proposing the dinner. I spent a miserable drizzling evening alone, walking in darkness between the four clusters of lights that lit that otherwise black part of the coast, killing time.

She did not turn up at 10. I stood in the dark by the sea, which dashed in on dark, laval rocks, stinging my cheeks. Before that foaming, boiling surf and black crinkled sea the anger and indignation I felt deep down came to the surface, and a separation took place between the warmth I knew I wanted and the woman who had given it to me until now. I did not go to sleep until 2.

The next morning was sunny with a blue sky, and the sea was a rough indigo. It was windy and I walked past red poppies and small blue irises to Daphne's parents' house. It was a Sunday and all the curtains were drawn.

I hung around on the waterfront and when I returned there were signs of life. I found Daphne and Caroline having breakfast on their own.

I said, "You didn't come at 10."

Caroline said, "No, we went back to the Officers' Mess at Luqa and we didn't get in until 2."

I said simply, "Last night's arrangement was not one of a woman who wants to get back to her husband." I turned and left the house and walked back to my room.

She followed and asked, "Will you be leaving Malta? Daphne's boyfriend is to take us on a tour of the island this afternoon."

Thinking of Nadia, I agreed to join the tour.

The tour took us round all the bays from Sliema to Cospicua. Daphne's boyfriend flew Canberras to photograph the Russian fleet. He was a quiet young Scot, and there was little opportunity to talk until I returned to my hotel, where there was a celebration in progress.

We talked in my room against distant drunken singing. Caroline said, "It's better if you find someone else."

That evening Caroline, Daphne, her boyfriend and I went to The Roundabout, and Daphne went and spoke to a bald-headed man sitting at the bar. Caroline could not take her eyes off him. I did not then know (though I could have guessed) that it was he who had joined Daphne's boyfriend the previous evening for dinner, and that Daphne was encouraging Caroline's relationship with him and our separation.

The next morning Caroline called for me wearing an RFC badge and Daphne drove us to a restaurant in St Paul's Bay that stands on rock that juts out into the sea, where we had drinks. Caroline was aggressive, and Daphne said, "This is a complete breakdown." On the beach outside the restaurant there were some *dghajsa*s, local boats with eyes printed on the prows, some with elaborate eyelashes.

We drove to Valetta and ate at the British, whose balcony overlooked the Grand Harbour and Fort St Angelo, and later we walked in Valletta. I visited the church of the Knights, St John's Co-Cathedral, and we took the bus back to St Paul's Bay.

I had another session with Caroline, during which she said she was no longer emotionally involved with me. She left, and I sat on, staring on my bed as dusk fell.

That evening Daphne, Caroline and I had dinner in the waterfront restaurant. I tried to feign high spirits. There were musicians present, and the ladies were asked to choose songs. Daphne chose 'Yesterday', Caroline 'Luglio' ('July'). Afterwards we drove to Mdina, the medieval capital which is known as the Silent City because there is never anybody on the streets. We had a harmonious midnight walk.

Next morning Caroline's mood had changed. We drove north until we could see Gozo, and with my departure imminent, she began to be forward-looking. Looking at the island where St Paul was shipwrecked, I quoted from Tennyson's 'Maud', "And ah for a man to arise in me,/That the man I am may cease to be!"[7] I said, "It sums up how I feel now, not shipwrecked, but emotionally wrecked."

Caroline said she wanted to write the quotation down. She asked me to bring some casserole dishes in July as "we'll need them".

Daphne said quietly to me, "I should think you'll get back together."

But Caroline's change of mood was short-lived, and after a final walk in Golden Bay that afternoon she picked flowers on a low cliff and wistfully told me to find a woman to look after me in Tripoli. At the airport I told her she rotated between three moods – aggressive, depressed, elated – and that she was like the three whirling disks in a fruit machine: "If you don't get the orange on each, you get nothing."

I flew back to Libya and lived alone and heard nothing for two weeks. Then I received two letters by the same post, one softly asking for a divorce and the other saying she had been to see a solicitor. By the next post I received a letter from Daphne saying that after I left she had seen little of Caroline as she was out with David, the bald-headed man I had seen at The Roundabout.

I communicated my knowledge of the situation to Caroline and received an angry letter saying we should communicate through solicitors from now on. I heard nothing from her for six weeks.

Purgation: terror and 'execution'

My Way of Loss was agonising. I was still attached to Caroline, and I did not fully understand that I had to become detached as the sensual attachments of my ego continued to be purged. If she had died, I could have adjusted. But she was there. I felt her like an amputated foot, and it was still possible that there might be a reversal of her position. I had a wound that would not heal, like Philoctetes, the greatest archer in Greece who bore Heracles' bow and was stranded on the island of Lemnos with a snake bite in a foot for ten years during the Trojan War. (In Edmund Wilson's interpretation in *The Wound and the Bow* Philoctetes represents a traumatised artist waiting for the healing power of insight symbolised by his mastery of the bow.) I had not yet emptied myself of hope, and my attachment was a torment. I had companions in Tripoli, a couple of nurses mainly who nursed me emotionally in their separate ways.

There were two more letters from Caroline, both pressing for a divorce, and I began to court danger. It was as if I was trying to destroy part of my ego that still hankered after her. I wandered into parts of Tripoli where I might be arrested.

During this nightmare I came across a quotation from Marcus Aurelius's *Meditations*: "If aught befall thee it is good, it is all part of the great web." I began to consider that what had seemed to be a catastrophe might be a hidden blessing, that what had befallen me had been for my own good without my realising it. A different perspective on the events I had been through from the point of view of the 'great web' might demonstrate that I had benefited by being put on a different path.

Ben Nagy refuses to meet Andrew Mackenzie
I saw Andrew Mackenzie on 15 April, and on 22 and 27 April, both at 8.30. He now wanted to recruit Ben, presumably so that Ben could attempt a pro-Western *coup*. Ben had told me that he wanted to get some money out to London, and I had reported this to Andrew, who said he would do what Ben wanted. Andrew wanted me to arrange a meeting between himself and Ben in my flat, a re-run of his meeting with Viktor.

I told Ben that I could arrange to transfer his money to London if he met "a friend from the Embassy". Ben refused to meet Andrew.

Viktor wants to transfer funds to prepare for defection
Viktor also asked me if I could help him get some money out of Libya. Andrew was now leaving Libya, his term of service having come to an end, and I was passed on to his secretary, Miranda, who was to act as an intermediary between Andrew and me regarding Viktor's transfer of funds to London when the time came.

Xenophobia, Italians to be expelled
The RCC now confronted Westerners. Its xenophobia worsened. The Libyan leaders had begun Robin-Hooding the American oil companies, making the first move to nationalise them, and they were preparing to expel 30,000 Italians. The RCC set up a new department within the Ministry of Interior "to watch the foreigners", and the system of fawn Volkswagens was now reinforced by a team of Arabs in maroon skullcaps who hung around the street corners. I was now watched again. The fawn Volkswagen returned and sat outside my gate again for large parts of each day.

I am asked to join the Mafia
To protect his bootlegging from the surveillance teams, Guido (one of the Italians facing expulsion) had begun wrapping up boxes of a dozen bottles of wine, which were larger than his boxes of "vegetables and potatoes" (Bavarian beer). He called them "dog meat" and handed them to foreigners looking for wine. The Mafia had bribed the armed soldiers on duty in his store, who never investigated wrapped boxes. I openly carried boxes to my car and played my part in distributing bottles to the foreign community.

I evidently did well as one day one of Guido's Mafia contacts approached me outside his store and asked if I would have lunch with him. Over lunch he asked if I would join the Mafia. He said I would be part of a network of 48 that really ruled Tripoli, and actively tried to recruit me by telling me how much I could expect to make. I politely declined.

Jerry Okoro of The Times *admits to being a Russian agent*
I had got to know Jerry Okoro, the Biafran Tripoli correspondent of *The Times*. He told me that he received most of his news from East-European Embassies. On 16 May he confessed to me, "I am a Russian agent. I get my whisky, and even girls, from my Soviet suppliers. But they insist on chaperoning me. I don't like that." I was wary of him, aware he might be reporting on me to the KGB, but I continued to see him as he had good contacts.

Set up by Okoro to meet Libyan Head of Security
One night he came round and said he had been invited to a big reception at the Uaddan Hotel. He said that, being black, he was nervous of going in by himself. Would I accompany him?

Not believing that so confident an African could really feel nervous, I accompanied him. There must have been a couple of hundred people in the large room. Almost immediately he said, "Oh, there's the American Ambassador. I must go and have a word with him." He strode across the huge room very confidently and chatted with the US Ambassador. He returned. Almost immediately he said, "Oh, there's the Head of Security in Tripoli. He's an Egyptian called Khalid but he has several names and passes himself off as a business man or an architect or a company director. I will bring him over."

An Egyptian Head of Security in Libya where there had been an Egyptian-inspired *coup* – he was someone I instinctively knew I should avoid. Egyptian intelligence was hand-in-glove with the KGB. Now suspecting that I had been set up, brought along by Okoro at this Egyptian's request, I resolved to avoid the Head of Security and began to make myself scarce.

To my horror Okoro spotted me and returned with him. He introduced himself as a Frenchman called Tony, and (not realising I knew he was the Head of Security) began interrogating me very persistently. He asked what work I did several times, and if I wrote for newspapers.

At first I gave joking replies – "You're very inquisitive for a Frenchman," I smiled – and then said I had to go to the "rest room". I left the reception as quickly as I could and headed for my car.

He followed me and tried to talk to me in the dark street. I turned a corner and hurried to my car. As I got in he reappeared and wrote down the number on my car's number-plate, which was now in Arabic. (Western number-plates had been replaced by Arabic number-plates.) I drove off into the night.

I was now even more wary of Okoro. The Soviet Union had supplied SAM-3 missiles to Egypt (*see* pp.276–277, 297, 301) and I wondered if the KGB had now moved in on Libya and were working with the Egyptian Head of Security. Okoro seemed to be helping the Egyptian Head of Security along with the KGB, and I was convinced he had invited me to the reception at the Head of Security's request so that the Head of Security could interview me. I was convinced Okoro had set me up.

Regime terrorises journalists – Gaddafi: "Journalists will be executed"
Two days later, at a seminar in Tripoli, Gaddafi was reported as saying: "Since journalists are part of the people, I would like to say that some will be punished, some will be imprisoned and also others will be executed as members of the people." The statement was in answer to a question put by the publisher of *Sha'ab* newspapers.[8] There were rumours that a Reign of Terror was about to start.

Arrested by Mohammed Barassi, powerful figure behind the RCC, and threatened with execution by Luger
Gaddafi's terrorising of pro-Western journalists targeted me seven days later. One hot night (27 May) I was at the villa of the couple Caroline had stayed with over Christmas. They had invited me to share their bootleg wine. It had got very late and it was after 2 a.m., just as I was about to leave, when the gate bell rang. I answered it while the others hid the wineglasses.

A *tarboosh*ed Arab pointed to my car, which was parked outside. He had a note of my number, which may have come from "Tony". He showed me a card saying "Ministry of Interior, Security Forces". He said, "Is that your car? Come to prison."

He said he was working in the new department "to watch the foreigners". I was sure that the Head of Security, who had used Okoro to set me up, was behind this Arab's request that I should accompany him to prison.

Behind him a lean, vigorous, fair-skinned, curly-fair-haired man of about 30 was sitting in the driver's seat of an enormous car. He called from the other side of the gate in English: "I want you to get in this car. You come for questioning. I will save you from prison if you come with me." I saw that he was wearing a Western suit and a tie.

I went to the gate and asked, "Who are you?"

"I am not permitted to disclose my identity. I am connected with the Revolutionary Command Council. The man from the Ministry of Interior is here at my instructions, so you must comply. I know you are with some friends, they will come too." The husband staggered to the gates in shorts. He was very drunk. "You will all come with me for questioning. I will give you a beer. I have the supply we confiscated from Guido's on the first day of the Revolution."

And so the four of us – the couple, a Chinese girl and me – got into the back of his wide car. The official from the Ministry of Interior sat in the front, still wearing his *tarboosh*.

The fair-haired Arab – was he a Berber? – drove us to a villa in a nearby sandy lane. Four Arabs opened the door to him. They were in Western shirts. He sat us round a circular table near dozens of crates of Oea beer which looked as if they had been quickly dumped there after the *coup*.

"I am not permitted to disclose my identity," he repeated. "You may call me Mohammed. Now my questioning. We have had this evolution – not revolution – to restore the dignity of Libya. What is your opinion of it?"

At first we were silent, but he insisted, "I want your opinion."

I said, "You want me to speak the truth? There's no freedom for the Libyans. It's a police state. And it's intolerant to prohibit drink."

At that point the husband whose villa we had been in, the colleague of mine at the University who Caroline had stayed with, swayed and fell off his chair with a crash onto the marble floor. There was a long silence. Mohammed leapt to his feet.

"You have been drinking," he shouted. "I know you" (he pointed at me) "have done some journalism, I know you are a spy. You had twenty-five litres of wine from Guido's four days ago." (This was true.) "There are 48 members of the Mafia in Tripoli and Guido is one of the most powerful of them." (This was true as I had heard from the member of the Mafia who had taken me to lunch and asked me to work for the Mafia.) "I have had your flat searched, and I know you have a gun, which is a capital offence." (This was true. I knew I was taking a risk when I bought the air rifle to use if a mob stormed Westerners' homes.) "I know you have been writing against Libya both in newspapers before the Revolution and now." (I had not written any newspaper articles since two weeks after the *coup*. But he knew about my journalism and, recalling Gaddafi's threat, "Some journalists will be executed," I sensed that Gaddafi was behind his interrogation.) "I know you are a spy." I naturally protested that I wasn't. "Don't argue. The others I will deal with later, but I am going to have you executed. I will arrange it now." He strode out to the telephone and started dialling.

We all looked at each other. The husband picked himself up from the floor and crawled back on his chair. The Chinese girl ran after Mohammed, apologising hysterically. Mohammed shouted at her. She returned sobbing uncontrollably. I left the room and tried to reason with Mohammed who was gabbling in Arabic on the phone.

He rang off. "No," he said, "if I decide you'll be executed, you will be. I will telephone the British Ambassador now." Clearly the Arab he had just spoken to had told him he must report news of my execution to the British Ambassador in advance.

Mohammed hunted in a book, found a number and dialled. It was now nearly 4 a.m. and there was no reply. Donald Maitland was presumably asleep and there was no answering service.

Mohammed slammed down the receiver and said with terrifying finality, "I am going to execute you myself." He strode into the next room.

At the door the Chinese girl cried out in panic, "He's got a gun."

Mohammed returned brandishing a revolver in his right hand. "It's a Luger," he said. He motioned with his gun that I should retake my place at the circular table. He sat back in his chair and pointed the gun at me across the table. Everyone else sat very still.

I did not feel afraid. I knew it was important to talk and keep talking for that was my only chance to control the situation. "It'll leak out and it'll be bad publicity for Libya," I said. I carried on talking, monologuing, saying the first thing that came into my head. I was aware that any moment Mohammed could squeeze the trigger, but I had no feeling of wanting to resist. I felt a tremendous peace, as though I had surrendered to the situation. I felt serene, and honestly did not care if I was shot. I thought of the inscription on the lintel over the front door of T.E. Lawrence's house at Clouds Hill, Dorset, 'Ou phrontis', 'I don't care' (words attributed by Herodotus to Hippocleides who, failing to complete a dance before the King of Sicyon, forfeited the prize of a bride and was told, "You have danced away your bride").

I also thought of the words in *Luke*: "Whosoever will save his life shall lose it. Whosoever will lose his life for my sake, the same shall save it."[9]

As I carried on talking I was aware that I had stopped saving my life in the sense of clinging to it, being attached to it, and I felt glad that Caroline and Nadia were safe. In some way I felt that by surrendering my life it would somehow be given back to me.

"You believe in the sword," I said. "I represent the word. You believe power's down the barrel of a gun. I believe it is in the nib of a fountain-pen."

I half-expected this to push him into pulling the trigger, but he did not. He replied angrily: "I am definitely going to execute *you*."

As I spoke I was aware that he was terrorising me, that I had been picked on as a pro-Western journalist – and if Gaddafi was behind it, as an instigator of the 5-September *coup*. I realised I was being subjected to calculated terror. Libya was a terror-state, and as a representative of the RCC Mohammed was waging psychological terror against what he regarded as a representative of the West, a Western target, while implementing Gaddafi's policy on executing some journalists.

Ordered to return to 'executioner'
At 5 a.m. Mohammed suddenly said, "All right, you are free. You can go, all of you. But I warn you, I'm going to have you watched." To me he added,

"You must come back tonight. You can go now but you must come back here at 7 o'clock alone or you'll be arrested."

I was disturbed at the prospect of returning but said nothing. Relieved, we were driven back to the villa where we had been arrested and I drove straight home. I felt I had undergone a kind of death. For an hour I had lived through a new self and had known a thrilling intensity.

I gatecrash reception at British Embassy for Queen's birthday and inform Donald Maitland, British Ambassador, on my way to 'new execution'

I went to work on no sleep and told my colleagues what had happened. They were alarmed and said I should not go back that evening. My Acting Head of Department (who had replaced the expelled New Zealander) said I should visit the British Ambassador. He said that there was a reception for the Queen's birthday at 6 p.m. that evening.[10]

I deliberated all afternoon. I decided to visit the British Ambassador on my way to Mohammed's villa.

I arrived at the venue of the reception (to which I had not been invited): the British Ambassador's residence. I made my way through large grounds with palms and shrubs to the end of a very long queue of about 200 guests, the men in suits and ties and some in evening dress, waiting to be greeted by the Ambassador in the distant entrance hall. The queue stretched 50 yards to some 20 wide steps and continued up the steps on the right side. I was not in a suit or evening dress. I walked alongside the queue and, braving the indignant glares, up the steps to the entrance hall where Donald Maitland stood with his wife in evening dress. Had the 5-September *coup* taken place, it could have been me doing the greeting. I had met him twice before. The second time he received me at a reception after my wife had gone, and talked to me for the full half-hour he was there.

Although I had queue-jumped and was casually dressed, he greeted me very warmly as though I had been invited and was next in the queue: "Hello, how nice to see you. How nice of you to come."

I asked if I could speak to him alone as something had happened.

"Certainly," he said, and after a word to his wife led me to a room off his residence's entrance.

I told him how I had been arrested and threatened with execution, and how an attempt had been made to telephone him at 4 a.m. He listened very intently. I explained that I had to go back at 7 p.m. "What do you think I should do?" I asked.

Looking up at me (for he was much shorter than me) and no doubt thinking of the 200 formally-dressed people who were waiting to shake his hand before going through to take their ice-cold drink, he said: "The RCC *are* the Law. After the *coup* all laws were suspended and remade. The RCC did the suspending and remaking. The RCC do actually have the power to execute people. They can do whatever they like. If he said you must go back, you *must* go back as the RCC's word is law, and if you break the law you will be arrested. It will be worse for you then. You must go back now but I will know where you are."

'You must go back now' sounded like 'Go off and face execution, just let me get on and shake all these people's hands, which is my priority now.'

I said, "Thank you for listening. I'm sorry to have taken you away from your reception."

He said, "Good luck."

Smiling at the glares, I walked back past the queue of formally-dressed Westerners who were bristling that I had queue-jumped my way to the Ambassador's attention and held up the formal greeting and their convivial evening. I sauntered through the grounds back towards my car. Miranda, Andrew Mackenzie's secretary, had seen me. She hurried after me, and out of view of the guests I handed over a typed account of my encounter with Mohammed, which I had put in my pocket in case I saw her. I told her what the Ambassador had said. She asked me to find out as much about the group as I could and let her know. Then I drove to the villa and the prospect of solitary interrogation, beating-up and execution. I looked in my rear mirror but was not being followed. I was on my own. The Ambassador had said "I will know where you are", but I suspected he had no idea of the address I was heading for.

Mohammed was waiting for me at the front door with three accomplices. He directed me to the circular table. He put a bottle of whisky in front of me and a jug of water. He brought me a glass. He invited me to help myself and stood menacingly over me, looking for an excuse to attack me. I wondered whether to decline but thought better of it. I had to stay clear-headed. I poured a tiny amount of whisky and a lot of water.

He went berserk. He shouted, "You are having your whisky too weak, you are in a conspiracy with other foreigners." He seized me by the throat and belaboured me around my neck and shoulders. I tried to fend him off as he hit me, shielding my head with my arms and hands.

The others joined in. They dragged me into a larger room and punched me and kicked me. They all said, " We are going to execute you, you are a spy."

Mohammed beat me up, not very effectively. I was able to ward off many of the blows. He talked to me between attacks. "We are Baathists. We are in charge of the RCC."

I knew that Baathists were cruel and believed in execution as an instrument of government. I said, "You can't be in charge of the RCC as the RCC is the supreme authority."

He said, "I am in charge of presenting the RCC on the media and I am in charge of the department for watching foreigners in the Ministry of Interior." Miranda had asked me to find out who they were. I asked his name. "Mohammed Barassi. My name is Mohammed Barassi. I am editor of *Al-Thawra*, the Government newspaper, the only paper left following the closure of the press. I am an adviser to Jalloud. I present the RCC to the public. And I defend them from their enemies. And I know all about you. I know you are an enemy, a spy."

Al-Thawra ('The Revolution') was the Revolution's newspaper. It censored all anti-Revolutionary news and reflected the program of the Revolution. I learned that his three accomplices were all Baathists: a Secretary in the Syrian Embassy; a Syrian journalist; and the Director-General of Libyan TV, who as Kaseem's Director of TV in Iraq had witnessed the execution of Kaseem in the TV studio in 1963.

Now Mohammed went berserk again. He had a dagger in his hand. He was shouting and held the dagger up as if to stab me.

I leapt up, kicking the chair over, and dashed for the front door. I got out. I ran to my car with Mohammed pursuing about twenty yards behind. I leapt into my green Volkswagen and drove away.

I returned home a little afraid. He was in charge of the department that watched foreigners and could find me at any time. I felt a little terrified. Then I thought: this is part of the Revolution's terror. They intend to make foreigners feel terrified. Their aim was to terrify, from Gaddafi (who had appeared at the Wheelus entrance with a gun) downwards. So I decided I would not be terrified, and they would therefore not succeed in their aim. I went up on the roof and spent an hour basking in the sun.

Return visits to 'executioner': psychological terrorising
The next day Mohammed called at the villa where I had been arrested to demand that the four of us should visit him that evening. There was no escape for me, yet. Mindful of what the Ambassador had said, I agreed to return with them.

Mohammed greeted us with his three accomplices. He made no mention of my flight the previous evening. He placed beer and whisky on the circular table. The conversation soon turned to executions. He said firmly: "I can execute you if I think it is justified, and I may have you executed." Then the phone rang.

The Iraqi answered it, and said to Mohammed: "Abdul Salam Jalloud." (Jalloud was Gaddafi's no. 2.)

Mohammed had a conversation for about three minutes and then said he had some work to do. We should remain with the others.

He was gone for two hours. I probed, and the Iraqi said that Jalloud was announcing a new land revolution – the seizure of the lands of the 30,000 Italians who were to be expelled – and he needed Mohammed's help.

When Mohammed returned I said, "We expected to see you on TV with Jalloud."

Mohammed became angry. "Who said I've been with Jalloud?"

The Iraqi owned up.

Mohammed took the three accomplices into the kitchen and spoke sternly with them. He returned and said, "I have not been with Jalloud."

I said, "And there's no land revolution?"

That set Mohammed off: "There's no land revolution, and I'm warning you, I shall have you executed." At one point he said, "We are against civilised values."

To which I retorted, "So you are, by definition, barbarians."

At this he became very angry. But we were allowed to leave at 3 a.m.

The fawn Volkswagen Beetle now returned. Sometimes a white Volkswagen Beetle sat at my gate. I had a minimum of four plain-clothes men watching me. Sometimes there were seven. I had a man who sat permanently in my garden. Another man rang my doorbell and asked me in French how I was getting on with selling my furniture and leaving Libya. He told me in French that his job was to *"regarder les étrangers"*. Terror was now psychological pressure: urging me to hurry up and leave Libya.

The Chinese girl was being tailed everywhere. She insisted on returning to Mohammed's villa to ask Mohammed to call off his surveillance. I tried to dissuade her but she would not listen. When she arrived at Mohammed's villa Mohammed ordered her to return with the couple and me.

The last place I wanted to go to was Mohammed's villa, but as the RCC *were* now the Law I considered it safer to comply – and perhaps the fawn Volkswagen Beetle would be removed from my gate. And Miranda *had* asked me to find out as much as possible about the group.

As soon as we all arrived the Chinese girl complained about her police scrutiny. Mohammed said it was necessary that we should be watched, particularly as I had been a journalist and was a writer. "Do you deny that?" he asked me.

I said again: "You represent the sword, I represent the pen. The written word will prove stronger than your regime."

I did not know that my book *The Libyan Revolution* would outlast Gaddafi's tyranny.

Mohammed said, "I'm not listening to this." He went off to bring his Luger to shoot me, but thought better of it and came back.

No promise was given to call off the surveillance, and we were all ordered to return on Wednesday 3 June. The Chinese girl offered to bring Chinese food.

I met Miranda to bring her up to date.

We all returned to Mohammed's villa about 10 p.m. on 3 June. The Iraqi left as we arrived. By way of explanation Mohammed said that a state of emergency had been announced in Libya the previous evening, and any car on the streets after midnight would be stopped. I asked, "Why? Is there about to be a *coup*?"

One of the Syrians said, "The *coup* is tomorrow, June 4, at 7 o'clock, starting with the police immigration building opposite Istiqlal. Don't be around in Castle Square or Post Office Square then."

There was general conversation while the Chinese girl dished food from casseroles she had brought. Then suddenly, without provocation and for no apparent reason, Mohammed asked to taste my whisky, and threw it onto the floor, saying it was too weak. He rushed at me, grabbed me round the throat and hit me six or seven times. The others restrained him. He said heatedly, "I am the Libyan representative to the UN after July the seventh. You must respect me." He broke free and ran off for his revolver.

I fled into the garden and crouched behind the parked cars in his sandy lane. The Syrians followed Mohammed out and disarmed him of a dagger.

I returned very warily, but he flew at me again and (literally) kicked me out. Terrified, the Chinese girl fled with me, leaving the casseroles behind.

I drove her home through the state of emergency just before midnight. The couple stayed behind, worried about driving back in a state of emergency. Later that night the Syrians tried to recruit the husband into Syrian intelligence and the wife was ordered to submit to rape and thought it best to comply.

The next day there was no *coup* attempt.

I wondered if Mohammed and his dreadful posse of Baathists would come to my door and arrest me for immediate execution. He never came, and I saw no more of him. But I later found out that he was one of the most dangerous men in Libya. Mohammed Barassi *was* in charge of presenting the RCC on the media and in charge of the department for watching foreigners within the Ministry of Interior. He *did* work with Jalloud. And he *did* become Libya's Ambassador to the UN. He was a shadowy figure behind the RCC's dictatorship and he had the outlook towards execution of Robespierre, with *carte blanche* to execute. His mentality was the closest to Robespierre's that I have met. He could have executed me with impunity. I had taken a huge risk in going back to him so many times to stay within the RCC's law.

Separation: defections and the KGB

Now I was harassed wherever I went. The fawn Volkswagen was always in attendance, waiting nearby while I spent hot boring mornings invigilating and tedious afternoons marking scripts. It came with me when I went to a show in honour of the leaders who were attending the Arab Summit and I was badly jostled by Libyans in the crowd.

I attended a big rally in a sports stadium and stood ten feet from the 'Royal Box' in a large crowd. After an hour's military music Col. Gaddafi arrived in a Jeep and toured the stadium, waving at the crowd. He strode up to the 'Royal Box' and made a long speech. All round me were skull-capped, *barracan*ed Libyan workers.

I was seized by two plain-clothes men. Each held one of my arms. "You have a gun in your pocket," one said, patting me.

He plunged his hand into my trouser pocket and removed: my dark glasses.

I submitted to incidents like this as if to a Zen priest's stick, mortifying my old self in purgation and remaking it, preparing for the act of surrender that lay ahead. I wondered if I had subconsciously willed Mohammed to berate my old self, which I was casting off.

Viktor prepared to defect: transferring Viktor's savings – I sign a receipt and lob Viktor's cash to Andrew Mackenzie's secretary in a supermarket

Viktor was now preparing to separate from his Czech culture and background and defect to Britain with his family. I had already reeled him in by establishing his disillusion with Brezhnev's Soviet-occupied Czechoslovakia. I had discussed the nuclear knowledge that he was expected to bring with him with Andrew. Andrew had said that the knowledge he would bring was very important and that it was vital he should defect. We had agreed that he might be a second Penkovsky, who had handed the West details of Soviet nuclear missiles in Cuba in 1963. It was believed that Penkovsky was executed in Moscow before he could defect, and I was clear that Viktor should defect before he suffered Penkovsky's fate.

Viktor was now ready to transfer £400 from Libya to Switzerland, his hard-earned savings in Libya on which he would draw to set up his new life. The £400 was a huge amount to Viktor (the equivalent of thousands of pounds today).

There were strict exchange-control regulations in force at that time, both in Libya and in the UK. A banking transfer by an East-European might alert the Libyan authorities (and therefore the Egyptians, the Czech authorities and the KGB) to his plan to defect. He thought it would be risky to travel with £400 in undeclared cash on his person or in his luggage as it might be confiscated if found during a search. On 16 June (when I met her at 9 p.m., after giving my plain-clothes men the slip) Miranda asked me to collect the £400 from Viktor in a private room at the University – Andrew had suggested the 'washroom' – and hand it to her. She said Andrew Mackenzie had said that on no account should I sign anything. The equivalent would then be paid into a bank account in Switzerland.

By arrangement I duly met Viktor in a University 'washroom', a large empty room with basins. Viktor was more than six feet tall, had broad shoulders and a very authoritative way of speaking. He was about fifteen years older than me. He knew his mind and was very definite in what he wanted. He produced an envelope containing the £400 and said very firmly, "I want a receipt. It is a lot of money. What if you disappear and the money does not reach Switzerland?"

I explained that Andrew had said I should not sign anything.

He stuck out his chin and said very aggressively, "All future operations are cancelled unless I have a receipt."

Either he had his receipt or he cancelled his defection and the West would not benefit from the nuclear knowledge he was expected to bring with him.

I had to make a decision there and then. I was completely on my own and had to choose a course of action in an Existentialist free choice that would: keep Viktor defecting (which I saw as the priority from the SIS's point of view, for the Americans wanted him to defect to the US); address his worries that I might disappear with the £400; and maintain my ability to function as an agent.

I could have refused to give a receipt and walked away from Viktor's plan to defect. I could have explained to Miranda that the defection was off, and put up with being criticised for messing up the defection and losing valuable nuclear intelligence. In that case he might defect to the US instead. However, if I were dealing with Penkovsky I would make it a priority that the defection took place. It was reasonable for Viktor to want a receipt. Would I give money to the Russians without a receipt if the roles were reversed? No.

The question was, could I trust Viktor? I took the view that I *had* to trust him if I was to keep him defecting. He was supposed to be bringing with him nuclear intelligence that Czech intelligence and the KGB did not want to pass to the West. If he was working for, and remaining loyal to, Czech intelligence and the KGB his nuclear intelligence would be worthless. That was not how Andrew had evaluated it. I had to believe that his defection was genuine.

I said to him, "If this is a trap, I think it's a pretty shabby one." He looked at me and averted his eyes. He could not look me straight in the eye, and I knew I was taking a risk.

I took the envelope containing a wad of notes from him, counted the money, hand-wrote a receipt for £400 on a page torn from my pocketbook and gave it to him. Then I wrote a copy of the receipt and tucked it into the envelope. I tucked the envelope inside my shirt, went out into the car park and stored it under the front seat of my car, ducking down so my minders in their fawn Volkswagen could not see.

Because all foreigners were watched – especially me – it was not safe to take the £400 to Miranda's home. She had arranged to meet me in a tiny supermarket-style store, the International, which faced the sea on the way to Giorgimpopoli. I drove to the International, parked and transferred the bundle of notes back to the inside of my shirt, which was tucked into my trousers.

I entered the small self-service store and picked up a wire basket. In those days stores were not equipped with CCTV cameras. The store had a central five-foot-high wire rack and on each side several two-foot-deep shelves that were stacked with packets and tins. There was an aisle each side of the rack. In the aisle nearest the road, which was visible through the window, stood Miranda (the only shopper in the store), putting a tin in her wire basket. She ignored me, giving the impression that she did not know me. Holding my wire basket I headed for the other aisle that had more shelves with stacked packets and tins on the back wall. Miranda and I were now separated by the central rack.

There were two white-coated assistants near a till by the door. My four minders had followed me in. Two stood at one end of the two aisles and two at the other end. Each man was able to see everything within his aisle, and all angles were covered. Apart from Miranda and me there were no other shoppers, and we were being watched by four minders.

I put my wire basket down by the central rack, out of sight of the two staff operating the till. The minders at each end of my aisle were staring at me. I pretended to bend and examine what was on the shelves. Through a chink in some tins I could see Miranda examining tins the other side of the rack. I could see the wire basket over her arm. I glanced at the two minders at each end of my aisle. They were both looking sideways, their attention temporarily distracted by the two assistants near the till. I stepped back and saw the two minders the other side were also distracted. The two staff on the till were preoccupied.

I quickly opened my shirt where I had hidden the envelope containing the wad of notes, gripped the envelope and, near the top of the rack, lobbed it over. There was a slight thud the other side.

Through my spyhole I saw it had landed in Miranda's basket. My aim had been true. Miranda was covering the envelope with a box of soap powder. A few seconds later she surreptitiously transferred it into her bag. She took her wire basket to the check-out.

I had taken an appalling risk. If the envelope had missed and landed on the floor, my four minders would have rushed and picked it up and Viktor's money would have been seized – and so would Miranda and I. I had got the money on its way to Switzerland via Miranda and Andrew under the noses of four plain-clothes men. The slickness of the operation and the accuracy of my lob (which owed something to my cricketing) when under surveillance was one of the high spots of my intelligence career.

Viktor "linked to Czech intelligence"
I saw Miranda one more time, on 18 June at 9 p.m. She had found the copy of my receipt in the envelope. She said there was disquiet within the Service that I had issued a receipt as it was highly likely that Viktor was "linked to Czech intelligence" and therefore with the KGB and might show them the receipt to cover his traces if put under pressure by them. Miranda said that it was highly likely that Czech intelligence was extremely interested in me.

I could understand this. Before the *coup* a Czech had lived in the ground-floor flat opposite ours, and I had been warned by Andrew Mackenzie that he was one of half a dozen Czechs in Tripoli who were connected to Czech intelligence. One night his wife had rung our doorbell and asked me to look at him as he had been taken ill. I had examined him and diagnosed a stroke. I had arranged for an ambulance to come.

My diagnosis was confirmed by hospital tests and the hospital said that my prompt action had saved his life. He was told that he and his family were being sent home. In gratitude his wife had given us the ultra-modern air-cooling propeller blade from their ceiling. Before this episode my Czech neighbour had apparently reported on me to Czech intelligence and to the KGB, Andrew had told me, as, no doubt, had one of the engineers of the Czech Road Company I stayed with on the way to Ghadames.

Andrew had not told me that Viktor was probably connected with Czech intelligence and the KGB. I had always considered the possibility, and had Andrew told me this earlier I would probably have refused to issue a receipt in the University 'washroom'. (I had not been told on a 'need to know' basis. It had been assumed that I did not need to know, I just had to persuade him to defect. The SIS had misjudged the situation by assuming that Viktor would defect without a receipt.)

Given what I knew at the time my decision was right as it made the defection possible and benefited the West, and the defection was arguably more important to the West than the compromising of my security. However the receipt would cause me a problem. It was evidence that I had taken Viktor's money and arranged to pay it into a Swiss bank account, which, as an individual living in Libya I would not be able to do without Embassy help. From the receipt and Viktor's explanation for it, it could be construed that I had been engaged in an SIS operation if Viktor chose to pass it on to Czech intelligence with such an explanation.

I escape arrest for "stealing five bunches of grapes"
I now began to struggle round a dozen Ministries and collect all the signatures I needed to allow myself, my car, my goods and my money to leave Libya at the end of my two-year contract. The most bureaucratic office was the Electricity Office, which passed me and re-passed me between its numerous departments. All the while I was followed by my four minders, at least two of whom came in with me if I went into any building outside my own home.

The day before I was due to leave Libya there was an attempt to arrest me. When I returned home I opened my double gates and reversed my car under the grapevine. My faithful *ghaffir*, Milud, who spoke no English and wore a white skullcap, knocked on my window. He pointed at the grapevine and at five bunches of grapes that lay in the dust alongside where I had parked. He jabbered in Arabic. I turned off the engine, pocketed my car keys and got out to look at the grapes.

One-eyed Mohammed came across from his greengrocer's and said, "He say you stole these grapes. For sure, I see you last night, ten o'clock. These police take you to prison."

Two armed uniformed policemen then stepped out from behind bushes where they had been hiding, wearing revolver holsters on their belts, and motioned me to go with them. They had clearly told Milud and Mohammed what to say.

Thinking quickly, I edged nearer my car under the grapevine and kept them talking. I said they were my grapes to pick.

"No, they Libyan grapes. They belong Revolution for sure."

The double gates were still open. I said I had to get something from the front seat. I had taken my keys from my pocket and I quickly opened the driver's door, jumped in, started the engine and roared out. The policemen jumped aside to left and right. I was away and heading for Giorgimpopoli.

I did not stop until I reached the sea. I got out of the car and took a long last look at the laval rock and sparkling waves. I wondered whether to return to the British Ambassador, but the last time I did that he had said I must go back into the lions' den and as a result I had been mildly beaten up and nearly shot and stabbed. He would urge me to give myself up to the police and I would not get out of Libya. I decided to visit my landlord and fellow *coup*-plotter, Ben.

To Ben Nagy
Ahmad, his Egyptian servant, let me in. Ben greeted me warmly. I told him about the five bunches of grapes. I said, "They're your grapes, not the Revolution's grapes. Can you get the Revolution off my back? I'm supposed to be leaving Libya tomorrow. Gaddafi used to be your bootboy. Can you

tell your former bootboy to call off the police who are trying to arrest me for stealing five bunches of my landlord's grapes."

Ben looked shifty. He said he could do nothing: "Since the Revolution, we Libyans have become powerless. There's nothing I can do. Your paperwork is in order. You must get out of Libya as fast as you can. Now."

But, I said, I had to pack.

"Collect your possessions, leave the key under the brick and then get out of Libya."

I said I could not return to my flat until *after* Mohammed the greengrocer had closed. Otherwise he would report me. It would be better to go the next morning.

I asked if I could stay the night at his villa, but he shook his head. I could see he felt I would be endangering him. We had both been involved in the 5-September *coup* and he wanted to keep his distance from me just as he had refused to see my "friend in the Embassy" (Andrew Mackenzie) who would have helped him transfer some money.

To Okoro

I deliberated and decided I would visit the Biafran, Jerry Okoro, the Tripoli correspondent of the London *Times*. I had misgivings about going to him as he had told me he had links with the KGB, but I decided to take the risk. He would be able to report my arrest and the publicity would alert Maitland, the British Ambassador.

I drove to Okoro's flat. He opened the door, seemingly delighted to see me. I told him what had happened. I said I didn't want the Head of Security to know. He said that if I were arrested there would be a front-page news story in *The Times*.

I spent the rest of the day with him. He poured me some of the whisky the KGB had given him. We discussed how the US had vacated Wheelus Air Base on 11 June – the result Gaddafi had wanted to achieve on 18 October 1969 – and how the British Ambassador, Donald Maitland, had just been made Chief Press Secretary to Edward Heath, who had won the British General Election on 19 June. I had in fact just written a letter to Maitland congratulating him on his new position.

In the evening I drove past my flat at high speed. There was no sign of any armed policemen and the greengrocer's was closed. I turned and drove back. The double gates were still open from when I escaped. I reversed my car in under the Revolution's grapevine, squashing one of the five bunches of the Revolution's grapes.

I had already cleared my flat. My possessions were stacked in neat piles on the kitchen floor. Stealthily I entered by my front door, opened the back door and threw all my belongings into the car. I threw the clothes in loose. I locked up and left my key under the brick as Ben had directed.

I spent the night at Okoro's, sleeping under the stars on a huge veranda and hoping that the KGB would not alert the police to take me to prison.

I escape to border and leave Libya

The next morning I said goodbye to Okoro and left Tripoli. I was sure he would be telling the KGB, and probably the Head of Security, about my stay and where I was crossing the border. Feeling like a defector, separating from my home of more than eighteen months, I headed west, expecting to be pursued, looking out for police or Security who would flag me down and take me back to face charges for picking five bunches of my own – no the Revolution's – grapes. I reached the Tunisian border at 5 p.m.

I had to leave my car to present paperwork to the border guards. One of the Libyan border guards eyed my possessions through my car windows with suspicion. The strewn clothes did look as though I had left in great haste. He exuded hostility towards me and I wondered if the Head of Security (alerted by Okoro) had telephoned him about me. When I was not looking he drove two nails into one of my rear tyres: the Revolution's farewell.

Flat tyre: I change a wheel in the desert among Tuareg

I crossed the border and came to a halt with a flat tyre in the Tunisian desert at dusk. I was utterly alone in the desert – I had become the man in the desert. The spare wheel was beneath the back seat, which was piled up with clothes. I had to lift the piles of clothes onto the sand, raise the back seat and remove the spare wheel. While I found my tools a camelcade of Tuareg nomads approached. They watched menacingly, eyeing my possessions and the clothes on the sand from a distance of five yards.

They outnumbered me. Until the 1930s the Tuareg had made a living by attacking lone travellers and stealing their possessions. They stared at me behind their veils. I stared back and smiled reassuringly. I pointed to the flat tyre, shrugged and made wheel-changing gestures. It occurred to me that they may never have seen a car.

I completed the wheel-change without being attacked, put the old wheel where the spare wheel had been, piled my clothes and belongings back onto the back seat, shut the door and drove off, heaving a sigh of relief. It was now virtually dark.

So ended my long exposure to Gaddafi's anti-Western measures and to the growing extremism of the Libyan Revolution. Looking back, I believe that Barassi's threats of execution were a consequence of my involvement in the 5-September *coup* and of my arrest and questioning at the Tripoli radio station. I was sure that Gaddafi knew about my involvement with

Bushwerib and the 5-September *coup*, and was behind the incidents.

Libya was pro-Western and orderly when I arrived. I had offered technical help in improving the Arabs' English, and the Arabs had wanted to improve their English. There were no suicide-bombers or Jihadists in those days. I had tried to help forward a succession to the King's rule that would have continued a pro-Western Libya, but Gaddafi's *coup* had put an end to that. When I left, Libya was anti-Western and under army rule. Now, more than 40 years later, Libya is in anarchy, ruled by feuding armed militias with no central control, and home to terrorists. Like Iraq, Libya seems worse off today than when I was there.

The extremist terror of the Revolution had intimidated my wife and sabotaged my marriage. It had compounded the dreadful Dark Night which was purging my soul of its attachments and made it more terrifying. The process of purgation during my separation still had a long way to go.

CHAPTER 5

Transformation: the Illuminative Way

"Strong in will
To strive, to seek, to find, and not to yield."
Tennyson, 'Ulysses'

Libya accelerated my drastic purgation and remaking of myself. I was on the universal Mystic Way without really realising it. I did not know at the time that my Dark Night of the Soul, or more strictly my Dark Night of the Senses, would help me back onto the right path of detachment, illumination and transformation – onto the Illuminative Way and self-remaking – but that I would have to traverse Hell before I could reach inner serenity. Bewildered, I now felt more intensely than ever that I had lost my way in a dark wood and was still searching for my right path.

Episode 13:

Ambassador and Journalism

Years: 1970–1971
Locations: Rapallo; London; Loughton; Sandgate
Works: *The Gates of Hell*; 'The Silence'; *The Flight*
Initiatives: articles for *The Times*; becomes Heath's 'unofficial Ambassador' to African liberation movements; operates openly

"An ambassador is an honest man sent to lie abroad for the good of his country."
Sir Henry Wotton, 'Written in the Album of Christopher Fleckmore' (1604)

My intelligence work was about to be stepped up within the Cold-War atmosphere of the time and I was about to become an 'unofficial Ambassador' while writing journalistic articles. The tension between my two new roles intensified the strain and suffering within my Dark Night.

Ambassador and poetry

I have no doubt that I was traumatised by the events of Libya. I had not been a hostage in the sense of being confined in a small dark room, but I had been kept under virtual house arrest in an open prison with no possibility of leaving Libya for good until my contract expired. I had been at the mercy of young revolutionaries and potential executioners and, separated from Nadia, I still yearned to have my family back. I knew it was impossible but deep down hoped for a miracle, a change of heart on Caroline's part.

Return to UK

This was how I felt during the long drive back. I drove all day and slept at Medenine. The next day I drove on to Gabes and spent the next night in Hammamet, where I stayed three days. I lay on the windy beach and thought, 'The sun is shining, the sea is blue, the hills are beautiful, but....' The natural beauty mocked my emotional terrain, which was a region in Hell, and I felt a fissure across my being. I wrote a poem that would appear in my sequence *The Gates of Hell*.

I drove on to mountainous and beautiful Algeria, stopped at Souk Ahras and spent a night in Constantine. In pursuit of Camus, I drove on to Algiers and Oran, where I wrote another poem. I crossed Morocco to Tangiers and drove up Spain. I spent three days in Marbella at the Melia Don Pepe, and then drove up the coast via Barcelona to the Italian Riviera and Rapallo.

With Ezra Pound in Rapallo

I had written to the American poet, Ezra Pound, from Libya, having spent part of June thinking about the epic I knew I would one day write: a long poetic work in the tradition of Homer, Virgil, Dante, Milton and Pound that would become *Overlord*.

I had identified Ezra Pound as a suitable person to give me advice. He had arguably been the originator of the Modernist movement in 20th-century English literature. At 24, while acting as his secretary, he had turned the 48-year-old Yeats into a Modernist poet, and he had cut out half of Eliot's 'The Waste Land'. He had written a long work – he had been writing his own 20th-century epic, *The Cantos*, for 57 years – and had helped Joyce and Hemingway. In 1970 Pound was 85 and was known to be largely silent following his incarceration for twelve years without trial at St Elizabeth's Hospital, Washington DC, for his "treason" in broadcasting in Italy during the Second World War that the US Government was controlled by Jewish bankers.

On 16 July I found a hotel and then drove to Sant' Ambrogio and asked directions from passers-by. I was told to go to a *"casa rossa"* (red house) on top of a mountain. I arrived about 7 and knocked at the back door. Pound appeared, bearded, in his slippers, at the foot of stairs. He turned away and went back in for his companion Olga Rudge was coming up the garden behind me. Yes, she said, she *had* got my letter (which was simply addressed 'Ezra Pound, Rapallo') and it *would* be convenient to see him immediately. I followed her in and up the stairs and was shown into a large room with many books, some sculptures and a circular table covered with papers.

Pound sat apart beside a window in great silence. He had a serene face and troubled eyes. I sat on a sofa the other side of the room from him and spoke about my reason for consulting him. I spoke of my knowledge of Japan and China, including the Cultural Revolution. I said I knew he had persuaded Yeats to look at Japanese *Noh* plays and had inspired Yeats's own plays, and that he had been given the idea for *The Cantos* from China through Ernest Fenollosa's posthumous papers sent to him by his widow in 1913, and I detected his interest in his eyes. I spoke about my interest in developing his innovations and my plans to write a poetic epic, and said: "You've been writing *The Cantos* for 57 years, so you're the best person to ask about a method which is going to involve me in many years of work. You compressed 26 lines into two: 'The apparition of these faces in the crowd;/Petals on a wet, black bough.' Is it possible to compress at length over twelve books?"

He listened to me for 15 minutes in complete silence – he was like the Delphic Oracle, you asked a question and listened to the silence which revealed your own heart – and then he said: "Wait until Antonio comes, he'll answer these questions better than I can. Or ask Desmond O'Grady or Graves." I persisted and asked my question again. He said: "It's worth trying."

His *Cantos* compressed at length, but I subsequently turned away from the compression of 'The Silence' to classical narrative.

I turned from technical epic method and style to epic subject matter. I said that the epic can sum up the culture of the last thirty years in twelve books.

Pound asked suddenly: "Have you had twelve experiences that sum up the culture of the last thirty years?"

I said, "Yes. For example, my experience of China."

At that point Olga Rudge, a violinist brought up in Italy, his mistress and mother of his child, returned with coffee. She was younger than he was, about 75 I judged, and she was rather rude: "If you put everything on a postcard, then he'll take you seriously."

Pound said: "T.E. Hulme said to me in 1915, 'Everything a writer has to say can be put on half a side of a postcard, and all the rest is application and elaboration.' Have you got the application and elaboration?"

I said I had.

Suddenly without warning in came an Italian neighbour and writer, who introduced himself to me as "Pescatore, like a fish". With him was his mistress and an Italian boy, and suddenly the room was filled with talk. Pound did not say a word. He sat in silence in the open window, a full moon over his shoulder, very sad and apart, blinking constantly, and I noticed a sculpted head cast by Gaudier-Brzeska and saw a copy of Yeats's *Mythologies*. I spoke about my visit to China and talked about my travels.

About 9 Pescatore turned to me and said, "You know, I've been visiting Mr Pound for ten years, but I've never heard his voice." He stood up to go, and I stood up to go with him, thinking that if he had not heard Pound speak in ten years there was not much hope that I would do a lot better in a couple of hours.

But as the neighbours trooped out with Olga Rudge and I lingered to say goodbye to the Oracle, unexpectedly Pound stood up, advanced rapidly towards me, dragged my arm and pointed to the chair in front of him. He said (just after Pescatore left the room): "Here, sit down, sit down, you don't have to go yet do you? I've been thinking and listening to you. You've been around a lot, I think you *can* do what you want to do: put the culture and the Age into twelve poems."

Inspired, I sat down on the chair at the circular table and told him I knew I could.

Sitting down opposite me at the circular table, he said, "Your long preamble about myself wasn't necessary" – he did not seem to want to acknowledge his technical innovations – and when I said I could *see* the pattern ahead ("I can *see* the poem") he said: "If you can see it, then you've already done it. Seeing it's half the battle."

We talked on. On the circular table, upside down as I looked, was his handwritten text of the latest canto – I could read "A place of skulls" – and as we discussed the technical side of writing an epic he said: "It doesn't matter where you begin. It's like making a table, it doesn't matter which leg you put on first as long as the table stands up at the end."

Olga Rudge kept intruding, saying at one point, "E-zra [the first syllable being deep, the second quite shrill], it's time for your orange juice," which she put in front of him, and later, "E-zra, it's time you went to bed." To which he muttered, "Leave us alone, woman." I asked him about many details in his study, including the bust by Gaudier-Brzeska.

Eventually, just before midnight I stood up to take my leave. He stood up too and we stood together. I was surprised he was so tall. I told him, "When I am 70 I will have a reputation like yours" – he looked at me queerly – "and I will think of this evening. I believe two eras are spanning each other, although this will not be apparent until the next century."

He shook me warmly by the hand – there was nothing feeble about his handshake – and he held onto my hand and looked intently into my eyes like a healer transmitting an energy and brightening my aura, like a poet passing on a seed from a tradition he has grown, and in what I took to be an endorsement of what I had said he repeated: "If you can see it, you've already done it." Then he lapsed into oracular silence and returned to his chair and sat as silent as the future, the full moon over his shoulder, and I left.

As I closed the door I could hear Olga Rudge scolding him (and by implication me) for staying up so late. I thought it sad that the founder of Modernism in literature and all his questionings should have ended in a silence.[1]

I returned to my hotel after midnight transported into another world, having glimpsed my true path and direction and therefore my destiny, feeling in Paradise rather than in Hell, full of purpose and meaning, far removed from the pain and littleness of Libya. I wrote my *Diaries* entry into the small hours.

Geneva

The next day I drove to Geneva and on to Annemasse, where I stayed at a small hotel kept by the parents of a girl we had met on Djerba, Les Pleiades. The following day, guided by her, I drove into the mountains so that I could appreciate the spectacular view of snow-covered Mont Blanc above Lake Leman. I was in the footsteps of Shelley, who wrote 'Mont Blanc' – and also of Eliot, who drafted 'The Waste Land' by Lake Leman.

I had seen that Pound had called me to be my Shadow, my future self, and as we sat in my car I spoke of the mountain as the measure of man and told her my future task was: "To search through everything, through literature, art, philosophy, every culture, every country, different people, until in the end I have a total knowledge about what man is, i.e. in terms of himself. Then I shall hope to know what he is in terms of Nature and his society and context [i.e. the universe]." I distinguished vertical and horizontal living: living in relation to Reality and in relation to society. I spoke of "my huge 40-year task".[2] More than 42 years after writing these words I look back with approval at the definition of my task under Mont Blanc.

Inspired by my meeting with Pound I was groping towards a Universalist vision. I saw my true path very clearly that day.

London: reunions

My visit to Pound had buoyed me up, but my return to England was dismal. I drove all night and arrived on a cross-Channel ferry on a wet Sunday morning, 19 July. I drove to London and unsuccessfully looked for a room off the Brompton Road. I saw a card in a window and went to 13 Egerton

Gardens, a short walk from Knightsbridge, where I was shown an upstairs room with no view and walls covered in silver foil. I rejected the room. I rang Caroline but she was "not in". It rained and rained and in the end I drove out to Loughton and spent the night at my mother's.

I got through to Caroline about 10 that evening. She said, "I don't see any point in seeing you, there's nothing to discuss. But if you insist...." She added: "I haven't told you this because he only proposed recently. But I'm definitely marrying David when he gets his divorce in 18 months' time. I've told Nadia that you will not be living with her any more."

That bleak night I slept in my old room. I had swung from complete exhilaration to total despair. I awoke the next morning, the sun hot on my cheeks.

I met Caroline in London. I saw her golden hair up Sloane Avenue. We sat in the King's Arms, Sloane Square (the Royal Court theatre pub). We had a gentle talk in which she pleaded for a divorce. I drove back to Loughton feeling as if the dark wood had closed round me again. I visited a solicitor to discuss divorce proceedings. His name was appropriately Payne.

I was reunited with Nadia outside the Dulwich Crown and Greyhound, near Dulwich Park. She jumped out of the red MG Caroline had borrowed and, still wearing her school uniform, ran to meet me and held my hand. Then she went shy. We all had lunch in the Crown and Greyhound garden and Nadia remained within earshot and talked intelligently, almost too politely. She chatted a lot and was outgoing.

I drove her to Essex and she asked why I had chosen not to live with her any more. I had to explain that it was Mummy's choice, not mine. "But can't you still come and live with Mummy?" she asked. "I'm sure it'll be all right if I ask her."

We spent a week at my mother's and I took her swimming in the local pool, walked with her in the Forest and guided her round the Tower. I always put her to bed. I took her back to the Crown and Greyhound where Caroline was waiting, and she went to Yorkshire for a fortnight.

When she returned I drove her to Sandgate, where my mother was spending a fortnight on the front. At high tide the sea flung great fountains of spray onto the promenade, and sometimes the road was awash. At low tide we went down onto the shingle and paddled near the rocks and she found a green crab. One dawn I took her to the harbour and showed her the fish market where plaice and skate were being auctioned while the fishermen stood smoking near their nets. Another morning I took her to the Amusement Arcade and she went on a roundabout that whizzed round too fast and she clung to a painted horse, a look of happy terror on her face while I stood feeling the sickening lurch in my stomach that a parent feels when a child is in danger. At bedtime the sea crashed outside the window, and there was a long drag of pebbles. I would whisper "I love you" and she murmured back, "I love *you*."

Soon afterwards Caroline went to Malta for two weeks to be near her future husband. Nadia stayed in Essex. I took her shopping and to visit her old school friends, revelling in the freedom to lead a normal life after the privations of Libya. We looked for conkers. Caroline stayed on an extra week in Malta, and on the first afternoon of the September term I drove to Nadia's school and took her for a walk in Dulwich Park. After that, as autumn turned golden-reds to yellows, and apples fell in the Essex garden, I took her for a weekend in Essex every fortnight. We collected leaves and holly with red berries and observed the wood mushrooms and red toadstools and puffballs that grew in the beech woods. In the evenings I put her to bed and slipped out for a quick drink in The Owl or Turpin's Cave (a very old house where Dick Turpin was reputed to have hidden) and when I returned I always checked that her covers were over her. Sometimes I picked her up from school and drove her to the Park and we fed the squirrels. I was a permanent protective presence in relation to which she could feel secure.

I take a room in 13 Egerton Gardens, London SW3
Meanwhile a room had become vacant on the first floor of 13 Egerton Gardens, London SW3, near Knightsbridge. It was a double room with two beds that overlooked the gardens and beyond it Egerton Crescent (now the most expensive street in Britain). The room had long French windows and a balcony opposite a plane-tree. It let in the morning sun, and the rent was £10.50 per week. I could not face living at my flat in Loughton, so I had taken the room. I brought two suitcases with clothes and personal papers and nothing else so that I could simplify my life and finish my paring-down.

Here I established a routine. After a gloomy breakfast with wrecked people in the basement, I sat at my desk and wrote 'The Flight', a poem I had begun in August, and a draft of *Chains*, a novel set in Libya, and occasional poems, and gazed out at the huge plane-tree and the white Georgian terrace of Egerton Crescent. Sometimes I put on the radio, sometimes I boiled coffee on the hotplate. I had no television and there was a communal telephone extension, for incoming calls only, outside my door. I lunched in South Kensington (sometimes at Dino's, a haunt at one time of T.S. Eliot's) or in the King's Road, or in one of the Knightsbridge pubs, and I sometimes walked round one of the museums, The Victoria and Albert or Science Museums. Then I worked until evening when I went out and ate in a small inexpensive restaurant like the Chelsea Kitchen.

The Spanish psychiatrist had told me I would be more independent: "You will have a narrower range of feelings: you will suffer less but you will enjoy less. You will have relationships you like but do not need." Such a shift is consistent with a shift from the ego to a new centre. I did not want to get involved again until I was firmly on my true path and heading in the right direction. I fled involvement with one by consorting with several. There was safety in numbers. I was still in Hell for I lived in the past and was merely passing the present. I lunched with Tuohy in a Greek restaurant near his London base. He was going to live in Somerset, alone, and he suggested I wrote some articles on Libya.[3]

Journalism on Libya: articles for The Times *and* The Sunday Telegraph
I duly contacted the national newspapers and was asked to write articles on Libya for *The Times* and *The Sunday Telegraph*.[4] The *Times* article was commissioned by Brian MacArthur, who I visited at John Ezard's suggestion. We had a drink together. Tuohy's literary agent referred me to MacArthur's boss, Charlie Douglas-Home, the Features Editor, and I met him as well and fixed up an article on Libya. I met George Evans, Assistant Editor of *The Sunday Telegraph*, and fixed up an article with him. Both these articles were commissioned on my own initiative.

My *Times* article spoke of the Libyan Revolution as an "armed sit-in on the throne" by a group of 28-year-olds, and Brian MacArthur said there would be freelance work with *The Times* when the article had appeared.[5] My *Sunday Telegraph* article predicted, in the text I submitted, that Gaddafi would be in power for 40 years. *The Telegraph* did not want him in power at all, and my prediction was sub-edited out. (It turned out to be accurate for Gaddafi would rule for 42 years until he lost power to rebels and was assassinated in 2011.)

London poets. Poetry Revolution to restore grand themes, seriousness, prophecy and vision: three visits to John Heath-Stubbs; Ted Hughes
Through John Ezard I got in with the London poets. He took me to a party at Bernard Stone's bookshop, Turrets, off Kensington Church Street, and the next day, 30 July, he arranged for me to meet blind, grey-haired John Heath-Stubbs.

Heath-Stubbs lived in a shabby room with a faded patterned carpet in 35 Sutherland Place, Notting Hill. I was on my own, and with the independence of the blind he insisted on pouring my tea from a tea-pot. He missed my cup and tea cascaded onto the table and floor. I told him how I discussed epic poetry and culture with Pound. He said of Pound: "You don't have to have been anywhere to write about culture, you must go in your imagination, not physically." He added, "Pound isn't discursive enough, his images don't communicate,"[6] a traditional writer's swipe (with which I now agree) at a compressed Modernist.

He gave me a flimsy booklet of the first book of his *Artorius*, an epic he had started. He was suggesting that he was a better person than Pound to advise me on epic. After tea we walked around the corner to the pub, the Pavistock. He talked all the while and groped with his white stick. We sat and discussed mythology in poetry at a small table while he peered in my direction and fumbled for his beer.

There was always a meeting of poets (or poetasters), and several listened to what I had to say. I called for a Poetry Revolution that would restore grand themes, seriousness, and prophecy after a Movement-dominated time of triviality and smallness. This Revolution would be like the 1798 or 1912 literary revolutions, both of which were conducted by two men (Wordsworth and Coleridge, Eliot and Pound). It would move away from the social themes of Larkin to the unity of the universe and the meaning of life. I said a poet is a man with a vision of the Whole, not a dreamer in private. The Revolution would get in touch with common people again: metre, diction and rhythm must be close to the rhythms of common speech, and I called for incantation in some poetry to differ from the Movement's argument. I spoke with conviction for I believed in myself and I was anticipating a neo-Baroque poetic revolution. I again resolved to write a hundred poems by being open to write a poem a day. I began revising 'The Silence'. Daphne and Ursula both appeared, separately, in Chelsea, but I was so involved with the poets I had little time to see them.

On 8 August I went with John Ezard to a party at Heath-Stubbs's and talked about the Poetry Revolution with the young poet Bernard Saint, a precocious 19-year-old who had lived with George Barker, Heath-Stubbs and others since he was 16. He had a lean face and wore a black velvet jacket. Towards midnight he read a poem by Vernon Watkins, 'Ballad of the Mari Lwyd' (the Mari Lwyd being a Welsh midwinter tradition that may have celebrated the New Year), which contains the lines "Midnight. Midnight. Midnight. Midnight./Hark at the hands of the clock."

I spent the next day with Bernard Saint at his rooms in Balham, where he lived with his older BBC wife, Jeanne. He told me he was a Nature poet and that, in terms of the sun, man is not a city being. He said: "I go into an ecstatic trance, a reverie, and write a poetry of high dream and celebration. The images come out in an order and rhythm that must not be disturbed. Anything else is stilted or, like the Movement poets, very weak." I told him that like Keats he was writing of "joys" and that he had to progress to "the agonies, the strife/of human hearts". He disagreed.

On 17 August I met him and his wife at the Chelsea Markham, and we travelled to Heath-Stubbs's. Blind Heath-Stubbs tap-tapped the road with his stick as we walked to the Pavistock. There he told me authoritatively, gripping his beer, "Pop music is inferior to poetry in the same way that

Victorian ballads were inferior to the *Lyrical Ballads*."[7] We went on to Maxim's, drank *ouzo* and *retsina* and watched a Greek dance.

I stayed with the Saints for a couple of nights, and sat on the sofa while Bernard typed up a poem he had just written. Bernard took me to meet Martin Green for a literary conversation. I met the Saints in a Knightsbridge pub, The Bunch of Grapes, and Bernard suddenly said, "Look, that man's blessed with a rainbow and doesn't know it." I looked and saw a rainbow thrown by the pub's stained glass on a man's knee. Bernard seemed at the time to be a new Rimbaud, and he told me, "I've developed beyond George Barker and he doesn't know it." In fact, he produced one volume, *Testament of the Compass* (1978), and then returned to the Bristol area to teach.

I attended poetry readings organised by Leonie Scott-Matthews at the Freemason's Arms, Hampstead. There I first encountered Ted Hughes, drinking on his own at the bar. Every day poets visited each other and met somewhere. Bernard Stone put on wine evenings where the drink was free and poets like Dannie Abse, Michael Hamburger and Edward Lucie-Smith could be met. Sometimes the poets met in the Elephant in Kensington.

I met Asa Benveniste, a dark-haired printer who ran Trigram, a small press that he was keen to sell to me. I went through the motions of endeavouring to buy his business, planning to publish an anthology of poets who were implementing the Poetry Revolution. However, I was soon dismayed that most of the poets had no understanding of the poetic tradition from Chaucer to Eliot, but lived in a modern bubble in which scanning and rhyming were non-existent. Deep down I was discontented that I was lurching from one meeting with marginal people to another, fleeing inner concentration.

In the course of August I had written *The Flight*, but I was aware that I had not finished enough poems to run a Poetry Revolution – I was still revising 'The Silence' – and that I was still groping towards the metaphysical vision that would distinguish my Poetry Revolution from the Movement. I longed to withdraw from the time-wasting social round and pare my self down. I was not an instant poet who came across best at a poetry reading, but rather a literary poet with a perspective that went beyond the reason.

Letter from Donald Maitland, now Heath's Press Secretary

I had written to Donald Maitland, Heath's Press Secretary,[8] recently Ambassador to Libya, who replied on 14 July[9] that he had passed my letter to the Political Office in 10 Downing Street. I then received a letter from Douglas Hurd,[10] Political Secretary, saying that he had passed my letter on to the Director of the Conservative Research Department, Brendon Sewill,[11] who replied that the department was being cut back and there were no jobs.

Andrew Mackenzie had asked me to contact him by finding his number in the London telephone directory.

I meet Andrew Mackenzie in Trafalgar Square and through Maitland become Edward Heath's 'unofficial Ambassador' to representatives of African liberation movements

I met him on the steps of St Martin-in-the-Fields just before 1 p.m. on 24 August. We sat in Trafalgar Square with pigeons round our feet, and he told me how he had met Viktor immediately after his defection to England. He said that the first person they had seen was Enoch Powell, a man Viktor despised, and that he was afraid Viktor would call the defection off. We chatted as freely as in our car meetings in Tripoli, and he reviewed how we had done and said self-congratulatingly, "We didn't get caught."

He said he had enquired if there was something I could do, and that it had at first been suggested that I should work with some of the exile movements in London. He mentioned as possibilities: the Palestine movement; the South African and Rhodesian movements; the anti-Portuguese movements; the Free Czechs; the Free Poles; the Free Greece and the anti-Vietnam movements. All these were movements the Russians might be interested in, and also the Chinese. He explained that in this phase of the Cold War the battleground between East and West was in Africa, Europe and Asia. The movements had all been infiltrated or penetrated by Soviet or Chinese Communists. I would really be finding out about Soviet and Chinese attitudes.

Andrew said it had subsequently been decided that I should concentrate on Africa. I should go to the Africa Bureau for a briefing as a freelance journalist. I should read *X-Ray*, a new publication, and he suggested three people I should visit. He said I would have to start again and prove myself anew, but that I would receive expenses. I continued to receive my salary of £50 per month after tax. He said the "rules of the game" included "no recruiting".

He said that the British Prime Minister, Heath, was in favour of selling arms to South Africa to combat growing Soviet and Chinese power on the African continent, and he wanted an "unofficial Ambassador" (his words) to the black Africans so that a line could be kept open to them. The "Ambassador" would represent Western freedom on the African continent. He would be an 'Ambassador for freedom', but he would relate to black Africans as they were. He said it had been proposed that I should be the Ambassador.

I am to defend the West against Soviet and Chinese Cold-War expansion in Africa and pursue link with Chinese

The idea was that if any of the liberation movements succeeded, I would be a line to them in the future. I would defend British interests in Africa against Soviet and Chinese interests and – at a time when the Soviet Union was becoming entrenched in Mozambique and Angola, when Communist-backed guerillas were fighting in Namibia and Rhodesia, when the Russians had armed Uganda and might be arming Namibia and when the Chinese were involved in Tanzania and now Angola – I would oppose attempts by the Soviet Union and China to prise African countries away from the West. I would find out what the Russians and Chinese were doing to the liberation movements – by being recruited as a pro-Chinese agent.

He said that Heath wanted unofficial links with China with a view to one day allying with China against the Soviet Union, and as an "unofficial Ambassador" to the Chinese I would improve Chinese-British relations and pave the way for normalising relations between Britain and China.

I had some misgivings about appearing pro-Communist. I had come out strongly against the Chinese Cultural Revolution and I did not want to pretend that I was for it. I did not believe that I *would* be recruited as a pro-Chinese agent. I was confident that I could be an 'unofficial Ambassador' and retain my integrity. I told myself that my attitude to the Cultural Revolution was within a bigger picture of being an 'unofficial Ambassador'. I had looked up to Churchill and would be happy to work with his successor, Heath.

I intuitively grasped that Donald Maitland, the ex-British Ambassador in Libya, now Heath's Press Secretary, was instrumental in my being offered this Ambassadorial role. What I was being asked to do was close to the "policy-forming" job I had asked Maitland to find. It was as if my letter to Maitland had resulted in my being made an 'unofficial Ambassador'. I was sure that Maitland had told Heath about my work in Libya, and how Libyans had wanted me to be British Ambassador after the 5-September *coup*. He may have been making amends for the SIS's role in the end of my marriage and for abandoning me to possible execution. I felt grateful to Maitland for fixing this job behind the scenes and I hoped to have an opportunity to thank him, but I never saw him again. (He died in Wiltshire on 22 August 2010, aged 88.)

Looking back, I can see that I had been head-hunted, and why. I had been active in China in 1966, had been the first to discover the Chinese Cultural Revolution and had been proved more right than China-experts such as Edward Crankshaw. I had demonstrated a detailed knowledge of China's internal politics. I was anti-Communist, had seen through the Soviet and Chinese ideology and understood that both the Soviet Union and China were expansionist. I had written 'Archangel' about my opposition to the Soviet Union and China. I had gained knowledge about African *coups* during my involvement in the 5-September Libyan *coup* and had been within four days of becoming British Ambassador in Libya. Biggs-Davison, who had given me a ticket for the main Suez debate, could vouch for my pro-Britishness as could Maitland, Heath's new Press Secretary, who knew I had been blooded in Libya during the night of my 'execution'. My clandestine work in China and Libya had recommended me for the position of 'unofficial Ambassador'.

I can now see that my known views would have resonated with Heath. I was pro-African and anti-*apartheid*. I saw Africa as a zebra with black and white stripes that co-existed. I had seen behind the idealism in liberal circles about the African liberation movements, and had grasped they were instruments of Cold-War, Great-Power manoeuvring. I had seen that the Cold War in Africa was a phase of the Third World War that had begun in 1944, and I stood for the freedom of the West, my stance in my 1966 poem 'Archangel'. My views coincided with the role Heath could be expected to want.

My weakness, from the headhunters' point of view, was that I had already gone beyond nationalism in my thinking. In Japan I had undergone an 'inconvenient' transformation and had come to see the universe, and the world, as a unity, which I wanted to explore in literature, philosophy and history. I had too great an interest in the works of Wordsworth, Whitehead and Toynbee, and an 'unhealthy' interest in a coming World State rather than nationalistic ascendancy.

There was the whole question of whether journalism should be a cover for such nationalistic intelligence work. I raised this with Andrew Mackenzie, who said, "Many journalists do this. They collect information for their story and hold some bits back for us. Then they write a freelance article for us rather than for their newspaper." The Admiral had said as much at my first meeting with him in 1960 (*see* p.122). It had been drummed into me from the outset that it was standard practice for a journalist to gather intelligence for an article and to hold some information back for the SIS. Ian Fleming had been in charge of more than 80 foreign correspondents, many of whom were thought to work for the SIS.[12] And Jerry Okoro had admitted to holding stories back for his Soviet masters.

Visit to Africa Bureau: meeting Africans

At the end of August I went to 2 Arundel Street, WC2, and visited the Africa Bureau, which advised Africans wishing to oppose political decisions by constitutional means. I met its 1952 founder, Rev. Michael Scott (a British anti-*apartheid* activist and promoter of Namibian independence who had co-founded the anti-war Committee of 100 with Bertrand Russell in 1960). He was very eager to help me. For a couple of hours, sitting behind his desk, he gave me an overview of the African liberation movements and their London representatives. He characterised each movement's main features and problems, and gave me a list of people to contact: he wrote in my pocketbook[13] the phone numbers for the Secretary and Executive Secretary of the Anti-*Apartheid* Movement, and for the representatives for the ANC (African National Congress) and PAC (Pan-African Congress). He wrote out the addresses and contact names for ZAPU (Zimbabwe National People's Union), ZANU (Zimbabwe Africa National Union), and the anti-Portuguese FRELIMO (Frente de Libertação de Moçambique, the Liberation Front of Mozambique) and Committee for Freedom in Mozambique, Angola and Guinea-Bissau. Africa was a Cold-War battleground, and the liberation movements spearheaded Soviet and Chinese expansion in the continent.

Visits to representatives of African liberation movements
For the next three weeks I visited these representatives and gathered material about their movements, acquired their booklets, learned about Africa and did my research. There had been little interest in the liberation movements and the representatives embraced me with open arms, delighted that a journalist was taking an interest and could project their views. I visited Richard Hové of ZANU and Kotsho Lloyd Dubé of ZAPU, who were both London representatives of their movements, and Polly Gaster, the Secretary of the Committee for Freedom in Mozambique, Angola and Guinea-Bissau. I visited Vrisumuzi Maké of the PAC and David Sibeko, the representative of the PAC. I visited Peter Katjavivi, the representative of SWAPO (South-West Africa People's Organisation). I also met the representative of SWANU (South-West Africa National Union), Tunguru Huraka.

I met Andrew again at Charing Cross tube station on 14 September at 2.30. We again walked to Trafalgar Square and sat on a seat near pigeons. My two articles on Libya had come out at the end of August. He said that they had been praised by his superior.

My three-column article in The Times *on World Council of Churches' grants to African liberation movements – first mention of UNITA in* The Times
Meanwhile, Brian MacArthur of *The Times* had written me a note on headed paper[14] asking me to call him. He requested a 1,500-word article for *The Times* on the criteria for the World Council of Churches' decision to help Southern-African liberation movements. I should visit the representatives of all the liberation movements.

I had a drink with Dag Dawood, a lawyer from Ceylon who had researched the World Council of Churches (WCC). He knew I was writing an article for *The Times* and he said he would hand me a hitherto unpublished, confidential document from the WCC's Programme to Combat Racism detailing the World Council of Churches' grants to the liberation movements and exactly what the sums were to be spent on, a scoop.

Dawood duly kept his word.

I wrote my article and attached the confidential document. Charlie Douglas-Home, the Editor of *The Times*, extracted the document and published it in three whole columns on the centre page on Saturday 3 October under the heading 'The war against racialism'.[15] (*See* Appendix 5, p.522.) The article was illustrated by a photo Dawood had given me, of a training camp in Angola run by UNITA (União Nacional para a Independência Total de Angola), the first time UNITA had been mentioned in *The Times*, I was later told by its London representative. I felt hard done-by because much of my research had not been used. There was a considerable reaction, and MacArthur told me later that the article had changed the Archbishop of Canterbury's mind.

Meeting with Andrew Mackenzie in Trafalgar Square: new terms
I met Andrew Mackenzie on the steps of St Martin-in-the-Fields on 9 October at 1 p.m. I handed Andrew my researched article, which had been superseded by the document. He later told me that his superior said it was a "good article". Andrew told me my probationary month was up and that I had passed it satisfactorily. He said uncomfortably, "I'm very aware that we are responsible for the end of your marriage." He said I would be paid £100 a month after tax until the end of December and thereafter £50 a month after tax. I should find a job starting at the beginning of January that would provide good cover.

UNITA
Through Dawood I had met a Hertford printer, Mike Marshment, who had walked 1,200 miles into Angola to interview UNITA's leader, Jonas Savimbi. He gave me a written account of his visit. UNITA's London representative and Minister for Foreign Affairs, Jorge Sangumba, was present. He was known to have links with Chinese intelligence.

I had begun writing an article for *The Times*, 'Angolan Spider's Web',[16] about UNITA. This was not taken by *The Times* or *The Observer* because the facts could not be confirmed: there had been no mention of UNITA in these newspapers until my publication of the WCC's confidential document and they were understandably cautious.

New controller, Martin Rowley: more articles for The Times
Andrew now told me that I was to be passed on to an African specialist, who would be running me as my controller from now on. He introduced me to Martin Rowley at the Black Horse, St Martin's Lane on 14 October at 12.30. Martin was a stocky, chubby fellow with coppery fair hair and freckles and an engaging manner, and I immediately liked him. I handed

him a confidential circular[17] that had been put out by the MPLA (Movimento Popular de Libertação de Angola), saying that the death penalty would be imposed on all who did not pursue GRAE (Governo Revolucionário de Angola no Exilio, later the FNLA) in Angola. Martin said, "This is straight intelligence." He said to me: "If you're caught we shall disown you and say you're nothing to do with us."

He gave me a new telephone number, and I used this and a new code-name for identifying myself when I rang the new number: "'Seymour'," he said, "because all blue-blooded Englishmen see more legs." Eventually the number was suddenly changed to the Century House number given in a *Time-Out* interview with Kenneth Littlejohn, the self-proclaimed anti-IRA British agent who escaped by helicopter with his brother from a top-security Irish prison after being convicted of armed robbery in 1974. (That Littlejohn knew this number is proof to me that he was genuinely in contact with the SIS as he said he was.)

Kenneth Kaunda, the President of Zambia, was coming to London at the weekend and Martin wanted me to interview him. Kaunda was visiting Grosvenor House, but my arrangement to join the WCC delegation collapsed as Dawood was not with them. I was not able to see Kaunda.

I now had regular work freelancing for *The Times*. Soon afterwards an article of mine appeared in *The Times Diary* on the Quebec Liberation Front,[18] and another one on the merging of two London clubs.[19] I had to keep the momentum going for Martin Rowley, and I had less time to meet the poets.

George MacBeth
However, I did go to a party given by George MacBeth at Turret Bookshop, Kensington Church Walk (near where Ezra Pound was living in 1914), to which I had been invited by Bernard Stone. I spoke at some length to Michael Hamburger and discussed the long poem with him. I ended up having dinner at the Chelsea Kitchen in the King's Road with MacBeth, who had a drooping moustache. We went on to a *discothèque*, Le Kilt in Soho, and I can still see him skip-dancing up Dean Street.

But this was an exception as I was now spending time with Marshment and Sangumba. Politics had replaced poetry, and I thought about 'the wretched of the earth'.

Purgation: detachment and renunciation
I was also entrammelled in my domestic situation. When I returned Nadia on a Friday afternoon I discovered that Caroline had returned from Malta with David, that he had a month's leave and that they had moved into the Dulwich house.

One morning Caroline told me over the phone that in a year's time she would be taking Nadia up north to live near David, who, as a navigator of Phantoms, was stationed at RAF Coningsby in Lincolnshire. (The Phantom was a US-made plane that featured in Britain's defence as an interceptor and low-level strike bomber after 1969.) She said: "David needs to get to know Nadia better so I don't want you to see her at weekends now, and I want to start divorce proceedings immediately."

Suddenly I had been denied access to Nadia. Access would be legally protected under a divorce. The strain of the situation was tearing me apart.

Agreement to divorce to protect access
On Saturday 10 October I drove to Essex. It was misty and my mood darkened with the evening. I sat alone in the dining-room at Journey's End. In that room, with a statue of Beethoven in a picture over the piano and a ha'pen'y-ship toasting-fork in the fireplace, I knew with Buddhist knowledge that my attachment was causing me to suffer and that the cure was detachment. I wandered out into the garden, and my agony is captured in my poem 'Journey's End'.

That night I drove past the prehistoric pillow mounds at High Beach, walked down to Turpin's Cave and sat before the log fire. The publican, massive as an oak with two fingers missing, shuffled into the back room and returned carrying a pint of bitter. I sat with my feet in the hearth, the glow of the fire on my cheeks, and gazed at the knobbly locals who laughed happily round drinks in groups.

I awoke early and from 5 a.m. to 10 lay alone, thinking. It was exactly six months since my visit to Malta, and the situation had dragged on and could not be allowed to continue now that I was being denied access to Nadia. A resolve came into my despair. Either I was married to Caroline or I wasn't. It had to be all or nothing.

That morning I telephoned the Dulwich house. Caroline's mother answered. As usual Caroline was "out". "Tell Caroline," I said, "either she presents herself in the Crown and Greyhound at 7.15 or every undertaking I've made in the past is invalid." "Oh, all right," she snapped.

Caroline came to The Crown and Greyhound with David. She looked matronly, with her hair up, wearing a thick coat. He was stolid in a sports jacket, balding and sandy-haired, the man I had seen in Malta at The Roundabout. He sat in silence.

I told her that I was making a final attempt at a reconciliation. I said we'd have separate holidays, meet in Italy for three days and then live together for a trial period of three months, which we could do legally without preju-dicing our chances of divorce.

She looked down and said, "No, definitely not."

In that case, I said, there would have to be a divorce and I would have legally-protected access to Nadia.

I left the pub and stood on the kerb. Through the coloured glass I could see them sitting together at the crowded bar. They were talking together. They wanted to be happy. Only I stood in their way. I simply had to choose to lose Nadia, to surrender her to her mother and let her go north and have legally-protected access. For her sake I had to stop being attached.

There is no greater Hell than to choose quite freely to lose someone who you care about more than your own life. My Way of Loss had become a Way of Renunciation. Standing on the kerb I accepted the situation behind the coloured glass, and, acknowledging I could not have tried harder or done any more to stay married for Nadia's sake, I detached myself, walked away from the trauma of Libya, put it behind me, and began a permanent move into the new centre within myself.

Journalism: Angola and Chinese

My Way of Detachment reversed my Way of Involvement. I sat in my room and reflected, and often contemplated. My article on the WCC had been deemed a success and my *Times* editors pushed me in the direction of the African liberation movements. I was asked to cultivate the London representatives of SWAPO (Peter Katjavivi) and of UNITA (Jorge Sangumba). I now discovered that *The Times Diary* were always willing to publish any story I had about the liberation movements' on-going drive for the freedom of Namibia, Angola, Zimbabwe, Mozambique and the rest.

Mike Marshment plans a trek into Angola to include Jean-Paul Sartre and me
On 19 October I met Martin Rowley at 12.30, again at the Black Horse. That evening I met Marshment. In October 1969 he had walked 900 miles, spent six days with UNITA's President, Dr Jonas Savimbi, and had left on 15 December. He was now planning a return trip to Angola. This time he planned to go with Dawood, Sangumba and me. He wanted to take in between 2,000 and 3,000 rifles, which Dawood had promised to supply. He said that Sartre should join our trek into Angola.

I met Jorge Sangumba and discussed his links with China. He told me the Chinese trained groups of 150 UNITA commandos. I met Martin Rowley again on 28 October at 2 p.m., and he urged me to carry on with the plan to visit Angola.

More articles, room searched, papers strewn
MacArthur had asked me to write another article on the African liberation movements. I wrote 'The African Liberation Movements in London: Rebels with a Cause', which covered all the groups who were receiving money from the WCC. I was dismayed when Charlie Douglas-Home, Features Editor,

wrote saying I had not dealt with them "quite comprehensively enough for us". He asked for more detail about the financing of the liberation movements, a subject on which the representatives were very guarded and were reluctant to share with me.

I later heard from MacArthur that South Africa had booked advertising in *The Times* costing £26,000, and that a decision had been taken within *The Times* not to print anything about the anti-South-African liberation movements until the advertisement had appeared.

On 4 November I met Martin Rowley in the entrance to Harrods. He took me up to the Way In, a coffee bar on an upper floor. (Again the wording of our meeting place was symbolic.) We discussed what work I would do from 1 January and little by little I began to grasp the importance of what I was doing. He said, "You should be devouring all the newspapers each day and seizing on anything connected with Africa." Later he said: "Your file is labelled 'Top Secret', the highest classification there is, and only four people see it from the top downwards." By 'the top' he meant the Prime Minister, Edward Heath.

He said that the 'Top-Secret' classification was because the British Government were planting me on the Chinese, and that this could cause a breach with China if it came out. (There might have been a rift with Maoist China in 1970, but today post-Maoist China is completely different, having diluted Communism with capitalism.) Heath wanted to have someone close to the Chinese leadership who could be a window on them, seeing China as a potential ally against Russia. I pointed out that although my diplomacy regarding China would be within a friendly atmosphere, I was actually opposed to Chinese Marxism.

I told Martin Rowley that I had a genuine sympathy with the Africans. I was against *apartheid* and believed that there should be no foreign inter-ference at all in Africa. I was a genuine force for change in reporting the need for a new approach to Africa. I said that though I was Heath's 'unofficial Ambassador' and was forging links with the representatives of all the liberation movements, I would be working to implement 'Africa for the Africans'.

I returned to Egerton Gardens to find the door to my room damaged and my room wrecked. My bed was rucked up and there were papers strewn across the floor. Nothing had been stolen, but someone had blatantly gone through my work with a very heavy hand. It could have been a represen-tative of any of the nations I was writing about – Libyans, South Africans, Rhodesians, Russians, Chinese (or Sangumba, or Marshment). John Ezard said, "Good old Special Branch." I said, "No, this crowd haven't any finesse. They used brute force. These were foreigners." I called the Chelsea police, but they said there was nothing they could do.

I met Martin Rowley again at the Way In on 16 November at 3 p.m. We discussed the searching of my room, and Martin felt that it was a very amateur job. He was more interested in developing the idea of Dawood and me visiting UNITA in Angola with Marshment.

I met Martin again at the Grosvenor Hotel, Victoria on 30 November at 5.45 p.m. Martin showed me how I could shake off a tail by walking into the front entrance of the hotel, hurrying down a passage at the back and emerging from the back entrance onto Victoria station, where I could lose myself in the crowds.

Jorge Sangumba, UNITA's Foreign Secretary, and trek with Sartre
He reiterated that I should concentrate on Jorge Sangumba, UNITA's Foreign Secretary. My aim was to meet his Chinese contacts and be recruited as a Chinese agent, which would make me a double agent. This might in turn lead to information about the Soviet Union. Martin said that this would be a long process because the Chinese would not be rushed. On the way I would find out the Chinese intentions on Africa and details of their aid to liberation movements. He said, "When the Chinese are taking the bait we will pull away and leave you alone."

I still did not want to be a Chinese agent. I was content to be Heath's 'unofficial Ambassador' and relate to all the Africans on that basis, and I thought I would never be approached by the Chinese.

I reported that I had been with Marshment and Jorge the previous evening. I said that Jorge had contacted Savimbi about our visit, and that Savimbi had replied: "Both Hagger and Dawood are welcome to come to UNITA-held territory." I said that Marshment had proposed sending in a Land Rover: there would be space for Sartre, a pro-Maoist, and Jorge had suggested that I should contact Sartre and persuade him to go. They both agreed that the Land Rover would seat: Sartre; Dawood; a photographer called Ivens; me; a camera technician; and an armed driver. Sartre would only walk a token distance into Angola. The rest of us would have to walk 800 miles. I said that Jorge had spoken with great loyalty and devotion about Jonas Savimbi's "state within a state" in Angola. The trip would cost me £450, of which Marshment offered to lend me £100.

On 7 December I met Jorge, who told me that it had been decided within Angola that Sartre would fly from Paris to Katanga, would go by car to the Angolan border (a journey of ten hours) and sleep in a UNITA safe house near the border. He would then walk 15–20 miles a day for three days to meet Savimbi. He would spend one or two days with him, leave and then walk out of Angola for two days. The expedition would counter Basil Davidson's propaganda on behalf of the MPLA, the rival liberation movement seeking to rule Angola.

On 1 December three fellows from *The Times Diary* (Nick Ashford and two colleagues) invited me to a very civilised lunch in a private room in the Black Friar, the pub near Blackfriars Bridge, which was round the corner from where *The Times* was then housed in Printing House Square. I had supplied them with short articles on liberation movements and the lunch was a kind of 'thank you' and a getting-to-know-me-further. The four of us stood with drinks and chatted before a roaring log fire.

Jorge says he will introduce me to the Chinese Chargé
Martin Rowley had asked me to "winkle out a Chinaman". There was a plan for me to return to China. At Jorge's party on 12 December I asked him if he could recommend a Chinese who would help me obtain a visa. I said I wanted to go to the Chinese Mission to discuss this, press UNITA's case and explain the visit by Sartre to Angola.

Jorge told me that he had visited the Chinese Chargé twice and that he would introduce me to him. He was going to Geneva in a week's time to see Dawood and organise the WCC's payment for our visit. There were several Namibians at the party, and a number of Zimbabweans, including Chen Chimutengwende, a charismatic Maoist. (He later became Minister of Information and Minister of State for Public and Interactive Affairs in the Office of the President and Cabinet, and was heavily involved in the confiscation of land from white farmers in Mugabe's Zimbabwe.)

I met Jorge a couple of days later and he asked when I was going to the Chinese Mission.

I said, "When I've worked out when I can visit China." I asked again if the Chargé would see me.

He said: "Yes, and he may have your file as well." He said he would accompany me.

Visit to Angola disallowed
I was now ready to go to Paris to ask Sartre to agree to visit Angola. I intended to return to the apartment where I had encountered him in 1959. I had already formed the view in Japan that Sartrean Existentialism had disintegrated into left-wing Maoism, and I planned to tackle Sartre on the corruption of Existentialism during the trip. I intended to argue the case for the West.

I would have to walk 800 miles across a lawless open sandy plain dotted with trees and a few shrubs, with little cover from the sun and a shortage of water, and I would have to go into training in London. I wrote in my secret diary for Martin Rowley, "Do I really have to go? Can I go ill with bunions at the last minute?"

Soon afterwards Martin Rowley exonerated me. He said that there had been a meeting and the SIS would not allow me to go to Angola because it was too dangerous. They could not guarantee my safety. I might be shot by the Portuguese or any number of people. I must now appear cool towards Jorge and continue to "winkle out a Chinaman".

In my personal life, my Way of Detachment was working. I was now aware of my true path. I had been exposed to the disease of the Age – my ascetic soul had been entrammelled in the permissive Age of Want – and I was now extricating myself from its clutches. I ate in the Chelsea Kitchen and had a drink in the Markham or the Admiral Codrington, and occasionally attended poets' parties. Actresses, poetesses, secretaries and journalists were plentiful, but I avoided them.

I focused on Nadia. I bought her a watch and a bicycle. I took her to *Scrooge*. I drove through thick fog to visit her on her birthday, and at Christmas I drove her to Essex and we went for walks and looked at the snow sparkling on frozen grass, fences and boughs and starlings shuffling on white roofs.

My green Volkswagen Beetle, nicknamed "Saturnalia" (a reference to the unrestrained merry-making associated with the pagan festival that preceded Christmas), still had its Libyan number-plates. I had found that if I parked it on a double-yellow line in the most policed London thoroughfare and went into a department store, the police merely put a note under the wipers saying, "Dear visitor, the laws in this country do not permit car drivers to park their vehicles on yellow lines." For several months I had had the freedom of London and parked at will in Oxford Street, Kensington High Street and Charing Cross Road. Then one day after an act of Arab terrorism there was a screaming of police sirens and I was stopped and hauled out of my car and questioned as to why I had Arabic number-plates. I explained I had returned from Libya and had not yet had them changed. I was told that in future I must use English number-plates.

Cover job in ESN school in Greenwich: Riverway
Martin Rowley had stressed that my income from freelance journalism should be supplemented by a cover job that would leave me free to do my intelligence work and write articles in the late afternoons and early evenings. Only a teaching job without any marking satisfied this requirement. The marking issue eliminated higher and secondary education, which would involve lengthy preparation for which I was anyway not yet ready.

I went to County Hall and was interviewed by an inspector, Mr Lewis. He told me I could start the following Monday at an ESN (educationally subnormal) school. In those days pupils assessed as being educationally subnormal were taught in special schools located apart from State secondary schools. Today pupils with learning difficulties would be integrated within the State system. I would be teaching 'backward' boys from Deptford on the edge of Greenwich, and the commitment would end at 3.30. There would be no marking.

I thought of the job as cover for my real work, but the routine would also numb the feelings that caused me pain. It would be like T.E. Lawrence's "mind-suicide" in the RAF. It would still my mind and allow my soul to grow. I saw the job as an important step in my Way of Detachment. "Except a corn of wheat fall into the ground and die, it abideth alone: but if it die, it bringeth forth much fruit."[20] I would stop abiding alone. I would die into the ground of serving my fellow human beings and in doing so I would find myself, my new self, and bring forth much fruit.

I accepted the job there and then, without any further thought. It fitted Martin Rowley's requirements perfectly.

The school, Riverway, was near the Thames in Blackwall Lane at the Blackwall-Tunnel end of Greenwich. Here on 11 January 1971 I found myself taking the top class of 14- and 15-year-olds. (The school-leaving age was 15 until 1972.) Many of them had been expelled from their normal schools for violent and maladjusted behaviour (such as throwing a chair at a teacher). I also patrolled a playground where 150 tearaways rushed about between river mists. They were poor and ragged, underprivileged and disadvantaged orphans, thieves and village idiots.

No one understood why I had taken a university professor's skills to "the dregs of society", but to me it made perfect sense: mixing with the poor and the downtrodden had always been an essential part of purgation – St Francis of Assisi gave up wealth to mix with beggars – and apart from providing cover for my intelligence work it allowed me to get beyond words and relocate the silence in myself, pare away academicism and, like Blake, immerse myself in latter-day chimney-sweeps and little boys lost. "Blessed are the poor in spirit": I soon found a happiness in caring for my charges, taking them for football and on outings, healing their deprived and damaged lives with such caring love as I could give them. I earned £136 a month, less £51 deductions, and had to live on £85 and the rent I received from 9 Crescent View.

I gave the Head, a shock-haired Welshman called Mr Macho who also lived in London, a lift to and from school, at his request. I picked him up near Embankment station and drove him to Greenwich. Each afternoon I returned him to the same station and went on through Trafalgar Square and along Piccadilly to Knightsbridge. We had discussions in the car, and it was soon apparent that he was extremely left-wing. He hated Edward Heath. He called him "an overweight slob". On one occasion we passed a small anti-Heath demonstration and he leaned over and tooted my horn several times and bawled out of the window (as if calling rampaging boys to order in the playground), "Good for you, brothers. Heath out!" I said nothing, not wanting to jeopardise my position as Heath's 'unofficial Ambassador'.

The staff were a blunt, dour, proletarian crowd whose hearts were in the right place and who sat around discussing *minutiae* in the small staff room at break and lunch-time. In the late afternoons I began my newspaper work with phone calls and meetings.

Jorge asks Edgar Snow to arrange for me to interview Mao
I had heard that the American Edgar Snow – the first Western journalist to interview Mao in 1936 and author of a 1937 book on the rise of the Chinese Communist movement – was fixing up a new interview with Mao. (In that interview Mao told him that President Nixon was welcome to visit China either officially or as a private citizen.) To bring forward a meeting with a Chinese I now told Jorge I wanted to interview Chairman Mao like Edgar Snow, and was looking for an introduction to a Chinese who could arrange this. He said Snow would arrange an interview. I saw Martin Rowley at the Way In at 4.30 on 13 January, and he urged me to follow this through.

Jorge to introduce a Chinese First Secretary
The next day Jorge mentioned a Chinese who would see me out of office hours, a Mr Hué (pronounced 'Who-ey'), who was a First Secretary. Martin Rowley later established that the name he gave me was a fake: there was no one of that name in London.

Marshment held a moving-in party on 13 February, and asked me to drive Jorge and his girlfriend Clair. Marshment had only just moved in and his new house was bare, with no carpets and little furniture. There I met Paula Seymour, who was older than me and heavily made-up. She told me she worked in telecommunications in Regent Street where she gave expert advice on telephones and telexes. I noticed that her surname was the same as my code-name and wondered if it was her real surname. Had she been told to use it to get in with me and report on what I was doing? She told me that she always told the truth and that she worked for the KGB. She said she had a boyfriend with a Russian-sounding name.

I met Martin Rowley on 8 February at 5 p.m. and on 10 February at 5.30. He was still urging me to meet a Chinese.

On 19 February I met Jorge. He said he had visited a Chinese that afternoon. He gave me a piece of paper on which was written in blue felt pen: "Chang Chi-hsiang (1st Sec)." Beneath there were two telephone numbers.

I said that I wanted to postpone my visit to China until I could be sure of a meeting with Mao. He said (taking up my mention of Snow's coming interview with Mao) that he had been staying with Edgar Snow in Geneva and that Snow was confident he would be able to fix a meeting between Mao and me. In fact Edgar Snow had just died of pancreatic cancer on 15 February 1972, in the week President Nixon was travelling to China. He was looked after to the end by Chinese doctors sent by Chou En-lai (or Zhou Enlai). (His remains are now buried alongside a lake on the campus of Peking University where I discovered the Cultural Revolution.) Jorge must have had discussions with him about me a few days before his death. Jorge said that I should discuss my visit to Angola with the Chinese Chang Chi-hsiang and not mention Mao at this stage.

I met Martin Rowley in the Grosvenor Hotel, Victoria on 25 February at 5.30 and again the next day at 12.30 (it being half-term). I had winkled out a Chinese name, but was instructed not to ring him. I had to wait for him to contact me.

A week later I had a drink with Ezard and on 1 March a long drink with Brian MacArthur of *The Times*. He gave me a list of press contacts and invited me to submit articles on abortion and Africa. I saw Charlie Douglas-Home, his boss, for an amiable chat afterwards. I busied myself with researching the Lane Committee's report and writing an article on abortion, which I regarded as cover.

Attack on my car

On 7 March I had dinner with Marshment. He told me that he was printing an Anglo-Portuguese magazine and that he had access to the Portuguese Embassy once a month with his van. He said that he could (if so minded) blow the Embassy up with a van bomb. He asked me if I would be interested in exploding a bomb. I looked at him, and wondered if he was testing my resolve without having any intention to carry out a bombing, or whether he had a serious intent and was asking *me* to carry out a bombing so *he* would not be caught. I had no plans to plant a bomb like the Angry Brigade and spend decades in prison, and I was noncommittal.

After our meeting I returned to my car and found the small window smashed and glass all over the seats. My property, including a suitcase I had hidden, had been searched but nothing had been taken.

The next day, 8 March, I saw Martin Rowley and discussed the attack on my car. He blamed Paula's boyfriend, but I thought his tone was too casual and I did not believe him. I thought he was covering up something more sinister.

Jorge urges me to obtain Portuguese war communiqués, *as does Polly Gaster; and wants to introduce the editor of* Hsinhua *News Agency*

I had been asked by Brian MacArthur of *The Times* to write a new article on the liberation movements and the Portuguese war in Africa. This would mean interviewing a representative of the anti-Portuguese MPLA. On 11 March I met Jorge and told him I would have to visit a representative of the MPLA.

Jorge said that I should obtain the MPLA war *communiqués* as sources for my article, which I could obtain from Polly Gaster; and the Portuguese war *communiqués*, which I could obtain from the Portuguese Embassy. He told me that the Chinese expert on liberation movements, Chang Chi-hsiang, was now back and that he would introduce me in a week's time. He also wanted me to meet the editor of *Hsinhua* News Agency.

On 15 March I visited Polly Gaster and discussed my new article with her in her kitchen. She would not hear of my having any MPLA *communiqués* and said I should obtain the Portuguese *communiqués* from April to December 1971 and go through them. She said, "That would be useful, we've often meant to do it, but haven't got round to doing it." She talked at length about the article she felt I should write. In her version the MPLA came out on top of everything. I had to point out that I was not dealing in propaganda, but in historical, evidential fact.

Martin Rowley introduces me to a China expert
On the last day of term, 6 April, I had driven straight from school to Victoria and met Martin Rowley at the Grosvenor Hotel at 5.30. With him was an expert on China who worked with the SIS, a tall, thin, youngish Englishman with dark hair who wore a dark suit. We all walked to a flat round the corner. There, and later in the streets outside, I was given training in how to detect when I was being tailed.

I was taught to saunter to a street corner and then sprint to the next corner and hide myself so that those tailing me could not see where I had gone. I was taught to jump the traffic-lights as they changed from amber to red to throw off any car that might have been following me. I was told that sometimes there would be a squad of three or more cars following me. (In those days there were no cameras on traffic-lights.) Car no. 1 would peel off and be replaced by car no. 2, which in turn would be replaced by car no. 3. Then car no. 1 would replace car no. 3. I should listen to the number of beeps on a car horn as a car might communicate with car no. 1 with one beep, car no. 2 with two beeps and car no. 3 with three beeps. (In the coming months I often heard this communication between squad cars when I was out in the evenings.) I was shown how to use shop-windows as mirrors to see who was behind me. I was told how foreign intelligence squads might operate while following me. I was again given practical training in how to give a tail the slip by entering the front entrance of the Grosvenor Hotel and emerging from the back entrance onto Victoria station, then heading fast for the underground. I was also briefed on how to present myself to the Chinese.

Both the MPLA and UNITA wanted me to visit the Portuguese Embassy at 11 Belgrave Square and ask for the war *communiqués*. Urged on by Martin Rowley, I did this on 13 April. (I was still Heath's 'unofficial Ambassador', and I wondered if, technically, this made me a double or triple agent.) There I was asked to submit a written request to the Ministry of Defence in Lisbon. A month later, on 13 May, a first batch of bulletins was sent to me c/o the Office of the Military Attaché of the Portuguese Embassy.

I meet Chinese First Secretary, Chang Chi-hsiang, expert on liberation movements, with Jorge
On 16 April, at long last, I finally visited the Chinese Mission with Jorge and met Chang Chi-hsiang, who was in charge of dealing with the African liberation movements. I remember little of our meeting. He made little impact on me but I remember him standing behind his desk in a cramped room. I described the Angolan venture and asked him to help. I also asked him to help in getting me to China to interview Mao.

Exposed to the KGB: news that Viktor has shown Czech intelligence/KGB my signed receipt – I am now operating openly like James Bond
The next week, on 21 April, Martin Rowley gave me lunch. I described my meeting. He said that my pushing of Jorge to get to Chang was "a brilliant operation".

At that lunch I found out why I had been given training in avoiding surveillance. Martin told me that the KGB knew what I was doing. Viktor had felt that the Russians were closing in on him and had decided to volunteer information to save his own skin. My connection with the SIS was one fact he volunteered. Martin said that things might get "difficult or rough" from now on. This was the explanation for the attacks on my car. The KGB or one of its subcontracted proxies had broken into my car. Martin changed my code-name to 'Francis'. From now on, when telephoning the SIS, I should identify myself as Francis.

So now the KGB knew about me. No doubt they had the receipt Viktor insisted I signed. I now had to operate without cover, like James Bond himself. Soon afterwards Paula asked me if I was a spy. She seemed to be at all the events Jorge was invited to and I was sure she was working for an organisation. She claimed to be working for the KGB *and* for a branch of the Secret Service, and her question either reflected the KGB's interest in me or an SIS check on my confidentiality. I had to conclude that I was a marked man. But, telling myself I was merely an 'unofficial Ambassador', I resolved to carry on and not worry about my lack of cover. I would go on doing the job for Heath that I was expected to do.

Now Martin said that the secret diary I had been writing for him in instalments for our meetings had to stop. It was now too risky to write anything down as the KGB might search my room. Martin said there should be nothing sensitive in my room.

The British Council had written to ask if I would consider taking up a lectureship in Moscow. I had been tempted and I had gone so far as to apply. Martin told me it was too dangerous for me to take the job as now that the KGB knew what I had been doing I might not get out of the Soviet Union. I wrote to the British Council withdrawing my application, and their annoyance was evident in their reply.[21]

My position now seemed very precarious, and the lunch seemed to mark the end of a phase, as if Martin was saying "thank you" for services rendered, the continuation of which were now in doubt.

Divorce: legally protected access
With all this going on I had seen very little of Caroline. I rang her merely to make arrangements to collect Nadia. She now called me "darling" but it was as if a tender word were shouted across a great chasm. Under the circumstances it seemed public relations.

The divorce took place on 29 April at the Law Courts. It was a sunny day. I was on my own. I parked on a double-yellow line in Lincoln's Inn Fields, not caring, and waited outside court 44. My solicitor Payne's managing clerk said to me, "I've studied all the documents, and I can tell you, the reason your marriage failed was your wife's withdrawals." He was telling me that I was not aware of the full situation. I answered questions in the witness-box while Caroline sat with David at the back of the court. Their discretionary statement stated (I later found out) that she was a separated woman when she went to Malta (resting on the Evidence of Agreement that had secured her an exit visa from Libya), and costs were awarded against me. I would pay maintenance.

She was given custody of Nadia, I had legally-protected access.

After the *nisi* was granted I acknowledged her sad smile with a depressed wink, then went out and sat in Lincoln's Inn Fields for the rest of the afternoon, listening to sounds from the land of the living – a motor mower, a plane – and feeling limp and drained. When I finally returned to my car I found it had not been fined, and I wondered if in spite of everything Providence was still looking after me.

Hostile surveillance: Egerton Gardens filled with police
Now I was among the Chinese. The day after an article of mine on Chen Chimutengwende, the Rhodesian revolutionary, appeared in *The Times Diary*,[22] on 8 May, I visited Yu En-kuang, correspondent of the *Hsinhua* (now

Xinhua) News Agency of Peking without Jorge. Again, I can recall little of our meeting. I discussed the African liberation movements at length.

At Martin Rowley's suggestion I had bought the "little red book" which had been brandished by all loyal Chinese during the Cultural Revolution. I left it in my room rather obviously in case the room was searched. (I told myself this was necessary to do my Ambassadorial work and that it did not suggest I was on the side of the Cultural Revolution I had despised.) I was now attracting the attention of several foreign surveillance squads, and often when I went out on my own teams of Palestinians, Africans or Chinese would come and drink near me and follow me out, a throwback to the fawn Volkswagen that simulated the conditions of house arrest in Libya in the very centre of London. I took all this in my stride. My training had prepared me for it.

On 14 May I was aware of exceptionally hostile surveillance, presumably by agents of the KGB. I had parked my car in the dark a few doors down from 13 Egerton Gardens. A team of swarthy Palestinian-looking men got out of a Volkswagen very aggressively and tried to intercept me – interpose their bodies between me and the house – before I opened my front door. I thought one of them held a gun. I managed to open my front door and, as in a nightmare, shut it in their menacing faces. I ran upstairs to my room and lay on the floor with the lights off, peering under the long curtain that draped above the bottom of the French windows. Through my balcony railings I saw them loiter in the dark by the railings surrounding Egerton Gardens for a good half hour. Now the streets had become a nightmare.

I went to the landing outside my door and rang Martin's number. He answered. I described the situation softly (so no one else in the house could hear) and said I expected an imminent attack, either through the front door and up the stairs or shots from across the street. Martin said that it was too late to do anything that night, that I would have to fend for myself. He advised me what to do if it got "rough". Luckily no one burst in that night.

The next day I drove to work as usual. Coming home I turned into Egerton Gardens as usual and was stunned. Both the road in front of my house and the Crescent the other side of the Gardens were filled with a couple of lines of policemen in uniform. There seemed to be dozens – indeed, hundreds – of uniformed police. I wondered if there had been an incident or a demonstration. I parked my car as usual and walked the gauntlet of a long police line. All were standing still in surreal silence.

I reached my front door without hurrying. As soon as I reached my landing I rang Martin and told him what I had just seen.

He said, "We let them know they can't touch you on our own territory."

I understood that all the policemen outside had been directed to stand in lines. I was not sure if they knew they were doing it to support me.

Next time I saw Martin he expanded. He said: "We can do anything we want. Anything. For example, not long ago we needed to make an arrest in a London square. The square was bustling with people in different dress, there were 25 or 30 different people walking to and fro, doing things. Everyone in the square was one of us. We have a huge wardrobe, and they were all in costume. It was like a stage in a theatre, only it was a London square. There was a window-cleaner up a ladder with a pail and leather. There was a nun in a black habit. Suddenly they stopped being their pretend characters and rushed to help apprehend the person we were trying to arrest." He added of my car, "It's got to be the most photographed and recorded car in the world. Every intelligence agency knows it. It is very recognisable to surveillance squads."

My purgation proceeded. I spent many evenings on my own "in the Devil's Chelsea" (as I spoke of it). I wrote in my *Diaries* laconically: "I am seeking God the hard way, in the Devil's Chelsea." Again: "I am the monk *manqué* of the medieval *Carmina Burana* who sings his rollicking Don't-Care songs in the tavern and cheerfully complains of the wheel of fortune (*'Quicquid enim flori/felix et beatus/tunc asumo corrui,/gloria privatus'*)." Like the Desert Fathers I struggled to overcome the temptation in the King's Road that summer.

To complicate things the surveillance squads were now a matter of course. I was tailed everywhere and, eating out every evening as I did, I found war correspondents and strange, suspicious-looking people turning up opposite me or next to me in the Chelsea Kitchen. They accosted me in the Markham in the King's Road or drank at my elbow and eavesdropped. Two Chinese engaged me in conversation in the Markham. Yet another China expert I was introduced to, a woman, thought they might herald an approach by Chinese intelligence.

Pussy-cat, Portuguese linguist, becomes housekeeper at 13 Egerton Gardens
I sat in my room overlooking Egerton Gardens and waded through the first batch of Portuguese war *communiqués*, which had been sent by the Portuguese Embassy to me at 13 Egerton Gardens and which I had just received. It was a nightmarish summer and I wondered if there would ever be deliverance from my Dark Night.

I was living in a madhouse. In the next room to me was an ex-Miss UK, now a whore who used the room occasionally for elderly clients whom she beat with a cane. (I could hear the cracks of her stick through my wall.) Below was a Black-Magic warlock and his white-faced blonde witch-wife. He told me he had been crucified upside down on Hampstead Heath. There was a security guard at Harvey Nichols who regarded the whole house as under his protection. He would have been useless if I had asked to be protected against the aggressive spies in the street. There was an elderly aristocratic lady who showed documents to prove she was "a cousin of the Queen". On inspection the documents turned out to be doctors' prescriptions. And there was an elderly Puritan who regularly prayed, standing motionless on the stairs. Residents had to squeeze past him as they came and went.

All these people gathered in the basement for breakfast which was served by the landlady who also ran the telephone system. She was drunk after midday, and she was then not averse to giving incoming callers a piece of her mind for disturbing her. "This isn't an office, you know," she shrieked at Charlie Douglas-Home, *The Times'* Features Editor, when he tried to reach me urgently one teatime, and when he said, "I'm sorry, I didn't know," she added, "Well, you know now," and slammed the phone down on him. (He told me this when I next visited his room at *The Times* and sat at the long table at the end of which he held court.)

One morning I went down to breakfast and the aristocratic old lady said: "Good news, Jimmy's in charge now. Mrs. Wilson's out. She was drinking three bottles of Scotch every day on money she took out of our rents." But my delight was short-lived as she was replaced by a brilliant Portuguese lady who wore tinted spectacles (which meant that it was impossible to look into her eyes), spoke eight languages and had refused a Portuguese Government scholarship to study poetry (she said, signalling that she had a love of poetry). She looked so innocuous that I nicknamed her "Pussy-cat". She appeared with unaccountable immediateness and suddenness, as though her arrival was the cause of the change.

Pussy-cat controls incoming calls, cleans and cooks – and bugs my room
She was now our landlady, kitchen chef and chambermaid. She served our breakfast in the basement and cleaned my room when I was at school. She took all my incoming calls and put them through to my landing. It took me no time at all to work out that besides sending me their war *communiqués* the Portuguese had placed their own intelligence agent in a position to go through my papers and listen to my telephone calls each day, and have access to my food.

Soon I found a small electrical-wiring box on the floor inside my French windows which had been freshly installed. A wire ran out to the balcony and down the side of the house to the basement area where our new landlady lived. She had bugged my room and was listening in to all my conversations there, I was sure of it.

I told Martin Rowley about it when I met him at 5.30 on 25 May. He came back with me. He put his finger to his lips and quietly said "Shhh" as we entered my room. He had a look at the box and suddenly tugged and yanked the wire out and threw it over the balcony so it trailed down the wall.

He had debugged my room, but I told him I was going to leave the house. He urged me to stay as both the Portuguese and the Chinese reckoned they controlled me there.

Soon afterwards my room was raided again, less heavy-handedly this time. Was it the Portuguese, the Chinese, the KGB or another group?

The nightmare had spread from the streets to my room. The only sane place was at school – among the ESN boys, and most of them behaved as if they were mad. I was like Lear on his heath, surrounded by madness and trying not to go mad myself.

I become a coach-driver for Riverway outings

And yet I had to admit I found much relief in taking the 'backward' boys out of school. I had a coach at my disposal. Mr Macho had told me I would have a "scale-2" post (promotion to a higher rate of pay) with responsibility for outings from September. One day I was called to his office and he said: "I want you to be able to drive the coach. You've got your test in 15 minutes' time." I said I had never driven a coach before. He said, "The examiner is sitting in the passenger seat waiting for you. Just switch on the ignition and you'll be fine. Treat it as if you'd just picked me up at Embankment station."

I went out and climbed into the driver's seat and with no practice at all drove the coach out of the school and towards Greenwich. As I turned right from Blackwall Lane into Trafalgar Road the end of the coach knocked over a bollard. The examiner did not seem to notice. I drove all round Greenwich, following the route he indicated with his right hand. Incredibly I passed, and was certificated to drive the coach.

One day a week my class climbed into the coach and I drove them somewhere for the day, keeping order at the back while I watched the road. I had no help.

We went to the Serpentine on a warm day, and the boys went out in the rowing-boats. One boatload of boys lost both oars, which were floating in the water, and I had to shout directions from land – in a clear, simple form they would understand – to paddle with their hands towards the oars, retrieve them and row the boat back. It was a spectacle watched by several hundred sunbathers (who quickly sat up to get a better view) and passers-by.

On one occasion I walked with a group near Trafalgar Square and turned round to find one of my party was missing. We retraced our steps and I saw him standing at an unattended news-stall calling, "*Standard, Standard.*" He was selling the pile of evening papers, giving the right change and pocketing the proceeds like an experienced market trader although officially he was too 'backward' to be in a normal school.

By and large I civilised and socialised my class on these outings, got them to behave like normal souls. Occasionally there were ferocious conversations in which one accused another of being a "wally" or a "div" or a "lake" (Deptfordese for 'backward' on account of the association of 'river' in 'Riverway' with 'lake') and the one accused would come to me, hurt, and say, looking mad, "Sir, I'm not a wally, am I?"

John Ezard's interview: "John Ezard of MI5"
John Ezard had *rendezvous*-ed with me on one or two of these outings and had spoken to the boys. He asked if he could tape-record an interview with me about how I "normalised" 'backward' boys.

We met at the Cutty Sark (which had been launched in 1869 and was not far from Riverway) and sat on a low wall. He told me he needed to put a heading on the tape, and in front of me, quite brazenly, he dictated without any trace of humour or irony, "This is John Ezard of MI5 interviewing Nicholas Hagger about his class of educationally-subnormal boys." Neither of us ever referred to that heading again, which seemed to be straight and which he seemed to be sharing with me.

My Oxford friend Ricky Herbert was living in a South-London square and he sometimes met me at the Markham or in the Chelsea Kitchen, where the wooden tables satisfied our monastic craving for simplicity. The Admiral had asked me to seek the advice of both John and Ricky about doing secret work, but I did not let on to either of them that I was now doing it. So the secret State cuts through and divides friendships in the land of the Mother of Parliaments.

Targeting Chinese: with four China experts in Harrods' Way In, six Chinese targets
In June Martin Rowley passed me on to James Appleton, who was to be my next SIS controller. Martin introduced him to me at the Way In, Harrods, where he was sitting with the China expert who had taught me to throw off tails and the lady China expert who thought that the Chinese might be about to approach me. The five of us sat in a corner, and there was a conference on how I would be recruited by the Chinese. James, a short, slight man of few words and always to the point (in contrast to Martin's expansive love of a good gossip) showed me photographs of Chinese diplomats in London, picking out the ones I might meet. They made me learn their names and faces, jumbled up the pictures and tested me. I was given a list of six who were targets, which I had to memorise. I was to take nothing in writing away with me that "Pussy-cat" could find in my room.

The lady China-expert, said, "We know very little about how they operate in London." She added: "We'll give you some photocopies of sensitive documents to slip to Jorge, to let him know that your sources are good." This happened. She also said: "We'll give you some dirt on some of the liberation movements to feed to the Chinese, and they will be grateful to you." This did not happen.

Interviewing Africans
Meanwhile I was to continue interviewing representatives and associates of the African liberation movements to come to the attention of the Chinese and Soviet intelligence services: Chen Chimutengwende, a pro-Chinese Zimbabwean mixed up in a dozen different movements and known for his Chinese sympathies; Jorge, who had his own Chinese links; Dubé; Dawood; the Kenyan Osumba Langi, who was a supporter of Oginga Odinga; and Polly Gaster, whose links with MPLA as Secretary of the Committee for Freedom in Mozambique, Angola and Guinea-Bissau would have made her known to the KGB to whose attention they wanted my interviews to come. They repeated that on no account was I to take a British-Council job in the Soviet Union. James said: "Viktor's information means that the Russians will be very interested in you, and if you go to work there you might be detained." (*See* pp.355–356.) And I broadened my writing for *The Times*. My article on abortion filled half the centre (Features) page and finally appeared in *The Times* on 17 June.[23]

'Portugal's African War': I am paid for The Times article not used
I continued to work through the Portuguese military bulletins, and the Portuguese Embassy sent me two more batches on 19 and 31 July. I went over them with both Jorge Sangumba of UNITA and Polly Gaster of MPLA, who between them reflected the Chinese and Russian attitudes to Angola. I also obtained the *Portuguese and Colonial Bulletin* and wrote an article on the bulletins for *The Times*, 'Portugal's African War'. Douglas-Home's secretary told me he was very enthusiastic about it and said that it contained a lot of new material. The article was turned into proofs dated 1 September 1971. (*See* Appendix 5, p.527.) However, it never appeared. Douglas-Home paid me £20 for this article.[24]

New controller, James Appleton
In July James Appleton finally took over from Martin Rowley, and the method of operating changed. Between April and July Martin had taken notes on my oral reports rather than taken delivery of an instalment of my secret typewritten diary so that Pussy-cat's daily searches of my room and papers would not turn up anything incriminating. Now James Appleton gave me specific questions.

He expected me to conduct my interviews with the representatives of the African liberation movements to find the answers, and how I did it was up to me. "You find a way," he said, "that's what you're paid for." He would ask me to find out impossible things, for example to ring Polly Gaster and ask for the breakdown of the Soviet funding of MPLA. She would clearly slam the phone down and complain to *The Times* about me. Was that what he was trying to achieve? If so, I did not want to be doing it. His lack of sensitivity and psychology reminded me of Malcolm Hall.

My Top-Secret file (I had been told by Martin Rowley) could then only be seen by four people: my controller; the Chief of the SIS; the Foreign Secretary; and the Prime Minister, Edward Heath. The others had been brought in to give general advice. It could be that the new approach involving questions came from a new direct involvement by one of these four people.[25]

Meetings now took place in a flat in Chelsea by the River Thames. It had a very white carpet which must not be dirtied, and James Appleton carried a small piece of carpet like a prayer-mat for me to put my feet on. (He would not hear of my taking my shoes off at the door and I had to scrub them backwards and forwards many times on the doormat before tiptoeing to an armchair where I would sit and raise my feet so the prayer-mat could be carefully put in place beneath them.) Sometimes we met in the Golden Egg, Trafalgar Square.

There was to be a 'Photo Exhibition of China' at the end of September, sponsored by the Chinese Chargé d'affaires, Mr Pei, and I was to try and obtain an invitation from the Cultural Attaché, Mr Liu, as all my six targets, whose names and faces I had memorised, might be present.

My Ambassadorial role had been in conflict with my journalistic role, and now a new episode brought new conflict to my life.

Episode 14:

Illumination and Nationalism

Years: 1971–1972
Locations: London; Loughton; Worthing; Brussels; Arnoldshain
Works: *The Gates of Hell*; *A Bulb in Winter*; *A Spade Fresh with Mud*
Initiatives: illumination; Second Mystic Life

"I entered [within myself]. I saw with the eye of my soul, above [or beyond] my mind, the Light Unchangeable."

St Augustine, *Confessions* (c.AD400)

In my next episode illumination broke into my Dark Night and shone on my true path. It brought with it a host of visions, raptures and ecstasies that I at first saw as a bubbling-up from my imagination, from the spring of my inspiring Muse. As I progressed along the Illuminative Way I had a growing sense of the unity of humankind, an internationalism that was in conflict with, and superseded, the competing nationalisms of the world of intelligence.

Illumination: Second Mystic Life (3 September 1971–28 April 1972)
Mystic and artist Margaret Riley at 13 Egerton Gardens
Among the extraordinary collection of people who had breakfast in the basement of 13 Egerton Gardens appeared Margaret Riley, a painter, potter and (I was to find out) mystic. She was probably in her early 50s and had left her millionaire husband to live in a room on my floor at the back of the stairs while she pondered what to do next. We all celebrated our liberation from the tyranny of Mrs. Wilson's drunken tongue by chatting over breakfast in a way that had not happened until now. From the next table she told me she was Austrian, from Vienna.

She invited me to look into her room. It was a palace of art: every available inch was taken up with stacked and leaning canvases of her peaceful and symbolic landscapes. She had brought her life's paintings with her, and her door was permanently ajar. She looked into my room for short chats, often to borrow coffee. She told me she looked back to the Austro-Hungarian Empire and that at the time of the Hungarian Uprising of 1956 she had had a love affair with a Hungarian General who had been executed in a railway yard by the occupying Russians. She was religious and urged me to withdraw from all the extraneous people in my life.

Pottery pyramid of chains
One day I told her that I saw events as chains. She said, "I will make you a pot of chains at the Pottery." A few days later she took me to the Chelsea Pottery, where there were several wheels and potters kneading red clay. There were shelves of pots awaiting firing in the kiln. She was about to fire a pyramid without a top, and she showed me without explanation. A few days later she brought it to my room in a white plastic bag and gave it to me.

It was a clay pot shaped like a pyramid. It had a red clay base and comprised 15 narrowing triangles, one above the other. Each triangle was made of a round tubular-shaped excrescence which she had rolled like plasticine in the palms of her hands. Looking back now, I cannot but see the 15 triangles as 15 episodes, each with a pair of opposites.

"You see," she said, "the self, made of chains. Smash one side and what's inside gets out, it's all one."

The Way In was the Way Out, I saw. Smash the 'I' and get inside yourself, and you're at one with the trees and the sky. I knew that the wanting 'I' must die, and I noticed the paring-down, the search for simplicity in her work: the triangles got smaller and smaller as they approached the open top of the pyramid. Chains of events, works of art – they got sparer as they were accumulated and pared down.

Later, gazing at the pyramid of chains I saw that there were two ways of living. The Way of Involvement included chains of cause and effect, a mesh of accident in which the inner self was separated from the world, and the 'I' selfishly faced outside and indulged itself, doing what it wanted and shutting out the flow. The opposite Way of Detachment involved a flow and a purpose. It was free from chains of events, and there was a unity between the inner 'I' and the world outside just as there was a unity between the air in my pot and the air outside. The inner 'I' had the self-discipline to release the people it had been attached to and to love selflessly, as it should, and to experience eternity as a timeless flow, living through the real self which was indivisible from the One. I saw the distance between the two Ways was the difference between false values and true values.

One direction

I was now a flowing stream that appears still on the surface but is flowing in one direction underneath as in my poem on the Waltham stream, 'An Inner Home'. During each visit she made to my room Margaret kneaded and shaped my soul like the clay she used to make a beehive. I felt like a Zen seeker who had found a spiritual teacher in an unexpected place and was progressing along the path to enlightenment. My Sisyphean endurance seemed over.

She said: "Something tremendously important is happening inside you. I can see it and you don't understand it. Ponder it while I am away. You are seeing the truth."

Margaret went to Vienna for a holiday and sent me a card of a church seen through an arch. I did not want to be told to go to church, and I ignored it.

Dinner with Toynbee's granddaughter

I was invited to a dinner for Claire Toynbee, the granddaughter of the historian Arnold Toynbee who had written A Study of History, which I had taught in Japan. The dinner was thrown by Ricky's friend Bertie. We all met in the Churchill and ate in a small restaurant nearby. I discussed Toynbee's history with Claire, knowing she had to leave early. After dinner we walked by the Thames. Bertie behaved outrageously: he threw his shoes in the Thames because they were uncomfortable. We all walked back to his

London house (Bertie hobbling in his socks) and drank wine in his small back garden.

Ricky arrived, late, and immediately asked for my view of "*wu wei*" (action being non-action) and of Goethe. "You're like Faust," Ricky told me, "always seeking beyond the horizon,... like Tennyson's Ulysses seeking 'beyond the sunset, and the baths/Of all the western stars'."

On another day Ricky took me into a church near Kensington High Road and read aloud Psalm 22 from the *Bible* on the lectern: "'My God, my God, why hast thou forsaken me?... O my God, I cry in the daytime but thou hearest not.... But I am a worm, and no man.'"

Poetry of Search

I suddenly knew I was back on my quest. I wrote in my *Diaries*: "I want to reject the King's Road for ten years of art – for the search and quest of Baudelaire and Faust. The Flight has ended: I want to resume my Search." I told Ricky that I would write "a Poetry of Search" and that we might be "the Beardsley and Dowson of the 70s".[1]

Nadia was going to Scarborough for much of the summer holidays. I visited her school fête before she went – she was dressed as an Elizabethan page-boy and I bought posies from her – and later we visited the toucan that lived in the aviary in Dulwich Park. I was delighted to be away from intelligence work.

A sibyl's prophecy: predictions of an American psychic

On 26 July I looked in at the Markham and was almost immediately approached by an American in her 30s. She said: "Hi, my name's Michelle. I am a psychic, I see things. I just want you to know that I've seen your face on the cover of *Time* magazine. You're going to be involved in some sort of a revolution, and you will be famous. I knew your father was dead as soon as I saw you. And I knew you'd be famous." She told me, "You will be approached by a man with an offer. I see £5,000. I can see you waving a yellow piece of paper. By the end of the next twelve months you will consequently have moved out to a big house. You will be engaged and married within a year and a half of that. In due course you will do no teaching and you will have a lot of money. You are going to buy a big house. I can see it, but there's sadness on the way, a death. You will be fomenting revolution and will be in *Time* magazine. Famous. You'll have a long, long life and die very old. You'll have a little illness with your lungs, for example pneumonia, bronchitis. You've got something in your room right now, some writing you've done. You've no idea how famous that's going to be once you've had the revolution you're going to be involved in. You will have a long, long life and die very old."[2]

I had not had to go to Cumae to visit the Sibyl, she had found me. The writing she referred to might be 'The Silence' and the revolution might be the Universalist Revolution. Who knows.

Fascinated, I probed her sibylline gift. She explained she could pick horses to win races for other people but she couldn't do it for herself. She then excused herself as she had to rush away, and she left, having set out my future life in a couple of minutes with (on the bits that have happened) an accuracy I find incredible.

A Negative Way, spiritual teaching

Margaret returned from Vienna and told me I had been mixing with the wrong people. She immediately set out a Negative Way and general principles. "Stop talking, work." "Don't tell me about it." "Be now here, not beyond." "Don't force it, let it come spontaneously, from underneath." "Don't explain." She was expressing an instinctive Taoism. "Don't give it a name, don't say it.... Don't act, it will happen spontaneously. Don't cut the evening up. Don't chase. If you do no work today, it doesn't matter. The bees can't make honey all the time. I can't push my flowers to grow." I came to feel that the way forward was the way back, a Negative Way in which apparent redress was in fact progress. *Wu wei.*

In August I had a couple of meetings with James Appleton in the flat with the white carpet, on 6 August and 26 August, both at 4 p.m. They were supposed to focus me on the 'Photo Exhibition of China'. But I was completing my purification by implementing the Negative Way. I wrote in my *Diaries* for 8 August: "I have found a direction, rediscovered my identity as an artist, returned to the Eastern *Tao* below the will."

I dismantled the superfluous things like unnecessary drinks. I began to discard, declutter the remainder of my unnecessary words and ideas. I saw that there is a flow and that time cuts up; that the feelings are ruined by time. I realised I had a river of days flowing through me. It flowed in one direction, not hearing the people shouting from the banks, detached from everything. I had been like a river with tributaries branching off at the sides, and now all my energies were going in one direction.

I was practising a catechism of "Don'ts" which I listed as follows:

Don't say it, it will kill the feelings.
Don't put it into words, silence is better.
Don't read, sit still and feel.
Don't compare, it exists by itself, it is unique.
Don't act, it will happen spontaneously.
Don't struggle, it will happen unconsciously, you cannot push the flowers to grow.

Don't try, never control events.

Don't work if you don't feel like it, you *will* feel like it.

Don't get upset if it turns out badly, it doesn't matter.

Don't chase it, it will come to you.

Don't run, be still; let go.

Don't go towards anybody, wait.

Don't expect quick results, a tree grows 365 days a year for a crop that lasts four days.

Don't accept unnecessary invitations, they are messy.

Don't waste energy, keep it inside you as a force.

Don't let people trample on the garden of your soul, protect your flowers.

Don't let people tread mud all over your carpet and disturb your peace.

Don't let others tell you about their mess, you are the one that has to sweep it away, you are not a dustman.

Don't do bitty things, do one thing and one only.

Don't be dependent on riches, live among them but be able to walk away from them.[3]

Great Flow

I was aware of the timeless flow underneath that continues from day to day, which schedules and timetables chop up, which the world of 'I' shuts out, depriving the being of inner unity. Slowly I found myself preferring silence or classical music to speech. Slowly, like a blind man, I *felt* the world round me rather than saw it. Slowly I started to live through my heart and soul, and became the mouthpiece of my unconscious depths.

I had discovered the art of living which a wanting generation had lost, and I saw it was my role to point the way. I saw another meaning in my pyramid of chains. The triangular tubes showed empty triangles like my triangle with Caroline. They were all empty, there was nothing inside them. And yet at a deeper level they had shut in my inner being and had prevented me from getting access to my self. I saw that I had to undergo a profound shift in my way of looking at the universe, and of seeing myself.

Margaret said to me: "You are like a man twenty years older than you are. In ten years you have crammed twenty or thirty years' of experience. You must stop now. No more going towards.... Be still. Sit still. Watch. Don't go towards anybody. You will see the difference. You broke with Caroline because you had the silence of your poem and she did not. You had the silence in Japan, that is your strength."

I saw now that the Way Up and the Way Down were different for me, and yet the Way Down had led to the Way Up and in that sense they were one and the same Way. "The chains shut in your flow. You can't shut it in. But there is no top now." Then she added: "You are like a flower, that flower on my veranda. It was beautiful but when I came back from Vienna it was nearly dead. I nipped off these parts and discarded them and now it is growing again. I have not wasted my time with you. You are quick to understand. You will have few words now. If there is a flow I get angry when unimportant things interfere, when things from outside spoil the flow."

I now saw that perhaps Providence had wanted me to push Caroline away all along so that I could be reunited with my deeper self. I saw that there was my flow and the Great Flow, and that my flow was part of the Great Flow. To express it in terms of the Stone Garden, my stone was one of the stones in the Stone Garden. I had to surrender to my instincts, let go, not analyse or control.

Margaret said to me: "You should not want, that is not the real self. Don't want and then you'll feel the flow." Of my visit to Ezra Pound she said: "He understood, he showed you by example. Why should he speak to boring people, why should he? You talked about the silence, he replied by example. He knew you were not ready for it, so he said what he could."

Then she spoke of her pottery: "It happens, it just turns out…. It is in the firing. The beehive got lost. Your lid got lost. I knew I should leave the pyramid open, for that was my message to you."

Margaret was giving me the precise instructions of a spiritual teacher. In the Zen tradition I had not found my teacher in a temple or church but hidden in a bizarre house near the Devil's Chelsea.

"You must be master of everything," she told me, "not its slave. You must find the centre of yourself, your heart. Do not ask why or when or where, it cuts the flow. Don't compare, and then you will live through your heart." Pondering these words, I realised that I must see my depths not as something still but as a moving flow. I wrote in my *Diaries*: "I have so far seen the ground of my being/the silence/God/the Sahara pool as something still…. I now see it as a flow/as the bottom of a river/as *Tao* – a way. As something moving. God is a process – the flow."[4]

I took Margaret to Essex to see the Strawberry Hill pond with its fallen beech tree. Heather grew on the patch of open grass. Margaret said, "This is your heart, you're silent here."

I felt well. I wrote in my *Diaries*: "I've turned round for the Way Back…, the Way of Discarding…. A momentous day…, the consequences will reverberate like Saturday's thunder for months to come, possibly years. I am whole again, myself, other people don't matter…. I am in touch with the ground of my being. I can be still."

I thought Margaret's paintings belonged with the visionary landscapes of Palmer, Blake and van Gogh, and wondered if she would paint the pond and fallen tree.

I was aware that I was locating a new energy within myself. I wrote in my *Diaries*: "Move… and you are aware of stillness beneath you. Be still… and you are aware of movement beneath you…. See the underlying flow."

Margaret said that my poems would belong with the work of the Metaphysical poets: "You've got it there, you can do it." I thought of Ezra Pound's "If you can see it you can do it". I wrote: "My soul is suffering from malnutrition."[5] I longed to be clear of intelligence work.

Increased intensity

Now the natural world took on a more vivid, intensified hue. I went to Worthing for five days. I took Nadia to Sompting Abbots, a neo-Gothic school where she was holidaying with children of her own age, and I stayed nearby in the Anchorage on the front.

On the beach I found pebbles shaped by the flow of the tide, and saw the flow in each pebble and some pines bent by the flowing wind. I watched the hotel flowers bent double in the wind, red and yellow roses, red roses nodding their heads and yellow roses shaking theirs under great clouds whirled by a high-tide wind which flapped the red flag. I took Nadia up on the Downs and we picked a bunch of poppies in a wheatfield. I felt at one with the grass and the earth, the trees and the beetles, the flies and the sky. I was sorry to leave the simplified life of Worthing: its silence at meals, the birds, sea, sky, pebbles, flowers, Downs and rural local settings.

Back in London I wrote in my *Diaries*: "I was lost in a forest, a dark wood, and I went from tree to tree, wandering, enquiring if different concepts contained truth."[6] I felt my volcano, which had been dormant for four years, rumbling poetry and suggesting a coming eruption. I knew I would soon be writing poems each day again. I felt whole and very creative, I knew that ahead of me was a poetry of vision.

I took Nadia to Essex for a few days and spent an hour watching the destruction of a wasps' nest in a grille in a brick wall at Journey's End. A man puffed white chemical from a canister and the wasp guards sent out radar signals. A dozen wasps came flying to the grille and entered the nest, to emerge with chemical on their wings, become sleepy and die.

In London Margaret spoke of the pyramid in terms of the work ahead of me: "You have a solid base out of experience. You have fifteen works to go before you get to the top." She said that the pyramid shape, besides being a tomb, was a triangle: sexual triangles behind sexual triangles. "It is also about containing and releasing – God cannot be contained by chains. A pyramid of chains that is waiting to be smashed."

She insisted on not knowing about Dylan Thomas: "I don't want to know, don't tell me about Dylan Thomas. He is on the bank. He is not my river, my existence. It doesn't matter what others have written or thought." I again felt a poetry eruption ahead, and she told me: "You are so lucky, you don't know how lucky you are. You are alive." She took me round the corner to the Brompton Oratory and she pointed out the eternal light in the basket and asked me to light a candle, and as I placed it in the candle-holder, she said, "God is Light."[7] Her message was that I had finished with physical beauty. I should be focused on spiritual beauty now.

After that she took to sitting in solitude in her room with her door closed, and she went to bed early, "to be fresh for work". She did not visit me in the mornings any more, and she took to conversing with a priest at the Brompton Oratory. She was returning to her Viennese Catholic faith and she now spent much of the day in mystic prayer. I found that I too was going early to bed. "Detachment puts something into the eyes that others want," Margaret said. I found myself embodying a detachment from the King's Road. One evening Margaret looked in and said: "You have learned more in the past two months than in the last five years. Don't talk about the past now, be forward-looking. Never try to keep people or control events, they disappear as soon as you do." But after that she said more and more: "Leave me alone, I want solitude and silence."

I took Nadia out to Essex again. We flew her kite and caught purple and maroon grasshoppers on the Stubbles and she caught a brown frog which she carried home in cupped hands. She also put some acorns we had found in a medicine jar so we could watch them sprout roots. I took her to Paddy Manning's house in Moreton so she could play with her daughter. I fished a dead tench out of the pond and helped fell seven elms that had the beetle that causes Dutch elm disease. I hewed the wood with an axe and burnt the branches in the field. ("If it's no good," Margaret said later when I told her, "cut it down.") I walked on my mother's lawn and thrilled at the mystery of a pear. I wrote in my *Diaries*: "Earth, roots, sap, flow, buds, sun, water, air, sun, and – hanging supreme, still in the twilight – a pear! For me to eat!"[8] I looked on Nadia as a miniature rose, some of whose blooms were fresh, others dead; and I was a gardener with a watering-can.

Beginning of Second Mystic Life (3 September 1971–28 April 1972)
In early September I returned to Worthing for a weekend. I saw with a new intensity. On the Friday, in the sun, the sea was like shoals of fish, leaping and tossing. I thrilled to trees bent in the wind, and to the flow of the wind in the sea. There was a tortoiseshell on the pebbles. On the Downs there were forget-me-nots on the chalk. Night fell over a cornfield and the moon was round, like a balloon over the corn. The moon had a strange white glow around it, and I noticed it was the same with the horizon the next day. There was a whiteness between the sea and the sky I had not seen before, and I felt ecstatically peaceful.

I read Underhill's Mysticism

On the Saturday morning I read Evelyn Underhill's *Mysticism* (which I had happily packed) in my Worthing room and read of the Dark Night as "this last and drastic purgation of the spirit." I reviewed my mystic life and felt that after a first glimpse of Light in Japan I had plunged into an exhaustion which had led to the mess of Libya, from which I was only now emerging. I wrote in my *Diaries* there in my Worthing room: "I am on the journey and I am not sure how far I have gone, how far I have got to go.... Something is happening to my perception: the glow that unites the moon and the corn.... The white that unites the sky and sea – yet it is hardly there.... Something is happening to my way of *seeing*, and I do not understand." Later I wrote of "this mystic glow around beautiful everything, this strange white light round the sea, the sky". The experience found its way into my poem 'Flow: Moon and Sea'.

On the Sunday morning I woke and lay with my eyes closed and was surprised by two visions: one of a cross with a white light behind it, and one of a small figure of the Virgin Mary. I thought nothing more of these. I drove to Brighton and lay on the pebbles in the hot sun and later went up the Devil's Dyke, which I had visited as a child. I returned to London and mentioned some of this to Margaret who said enigmatically, "God is always the same."

The next day the autumn term began at school and I had little time to contemplate this experience until the following weekend. One evening during the week Margaret said, "You're like a beautiful garden that is overgrown,"[9] and I thought of how Tuohy and I were symbolically set to hoe weeds in the Zen temple in Japan.

I was on the verge of the two most intense months of my life. I had begun my Second Mystic Life (*see* Appendix 1, p.490). I was whole, alive, fresh and had had a glimpse of what was to come. A spring in my clear consciousness was about to wobble visions up, like the bubbles in the spring Ain el Faras at Ghadames.

Illumination and visions
Illumination on 10 September 1971

I now come to the momentous day, Friday 10 September 1971, the equivalent for me of what Monday 23 November 1654 meant to Pascal, who wrote down his experience and sewed the parchment into his doublet and *wore* it until he died, so important was his illumination to him.

The day began unpromisingly as an ordinary school day, the last day of the first week of the autumn term. I returned home, wrote a letter (to my solicitor agreeing to the decree nisi being made absolute, the final surrender) and posted it. I washed two shirts, underwear and socks in the bathroom and hung them up to dry, and had a bath. I shaved. Margaret knocked on my door, came in and sat on the bed nearest the French windows. I picked up Underhill's *Mysticism*, opened the book at random and sat on my bed so that she was next to me on my left. I read aloud a passage about the philosopher's stone, how it turns metal into gold.

At 5.30 there was a knock on the door. Ex-Miss UK called, "Phone call." Pussy-cat, who had put the call through to my landing, was standing half-way up the stairs within earshot, having come up as no one had answered. She went back down again and I assumed she would be listening in on the line. I went to the wall phone on the landing. It was John Ezard giving me his sceptical journalist's view of Margaret, whom he had met the previous evening: "I don't think she's a mystic, I think she's wearing mysticism as a hat."[10] (Later, long after grasping the situation into which he had rung, he would write that I must have seen his call as being like Coleridge's "person from Porlock" who interrupted 'Kubla Khan'.)

I received his words without expressing an attitude, returned to my room and carried on reading to Margaret. I read passages on different mystics: St Teresa and Mme Guyon. There was more on the philosopher's stone and mention of the Light.

Experiencing the Flowing Light, an encounter with the metaphysical
I felt a quickening within me. Margaret said, "It's a Flowing Light, it flows upwards. Just sit and feel the peace." We sat side by side and looked at the plane-tree for about half an hour. Then she said quietly, "Lie down." I lay down behind her – the pillow was at the end of the bed nearest the French windows – so that she was now on my left side. She said, "Shut your eyes."

I shut out the world, and waited, watching within. At her direction I gave my breathing to the twilight until I fell into a trance. And from behind my closed eyes, looking *into* my closed eyes I saw white light flowing upwards: a tree, white against the black inside me, a bare winter tree of white fire, flowing, rippling as if in water. I put my hands over my eyes, I wanted nothing outside to spoil the brightness of what I saw within. Then a spring opened within me like the spring in the Sahara, and for a good hour and a half visions wobbled up inside me like the wobbling bubbles in Ain el Faras. I remember the first two most clearly: a centre of light shining down from a great height, and then a white flower, like a dahlia or a chrysan-themum, with very detailed, breathtakingly beautiful cells. This was my first glimpse of the celebrated Golden Flower, the centre and source of my being.

There were too many visions for me to remember one quarter of what I saw. But almost immediately a sun broke through my inner dark and hung in the 'sky' with a dazzling whiteness. Then I saw a fountain of light. Then all was dark and I saw stars, then strange patterns, old paintings I had never seen before, old gods and saints. When I came out of my contemplation I was refreshed. I felt turned inside out and wobbly at the knees.

Having been born a Catholic, Margaret left the room to pray. Alone, I fell on my knees in the dark. I screwed up my eyes to shut out the outer world, and there was a white point, a small circle of light that went deep up into the heavens behind my closed eyes. I said aloud, "I surrender," and the light moved and changed until it became a celestial curtain blown in the wind, like the *aurora borealis*. I felt limp, exhausted. I had to stop. I was filled with an afterglow, and my fingers were moist. I felt blissfully happy.

I put on my desk-light and wrote in my *Diaries* at 8.20 p.m.:

It came in me: a tree, white against black inside me, a bare winter tree of white fire, flowing, rippling as if in water.... And more. A centre of light shining down as if from a great height, rays coming down like rocket blasts or fireworks. Then a white flower like a chrysanthemum (detailed cells). And so much more.... A sun, breaking through cloud (a moon?). Stars. And a fountain of white light. Patterns like my *mandala*. And I was behind my chest – in my *heart* – lying down, breathing slowly and deeply with half-closed eyes, near sleep as at Worthing when I had two visions.... When I sat up I felt... refreshed, turned inside out, and wobbly at the knees. I asked to be alone. Margaret had seen a bishop with a crozier ('God', she said) and a painting with 'God sitting on a throne'. She went to pray.... It was dark, my window was open. The clock ticked. Some traffic roared. I fell on my knees in the dark, hands clasped and there was a white point, then a circle of light that went deep deep up into the heavens. I said, 'I surrender', and the light moved and changed till I felt exhausted.... I want to push it away now, forget about it and have a drink in The Bunch of Grapes. I feel relaxed. After all my seeking, I have found my heart, my centre, my soul, I have found my white light. I feel exhausted but blissfully happy. Full of love.... A round blob, sometimes like a jellyfish, sometimes like a celestial curtain blown in a wind – the *aurora borealis* in *Marvels of the Universe*. That is what I have found. Feel too limp and exhausted to write any more. Or to communicate my weary jubilation.

I began to interpret:

Me and my Flowing Light. Nothing else. Everyone has it.... I was like a child that does not know it can walk until it has been told it can..., until it has been taught.... I am quite drunk with it. So wobbly on my knees. Drunk with love. Can't take any more now. Too tired. At great peace.[11]

I was fortunate that I had been reading Underhill's *Mysticism* immediately before my illumination and so understood that this was an experience that begins the ending of the Dark Night along the Mystic Way.

Visions: images and symbols
I was fortunate that I knew what was happening to me. I also realised that the energies I had seen, which seemed symbols from the beyond, were what a poet sees in the genuine poetic vision. I had been seeking the poetic vision in Japan, and had glimpsed it there. I knew from personal experience about the Light and the images or symbols that accompany it. In a time when poets have become separated from the traditional vision and become social rationalists I had rediscovered the vision that was known to Eliot and Yeats. I had seen Reality.

I grasped that my journey was unique among 20th-century poets as it had taken me to this vision and culminated in a room that had been bugged and raided by intelligence agencies and overlooked streets where surveillance squads followed my every move. My vision of truth was in conflict with the deceptive world of intelligence.

More visions; Brompton Oratory
The next day I closed my eyes, buried my eyelids in the crook of my arm, and it happened again. I saw a beautiful dome made of light like a spider's web, and then a sumptuous yellow and purple tomb. Then, like an old gold death-mask on a primitive shield, the magnificent face of God. When I finished I felt shaky again, like a child taking its first tottering steps. I made another attempt to define what had happened in my *Diaries*:

> At peace. Feel turned inside out still, infinitely relaxed…. I have been loved by a great light…. This is enlightenment. *Satori*. Illumination.

And again:

> Fingers wet after vision: inside a cave, which became a beautiful dome seen from inside in spider's-web-like, filigree light. Also, earlier a sumptuous tomb (yellow and purple here). An old primitive OE (Old English) shield with a face, looming up – the face of God, like an old gold death-mask…. All this after Margaret returned from confession at the Brompton Oratory and we talked about the Way.

Margaret knocked on my door and asked me to accompany her back to the Brompton Oratory. Its Italianate baroque splendour always uplifted me. (I was appalled when the KGB later used St Patrick's Chapel as a dead-letter box.) As usual I was tailed by a surveillance squad. For some time I stood in the aisle. At length, for the first time for years I went into the pews and knelt and gave myself to the silence. I blotted out the tails who were standing around the entrance and concentrated on the point of white light between my closed eyes, and observed the eternal light in the basket, the light which is never put out and from which all candles are lit. And I felt an immense peace. But I was not putting a Christian gloss on my experience. I was in touch with Reality and had had a true mystic and poetic vision, but I did not interpret my vision in terms of the teachings of the Catholic Church, as Margaret did.

That night I lay again for an hour and a half. I saw a silver egg, which I thought was the philosopher's stone; a round mirror; a shadowy Christ on a cross; a flaming devil in white light; a saint with a halo round his head.

The visions poured up: a yellow rose; black thorns against squirming, moving white lines; a child that looked foetal; a high death-mask, like an Eastern god, with a high crown. And then, with breathtaking clarity, Christ: a man with dark-brown hair, a crown of thorns, and a reddy-brown robe worn round his shoulders and gathered by a pin under his chin. It was a direct frontal view, the vision gazed straight at me. I received it as a poetic vision and did not give it religious significance. Then there were more patterns, like frost on glass. And all the time there were hints of a white flower, suns and shafts of light.

My arm was across my eyes to black out the dusk, and every so often I had to stop and rest. Then I saw a starless night, with an outline of something at the top, as though I were looking up at the universe from the bottom of a round pit. Through this a point of white light always broke, and as it got larger everything started again. In the end I saw a long white-hot line like the trunk of a tree, down the centre of my being, and I again knelt and said, "I surrender." And as if in answer the point of light swelled into a vivid moon.

Again I should record what I wrote in my *Diaries*:

Shaky, moist fingers, cold feeling on forehead after spending 6.30–8 p.m. lying on my bed with Margaret, having visions. An egg, in silver, empty inside – I thought it was the philosopher's stone; a round mirror; Christ on the cross – shadowy, and a flaming devil or demon in Paisley blotches of white light; a saint with a halo round his head in full length facing to the right; and then – how can I remember out of the abundance of images – a yellow rose; black thorns against squirming, moving white lines; a child – a foetus; a death-mask, like a Buddha, with a high crown, probably in gold though it looked white of course; and, with breathtaking clarity, Christ – I think an effigy: with a crown of thorns, brown – dark-brown – hair and a Roman robe gathered at a pin under the chin (he looked straight at me) and worn round the shoulders; then.... What? Patterns? Like frost on glass. And a primitive shield. All the time there were hints of a white flower and suns, and shafts of light fell towards me. Sometimes after a rest, for my arm was across my eyes to black out the dusk outside and it ached every so often and I had to rest, I saw a starless night, I was looking up into an empty universe... very aware of distance and space. Then it would all begin again, starting from a point of white light which got larger, then broke, like a moon through clouds, scattering spider's webs of shapes. The long white-hot line like the trunk of a tree in the centre. After Margaret went to her room I fell on my knees and covered my eyes with my palms and said again, "I surrender", and the still point came up and broke through the night into a vivid moon, as if in answer. Then worn out and wobbly on my knees, I knew it was time to stop. I have found my heart, the centre of my self. *Practice*, knowledge is not enough, there must be practice.[12]

After that I had several evenings of visions. I saw the Flower a number of times. I saw the philosopher's stone – an egg in the heavens above a tree. I saw prison gates, and, gathering in a majestic splendour among stars and floating down, nearer and nearer and nearer, looking slightly to the right, full of experience-frowns and bearded like a Greek sculpture or a Rodin, the magnificent aged face of God. I saw the sky as van Gogh painted it, and a recurring vision of a river of Flowing Light. This made me say: "Time is the cutting-up of eternity, which can be known through the Silence."

Yet when it came to evaluating what had happened to me, I was reluctant to give it any metaphysical significance. I now preferred to think, 'I've made direct contact with my imagination.' I regarded my visions as no more metaphysical than the opium vision Coleridge had of Xanadu, although I did attribute metaphysical significance to the white light, the Flowing Light.

I fell asleep on the Saturday night exhausted and in the interest of faithfulness to the visions I experienced when I awoke the next morning, I quote from my *Diaries* for 12 September:

This morning more visions: a red flower and, after streaks of white, then red light across the centre of my being – the great cable of my soul: prison gates with arrows, in black; an egg in the heavens above a tree, an egg which turned into the philosopher's stone; and again, gathering in majestic splendour among stars and then floating down nearer and nearer, the magnificent aged face of God, looking slightly to the right, all experience-frowns and bushy moustached and bearded, like a great

Rodin or Greek sculpture. And so much more, I have temporarily forgotten. Now do not feel so weak on my knees. I am learning to walk. How long will this period of illumination last?

On that Sunday "both my clocks stopped within a quarter of an hour of each other." Looking back, I am sure the intensity of the energy that flooded in stopped the clocks. And again:

> Before lunch. Lay on my bed, hands over my eyes. More visions. In colour against skies, paintings in blues and yellows and reds and browns. The face of God again, as an old master. Again, as a Russian icon. Earlier, a white wheel. I emerge from these contacts with my imagination and soul fresh and whole in my centre.... Still the images come. A tree, wide trunk, a white light behind it.... Earlier red lights – red for my throbbing passion.... And more: the night sky and star seen through a crown of black thorns. A yellow mountain range sloping down and a blob of a moon. And hundreds of van Gogh rings round the stars – all in white. Perhaps I should become a painter of these visions. Also, life spreading like roots or nerves round blobs – in thin and white map contours.... Visions: thorns like a whale's backbone and light from behind. A Greek theatre, yellow column on left and a yellow window in middle, otherwise a purple drape.

And again at 3.30:

> Vision: a golden star (two triangles?) on a blue wall, golden rays pouring out of it. Then a silver star in the heavens, white rounded, turning into an amoeba? A jellyfish? An iced-cake ceiling melting into a sky and whirling stars.... Back to visions: Tudor suns, bamboo leaves, wrought-iron gateways.[13]

The next day was a Monday, and I spent most of it at school. My *Diaries* record of the evening: "Vision: Tudor rose." And the following day: "Vision abating."

I now understood that I had an inner television in my soul, and I understood how life was lived before the 1880s, before electricity when there were dark nights and no external television and merely inner contemplation to keep one feeling at peace. And I did feel at peace. I had the Mystic Peace. I was not in Hell now. I sat utterly still, and gazing at the plane-tree outside my window brought an ecstatic serenity. I felt at one with my surroundings and the universe. I was a stranger to nothing. I had found that joy and love of everything which is the highest meaning and the justification of suffering.

"Stop looking and you will find," Margaret told me with instinctive Taoism, meaning I would find my heart. I had found.

It was now apparent that something fundamental had happened to both Margaret and me on 10 September. At the very same moment that I saw Reality and made the breakthrough into a life of genuinely-poetic, imaginative vision, Margaret felt a call back to the Church. My poetic vision could now take its place alongside the work of the 17th-century Metaphysical poets. Now she spoke more and more of the Church, telling me it was the centre which stopped one from "pulling people to pieces", and she urged me to speak to a priest.

But I knew I wouldn't. I was still not interested in relating my experience to any doctrinal belief. The Catholic Church was a social institution, and I did not trust it to interpret my vision.

I was on my path, and it was for me to interpret what had happened to me. Margaret said that I might become a priest, but I knew that was wrong. She told me: "Your task is to teach the younger generation, be a prophet to the younger generation. They will take it from you. Then you can say: 'I did it the hard way – at my school.'" I knew that I had a role in relation to the younger generation, but I felt it should be as an artist now, as a poet, not as a priest. "No more mountains for you," Margaret said. "You've climbed the last one." And I knew she was right on that, but I was aware I had many mountains still to climb: ranges of books to write with hidden peaks and summits, which, seen as a whole, looked daunting and exhausting.

There was a lull for a few days while the outer world crowded back in. On 24 September I arrived back with some dahlias and was thrilled at how like my golden flower they were. Over that day I had more visions: "The flowers in my soul. Streaks of white light inside me. The picturebook of my imagination – leafing through it like an old scrapbook of strange patterns." The next day I wrote in my *Diaries*:

> After the suffering, the gain that justifies the suffering, the meaning.... I have found the source of my being, the fountain of my imagination, the spiked dahlia of the golden (white) flower.... The meaning of life – the highest meaning – is to be found in joy, to get which you have to suffer. A stern message to the young.... To find the joy, and live, you must suffer.[14]

I meant that one must suffer at a deep level, at the deep level of losing everything, for it gives meaning.

I now saw that we are on the threshold of a new epoch. A European rebirth was in the air, and might restore the soul after a time of doubt. A new view of man and of the universe was ahead, and consequently a new philosophy that would recover the inner life our age has lost. I knew that man must change his perception so that he perceived the unity of the universe. Crucial to this new perception were: self-stripping, not-wanting (detachment), discarding (or purifying), growing, flowing and peace. Mine would be a lone voice crying in the wilderness for this new outlook that went against what the world stood for.

The imagination – I am in a process of transformation
The Illuminative Way is tidal. The beyond approaches and for a while covers the sand and shingle of the social ego like the tide, but after the tide has receded the sand and shingle are there again, and the ego is apt to explain the encroachment in terms that do not threaten it. So it was that my rational, social ego, when faced with interpreting my visions and the Light in my *Diaries*, immediately saw it in terms that were familiar to itself: the imagination. I had been united with my imagination and my inspiring Muse. That explanation enabled me to assimilate what had happened, adjust to it.

Looking back now I believe my interpretation was only partially correct. For although the visions were from my imagination, my imagination itself was part of the tidal flow of the Light from the beyond, the tidal current which was always behind the white crests and surf of the visions. Beyond all the visions was the Light. To change the image to the Ghadames spring, the visions were the bubbles but the Light was the underground spring from which they wobbled to the surface of my gazing mind.

It was only as time went by that I realised that the events of 10 September appeared to "turn me around" from a materialistic outlook to a metaphysical outlook. But in fact those events were themselves part of a process, much of which was subterranean, unconscious, so that when the events of 10 September happened they seemed to my rational, social ego to be of the order of an accident which had happened to me rather than the culmination of a process, of a movement towards something I had been seeking, something for which I had been striving. When seen historically in this account, that is how they must appear. Would the breakthrough have happened if I had not undergone the trauma in desert Libya? I doubt it.

Nationalism: Russians and Chinese
I had found spiritual Reality, the Light, but my Dark Night was by no means over. The intelligence world closed in on me.

Nearly exposed by Philby in retaliation for Heath's expulsion of 105 Russians
On 24 September 1971 Heath, the British Prime Minister whose 'unofficial Ambassador' I had been, expelled 90 Soviet diplomats – 105 Russians in all – after a KGB defector gave secret information on spying in Britain. I heard

the news while driving and immediately wondered if the defector was associated with Viktor.

I believe it was the same day that James Appleton contacted me urgently and told me that the SIS had information that I might be named in retaliation within the next 24 hours. He said, "The retaliation will come from Kim Philby, who is now a KGB General, in Moscow. He will retaliate by naming British subjects as spies. Our information is that he has a dozen names, and that your name is one of them. He will name you as an SIS intelligence agent to retaliate."

I grasped that to retaliate against Heath's expulsion of 105 Russians Philby would name me as the KGB knew I was Heath's 'unofficial Ambassador'. I immediately wondered how the KGB and Philby had linked me with Heath. Had they found out from what Viktor had told them?

James Appleton continued: "If that happens, it will be Viktor who is responsible. Martin Rowley told you back in April that Viktor had given the KGB your name. He did not tell them your name to hurt you but to protect himself, so don't be bitter. Every newspaper in town will be ringing you up. Just laugh it off."

He did not seem to realise the logistics and implications of twenty calls being put through to my landing extension by Pussy-cat, possibly answered by ex-Miss UK if she got to the phone before I did, and then of my "laughing it off" on the landing within earshot of anyone who happened to be on the stairs and of Pussy-cat, who would be listening in.

The defector was in fact a KGB officer, a Major, in the Soviet Embassy in London. I had no evidence that Viktor was associated with him or had led the British intelligence services to him. Had Viktor brought with him information that identified the KGB Major in the Soviet Embassy and confirmed his willingness to defect?

After I left James Appleton I pondered the Soviet plan to name me in retaliation. I tried to understand what had happened. Andrew Mackenzie had told me in Tripoli that Viktor had important information he would bring with him when he defected. I had been told that Viktor had named me "to protect himself". I had been told that Philby was set to name me only hours after the announcement that Heath was expelling the 90 Russian diplomats. I must have been linked with Viktor for some while in KGB circles for there to have been such a rapid Soviet reaction. The KGB and Philby knew of my link with Viktor but did they also know of my link to Heath? Was I part of the expulsion story? Like K in Kafka's work I was in the middle of nightmarish circumstances I did not fully understand.

Throughout that long weekend I held my breath, expecting the world's press to gather beneath my French windows. Then early the following week James Appleton saw me and said that I would *not* be named. The danger was over. For some reason, perhaps because they did not want to reveal that they knew about my links with Viktor, the KGB and Philby had changed their mind. The earlier information that James had received had been countermanded. In due course he gave me a photocopy of an article about Philby that, he told me, had appeared in *Pravda* on 2 October 1971.[15] I was told that Philby had mentioned "two or three" British names, but that no mention was made of me. I was not in the article. I have since established that Philby revealed names in *Izvestia* on 1 October 1971.[16] I have not managed to track this article down. I have obtained a copy of an interview Philby gave to the Estonian *Kodumaa* on 13 October, in which Philby named 21 British agents.[17] I was not among them, and assumed that I was not mentioned in *Izvestia*.

The next time I saw him James said he thought that the KGB might be interested in how I was getting on with the Chinese, and that they might prefer me to be at large targeting the Chinese than to be exposed and discontinue my work. But the prospect of being named unsettled me as once again I faced the reality that I was operating under my own name, with no cover, like James Bond, and that I was extremely vulnerable. There was no getting away from it, Philby, who had written for *The Observer* while working for the SIS before defecting to Moscow, knew what I had been doing. I now spoke of "the long arm of Kim Philby".

Invited by Yu En-kuang to 'Exhibition of Photos of China'
While all this was going on, I received a letter from Mr Yu En-kuang of the *Hsinhua* News Agency sending me a ticket for the 'Exhibition of Photos of China' which was opening at 49 Portland Place, London on 29 September and running until 9 October. I was still coming to terms with the Light and found the juxtaposition of Reality and surveillance squads bizarre.

Now I was briefed by James Appleton in the flat with the white carpet on how to react at the Exhibition. As I had been requested at the conference in Harrods' Way In, I was to be reticent, not to press. I was to let them come to me, not to frighten them off. I was to say that I found the Exhibition very interesting, get across that I was fascinated by China, talk about myself and my interest in African revolutions, say they could not be understood without a study of revolution in China, explain where I thought the Russians had gone wrong and profess to want to improve my knowledge of Russian-orientated movements. I was to ask about the family of any Chinese I spoke to, ask what they were doing in London and before, and, most importantly, obtain the card of everyone I met. I had six targets: Mr Chang Chi-hsiang, the First Secretary; Mr Liu, the bespectacled Cultural Attaché; Mr Pei, the Chargé; Mr Chang; Mr Ku; and Mr Li.

There was great anticipation that at last I would be recruited by the

Chinese at the Exhibition. However, in the event I went on a day Jorge arranged during the time the Exhibition was open (5.30–9 p.m.) and found none of my six targets there. I was only able to speak to one Chinese, a woman.

I reported this to James Appleton, thinking that the whole visit had been an anti-climax. However, there was intense interest in this contact. James was sure that the woman was part of the operation they had been planning. He said, "Once they are interested in you, we will leave you alone, and let them come to you." I now found that as many as eight men lurked near my elbow when I was in a public place.

I was secretly relieved that no formal approach had been made to recruit me. I was engulfed in researching illumination and what had happened to me, and did not want to pretend that I was on the side of the Chinese Communism I had despised so much in 1966. Somehow I had managed to continue operating as an 'unofficial Ambassador' without betraying the internationalist principle of the Light for narrow nationalistic ends.

Illumination: accepting the One law of the universe
I now entered a confused time of gains and fallow consolidation. There were more tangled confusions. At the time I had little understanding of why, but weirdly the more I accepted that I was losing Nadia, the more I became aware of the underlying law of the universe.

Understanding the universe as Nadia leaves for Lincolnshire
I was waiting for Nadia to move to Lincolnshire with her mother. In October I had begun to look for a flat I could buy on mortgage to escape the house of rooms where I was living. It would be somewhere where I could have Nadia to stay when she visited me. I looked in Islington and Chelsea, and recoiled from dark squares which were depressing. I took Nadia to Essex for a weekend and among the Forest ponds let the whole world into my soul, felt it through my heart. "What's the toadstool feeling?" I asked her. "'I'm peaceful in the shade.' What are the bullheads feeling? 'I'm happy under my bank.' What is that leaf feeling? 'I'm so tired I can't hold on any longer.' What are the fallen conkers feeling? 'We're snug under these dead leaves and full of flowing lines.'"[18] In my *Diaries* I wrote about "holism…, the need to be whole…. The mysticism is a consequence of growing into a whole."

Law of Nature: Law of the Seed
And, explaining the universe to Nadia, suddenly I felt with the shattering force of discovery the law of Nature, the Law of the Seed. I drew a diagram in my *Diaries* and labelled it "one law of life". I put the diagram on my school blackboard the next day and explained it to my 'backward' boys:

The earth, the air, the sun and the rain are all there to help the seed to grow. The wind blows the seed to the earth, the sea makes rain and waters it, the sun warms it. Everything has its place in the Great Plan. Animals, birds, fish, men hunt each other, eat fruit, plants, vegetables, to help their seed to grow. Trees, flowers and humans flower to be fertilised, so that their seed can grow. There is never an accident: no man has five heads or seven legs, the corn never ripens in December, the trees never go bare in the summer.

It was one law we cannot see: "You can't see the moon by day, but you can by night." It was one law we cannot touch: "You cannot touch the wind." I was so struck by my insight that I took my Riverway boys to the Natural History Museum and spent an hour showing them diagrams of how a flash of lightning hit the sea and made the first living cell.

My insight was a breakthrough. It took me right outside myself, I saw from the point of view of the whole. Now I saw it was useless to ask *why* anything happened, *why* one hazelnut grew and others did not. Why did the wind blow this sycamore wing here and that one there? There was no why, it just had to be accepted. And human life followed the same law. Things happened in the course of the working of a law, and a girl going north had to be accepted like prematurely fallen blossom. I wrote in my *Diaries*:

Why, why – do not ask why. The moon pulls the sea, the sea tides help water the shore and make plants grow, they left behind the earliest forms of life.... Seaweeds put down shoots on wet ground, the sun made them grow, sea animals put seed in wombs, then ate the plants, the fruit.... Everything has its place in the Great Plan, the great mystery, and technology merely hides the Mystery, cities hide it. The wind (air) fertilises and blows the poplar seed and the sycamores to the ground (the earth), the sea (water) makes clouds and rain water the earth so that the seed grows, and the sun (fire) warms it up. The whole plan and Mystery involves: growth. The elements are there to help the seed grow.... Hence the family urge – feeling for the mate and the child.... So what is God? The Unknowable, the Mystery, the Law of the Seed.[19]

Thirty-five years later my perception of the Great Plan, first outlined to my 'backward' boys, would find expression in *The New Philosophy of Universalism*.

Acceptance of events and the Great Flow
Then I made an enormous acceptance. Looking out at the autumnal gardens from my room, I felt an immense law rolling through all Nature and human

life. It moved imperceptibly slowly, "at the level of eternity", a "long splendid flow of generations upon generations". Families succeeded one another, each with its sufferings, through bud and flower and fruit, now revelled-in and now forgotten. There were accidents and separations, but these were only at the level of time. Underneath the process was inexorable as the seasons. And, sitting opposite my plane-tree, I felt for a short while that everything was for the best. Did not the falling of the blossom herald in the fruit? I felt that the events would happen regardless, so I should surrender to the Great Flow. I should not fight to control events. I was not sure whether I believed in the goodness of the Great Flow, but I wrote: "There is nothing more I can do, so I shall do nothing and accept my suffering and wear it silently and have faith in what happens. I shall trust in the Great Purpose. I will surrender Nadia to the Great Flow."

I meet Ann Johnson in Greenwich
I had accepted everything. I felt instinctively that at the level of flow there are no accidents. Events are only perceived as events at the level of the ego. In fact, I felt, we are all seeds and some grow in good earth and some fall by the wayside onto stony ground, and there is no why as to what the great rolling law of God ordains. I spent a long time staring at *John* 12.24: "Verily, verily, I say unto you, Except a corn of wheat fall into the ground and die, it abideth alone: but if it die, it bringeth forth much fruit." I saw from the point of view of the whole, and in my *Diaries* I wrote down: "Unitism" as the philosophy that would catch this.

I was groping towards Universalism. I was contemplating through my real self which was connected to, and inseparable from, the whole. On 18 October I had a vision of "a very bright diamond with an egg in it".[20] I recorded this in my *Diaries* at 6.30 a.m., and was sure it was a symbol for the Light with the universe in it.

My acceptance of the universe was deep, fundamental, profound. Strangely, now I had accepted Nadia's departure it was suddenly postponed. Caroline rang me on 21 October and told me things had not worked out and they would not now be going until April. I was overjoyed and redoubled my efforts to find a flat with two bedrooms so that Nadia could come and stay.

I had accepted the future and placed a blind trust in the universe. And in return, as it were, the universe gave me Ann. I took the 'backward' boys swimming at Greenwich Baths, and while I got them out of the water and changed I chatted to a young teacher who patrolled the swimmers from the school that had the next slot, All Saints' Church-of-England primary school, Blackheath.

The day I heard that Nadia was staying I had a drink with Ann, keeping a discreet eye on the Arab surveillance squad that had tailed me. She was a young girl of 21 and shared a house in Greenwich – at 136 Humber Road, SE10 – with other girls. Her room was on the ground floor. She was a spirited girl, and I took her back to Egerton Gardens, where she met Margaret. I did not know that she would become my second wife. It was as if Providence had accepted my most recent surrender of Nadia and had given her back *and* a new wife for good measure.

Margaret gave me another pot she had made, a small urn of tubular rings with four snails on the outside, clinging like limpets. "The snails make it look ugly, it is more perfect without them," Margaret said. "They are four people who need to be flicked off, discarded." She did not say who the four were, but I reckoned they were Caroline, Paula (who still rang my landing phone, asking questions an intelligence agent might ask), Pussy-cat – and perhaps from her viewpoint Nadia or perhaps herself, for she saw me as a soul that did not need people any more and was preparing for creative work.

Exhausted by my recent gains, I was plunged back into darkness with the exception of one gleam: I wrote in my *Diaries*, "Vision – saw the Flower again yesterday," but I had few visions now. I had lived at an intense level and needed time to relax and recuperate. I pondered the snails and accepted everything. "Don't ask why," Margaret had said, "accept."[21]

Nationalism: Portuguese
To me, the intelligence world of Pussy-cat and surveillance squads were snails that needed to be flicked off.

Food poisoning at 13 Egerton Gardens, under Pussy-cat: Margaret "poisoned"
In late October Margaret fell ill. For several days she complained she had vomited repeatedly and had a temperature, and that she was feeling worse. She went into a decline. She said, "I'm being poisoned. There's no other explanation." She was suspicious of Pussy-cat, who still cooked the fried breakfasts we all had in a little kitchen just out of sight of where we all sat in the basement breakfast room.

I was very wary of Pussy-cat. She still cleaned our rooms every day. Things had disappeared from my room, including a tie-pin with a green emerald given me as a leaving present by Prince Hitachi, which I sometimes wore to work. In my bedsit the only place to store the Portuguese military bulletins was the bottom of my wardrobe. They were in a pile, covered by clothes but easy for Pussy-cat to inspect during her daily cleaning of my room.

It was widely assumed that the Portuguese casualty and death figures were untrustworthy and that the Portuguese African wars had strained Portugal's economy. The Portuguese Ministry of Defence in Lisbon and the

Portuguese Embassy in London kept sending me the latest batch of bulletins as they were propaganda, I thought, and they hoped I would convey them as accurate. If Pussy-cat was a Portuguese intelligence agent, as I suspected, she needed to see that I was working on the bulletins, and I made sure she would detect such work when she was alone in my room.

Visit of Amilcar Cabral and exposure – Philby's information reaches The Times
In November Amilcar Cabral, the Secretary-General of PAIGC (Partido Africano da Independência da Guiné e Cabo Verde), the liberation movement in Guinea-Bissau and Verde Islands, visited London. He was to speak at Westminster City Hall. James Appleton, sitting in the flat with a white carpet, casually set me the task of meeting him and asking him some difficult questions. I made phone calls from public call-boxes and established that his itinerary was in the hands of Polly Gaster. I rang her and asked if she could timetable a slot for me to meet Cabral. Over the phone she refused point-blank.

When I told James he told me to be persistent. He seemed to be acting on orders from higher up. I rang her again and persisted, with a predictable outcome.

Nicholas Ashford, my contact on *The Times Diary* and my host at the Black Friar, informed me that she had rung *The Times* and accused me of being a secret agent. (Coincidentally, in due course he would report for *The Times* from Angola.) To me, the very fact that she could say this so confidently meant that the information Philby had access to had reached the Soviet-backed MPLA. It seemed likely that the KGB were allowing me to operate against the Chinese to see what I discovered but were blocking my attempts to obtain information from the pro-Soviet anti-Portuguese liberation movements, and were also trying to block my outlet through *The Times*.

I went to the rally in Westminster Central Hall and sat near the back in a packed audience of several hundred. Basil Davidson, a pro-Soviet writer on Portuguese Africa, made a speech. Then there was a collection. Helpers went into the audience and shook tins for donations. Polly Gaster headed towards where I was sitting and thrust her tin very aggressively under my nose and shook it heavily up and down. I looked her in the eye and declined to make a donation. Then Cabral spoke. I had a strong feeling that he was about to meet a violent end. (He was assassinated on 20 January 1972.)

One day soon afterwards while I was at work my room was broken into again, and papers were strewn everywhere. I discussed this latest break-in with James Appleton. He said that it might be action from the Portuguese following my visit to Cabral. But Pussy-cat did not need to scatter my papers as she had access to my room whenever she wanted and could have searched it every day for several weeks without my being aware. I wondered if it was a KGB proxy.

While all this was going on Paula kept ringing me. I did not want to see her, and reported this to James, who said, in a clear hint that she might be an intelligence agent: "Her interest in you may exceed the personal." She rang me for the last time on 15 February 1972 to say it was a year since we met and that she had recently had two marriage proposals, one by her hairdresser, who was 25 and ten years younger than she was, and the other by her long-term Jewish boyfriend. She married her hairdresser and her intelligence-like telephone calls stopped.

I am ill with food poisoning: Margaret moves out
Not long after Cabral's visit I too fell mysteriously ill. I felt dreadful. I was persistently sick and had a very high temperature. For a couple of days over a weekend I was delirious. I had not been so ill since I had sandfly fever and a temperature of 107 in Baghdad. I stayed in bed, sweating, tossing and turning feverishly, and was too ill to attend a surgery. Margaret, who was feeling rough herself, called the doctor.

The doctor told me: "You have food poisoning."

Margaret, standing by my door, heard the diagnosis and was again concerned that she was being poisoned as well. After the doctor left, she said, "It's definitely Pussy-cat. She is poisoning both of us. I'm going to have to leave this house."

I recovered. I was not well enough to eat breakfast for a couple of days, and I made sure I told Pussy-cat that a doctor had said I had had food poisoning. I said this at breakfast so that Pussy-cat would have to stop what she was doing if she was doing it. She looked at me, her eyes evasive behind her tinted spectacles, and said, "You must have eaten something unhealthy outside. This kitchen is too hygienic for you to have got food poisoning at 13 Egerton Gardens."

I reckoned she would have to stop tinkering with my food for a while, and resumed having breakfast. However, I changed my table so that I could watch her cooking breakfast in a frying-pan on the stove. I reassured myself by telling myself that she could not be poisoning Margaret and me. I did not believe she was trying to drive Margaret out of the house so she could concentrate on poisoning me for consorting with Portugal's enemies while I combed through Portugal's war *communiqués*, a task the Portuguese Ministry of Defence wanted me to complete. She was there to report on me while I read the *communiqués*, and was surely not responsible for any illness. I resolved to continue as I was. However, there was no getting away from it, according to the doctor I had had food poisoning.

I invited Ann to spend a weekend with me. We visited the Markham and the Chelsea Kitchen. I was followed wherever we went. We looked in at the Trafalgar, and six Arabs came with me. On 11 November I said to her, "The streets are a nightmare" and she, not knowing about the surveillance squads I had endured for months, said, "What a strange thing to say." I was trying to be normal with her amid chronic abnormality around me.

I tried to spend evenings south of the river or in East London, where there was less surveillance. We spent an evening in Greenwich. We crossed the Thames and visited the Waterman's Arms and the 1520 Prospect of Whitby in Wapping, where I was free from surveillance squads. As soon as I ate alone in Chelsea strange people came and sat next to me: an ex-war correspondent who struck up conversation and asked me detailed questions about Africa, and a Russian expert who opened a conversation on the Soviet Union.

I longed to escape the drifting picaresque existence among human flotsam one meets when living in a bedsit, and I renewed my efforts to find a flat. I took Ann to Essex to visit my mother one Saturday afternoon and returned to find that all the tenants at 13 Egerton Gardens had been given a month's notice.

Even as I read the letter, on 20 November, Margaret moved out. A taxi came and waited, throbbing outside the front door. The driver made several journeys up and down the stairs and stacked the taxi with her paintings and belongings. I looked out of my door and saw his arms bulging with loose canvases.

Then Margaret knocked to say goodbye. She gave me a painting of Manarola in Italy: a black rock with a sea and sky, a red church at the top and a splurge of sunlight on a cliff half-way down. She returned and thrust some plants into my arms, saying, "It ends in growth." She would not say where she was going. Her last words to me were reproachful: "Visions such as yours only happen to someone with a calling." By 'calling' she meant 'calling to the Catholic Church'. "The spirit needs solitude to grow in the heart. When you need it, you will find it." From my French windows I saw her drive off in her Aladdin's cave of a taxi.

Illumination: Reality
The notice to leave 13 Egerton Gardens was generally ignored. Everyone simply stayed on as if the notice had not been issued.

Poetry and visions; Tuohy's persona
The next day I lunched at Dino's with Ann. I told her I was a patriot but that I also cared about the wretched of the earth and all humankind. That night I had visions again, and my *Diaries* record: "Visions again. Diamond. Fire. Then a whole succession, including vertebrae (of an old fish) and a constant

golden glow, the size of a large sun. Diamonds. Laurel wreath."[22] I associated the laurel wreath with the poems I had ahead of me.

I took Ann to the Colony Room, the afternoon drinking club in Soho, and encountered Peter Jenkins, the *Guardian* journalist, sitting on a stool at the bar. I reminded him of how we had met in Japan.

I met Ricky a couple of times and told him I intended to unite all my opposites: deed and reason, sensuality and mysticism, "the four faces of my being". I told him, "There is a sea of cause and effect, but if one makes the move and detaches oneself one becomes an island and it washes by." To which Ricky replied: "You are very near the Kingdom of Heaven."

A week before Christmas I took Nadia to a Christingle Service at All Saints', Blackheath, near the school where Ann taught. A christingle is a lighted candle, on that day placed in an orange (representing the world) with a band of red 'blood' round it.

The Dean of Southwark gave a sermon on the Light of the World. He told the children, "You are candles, waiting to be lit inside by the Holy Spirit," and each child was given a candle to take away. I found the service strangely moving, and I wrote afterwards: "It requires immense effort to keep the inner Light there amid the world of action."

I spent that evening with Tuohy in Soho. We went to the Swiss Tavern and then to the Greyhound; then to an Italian restaurant in Greek Street; and finally to the Wellington. He talked about the US and Portugal, and he said of the African liberation movements: "Revolutionary governments are always underequipped with information about human beings, so I've changed sides." He meant that he was now on the side of the British Empire and colonial Africa.

We discussed the breakdown of the West. Tuohy dated it to 1870 or 1880 because: "Men stopped writing novels because they were good at them and became self-conscious (Proust, Joyce). The mechanical side of the West went on developing, but not the arts. And men started to collect antique furniture – things became imitation." We discussed mysticism and he said: "I am too much of an Existentialist to be a mystic, I believe in choices." To which I said, "So you are trapped in your persona, in the 'I, I, I', the outer world."[23] I began to tell him about my experience of 10 September but he changed the subject.

At that point a strange Chinese appeared near us. He was evidently listening to what we were saying, and, noticing, Tuohy suggested we moved, not wanting to know about any experience that threatened his way of changing the world in social terms. That night I had a vision of "golden ears of corn".

That Christmas I took Ann to Essex for a couple of nights as Nadia was spending a week with my mother. We fed the mallards and geese on

Connaught Water, went to Queen Elizabeth's hunting lodge and visited the church in the Forest at High Beach. I took Nadia to dancing classes and attended the final dance, smiling at her erect, stiff-legged waltz.

On 3 January I reported in my *Diaries*: "Visions. Bleary eyes from inward-looking. A lot of patterns. Snowflakes. Saints, Pope's head, monk, altar, Cathedral – ...white light – began and stopped."

At the end of January I took Ann to Essex. We parked in the Forest and talked, and when I looked out of the window the Forest had turned white with snow.

In early February in Greenwich I felt the call back to be a poet. I wrote in my *Diaries*:

I am above all a Romantic poet – an isolated artist carrying on in a philistine and alien society, using image and organic form, interested in such Romantic causes as liberation movements, wanting to change the world. Yet at the same time, killing my soul in a studied suicide of politics.... Action – for me it is what abstract metaphysics were to Coleridge. An escape.... "We Poets in our youth begin in gladness;/But thereof come in the end despondency and madness." Because poets feel more intensely, they feel the gladness and the despair more than others.... I will continue to reflect the natural world.... Seeing everyday life – and Nature.[24]

Soon afterwards I spent another evening with Tuohy, meeting him at 2 Aubrey Road in a relative's sitting-room, eating at Costa's and returning for final drinks to the house. There I met his relative Lady Flavia and heard about her boyfriend Colin MacCabe, a structuralist who had written on semiology. I reaffirmed my identity as a Romantic poet and Existentialist who is interested in "dynamic growing" ("the upward thrust of the sap")[25] and "rooted growth", rather than analysis in terms of any social theory such as structuralism or class.

I spent a weekend with Nadia during the February half-term. I took her up the Monument and to the zoo, and on the Sunday we went for a walk in Epping Forest. In my *Diaries* I wrote:

The buds were nearly out: hawthorn and beech. The great tit sang "see-saw" from near its nest. A squirrel sat still on a branch. I stood on a mossy knoll and looked at the lacy pattern of twigs against a white sky, and later, scuffling through last year's leaves, I felt the scales unfold from around my heart, I burst into happy bud.[26]

The account went into my poem, 'February Budding, Half Term', with very little changed.

Reality as a Void: the Silence, centre-shift beneath 'I'

I began a further development, a further undermining of my 'I'. The next evening Ann happened to remark in the Chelsea Kitchen that at school she was illustrating the Creation as it is described in *Genesis*. I said: "Light and darkness come out of a Void." And suddenly I glimpsed deep into Reality. Thoughts came up from within me "like bubbles from the Void at the bottom of the Sahara spring", and I told her with absolute confidence that God is a Void. For half an hour I explained to her that to approach God "you must be negative, you must discard the world of time, of timetables and journalism and money-earners. You must empty yourself of it. Then you get back to the Void underneath. You are filled with a level of living which is eternal, for it has been going on for centuries." So, I said, an emptying is a filling, and the more emptying, the more filling; a loss is a gain, the more loss, the more gain. "But both time and eternity are parts of the same unity, like the top and bottom of a river, or as light and darkness are part of the same Void." I repeated that "Time is the cutting-up of eternity".

We went for a final drink in the Southwark George, and the thoughts went on pouring up from the depths of my being. I believed in a great deep presence of a Void that can be known by losing the sense of time, by a deepening in the living. I believed that the artist should be a mere shaper, like the big walls round the Ain el Faras which shape the spring and that his function was to rediscover truths which his time-bound Age had forgotten. Above all, I said, "I-I-I is at the level of time, 'I' am not important to eternity but an echo under a silent railway bridge." I insisted that therefore the really important pastimes, from the point of view of eternity, were "leisure and ruminating and sitting in the Brompton Oratory and walking in Epping Forest and writing poetry". I wrote in my *Diaries*:

> I saw that eternity and time are part of a unity which is a Void, in its negative and positive aspects.... By discarding the positive phenomena the mystic can become one with the Void.... My soul thirsts for real things, not for the cheap and vulgar.

I was confronted with belief in God. I saw my Void-like Reality could be regarded as God. I wrote:

> It is the Silence I found in Japan, the spring in the desert I found in the Sahara, the visions I found through the distractions of Egerton Gardens. There is a richness and a deepening, a purpose that can be known and felt, but about which there are no facts. God is a Void that can be felt

beneath the bustle of temporal phenomena and events; God is a flow through the temporal phenomena and events. God *is*, at the level of Being, whereas the temporal phenomena and events are at the level of Becoming.

I ended: "The artist... as hero, rediscovering truths which his time-bound Age has forgotten." I urged myself to get back to poetry as soon as possible and wrote that "my development as a writer is from the level of time to the level of the eternal".[27]

Nationalism: Portuguese and World Council of Churches

I had been writing articles about Africans known to the KGB. I had met two guerillas from the Eritrean Liberation Front (ELF), and wrote about Eritrea. I wrote about SWAPO and the Zimbabwean movements.

Articles on Africa, receptions for Bishop Muzorewa

I had met a Portuguese exile, Dr Alberto Noronha-Rodrigues, Secretary of the FLNC (*Front de Libertação Nacional e Colonial*, or Portuguese and Colonial Liberation Front), who was linked with bombings by ARA (Armed Revolutionary Action). This organisation had been founded by members of the Portuguese Communist Party who escaped from prison in 1960, and Noronha-Rodrigues had announced the first ARA explosion at the Telecommunications Centre, Lisbon, in September 1970 before it happened.[28] In 1971 ARA bombed a Portuguese ship off the coast of Mozambique, killing 23. We discussed the latest batch of Portuguese war *communiqués* which the Portuguese Embassy had sent me on 7 December. (*See* pp.353–354.)

I learned that Jerry Okoro was staying in London. I obtained his phone number and met him. He appeared overjoyed to see me again and knew of my work among the liberation movements. We talked about Libya. I never saw Okoro again. He died after a brief illness, in 2004, aged 62, in Enugu, Nigeria – the Igbo capital of Biafra that had seceded from Nigeria in 1967, triggering the 1967–1970 war between Nigeria and Biafra in which the KGB were actively involved.

I had fallen into a pattern of scribbling down James Appleton's questions and working them into my meetings with liberation-movement leaders and terrorists. I had some articles in *The Times Diary* – I had written about a Guyanan Black Power leader, Roy Sawh,[29] and a former Ghanaian High Commissioner, Kwesi Armah[30] – and I found new outlets in *Africa Confidential* and *Africa Features*.

Africa Confidential was a subscription eight-page, two-columned, blue leaflet filled with intelligence about Africa. It monitored issues *before* they were picked up in the general media and analysed their real significance. It carried news that did not appear in the national press, and it was ahead of the national press in knowing what was going on in different parts of Africa. It was a commercial enterprise that drew on all the available intelligence and channelled exclusive reports, like my own, to readers' breakfast tables through the post.

Africa Confidential asked me to write a long article covering all the African exiles in London. This took me round all the organisations in exile in London, including the Eritrean ELF and the Sudanese SSLM (the South Sudan Liberation Movement), and such deposed ministers as the ex-Prime Minister of Sierra Leone Sir Albert Margai and the ex-High Commissioner of Ghana, Kwesi Armah. This article appeared under the headline: 'London: Still the Exiles' Mecca'.[31] I wrote an article on a SWAPO strike for *Africa Features*,[32] and had a scoop on the London-based Rhodesian ANC (African National Congress).[33]

In February 1972 I interviewed Bishop Abel Muzorewa, chairman of the ANC, and my piece went into *The Times Diary*. As a result of my article Muzorewa wrote a letter to *The Times* explaining that Eshmael Mlambo, the ANC's London representative, was opposing the Rhodesian settlement.[34] Meanwhile I had attended a reception for Bishop Muzorewa in the Liberal peer Lord Beaumont's basement. I attended another reception for Muzorewa in a church hall the next day.

Soon afterwards Biggs-Davison rang and invited me to the launch of his book *Africa: Hope Deferred*, which took place in a room in the Palace of Westminster. Biggs-Davison sat at the end of a long table and talked about his book. He insisted I sat next to him in the seat of honour on his right (possibly because he knew I was linked to Heath) and Adrian Berry of *The Daily Telegraph* sat next to me. Biggs-Davison asked me very publicly if I would cover the book for *The Times Diary*. His book was pro-Portuguese, pro-Rhodesian and pro-South-African and would be considered extremely right-wing by the anti-Portuguese, anti-Rhodesian and anti-South-African liberation movement leaders I normally wrote about. I saw Biggs-Davison, who was universally proclaimed the "best-read" MP, as the past. I could see the future – I had felt the wind of change and knew that the Portuguese, Rhodesian and South-African whites would lose to the black liberation movements. I saw the transition which Biggs-Davison, in denial and preferring to believe it was not taking place, did not address. I wrote a piece, sent him a copy and was relieved that it was never published.

Coach and Douglas-Home

I had at last completed my study of the Portuguese war *communiqués* and had written a long article for *The Times*, 'Portugal's African War', updating the article I had written earlier. (*See* Appendix 5, p.527.) I had again submitted it to Charlie Douglas-Home, Features Editor of *The Times*. (*See* p.362.) On the day he had asked me to ring him for his response, a Thursday towards the end of February, I was driving my class in the grey coach and became stuck in traffic on the Embankment near an empty red telephone kiosk. Calling *The Times* was difficult: I could not ring from my landing phone as Pussy-cat would be listening, and I could not walk to a phone box from 13 Egerton Gardens as a six-man surveillance squad would tail me, two of whom would occupy the next kiosk and peer through the glass to make out the number I was dialling. The traffic was completely stationary.

Shouting to the ESN boys to behave, I jumped down from the driver's seat, ran round the front of the coach to the empty kiosk, pushed my four pennies into the slot one at a time, dialled Charlie Douglas-Home's number and when a secretary answered pushed the button that made the coins drop (which is how the red telephone boxes worked in those days). I was put through to him quickly. He said: "Your article's very good. It has a lot of information that's new but you draw conclusions. Never draw conclusions, Nicholas. Never apologise or explain, and never draw conclusions." He then told me how busy he had been and what meetings he had been in and what he had said to the Editor, and I felt he was sharing something personal with me, which increased my loyalty to him.

I was watching the coach as I spoke to him. I waited for him to finish, rang off, ran back into the road and round to the driver's door, climbed back into the driver's seat and resumed my control of twenty ESN teenagers, who, having been trusted, had been trustworthy and well-behaved. As I switched on the engine the traffic began moving. I had made my call without surveillance squads trying to listen to my conversation, and I now knew Douglas-Home's reaction.

However despite Douglas-Home's praise, the article never appeared.

I cover World Council of Churches' symposium on Cunene River Scheme, Angola for The Times, *commissioned by Louis Heren*

The World Council of Churches was sponsoring a symposium on the Cunene River Scheme in Angola. The symposium had been arranged by Dawood, and I had been invited. I had visited *The Times* to ask if I could cover it as a news story. I was shown through to the foreign-news desk and found myself talking to Louis Heren, a very distinguished former *Times* Washington correspondent: he had been first to report that President Kennedy had sent US combat troops to Vietnam, and had accompanied Martin Luther King on some of his Freedom Rides. He was widely regarded as having inspired Thomas Fowler, the journalist in Graham Greene's *The*

Quiet American. (Greene stayed on his houseboat in Singapore.) He was now deputy editor. I said that I had been responsible for the article on the World Council of Churches' aid to African liberation movements and I explained that my fares would be paid by the WCC. I asked for accreditation to *The Times* for a retrospective article.

Heren said he could not commission me, but there was a tiredness in the way he turned me down, his 'No' lacked conviction. So I asked him again. This time he sighed and said, "You are very persistent. You wore me down. Yes, all right." I was to be away from early in the morning on Wednesday 1 March to Saturday morning, 4 March.

I flew to Frankfurt and caught a bus near the Messe to where the symposium was being held in a pine forest at Arnoldshain in the Taunus mountains. I had a longish walk through a German village and bracing mountain air to the conference centre, where sixty African liberation movement leaders, guerillas, Communists and organisers met, having had their fares paid by the World Council of Churches out of funds people had given in church.

Dawood handles complaint by Polly Gaster

I arrived at the conference centre, during coffee, and was confronted by Polly Gaster who asked: "What are you doing here?" She crossed to Dawood and complained to him (as she had to *The Times*) that I was a British intelligence agent. She threatened to leave unless I left. Dawood came and had a few words with me. He told me what she had said and was clearly on my side. He then returned to her and told her very firmly on behalf of the World Council of Churches and the organisers of the conference that I was staying. She argued and there were raised voices but she did not get her way.

She then organised an attempt to exclude me on the grounds that the proceedings should not be reported. But Dawood wanted a report in *The Times* and overruled her. She then came to me and insisted that her movement and no others should be mentioned in my article. I said I would be giving the conference objective coverage. I wrote in my *Diaries* of "a sinister reception I got".[35]

Plato's 'symposium' was a meeting of friends who made speeches at a party held to mark the impending death of Socrates. The guerillas all made speeches at this party in Germany. Looking back, I wonder how near I came to *my* impending death when among the guerillas – terrorists – near the dark, forbidding Arnoldshain woods.

The first session after coffee began with a prayer. At their paymaster's request the guerillas, Communists and terrorists unwillingly stood in prayer, some looking outraged, impatient to get on with the serious business of opposing Portugal's dam and the effect it would have on the guerilla wars in Angola and Namibia.

For the next couple of days my role as an intelligence agent was in direct conflict with my role as a journalist. I kept myself to myself, fighting off thirty different groups which wanted me to give them exclusive publicity.

At the end of the conference the General Secretary of the World Council of Churches asked all the guerillas to stand and pray. Lolling back in their comfortable seats, some looking appalled and indignant, others looking knowingly at each other, weighing their Communist principles against the cash the World Council of Churches would be giving their movements, one by one, they reluctantly stood to pray.

I made my article a scrupulously accurate summary of what was said at the conference. I had written it in the evenings: 'Church call to block finance for Angola' (see Appendix 5, p.530).[36] After it appeared I heard it was praised by all factions for its fairness.

Dr Noronha-Rodrigues and Pussy-cat
On my return to London Noronha-Rodrigues rang and told me he had sent me some important confidential documents to 13 Egerton Gardens. They never arrived. He came to see me to investigate.

I thought of him as 'The Elusive Doctor' as he met me in the depths of cafés or materialised out of thin air, his henchmen having given him the all clear. Sporting an assumed identity and apparently running a terrorist organisation of his own, he materialised out of nowhere in the street next to me as I walked back towards my front door. Thin, grey-haired and bearded, and resembling a Russian anarchist, he said, "I am convinced the documents have been intercepted. Is there any Portuguese where you live?"

I mentioned Pussy-cat. He asked to see her. I devised a pretext to bring her to the front door while he lurked in the street nearby. I rejoined him. I said I thought she was probably pro-Caetano, but wondered whether she was in the KGB. He looked shifty, and I sensed that his organisation had links with the KGB.

World Council of Churches' God
Back in London, I reflected on the God of the idealistic Christians who wanted to liberate Africa from colonial rule. Their God was very different from the Void-like Reality I had sought. I wrote in my *Diaries*: "God is an itness that can be known through silence (eternity), not noise (time)."

It seemed I had achieved a sudden unification of myself: "I cannot live wholly in eternity, I cannot live wholly in time – I have to have a foot in both…. My journal – this *Diary* and dustbin – is the level of eternity contemplating the level of time…. As a writer I get my material from time but depth from eternity." And again: "I have immense purpose, a river of will in me compared with which I am nothing…. There is a force flowing through me, like water through a pipe. I could do anything in this mood, absolutely anything." Again: "It is the experience that I go for – the experience of gaining the eternal and growing for I am an Existentialist." And again, thinking of the Void-like Reality but using the terminology of the World Council of Churches' God, I wrote: "The force is greater than me and 'I' is small…. Like electricity it is + and – , through loss…. I lost the world but gained God as a compensation (in the spirit of *John*, *ch.12*)."[37] By 'God' I meant Reality.

Illumination: moves and more visions
I buy Flat 6, 33 Stanhope Gardens, London SW7
I had visited, and made an offer for, the top flat (Flat 6) at 33 Stanhope Gardens, SW7, in a 19th-century Belgravian-style terrace. I now heard that a building society had offered the money for the 17½-year lease: £5,000, the exact figure that Michelle, the psychic, had forecast the previous 26 July. I would be moving in in April, within the 12-month period she had forecast. It was uncanny, but the estate agent's leaflet was yellow, the colour she had forecast.

Time and eternity; Bronwen Astor
The same evening on the radio I heard Lady Astor's account of illumination at the age of 28:

> I believe we are all on a journey to God, whether we know it or not…. At 28 I was like an 18-year-old, gay and busy, then in despair…. Then a brilliant Light enveloped me. Everything was a unity. I understood the mystery. God is not remote, he awaits us…. There is a power within each one of us that will transform our life, like a lamp switched on.

I did not then know I would meet her, and learn that she was already illumined when the Profumo Affair took place at Cliveden, the seat of her husband, Lord Astor, in 1963.

All night I lay awake near Blackheath, thinking about the Light. The next day I showed a film at school about "the hermit-crabs and starfish between the tides, and – wonder upon wonder! – the self-planting of the corn of wheat which falls to the ground and actually winds itself downwards into the earth and dies." Straightaway I sent one of my boys to the local library to check the quotation I was reminded of (*see* p.385), from *John* 12.24: "Verily, verily, I say unto you, Except a corn of wheat fall into the ground and die, it abideth alone: but if it die, it bringeth forth much fruit." I felt I had died into the ground of eternity and was now ready to grow again.

I spent a weekend in Essex with Nadia and Ann. We visited the church of the Holy Innocents, which is in the heart of the Forest, and I gave myself to the peace of the ferny graveyard. I mused to Ann: "Eternity is not having anything dumped on you from the world of time, no handfuls of earth thrown on your spring.... Instead you live in blissfully undisturbed communion with the white Inner Light." Later I spoke of love as being "at the level of eternity, it has nothing to do with timetables, it is always there".

The next evening we drove back to Egerton Gardens. I stopped to walk among the crocuses of St James's Park and heard the call of my destiny from beyond myself: "A huge work that would be a vast fulfilment of myself as an artist, a capturing of the eternal world clothed in time."[38]

I expanded in my *Diaries*: "Today I heard the call of my destiny, among the crocuses of St James's Park: I was driving along Birdcage Walk towards the Palace and stopped at Ann's request for a stroll. Behind me I felt the call of my future: to clear the way for my long work – which will be like *Paradise Lost* and *Pilgrim's Progress*.... Eternity and time: 'As when the ruffled surface calmed/... You saw the clouded ground' ['The Silence', lines 1163–1165].[39] That is the union between eternity and time I dream of."[40]

Article on Portuguese war communiqués *blocked*

Time intruded on these subterranean ruminations. At one of our meetings in the Embankment room with the white carpet James Appleton had urged me to update my article on the Portuguese war *communiqués* and resubmit it to *The Times*. (I had been sent further batches every three months since September, most recently on 16 March.) I still did not know why *The Times* had not published my original article on the war *communiqués*. (*See* pp.353–354, 393, 394–395.) On 20 March Charlie Douglas-Home wrote to say that it was "not quite suitable for *The Times*". *The Times* paid me a half-fee for the article. I sent the article to *The Guardian*, and had letters from the editor (who surprised me by regretting that he could not offer me salaried employment to write on liberation movements) and the foreign editor (explaining that *Guardian* readers already mistrusted Portugal's casualty figures, and recommending I stayed in touch).

Strain

The strain of the last few months and of the recent visions had exhausted me. Now I began to feel ill again. I was run down and energyless. I felt just as I had done shortly after Cabral's visit. I wondered if Pussy-cat had resumed poisoning my cooked breakfasts. I visited my Chelsea doctor. He arranged for me to have a complete check-up.

I went back to see him, and he told me: "There's nothing wrong with you. The doctor who checked you can smell disease. You haven't got a disease. I just can't understand how a chap of your age can be going into a decline." The same word 'decline' had been used of Margaret. The flat I was buying was now mercifully ready. I did not eat breakfast in 13 Egerton Gardens until I moved.

No pay increase

Moving into my flat would be expensive. I knew the SIS did not like being asked for money as Andrew Mackenzie had told me in Tripoli: "They like you to be good about money. That means, you don't ask. It seems as though you're doing it for love, and the money is a little extra, a token of gratitude." This was an outdated attitude in the modern world. Removal expenses and furnishing a new flat were costly.

At my next meeting with James Appleton in the Sherlock Holmes, Northumberland Avenue, I asked for a pay rise. I pointed out that spies had no trade union. James looked at me as though I had crossed the white carpet in the Embankment flat with muddy feet and said, "We feel we're paying you what you're worth. You were overpaid before. When you started in London it was sheer charity." There was clearly going to be no financial help from those who expected me to live among surveillance squads, risk being poisoned at breakfast and know my place. The message was: 'Get on with it.'

Period of Dark Night

On 2 April I had an insight into my past: "I got lost in 1966 and experienced darkness from the end of 'The Silence' (mid-1966) until my disquiet at the end of 1969.... Could they be my Dark Night, those three years, and could it be that my marriage break-up was necessary to me to take me through to find unitive life?" And again: "My lost years, 1966–1969.... When the Dark Night ends, affirmation takes the place of negation.... Vaughan: 'I saw Eternity the other night/Like a great Ring of pure and endless light,/All calm, as it was bright.'"[41] (With hindsight, my Dark Night of the Soul began on 19 October 1965 and continued to 2 September 1971, see Appendix 1, p.490.)

Nadia moves north

I spent that Easter with Nadia in Essex. She knew most of the situation: she had seen her new school and the furnished flat in the grounds of Harrington Hall where she would soon be living. She knew that Caroline was remarrying. She knew that she would miss her Daddy, though, and she said when I tucked her up on the first night: "I wish you could still live with me." I reassured her: she would be spending part of her holidays in my new flat. Taking her swimming and to her friends, catching frog-spawn with her and holding her hand all round Chingford Fair on Easter Monday, gazing up as she sickeningly whirled round at terrifying speed in a flying chair, I felt a peaceful resignation I never dreamed I would feel.

On Easter Monday I saw the Light again. My *Diaries* record: "The Flowing Light again, as I lay with my hands over my eyes. A golden head of Christ and, separately, twice, a crown of thorns, also in golden light." I had more visions: "I closed my eyes and saw a brown Roman effigy of God. From an old master (I could see the paint cracks) it looked massively solid, eyes closed. Then a white sun, not very bright, and disappearing when I 'looked' at it, but re-emerging when I looked to one side. Then two stars.... Did it again, in broad daylight still, and saw a white ageless face."[42]

Early one morning, I prepared to drive Nadia from Essex to Dulwich to go north. From bud-dust the trees were now in blossom. She got into my car and waved goodbye to my family, and burst into tears. I said very softly, "You'll see them all again, don't worry. You'll go to your new home and you'll think of us, yes, but we'll still be here. We'll come and see you and your new friends, and think, you won't just have a hamster now, you'll have peacocks in your garden." I told her animal stories during the journey. When we arrived I gave her a brief kiss at the gate, squeezed her hand, made a joke, then got into my car and drove off.

My parting had not been agonised. My love considered only what was good for her, it focused on her as a Kew gardener focuses his care on a miniature rose, and I was sure she would be happy. My love for her was now the selfless love which can only truly be known through loss, the love which is the highest meaning of love. What *I* wanted, I now felt, was irrelevant to the situation in Lincolnshire.

I spent the rest of the day in London busying myself with the imminent purchase of my flat. I visited the electricity and gas offices. Later I phoned Caroline. She claimed she had married David. After that I met Ann, who had been visiting her mother in Cornwall. She gave me a bunch of spring violets she had picked in Cornwall. She said they might help me forget Nadia. Standing in my window, looking out at the plane-tree, I held the bunch against a sky like a purple bruise and murmured some lines from Tennyson (who had visited Harrington Hall): "'And my regret/Becomes an April violet/And buds and blossoms with the rest.'"

For about a week I prepared to move to 33 Stanhope Gardens. I collected my possessions and books together in Essex and cleaned and hoovered my new flat, washed the skirting and swept the stairs.

Visions: rapture
I was still having visions. The day after Nadia left I was "rapt": I felt the 'divine presence' steal up suddenly from below and fill my soul, slow my breathing, lock my body rigid as a fakir's. I lay down on my bed and closed

my eyes. I surrendered the deepest crevices of my soul and was given more visions: of beautiful golden furniture, of temple columns, of a brown statue head, of the celestial curtain, and then, marvellously, of the diamond in luminous blue light. This was the first time I had seen the colour blue in my secret journeys, and it stood out in my memory afterwards, even though it blended into the Golden Flower and was followed by perhaps half an hour of light flashing up into my inner night like a dawn.

Later I wrote in my *Diaries*: "Visions again. So many I can't remember them.... There were gold items of furniture (e.g. table leg) and a lot of old masters and temple columns, one old brown statue head, a celestial curtain, the diamond in blue light, and a yellow flower. A lot of light breaking, like a dawn turning into morning or like the sun coming out." Later still I wrote: "This *Diary* is a kind of newspaper of the eternal." Also: "The spirit is the force that says 'Don't'."[43]

Maltese cross
On my last night in my room in 13 Egerton Gardens I stared at the ceiling for a long time, trying to decipher the pattern that I had always referred to as 'chains'. Suddenly I said aloud: "It's a diamond.... No, a Maltese cross. My monastic cell with a Maltese cross on the ceiling, hidden by chains."[44]

Within the chains on my ceiling was a hidden symbol of Malta, the consequences of which had removed my daughter to the north. I had thought its decorative *motif* was chains but now I discovered that a Maltese cross was hidden within it: four diamonds linked with chains.

I move to 33 Stanhope Gardens
I moved into my new flat and spent the first afternoon projecting my vision onto the walls. Being at the top of the house, the flat had a red ladder on the wall above the stairs that led up from the front door, to comply with local-authority fire regulations. Over one end I hung my Tibetan *thanka* of 'the Devil' (a blue ape-like god – Yamantaka, conqueror of death – clutching several women) and at the other end, high up near the skylight, I hung my 400-year-old Tibetan *mandala*: a round orb in gold work that suggested the halo of the Inner Light. Next to this I hung a photograph of a sun halo from the outer world. I was obsessed by circles, and I covered my bedroom walls with pictures of rose windows, and with views into the deepest orbs of domes.

Visions: three more raptures
At twilight I ate peacefully at the dining-table and looked across Chelsea at the lights in dusky windows. I sat rigid for a while, then stood up and left Ann, went through to my bedroom and lay on my bed in the dark. Soon I

was breathing slowly and deeply, possessed, in union with the Light. After perhaps a quarter of an hour my breathing became heavy and reached a kind of sighing climax. Feeling thirsty I put out a hand. As my body recovered its sensation I felt satisfied behind my lungs. I felt as though a voice had said, "Your loss is not in vain, I will give you greatness," and my eyes were so nearly filled with tears that I could not go through to Ann for several minutes.

I recorded this experience in my *Diaries*: "I am aglow with the mystic Fire." Two days later, on 19 April, I wrote in my *Diaries*:

> I feel like St Paul – after reading passages from St Augustine and St Gregory in Dom Cuthbert Butler's *Western Mysticism*. Both speak of the inner Light as the aim of mysticism, as God, as Being which is unchangeable.... I have had it what? Some twenty times since September?... Contemplative and active lives.... 'Rapture' is being snatched up.

After that quite abruptly I stopped going out. Instead I sat in my window at my leather-covered antique desk and looked down at the new plane-tree beneath me, behind which, like a heart, was hidden a magnolia. I drank gunpowder tea and pottered among my old papers and possessions, rooting myself and paring them down.

I was again 'snatched', this time while finishing a Saturday lunch on 22 April. Looking out over Chelsea, and feeling the peace rising up around me and enfolding me, I put down my spoon, pushed back my chair and sat cross-legged, hands clasped. Soon I was breathing deeply and sinking into a trance that made me rigid, so that I felt no discomfort in what would ordinarily have been an uncomfortable position. As I sank deeper I saw a wonderful pale blue light that blended with a dazzling white light like a diamond shining in the sun. I sighed in ecstasy. Stiffly I walked through to my bedroom and lay on the bed and the Light came and went again, only more faintly this time. I came slowly out of my trance. For the rest of the day I felt very creative, very alive, full of intimations of inner power.

I later wrote in my *Diaries*:

> The second time this week I have been 'rapt'.... Again I was sitting at my sitting-room table, looking down on the world beneath me, and again I felt an immense well-being come over me. Everything was good, I felt contented – at peace.... There was a glorious light blue light that blended with a dazzling white light of much greater circumference than I've ever seen before – almost like a diamond shining in the sun. It was not with me for long, but I went and lay down on my bed and the light came and

went, faintly, again, and then I came slowly out of the trance. I had not felt my body at all, for about 45 minutes, and now I finished my pudding: raspberry fool.[45]

I had another visitation a few days later, on 28 April. After a long silence from Lincolnshire Caroline had written to cancel a long-standing arrangement that I would spend a whole weekend with Nadia. Instead I would just have a Saturday afternoon. As if to help me through my sorrow, the presence revealed itself again on the Friday evening. My breathing slowed and my fingers locked so that I again could not hold a spoon without difficulty. I closed my eyes and wandered into my bedroom. The white light came up with blue tints. I felt an ecstasy grow in me. I began to catch my breath and the white light grew brighter and bigger and brighter. Suddenly, there was a round halo before my closed eyes like a hoop of light, exactly the same as the sun-halo I had pinned near my Tibetan *mandala*. I gave a gasp and fell away. It was then shortly after 10 p.m.

The four visions of 8, 17, 22 and 28 April became poems: 'Visions: Raid on the Gold Mine'; 'The Furnace'; 'Vision: Snatched by God, A Blue Light'; and 'Vision: Love like a Grid'.

Harrington Hall
The next day I had my Saturday afternoon with Nadia. I drove to Horncastle Market Square and received Nadia from Caroline and David, who was in RAF uniform. I drove her to her new school and had a chance meeting with the Head, who walked me round even though it was a Saturday. I lingered in Nadia's classroom and then took her to lunch at the Magpie.

Nadia chatted happily about her new life. Her flat was in the grounds of Harrington Hall, where, in one of those strange coincidences which suggests a Providential pattern in the sequence of events of my story, lived Sir John and Lady Maitland, descendants of the Maitlands of Loughton Hall from whom my father had rented two houses and bought the second one, Journey's End, at the end of the war. Nadia played with Lady Maitland's twelve grandchildren when they were home and helped Mr Knight, the gardener, plant the seedlings. Sometimes she walked up the road to a neighbouring farm for eggs, and saw hares and pheasants. Once she had woken out of a nightmare at 3 a.m., with the wind moaning and the window clattering, and she said to me, "You weren't there," but otherwise nothing had been wrong. She seemed very natural.

After lunch we drove to Skegness and found a fair on the front. She rode on a merry-go-round horse and then went on the big wheel. I got into the float with her and for five minutes gripped the belt of her raincoat in sick tension while we soared up to sixty feet and down again. Afterwards we walked over a dune to the deserted yellow sand. The sea was a quarter of a mile away under a squally sky, and Nadia ran off until she was a mite crouching over some oyster shells. It began to drizzle and I watched how she was utterly involved in the present.

As I drove Nadia along a winding lane in the countryside to return her to Horncastle she gave a shout: "Look, here's where I walk for eggs, I live just down there." And, looking across hedges and green fields, I saw Harrington Hall's massive and splendidly ancient grey 17th-century façade. It had umpteen windows and a line of cars in the drive. Nadia directed me through the great iron gates to the flat over the garage, and she was immediately out of the car and knee-deep in daffodils, "finding leaves to weave into a Palm-Sunday cross". Knowing that the semi-walled garden was thought to have inspired lines about Rosa Baring in Tennyson's 'Maud', I stood among the daffodils and quoted:

Come into the garden, Maud,
For the black bat, night, has flown,
Come into the garden, Maud,
I am here at the gate alone.

(I was aware that Tennyson's home in the Isle of Wight, Farringford, was also thought to have inspired Maud's garden.) From 'Maud' had come the lines I quoted in Malta which Caroline had wanted to write down: "And ah for a man to arise in me,/That the man I am may cease to be!" I felt that that "man" had already arisen in me.

At that moment Caroline and David appeared in the drive. They were setting off to meet me in Horncastle, and were evidently taken aback that I was inside the gates. We all stood and talked briefly in light rain. Then way back at the Hall the front door opened and three tiny figures emerged by the parked cars. Caroline said, "You'll have to move, you're blocking the drive."

I went over to the daffodil bank and kissed Nadia, who was totally absorbed in the leaves. Then I got back into the car. From up the drive Lady Maitland's *cortège* hissed on the gravel. Abruptly I reversed out of the gates.

Intensity
I felt on the mend. In Essex my aunt Argie remarked to Ann while picking rhubarb, "Nick has looked so much better since he got his flat." I certainly felt an increased intensity and sense of meaning.

In May I took Ann out to Essex again. The woods were full of chestnut candles and bluebells, and I rejoiced in the may. In my *Diaries* I wrote:

Like a great tree I have several branches, all of which are me. My sap can put out leaves in poetry, journalism, novels, politics, teaching, religion etc. I am like the great plane-tree outside my window, and Nadia is the magnolia white and pure, hidden behind it. Or, I am like the chestnut tree, full of candles, each one an illumination.

In London I planted a window-box of red geraniums, and thrilled to a blackbird singing in the trees in Stanhope Gardens.

I took my 'backward' boys to Southwark Cathedral and gazed at the saints behind the altar, which included St Augustine of Hippo; at the tombs of the poet John Gower and the sermoniser Lancelot Andrewes; and at the 15th-century bosses on the ceiling which showed the medieval faces of gluttony and lying. I wrote in my *Diaries*: "The Church... is the world of eternity, the house of selflessness, outside which you leave behind 'I, I, I', in which you are clean – the world of eternity – and the world of time."[46]

Exhaustion, strain: end of my Second Mystic Life
The Mystic Way is full of instances of the swing back from Light to Darkness through exhaustion. The Light had burned away the impurities that had encrusted my soul, and had accelerated my transformation. But it had taken a toll on my health. I was in a feverish state of mind and again felt ill. I wrote: "I have great swollen glands and a sore throat."

On 17 May I had some sort of attack in Cliveden Place, near Sloane Square. I was driving back from school with Ann and felt ill. I couldn't breathe and felt peculiar. I felt myself blacking out. There was a singing in my ears, everything rippled away into remoteness, there was a twisting pain in my heart and pressure on my skull which I connected with my spine. I stopped the car and got out, and, thinking I was about to die, walked about. I was shaking and felt breathless.

I drove to a doctor, and a second attack began as I waited in the waiting-room. I was trembling and shaking and gasping. The doctor laid me on an examination bed and examined me. He said: "It's not a heart attack but exhaustion, strain. It's a warning, a finger from Heaven. You've been doing too much." I immediately grasped that my four April visions had left me with psychological wear-and-tear. The doctor prescribed equanil.

The next day there were more heart pains, and I visited my own doctor. He wanted to know what was causing my "overtiredness and overstrain",[47] and he sent me for a check-up at St Stephen's Hospital, which confirmed the diagnosis of the first doctor. I could not say that I had been operating as a British intelligence agent under the intolerable strain of surveillance squads and possible poisoning for months, and I carried on as if the attacks had not happened. But they had done something to my nerves, and I started to shake abominably. My hands shook. Two days later I still felt shaky.

Thinking I had nearly buckled under the strain of surveillance I wondered if the Elizabethan dramatist Christopher Marlowe had felt like this after his years of espionage, and had longed to fake his death and escape to the Continent. I wanted to get away from the world of intelligence to stabilise my health, but told myself that now I had a flat and had escaped Pussy-cat I was fine.

My Second Mystic Life ended with my exhaustion and visit to the doctor.

Nationalism: Rhodesia and Namibia

My nationalistic intelligence work had redoubled. In the course of April James Appleton was replaced by Joseph Winter, a tall, broad-shouldered, bluff fellow who always wore a dark suit, white shirt and tie and came across very confidently as though he were in charge of the entire Civil Service.

After my last meeting with James Appleton on 17 April some of my meetings with Joseph took place in Chelsea Cloisters, Sloane Avenue. (He told me how to avoid being followed to his front door after entering the block of apartments.) At the meetings there he placed a large, bulging, yellowy-brown, leather briefcase (with a handle at the top and brass locks on either side) on the carpet by my feet, and I wondered if it contained a tape-recorder. Some meetings with him took place late at night, sometimes in a pub at the top of Whitehall (I presumed near his office).

I believe that it was around this time that I was asked to change my code-name. I chose the new name of 'Esau', quoting the child's rhyme "I saw Esau sitting on a see-saw, how many 's's in that?" I added ironically, thinking of my supermarket bill in Tripoli and the pittance I was being paid, "Esau sold his birthright for a mess of pottage (lentil soup) when he was faint and 'at the point to die'."[48] At the time I did not explain what I meant. By 'birthright' I was thinking of my family and possible future children, and by 'mess of pottage' I meant 'earning enough for my family to survive'.

Rhodesia: Rev. Canaan Banana

I had been heavily involved with the Rhodesians: the various factions of the ANC, ZAPU and ZANU who were seeking to take over the emerging Zimbabwe. Through an Indian at Riverway, Saxena, I had met Eshmael Mlambo, the Rhodesian ANC representative (or "correspondent" as the ANC preferred to call him). I rang him a number of times and scooped the formation of the ANC. An article by me appeared in *Africa Confidential*, 'Rhodesia: ANC and others'.[49]

I had got to know the Rev. Canaan Banana, Bishop Muzorewa's Deputy, at the drinks party given by Lord Beaumont. Banana invited me back to his bedsit. He sat on the edge of his bed in his socks and told me how the ANC would take over Zimbabwe after a guerilla struggle. I passed this on to Joseph Winter in the Denmark, Old Brompton Road. I was later told by Joseph that this information had been described by the Foreign Secretary, Sir Alec Douglas-Home (Charlie's uncle), as "invaluable".

My attitude was that I was presenting the African point of view truly and accurately to the SIS and ultimately to Sir Alec Douglas-Home as Heath's 'unofficial Ambassador', and that I was therefore helping to shape British policy towards Rhodesia at a time when it seemed as if a deal between the UK and Rhodesia might leave the Africans out in the cold. By warning the British Government of the possibility of guerilla action in Rhodesia I was modifying British policy towards Rhodesia for the good of all parties.

In the first week of May Banana, Vice-President of the ANC, and Ronald Sadamba, the ANC's Deputy Secretary for External Affairs, met the British Foreign Secretary, Sir Alec Douglas-Home. The background to their visit was the Rhodesian settlement: Rhodesia had agreed to make concessions to African nationalism in return for its unilateral declaration of independence being recognised by the UK, and the Pearce Commission had to report on whether the settlement proposals would be approved by the Africans in Rhodesia. Banana and Sadamba had assumed that the Pearce report, which Lord Pearce had just handed to the British Government, would answer "on the basis of No" and were pressing for a constitutional conference with full African participation. I went to the Commons to hear their account of their meeting with Douglas-Home.

SWAPO's Namibia International Conference in Brussels
James Appleton had wanted me to attend a big Namibia International Conference in Brussels at the end of May, and I had visited SWAPO's London representative, Peter Katjavivi, and obtained an official invitation. I had written an article about the conference, which appeared in *Africa Confidential*.[50] There were many arrangements to make. Now I was in a flat I was more secure: a telephone had been installed immediately – although some people had to wait 18 months there was no wait if you were an agent – but I presumed it was bugged.

I booked a hotel for four nights. I met Joseph Winter at 4.15 on Wednesday 24 May and he went through a typed sheet of points he wanted me to investigate. The main one was the work of the UN Committee on Decolonisation: the Committee of 24 established by the General Assembly in 1960 to end colonialism and monitor independence in colonial countries. He did not tell me which 24 nations were represented, and in those pre-Google days I had virtually no background on what I was trying to find out.

I had told Mr Macho I could not be in on Friday as *The Times* had asked me to go to Brussels. As I drove him to and from school he was in no position to oppose me. I flew to Brussels by BEA at 7.15 p.m. The next day, 26 May, I attended the opening of the conference in the Palais des Congrès, seemingly among hundreds. It was a relatively high-level conference with many governmental ministers and leaders of movements. Its aim was to persuade the Western world and the UN to support the independence of South-West Africa as Namibia with Sam Nujoma, President of SWAPO, as leader. The two stars were Lord Caradon, a former UK Representative to the UN, and Bishop Colin Winter, an affable and idealistic Church leader who voiced the Church's support for SWAPO.

I had a lot of interviewing to do for my articles. Following my inner exhaustion it was good to recuperate in the outer world and to have some respite from further visions and raptures which would have increased my inner strain. I found the time very therapeutic, an escape from inner tension. I teamed up with the BBC representative, Michael Popham, who left a trail of hilarity in his wake. In the lift he told a funny story about Lord Caradon. The lift stopped in the middle of his story, and in walked Lord Caradon. We both went to interview the Action Commission and found it a model of inaction: one man snoozing and no one else there.

Everyone wanted to be interviewed, and Popham was permanently in the corridors, sound equipment massively bulky on his back, huge earphones over his ears, holding a large microphone under his interviewee's nose, his eyes meeting mine in unspoken irreverence. He had them queuing to be recorded, and as fast as he finished with one, I took over with my reporter's pad for The Times. I interviewed at least a couple of dozen after they had talked to him: an Ambassador from Guinea; ministers from Liberia, Kenya and Egypt; various members of the UN and of the Council for Namibia; the Secretary-General of the OAU (Organisation of African Unity); Marcelino dos Santos, a Mozambican poet, revolutionary and founding member of FRELIMO and subsequently Vice-President; Krishna Menon, the Indian nationalist, statesman and architect of non-alignment; and Sam Nujoma, President of SWAPO from 1960 (to 2007, and in due course of Namibia from 1990 to 2005).

I soon found there was no information to be had about the UN Committee on Decolonisation. Most of those I asked seemed to know nothing about it. I eventually found a representative of the Committee, a Mr Rosé, and interviewed him in French but he said so little of substance that I took no notes at all. Dos Santos congratulated the Committee on recognising the PAIGC, but that was known anyway.

On the last day of the conference I interviewed D. Arslan Humbaraci, who had just resigned as Director of External Relations on the Conference of Human Environment, Stockholm. He told me there was a deal between

UN Secretary-General Waldheim and the South-African regime under which South Africa would not transfer power over Namibia to the UN. I wrote a story on this which I offered to *The Times*, but when it was rejected by (according to Nick Ashford) a known South-African intelligence agent on the paper (Jerry Caminada, who went on to become foreign news editor before he died in 1985), I had it published in *The Guardian*.[51] SWAPO, and Nujoma, had been dreading a South African refusal to transfer power to the UN, and in his closing speech Nujoma announced that Lord Caradon would lead a delegation to the UN on behalf of the International Standing Committee of the Conference. I put this in an article for *Africa Confidential*.[52]

Invited to Tanzania by Minister of Foreign Affairs

My greatest triumph involved Tanzania. Early on I had interviewed John Malecela, Tanzania's Minister of Foreign Affairs. He seemed to know that I represented Heath and he invited me back to his hotel, the Hotel Metropole, for a long interview on the last evening. During this interview he invited me to Tanzania in the autumn if *The Times* would send me. I wrote a piece on him in *Africa Confidential*[53] and wrote a paragraph about him into an article in *The Times*.

I flew back to London on 29 May and saw Joseph Winter at 10 a.m. the next morning. (It was now half-term.) I thought I had done well at the conference, having covered it in articles, interviewed a couple of dozen high-profile people, scooped the UN-South Africa deal and received an invitation to Tanzania, but all Joseph Winter wanted to know about was the UN Committee on Decolonisation. He said I should have found out more and warned that there would not be any further trips abroad if I could not obtain fuller answers to questions I was set.

I was indignant. There was nothing on decolonization at the conference, and I had shown initiative in latching on to the big issues. There was now a rigidness somewhere in the SIS – in his superior? – that contradicted the realities of gathering intelligence which cannot be approached with preconceived, inflexible ideas. It looked as if someone had apportioned what the SIS needed to know and arbitrarily doled it out between several agents without telling them to ignore all other topics. I had not been told to concentrate on half a dozen minor questions – *minutiae* – and exclude all others.

I was an independent, which is why I was only paid £50 a month. I would not be treated as if I belonged to their bureaucracy on several hundred pounds a month and was controlled by them. In Libya I had been in charge and had shared what I found out with Andrew Mackenzie. There was a weakness in the SIS's communication: I had not been told to ignore everything except the specific tasks I had been given. I communicated some of this indignation to Joseph Winter, who later told me he had fed it back into the system.

Rhodesia: I collect four ANC Zimbabweans from the Foreign Office
Joseph Winter now wanted me to clinch the invitation to Tanzania. He asked me to write to Malecela and to Tanzania's High Commissioner in London. I had to obtain a visa, and I made it clear that the Tanzanian Government would have to pay my fares.

While I waited for my visit to Tanzania to be confirmed I saw Mlambo, who told me that the ANC would press for a constitutional conference. I put this in an article in *Africa Confidential*.[54] I met Noronha-Rodrigues and Chen several times.

In June I followed Nujoma's trip to China and visited Mr Yu En-kuang of the *Hsinhua* News Agency again. He gave me a story about the Chinese Ambassador to Morocco, and I wrote a short article on him which was not taken by *Africa Confidential*. I sent the article to Mr Yu.

On 18 July Jorge gave me a confidential story of a global deal between President Nixon and the Soviet leader Brezhnev. He told me that the recent reconciliation between Angola's MPLA and GRAE (now FNLA) had to be seen within the context of this Nixon-Brezhnev deal. I wrote an article for *The Guardian*, which was enthusiastically accepted and mysteriously never printed. It eventually appeared in *Africa Confidential*.[55] I reckoned the story was probably Chinese anti-Soviet propaganda, given to Jorge by Mr Yu, and probably true.

(I next ran into Jorge in Foyles on 11 February 1974, when he was still UNITA's Minister for Foreign Affairs and running UNITA's war in Angola. Weirdly I was browsing in the same first-floor bay of shelves as Orson Welles, who was massively studying titles looking like Harry Lime, who he played in the 1949 film *The Third Man*. Jorge greeted me, and we had a short chat that Orson Welles could not fail to have overheard. It was the last time I saw him for in 1983 he was hacked to death in Angola and his body burned. It was reported in the press that Savimbi regarded him as a rival for the leadership of UNITA.)

I was again involved with the Rhodesian ANC. At the end of July Eshmael Mlambo told me that he was taking two of the four founder-members of the ANC, Michael Mawema and Edson Zvobgo (who had recently been released from prison) and another Rhodesian to the British Foreign and Commonwealth Office to have confidential talks with Baroness Tweedsmuir, Minister of State (who in 1948 had married author John Buchan's heir). The four ANC Zimbabweans were to discuss the settlement and the Pearce Commission's report. They hoped to extract a statement that the British Government would not accept Rhodesia's "underhand manoeuvring" regarding the settlement.

Mlambo asked me to collect them all from Lady Tweedsmuir's door after their meeting as they had no transport. I was granted a permit to enter the Foreign Office and go upstairs and wait for them. I greeted Mlambo, Mawema, Zvobgo and their colleague as they came out of the Minister of State's door and led them downstairs. All four of them piled into my green Volkswagen. One sat in the passenger seat and three sat along the back seat, their heads bent forward because of the low roof. I debriefed them as I drove them across the river.

I put their interview with Baroness Tweedsmuir in *Africa Confidential*.[56] After that I wrote a story on the banning of SWAPO's acting President, Nathaniel Mahuilili.[57] Then Chen rang me and gave me a story about Roy Sawh, the pro-Maoist Guyanan, which I put in *The Times Diary*.[58]

I had won through to illumination and unitive living despite being compelled to think nationalistically and patriotically in my work. I longed to withdraw from my interviewing and journalism to reflect my inner visions in poetry and become a literary writer. But I was locked into the world of intelligence, and I could not see how I could escape.

Episode 15:

Meaning and Disenchantment

Years: 1972–1973
Locations: London; Dar es Salaam; Tanga; Zanzibar; Mlimba; Cornwall
Works: *The Gates of Hell*; *A Bulb in Winter*; *A Spade Fresh with Mud*
Initiatives: invitation to Tanzania; Nyerere permits visit to restricted section of Chinese Tanzam railway; countering Chinese influence in Tanzania

"The One remains, the many change and pass;
Heaven's light forever shines, Earth's shadows fly;
Life, like a dome of many-coloured glass,
Stains the white radiance of Eternity."
Shelley, 'Adonais'

In my next episode the meaning I was finding in life was in conflict with my growing disenchantment with my intelligence work.

Disenchantment: preparations for Tanzania

My Second Mystic Life in which I had been at one with the universe and truth had come to an end in May 1972, with my exhaustion and visit to my doctor. Suddenly I was plunged into a new intelligence experience of mendacity, division and disunity, which I abhorred.

My impending visit to Tanzania required a Heraclean effort of determination, will-power, memory and initiative, but as events unfolded I progressed more deeply towards a vision of the unity of the universe and of the meaning of life – and became increasingly disenchanted with my secret work and the increasing insensitivity and ruthlessness of the intelligence world.

I meet Pita-Kabisa again at the Tanzanian High Commission: visa for Tanzania

I was at last asked to go to the Tanzanian High Commission. Joseph Winter had told me that they would vet me, and that if I passed their vetting I would be granted a visa to go to Tanzania. I arrived at the High Commission and was shown into a downstairs room with a desk.

A coal-black young Tanzanian in a suit rose and shook my hand and said, "Hello again from Worcester College."

"Pita-Kabisa," I said. "You were in the Riding Stables. (*See* p.91.) You left the college, and I moved into your room."

It was extraordinary, I was being vetted by my fellow-undergraduate, Pita-Kabisa. He had read Law under A.B. Brown during his first two terms, as I had. We recalled our days at Oxford under Masterman. He told me that his parents had recalled him to Tanganyika, and that Tanganyika and Zanzibar had united in 1964 to form the United Republic of Tanzania. He told me he was living at 29 Mayfield Gardens. He passed me on to Msolomi of the High Commission, who asked me questions.

Pita-Kabisa had me to lunch on 7 August. He booked a table at a French restaurant in Jermyn Street not far from Piccadilly Circus. He told me that Msolomi was from a different faction and was his rival. Coincidentally, at the next table sat Robin Blackburn, another of A.B. Brown's Law undergraduates, who had become a solicitor. Three of that 1958/59 year at Worcester College were sitting within talking distance, and again I wondered if our coming-together was accidental or Providential.

I was now told that I would be receiving a visa to enter Tanzania in mid-September. Joseph Winter asked me to visit Mr Yu again and ask him for a contact in Dar es Salaam who would help me go on the Chinese Tanzam railway, which *The Guardian* had asked me to cover. Mr Yu eventually gave me the name of Mr Shu, who was on the NCNA (New China News Agency).

Course on Report-writing

Joseph Winter now arranged for me to have a two-day course in Report-writing. It was a two-day-long, one-to-one tutorial, and was conducted by an elderly academic in the Embankment flat with the white carpet. Joseph Winter introduced us, made sure we both knew to keep our feet on the carpet-pieces and left for the day. As Nadia was staying with me in Stanhope Gardens and Ann was visiting her mother in Cornwall, Joseph's secretary looked after Nadia during each of the two days.

The tutor and I sat next to each other in comfortable armchairs so I could see the model reports on his knees. My feet were on a small piece of white carpet and he had a small piece of white carpet – a prayer-mat – under his feet too. He knew I was going to Tanzania.

He said I would have to write half a dozen reports and gave me their titles. He showed me the civil-service lay-out for each report. At the top of each report there was a sub-heading 'Sources'. The paragraphs all had to be numbered. Fact had to be separated from opinion. I was taught to summarise the five newspaper articles I proposed to write in one report; and to present my day-by-day programme in Tanzania in chronological order in another. In a third report I was taught to list all the personalities I would meet in Tanzania under different headings: 'Ministry of Foreign Affairs'; 'Ministry of Information and Broadcasting'; 'Zanzibar'; 'Tanga region'; 'liberation movements'; 'Tanzam railway'; and 'Miscellaneous'. I was taught how to present reports on: the Chinese; decentralisation; *ujamaa* villages; guerilla camps; and TANU (the Tanganyika African National Union). In some cases one report would include several such headings. The course covered the areas I would be focusing on, which, I was told, I would be asked to memorise. I was given instruction in how to memorise 30 sentences, by linking them to rooms in a very large house.

It was a very comprehensive course, and I was on quite familiar terms with the tutor by the end of the second day. After we had finished and were chatting, I said to him: "I sometimes wonder who I'm really working for. In Libya I was confident that it was the SIS because my controller corroborated this. In London, I'm not so sure. There seem to be different methods. I'm being asked to target specific points and you have been teaching me how to write my intelligence up. But who is ultimately seeing what I am producing? The Chief of MI6? The Prime Minister? Who ultimately is behind the organisation I'm working for?"

Told I am working for 'Rothschilds'

I was seeking to establish who I was primarily working for: the SIS or Heath. I had not thought there would be another organisation in the background. He said, "It's not widely known that the Rothschild family control MI6. They also control the Bank of England. That's been the case ever since the Battle of Waterloo in 1815. You are ultimately working for the Rothschilds."

His reply stunned and shocked me. At first I thought he might be teasing me, but he was deadly serious. I was flabbergasted. What did he mean?

At that moment James Appleton looked in. I had first met him in this same white-carpeted apartment. He had come with Joseph's secretary, who was returning my daughter, to escort us out and lock up after us – and make sure we had not marked the white carpet. He asked how the course had gone.

The tutor said, "Very well. He's got the hang of what he has to do and will be able to write reports in the correct format. But we've had some questions. Just now we had, 'Who am I ultimately working for?'"

James Appleton smiled but said nothing. No more was made of my question. But I took the tutor's answer away with me and pondered the implications of my working ultimately for the Rothschild family, if what he had said was true. It was as if an earthquake had brought my assumptions about the SIS crashing down.

I collected my daughter from Joseph Winter's secretary and took her back to my flat, and that night I was full of disquiet. In Libya it had been so clear-cut. I was working for my country, the UK, first of all to control Libyan oil and then to oppose Gaddafi. In London I had been told that I was Heath's 'unofficial Ambassador'. Victor, Lord Rothschild was head of his think tank. But who were the Rothschilds, and how did they come to have such influence over the British State? I wanted to delve into history and find out how they could wield such influence that they were in effect my employer. Had James Bond been working for the Rothschilds without realising it? I had thought I was taking risks among surveillance squads to help Britain – my England – even though I now had an internationalist outlook. I did not want to be working for the Rothschilds. The tutor's answer nagged in my mind and led to the research that produced *The Syndicate*.

Briefing for Tanzania
I was not too happy at being asked to write reports in a bureaucratic format and lay-out. I saw my job (for which I received £50 per month 'after tax') as to gather intelligence, not to assemble it in a form that would be palatable to Whitehall mandarins. It still irked that they had not helped with my removal expenses. I said some of this to Joseph Winter when we next met in the Denmark one evening so he could brief me on Tanzania.

He quickly said that while the Tanzanian Ministry of Foreign Affairs would be paying for my air tickets and hotel bills during my visit to Tanzania the SIS would be paying my normal school salary for the time I was away plus their own salary and "initiative bonuses" (a term that had not been mentioned before). He said that a priority was to reach the restricted Mlimba-Makumbako section of the Tanzam railway. I raised the question of safety. He said it would be safe for me to go because I had the word of the Minister of Foreign Affairs, John Malecela, as my bond. I was under his protection.

Joseph Winter then gave me a list of some three dozen questions to memorise. I had to study the typed sheet, memorise every word, applying the techniques the tutor had taught me, and then repeat every word on the typed sheet of paper before giving it back to him. It took me half an hour to memorise everything. Joseph tested me. He listened as I recited what I had remembered, and at the end he said: "I reckon your memory is bloody brilliant."

At the end he said I should try to secure an invitation for Edward Heath, the Prime Minister, to visit Tanzania. "Try and get Malecela to invite the Prime Minister." From a bag he supplied me with a cassette-player and a camera that took good pictures of interiors.

A telex was sent from Tanzania to say that I must be in Dar es Salaam by 14 September. Mr Macho had left Riverway at the end of the summer term, and I now had the embarrassing – indeed, irksome – task of visiting the new Head at his house in London SE9 and (after introducing myself) of explaining that I needed to be released from school for the first two or three weeks of the coming term.

The new Head, Mr Wright, turned out to be a bespectacled, shambling, stooping man in his late fifties. He seemed to know what I was about to say and immediately encouraged me to go to Tanzania. I would have to forego my teaching salary while I was away, but I had already been told this would be made up by Joseph Winter's organisation.

I give John Biggs-Davison a lift
About this time I was driving my green Volkswagen Beetle in the Cromwell Road when I spotted my local Epping-Forest MP Biggs-Davison walking very slowly. I stopped and wound the window down and called to him, "Want a lift?"

He said he was going to the Brompton Oratory. He was living in Hereford Square, and he went to the Oratory to pray.

He got in and I told him I was going to have a look at Tanzania. I stopped outside the Oratory and he asked rather disparagingly before he got out, "Are you taking this car to Tanzania?"

I had not been able to publicise his book, but I had alerted him of my impending departure and if anything happened to me in Tanzania I was sure he would raise my name in Parliament as he had done in Libya.

'Security'

Meanwhile my Way of Detachment had brought me into harmony regarding Nadia's situation. There was still disquieting conflict, but I neutralised it by reacting to it harmoniously.

Towards the end of half-term on Friday 2 June Ann and I drove to Horncastle in Lincolnshire, booked in at The George, received Nadia and took her out for the day.

It was raining when we returned her at 6 p.m. Caroline and David were waiting in their car outside the churchyard. They both got out and we all had a few words in the rain, during which I, trying to be pleasant, said (recalling what Caroline had told me) that I gathered they were now married.

David said curtly and defensively, "You don't need to know. That's an unreasonable thing to say." He went on to say, "I know what work you're doing in London, I know all about the Africans you are meeting."

It was raining more heavily and, taken aback and wanting to learn more, I suggested we walked to the nearby George. Caroline, Ann and Nadia sat down by a log fire and after I carried their drinks over and returned for our drinks, David said to me, standing by the bar, "I'm in Red Security."[1] I had never heard of 'Red Security'. Had I heard correctly? "I know about you through my work in Security. As I see it, one of us will have to leave our job."

To me 'Security' meant MI5. As he was under the Ministry of Defence I wondered if it meant Defence Intelligence Security 5 or DI5 (often referred to as 'Security'). I was not sure what he had meant, or whether he really knew about my intelligence work. I wondered if 'Red Security' identified Communist threats during the Cold War at that time, and if he thought I was a Communist because I had been interviewing Communists.

We had to rejoin the others but Caroline and David suggested that Ann and I should join them at Harrington Hall after dinner. (It was now too late to eat – in the provinces, dinner was really early – and Ann and I found take-away fish and chips.)

At Harrington Hall

Ann and I drove to Harrington Hall and sat in their rented flat over the garage and near the walled garden. It was strange to be sitting opposite my ex-wife, who looked very blonde, among our old rugs and pictures. It did not occur to us that she might be pregnant. After a while David said that he and I were going out for a drink. Leaving Ann with Caroline, he drove me to a nearby pub. There he explained that besides being a navigator of Phantoms he was in 'Security' and that he knew about me through his work. He said he had to declare who he came into contact with, and he would have to declare our meetings that day.

From what he told me I concluded that 'Security' *did* mean MI5. I asked him about his meeting with Caroline on Malta, wondering if MI5 had asked him to interview her. He seemed to miss the point. He said, "For her, Malta was important. It was a way of saying 'No more'."

I did not point out that he had interfered. I asked point-blank, "Did Security put you up to getting to know Caroline on Malta, as a window on me?"

He changed the subject without confirming or denying that MI5 had put him up to meeting her.

I thought of all the people linked with the KGB I had been involved with in Libya, such as Viktor and Okoro, and all the African guerillas with links to the Soviet Union or the Chinese I had interviewed in London, and I could understand why, if they had not been told otherwise, 'Security' might think I was a Communist. But I could not explain to him that I was Heath's 'unofficial Ambassador' or discuss my role with him. My lips had to remain sealed.

We returned to Harrington Hall. After an hour Ann and I returned to The George.

Meaning: great spring of time and eternity
The meaning of life

The next morning, a Saturday, Caroline and David brought Nadia to The George at 10. Ann and I took her to Skegness and spent the morning on the beach. On the way back we drove round Tennyson country and visited the Old Rectory, Tennyson's birthplace.

At the end of our day out, Caroline and David met us for a drink and safe small talk in a pub near Somersby, which had a garden. Leaving Nadia with them, Ann and I drove back to The George and were just in time for dinner.

The next morning we all drove to Tattershall Castle and walked through woods full of sunshine and bluebells to the Bluebell. Caroline and David walked ahead, sometimes holding hands, and Ann and I walked behind with Nadia, listening to the flowing call of a cuckoo. There were skylarks over green corn. Nadia stopped at a fallen tree and counted the rings. She said, "It's 33 years old." (I had just turned 33.) I was no longer attached, I had let it all go. I soaked in the slow rhythms of eternity among the bluebells in the countryside and felt free of the past.

I was now full of meaning and purpose. The next week I took my ESN boys to All Hallows, which is on the Thames estuary. The boys caught crabs and I stopped them trying to pull their legs off. I spent a long time looking out to where the river becomes the sea and thought of my life as a river that opened to a universal expanse.

In June I had a card from Tuohy, who was in Australia: a Flemish tapestry of a unicorn being killed by hunters. I knew he saw the unicorn as representing the artist and I wondered if he had an insight into the surveillance squads that hunted me.

I met Ricky in the Denmark, who told me: "Your 'eternal side' is very Wordsworthian – 'a dim and undetermined sense/Of unknown modes of being' and 'a spirit that rolls through all things'."[2] He said that like Goethe's Faust, I practised "solution by action".

Soon afterwards John Ezard asked how I thought my poetic work would be received by the Age, and I replied by quoting Pound's 'Hugh Selwyn Mauberley':

> The age demanded an image
> Of its accelerated grimace....
> Not, not certainly, the obscure reveries
> Of the inward gaze.

I was saying that the Age demanded the meaninglessness of a Francis Bacon, not images of soulful meaning which the true artist produces. I said we were living (to paraphrase Hamlet) in a time that is out of joint, and "there are more things in Heaven and Earth, Horatio/Than are dreamt of in your philosophy". I told him that my work would defy the Age.

In early July I was pondering opposites. Nadia came. I took her down into the Gardens beneath my window and we walked round the white magnolia. We see-sawed and I put her on the swing. I heard about her school. When I returned her to Dulwich, Caroline came to the gate in a maroon velvety dress, nursing a swollen belly.

The next day I met Ricky, and as my *Diaries* record I approached the meaning of life through opposites:

> By the Socratic method I got him to agree that in Nishiwaki's words, $(+A) + (-A) = 0$. He wanted the negative Beckett way and the positive Faustian way substituted in the first side of the equation, but after careful questioning finally conceded that it was the World of Time (Beckett and Faust representing different aspects) + the World of Eternity = the Whole, i.e. that time and eternity are in an indivisible unity, a synthesis. Cf Blake, "Eternity is in love with the productions of time." So it is not pain *versus* joy, but pain *plus* joy – so Colin Wilson is to that extent wrong. Ditto Sartre (Being *versus* Nothingness). There is life, and so there must be death – for without death there could not be life. One cannot find a meaning in the world of language (which is time), the world of eternity has no language. The Whole is therefore indescribable, and one should

not explain it to Faust. Everything is opposites. cf Pascal. So Beckett is wrong, for there is neither pessimistic nor the simple Christian optimistic, but both together.... Life is a unity formed of a dialectic that is eternal.[3]

I went back to my flat and pondered my insight. My lost family and my inner peace – the two were contradictory. Pondering on my mixed feelings, I felt again that life was an eternal dialectic between misery and joy, despair and hope, the world of time and the world of eternity. There would be a thousand agonies ahead, but there would also be perhaps fifty joys, and the opposites could not be understood in terms of each other. They had to be seen as parts of a greater whole. Or, as Nishiwaki had told me in a shabby restaurant with sawdust on the floor, $(+A) + (-A) = 0$. "Zero,... Great Nothing."

Immediately I was trembling on the verge of a great insight. Life's mysteries suddenly fell away. There was plus *and* minus, time *and* eternity, life *and* death: they were necessary to each other, there could not be one without the other. But it was the whole unity that gave the meaning. I looked out at the Gardens and my reasoning gave way to existential perception.

Then I saw a postcard that Nadia had left on the bed, of the Zen Ryoanji Stone Garden. (She had brought it with her, and years later it appeared on the back of my *Selected Poems*.) It showed pebbles round three rocks, and I already knew that it could be interpreted as earth or clouds and mountains; or as sea or sand and rocks. All stones were parts of one stone, and in the same way, all existence came down to a unity that was infinite.

I looked back at the Gardens. The foliage of the great plane-trees obscured the white magnolia, and I felt a hint of a similarity. All the many trees and plants and crawling things in the earth came down to a unity.

Suddenly everything was blindingly clear. The Gardens were like a *spring*, a spring of leaves and seeds, a teeming, abundant, never-ending flow of opposites that went on gushing from nowhere, like the bubbles that wobbled up for thousands of years from the Saharan spring. All life was a spring from a void, a spring of water, of seeds, of creatures, of people, of words.

In an instant, I grasped the meaning of life for the first time. Seizing my pen I wrote in frenzied haste:

If I look at a Chinese character it has significance. If I understand Chinese, it has meaning. If I look at the Stone Garden, it has significance. If I under-stand the idea of unity, it has meaning. So it is of life. If I look at the world it has significance. If I feel the flow in it, it has meaning. Wordsworth sees the ideogram and describes it, but does not give us its meaning. He doesn't know it, he guesses at it.... *Tao*, the Void, produced the One which produced multiplicity. The Void, negative and fertile, is the spring.[4]

I had seen that significance is a two-way relationship (as, in Japan, Fitzsimmons had once remarked), and that meaning has a third dimension concealed within it. Now I knew: all images have meaning, all images teem from the Great Meaning, the One which is also a Great Nothing, a fertile Void.

Then I felt very deeply that the miseries and joys were all reconciled in the Great Spring that flowed through everything and would gush opposites and contradictions for thousands of years to come. I realised that to that fountain of abundance there was no difference between misery and joy which, being parts of the same, were ultimately the same. I felt the griefs would not have the same hold over me, I would be free of them. And as for my raptures, I felt they would be unions with the One. I would know what was going on now. I felt I would live in the peace which passeth all understanding, largely beyond emotions.

I felt that a part of me belonged to the whole. And though I had no idea what might happen to me when I died, I believed so instinctively in the importance of the Great Spring that I did not think it impossible that my "eternal self" might survive in it, in some form. That, however, was mere speculation. What mattered immediately was that I had escaped the chains of emotion and self, I could fulfil my destiny. I felt I could go no further in my inner life for the time being. I had found.

I symbolised what I had found in my present for Ann's birthday. I gave her an onyx marble egg from Italy, which was like the Chinese *Taoist* eggs I had seen in Peking. The egg was an image of the One with many opposite lines and colours, wavy lines of the sea, the furrowed earth, clouds and contours, and somewhere, it contained the fleck of a seed, an egg, a mountain top. The egg symbolised the universe, Reality, a heart, though only he who has eyes to see could see it. The egg reflected the world from its centre. It united time and eternity, now and forever. Ann now began collecting interesting specimens of different stones.

Cornwall: return to Portmellon
In August I took the train to Cornwall and spent three days with Ann and her mother, who lived in a bungalow on the outskirts of St Austell. Ann's late father's car was still in the garage, and the first evening she drove me a mile and a half to Charlestown, a 1790s village which still had a working harbour with a dock and china-clay chutes.

We went on to Portmellon and drank at the Rising Sun by the watersplash where I told Colin Wilson in January 1961: "I shall become a wanderer, an exile, for ten years." It was like a homecoming. Now, eleven years later, I felt I had returned. We drove to the end of Colin Wilson's lane, where there was now a forbidding notice: "No Visitors Unless by Appointment." We came back via Porthpean, where the stars were very bright and we identified the Pole Star and the Plough. I did not know until years later that on that day, 9 August, Caroline married David at Spilsby Register Office.

The next day we spent roasting in the sun on Charlestown beach under the Harbourmaster's House, and watching crabs like armoured tanks in a large rock pool. We went on to Carlyon Bay where waves boomed in the caves beneath and gulls shrieked round the gorse points. We lay on the cliff tops where bees hummed in the wild flowers and the sea sparkled. In the evening we went to Fowey and walked through the tiny streets and took the ferry to Polruan, a village set on a hill. It grew dark as we returned, and the sea was black and silver.

Health
When I got back to London, Nadia came to stay again – she had spent some days with me in July – and I felt ill. I recorded in my *Diaries*:

> Giddy, as though I am about to faint. Overwork.... Ever since I had these experiences... my psychic life has been brittle.... 1972 is above all the year of ill health for me when I found, when I ended my search, when my health began to suffer after all the demands I have made on my nervous system.[5]

I took Nadia to Worthing again so she could stay at Sompting Abbots, a great house where children could have a few days of activity courses. I again stayed at the Anchorage, and recuperated. I visited the rose garden in Sompting church and saw each rose as a living, rooted person. I took Nadia back to Peterborough.

At the beginning of September I suddenly and impulsively decided to stop drinking alcohol. I resolved to go on to soft drinks, to drink alcohol occasionally but not regularly to lengthen my evenings, break another chain, free myself from craving and advance the purposive life. This decision, which I implemented, was a further consequence of my illumination and four April visions, and marked a further purgation, a further cleansing and detaching of my spirit from my senses.

Meaning and disenchantment: replacing Chinese influence in Tanzania
I leave for Tanzania
I left for Tanzania on 10 September, having bought suitably tropical clothes from Airey and Wheeler (for which I was given a clothing allowance). Joseph

Winter made sure I had anti-malaria tablets and stressed that I should take talcum powder for "daily dusting" in the hot, insanitary conditions I might encounter round the Tanzam railway. Pita-Kabisa came to the airport to see me off.

We flew through the night non-stop to Nairobi, and descended in an orange dawn. We flew on to Mombasa past Mt Kilimanjaro, a black blanc-mange with icing on its top. Mombasa was sticky and an orange bird sang from a giant tree. We flew on over beautiful Indian-Ocean islands and arrived at Dar es Salaam, where I was met by a young official of the Ministry of Foreign Affairs, Milao. A chauffeur drove us to the Twiga Hotel in Independence Avenue.

Dar es Salaam
Dar es Salaam (which means 'haven of peace') was really an arched yellow-and-white village on the coast with a lot of coconut and mango trees. Its outskirts merged with the surrounding bush and contain rural encamp-ments and markets. My chauffeur drove me to the Ministry of Foreign Affairs at 8.45 on the first day, 12 September 1972, to meet John Malecela, the Minister of Foreign Affairs, who had been appointed the previous February.

The Cold War, a covert 'Third World War' fought as a series of limited local wars by Communist and Western enemies armed with nuclear missiles, had become world-wide since its start in 1944. Tanzania had been Marxist and Moscow-aligned since 1964. In 1972 there was a Soviet threat in the Indian Ocean, and Chinese influence dominated Tanzania through their building of the Tanzam railway. My task was to counter the Soviet and Chinese presences by strengthening Western – i.e. British – influence in Tanzania during this hot phase of the Cold War. Tanzanian-British relations had been very bad since President Nyerere visited London in 1970 to oppose Heath's plan to sell arms to South Africa. His visit was unsuccessful – it ended in "irreconcilable differences" – and resulted in a Tanzanian embargo on British aid. Another of my tasks was to get the embargo lifted.

I waited an hour and a half to see Malecela, and then saw him for a minute as he was leaving for a Cabinet meeting. He asked me to return in the afternoon.

I asked my chauffeur to drive me to Pita-Kabisa's brother-in-law and to the Chinese Mr Shu of the NCNA (New China News Agency) so I could ask him to arrange for me to go on the Tanzam railway. He was out, and I left him a message.

Interview with John Malecela, Minister of Foreign Affairs
In the afternoon I interviewed Malecela for two hours. Wearing a round-necked, colourless, short-sleeved top, he said that a programme had been

drawn up for me which allowed one day for the Tanzam railway – he said I would not be able to go on the railway as it needed seven days' clearance from the Chinese – and that I would not be able to get into "a freedom-fighter camp".

But he still seemed to assume that I had a direct line to Heath, and he spoke to me very frankly as if talking with the British Government. I soon grasped that Tanzania was virtually bankrupt and that, having got the Chinese to build the Tanzam railway, was trying to winkle further money out of the West (though being intensely proud and independent). It was clear that I had been invited to inform the British people that Tanzania was not a Chinese province, that the Tanzanian *ujamaa* ('co-operative farm') system was different from the Chinese commune system, and that Tanzania needed aid from other countries besides China.

Malecela told me that Tanzania wanted to repay the loan from China that built the Tanzam railway as early as possible. (Milao told me two days later that Malecela had refused a new loan from China when he was recently in Peking.) I proposed that Sir Alec Douglas-Home, the British Foreign Secretary, should visit Tanzania to discuss giving British aid to help Tanzania become less dependent on China, and that there should be a further visit by Edward Heath, the British Prime Minister, to let the world know that Tanzania was now in the British rather than the Chinese camp. Malecela agreed to my proposal.

Throughout our two-hour conversation Malecela gave the impression of assuming that I was Heath's 'unofficial Ambassador', and I wondered if word of my activities had spread from the KGB to the Tanzanian Government. Once again, I seemed to be operating openly, without cover. I was now convinced that I had been invited to Tanzania as a known British agent who could inform Heath and the British Government that Tanzania wished to move towards the West. Out of this interview I wrote an article for *The Times*, 'Tanzania gets off the Peking gravy train'.[6] (*See* Appendix 5, p.533.) In this and other articles I reflected the will of the Africans and tried to tell the truth about Tanzania's situation.

Ujamaas *near Tanga*

The first part of my programme had me flying to Tanga, which is on the Tanzanian-Kenyan border. There I was to visit *ujamaa* villages and see for myself that they were different from Chinese communes.

The next morning I was up at 5 a.m. but my chauffeur did not turn up. Milao, who had my ticket, phoned from the airport to say we had missed the plane. I had a free day in Dar, and we travelled the next morning, on 14 September. The chauffeur again did not turn up, but this time Milao collected me in a taxi.

In Tanga we checked in at the Sea View Hotel. I was taken to meet the Regional Commissioner and in the afternoon I toured the bush in a TANU (Tanzania African National Union) Land Rover. We visited Kicheba and Mbambara *ujumaa* villages: co-operative or collective farms that looked like glorified allotments run on socialist principles. The *ujamaa* system brought groups of 100–200 or more families together, the theory being that only when families live and work together could land be developed, incomes raised, schools and hospitals built and economic use made of tractors. The next morning we visited Vuo and Moa *ujumaa* villages. They were mainly fields of head-high sisal and maize.

In all these *ujumaa* villages Africans planted crops and shared them out according to the work they put in. I spoke with local TANU officials and saw how the Party controlled the villages. We visited clearings with thatched huts, from one of which the local witch-doctor ran out to greet me, shaking his bones.

Back in Dar, blocked from going on the Tanzam railway: Makumbako, second rebuff
When I returned to Dar it transpired that one of the reasons I had been invited to Tanzania was to cover a *coup*, if it succeeded, by supporters of Milton Obote, President of Uganda until he was overthrown by Gen. Amin in 1971 and fled to Tanzania. On 16 September Malecela left for New York so that he could be there when the *coup* took place. There was Tanzanian involvement in the *coup* as Malecela knew in advance that it would happen. The *coup* was attempted almost immediately, and failed.

Malecela stayed on in New York to limit the damage, and in his absence my position deteriorated: I now received little help from the Ministry of Foreign Affairs. My chauffeur disappeared ("sacked", Milao told me) and Milao himself became hard to obtain over the telephone. I was frequently told there was "no line" or "that number is out of order".

I had ignored Malecela's statement that there would not be time to see the Tanzam railway properly, and I had asked Milao if I could go to Makumbako on the Chinese railway. To go there was one of the tasks Joseph Winter had set me. My request was rejected by Milao (the second time I had been rebuffed on Makumbako, Malecela's rebuff being the first). The Ministry of Foreign Affairs saw me as having been inflicted on them by Malecela. To the Ministry of Foreign Affairs I was in Tanzania solely to arrange British aid and should not be seeing the Chinese railway.

I visited the NCNA (New China News Agency) again and this time I was swept in by Mr Shu himself with cries of mirth, was seated in an armchair and offered Coca-Cola and cigarettes before I had even said hello. Mr Shu was full of smiles but with elusive eyes that hid behind his horn-rims.

I explained: "*The Guardian* want an article on the railway. Mr Yu suggested that you might be able to help. The Ministry of Foreign Affairs is being difficult: Mr Malecela said I would not have time to see the Tanzam railway properly. I want to go to Makumbako."

Mr Shu was sympathetic but said, "You must try again with the Ministry of Foreign Affairs, there's nothing I can do. And I don't know anybody on the railway. So many Chinese work there. Have another Coca-Cola."

I pushed the idea of Makumbako temporarily to one side. One of my briefs was to get into a guerilla camp. On this I had also been rebuffed by Malecela. I spoke to the key figure in the OAU (Organisation of African Unity) in Dar, Major Mbita, over the phone on 16 September, but he was just off to Lusaka and "too busy" to see me until he returned. The same day I met Laban Oyaka, the Assistant Executive Secretary of the OAU in the Twiga bar at lunch-time.

Interviews with guerillas and terrorists: Chitepo and Moyo
As a means to the end of getting into a guerilla camp, I had drawn up a programme of interviewing the representatives of liberation movements such as FROLIZI (Front for the Liberation of Zimbabwe), FRELIMO, MPLA and PAIGC. On 17 September I met the two Rhodesian leaders of ZANU and ZAPU, Herbert Chitepo and Jason Moyo, who together formed the Patriotic Front that had been responsible for several explosions and deaths inside Rhodesia. They lived in rooms next door to each other at the Forodhani Hotel, and met me together. Moyo – then the most wanted Zimbabwean, as notorious as the Head of the IRA – was tall, slim and quiet while the bespectacled Chitepo was chubby and more talkative. They suggested we went for a walk.

My predicament as an intelligence agent could not have been brought home to me more starkly. I was on my own. There was no back-up or support. I was thrown back on my inner resources. I was with the heads of two feared terrorist organisations who had killed many times. I was unarmed and at their mercy, with only my nimble wits to protect me.

For half an hour I walked between them out into the bush. Although they were both notorious terrorists and I was putting myself into harm's way, indeed great danger, I trusted my instinct that they would not harm me. I was in a rapport with them and was a journalist, and could be of use to them. I pointed out that I felt as if I were walking between two Russian Nihilists, anarchistic terrorists such as Bakunin and Kropotkin in the 1860s and 1870s. I asked them whether they did not feel responsible for the deaths they had caused and what it was like living on the run. Moyo talked at some length about planting a bomb on a railway line in Rhodesia. I said that the British intelligence agent T.E. Lawrence had blown up railway lines while leading guerillas against the Ottoman Turks, and they were both aware of this. After a while they were speaking to me on an equal footing.

I asked if they could get me into a guerilla camp. They both said they couldn't as they did not operate camps. I found them both highly articulate and polite, and was inclined to believe them.

I arguably took a great risk as they could easily have killed me and left me in the bush and no one would have known where I was. I would have disappeared without trace. Both were murdered not long afterwards. Herbert Chitepo was killed when a car bomb placed overnight in his Volkswagen Beetle exploded with him and two bodyguards inside in 1975, and Jason Moyo was killed by a parcel bomb in 1976.

Nujoma and Leballo

The next day, 18 September, I visited Oyaka at his OAU office. He told me it was quite out of the question for me to get into a guerilla camp. I interviewed two more leaders of liberation movements: Sam Nujoma of SWAPO, now in military fatigues instead of the pinstriped suit he wore at the Namibia International Conference, and Potlako Leballo of the PAC (Pan-African Congress), both of whom were surrounded by half a dozen subordinates. Both denied having camps that I could visit.

Makumbako: third and fourth rebuffs

Universally rebuffed on camps, I returned to the idea of Makumbako. I did what Mr Shu had asked, and tried a third time to obtain permission to go to Makumbako. I pressed Milao of the Ministry of Foreign Affairs for a permit to go there but received another rebuff. He asked me, "And who is going to pay for you to go to Makumbako?"

I did not accept No as an answer, and to turn it into a Yes I visited the Senior Information Officer of the Information Services Department in the Ministry of Information and Broadcasting, Mr Rweyemamu, whose name Pita-Kabisa had given me. I made a fourth attempt to go to Makumbako. He said he would challenge the Ministry of Foreign Affairs on my behalf. But he fared no better than me.

He rang later that day to say I could not go to Makumbako. He told me there was no hope of my going as it was definitely a "restricted area", and besides, the Ministry of Foreign Affairs had decided that 22 Scandinavian journalists would be accompanying me to Zanzibar and that they should definitely not visit Makumbako. No exception could be made for me.

My request to go to Makumbako had now been turned down on four separate occasions by the Ministry of Foreign Affairs and had been confirmed by the Ministry for Information and Broadcasting. I had the whole Tanzanian State against me, and if I were to go I would have to outmanoeuvre the whole Tanzanian State.

The 22 Scandinavian journalists who I was to accompany to Zanzibar had booked in at the New Africa Hotel. I was supposed to move in and join them there. I waited two hours in the foyer of the Twiga, sitting with my luggage and waiting for Milao to appear, and eventually got a lift with a UN man who was an expert on cashew nuts. At the New Africa I waited another two hours for Milao to arrive and authorise my check-in. I ate at 11 p.m. with the Scandinavian party.

I go to Zanzibar: Jumbe and the slave market
The next morning, 19 September, we were up at 6 a.m. We were driven to a military airport near Dar and had another two-hour wait because all planes were grounded as a result of the situation in Uganda. At the airport I noticed about five chest-high piles of six-inch-deep boxes containing what (in two places where the wood was not nailed together properly) looked like grenades. I reckoned they were being sent in the direction of the border with Uganda. We eventually flew to Zanzibar.

In Zanzibar we were driven through palms straight to the headquarters of the Afro-Shirazi Party (ASP) for a meeting with Zanzibar's President, Aboud Jumbe. The 22 journalists and I were seated on either side of a long table. I sat nearest the chair at the end. Suddenly there was a commotion and Jumbe arrived surrounded by four armed guards in berets pointing weapons at us (identical to the protection squad Gaddafi had used) along with officers in peaked caps who were in the Revolutionary Command Council. There were a dozen civilians who seemed to be a part of his regime.

Jumbe sat in the chair next to me. A picture of his predecessor, the former leader Karume, hung behind him. Jumbe wore a white shirt and throat scarf and after a halting but rational account of how he had taken over following the murder of Sheikh Karume at the ASP headquarters (where we were) he invited questions.

I had my tape-recorder on the table in front of me, and of him, and I asked the first question: "Who killed Karume?"

There was a stunned silence. Jumbe said, "Er, um, um, I don't know," and gave a lengthy but vague reply.

After a few more questions Jumbe left with his entourage and tea was served. Zanzibar's Attorney-General approached me, a young man of about 40. "I was educated at Oxford," he said. "You were very brave. Your question is one that no one in Zanzibar would dare to ask. It is rumoured that Jumbe himself killed Karume." And I realised that it was as if I had asked Macbeth who killed Duncan.

We were taken to lunch at Uwanjani Hotel opposite the stadium, where a crowd was gathering to celebrate Free Education Day. We were staying there and were given our room-keys. Jumbe had said in answer to another of my questions that he would open Zanzibar to journalists, so that afternoon I took my cassette-recorder with me.

We were taken by coach for a complete tour of the island under the care of the sinister, moustached Mr Jecha of the Information Office. He viewed my cassette-recorder with deep suspicion. His role was to arrange for us to see what we did not want to see and prevent us from seeing what we wanted to see. We looked at the clove harvest and cigarette, shoe and sugar factories.

For an hour and a half the Scandinavian journalists and I tried to persuade Mr Jecha to take us into Zanzibar town. Eventually he weakened and we were allowed to walk in the slave market where in past centuries Africans were sold as slaves. We were being shown the wickedness of colonialism, and I walked around freely interviewing on tape anybody who would stop and talk. Mr Jecha told me to stop interviewing, but I explained (much to the approval of the Scandinavians) that Jumbe had given us permission. In the slave market Mr Jecha asked to listen to a couple of the interviews, and I played him snippets, so we both knew that the cassette was packed with interviews.

We returned to our hotel to eat. The meal was part-buffet and my equipment was too bulky to take into the dining-room. I left it in my room, hidden under clothes at the bottom of the wardrobe. When I returned I found most of the cassette had been wiped clean.

I indignantly reported what had happened to Mr Jecha, saying that Jumbe would be very angry as the wiping of my cassette broke his undertaking that there could be free journalism in Zanzibar. He looked very uncomfortable and visibly squirmed.

Mr Jecha now announced that President Nyerere would receive us all the next day. I knew I should ask Nyerere if I could go to Mukambako and so I proposed that three of us – two of the 22 Scandinavians and I – should write out questions to Nyerere which would have the consent of all, and that we should agree the order in which questions could be asked.

Over dinner I spent two hours with two Scandinavians drawing up a master list of questions for President Nyerere which would be acceptable to the 22 journalists. I was able to get all my questions on the agreed list, and it was accepted that I could ask the first question. My questions did not refer to the Tanzam railway.

The next morning, 20 September, our bags were loaded onto the mini-bus before 6 a.m. We had arranged with Mr Jecha that he would take us back to Zanzibar town to take pictures before we went on to the airport. Mr Jecha did not turn up, and the Tanzanians with us said that only he had the authority to take us. We all protested, and towards 7 a.m. Milao's assistant took it upon himself to take us. We wandered round the slave market again, and again I interviewed any Zanzibaris who would talk to me.

At 7 a.m. Mr Jecha mysteriously appeared by our mini-bus and tried to hustle us off to the airport. When I said goodbye he said darkly, "I am visiting Dar this afternoon." I thought he might lodge a complaint at the Ministry of Foreign Affairs about my taping activities. On the flight back I wrote an article for *The Guardian* on my visit to Zanzibar.[7]

Dar: I ask President Nyerere if I can go to Tanzam railway's restricted area
We arrived in Dar in time to change and meet Nyerere at State House at 1.30 p.m.

It was a house in the outskirts of Dar. It had a view of the sea across gardens, and we sat on the veranda in the open air. The 22 Scandinavians filled the veranda but there seemed to be more Tanzanians sitting around a very grey-haired Nyerere in the room which was open to the veranda. There may have been 60 people present: in terms of decision-making the entire Tanzanian State that was preventing me from going to Makumbako.

Nyerere talked to us gravely and impressively against a background of wild-animal screeches and whoops and a screaming peacock. Several ministers, including the Minister for Information, sat alongside him. Nyerere condemned President Amin of Uganda, whose planes had attacked Bukoba, a town near the northern border of Tanzania. (Amin was probably retaliating for the *coup* attempt by supporters of Obote, which was assisted by Tanzania.) Then he asked, "Any questions?" The Scandinavians looked at me.

Now was my chance to take on the entire Tanzanian State that was preventing me from going to Makumbako. Departing from the question we had agreed the previous evening that should be asked first, I asked, appealing to the President as a last resort after being blocked four times by the Ministry of Foreign Affairs and knowing that the Mlimba-Makumbako section of the Chinese Tanzam railway was a secret, restricted area: "Can I go to the Chinese railway and see the new section between Mlimba and Makumbako?"

Nyerere said, "Er, um, er, I don't know. I don't see why not." He conferred with his ministers.

A few Scandinavians asked some of the questions we had devised at dinner the previous evening. Then suddenly, without explanation, the conference was terminated. All the Tanzanians stood up at the same time, and we were expected to leave.

Going to Makumbako
A very senior official in the Ministry of Information and Broadcasting who had accompanied us to Zanzibar and was nicknamed 'Uncle Ho' because he

had been in North Vietnam and looked like Ho Chi Minh detained me in my chair while the Scandinavians returned to our coach. He made me write out the newspapers I had written for together with a short autobiographical sketch. The Scandinavians were held up for five minutes at the President's front door, and when I rejoined the coach one of them said, "We thought they'd arrested you."

I had seen Rweyemamu of the Ministry of Information and Broadcasting sitting near President Nyerere but had not been able to speak to him. Later that afternoon he rang me and said, "Would you like to go to Bukoba, the village Amin's planes bombed, and see the damage caused by Amin's planes rather than go to Makumbako? You can't go to both, it's one or the other."

Bukoba did not feature on Joseph Winter's list, whereas Makumbako was his priority. I said, "I'll stick to Makumbako, if that's all right."

The Ministry of Information and Broadcasting may have been trying to tempt me away from the secret Mlimba-Makumbako section of the railway by offering me the opportunity of a scoop on Amin's attack.

In the afternoon a visit was laid on for the 22 Scandinavians and me to the Tanzania-Zambia Railway Authority: we were to visit the locomotive-and-rolling-stock repair workshops, hear a talk by the team leader of the Chinese Railway Working Team, and make a short journey on a train. I went to the Dar railway and met Mr Chopeta, the Deputy Executive Officer of the Tanzania-Zambia Railway Authority. I told him that Nyerere had given me permission to go on the Mlimba-Makumbako section. We met the Chinese Working Team of six: Mr Han Kuo-en; Mr Wang, Chief Engineer of Construction, and his interpreter (Mr Chou); Mr Han, Chief Engineer of the Traffic Operating Team, and his interpreter (Mr Kuo); and Mrs. Wang. We heard how the construction of the railway began in 1970 and the progress since then, and went on a very short train ride. I came away without being told that I could go on the Chinese railway.

When I returned to my hotel I received a call from the Ministry of Information and Broadcasting's Senior Information Officer, Mr Rweyemamu, who had been so obstructive two or three days back. He had attended the interview with Nyerere along with Milao, and he said over the phone, "There's an Australian TV team who want to visit the Chinese railway line. Contact them and see if they will agree to go to Makumbako."

His proposal answered the Ministry of Foreign Affairs' question, 'And who is going to pay for you to go to Makumbako?' The Australian TV team might do the paying. I took their number and rang them from my room and spoke to one of them.

And so it was that I met a silver-haired John Temple (Reporter) and his two Australian colleagues Ray Byrnes (Camera) and Peter Lipscomb (Sound), all of ABC TV. John Temple told me he was making a film that would be shown in Australia, and that they had been given permission to go to the Mlimba-Makumbako section in their Land Rover provided they took me with them.

That evening I was invited along with the Scandinavians to a reception-dinner given by the Minister for Information at our hotel, the New Africa. I talked to the Minister, Mr Mwakawago, about the railway for five minutes. He introduced me to the Deputy Director of Information Services Department, Krispin S. Mwambenja and to his boss, Riyami, who was seated next to me at dinner. Mwambenja asked me to visit him the next morning.

The next morning, 21 September, with the three Australians I visited Mwambenja. He said to me: "You can go to the Mlimba-Makumbako section of the Chinese railway this afternoon but you must travel by a hired Land Rover with this Australian television crew."

Mwambenja of the Ministry of Information and Broadcasting gave us a letter to take to Mr Chopeta of the Tanzam Railway company, who I had visited the previous afternoon. We took the letter straight to him. He said we would have to travel at our own expense as the Ministry of Foreign Affairs had refused to fund our journey. We were now free to begin our journey.

As Malecela had said, normally it took seven days to get clearance from the Chinese for a site visit to the Tanzam railway. I had circumvented this constraint, and reckoned that my question to Nyerere and my contact with Mr Shu had between them defeated the Tanzanian and Chinese bureaucracies. I, an individual, had taken on the Tanzanian State and had won. Of all my operations for the SIS, overcoming the obstacles to get to Makumbako was the one that would have impressed James Bond the most.

The four of us set off with a driver for Iringa at 2 p.m. We arrived at 11 p.m. and spent the night at an inn near blue jacaranda trees.

I visit the Tanzam railway's Chinese-run Mlimba-Makumbako section
The single-track 1,150-mile-long Tanzam railway from Dar es Salaam harbour to Kapiri Mposhi was central to the Tanzanian economy. Repayments for the money China was lending would be spread over thirty years from 1983. The second phase covered the 98 miles between Mlimba and Makumbako. The difficulties included broken escarpments (long steep slopes) in the low plains of the Kilombero valley and mountains as high as 6,000 feet, and the railway had to cross precipitous ravines and quagmires and go through 18 tunnels, one half a mile long. Mountain springs poured through some tunnel roofs.

Makumbako: Lugema
We arrived at Lugema base camp around midday on 22 September. There we were greeted by the jovial leader, Mr Li, his silent deputy Mr Yang, their

interpreter Mr Wu and an engineer, Mr Lien. We had a Chinese lunch washed down with a lot of beer. Mr Li carved, and we chinked beer-glasses. I gathered there was a more relaxed attitude to drinking than I had found during my visit to China in 1966.

We visited the Great Ruaha bridge, which was built in 89 days, and watched a crane hoist wooden sleepers to a posse of bustling men. We then went to Uchindile bridge, at one end of which the Chinese had moved a mountain. Two hundred African and Chinese workers swarmed over the base of the mountain like flies on a great pyramid, cementing concrete slabs on the sloping earthwork walls with great urgency. Wherever I walked the Chinese took great pride in telling me they had conquered the environment. They had a kind of ant-mentality: they were proud to be part of a collective effort, to be tiny scurrying ants on a dwarfing mountainside.

Mlimba: Mkera, I sleep in a Chinese camp
We went on to Mkera base camp near Mlimba, and were given a progress report. We ate and drank beer with the Chinese: Mr Lao-Zhe, the leader, who had revolting manners, spitting out food onto the floor, belching and tolerating a stinking lake outside (the communal urinal); his deputy Mr Lao-Ma; their Chinese-Swahili interpreter Mr Chou, whose English was good enough for me to have a conversation with him about *Taoism* and who said he would see me in Shanghai; and an engineer, Mr Lao-Chen.

We spent that night in a mud hut in the Chinese camp. Our beds were wooden boards with enormous mosquito-nets round them – I was glad I was taking anti-malaria tablets – and all of us tossed and turned all night. When I dropped off I dreamt that Nadia had returned to me with Caroline.

I woke to the cold reality of a bush dawn and the Chinese doing exercises near the ablutions, which were the stagnant shallow lake with a fetid stench. The Australians were humorous at the expense of Chinese hygiene.

After breakfast we walked through tunnel 13, which still leaked a ton of spring water a day at the exit. We squashed against the wall as a train trundled through. Stepping from sleeper to sleeper we trudged a mile between two mountains past several groups of Africans working flat out, and inspected the highest bridge, no. 25, which balanced on two columns 150 feet high.

We found track-laying in progress near Iringa. Most of the stone-laying had been done, and the tracks were laid at a rate of about two miles a day. A great track-laying machine suspended a length of railway line against the hot sun and lowered it towards the causeway of stones. A Chinese in a blue suit and a yellow coolie hat blew a whistle and waved a flag, and 30 African workmen prised it into place with levers and others flicked nuts and bolts.

Then with a hoot and a roar the track-laying machine edged forward and hoisted another length of line from its back and ran it along a girder so it hung in mid-air.

Here I met some Chinese of the Railway Formation section: the Director, Mr Chung, who wore a large Chairman-Mao badge (the only Chinese I saw wearing anything with Mao's head on it), a greying commissar who was at first friendly, then cold and brusque; his interpreter, Mr Chang; and the engineer who designed and built bridge no. 25, Mr Huan. In due course I wrote an article for *The Guardian* about the track-laying on the Tanzam railway.[8]

We returned to Lugema base camp and lunched with Mr Wu, the interpreter. We left for Iringa after lunch and arrived back at the blue jacaranda trees before dinner.

Mikumi National Park: lion and tsetse

We spent that night in Iringa and the next morning, on 24 September, we picked up the Assistant Superintendent of the local police, who was to escort us back to Dar. I asked him if we could visit the MPLA guerilla camp at Iringa. He consulted the local Information Officer and was told a call had come through on 22 September, clearly from the Ministry of Foreign Affairs, instructing him to offer no help to us whatsoever. I assumed that the Ministry of Foreign Affairs were piqued that I had gone over their heads and had reached Makumbako. The answer as regards the guerilla camp was clearly No.

The six of us – our driver, the three Australians, the policeman and I – all headed off in the Land Rover to the Mikumi National Park. During the next few hours we drove past lions, elephants, hippopotami, leopards, cheetahs, giraffes, zebras, impalas, wildebeests and warthogs.

It was extremely hot, and as the day progressed, it was clear that our policeman was ill. He was suffering from malaria, and halfway through our tour he retired to the back of the Land Rover, pushed our bags aside to make a space and lay down, feverish, shivering and sweating. We stopped in an open part of the bush near two trees which threw little pools of shade, in one of which two yards away lay a huge lion with a great mane. At that moment the malarial policeman sat up and shouted from the back, "*Tsetse, tsetse,*" pointing at the ceiling of the Land Rover two inches from my head. And there, yellowish-brown, wings folded back, upside down, sat a *tsetse* fly. The parasites passed on by a *tsetse* bite transmit sleeping sickness which infects the brain and the meninges, and if untreated is fatal. For this reason a century ago the *tsetse* fly was known as 'the white man's grave'.

I froze. As if in some awful Zen *koan* (riddle) I had a choice: to leave the Land Rover and be eaten by a lion; or stay in and possibly catch sleeping sickness from the *tsetse* fly's bite. I chose to stay in, reckoning that dying from drowsy sleeping sickness is preferable to dying from being mauled by a ferocious lion. For a quarter of an hour we all stayed still, not wanting to disturb the *tsetse* fly by starting our engine. Eventually the driver and policeman, with hunters' eyes and slow stealth, swatted and squashed the fly just above my head and we could then move on.

Soon afterwards the policeman became delirious. The Australians took his temperature. It was 106°F. We were concerned to return to Dar as soon as possible so he could have treatment, but I knew from personal experience that it is possible to have a temperature of 107 and survive.

I run out of money
Back in Dar the Australians and I counted the cost of our journey to Makumbako. My share was 1,000 Tanzanian shillings (at 17 Tanzanian shillings to the £), but I only had 250.[9] The Australians generously waived the remainder, saying they would not have got to Makumbako but for me. But I still owed them for two nights in Iringa, 148 Tanzanian shillings. I had to borrow.

I rang the Ministry of Foreign Affairs and spoke to a Mr Suedi, Deputy Chief of Protocol. He refused to pay my two hotel bills at Iringa. He said a refund would take a long time and that it could not be made to anyone else but me, and that would violate Exchange-Control Regulations. I rang the British Consulate. The Englishman in the Consulate merely said, "Oh dear." They would not agree to make me a loan next morning, so I visited Pita-Kabisa's brother-in-law and borrowed from him. I was glad that I did not have to find my hotel bill for the New Africa, which the Ministry of Foreign Affairs *would* be settling.

That morning I visited Chopeta and then Mr Shu of the NCNA. He was driving out, and we had a chat just inside the gate. I told him I had been to Makumbako. He did not seem surprised. I said I was leaving Dar. He said blandly, "Bye bye, and give my regards to Mr Yu." I sensed that behind the scenes Mr Shu had helped me to go to Makumbako. I visited the OAU to pursue guerilla camps, but Oyaka was in conference.

I had no money at all. Mr Suedi had told me that Malecela was returning from New York and that I could meet him in the airport waiting-room. He said he would send a car for me. I was driven to the airport.

I met Malecela in the VIP lounge. I detached him from obsequious men who bowed very low to him many times, and thanked him for my time in Tanzania. He asked what I had seen. I gave him a summary of all I had done, and reiterated that I would arrange for Sir Alec Douglas-Home, and later Edward Heath, to visit Tanzania. I said that I hoped that British aid would counter-balance the Chinese influence.

He was warm and friendly, and as he had paid for my air fares and hotel bills and I had overstayed my time by three days, I thought it would be churlish and ungrateful to complain that my Iringa bills had not been paid and that I had run out of money. I made no mention of this, and we agreed that my visit had come to an end. I asked him about Uganda. He said I could fly out later that afternoon.

I returned to my hotel and packed. A chauffeur collected me and my luggage from the New Africa and drove me back to the airport, where my ticket was waiting for me.

I flew out at 2.15. I had to change planes in Nairobi, and, having several hours to kill, made my way out of the airport. A large fellow spoke to me. It turned out to be Murray Sayle, a journalist for *The Sunday Times* whose articles I had often read. He asked if I would like to share his taxi. We went into Nairobi together and he took me round various tea- and coffee-bars he knew and we looked at the Government buildings. I left Nairobi after midnight on a BOAC Jumbo.

Return home, reflect on increase in British influence
On the plane I felt I had "seen" Africa very clearly. Essentially Tanzania's policy was "Africa first". Tanzania wanted freedom, independence and self-reliance, but needed aid, arms and the railway. Tanzania was afraid of becoming too dependent on China and wanted to turn away from China to the West. In my articles for *The Times* Features page and *The Guardian* I was able to present this with some clarity, and it was taken up at high level: Sir Alec Douglas-Home, the British Foreign Secretary, visited Dar in February 1974 and offered British money; and Edward Heath, the Prime Minister, was set to go soon afterwards, but cancelled at the last minute as he was overtaken by his loss of the 1974 election. A new British aid programme to Tanzania began with a £10m development loan after Harold Wilson's election victory in 1974, and President Nyerere visited Britain in November 1975. While signalling that Tanzania wanted to turn away from China to the West I had made possible an increase in British influence in Eastern Africa.

Biggs-Davison saw things differently. He was pro-South Africa and therefore anti-Tanzania. In March 1973 he would propose in Parliament that Sir Alec Douglas-Home should deduct aid from Zambia and Tanzania to compensate victims of armed attacks in Rhodesia mounted from the two countries. I had been behind the resumption of aid to Tanzania, and the armed attacks in Rhodesia had been planned by the two terrorists, Jason Moyo and Herbert Chitepo, with whom I had walked into the bush. Douglas-Home rejected Biggs-Davison's proposal, went on to visit Tanzania and implemented the resumption of aid I had set up. It is weird that Biggs-Davison, who had done so much to encourage me in my early years, tried to cancel my deal.

Disenchantment: lack of appetite for the SIS

I was weary when I returned to London. I thought I had done a good job in Tanzania, but the SIS did not seem to see it that way.

Grumbling

When he next saw me Joseph Winter complained that I had come home too early. I should have appealed to Malecela to pay the Iringa hotel bills and should have stayed on to visit a guerilla camp.

It was implied that I should have asked him to settle my hotel bills minutes after he had stepped off a plane and was being bowed to by flunkies, standing imperiously in the VIP lounge, and that I should have asked him in that VIP lounge to arrange for me to visit a guerilla camp even though he had previously said that I would not be able to "get into a freedom-fighter camp".

The truth was, the OAU had links with the KGB and knew I was a British agent, and I had been blocked by every guerilla I had asked, including Chitepo and Moyo, and it would have been well-nigh impossible for Malecela to overrule the OAU and order them to give me, a known British agent, permission to enter one of their guerilla camps, whose existence the OAU officially denied.

With regard to the British Consulate's refusal to lend me some money, he said, "We deliberately told no one that you would be coming." He took the view that it was for the Tanzanians to give me money, not the British. He then told me I would receive an incentive bonus of £30 for my initiative in getting on the Tanzam railway.

Now I looked back on my 16 days, on the risky situations I had been in – including operating as a known British agent in a country that had always been ideologically opposed to the West – and the turn-around in Western-Tanzanian relations I had effected, and I thought that I had achieved a lot. With the exception of getting inside a guerilla camp, I had achieved what I had been asked to do, and had 'done the business' of moving Tanzania away from the Chinese and back towards the West. The SIS had had a good deal for their outlay of around £72.50 (half a month's net ILEA salary, around £85, i.e. £42.50, plus the £30 initiative bonus). I knew their desk-bound operatives in their immaculate white shirts and dark suits could not have entered a guerilla camp without any cover.

There was a carping, grumbling presence in the organisation which Joseph Winter had to convey, which I did not like. There had been little official understanding of how difficult it was to operate in Tanzania after the departure of my protector, Malecela, when I was known to be a British agent. I had committed myself to defending the West against Communist expansion in Africa during the Cold War (the 'Third World War' fought clandestinely in limited local wars by two sides deterred from open warfare by each other's nuclear missiles). I had opposed Soviet and Chinese influence in Egypt, Libya, Angola, Rhodesia, South-West Africa, Tanzania and other African states. But I had lost my appetite for the work I had been doing.

Aftermath of Tanzania

For a couple of months I wrote my articles and discharged the aftermath of Tanzania. I sent cuttings of my pieces to Malecela, who replied, "I must say, your articles were really very good, at least for the first time Tanzania's side has been properly put";[10] and to the Tanzanian High Commission. I wrote articles for the *Railway Gazette International*[11] and *Africa Confidential*.[12] I also wrote reports on nine Rhodesian groups represented in London, including FROLIZI, and obtained information on a proposed international blockade of Rhodesia off Mozambique. Some of this material appeared in *Africa Confidential*.[13] In all these pieces I considered that I was modifying British policy by presenting the true feelings of the Africans while doing what I could to block Soviet and Chinese expansion.

This process was still continuing on 25 October when I appeared on the BBC World Service's live *African Morning Show*, and was interviewed by Pete Myers on the Tanzam railway.[14] Pete Myers was late, and made it to his desk five seconds before he began introducing me, and his first (breathless) question was, "How many kilometres long is the Tanzam railway?" I said, "1,150," but it was not the friendliest of opening questions. Incredibly, Mike Popham from Brussels was providing sound effects for the interview before mine, making Goon-like plopping noises by putting his forefinger in his mouth and pulling it against his cheek.

Exposure and review

I was told by one of *The Times* journalists that Michael Wolfers – an Africa correspondent on *The Times* and Marxist activist (*Times* obituary, 18 November 2014 – had been saying that I was a British agent. I raised this with Joseph Winter, who asked me to visit him to discuss the allegation. I did so.

Sitting in his small room at *The Illustrated London News*, wearing a suit, he confirmed that he was responsible for preventing the publication of the two versions of my article on the Portuguese war *communiqués* (see pp.353–354, 393, 394–395, 399) because "Polly Gaster complained that you are a British intelligence agent". I questioned when the complaint was made and grasped that complaints were made both before and after the Arnoldshain conference on the Cunene River. He said, "I think you *are* an intelligence agent." I neither confirmed nor denied his allegation. I was operating with the full knowledge of the KGB, and I assumed the KGB had leaked.

I felt my position was becoming untenable. I was now closer to Ann and the ESN work was becoming intolerable. I wanted to get back to 'A'-level work. I asked Joseph Winter for a review of my whole position.

Joseph said that a review was already under way: "We are trying to get inside your soul." He said, "It may be that you should have a rest. You have been doing intelligence work for four years, and it is very tiring."

Test of intuition

The review included a test of my intuition. I was invited to a party at 328A King's Road, Chelsea and seated in a corner with the editor of *Africa Confidential*, Godfrey Morrison, a tall, dark-haired man in his early forties. He asked me for my opinion on the other dozen people present. Without thinking I went through all of them, pointing out who was having a relationship with who and what their activities were. At the end I said, "That leaves Mitsy and her Yugoslav lover over there."

I had no evidence, but when I had finished Godfrey Morrison said quietly, "You were right in every case." I was convinced that following my illumination I had received a new power to look at a situation and see its underlying realities clearly; a kind of infused wisdom and knowledge which had come with the Light.

Switched from Africa to India and Japan against my wishes

Joseph Winter reported back. He said that I should continue to do the occasional African interview, for which I would be paid around £20 a time as an incentive, but that I should switch to India and Japan, two countries China was interested in. "If the Chinese see you near some of their targets there, then they will surely jump." Joseph said I would be promoting British commercial interests in India and Japan.

I was unhappy about this because my initial Indian contact was to be a colleague at Riverway, Saxena, who I did not want to involve, and my contact with the Japanese was to be a former employer of mine, JETRO (Japan External Trading Organisation), who had been good to me and who I did not want to exploit.

At the beginning of November I met a nondescript-looking elderly woman from the SIS. She was in her early sixties, wore a coat and carried a cloth shopping bag. She could have been anybody's aunt out shopping. Joseph Winter introduced her to me as "Auntie" in Chelsea Cloisters.

She said to me, "I've been hearing all about you. You have the kind of mind that can go into a room and sense what all fifteen people are doing," a clear reference to the party in the King's Road where everyone was an agent for someone. She said, "We will put you back into JETRO, where you once taught. You can teach there again, and we will instruct you so you can recognise certain files and we will give you a special camera so you can copy them."

I was extremely unhappy about this. This was a far cry from my ideal of contributing to the survival of the West against Communism. This sounded like industrial or commercial espionage. I was not interested in tariffs and quotas, though I recognised that Britain would suffer if India and Japan ran away with our markets. I was clear in my mind that I would not betray my former Japanese employers. It seemed that I had ceased to be Heath's 'unofficial Ambassador', and I did not fully understand what my new role was to be.

Joseph Winter was now replaced as my controller by Ronald Merton, a brown-haired man in his mid-to-late-thirties who was harder to talk to than his predecessors. He asked me to write out how I would present my transfer from Africa. I wrote proposing that the link would be the EEC. Europe would be a bridge between Africa on the one hand and India and Japan on the other.

I looked back on losing Africa with some regret. Africa was then a Cold-War battleground. I had been playing a small part in resisting Soviet and Chinese expansion in Africa, defending Western 'protectorates' there and helping the Africans. By and large our efforts had been successful. Now Africa harbours al-Qaeda and is a new front line for terrorism, and it is hard to believe that what I did helped Africans to achieve better lives.

Meaning: poetic spring
I rediscover my poetic spring
Deep within myself I felt an instinctive drive to return to writing poetry. I visited my mother in Loughton before her birthday. I drove to Baldwin's Hill and walked to the Lost Pond, which I found immediately. It was like rediscovering my poetic spring within the dark wood – an Ain el Faras in Epping Forest.

My new poetic activity was suspended while I had Nadia to stay. Ann and I drove to Spilsby to return her, and met Caroline and her husband in The George. Caroline had had a son while I was in Tanzania.

David shocked me by saying: "You could not have gone to Tanzania as a result of an invitation from the Minister of Foreign Affairs in Brussels as I have had a 'Security' report that the Tanzanian Minister of Foreign Affairs was not at the Brussels conference. I think you've made your visit to Tanzania up and should not be entrusted with Nadia."

I stared at him in disbelief. Did he really believe I was making up my visit to Tanzania? Had he actually received a wrong report from his 'Security'?

Was he seeking a pretext for denying me access to Nadia, inventing grounds for arguing before a judge that I was unfit to be a father? My lips had to be muzzled as to what I was doing in Tanzania, and I did not engage with him.

A few days later, on 6 November, I began writing poems again. I wrote in my *Diaries*: "Have started lyric poems.... For the first time... my grief has become sufficiently distant for me to ritualise it." I scribbled drafts, made fair copies in a green manuscript book Caroline had given me for my 1969 birthday in Libya and typed up perfected copies. On 10 November I wrote: "This last week, from Monday to Friday (today) I have been up at 6.30 a.m. every day, and have consequently written five poems out of 100, and have done five stories.... Now the loneliness of being an artist. No drinking – I have given up alcohol. Clean senses. Feelings in the moment."

A few days later I wrote: "100 pictures... of the same man, in different situations and from different angles. You get a picture of the whole."[15] On 19 November I had written 14 poems and 38 stories. My poems were the first of a cycle entitled *The Gates of Hell*. I based the title on Rodin's portal with three shades on top.

I discussed my new poetic activity with Tuohy a week later. Weirdly (in view of 'Auntie's' approach) he had written to ask if I would help him entertain four Japanese. On 24 November I went to Brighton and helped give them dinner. One of them, Professor Iwaki, was interested in Africa. Iwaki asked if we could stay in contact. The Japanese left at 11 and Tuohy and I talked until 3 a.m. about the technical side of writing prose and poems.

After breakfast we went for a long walk across the sea cliff, and were followed by a Chinese. Tuohy said, "A Chinese sat near us in Soho last December. Why are we being followed by a Chinese more than six years after our visit to China?" I assumed that the Chinese was following *me*, and made light of his presence. But the Chinese was in the way. He was coming between Tuohy and me as we discussed my writing of poems and stories.

We walked in Sussex Square Gardens, and I gave an indication that I would write a thousand stories: "If I were finding out why leaves die I would collect a thousand leaves and catalogue them. So it is in my stories, I am collecting a thousand people and presenting the evidence."

He agreed, and also agreed with my assumptions in my poems, that personal feeling is a better central idea than "Pound's tour of his library or Heath-Stubbs' mythology in *Artorius*";[16] and that the line of personal feeling in poetry runs from Catullus through Shakespeare's *Sonnets* to Tennyson's *In Memoriam* and Hardy. I said, with the Chinese still following me, pointing at a tree, that there is a trunk beneath the writer's branches – his novels, stories, poems, dramatic verse, essays and prose writings. Tuohy quoted Browning to suggest that others know what the trunk is whereas the artist himself does not know. (Browning was reported to have been asked by a lady what a poem of his meant – either 'Sordello' or 'Childe Roland to the Dark Tower Came' – and to have replied, "Madam, when I wrote that, only God and I knew what it meant. Now only God knows.")

In my poems I was groping towards a new view of man. I wrote in my *Diaries*:

Before Plato, body and spirit were united, but since then they have divided…: and by Rilke's 4th elegy the external world is a blur within the inner mind of the hero. Classicism: harmony with objects. Romanticism: troubled inner self. My work shows Romantic influence, e.g. inner world, imagination as opposed to reason, the value of the individual…. What is my subject?… Man's possibilities, i.e. the end of 1,000 stories…. We are measured in terms of our possibilities…. Man must live by realising his possibilities…. My 1,000 stories illustrate man's possibilities, and the poems show a man winning through to his possibilities, which is Existentialism within – and Romanticism that goes forward…. This idea after a night's drinking with Tuohy. My central idea, my trunk.

I was developing a theory of art which provided a context for my poems and very short stories. In my *Diaries* I wrote:

Art stages: soul-world muddled up (archaic); classical Age of Maturity, i.e. harmony, form as conceived by intellect and observation of world in balance, static; academic and Mannerist style, i.e. world of its own – sickness of styles; then Baroque, uneasiness and longing for freedom, full of rhythm, organic not intellectual: human passion and grief and pain, love and death, all ages of man: plant-like basis. The imagination drinks deeply of its forms, the cosmos itself seems to be throbbing in the soul (my stories). Mannerism – inability of artists to define themselves, upheaval of values…. So I stand for a new Baroque Romanticism (from self to world), man measured by his possibilities, no alienation from the outer world – the mannerism of Modernism (Baudelaire, Proust, Picasso, Rilke, Joyce, Eliot, Kafka, Mann, Sartre, Camus, Brecht) – but rather the self glorying in the outer world, full of possibilities within the unity, i.e. the *individual*. So Tuohy comes from a different tradition altogether, the outer world-Classicism. Possibilities: "The view which regards man as a well, a reservoir full of possibilities, I call the Romantic" (T.E. Hulme), cf Sartre. Future possibilities – at the end of 'The Silence'. So begin with an act of revolt against the whole tradition of philosophy and thought…. How to measure man: by his Shadow, by what is ahead of him. That is the liberation of man.[17]

442

This intense thinking about my view of art resulted in another illumination, after a day with a temperature:

> December 3rd–4th. A sleepless night after my fever, tossing and turning, seeing the white light again breaking through the universe – a white sun, dim in its centre, so that the light was evenly distributed.

On 9 December I took Ann to the Denmark and "poured out thoughts about… the deep will…. It is Everest or nothing. Do not be content with the Matterhorns or Snowdons or china-clay hills." I spoke of a Club of 600 members, all of whom had aspired to the highest possibilities. I was still getting up at 6.30 and writing before going to work:

> You have to keep the spring flowing. Get up at 6.30 and write and the spring is flowing for the rest of the day. Otherwise the spring is buried like the one in Coleridge's Xanadu caves…. So far, 52 stories, 45 poems.

I was so engrossed in creative work before I went to school and when I returned home that my work for Ronald Merton was a chore.

My work for Merton was a distraction for my poetic flow. I met him in The Bunch of Grapes, Brompton Road; or in the Chelsea Drugstore, King's Road; or at a wine bar near Charing Cross station with inward bad grace. I had reluctantly written to JETRO and asked for employment. A Mr Inoue said I could teach their personnel again, but not until the new fiscal year began on 6 April. Meanwhile, Saxena had told me about the India Development Association and I was waiting for an opportunity to go there.

My inner creativity was stimulated by a couple of chance meetings with the two friends I had been asked to consult about working with the SIS. As I drove back from school after a fire-drill I passed John Ezard waiting at a bus stop in Deptford, leaning on a crutch. I gave him a lift to the *Guardian* office. He told me he was Night News Editor now. I told him I had seen Tuohy, and Ezard said: "His obsession with technique ends in silence. He has nothing to say. *The Ice Saints* was heading that way." I privately agreed. I had something to say and was in a different position from Tuohy.

At the end of term there was a party for the ESN boys. Jelly and ice-cream was served in the lower hall, and stout Mr Wardlow surveyed the Dickensian scene like the Beadle in *Oliver Twist*. I left slightly early as Ann had asked me to accompany her to a carol service in Sloane Square. I found a pitifully small gathering opposite the tube station with almost as many box-rattlers as passers-by, and lo! in another 'accidental' encounter Ricky seized my right arm.

I detached myself from the carol service and we found a seat in Sloane

Square and discussed how the eternal can be reflected in literature. We agreed that it was outside all religions, and that the source of the spring was within each of us: "Neither shall they say, Lo here! or, lo there! for, behold, the kingdom of God is within you."[18] Ricky pointed out that there is no language for the eternal level and so it has to be conveyed in parables.

Vastation experiences
Following these two meetings I was back in my dark wood. In a swing from euphoric +A in which I grasped the unity of the universe and the meaning of life I was plunged back into −A: I suffered a bout of melancholia and pondered my own death. About 10.45 on 21 December I was filled with a deep sense of vastation. I felt completely laid waste as though my inner citadel had been sacked. I wrote afterwards:

> This has been like being in the middle of an ocean, drowning, no land near – for death is certain and all is a distraction from it. I experienced this utterly and totally…. This was the vastation experience, I see now, that Tolstoy and William James had; Nietzsche's hour of Great Contempt…. It was an attack – an attack of metaphysical giddiness as it were. Nothing was secure, nothing had value. All the works of man were as nothing. All were basically meaningless.[19]

The experience lasted until 1 a.m. I grasped that illumination does not immediately make one immune from sudden loss of meaning. Rather it brings one face to face with death and the denial of meaning in a way that can prepare the spirit for a triumphant overcoming of meaninglessness and confirm its sense of meaning.

I had Nadia for Christmas. I took her to see *Peter Pan*. I took her to Essex for Christmas Day. I returned her to Peterborough a few days later. I returned home to South Kensington.

The next day I had a different kind of 'accidental encounter' that took me away from poetic inspiration and plunged me back into my Libyan Dark Night. I was walking in Bute Street, Chelsea when I saw Ben from Libya in a suit and tie walking with his older brother. I crossed the road and laid a hand on his arm and said: "Col. Nagy, you are under arrest. I have instructions from Col. Gaddafi." He turned, and for five seconds there was horror – indeed terror – in his eyes as he believed he was being arrested. Then he recognised me and let out a large pealing laugh of relief.

He took me to his flat in Roland House, Old Brompton Road. He told me he was investing in hotels in London. He said his younger brother had married the daughter of the Minister for Petroleum and now had a steel industry, while the Minister for Petroleum now had an international business in Rome. The Minister of State for Prime Minister's Affairs now worked in an oil company.

I had a drink with the two brothers a couple of days later, during which he said of Caroline, "Her personality was too strong, she wasn't your type. Don't trust women with your secrets." What secrets? I came away feeling worse than when I had met him.

A few days later I spent an evening with him. We ate at the Chelsea Kitchen, where Ben chatted up a Russian waitress – how had a Russian waitress suddenly appeared in the Chelsea Kitchen? – very loudly so everyone heard, and he then insisted on taking me to the Hilton Hotel. He pointedly took me upstairs to the 007 bar, perhaps making the point that he knew of my link with Andrew Mackenzie. We sat and talked over a drink, and he said of Caroline: "You treated her kindly and well and politely and with respect, and so she thought she would find others who would treat her more kindly and well and politely, and with greater respect." I tried to get him talking about how Gaddafi had thwarted our revolution, but he would not be drawn. He dominated that part of our conversation and would not say anything negative about "our Head of State".

A few weeks later I received a postcard from Ben in Tripoli, on which there was a huge postage stamp of a Tuareg with a slit for his eyes, wearing a rifle on his back and standing by a camel. Ben wrote beneath: "Above is Nick and his camel in the Sahara." It seemed to be a reference to our revolution and also to my work for the SIS.

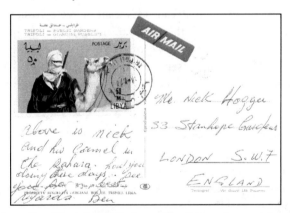

Postcard from Ben Nagy to Nicholas with stamp of a camel, referring to intelligence activities

Once again I felt lost in the dark wood. Perhaps it was because I wanted to leave the ESN school or perhaps I was depressed at the prospect of starting again among Indians and Japanese, or perhaps I was exhausted within from more than two months of getting up early to start writing at 6.30

a.m. before going to work and then doing intelligence work, but the vastation experience came again on 12 January 1973, late at night as I lay in bed:

> A creeping paralysis of the will, a feeling of the total futility of everything. The struggles of parents end in old age and silence, engagements and young love end in this loneliness in Kensington, nothing was secure or permanent.... It was a total vastation, a complete laying-waste of my sense of a future, of its worthwhileness. The smallness of 'I'.

The feeling slowly disappeared. Those on the Mystic Way learn to regard the vastation experience as a gift, for it teaches the smallness of the rational, social ego, which has to be transcended. I wondered if it was a call to sever my connection with the intelligence world.

The unity of the universe
Now I suddenly stopped writing poems and turned towards philosophy. I was thinking about authentic living.

I wrote in my *Diaries* on 23 January: "What is my Existentialism but a journey up the mystic ladder, allowing the deeper self to take over from the shallow self?" Inauthentic living involved "experiences at the bottom of the ladder" and "includes all English philosophy – which is trivial and dull".

Again:

> [In] moments the individual can appreciate a metaphysical reality – authentic Being... – and can therefore advance further up the ladder to the unitive life.... The inauthentic keeps men from Being, and in moments of intensity the inauthentic disappears, and Being is revealed as it really is. The inauthentic is therefore a barrier in our awareness, which prevents us from seeing pure Being.

Out of this insight came a focus on perception:

> *Percipere est esse*...: to perceive is to be. It means there is fundamentally no division between perceiver and perceived because both form part of a unity: Being.

By "to perceive is to be" I meant that the way we perceive can take us to Being as opposed to Becoming. I recorded that this was very different from Berkeley's *"esse est percipi (aut percipere)"*, "to be is to be perceived (or to perceive)" – that phenomenal objects only have existence when they are perceived.

The question then arose, what is "Being"? I groped towards it the next day:

> Being is there to be seen all the time, and if you see the One you must be
> a part of it, like a fleck on a marble egg. This brings peace – it is the art of
> living…. The negative anxiety is finished. Horror, dread. [I was thinking
> of the vastation experience.] These are what you feel… on the bottom
> rung of the ladder. All Being is one, and images – in which different
> aspects of multiplicity correspond – approach the One…. [When] the
> individual and his 'I, I, I' penetrates through his habits and murky
> consciousness to the part of himself which is a part of pure Being then he
> sees from the point of view of the whole.[20]

Ann returned from a course on religion to which her Head had sent her. I
connected her course with Being:

> The purpose of teaching religion is to [teach a] shift from the world of 'I'
> to the ground of our Being – the eternal world which is the ground of
> Being. That shift takes place inside you existentially, and parables teach
> you how to go through that shift…. Each being rests on the ground of All
> Being. The truth is that All Being is One Being…. What is right is what
> accords with Being, which we can all partake of, authentically, and what
> is wrong is inauthentic. For the first time in my life I can glimpse the
> Absolute. I write of inauthenticity and discover Being. I am emerging
> from the Dark Night of the Soul into the unitive life. My process is over
> – my shift.

And the next day:

> The unitive life sensing pure Being, uniting mysticism and
> Existentialism…. In it Being and Becoming are reconciled, within one
> nature…. The aim of life is to go through all the hardships of the journey
> and come through into *instinctively* knowing that all is pure Being.

I now felt I had achieved the unitive life. I wrote:

> I am almost at the top rung of the ladder. In my Dark Night I purged my
> selfhood further – I gave up drinking…. I am emerging with a strong
> sense of Unity…. I believe in purifying the senses…. I remade myself –
> my self has been remade…. With my new unitive life is coming a confi-
> dence…. I speak my opinion now, but it is not 'me' that speaks it but the
> Being that occupies me.[21]

Tuohy came to my flat and we then went to the Elephant. I told him about my ponderings on Being. He said, "You're absolutely right, but I'm trying to be a writer." I tried to explain that there was no division between metaphysical perception and being a writer, and (recalling Ezard's point) that a great writer had to have something to say, great subject matter. I tried to explain that inner developments relating to Being took one closer to becoming a great writer rather than farther away. But he took the conversation back to people we both knew and arrangements, and left for a dinner appointment in Gordon Square.

My fragile unitive life was broken into again the next evening, at 12.30 a.m. on 2 February. The vastation experience returned:

> A creeping depression, a paralysis of the will. Everything seems hopeless. Suffering. Sorrow. Some die, others don't, as in *War and Peace* and the seeds of trees.... A sadness, a vastation creeping up? Summer evenings, window open, all quiet at dusk, music... is playing somewhere – sadness. Chestnut leaves. Sad.

I realised that the basis of the vastation was that it was a view of the ephemeral world of the ego from the point of view of the soul. "We're living through the time of the dead-in-soul.... I am a describer of our deepest life. The authentic life in contact with Being." A few days later I wrote: "There is authentic Being and inauthentic products by inauthentic people (hideous lights, gimmicky novels)."[22]

My unitive vision was now beginning to see the unity between disciplines:

> The end of philosophy is religion – so philosophy and religion are part of a whole. And poetry, that is part of a whole too. I am holist.... You start off with philosophy (expressed through stories) and end with religion (expressed through poetry). Prose – the search; poetry – the finding.

Again:

> Prose describes the process of inauthenticity, poetry describes communion with the authentic.

And:

> Humanism deals with man's social self, Romanticism with man's aspiring self. The idea of 'beyond one's present reach' is very important to Romanticism.

I was looking towards Europe, and Existentialism. I suddenly decided to write an essay making a British Existentialism possible. I wrote:

> What my essay will say will be: we have lost our inner direction as individuals, and so society's problems reflect the outer 'I'.... The solution... is to return... to growth and improvement and betterment, i.e. to an Existentialism.... I am... an Existentialist who is using art to help [man] in his philosophical investigations that will result in... mystical communion.... Existentialism unites the many-sidedness, it's the trunk that unites my branches. In my life I act out my philosophy, my beliefs, my attitudes.... Existentialism... is about this life, and about living authentically and experiencing Being ('the world of eternity').[23]

Between 15 and 27 February I wrote an article, 'Why I am an Existentialist'. This focused on Perceptivism, my theory of perception, and besides restating the Existentialist tradition in deliberately personal terms that connected with my own living I also stated a need for a new European philosophy:

> We should create a British form of Existentialism.... I am an Existentialist because the old definitions are no good for me, I need a new definition for myself and the new definition must be about the whole of a man... and Perceptivism.... Why Europe needs an Existentialism that is Perceptivist. The old definitions are no good for Europe. She needs a new definition and that must be about the whole of man. There must be a revolt in European taste and art.[24]

Later this Perceptivism evolved into Universalism.

I sent my essay to H.J. Blackham, the leading British authority on Existentialism who had visited my Oxford college. In due course he replied, taking my view seriously and asking: "Is not your Existentialism nearer to Jaspers than to Heidegger or Sartre?"[25] Emboldened by being regarded as an Existentialist by Blackham, I sent the essay to Colin Wilson, who had brought out *Introduction to the New Existentialism*.

I was instinctively asserting my return to a writer's, as opposed to a journalist's, identity. I asserted this identity by brazenly handing a copy of my essay, and of Blackham's letter, to Ronald Merton when I met him on 27 March at 4.30.

I was still writing stories and was approaching 100. I thought about my stories in relation to Perceptivism, and became aware of their metaphysical nature. They brought out that what I perceived belonged to Being:

My stories are moments that are metaphysical, not psychological. All moments belong to a unity, like all flecks on a marble egg, and so the two moments when I visited the Portmellon water-splash belong to a unity, and are more important than moments this afternoon, i.e. they are now out of time, as images, and are therefore by definition in eternity and remembered for ever. So time is unreal and unimportant, it applies only to the "self of time". In a moment of intensity we see the world as it really is – we perceive truly and experience our oneness with the perceived, e.g. with the water-splash, we both belong to a greater whole. This experience of Being (i.e. of what we perceive belonging to a unity with us) means we are escaping the chains of time and are seeing something which, though changing (the tide), is a manifestation of something that is always there, something to which it and we belong. Therefore such a moment tells us about our shared belongingness to Being.... When we perceive truly and experience Being... we are out of time and in eternity.... The way we perceive determines whether we are bound by the chains of time (inauthentically) or whether we escape time for eternity. So I affirm a metaphysical Reality, which is the unchanging unity within which all changing Becoming is all moments, plus and minus, high tide and low.[26]

I was using some of the stories in what became *A Spade Fresh with Mud* to approach Being just as Wordsworth had used some of the verse in *The Prelude* to approach "unknown modes of being".

I was immersed in art and philosophy and had no time for Indians and Japanese.

I turn against intelligence work
My heart was no longer in the SIS because they had moved me away from my ideal. I no longer felt I was standing up to Communism and helping to keep Western Europe free. Suddenly what I was being asked to do had become ugly, and the new centre in my self would not stand for it. I was in conflict, and showing the essay to Ronald Merton had been a veiled protest.

Ronald Merton had given me some questions on Rhodesia. I had to find the answers and write a report. I also wrote another article on SWAPO.[27] Now Saxena took me to a meeting at the Indian High Commission at which John Grigg (formerly Lord Altrincham, who had controversially criticised the monarchy) presided.

I visited the Bank of Japan in London, which had given me work in 1967/68, and learned that my former pupil, Tadashi Sasaki, Vice-Governor when I was in Japan, had now become Governor and was coming to London. I had liked him and did not want to take advantage of him. The teacher-pupil relationship is special. Ronald Merton pressed me very hard to write to him to make an appointment to see him in London. I went through the motions, and was glad I missed him at Claridge's. He wrote to me that he had had to return to Tokyo, but that he hoped to see me in the near future.[28]

Ronald Merton was annoyed when I told him in The Bunch of Grapes at 10.30 p.m. He said, "I thought we were going to short-cut the whole slow business of getting established with the Japanese." He had no sense that I might have warm feelings towards Sasaki, having met him weekly for four years. Merton threatened, "You have six months to get established, from last November." I accepted his deadline and made a mental note that I might be free from his nightmare world in May.

Meanwhile Tuohy's contact, Professor Iwaki, introduced me to Yahei Taoka, who was 90 and the owner of an airline. He had worked in London in 1912. On 5 April he invited me to lunch at Hiroko's, a Japanese restaurant in London, and told me he wanted to start a 'Japanese Council', which would be the Japanese equivalent of the British Council. He asked for help. I passed him on to a British Council adviser, Tomlin's deputy, Alan Baker. (Taoka arranged for Baker to fly to Japan on his airline to assess the project. Baker later wrote to me that he was a most valuable contact.) I saw Ronald Merton at 5.30 on 9 April and explained that I did not see creating a 'Japanese Council' as part of my brief.

As part of my turning against the intelligence world I had sold my green Volkswagen Beetle, which Martin Rowley had floridly described as "the most photographed and recorded car in the world", and had bought a second-hand blue MGB GT. I had driven it up to Lincolnshire at half-term and met Nadia in Horncastle and had driven her to Skegness.

I also turned my attention away from the intelligence world to Cornwall. My mother had been to East Grinstead and had returned with some of Gwen Broad's paintings. (Gwen Broad had died the previous year.) She offered me 'Dusk at the (sic) Land's End' (a moody view of a tin-mine chimney on Cornish cliffs seen from the evening of life) and 'Kynance Cove' (in which rocks flow like clouds in a Zen-like unity). I still have both these paintings. Cornwall was home to Ann's mother – and to Colin Wilson.

Cornwall: with Colin Wilson, D.S. Savage
On Easter Sunday I took the train to Cornwall to join Ann, who was staying with her mother. She met me at St Austell station and I stopped at a call-box outside – the same one I had rung him from in January 1961, more than 12 years before – and rang Colin Wilson, who had received my essay. He was chummy: "Hello Nick, good to hear your voice again." He invited me to visit him on Tuesday evening.

Easter Monday was wet and Ann and I drove round the local bays, including the tiny china-clay port of Charlestown (the local harbour) and I spent a lot of time thinking about perception. It was as if the prospect of returning to Colin Wilson's presence heightened my consciousness. I felt there was a spectrum of learning-perception and I distinguished 9 modes of perception or levels of consciousness: passive blur; scanning; selection of detail; range-finding; seeing the whole situation at a glance or compre-hending; future-perception (or ambitiously perceiving an improved future); feeling-perception as in feeling the gorse or Nature; meditating-perception (feeling the sap rising in the tree); and unity-perception (feeling the unity of the universe).[29] These 9 levels of consciousness anticipated the 12 levels of consciousness I would identify in *The New Philosophy of Universalism*.[30] I visited Colin Wilson with my ideas sorted out.

On 24 April Ann drove me to Gorran and up the narrow lane to Tetherdown. We arrived at 5 and Colin peered round the door, now moustached, and said as though it was 12 minutes since he had last seen me and not 12 years, "Nick, can you go and find Joy behind the greenhouse and ask her where my underpants are?" The search for Joy and his pants took an hour. (His autobiography refers to the beginning of a breakdown he suffered from overwork soon after February 1973,[31] but there was no sign of this that Easter.)

In due course Ann and I sat in the familiar room before the log fire and sipped goblets of red wine, and with Joy sitting opposite him and talking to Ann, Colin looked at a few of my stories. He said, "They're a good form." I reminded him that I had told him in The Rising Sun (a name that evoked Japan) by the Portmellon water-splash that I would lecture abroad and become a wanderer and exile for ten years. I told him I had done exactly what I had said, and had been to Japan, and I told him about my illumi-nation. He was taken aback. He had not had the experience and had not referred to it in his work, and I think I disturbed him.

We discussed Existentialism and phenomenology. I explained my 9 levels of consciousness and he listened intently. (In his autobiography, published 31 years later, he listed 8 levels of consciousness.)[32] He said, "There are only two people interested in Existentialism in this country, you and me."

But then he attacked mysticism. He declared himself to be on the side of the reason and against poetry and mysticism. "I would gladly belong to a society to suppress poetry and mysticism," he said, conveniently forgetting he had written *Poetry and Mysticism*, which he had finished in January 1969. "Poetry is waiting passively for meaning whereas good thinking can solve the problem in half the time." He told me that to deny one's egotism for the Mystic Way was wrong: "When you have inner being the ego becomes like a wet suit of clothes. You don't want it, so it's a mistake to try and discard it." He modified his acceptance of egotism when I distinguished thinking from feeling and perception, and reminded him of his opposition to Blake's egotistical "Spectre". He darted up and returned with Husserl's *Ideas*, and said, "Husserl makes mysticism unnecessary, you can intentionalise meaning by inner being." He spoke with a passion and echo of the Colin Wilson I knew in 1961, but on other topics he was now less eager and more disillusioned. I was to use Husserl's method of "bracketing out the object" – not the aspect Colin had just mentioned – in *The Fire and the Stones*.

He said that he had not made a lot of money out of writing: "*The Occult* made £20,000 and saved this house – I owed income tax for years back – but now I have to pay the income tax on the £20,000."[33] He sat with his wife and three children before the log fire, talking about how *The God of the Labyrinth* was the dirtiest book he had ever written as his hero had 14 sexual experiences one after the other and his publisher said that was unbelievable and cut out two. He clearly regarded the book as a money-spinner, but in his autobiography he stated that the delay in placing it strained his finances.[34] I had abruptly, as part of my voluntary purgation, given up alcohol in early April. I made an exception for social drinking that evening, and we drank several goblets of red wine, which fumed in the head, and after supper, which was eaten on our knees, his daughter pointed out that his socks had holes in them. He tore them off and threw them on the log fire.

The atmosphere was very homely but we had progressed down different roads – I had been in the East and he had not – and there was a gulf between us. We had pulled away from each other. We were proceeding in the same direction – we were not going in opposite directions, and he said that our aims were "identical" – but we were on diverging roads, he on a rational path of psychological analysis and I on a poetic Mystic Way towards unitive vision. He generously gave me a signed copy of his book on Shaw. Because of the difference between us it would be nearly 18 years before I visited him again.

The next morning I took Ann to see D.S. Savage, who I had last seen in January 1960. He had moved from Lawn House in Mevagissey to Suffolk and back to a stone house across the road in Church Street, Mevagissey. He still had Russian black hair and a beard. He told me he was writing essays on Orwell and Greene, which would be more popular than the book he had written on *The Great Gatsby*. His wife nodded supportingly. He lamented the change of taste and the decline of the man of letters.

We returned in the evening and at his request he looked at my stories and read one or two, frowning. He said they looked a good form: "Because they are so short and have arresting titles, they make you read them. You're on to something here." A couple of lady academics were in the room, and one asked, "But are they stories?" Savage said: "Yes, they're stories."

The next day we drove to Trenarren and walked to the Black Head past A.L. Rowse's house. (I would meet Rowse in Tomlin's company at the

Athenaeum in 1985.) Ann picked some flowers, which she later pressed. On the train going back to London the next day I worked on 'The Silence' and wrote the Trenarren passages into the beginning and the end, aware that the harbour at Charlestown was the harbour I had glimpsed when I was at Oxford.

Disenchantment: leaving the SIS

There had been a minor dispute over the arrangement to collect and return Nadia before Easter. The usual arrangement to meet half-way in Peterborough had been suspended as "David would be working" according to Caroline. I had driven to Horncastle and collected Nadia in mid-April and had her to stay. I had returned her on 20 April. David's parents had met my car, and his father had said that David could not come as he was in hospital due to his "work in 'Security'".

I checked the access arrangement with my solicitor, who wrote a letter to Caroline confirming the half-way agreement. On 29 April I had a reasonable phone call from David making arrangements to meet me half-way at Peterborough in May and July.

Threat to expose me

But on 30 April, the next evening, he rang again and his tone had completely changed. He said he had taken exception to my handling of the access arrangement. He said that Nadia had asked him, "If you die in a plane, will I be with my Daddy again?" He said I must have put the idea in her mind while she stayed with me and that he was reviewing the access arrangement. I had not put the idea in her mind, and I said so.

He said he had found out about my visit to Colin Wilson from 'Security'. He said, "We do not want Nadia associated with people like Colin Wilson. Or Frank Tuohy. I have found out from 'Security' that he is a Soviet agent.[35] You are not a fit person to see Nadia unless there is a supervised guarantee that everything is controlled." He would not say what he found objectionable about Colin Wilson, but I knew that Wilson had had anarchistic tendencies in his early years.[36] He would not say what evidence he had that Tuohy was a Soviet agent. I remembered Keith Priest implying that Tuohy's friend Wittgenstein had been a Soviet agent – according to a minority view he had recruited the Cambridge Five while a fellow at Trinity College, Cambridge – and I wondered if his publisher, Donald Maclean's younger brother, was being used against him by association. I could not believe that Tuohy was working for the Soviet Union, and I wondered if 'Security' had in fact confirmed what he claimed. He would not define what he meant by "a guarantee". He said, "I have made my decision and you will have to apply to a Court if you want to see Nadia."[37]

I was shocked that his 'Security' might think for one moment that Colin Wilson and Tuohy were Communist threats, and that he was applying to Court to cancel my access to Nadia.

He said again, "You made up going to Tanzania, as I've already said. I know about Viktor from my work in Security. I found out from a friend, the old school tie within Security. I can go to *The Daily Express* about Viktor and prove that you made the defection up and have been living in fantasy. You made calls from phone boxes." This was true. When I was at 13 Egerton Gardens I used phone boxes so Pussy-cat would not be listening in. "And this proves you're paranoiac. You're not a fit person to see Nadia."

I was shocked that he knew Viktor's name, and was bewildered at being accused of "making up" Tanzania and Viktor's defection, and of using phone boxes for no reason other than paranoia.

I talked for 55 minutes to try to restore the *status quo* as regards access. He reiterated that he had applied to have the Court withdraw my access. I would not see Nadia again unless the Court gave me permission. He then rang off.

I was bemused. The access arrangements were between Caroline and me, not between him and me. He had interposed the Court between Nadia and me, arguing that I had "made up" my secret work and that he objected to my seeing writers, and was therefore unsuitable to be Nadia's father. I would have to return to my solicitor and spend more money renegotiating the access arrangement. I thought of Shelley's poem 'To the Lord Chancellor' after Harriet's parents had obtained a decree stating that he was unfit to have custody of his children: "Thy country's curse is on thee, darkest crest/Of that foul, knotted, many-headed worm...."

Leak?

But more immediately there was another issue. He had claimed that a friend in 'Security' had told him about Viktor's defection, and that he planned to expose me in *The Daily Express* as having made it up. I would have to report this to Ronald Merton.

I had an arrangement to meet Ronald in The Grenadier in Wilton Row, off Knightsbridge, on 2 May at 6 p.m. The pub's name suggested both the royal household infantry and a soldier armed with grenades: the military nature of my secret work and his own role as a grenade-bearing soldier controlling me.

I told Ronald that I had been told to apply to a Court for access to Nadia; that David claimed he knew about Viktor's defection from a friend in 'Security'; and that he had threatened to expose me to *The Daily Express* as having made the defection up.

Ronald Merton suddenly became animated. He said there must be an immediate investigation to see if there had been a leak within MI5. He terminated our meeting and said he would ring me later that evening at my flat.

He rang me half-way through the evening saying he had to visit me and that I should be alone in my flat. I explained that Ann was with me. He said I should drive her back to Greenwich and then return to my flat. I had to explain to Ann that there had to be an important meeting connected with my journalism and that she had to return to Greenwich for the night. She was understandably put out, not understanding what was going on. I drove her to Greenwich and returned on my own.

Ronald Merton arrived about 10.30 p.m. He now told me that an investigation was under way, and that it had already been determined that David could not have found out about Viktor's defection from a friend in Security, MI5. The only way he could have known about Viktor was through Caroline. He told me the decision had been taken to summon him to London and that he would be told that his job, and his future promotion in the RAF, depended on his silence. Ronald Merton left just after midnight.

I saw the writing on the wall and I was relieved. I had delved into the Cold War with relish but my heart was not in industrial or commercial espionage among Indians and Japanese. I wanted out. I had also had enough of the ESN school, which I had only taken on as a cover for my secret work.

New teaching job by Clapham Common

I had known for some time that I should leave the 'backward' boys. I was in a better frame of mind to take on more responsibility. They were very loyal and waited for my car to arrive each morning and surrounded me affectionately as I got out, but I knew it was time to move on to something better paid. I recognised that it would not be easy to jump back from ESN to academic work in one bound. There was not time to apply for university positions within the UK.

I had to find an alternative quickly, a job that would start in September 1973, not October 1974. I wrote 11 letters for advertised teaching jobs for which I was qualified. None of them appealed. I was invited to interview at two places. One, a girls' grammar school, offered a Scale 3. The second one, Henry Thornton on Clapham Common – Thornton was one of the Clapham Sect that included Wilberforce and Macaulay – offered a Scale 4 (£250 p.a. more) for Second-in-command in the English Department, which had a staff of 10.

I visited Henry Thornton to have a look and liked the Head of English, a quiet, elderly-looking man, Jim Doolan, who was very well-read in the classics. He asked me what I thought of Eliot, Yeats and Pound, and I explained that I had visited Pound. On 15 May I was offered the job. I would be teaching English at 'O' and 'A' level, and would be spending time each week teaching set books by poets which would feed into my own poetic work. I would have extensive preparation and marking, and little time for India and Japan. I accepted the job, to begin in September. I had also been offered the job at the first school and rang it a minute before the deadline, 4 p.m., to decline.

Last Riverway outings with ESN boys: signal-box, hospital mortuary, Windsor and the Royal family, St Paul's and Michael Horovitz

Although I had been appointed to a new job with 'A'-level work on poets whose writings would colour my own poetry, until the end of the summer term I had to fulfil my responsibility at Riverway to take my class of 'backward' 15-year-old boys out into the community in the grey coach so they could get to know different parts of London.

Now that I had to leave them I was struck by how devoted they were. They would do anything I asked.

One week we went to a British railway station, Dartford, to see the signal-box. We had the levers explained. I was then told that the way we had come in was now closed and that the only way back was across the railway lines.

"Just walk down to the crossing point and cross where the lines are shallower," the signal-box supervisor said. So I duly trooped my class down to the crossing point, where there was a wooden walkway of short sleepers between the rails, and stopped to look both ways for trains.

A railway worker came up and said, "You do know that the highest line is live, don't you?"

One rail was higher than the others and protruded above the wooden walkway.

"No," I said.

"Well it is," he said. "You're dead if you touch that one."

I explained that we had been told to cross by the signal-box supervisor and asked if there wasn't another way back. He said, "No. The other way is closed. You can't go back the way you came. You have to cross the lines."

I said, "I can't ask these boys to do that. They're not normal. You'll have to reopen the other way."

"We can't. You've got to cross this way. Otherwise you'll still be here tomorrow morning."

In those days there were no mobile phones and returning the boys to school on time was expected. So I lined the class up and told each boy to walk onto the wooden walkway and jump over the live rail without touching it. One by one they did so successfully. The last boy, 'Wally' Burke, a small unco-ordinated boy with a mad gleam in his eyes and tousled hair, mumbled with rolling pupils, "Sir, I'm not going to be able to jump over that line."

"You're going to jump it," I told him.

He walked slowly onto the wooden walkway and up to the line and stood, his toes an inch away from it. "Jump it, step over it without touching it," I commanded.

"I can't, sir."

"JUMP," I yelled, and in terror, with both feet together, hands by his sides and palms out like a penguin, he made a little flopping movement and landed with both feet together an inch the other side of the line.

"I jumped it, sir," he mumbled. In the distance I could see an electric train hurtling towards us.

"Run," I shouted. And he ran. I followed, leaping the live rail and getting clear of the path of the train.

Now that I had marshalled them successfully across the live track the full enormity of my predicament hit me. Several of the boys were brain-damaged. It was amazing that no one had trodden on the line. We should never have been told to leave by this route. But I had treated them as if they were normal and they had responded and behaved normally. They had all done exactly what I had asked of them, Burke albeit reluctantly.

Another outing was to St Nicholas's Hospital to see if any of them wanted to work in the kitchens or boiler-house or on the porters' trolleys. The Head Porter, a giant, asked us communally if we wanted to see the mortuary.

"Cor, yes," one of the more streetwise boys said, "I ain't squeamish."

I said I did not think it was a good idea, but the boys had been asked collectively and there was a clamour to go in.

The Head Porter said, "You all seem to want to see it, is it all right with sir?"

"Come on, sir, say Yes," chorused the boys.

The Head Porter had swept them along, so we went into a room with a scrubbed stone floor and wired glass. The mortician was beady-eyed with rimless spectacles. He said, "The dead bodies are in these fridges."

He opened a fridge door to disclose three trays. He pulled out a tray to reveal a man of 70 with a cut on his head and open eyes. He was in his own clothes with no winding-sheet.

"Touch him," said the giant, but no one dared. The boys had gone very quiet.

"He's just asleep, see? He died yesterday and fell, see? He's looking at you," he said and he closed the man's eyes.

He pushed the drawer back in and pulled out another on which lay a woman of 55, her skull bound in a bandage. He pushed that drawer back in and pulled out a woman of 70 with a wax-like face. He pushed that drawer in and finally opened another fridge door and pulled out a much younger woman. "She was alive this morning," he said.

The boy who had boasted he wasn't squeamish went out to be sick, while 'Wally' Burke asked mad questions, his eyes darting from side to side: "Was she alive this morning, sir? Did she have breakfast this morning, sir? Is she dead, sir? Yes, but is she dead?"

I left feeling faintly sick and, still smelling the smell of death, I felt it was all the more important to enjoy life now, today. I thought of all the moments that man in the drawer was missing. To be alive was not to be dead in that drawer. I revelled in being alive. Later I based my story 'A Smell of Leaves and Summer' on what I had seen and felt.

A week later I took the boys to Windsor. "I don't want to see the Queen," Derek la Rivière said, "what's she ever done for us? She doesn't earn her money." 'Wally' Burke was frightened of the changing of the guard: six soldiers in red with busbies and bayonets.

I talked to a royal chauffeur and Burke came in on the conversation and asked: "Will the Queen be coming out?"

"The whole family," the chauffeur said.

"Yes, but will the Queen?" Burke asked. The chauffeur gave me an odd look.

At 1.45 the Queen and the entire Royal family – in whose service I had during the past four years risked my life many times – left from the back gates on Long Walk in a fleet of black cars. They came out of the gates and drove slowly along the road across the Park, which was lined with waving people. They were on their way to Ascot, and the Duke of Edinburgh was in a top hat. The Queen, in green, looked strangely white and unreal. The other members of the Royal family smiled and waved like puppets.

On the way back London was full of large buildings occupied by companies such as Siemens and Honeywell. I had a clear image of our country: of capitalist companies under a puppet monarchy, represented in Parliament and local government, an existing order kept intact by the police. Recently I had been a tiny cog in the machinery of the Establishment's government.[38]

Strangely, my ESN boys had reconnected me with my poetic self. After an outing to the National Gallery the previous December I had looked in on St Paul's Cathedral with my ESN boys. A section to the immediate left of the entrance was roped off and a poetry reading was in progress. Someone was standing before a seated audience, wearing a sweater and jeans. He blew into a party tooter, one of those curled-up things that expand and toot simultaneously before retracting.

"Sir, what's he doing?" asked 'Wally' Burke.

With a shock I realised it was my old Oxford acquaintance, the Beat poet Michael Horovitz (*see* pp.96, 127). So far as I recollect he declaimed between toots: "The Committee of St Paul's Cathedral's Restoration Fund were blown away on a puff of wind." He tooted again.

"Sir, who's blown away?" asked 'Wally' Burke. "Sir, why's he blowing on that thing? Sir, how were they blown away? Was it the wind? And why's he blowing that thing?"

I found it impossible to justify Horovitz's statement to Burke's ESN mind, and I simply said, "It's a bit of fun."

"Sir, is he mad, sir?" asked 'Wally' Burke. I considered the merit in his point and I did not reply. But I had felt a call to return to the poetry I wanted to write, and that summer I was impatient to write poems again.

I looked ahead to July, when Riverway would break up and I would leave. It had been a cover for my secret work, and now that my secret work nearly did not exist any more it seemed natural that my cover should have fallen away.

Row between MI6 and MI5
I next met Ronald Merton in The Grenadier on 17 May. Before I could tell him my news, that I had accepted the offer of a new job, he informed me, "There's been a meeting between MI6 and MI5. There was an almighty row. MI6 told MI5 to 'lay off' probing Viktor's defection and to 'lay off' their agent. (You.) David was summoned to London and was told in no uncertain terms not to expose Viktor's defection in *The Daily Express*. Chastened, he undertook not to carry out his threat to go to *The Daily Express*. However, he defiantly said that the Court would determine whether you can see Nadia. There's a risk that he will expose Viktor's defection in Court."

"Never see your daughter again": I am asked to sign that I will not see my daughter again
Ronald Merton said to me: "We have looked at the situation in great detail and we are sure that your arrangements with your ex-wife over your daughter will eventually come to Court as she will want custody without access. In that case, though your ex-wife's husband has been warned not to expose you, he might expose you under the protection of a court of law, and we will therefore be put at risk. I agree it's a dirty trick on his part, but we are good because we don't take risks. The only way you can continue working with us is if you agree not to have anything more to do with your daughter, ever again – walk out of her life for good now. For in that case nothing would come to Court and there would be no risk. I feel terrible at having to ask you – but I have been told to ask you – if you will sign a document I have here in my briefcase agreeing that you will have no further dealings with your daughter, that you will never see her again. If you sign this document now, we can continue. If you don't sign it, then I am afraid we

will have to discontinue. I am sorry to put this choice to you in such stark terms, but that is what I've been asked to do."

I did not have to think. I knew immediately that I would never sign away my right to see Nadia ever again. I was aghast at the very thought, and saddened that a civil-service-like organisation that had once been so friendly, gentlemanly and civilised in the days of Keith Priest and Andrew Mackenzie should by degrees have turned into an organisation that had on its own admission: broken up my family by exposing it to agents from other organisations; made me function as a known agent after Viktor had exposed me to Czech intelligence and therefore to the KGB; made me ask blatant questions of people who knew I was an agent; told me off for not persuading guerillas who knew I was an agent to get me into a guerilla camp; ordered

Nadia feeding pigeons in Trafalgar Square, London, 1970

me to betray people I liked and regarded as friends; and was now – a ratcheting-up of its escalating ruthlessness – asking me to turn my back on my own daughter, walk out of her life for ever. It had placed its own security and freedom from risk above the human bond between father and daughter. Agreeing would involve me in the greatest betrayal of my life. I had not believed that the SIS would deliberately separate a husband and wife to suit their own self-interest, but now they were deliberately attempting to separate a father and daughter to suit their own self-interest.

Ricky Herbert had warned me: "You can start off thinking you can control them but then discover that they control you. It's like Goethe's Faust. He believes *he* can control Mephistopheles but in the end Mephistopheles controls *him*. You need to be careful that you don't suffer Faust's fate."

I had thought I was independent but now the SIS were acting as if they felt they were entitled to control me, by insisting that I renounce my daughter. I had made a more binding Faustian pact with Mephistopheles than I had realised, and now my daughter was required of me. I had been lured into a darker working relationship, a darker part of the wood, than I had initially understood.

I said, "I'm not signing. Nothing can prevent me from continuing to see my daughter."

Discontinuing: I leave the SIS

He said, "That would have been my reply. I completely agree with you that your daughter comes first. I felt very uncomfortable at asking you, but I was ordered to ask and I had to ask. So I'm very sorry, I've enjoyed working with you but we will have to discontinue. The situation has got to come to court. It depends on whether he wants custody without access and is prepared to try and get it. Don't press him too hard. He will be feeling one-down over this, having heard it through an official channel. That man will never get promotion. And he knows it." Then he asked, "What will you do?"[39]

I told him I was starting a new job on 1 September. He nodded and said he would pay me until the end of August and that I would receive a severance gratuity of £200, which would represent a month's salary for each of the four years I had served. I recalled that Christine Granville, the wartime SOE agent who had five years' service, received five months of half-salary as severance gratuity from the SOE in 1945.[40]

He said, "There is a lot of official gratitude. If it does come out, it will matter less as time goes by."

He took me to a nearby restaurant for an Indian curry – suggesting the work on India I had turned my back on. He said uncomfortably and enigmatically, "I'm very conscious that *we* are responsible for the break-up of your marriage,"[41] and would not elaborate as to *how* the SIS had broken up my marriage.

I now instinctively knew why Marlowe, a 16th-century intelligence agent, had written *Dr Faustus*. Walsingham's secret service had been his Mephistophilis, and it had come to control him (and would end his life). That was the true meaning of *Dr Faustus* to Marlowe, I was sure. When I came to write my poetic epic, *Overlord*, I would have a good knowledge of the way Satan worked in the world. I was relieved to have ended the secret service's control of me. I wrote a reproachful poem, 'Mephistopheles' (Goethe's rather than Marlowe's spelling), pointing out that there was good reason for Mephistopheles to blush.

I collected Nadia from Tattershall on 26 May to drive her to London for half-term. David handed her over in thunderous silence. He stood silent in the square on a hot day. I did not speak to him.

She wore the yellow smock I had bought her before Easter, and I called her "primrose". I had a close talk to her after I turned her light off. She told me she was afraid of people under her bed and of shadows, just as I had been at the end of the war. I was protective and revelled in the continuation of our relationship, which the SIS had tried to end.

I returned her to Lincolnshire on 30 May. This time David was in a "sand uniform, wearing [a] pistol".[42] I wondered if the pistol was loaded. Again, we did not speak.

The real reason

I had a brief meeting with Ronald Merton in The Grenadier on 3 July at 6.30 so he could give me my salary for June. Our final meeting was in The Grenadier on 8 August. He handed over my July and August salaries, and the £200 severance gratuity: £300 in all.

I asked him, "What's the real reason for my severance?"

He looked startled, then said: "The world's changed. Sir Alec Douglas-Home, our Foreign Secretary, has been to China in the wake of Nixon's visit. Our leaders can go and talk to the Chinese leaders, and we don't have to do it through intermediaries now. Nixon has reached an understanding with Brezhnev. Also Watergate has happened, and Heath doesn't want a Watergate here. Heath can no longer take the risk of having an 'unofficial Ambassador', and he does not need you to the same extent now."

He still felt uncomfortable at asking me to walk out of my daughter's life for good and I believe he was telling me the truth. Ronald Merton said, "If the Chinese try to recruit you, we will know. If you need us, you have a number to ring. Otherwise don't call us, we'll call you." He thanked me for what I had done and we parted for good.

Later I had mixed feelings. I had liked the excitement of the intelligence agent's life. Never had my sense of observation, awareness and alertness been so heightened as when I walked the streets of London being stalked by a surveillance squad and checking that they were not getting too close by peering at reflections in windows and parked cars. I was constantly aware of who was behind me, living in the moment to the full. Now there would be no more surveillance squads.

I reflected on Ronald Merton's description of "the real reason" for my severance. It made sense. The late-night meeting coincided with the replacement of Sir John Rennie as Chief of the SIS by Sir Maurice Oldfield after Rennie's son was arrested for importing a large amount of heroin into Hong Kong in January 1973. On his arrival Oldfield had ordered a fresh look at SIS policy. Henry Kissinger's talks with Chou En-lai of 9 July 1971[43] and 21 October 1971[44] and President Nixon's visit to China in February 1972[45] had begun the normalisation of relations between the US and China. Sir Alec Douglas-Home had visited China in October 1972 and had direct talks with Chou En-lai that included Chinese moral and material support for revolutionary movements occupying national territory.[46] Kissinger would have further talks with Chou En-lai on 14 November 1973.[47] These visits would mean that the British and Chinese Governments could talk face to face without having to use intermediaries such as myself. The Watergate scandal following the break-in at the Democratic National Committee headquarters at the Watergate complex in Washington DC in June 1972 had made all governments aware of the need to avoid scandals.

It may be that a threat to expose my role in the defection of Viktor to *The Daily Express* coupled with a wrong assertion that it never happened was seized on as a pretext for a more fundamental reason to sever links with me. It may be that I was doomed by the KGB's leak that circulated in Fleet Street, and that the SIS knew all along that I would never turn my back on Nadia and used their condition to achieve my severance from them, an outcome they wanted as I was now operating with the full knowledge of the KGB and was too much of a risk to continue working with. I have no means of knowing, but this was *not* how Ronald Merton thought.

Balanced view
I now took a balanced view of my four years of Government service.

On the positive side, I had stepped up when asked and, first in Libya and then as Heath's 'unofficial Ambassador', I had patriotically contributed to the defence of the West in the Cold War, the 'Third World War' being fought in Western Europe and Africa. It had all been interesting experience. I calculated that since May 1969 I had received (including one bonus of £30) £3,230 after tax, plus my teaching salary for the days I was in Tanzania. For that I had risked my life in Libya, Egypt, London, Brussels and Tanzania. To put it in perspective, according to the website MeasuringWorth.com £1 in 1970 was worth £12.10 (using the retail price index)/£21.80 (using average earnings) in 2010, so these amounts would have to be multiplied by between 12 and 21 to give today's equivalent. My Scale-4 salary would exceed the sum total of my ESN salary *and* what I was paid by the SIS.

On the negative side, there was a different kind of cost to me that would be life-long. If I had stayed in England in 1968 I would not have been approached by the SIS and would have been free to function as a normal writer. I would discover that this freedom would be denied to me, that my projects would mysteriously be denied publicity. A senior channel between politicians and the intelligence services would investigate and find that I had been subject to systemic, controlling *Totenstille*, 'death by silence', that my work had been deliberately surrounded by "walls of silence" – a consequence of my being wrongly grouped with the professional spymaster Peter Wright, author of *Spycatcher*, whose work had been suppressed on Government orders. He would tell me that he had negotiated a deal whereby I would be allowed to operate but with "limited" publicity. (*See My Double Life 2: A Rainbow over the Hills.*)

In a sense, I would be banished from the public eye as surely as Ovid who had been ordered to live beyond the frontier of Roman civilization in Tomis on the Black Sea for the rest of his life, a fate I show in my verse play *Ovid Banished*. If I had known that I would be allowed to operate as a writer in only a "limited" way as powers behind the scenes were bent on keeping me out of the public eye, I would not have agreed to undertake my secret work in the first place. It is partly to lay this ghost to rest, and after 40 years to set the record straight, that I have written this account.

My heart had not been in my secret work since my return from Tanzania. I had wanted to leave. I felt with relief as if I had at last emerged from a dark wood through which I had struggled to find a way since 1966, free from all thickets. I was clear and clean, and rejoiced in the sunlight. I still regarded the work of an agent as being necessary to the national interest, but it was no longer for me.

I had been transformed. I was living through a different centre now, and saw the universe, and therefore all humankind, as a unity. I no longer thought in nationalist terms. I had walked away from deception and returned to sincerity and art. I could now devote all my energies to my writing and getting ready for my new work in Clapham.

SIS judgement wrong

The SIS were "sure" that my arrangements regarding Nadia would "eventually come to Court" as my ex-wife would want custody without access. In fact, the SIS's judgement was proved wrong: the arrangements involving custody for my daughter did *not* come to Court and there was *no* further attempt to challenge my access or expose me. (The only Court involvement concerned an administrative change to the address to which my regular maintenance payments were sent.)

The SIS's premise was not right. We could have continued, although the six months I had been given to get established had run out and I suspect they were using Court as a pretext for terminating my employment due to my lack of enthusiasm for my new role. By now I was so disenchanted that I gladly consented to severing my links with what I had now come to believe was an insensitive and inhuman organisation.

David had been warned that he would not get promotion if he did not remain silent, that his future depended on his silence. Ronald Merton was right in saying that he would not get promotion. The row between MI6 and MI5 seems to have had a disastrous effect on his promotion prospects. I later heard that around 1976 he ceased to be a navigator of Phantoms, and he left the RAF in 1981. That evening in Malta when he sat at The Roundabout bar, keeping an eye on Caroline and me, had begun a chain of events that would culminate in the end of his RAF career.

No contact with SIS since 1973

Since 8 August 1973 I have had no contact of any kind with anyone in the SIS. I attended just two functions connected with my old life. The first was a reception at the Tanzanian High Commission on 26 March 1974 for Pita-

Kabisa's return to Tanzania, to which Pita-Kabisa invited me. The other was a reception on Namibia Day, 2 July 1974, when an empty sack of potatoes was raffled amid mirth to raise funds for Namibia.

I spoke with Sean MacBride (whose mother Maud Gonne Yeats wanted to marry and whose father John MacBride, the Irish republican Yeats wrote about in 'Easter 1916', was executed by the British in Kilmainham Gaol, Dublin in 1916). It was alleged that he had been Chief of Staff of the IRA in the late 1930s. I also found myself talking to Ruth First, the Communist anti-*apartheid* South-African activist whose husband Joe Slovo was a founder-member of the ANC. She was tried for treason between 1956 and 1961 and held in isolation for 117 days without charge under the 90-day South-African detention law in 1963. I described to her how I had seen a black-and-white television programme in Essex about her case in 1963. I still have a clear memory of her face from that programme. She denied that the programme ever existed and said, "I think you are a British agent." (She was killed by a parcel bomb addressed to her in Mozambique on the orders of a major in the South-African police in 1982.)

In June 1988 Heath came to my sons' school, Chigwell School, to distribute prizes, a ruddy-faced man with white hair, and my son Tony received a prize from him and shook his hand. Afterwards he walked with the Head, Brian Wilson. I stood beside him but backed away from speaking to him. In May 2008 I stood over the slab in the floor of Salisbury Cathedral that marks where he is buried. I pondered my connection with him, and the walls of silence round my work that seemed as tall as the towering Gothic walls of Salisbury Cathedral.

Now a picture hangs outside my study of Goethe's Faust sitting in *his* study and being confronted by Mephistopheles, a permanent reminder to keep Mephistopheles outside my closed study door.

For the last 40 years, to the best of my knowledge, I have been completely clear of any contact with the SIS. I have kept silent during the 40 years since my last contact with the SIS, and now feel (in the tradition of Sir John Masterman and Asa Briggs, *see* p.xxxi) that as most of the participants are dead and the Cold War is over the time is right to present a picture of what it was like being an intelligence agent during the very different Cold-War atmosphere of more than 40 years ago.

The vision of unity: first inklings of a neo-Baroque movement
Now that I had finished with the SIS, I threw myself into preparing for my new job in Clapham which would start in September. Now I would no longer be driving between Kensington and Greenwich, Ann looked to leave her Greenwich flat and move from her school All Saints', Blackheath. She was soon offered a job at another Church-of-England primary school, St

FAUST MAKES OVER HIS SOUL TO MEPHISTOPHELES.

Published by Jennings & Son, 2 Poultry Street, June 1820.

Engraving by Henry Moses of Goethe's Faust in his study being interrupted by Mephistopheles, 1820

James Norland, Holland Park, from September. This would mean that our lives would be lived between Clapham and Holland Park instead of South Kensington and Greenwich.

While I was severing my connection with the SIS my poetic flow had resumed. Poems had begun coming again on 6 May and for a couple of weeks I wrote the finished versions in my green manuscript book.

At the same time I had begun a drive to get my body fit. I began doing the Canadian 5BX exercises, which were devised for Canadian air-force flying crew. I started with one toe-touch, one lying-on-the-floor and sitting-up, one butterfly stroke, one double press-up and a few runs-on-the-spot, and built up to 28 toe-touches, 28 sit-ups, 39 butterfly strokes, 19 double press-ups and 650 runs-on-the-spot, all in 11 minutes. My aim was to get my weight down from 14 stone. Now 40 years later I am still doing a reduced version of these exercises and my weight fluctuates around 14 stone.

The Light I had experienced in September 1971 and so many times since then did not come into my inner night now and shine behind my closed eyes like a midnight sun, and the visions that accompanied it had abated.

467

At the end of July I noted in my *Diaries*: "I have not had illumination and picture visions for some months."[48] A few days later I "saw my imagination: Greek temples, an African mask, and the light nearly breaking and then not breaking...." I wrote: "I am a visionary and a mystic. The two are different. The visionary sees his imagination; the mystic feels the oneness of the outer world – having been helped to feel it by the oneness of the Light. I shall restore knowledge of the Light."[49] Later the same day I wrote my poem, 'Sunbathing'.

In August Margaret Riley, the older Austrian mystic artist who had brought my spiritual vision to birth and had disappeared after leaving the London boarding-house in Egerton Gardens, rang three times from St Ives in Cornwall. She said she had been painting and sculpting there and had had a new mystical period. She came to stay at my new flat at the top of 33 Stanhope Gardens on 15 August. She told me of "a vision she had of Jesus Christ (wearing white, dark hair) in the dark last October – so close she could touch him. 'It all comes from the heart. You discard from the heart, and the heart flows up when it is peaceful and becomes light in the head.' 'When I pray I feel at peace and go deep so I am not aware of anybody, and I *see* whoever I'm thinking of.'"

She was insistent that the Light comes through the heart: "'It is the heart that starts everything: love. If you are humble you are at peace.' 'Prayer is not speaking to anyone – don't talk.' 'The Light only comes when the heart is at peace, and visions I have thought day-dreams have turned out to be visions.'" I thought of the "burning *heart*" in St John of the Cross's poem about a secret stair.

She stayed the night, sleeping in my absent daughter Nadia's bed, and over breakfast next morning told me she would find a base in Shoreham, near her sister's family. Then "she brought through a small figurine in white Windsor-and-Newton clay, done in St Ives. A tall triangle, only the third side surprisingly reveals a side-on figure of the Virgin Mary – her vision. Margaret: 'It's about angles. Most people look along the line and see nothing, whereas if they change their way of looking and peep round the corner, there is this vision.'" I called this work 'Vision'. It was about changing your way of looking, peeping round the corner.

She gave me directions as if she were still my spiritual teacher: "No one owns me, and I own nobody." "Compare yourself with nobody." "Be yourself. Development is not reaching out for other people. Those who have lost their way are looking, searching, instead of staying and being themselves." "Overcome the conflicts – the heart feels all in One." "The heart is the fountain of all things."[50]

We walked in Stanhope Gardens. It was very hot and we discussed starting a new European movement in the arts, for which I drew up the following manifesto. We had had a neo-Romantic and Neoclassical movement in English poetry, and I thought that a combination of the two, a neo-Baroque movement, was ahead. I give the manifesto in full as my perception of a neo-Baroque movement in poetry and stories impacted on the way I wrote poems at this time.

1. There needs to be a new direction in all the European arts, which are stagnating.
2. This stagnation is caused by the fact that the values of the West and in the arts are wrong. They are based on the body and head. The soul of the West needs to be purified along with its perception.
3. All the clutter that has gathered like fungus on the soul of the West should be knocked off, and works of art should again come from the heart, which is the spring of peace, from which follow the illumination and visions of the mystical life.
4. The real world should therefore flood back into the arts, fresh and alive. This will be *a Baroque period* in relation to the cycle of art periods. Subject matter will have primacy, there will be an end to abstraction and the "technique-first" attitude.
5. Man is a Colossus in chains. When he has escaped his chains he will be seen as he is and as he can become, with all his possibilities – free, at peace, at unity with the universe, living by reality, truth and the meaning of life.
6. Art should therefore concentrate on these positive qualities. It should show examples of them, and if it shows someone who has lost his way, it should make it clear why he has lost his way.
7. Therefore the heart should dominate, not the head: there should be no rules except those which the heart demands. Paintings should not be worked out first, and from each work there must be a feeling, otherwise it will be a dud. The enemy is Rationalism, which asks questions, asks why: the reason is an obstacle to feeling peace.[51]

This statement encapsulated my aims in my poems and stories in the coming years and set down how I regarded the neo-Baroque. In point 5 I was thinking of Frank Tuohy's image of a unicorn in chains. He had just sent me a card from New York, identical to a previous card he had sent me, showing a unicorn chained to a post surrounded by a fence: the artist, unfree, on display as if in a zoo. He called to see me on his way to America at the end of May and we had lunched in the Denmark. He was in a melancholic mood. He said he had written some stories but they were "a failure" and: "My Somerset novel died on me. The structure was wrong. Too little happens in Somerset." Ezard had predicted (when I encountered him at a bus-stop) that Tuohy's work would end in silence. I recorded: "The ideal of the new Age of Contentment is the free, peaceful man, the Colossus of mysticism free from his chains."

I now moved back to shorter poems. I commented in my *Diaries*: "The long poem idea came from the idea of *searching*, which is now seen to be an enemy of peace. Now my aim is to… communicate peace, and this can be done in shorter poems. But stop rhymes. For now, no rules. Free verse. Let the heart control." I had arrived at a new aesthetic for my poetry, which was to take me away from the rigid metrical forms of the Movement for a few years.

I realised that my stories were neo-Baroque: "My stories are from the heart…. There are two ways [of writing stories], the sudden impulsive desire to do a story, or the contemplation at peace, 'emotion recollected in tranquillity'…. Something happens and I walk round and then it comes up and I write it. The heart is like a spring." (My ex-wife Caroline had once said to me: "I give you feelings [i.e. heart]; without them your writing would be arid.")

Margaret spoke of our roots: "The heart of the tree is in the roots. The trunk is the centre from there and it goes upwards, you paint it upwards. God is the ground of one's being – so the ground is in the heart…. The heart of the dahlia is in the roots. And if the roots are deep, it is strong. The deeper the roots the stronger." I saw that I had now become my own heart after a "painful way of loss".[52]

Margaret saw mysticism in terms of the heart: "It makes you see the beauty of virtue and the ugliness of vice, for example the beauty of humility and the ugliness of self-importance. And [it] also [makes you] appreciate the beauty of things you see as opposed to the dirt and squalor and foul breath and stale beer that Tuohy, who has lost his faith, writes about."

Her message now became one of work. She talked of arranging an exhibition in Vienna, which, I thought, would counteract and neutralise the wrong rationalistic view of the Vienna Circle. She spoke of my works, and I wrote in my *Diaries*: "Margaret: 'Never be afraid of failure, each work you do makes the next one easier.' She said that an artist can find that the first 50 paintings are no good, but the last 30 may be works of 'genius'. 'Your stories are flowing now. You do them quickly.'" She saw herself as ready for more work: "Last May I was confused. I did not know whether to take a religious direction, go into an organisation in the Church, but then I saw the European venture was right. You told me so two years ago: I was not ready. I am reaching the end of a religious period and now there will be a period of work."[53] Her message was that I should work to create images of my vision.

I saw that I had been transformed through suffering. Through it I had discarded the head-dominated manipulations of the intelligence world for poems from the heart. I had Ann, my partner, now to relate to heart-to-heart. In the course of my suffering I had undergone a centre-shift to a universal part of my self. I wrote: "It was necessary for me to suffer so that I could lose my head and gain my heart, from which all meaning is perceived. The justification of suffering is in this: that it gains the heart.... Suffering takes you from a heart involved with one person and not mankind to a heart that is free from the chains of one person, that is more truly itself, and which can more easily feel for all mankind – brotherly love.... Suffering came into my life and grew new places in my heart, and now I feel the universe more directly. Except a corn of wheat [the head] fall into the ground [of humanity] and die, it abideth alone [it stays the head]. But if it die, it bringeth forth much fruit [i.e. the heart]."

Margaret spoke of my illumination on 10 September 1971: "'It was Providence. But I had to get away from that place. It was suffocating me. I had to get away from Egerton Gardens.' 'No possessions (materially), the possession is here (in the heart).' 'You become strong through self-denial and self-discipline. The victory of giving (something you wanted for yourself).' 'It's not important if something breaks up, or if you lose somebody, for if it's lost, it was never worth it in the first place.'"

Eventually Margaret left after spending five days with me. She summed up her ideas on growth, community and work in vivid spoken images that lingered long in the mind. My *Diaries* record: "Margaret left this morning, nearly leaving behind her sketch-book and her [pottery] 'Vision'. This morning at breakfast she commented on the dahlias. Ann had thrown out the dead ones and left the young buds: 'With a little care these buds can develop into a better one than that good one.' Outside at the taxi rank: 'I am going to build another beehive, but one everyone can enjoy.... I am a bee flying back to the beehive.... The ploughman is at peace, he ploughs straight ahead, he has his direction, he doesn't look to left or right. Or over his shoulder. And when he reaches the end he returns. And there are seeds.'"

After Margaret had gone, leaving with me the ploughman's single-minded, methodical way of working, I began to implement the neo-Baroque idea in poems. I recorded: "Felt tired after writing three mystic poems and a story. Then wrote and got the title for (after typing): 'A Smell of Leaves and Summer'."[54] The title of this story eventually gave its name to the title of my second collection of stories. I noted that I was in a creative time.

There were just over two weeks left of the summer holidays. I prepared for my absent daughter Nadia to start at boarding-school in Yorkshire in September and for my new job on Clapham Common with a heavy heart.

Out of the dark wood with a vision
I was out of the dark wood now, and ready to ascend the hills ahead. I had

won a vision of the Light, the hidden Reality that manifests from the beyond, a vision of the unity of the universe. I understood the meaning of life, which can only be known when the universe and all living creatures including humankind are seen as being within the law of the infinite One which reconciles all opposites. I had a clear view of what the true values of the West should be. I had to restore knowledge of the Light and communicate my unitive vision in seven different disciplines.

Ahead of me were five decades of hard work in what I would come to see were the "seven hills of achievement". I had many books to write if I could create the leisure in which to write them. My seeking in foreign cultures was over, for I had found. My Way of Loss was over for I had transformed myself and had set about remaking myself.

Together with Ann I would embark on creating a new home, family and social position that would enable me to write works that would convey to a new generation what I had learned from my experience of nationalism: the need for Universalism. I had gone to Greenwich as cover for my secret work, and I owed meeting Ann to my secret work. For had I not agreed to work with Andrew Mackenzie I would not have met Ann in the Greenwich baths.

I had emerged from the dark wood with a vision. I was on the right path. But my true task in life had scarcely begun. I had left the nightmare of surveillance squads and deception behind in the thickets of the wood just as civilians I knew had left behind their distinguished war service, and I looked forward to living at a deeper level and with a writer's sincerity as I began to slog up the path to turn my vision into new deeds and more than 40 works.

Epilogue: View of the Path –
Episodes and Memories, Pattern and Unity

"For why? thou shalt not leave my soul in hell:... Thou shalt shew me the path of life."

Psalm 16.11–12

My story began in wartime. I quested for Reality in the Far East, found its concept in Tokyo – +A + –A = 0 – and experienced illumination in London while serving as Heath's top-secret 'unofficial Ambassador' to the African liberation movements. I extricated myself from intelligence work, emerged from my dark wood and was ready for the next stage of my quest, an ascent into the hills of achievement above which the call of my vision hung like a rainbow.

This part of my story has presented my double life, my path. In my double life I was first a lecturer and poet, then a teacher, agent and journalist. Throughout I lived in the social world and opened to metaphysical inklings in my writings. I earned a living and engaged with normal social life, but I also lived intensely in my imagination while composing works. I always had a +A and a –A in my double life, a *yang* and a *yin*, as befits a Gemini, but there was always an = 0 that perpetually reconciled the contradictions and opposites in my episodes. This part of my story has presented the path of just one member of humankind and the pattern behind my double life.

Pattern and unity in a life
Pattern and symmetry as design: life as a succession of episodes and memories, and pairs of opposites
Pattern is a "repeated decorative design", a "regular order or arrangement of parts" (*Concise Oxford Dictionary*). Looking down at the individual wood and the trees basking in sun, I reflect that pattern has much to do with symmetry, which is the "correct proportion of parts of an equal shape and size" (*Concise Oxford Dictionary*) in relation to the structure of the whole. Just as the trees are in correct proportion to the whole wood and the windows of a palace – Buckingham Palace, the Louvre – are in correct proportion to the whole palace, so the scales are in correct proportion to the whole structure of a spruce cone. I see a strange unifying symmetry in my experiences as the episodes and events in my life – its parts – are unified in relation to the structure of my life, its whole.

Pattern of transformation in 15 episodes and pairs of opposites: personal episodes and memories, pattern and unity – double helix

The pattern of a life is like the repeated decorative design on a carpet, wallpaper or dress. A decorative *motif* repeats at symmetrical intervals and is in correct proportion to the whole carpet, wallpaper or dress. The design has to be seen as a whole for the pattern to be recognised.

I see that the design in my life, and therefore its pattern, can be found in the succession of episodes I experienced. The episodes and pairs of opposites are like decorative *motif*s that repeat at symmetrical intervals and suggest a design and a recognisable pattern. I have said that each episode grows out of the previous episode and fades during the next episode. I have just described the first 15 episodes, in each of which there is a pair of opposites: a 'double' that meant that in each episode I lived a 'double life'. *My Double Life 2: A Rainbow over the Hills* will set out a complete list of all 30 episodes in my double life.

As time is a succession of events within episodes, and over the years memories of them accrete round the self in layers, the pattern in our episodic lives is reflected in our memories. If we detect a pattern in our episodes, that same pattern will be in our layered memories. Memories of the pairs of opposites in our lives – the pairs of conflicting sequences of events within episodes – accrete round our self in layers of photograph-like memories as (by analogy) scales form round the central stem of a spruce cone. The central self remembers them all. The earliest situations and memories of childhood are at the bottom, and are unconscious. The more recent and better-remembered ones are near the top, and more conscious. The more conscious situations and memories can be pictured vividly, and are images within space-time. (Sometimes – as in the case of my moments by the Strawberry Hill pond and the Worcester College lake – they have the force of symbols: images which point to a metaphysical Reality both within and outside space-time and have a life beyond everyday reality.)

Pattern can be detected in episodes and in the pairs of opposites they contain. Episodes and pairs of opposites are like decorative *motif*s that suggest a design that recalls the double helix of DNA, which its co-discoverer Francis Crick described in a letter to his 12-year-old son as "a very long chain with flat bits sticking out". The double chains formed pairs that entwined with each other. "Only these pairs can go together," Crick wrote.[1] The episodes and pairs of opposites can be seen as the DNA-like chain of a double helix.

It is now time to identify and reveal the pattern behind all the pairs of opposites in my life. I said on p.xxxi that after a long life we may be a succession of some 42 episodes and layered pairs of opposites. To recap, the first 15 of the 30 episodes and layered pairs of opposites I have lived through in my 'double' life, were:

- episode 1: family–war
- episode 2: Nature–school
- episode 3: archaeology–politics
- episode 4: Literature–Law
- episode 5: wisdom–intelligence
- episode 6: marriage–dictatorship
- episode 7: vitalism–mechanism
- episode 8: the Absolute–scepticism
- episode 9: civilizations–Communism
- episode 10: Establishment–revolution
- episode 11: liberation–tyranny
- episode 12: purgation–separation
- episode 13: Ambassador–journalism
- episode 14: illumination–nationalism
- episode 15: meaning–disenchantment

Pattern of progression and regression (+A + –A): transformation towards a vision of the unity of the universe

The episodes in my life show a progression – a transformation – from boyhood to maturity and an equivalent inner development. There is a pattern of transformation from episode 1 to episode 15. In each episode there is a conflict – a push-pull tug of war – between a positive aspect (the first in each pair in the above list) which impels the transforming soul and advances the transformation; and a negative aspect (the second in each pair in the above list) which impels the social ego that pulls against and restrains the transformation. The transformation, or metamorphosis, is a progress – a progression – in the soul towards a vision of the unity of the universe through a working-out of +A + –A = 0, in which the +A represents the positive aspect of each episode (the transforming power of the soul), and the –A the negative aspect of each episode (the anti-transforming pull of the social ego).

The positive aspects of the episodes (+A) reflect the soul's inner development. They have the following sequence within one helix:

family; Nature; archaeology; Literature; wisdom; marriage; vitalism; the Absolute; civilizations; Establishment; liberation; purgation; Ambassador; illumination; meaning.

In all of these there is a positive progression from my involvement with my family to my glimpses of the meaning of life via marriage, internationalism and illumination. All these positive aspects of the episodes advance the soul towards its awakening to the unity of the universe, thereby advancing the transformation.

The negative aspects of the episodes (−A) reflect the social ego's involvement in the outer world. They have the following sequence within the other helix:

war; school; politics; Law; intelligence; dictatorship; mechanism; scepticism; Communism; revolution; tyranny; separation; journalism; nationalism; disenchantment.

In all of these there is a regressive tendency – in relation to the positive progression – from awareness of the war to disenchantment via dictatorship and nationalism. All these negative aspects of the episodes pull against the soul's developing sense of the unity of the universe and return it to the social world of the rational, social ego, thereby restraining the transformation.

The positive and negative aspects are held in balance within episodes and the pairs of opposites and (when layers of memories have accreted round the stem of the self) within the reconciling power of memory that unites our divided memories. The deeper soul and ego have to be held in balance.

The episodes, then, belong to a pattern: a transformation in terms of the conflicting opposites of $+A + -A = 0$. There is a progression on the positive ('soul') side or helix from my involvement in my family to my glimpses of the meaning of life via marriage, internationalism and illumination. This is balanced on the negative ('social ego') side or helix by a regression from awareness of the war to disenchantment via dictatorship and nationalism. Both the positive progression and the negative regression of my transformation originated in the earliest episodes, indicating that in my life the principle is true that 'what we sow we reap': "whatever a man sows, this he will also reap" (*Galatians* 6.7). The episodes, and their positive and negative aspects, led me to the brink of an internationalism as will be apparent when my story continues in *My Double Life 2: A Rainbow over the Hills*.

As I reflect on the pattern of my double-helix-like life as a whole I see a pattern in the similarities between events within episodes. Everything I ever did has taken me further along my path to the person I am now, and my "Shadow", and my perception of the unity of the universe. What seemed at the time a wrong turning or a dead end led me in the right direction towards what I would need in the future. I took a bookkeeping exam and nearly 25 years later found I was a bookkeeper. I took a gardening job for a few weeks and nearly 35 years later found I was supervising gardeners. I worked in Baghdad, and nearly 45 years later found I was writing about the American invasion of Iraq. Each seemingly irrelevant direction I followed gave me experience I would be grateful for years later and prepared me for my future. Each direction and later experience are like a repeating *motif* in relation to the whole.

The similarities of these events are akin to repetitive design. Some events have led to later events as did my bookkeeping, gardening and working in Iraq. I see that many events of my youth were in some way essential to my life when it is viewed as a whole. Everything I encountered on my path was necessary to the shape of my life. Such linked events do not seem accidental or random when viewed within the pattern of the whole. They repeat at symmetrical intervals. Setting these linked pairs of events down at the end of this book's sequel, *My Double Life 2: A Rainbow over the Hills*, will reveal a further symmetry and pattern in my life.

The pattern of episodes and events I have detected reveals the unity in my life as each episode and event is unified in relation to my whole life as are scales in relation to a whole cone.

Pattern and unity in all lives
Looking back on my life I see that as I progressed along my path and experienced life as a succession of episodes that superimposed themselves on my self as a succession of layers of memories – or, to put it the other way round, as my self reacted to the episodes by growing a succession of layers in my memory – there was a 'dialectic' (a conflict between thesis and antithesis, +A + –A) in each episode. I see that layers accrete on the self like successive falls of leaves in a wood that bury previous years' layers of leaves, seeds, acorns and cones and turn them into rich compost. I see that the same is true of all humankind: everyone lives through a succession of episodes that consist of conflicting sequences of events and superimpose layers on the self that are pairs of opposites. The pattern of episodes and layers is a universal pattern.

As the underlying structure of the episodes in my life resembles the underlying structure of the episodes in every other human being's life, and as the structure of the layers of conflicting pairs of opposites in my self resembles the structure of layers and conflicting pairs of opposites in everybody's self, describing objective aspects of my life presents an exemplar – a model or pattern, and even a template – of the unity and pattern of all lives, a universal pattern.

As I reflect on my life above this wood I reflect on the pattern and unity in all lives. A pattern is a decorative *motif* that repeats at symmetrical intervals within a design (*see* pp.473–474). I have just claimed that a pattern can be detected in my first 15 episodes and that it unifies my life. It will be interesting to see if this unifying pattern will be continued in the last 15 episodes. Assuming it *is* continued, I believe that the pattern and unity of my life reflects the pattern and unity of all lives.

I believe that, like an archaeologist exposing the pattern in a mosaic floor that has been covered with turf, I have unearthed a universal chain-like (or double-helix-like) pattern and unity that is found in all lives. There are many walks of life and the exact nature of episodes and of the conflicting pairs of opposites in each episode will differ from life to life. But I believe that the *underlying principle* is present in all lives. Everyone's life can be seen in terms of episodes, and in each episode there is a pair of opposites. Whether one is a banker, a doctor, a teacher, a politician or a sportsman will determine the detail of the conflicting opposites, but the principle of a life of structured episodes and of conflicting episodes applies to all lives.

I hold that the pattern in everyone's life follows the same principle. I believe that in everyone's life the progression of positive and negative aspects can be traced back to the early episodes, and that in everyone's life 'what we sow we reap'.

Pattern of transformation in all lives: all lives have episodes and opposites and have the potential to progress towards vision of the unity of the universe
The principle behind the pattern I have detected reveals the principle behind the pattern in all lives. In my life, and potentially in all lives, there has been an archetypal pattern of transformation and progress through experience towards a vision of the unity of the universe. Many, through choice or lack of awareness, may seem to opt not to follow this pattern (or not to be given a chance to follow it). But even though they are not aware that their lives can include a centre-shift and transformation, they still have episodes, conflicting opposites and a progression towards harmony with the universe. Some seem to live ego-based active lives for hedonistic enjoyment. Some seem to live soul-based contemplative lives for purpose and achievement. But all have a mixture of the two: the positive progression to and negative regression from their development and growth. (*See* pp.475–476.) All have the principle of episodes and conflicting opposites in the pattern of their lives. And all at some time in their lives have had glimpses of the unity of the universe, and come to feel something akin to it as their lives progress.

A pre-ordained path? Free will + chance = Providential destiny; works like seeds of a spruce cone
If it is true that the universe is a manifestation of the infinite and has a law of order, and that the Light has spiritual powers, it is possible that we all have a pre-ordained task, instructions for which are contained within our genes at birth. If so, we have a destiny, a pre-determined or pre-allotted task. If so, our paths may not be chosen by accident but by our free will, which is driven by an instinctive knowledge of what Providential path we aim to be

on to fulfil our destiny.

My Double Life combines the opposites of free will and chance (+A + −A), and seeks to reconcile them in an underlying Providential destiny (+A + −A = 0), a unification anticipated by the 15th-century Nicholas of Cusa's "coincidence of opposites" (the infinite and finite). In all our lives events of free will (or choice) and chance seem to be reconciled within a Providential destiny. Some events along the path of my life were chosen by me and some were subject to chance, accident and coincidence, and some seem to have fulfilled a Providential destiny. And the seeds of my works – always latently within the layers of my memory like the seeds beneath the scales of a spruce cone – also seem to fulfil a Providential destiny. I will revisit this view after I have continued my story through the last 15 episodes.

The unity of each being
The principle behind the pattern of episodes and events I have detected applies to all lives, and reveals the unity in all lives. I have said (pp.476–477) that in my life nothing was wasted. My experience of the Law, my Trust Accounts and Bookkeeping and my time as a gardener all served a purpose in preparing me for skills I would need as we shall see when my story continues. I believe the same principle is true of all lives. In everyone's life, all that one does is unified as all 'scales' link to the centre. The principle behind the pattern I have identified indicates the unity of each being.

Universal episodes and memories, pattern and unity in all lives – analogy of a spruce cone; the unity of Being
As I reflect on my life I grasp that behind this study of the beginning of my life is an exemplar of a universal general principle concerning episodes and memories, pattern and unity. I have found an analogy for human experience and memory, pattern and unity in a spruce cone in which opposite scales form two differing spirals. In a cone:

- pairs of opposite scales are linked to a central stem and bear seeds;
- all scales form a unity as each scale is essential to the whole and is linked through the central stem;
- each pair of scales has perfect symmetry as the parts – the pairs – are in correct proportion to the whole;
- the scales form a pattern that can be seen as: similar pairs of scales; similar upward layers of scales; or a spiral of scales; and
- the closed, hard surface opens out to shed seeds.

I have felt intuitively that in human life:

- pairs of opposites (of conflicting sequences of events) are linked to a central self and bear the germs of potential creative works or projects;
- the pairs of opposites (conflicting sequences of events within episodes) and the layered memories of them within the self form a unity as each pair is essential to the whole and is linked through the central self;
- each pair of opposites (conflicting sequences of events in episodes) and layered memories has perfect symmetry as the parts – the pairs – are in correct proportion to the whole;
- the episodes and the pairs of opposites (conflicting sequences of events within episodes) and the layered memories of them within the self form a pattern that can be seen as: similar pairs of opposites within episodes and memories of them; similar upward layers of remembered episodes (with unconscious memories at the bottom and most conscious memories at the top); or a spiral of successive episodes and layered memories of them within the self; and
- the ego begins closed up and hard, and opens out to shed its potential works and projects when the right times comes.

I reflect that in all lives all experiences are essential to the final form of the self and to the pattern of its life. The same is true of all memories of experiences (or events within episodes). In all lives, the path through a dark wood to a hillside is arduous, and though each quest encounters different obstacles and copes with them with varying degrees of success, in all lives the potential for a successful quest is present. This is just as true of those who seem never to undertake the quest but remain in the bogs and thickets of day-to-day passive and hedonistic living. During the journey all have a central self that unites and reconciles all the episodes and conflicting sequences of events within their life, and all memories of them. There have been billions of conifer cones and all grow in the same way and obey the same law. Similarly, there have been billions of human beings, and all have grown in the same way and obey the same law. Behind the unity of each being is the unity of Being.

The structure of all human experience

The 15 episodes I have covered in this work offer a structure for the experience in all lives. They reveal the principle behind a pattern of transformation towards a vision of the unity of the universe, which is crucial for every quest for Reality, the One (*see* pp.475–477).

We all have projects of some sort to contribute to the world, which grow with us and seem to be stored within our memories like seeds beneath scales. All human memories shelter projects. The principle behind the episodes in *my* life is behind the experience of *all* human beings and is universal – a chain of episodes and of entwined pairs of opposites like a double helix – just as the principle behind the structure of *my* life is behind the structure of *all* human experience.

Gazing down at the sweep of trees beneath me, I reflect that as the universe is a unity the structure and arrangement of episodic human experience, memory and human projects seem to follow the same transforming law of Nature that governs the structure and arrangement of seeds in conifer cones. My quest for Reality has brought me face to face with the Oneness whose law of Nature transforms both natural phenomena and humankind.

I have described my finding and can now turn to the founding which followed from it.

Timeline

List of dates of key events in Nicholas Hagger's life
referred to in *My Double Life 1: This Dark Wood*

22 May 1939	Born.
2 Jul 1939	Christened.
Mar 1943	Bombs blow out windows of 52 Brooklyn Avenue, Loughton.
May 1943	Attends Essex House School.
Sep 1943	Starts at old Oaklands School.
Mar 1944	Bombs fall on cricket field and blow out windows of 52 Brooklyn Avenue again, including garage windows.
Sep 1944	Starts at new Oaklands School.
Apr 1945	Hears Churchill speak at Loughton war memorial.
Sep 1947	Starts at Chigwell School.
25 Oct 1951	Encounters Churchill in Loughton.
Sep 1953	Visit to France and D-Day beaches.
18 Oct 1953	Meets Montgomery.
July 1954	Experiences Oneness of the universe.
Apr 1956	On archaeological dig at Chester.
12 Sep 1956	Attends Suez debate in House of Commons as guest of John Biggs-Davison MP.
Mar 1957	Call to be a poet.
4–25 Apr 1957	Visit to Italy and Sicily.
Jul 1957–Jul 1958	Articled clerk at Gregory, Rowcliffe & Co., solicitors.
11 Aug–14 Sep 1958	Visit to Greece.
Oct 1958–Jun 1961	At Worcester College, Oxford.
Mar 1959	Changes from Law to English Literature.
1–10 Apr 1958	Visit to France.
23 Jul–23 Aug 1959	Visit to Spain.
Jan 1960	Visit to Colin Wilson.
14 Jul 1960	Writes to Major Goulding.
end of Jul/Aug 1960	Visit to Greece, encounters Col. Grivas.
6 Nov 1960	Sherry with Sir John Masterman.
1 Dec 1960	Meets Admiral Sir Charles Woodhouse.
6–9 Jan 1961	Stays with Colin Wilson and announces he will lecture abroad and find wisdom among foreign

	cultures.
16 Sep 1961	Marriage to Caroline.
30 Sep 1961–4 Jun 1962	Lecturer at University of Baghdad, Iraq.
13 Dec 1962	Birth of Nadia.
15 Oct 1963	Death of father.
6 Nov 1963	Visit to Dick Paul.
15 Nov 1963–18 Oct 1967	Professor at Tokyo University of Education and Keio University, Japan.
21 Dec 1963	Visits Junzaburo Nishiwaki.
22 Apr 1964–Mar 1965	Lecturer at Tokyo University.
26 Apr 1964	Lunches with Edmund Blunden.
Apr 1964–Oct 1967	Speech-writer for Governor of Bank of Japan.
20 Jul 1964–18 Oct 1965	First Mystic Life.
10 Jul 1964	Visits Ichikawa City Zen meditation centre.
20 Jul 1964	Visits Zen Kogenji temple.
5–6 Jan 1965	First visit to Kyoto (including Ryoanji Stone Garden) and Nara.
1965–1966	Writes *The Early Education and Making of a Mystic*.
Jan 1965–Jun 1966	Writes 'The Silence'.
1 Jul 1965–18 Oct 1967	Tutor to His Imperial Highness Prince Hitachi.
26–27 Jul 1965	Visits Zen Engakuji temple, Kitakamakura with Frank Tuohy.
11–12 Aug 1965	Second visit to Kyoto (including Ryoanji Stone Garden) and Nara.
11 Sep 1965	Visions: images.
5 Oct 1965	Junzaburo Nishiwaki writes out $+A + -A = 0$ to describe the manifestation of the Absolute and the wisdom of the East.
11 Oct 1965	Golden light.
17 Oct 1965	Centre-shift.
18 Oct 1965	Round white light, Zen enlightenment (*satori*).
19 Oct 1965–2 Sep 1971	Dark Night of the Soul.
3–23 Mar 1966	Visits China with Frank Tuohy.
19 Mar 1966	Interrogates Vice-President of Peking University and is first to discover Cultural Revolution (*see* Appendix 4, *see* pp.509–514).
Apr 1966–Oct 1967	Selects interpreters at Ministry of International Trade and Industry.
7–10 Jun/25–29 Aug 1966	Visits Soviet Union twice.
11, 20 Jun–23 Jul 1966	Writes 'Archangel', poem about Communism.
20 Dec 1966–13 Mar 1967	Writes 'Old Man in a Circle'.

18 Oct–6 Nov 1967	Tours south-east Asia and India, and parts of Europe.
25 Oct 1968–1 Jul 1970	Lecturer at University of Libya, Tripoli.
3 Nov 1968	Visit to Sabratha with Ben Nagy, discussion on a revolution in Libya.
15 Nov 1968	Visit to Leptis Magna with Ben Nagy.
3 Apr 1969	First article as Barbary Gipsy for *The Daily News*, arranged by Shukri Ghanem (later Prime Minister).
Apr 1969	Ben Nagy hosts parties for ministers.
30 May 1969	Is approached by SIS.
6–10 Jul 1969	Visit to Djerba.
18, 22 Aug 1969	Interviews Dr Muntasser, Libyan Ambassador to London.
24 Aug 1969	Article on Libyan-British relations appears in English and Arabic in Tripoli, read by Gaddafi.
28, 30 Aug 1969	Dinners with Beshir al-Muntasser, Minister of State for Prime Minister's Affairs.
1 Sep 1969	Gaddafi's *coup*.
5 Sep 1969	Scheduled date of pro-Western *coup*.
14 Sep 1969	Last article as Barbary Gipsy for *The Daily News*.
1969–1972	Writes *The Gates of Hell*.
6 Nov 1969	Viktor agrees to defect.
4 Dec 1969	Is separated.
25 Dec 1969	Sees Col. Nasser ride through Tripoli with Gaddafi and Numeiri.
1 Jan 1970	Knocks off Col. Gaddafi's peaked cap.
12–23 Feb 1970	Visit to Egypt.
19 Feb 1970	Locates SAM-3 missile transporter near El Alamein.
24–28 Feb 1970	Visit to Sahara and Ghadames.
11–14 Apr 1970	Visit to Malta.
27–28 May 1970	Is nearly executed.
28 May 1970	Holds up reception line for Queen's birthday to inform British Ambassador Donald Maitland.
28 May–3 Jun	Return visits to 'executioner'.
1–20 Jul 1970	Drives through North Africa and western Mediterranean.
16 Jul 1970	Visit to Ezra Pound in Rapallo.
30 Jul, 8, 17 Aug 1970	Visit to John Heath-Stubbs.
Aug 1970–15 Apr 1972	Lives at 13 Egerton Gardens, London.
24 Aug 1970	Becomes 'unofficial Ambassador' to Edward

	Heath, Prime Minister.
29, 30 Aug 1970	Articles on Libya in *The Times* and *The Sunday Telegraph*.
3 Oct 1970	Article on World Council of Churches' grants to liberation movements in *The Times*.
Jan 1971–Aug 1973	Teaches at Riverway ESN School, Greenwich.
21 Apr 1971	"Exposed to Czech intelligence and KGB" by Viktor.
May 1971–Nov 1972	Margaret Riley in 13 Egerton Gardens.
May 1971	Pussy-cat becomes landlady, chef and chambermaid at 13 Egerton Gardens.
3 Sep 1971–28 Apr 1972	Second Mystic Life.
5 Sep 1971–28 Apr 1972	Visions reflected in poems.
10 Sep 1971	Illumination.
24 Sep 1971	Told will be publicly exposed by Philby in retaliation for Heath's expulsion of 105 Russians.
1–4 Mar 1972	Attends symposium on Cunene Dam near Frankfurt for *The Times*.
15 Apr 1972	Moves into newly-purchased Flat 6, 33 Stanhope Gardens.
24 Apr 1972	Visit to Colin Wilson in Cornwall.
25–29 May 1972	Attends SWAPO conference in Brussels for *The Times*.
29 Apr 1972–12 May 1979	Dark Night of the Spirit: new powers.
10–27 Sep 1972	Visit to Tanzania and Zanzibar for *The Times* and *The Guardian*.
19 Sep 1972	Interviews Jumbe.
20 Sep 1972	Asks Nyerere for permission to visit Makumbako (restricted area).
22–23 Sep 1972	Visit to Mlimba-Makumbako section of the Tanzam railway.
24 Apr 1973	Visit to Colin Wilson.
17 May 1973	Discontinues with SIS.
3 Jul 1973	Ends all connection with SIS.
15–20 Aug 1973	Visit by Margaret Riley, first inklings of a neo-Baroque movement.
7, 20 Oct 1978	Asa Briggs urges the writing of this account.

APPENDIX

1

Light

16 experiences of the metaphysical Light or Fire, 2 Mystic Lives, 2 Dark
Nights: with visions, surges, sleep inspiration and Oneness ('showings')
in *My Double Life 1: This Dark Wood*

Page	Date	Experience
60	Jun 1954	Sleep inspiration: in a dream 'saw' the 'O' level Greek set book exam paper with four passages to translate.
60–61	Jul/Aug 1954	Experiences the Oneness of the universe on Merrow golf course.
92	Mar 1959	Experiences the Oneness of the universe by Worcester College lake.
103	Summer 1959	First encountered the Light in poems of the Metaphysical poets.
142	18 Jan 1962	Vision: received 'Life Cycle' in the air over Ur, Iraq.
160–161	13 Nov 1963	Experiences the Oneness of the universe by Strawberry Hill pond.
171	13 Jun 1964	Wrote first version of poem, 'Twilight', fire in cathedral square.

First Mystic Life: 20 July 1964–18 October 1965

Page	Date	Experience
173	20 Jul 1964	Koganji Zen temple, dawn glow on polished floor.
177	5–6 Jan 1965	Experience of the Oneness of the universe at Kyoto's Ryoanji Stone Garden.
177	24 Jan 1965	Fire in head when looking at sparkling waves.
184	11–12 Aug 1965	Second experience of the Oneness of the universe at Kyoto's Ryoanji Stone Garden.
185	11 Sep 1965	First experience of Light as orb of Fire. Visions: scrivenings in foreign language, corn stalks, whirlpool.
185	13 Sep 1965	Visions: gold heads, some Egyptian, diamonds.
185	13 Sep 1965	Sleep inspiration: centre-shift – in a dream 'saw' an earthquake, falling masonry, ruins, corpses dancing.

187	11 Oct 1965	Golden Light.
187–188	18 Oct 1965	Round white Light, dazzling like a white sun.

Dark Night of the Soul: 19 October 1965–2 September 1971
Second Mystic Life: 3 September 1971–28 April 1972

203	9 Jun 1966	Vision: enlightened world leaders in a World State's world government received in the Cathedral of the Archangel in Moscow (described in 'Archangel'); now stood for a World State.
371	3 Sep 1971	White glow round moon, whiteness between sea and sky.
372	4 Sep 1971	Strange white light between sea and sky.
372	5 Sep 1971	Visions: white light behind cross, Virgin Mary.
373–374	10 Sep 1971	Light. Visions: white light, bare winter tree of white fire, flowing, rippling (Flowing Light), white flower like chrysanthemum (Golden Flower), sun, stars, fountain of white light, white point, circle of light.
375–377	11 Sep 1971	Light. Visions: dome of light, yellow and purple tomb, old gold death mask, filigree light, face of God, point of white light, egg, Christ on the cross, devil, saint, crown of thorns, Roman robe, yellow rose, black thorns, child, death-mask, frost, white flower, suns, shafts of light, long white-hot line like trunk of tree.
377–378	12 Sep 1971	Light. Visions: (morning) red flower, streaks of white, red lights, prison gates, egg, face of God, white wheel, white light, yellow mountain range, stars with rings, blob of moon, blobs, thorns with light behind, Greek theatre; (afternoon) golden star, golden rays, silver star.
378	13 Sep 1971	Visions (evening): Tudor rose.
379	24 Sep 1971	Visions: streaks of white light, golden (white) flower like dahlia.
385	18 Oct 1971	Vision: very bright diamond with egg in it (symbol for the Light).
386	24 Oct 1971	Vision: the Flower.
389–390	21 Nov 1971	Visions: Diamond. Fire, golden glow, laurel wreath.
391	3 Jan 1972	Light. Visions: snowflakes, Saints, Pope's head, monk, altar, Cathedral, white light.

401	3 Apr 1972	Visions: Flowing Light, golden head of Christ, crown of thorns in golden light, Roman effigy of God, white sun, two stars, white ageless face.
401–402	8 Apr 1972	Visions: golden furniture, temple columns, brown statue head, celestial curtain, diamond in luminous blue light (first experience of blue Light), Golden Flower, light flashing up.
403	17 Apr 1972	Visions: possessed, in union with the Light, aglow with the mystic Fire.
403	22 Apr 1972	Visions: pale blue light that blended with dazzling white light like a diamond shining in the sun.
404	28 Apr 1972	Visions: white light with blue tints, hoop of light like sun-halo.

Dark Night of the Spirit, new powers: 29 April 1972–12 May 1979

| 443 | 3–4 Dec 1972 | White light, white sun, dim. |
| 468 | 31 Jul 1973 | Visions: Greek temples, African mask, light nearly breaking. |

2

Visits

Visits by Nicholas Hagger to countries/places
touched on in *My Double Life 1: This Dark Wood*
(For details see *Awakening to the Light, Selected Diaries*)

1953	September	France: Paris, Normandy (Cabourg, Caen, Ouistreham and the D-Day beaches).
1957	4–25 April	Italy: Rome, Licenza (Horace's villa), Naples, Pompeii, Herculaneum, Mount Vesuvius, Sorrento, Capri, Paestum, Syracuse, Catania, Mount Etna.
1958	11 August– 14 September	Greece: Athens, Thermopylae, Delphi, Mount Helicon, Thebes, Thespiae and the Veil of the Muses, Sunion, Marathon, Mount Parnassus, Eleusis, Dafni (Daphnae), Megara, Corinth, Patras, Olympia, Pylos, Sphacteria, Kalamai, Tripolis, Argos, Nauplion, Epidavros (Epidaurus), Tiryns, Mycenae. Crete (Knossos, Phaestos, Gourna). Rhodes. Mykonos. Delos. Return via Belgrade.
1959	1–10 April	France: Paris.
	23 July–23 August	Spain: Barcelona, Valencia, Malaga, Coin, Torremolinos, San Sebastian.
1960	end of July/August	Greece via Belgium, Amsterdam, Yugoslavia: Athens, Spetsai, Spetsopoula, Porto Cheli, Calchis, Sciathos. Return via Skopje, Dubrovnik, Split, Rijeka.
1961–2	30 September 1961– 4 June 1962	Iraq: Baghdad, Ctesiphon, Basra, Shatt al-Arab, Gourna, Rutba, Babylon. Visit to Holy Land: Bethlehem, Jericho, Dead Sea, Qumran, Bethany, River Jordan, Jerusalem (Mount of Olives, Gethsemane, Calvary, Garden Tomb, Via Dolorosa). Visits to Amman, Damascus, Beirut.

1963–7	15 November 1963– 18 October 1967	Japan: Tokyo, Hiroshima, Kyoto, Nara, Nikko, Gora, Kurihama/Nobe, Kamakura/Kitakamakura, Karuizawa.
1966	3–23 March	China via Hong Kong, Kowloon: Canton, Shanghai, Hangchow, Nanking, Peking.
	5–11 June/ 23–30 August	USSR: Nakhodka, Khabarovsk, Moscow. London via Brest, Warsaw, Berlin, Flanders. Same route in reverse in August.
1967	18 October– 6 November	South-East and Central Asia, Europe. Hong Kong. Macao. Vietnam: Saigon/Cholon, Bien Hoa. Cambodia: Phnom Penh, Siem Reap/Angkor Wat. Thailand: Bangkok. India: Calcutta, New Delhi. Nepal: Katmandu. Turkey: Istanbul. Hungary: Budapest. Austria: Vienna. France: Paris.
1968–70	25 October 1968– 1 July 1970	Libya via Avignon, Marseilles, Tunis. Carthage: Tripoli, Sabratha, Leptis Magna, Gourna (or Suk Al-Jum'a), Ghadames.
1969	6–10 July	Tunisia: Djerba.
1970	12–23 February	Egypt: Cairo/Pyramids, Memphis, Saqqara, Luxor, Alexandria, El Alamein.
	24–28 February	Libya: Tripoli, Nalut, Ghadames.
	11–14 April	Malta: Valletta, St Paul's Bay, Sliema.
	1–20 July	North Africa and Europe. Tunisia: Medenine, Gabes, Hammamet. Algeria: Souk Ahras, Algiers, Oran. Morocco: Tangier. Spain: Marbella, Barcelona. Italy: Rapallo. Switzerland: Geneva, Annemasse, Mont Blanc/Lake Leman.
1972	1–4 March	Germany: Frankfurt, Arnoldshain.
	25–29 May	Belgium: Brussels.
	10–27 September	Tanzania: Dar es Salaam, Zanzibar, Tanzam railway (Lugema, Mkera, Iringa), Mikumi National Park. Return via Nairobi.

3

Defence

Early article on defence against Soviet Communism

This comprehensive analysis of British defence in the Cold War was written by Nicholas Hagger in 1958 when he was 18, for a magazine *Right Wheel* which he revived. It brought him to the attention of his MP John Biggs-Davison. It is reproduced here (in an edited form) as early evidence of his informed view of the threat posed by the Soviet Union, and of how the Cold War weighed on the mind of an 18-year-old in 1958. Note that in 1958 Nicholas Hagger predicted German reunification, was alert to the predicament of Iraq (in which he was to live three-and-a-half years later) and advocated standing up to Soviet Communism.

Defence
Definition of terms for weapons used below:

Conventional weapons: weapons of the type used in the last war, i.e. soldiers, guns, aircraft, ships.

Strategic weapons: weapons whose range is such that from the Continent they could only be used against the homeland of an aggressor, and not against his armed forces on the battlefield (as at present deployed in the US and Britain).

Tactical weapons: atomic weapons to be used against armed forces on a battlefield, whose means of delivery depends on manned bombers (as at present deployed on the Continent).

NATO strategy
NATO strategy depends on the kind of war NATO must be prepared to fight, which determines the nature of weapons NATO will use. As NATO was originally created to preserve Western interests against Soviet influence, she takes her strategy from the Soviet Union, which is both the strongest continental land power and a global power. NATO thus has to guard against two threats: the physical invasion of Western Europe with conventional forces; and global war by serial bombardment directed against NATO-protected powers, of which only the US, Canada and Britain are separated from Russia by sea.

The West uses the same means to deter an aggressor from carrying out either threat: the deterrent of nuclear retaliation. Russian manpower and conventional forces are so vastly superior to those of the West that we could neither deter her nor defend ourselves without using the threat of nuclear resistance to aggression. If Russia has no reason to doubt our determination to use nuclear weapons against major aggression, there is no reason to believe she will risk a sudden attack. If she *is* given a reason to doubt our determination, then no large conventional forces on our part will eliminate the risk.

"The democratic Western Nations will never start a war against Russia. But it must be well understood that if Russia were to launch a major attack on them, even with conventional forces only, they would have to hit back with strategic nuclear weapons". (Defence White Paper.) And again "The strategy of NATO is based on the frank recognition that a full scale Soviet attack could not be repelled without resorting to a massive nuclear bombardment of the sources of power in Russia." In other words, our threat to use nuclear weapons in retaliation deters Soviet aggression. We are unable to match Soviet manpower. Whether Russia attacks with men or nuclear weapons an attack will be "major aggression" and our only means of self-defence is "to hit back with strategic nuclear weapons" (White Paper). These White-Paper sentences of Mr Sandys' [Duncan Sandys – British Minister of Defence] sum up the whole problem of nuclear retaliation, and have aroused three main criticisms:

(1) The criticism that Government's policy relies too predominantly on the threat of nuclear warfare. If we *are* deterred from using nuclear weapons because Russia also possesses them, then we ought not to base our defence plans on the pretence that we are *not* deterred. And if we possess such weapons with the intention of using them, our possession will not deter the Soviets from using theirs. Even if the Soviets believe we might use our weapons tomorrow, they will still not be deterred from using theirs.

The only alternative to announcing that we would *not* be deterred from using the only adequate means of self-defence at our disposal would be to announce to the world that we *are* deterred from using our weapons because the Soviets possess similar weapons. This would imply that we have no means of deterring or resisting a Soviet attack. And if we *are* deterred, we are not going to use our nuclear weapons whether or not the Soviets use theirs.

This standpoint is similar to pretending that we *can* deter the Soviets by possessing the bomb but swearing *not* to use it on any account. To say that we are not going to use the bomb although we have it is utter nonsense, for if we are not prepared to use it, it constitutes no deterrent whatsoever; and if we are not going to use it, why have it? It is a debatable point as to which is the more immoral: to have the bomb and say we *won't* use it; or to have the bomb and say we *will* use it. The hydrogen bomb is a moral issue, but it is just as evil for the Russians to have it and contemplate using it as it is for us to have it and contemplate using it.

(2) The criticism that nuclear weapons and other preparations for global war form no basis for defence. The change in our defence tactics and our reduction in conventional forces have altered the outlook of all three services:

- The role of the armed forces in Europe is now to hold the front line in the face of an attack until our nuclear retaliation takes effect. However since the West has no defence against a nuclear attack and is unable to launch a strategic nuclear attack of her own which could prevent a Soviet nuclear retaliation, a "major [Soviet] attack... even with conventional forces" (White Paper) would compel us to initiate a nuclear attack which we know will be reciprocated, precipitate global war and destroy ourselves and the world.

- So if we are attacked by conventional forces the aim of defence is not to defend us but to start a nuclear war in which both sides will be wiped out; and if we are attacked by nuclear weapons, the aim of defence is to revenge ourselves in our dying gasp by destroying the enemy. It is claimed that national defence is no longer possible and that there is no point in Britain possessing IRBMs (intermediate range ballistic missile, range 1,500 miles) and defending Europe's frontiers in global war that will bring about the death of the inhabitants.

- However, Russia does not want to be wiped out any more than we do; and so long as Britain possesses IRBMs and pledges herself ready to defend Europe against a Russian attack, Russia will not run the risk of being wiped out.

- As a result of the new role of the army, National Service is to be replaced by a 375,000-men-strong three-services armed forces in 1962. Eleven out of every 100 of the required age must then enlist as regulars, and although the infantry may be up to strength by 1962, recruiting for the administration corps is below requirements. The army alone will eventually require an annual recruitment from civilian life of about 20,000 men a year. (At present it is getting about 6,000, and 8,500 serving soldiers prolong their service.)

- On the assumption that there will be global nuclear war, the Navy is now to concentrate on an anti-submarine role. Yet "the overriding consideration in all military planning must be to prevent war rather than to prepare for it" (Defence White Paper). The view of the White Paper appears to be at variance with the Navy's policy of preparing for nuclear war in which the allied forces assist rather than prevent global nuclear war.

- However, the Navy's anti-submarine role curtails Soviet supremacy in conventional forces and deters Russia from using her atomic submarines (and she might not be deterred if we were unable to counter them).
- The role of our air defence is now based on the threat of our manned bombers carrying tactical nuclear weapons and getting through the enemy's lines in sufficient numbers to deter the Soviets from launching missiles against the West. British planning assumes the deterrent of the manned bomber will not be superseded until 1965.
- However, global war is an effective basis for defence if it is only used against its Soviet counterpart of global war. If we recognise the Soviet Union as a common enemy, we must assume that the Soviet Union looks on us as a common enemy. There is a balance of deterrent power (between the US and Britain against Russia) in which we have a political choice of participation (by possessing our own IRBMs) or acquiescence (by renouncing the H-bomb and leaving all determination of policy to the US). This logically promotes a global policy of one world, one enemy, one defence which is achieved politically by NATO, SEATO (South East Asia Treaty Organisation), and SHAPE (Supreme Headquarters of the Allied Powers in Europe, global high command) and militarily by the deterrent.

(3) The criticism that our nuclear deterrent will not deter "*limited* aggression". The deterrent is so absolute that it is only valid against its like, global nuclear aggression, but not against conventional aggression or local conflicts designed not to provoke nuclear retaliation. This "area in between" (the gap between a border incident which would not precipitate nuclear retaliation and a "major attack" even with conventional forces only which *would* do so) is defined by the size of the attack ("200 divisions") and by the country against which it is directed. (The bombing of London or Europe would trigger nuclear retaliation, but not necessarily the bombing of Norway or Greece, which are on the fringe of NATO.)

Facing up to whether or not massive nuclear retaliation is to be employed by the West leaves the Continental NATO countries veering between two systems of fear: that America will hesitate to defend them when she is vulnerable to nuclear attack herself; and that she will come to their aid but will ruin them in the process of defending them by setting off the nuclear deterrent. The hole in the policy of nuclear retaliation is that despite the preparations for global war on the part of the services there are insufficient conventional forces to fill this "area in between".

The validity of this criticism depends on a political and not a military judgement: where in the next 10 years is Britain likely to have to fight a "limited aggression" without allies at a strength of over five brigades? If the areas covered by our alliances are threatened by a great Power directly and in great force, this is no *"limited* aggression". Outside Europe great-Power diplomacy and UNO come into action, and Iraq or Yugoslavia would stand a good chance of resisting "aggression by proxy" (subversive Communist influence). There is no point in over-insuring with conventional forces in one area when an act of aggression means global war (the last thing that Russia wants at the moment).

The threat of nuclear retaliation involving global war is absolute and is applicable only to an absolute danger such as all-out aggression. There have been no recent assertions that improved tactical atomic weapons – which are less terrible than wholesale retaliation – should deal with situations short of global war. As a result an aggressor could well gamble that the West would shrink from blowing itself up to prevent a limited aggression.

Missiles
The American proposal to set up atomic stockpiles of IRBMs on the Continent under American control – after Britain has been supplied with them in 1959 – has led the European NATO countries to fear whether the weapons will be used, and if they are, whether retaliation will destroy Europe. The aim is to remove the present disparity between the areas of the non-nuclear NATO countries and those of Britain and America, and to make the suspicious Continental countries less dependent on the nuclear Powers.

The proposal arises from three military considerations:

- the assumption that Russia will have IRBMs by 1961 and ICBMs (intercontinental ballistic missiles, range 5,000 miles) by 1963;
- having developed the IRBM (range 1,500 miles) as a stepping-stone towards the ICBM (range 5,000 miles), the Americans must make use of IRBMs by placing them within 1,500 miles of Moscow;
- IRBMs are more useful than ICBMs because the longer the range the wider their inaccuracy.

The revolutionary aspect of this proposal is that so far only tactical weapons have been deployed on the Continental front. The 1957 Bermuda agreement that American IRBMs (strategic weapons) should be supplied to Britain did not affect this scenario as Britain was already a nuclear Power with strategic bomber bases. New strategic weapons with push-button delivery are now to be extended to the Continent, thus increasing the chances of accidental attack.

The West-German Government has agreed in principle to IRBMs (say Thor and Jupiter) being stationed in Western Europe provided it is agreed that this is necessary for the defence of the West. Considerations arise here. Because of their small ranges, unless IRBMs are stationed in a forward position such as Western Germany – Norway and Denmark will remain neutral until attacked – their contribution to the West's nuclear deterrent will be small.

There is a vast difference between placing missiles on German soil and arming German divisions. Politically it would be to the West's disadvantage to locate missiles in Western Germany with summit talks for disarmament round the corner, and deploying missiles is not essential to Western military security. Manned bombers will not be effectively countered by Soviet air-defence systems until 1965 and if the American ICBM (say Atlas and Titan) scheduled for 1962 is ready before the manned bomber is superseded it will not be vital to deploy IRBMs on the Continent.

The West is thus over- rather than under-insured for nuclear deterrence. The threat of missile attacks on Western bomber bases need not be taken seriously as the enemy would have to land a nuclear warhead within 7 miles of every base in the world to avoid retaliation. This threat has led to an increasing American dependence on early-warning systems in Europe and a major extension of air defences in North America. (But by the time these defences are wide enough to stop bombers flying round them, Soviet missiles will be able to fly over them.)

Unilateral renunciation
The 1957 agreement to station IRBMs in Britain involves no new principle as it merely extends the facilities granted to American bombers for several years. In fact the missile is merely a complement to, and later a substitute for, the bomber.

The considerations attached to such a decision are:

- It does not make Britain more likely to a nuclear attack than her bomber airfields have already made her;
- although it is regretted in some quarters that Britain entered the nuclear race in the first place, it is impracticable to throw away bombs and bombers already produced and rely on America;
- if we did renounce the bomb and became totally dependent on America, we could not refuse American access to British bases – we could not leave the whole burden of deterrence to the Americans and then refuse to allow them the facilities they deem essential for their task;
- if the Americans were to withdraw their IRBMs we would still be in a position to make our own;
- American strategic forces stationed in Britain are subject to dual

control with a right of veto on either side, an additional safeguard whereby the Americans have custody of the nuclear warheads and the British of the rocketry – until one is fitted to the other, the missile is useless;

- the aim is to counteract Soviet ICBMs with IRBMs to preserve the military advantages of the deterrent;
- by accepting the American offer we are fulfilling our NATO commitments – NATO is far more than a one-sided American guarantee to defend Western Europe – to do which is worth spending £10 million on launching sites; and we are avoiding duplication in accordance with the recent political doctrine of interdependence made possible by a relaxation of the McMahon Act (which prevents the exchange of atomic information);
- having US IRBMs is better than Western-European nations' developing their own as once the Western-European armies possess their own nuclear missiles they will never be persuaded to give them up and Russia will never withdraw from Europe under those circumstances;
- having American bases means that when the time comes for disengagement it will be far easier to thin out and withdraw;
- we cannot afford future experimentations in missile production based on an offensive policy, and there will always be a better missile or antidote round the corner to be duplicated by America and Britain;
- incidents of nuclear devices dropping from training aircraft can be defended as to date no harm has resulted – crews have to be trained and made ready, and weapons have to be transported from one airfield to another.

Unilateral disarmament by Britain would entail wholesale preparations for resistance against invasion by conventional Soviet forces. It has been said that preparing to resist invasion is the only way to find safety from the H-bomb without the immense economic sacrifice of duplicating American nuclear weapons or depending on America. Disarming is quite different from renouncing the *use* of the bomb we possess for once we disarm the Soviet Union will know we have no defence and what is more, we will be saying that we have no defence.

Disarmament is nonsense. Handing Europe over to Russia on a plate resembles a gloveless boxer going into the ring to abide by the rules and the referee's decision after making sure that a stretcher is on hand. It does not lead to "strength through weakness" (King-Hall) but to weakness through weakness. It would have no effect on Russia; the rest of the world would feel weaker and less secure; and America would pay less consideration to British views. There is no evidence that unless Britain renounces the bomb, first France, and then smaller countries, will make their own. We have already given far too much away to Russia without getting anything in return in post-war conferences. The present arrangement involving US IRBMs *does* deter invasion and maintains a higher spirit than would a prostrate Britain overrun by Russia. Since plans for unilateral disarmament do not include the USA the danger of an eventual nuclear war between America and Russia is in no way alleviated by such a damaging and degrading disarmament.

Disengagement

The military aspect of the ideal of disengagement is contained in proposals put forward in the U.N. on 2 October 1957 by Mr Rapacki, the Polish Foreign Minister, and supported by Russia, under which a zone free from all nuclear weapons would be created in Poland, Czechoslovakia, and both Germanies, where the manufacture and stocking of nuclear arms would be forbidden.

The military considerations are:

- as a nuclear weapon consists of the nuclear warhead (bomb or shell) and the means of delivering it (missile, aeroplane or gun) it is not clear whether the Rapacki proposals include the prohibition of ammunition *and* the means of delivery;
- in spite of control by inspection, stocks of ammunition can be concealed though the means of delivery will be harder to hide;
- as explosives are getting smaller and aircraft and guns incapable of delivering nuclear weapons today are potential nuclear weapons tomorrow, a nuclear-free zone would exclude artillery larger than rifles and it would be necessary to divide nuclear weapons into calibres and discriminate between their means of delivery, (say) bombers and fighter aircraft.

To accept disengagement NATO would have to build up an effective conventional defence force capable of coping with anything short of all-out aggression, on the basis of a successful attacking force's having a three-to-one superiority. Effective defence should have:

- a full range of conventional weapons (artillery and tactical aircraft);
- accommodation for nuclear weapons outside Germany on the Continent to deter local aggression;
- the continued presence of Americans in Germany to control the deterrent;
- no removal of nuclear weapons from Germany until she has

501

satisfactory conventional strength.

It would be to our military advantage to keep the NATO front-line area in Europe free from strategic weapons, and this could lead to an alternative strategy to massive retaliation (e.g. tactical weapons capable of firing atomic warheads). But we could not afford to accept the full military Rapacki proposals immediately because the withdrawal of American troops (whose presence is needed as an open pledge that America would not remain neutral if war broke out in Europe) and of NATO troops (who keep Western sea communications on a par with Soviet interior communications) from Europe would be too high a price to pay for a united Germany and liberated Europe.

The political argument is represented by Mr George Kennan's Reith lectures and by Mr Denis Healey MP [Labour defence spokesman] whose "neutral belt" completes the Rapacki plan. (Mr Bevan has been advocating a neutral belt for some years.) The withdrawal of Russian troops from Eastern Europe would be achieved in return for the withdrawal of American troops from Western Europe, by offering new terms for German reunification that would specifically exclude a united Germany from NATO and allow her to decide for herself whether to join the East or the West.

If the Soviet Union rejected the offer, the West would have to go ahead with plans to equip each of the available countries on the Soviet border with atomic weapons. The considerations are:

- the increasing destructiveness of atomic weapons;
- the folly of providing our Continental allies with such weapons;
- the division of Europe into two rival nuclear-armed camps – it is doubtful whether there can be a less dangerous arrangement;
- the ineffectiveness of military alliances and of building up the Rhine army as an answer to Soviet influence in Europe and the Middle East;
- the surmise that the Russians have an equal interest in gradual disengagement in Europe on the grounds that Soviet satellites, far from being a source of military strength to Russia, are a military danger and an economic burden.

Such a plan for disengagement is bound to have advantages for Western security. A nuclear-free area promotes disarmament as the West can safely abstain from setting up IRBM missile bases in Western Germany without any loss of security. And it would be difficult for Russia to reject such a proposal without appearing to be against disarmament in any form. In return Russia would not abstain from keeping strategic missile bases in all the satellites except for East Germany, which they would vacate. If Russia already has secret bases in East Germany, the West would be offering to refrain from doing something in the future while asking the Soviets in return to undo something that already exists. Western Germany would be relieved of the nuclear arsenal on its soil, and of the threat that Germany will succeed Belgium as the cockpit of Europe in the event of a war. The satellites would have no grounds to fear a militarist Western Germany equipped with nuclear weapons. There is nothing to lose and everything to gain. However there is a grave threat that if Germany were at the mercy of the Soviet Union and without weapons she would suffer a moral collapse, accept Soviet trade offers and become a Soviet satellite without a war.

Disengagement is also bound to have advantages for world peace. Despite the dependence of the satellites on the Red Army (which makes a Soviet withdrawal unlikely) disengagement would establish peace and security by liberating the satellites and thus avoiding repetitions of Hungary and Poland which might lead to war. It would separate the two chief combatants and remove the cause of tension, a divided Germany. An American withdrawal from Europe (to the delight of American isolationists and mothers) could be matched by a Soviet withdrawal to behind Soviet frontiers, whence Soviet troops could invade a vacated Germany without coming into contact with, or declaring war on, America.

If the Soviet Union did withdraw from Germany, she could not be prevented from returning at will unless the Americans retaliated with nuclear weapons or unless Germany possessed sufficient conventional forces to repel an invasion. A united Germany with a strong army of its own might pose a greater threat to peace than the present European arrangement. A unified Germany excluded from NATO to secure Russian approval for disengagement would be outside every alliance, and there is no guarantee that the West would risk a nuclear war to assist a country that was not an ally. Underground resistance against conventional invasion is a poor substitute for IRBMs as a deterrent.

NATO could not survive without German membership, first because of the military difficulty of America's maintaining an effective foothold without the use of German territory, and secondly because it would be difficult for America to continue her close cultural and economic co-operation with the West if Germany was militarily out of NATO. Germany could not be of the West but not in it.

In any summit negotiations it should be rememberd that:

- being a dictatorship, the Soviet Union can control its public opinion while making a show of talking peace, whereas the West is held responsible by its public for any failure to reach agreement;
- the Soviet Union's attitude towards the West will not be reformed

by an offer of German reunification for Soviet hostility did not spring from the present European division: the present division sprang from Soviet hostility displayed at Yalta.

If after a summit conference Russia rejects the offer of disengagement, the West must put into practice its threat of stationing weapons on the Soviet border for Russia's destructive motives will then have been fully revealed.

4

China

The first evidence of China's Cultural Revolution

Extracts from an account of two visits to Peking University on 16 and 19 March 1966, including a transcript of Nicholas Hagger's interrogation of Professor Wang, Vice-President of Peking University, on remoulding.

Frank Tuohy was in attendance. The analysis of the 'Transcript' on p.509, dated 19 March 1966, established the first evidence of the Cultural Revolution, news of which broke in August 1966. Nicholas Hagger (NH) asked the questions.

The car leaves the People's Square and the Forbidden City and after a few minutes turns north-west. Soon we are driving down an avenue. There are new trees on either side, and through the trees on the right we can see a road for bicycles and pedicabs. On the hard mud to the left new apartments appear, then a few large buildings, for example the Institute of Chinese Socialism and the Friendship House Hotel for foreign experts. Then come the Institutes of Higher Learning, such as the China People's University. A squad of students is doing rifle drill. Now the fawn mud is cultivated, and maize screens shelter small crop, factory hens peck at the side of the road. We turn left at a bus-station. On the left, farmland stretches away towards the western hills. On the other side a traditional white wall runs into a yellowy flinty wall, and we arrive at a traditional red gate. This is the entrance to Peking University's campus.

We go through the gate and cross a humped bridge over the silent moat. Ahead of us, divided by a path, are two hedged lawns on which stand two traditional columns representing lions on clouds. Beyond and on either side of these lawns are three traditional buildings with tiled roofs and red columns. The eaves are in imitation Ching blue and green, and each beam has a picture of a landscape or natural life. These three buildings are the department of oriental languages (left), the Administration building (centre), and one of the buildings in the school of sciences (right). We drive behind the Administration building. Adorned with red flags and paper roses is a notice board containing a list of teachers who have the right to vote for the Party. At the back of the science building is the central library, another traditional building with tiled roofs and red columns. We drive on through hillocks and pines and other kinds of trees, past long, curved walks. Magpies fly to and fro. We get out within view of the lake. From here we command an incomplete view of the campus. To the left is the house that Dr. Leighton Stuart lived in, when he was President of the American missionary university of Yenching, which occupied this campus until 1949. To the right, in new blocks, are the buildings of the English and Russian department. Way across the lake is the gymnasium, and in the distance the water-tower, which blends well with the surrounding trees. The reddish teachers' dormitories are at the back of Stuart's house, the grey students' dormitories being away over the lake, hidden behind the trees. It is a lovely campus, marred here and there by piles of bricks and leaden piping, perhaps, but still lovely. There is only one thing wrong: the campus is deserted. It is a Wednesday morning in the middle of term, and there are no students.

They must all be in class, Frank Tuohy and I conclude. And at that moment we are greeted by an elderly English-speaking Professor who taught in Peking University long before it was moved to its present site in 1949. After a few words he says: "We must visit an English class straightaway, for it will be over by nine." Strange, we think. This is Peking University, and there don't seem to be any English classes after nine.

We walk to the English building. A month previously, about the middle of February, the Professor tells us on the way, English and Russian were merged into one department. The English building is rather grey, and is quite different from the majority of department buildings on the campus, which are traditional in style. Classes have just begun and no one is about. We go up to the second floor, noting the green posters on the walls: Lei Feng and Wang Chieh, the two national heroes, both recently dead, and instructions on rifle drill. "Let us go in here," says the Professor, and we go into a small, oblong classroom. Two rows of 2nd-year students stand up and applaud us. When they sit down we notice the segregation: men in the back row – six of them – and five girls, all with braids, in the front row. All are wearing blue boiler jackets and trousers.

The class goes on. The teacher stands at the front, consults the notes on his desk, and proceeds with pattern drills. He is a young man – in fact he could be mistaken for a student. He too wears a blue boiler jacket, but he has the red tag of a teacher on his breast pocket whereas most of the students have white tags. Only one is wearing glasses; few wear glasses in China. The students do not seem to be using texts. In fact, the emphasis is almost entirely on oral work for the first two years, and all English classes are conducted in English, the numbers generally being limited to between 15 and 20. There is a constant dialogue and the results are extraordinary: not one of these 2nd-year students had learnt a word of English before University; at school they had learnt Russian; and yet their fluency was surprising.

"Due to," the teacher is saying with a flawless accent and in a sympathetic, persuasive tone. "'It was due to the building of reservoirs and the cadres setting an example by working in the fields.' Now listen to this sentence. 'Agriculture has developed a great deal since the People's communes were set up.' Use 'due to'. Comrade Wu." And Comrade Wu, in his second year of English, says: "The development of agriculture is due to the setting up of the People's communes."...

Outside the classroom I ask if we can see a 3rd- and 4th-year class. The Professor replies guardedly, "They have been in the countryside since August."

"All of them?" we ask in surprise.

"Yes, all. And some 5th-year too. It is socialist education," the Professor adds uncomfortably.

"When will they be back?"

"Oh, soon."

There is a silence. We go down the stairs. Outside the English building some forty students in boiler suits are doing P.T. There is one squad, but most are doing it on their own. We are told vaguely that these are all English students, but we are not satisfied. It is the middle of term, and the campus is deserted, and there don't seem to be any English classes after nine, and the 3rd- and 4th-year students have been in the countryside for the last seven months.

*

We go to Dr. Stuart's house. From the outside it looks rather like a temple with steps leading up to the front door between two red lacquered columns; there is a cluster of bamboo on the left. Here we are given a history of the University.

It was founded in 1898 under the name "Imperial University of Peking". In 1902 its name was changed to "National Peking University". In 1916 under the reforming Chancellor, Tsai Yuan-pei, the University's four schools – letters, science, law and engineering – were remodelled on the American pattern. It has a glorious revolutionary history and led the "May-4 movement" of 1919. In 1937 it was closed when the Japanese took Peking. Between 1945 and 1949 there was hostility between "Peita", as it is known, and the Kuomintang. All this time Peita was situated near Coal Hill, just behind the Forbidden City – it was here that Chairman Mao worked in the library – and the building on this, the old campus, today looks more like a hospital than a university. In 1949 Peita was moved to its present site. This site was already a university, the U.S. missionary University of Yenching. In 1952 the Schools of Law and Engineering were moved to other universities, and now only letters and science remain on the campus. These comprise nearly 10,000 students. In 1949 there were 1,500 students and 300 teachers. In 1965 there were 9,000 students, 200 postgraduates and 400 overseas students (I did not see, or hear mention of, any Africans), and 2,000 teachers....

Now we come to the purpose of the University. "We have gone work-study," the Professor says, "and the philosophy and history faculties have moved permanently into the countryside. Work-study has been tried since 1958, and it began here in 1965. It will not be generally applied here until 1975." And I recall the phrases from elsewhere: Futan University – "through work their skins grow dark but their hearts remain Red"; Nanking University – "return to grass roots levels and share the will and the wool."

Then, a little later, just as all our former suspicions are being allayed, the (male) secretary to the Administration speaks in Chinese. He is interpreted as saying: "We have two tasks. One is to wipe out imperialism, and some subjects which spread reactionary views have been cancelled, for example History, Philosophy and Literature, both Chinese and foreign. Attention must be focused on the present, and we must redeal with these subjects to get a Marxist view of them. The other task is to remould ideology and wipe out the bad influence of the past. In 1958 we began a new educational policy with the Big Leap Forward. Education must serve the proletariat and be combined with labour. We are struggling to carry this through."

We reflect. On the one hand, Philosophy and History have moved permanently into the countryside. On the other hand, Philosophy and History are subjects which spread reactionary views and "have been cancelled". Cancelled. And what of Literature? Is there perhaps a deeper explanation for the seven months' absence of the 3rd- and 4th-year students than work-study? Is work-study the official explanation, and is their absence really connected with "remoulding"?

"Are there many bourgeois reactionary influences on the campus?" we ask.

After a silence the English teacher whose class we have attended replies: "Yes."

"I was told there are a lot in Futan University," I say.

"There are probably the same here," he replies, and there is a silence.

We ask for further details of what the 3rd- and 4th-year students are doing.

It is a 5th-year student who replies. The 3rd- and 4th-year students, he says, have each been sent to different villages. There they each live and eat and work and talk with the peasants. There may be more than one in a village. They have no books, and have done no study at all for seven months. The teachers have not gone too, and they have had no classes for seven months. The students are supervised by the peasants. This 5th-year student might have been in the countryside himself.

"Why aren't you in Sinkiang?" I ask, seeking to locate the whereabouts of the 3rd- and 4th-year students.

"Because I have a medical certificate," he replies. (*See* p.513.)

Now my suspicions are acute. First, could it be that the 3rd- and 4th-year students are really in Sinkiang? And secondly, is it compulsory, since it requires a medical certificate to exempt? I think this 5th-year student has probably told me the truth.

I find out no more from this 5th-year student. Our meeting has taken place in one of the students' dormitories, and apart from my guide and the secretary to the Administration there were no inhibiting presences. He has spoken in English, and my guide has listened without comment....

Transcript

After I leave the campus I am troubled. I want to know more about the 3rd- and 4th-year students. I want to know whether there is anything punitive in the operation. Seven months' work without study in the middle of a university course does not seem very sound from an educational point of view. What is behind it? I decide to find out, and while returning to Hsin Chiao hotel from a cinema, I tell my guide that I am very unhappy as I have found out that intellectuals at Peking University are being purged. I say that my faith in China will not be restored until I have seen the Vice-President of Peking University and had a full explanation.

After two days of extreme pressure up and down Coal Hill, in and out of the Forbidden City; two days of blatant lies from my guide – for example "You were mistaken, the 3rd- and 4th-year students were on the campus during your visit" – I win. I meet Professor Wang, the Vice-President of Peking University, for an hour and really grill him, and his answers are extremely revealing for such questions as the purpose of the University and student rebel movements.

On our way to Dr. Stuart's house, where Frank Tuohy and I are received by Professor Wang on the Saturday morning, we see a squad of between 20 and 30 students, each of whom carry two rifles. All students at Peking University are members of the militia, the amateur army which is nearly 100 million strong. They march at the double away to the lake, past the air-raid shelter which gapes among the teachers' dormitories. I do not see any signs of an air-raid shelter near the students' dormitories.

Professor Wang is very civil in spite of a troublesome cough and my outspokenness. He speaks through a lady interpreter and he is evasive. I am able to take down what he says, and I give a cleaned-up transcript of the interview:

NH: Where are the 3rd-, 4th- and 5th-year students and what are they doing?

Answer (after a shocked silence): It is laid down in the directives of our socialist educational policy that our students must take part in physical work, so they are often coming and going. According to the regulations the students have to take part in physical labour for five times one-and-a-half months. That means they have to take part over five years in 5 x 1½ months, which is 7½ months during their student career. Sometimes they concentrate the periods of time.

NH: Why? Is this connected with socialist re-education?

Answer: My friends, according to Chairman Mao's thinking our education must serve the policy of the proletariat, be combined with productive labour and train cultured labourers with social consciousness. Our policy is fundamentally different from that in bourgeois countries. In bourgeois countries the policy is to train not labourers but intellectuals. But our ideal is the intellectual-labourer. We want to eliminate the three differences: the difference between mental and manual labour, the difference between industry and agriculture, and the difference between town and country.

NH: Are the students teaching the peasants or *vice versa*?

Answer: Each teaches the other. For example the peasants teach the students how to grow plants.

NH: You say the students sometimes "concentrate the periods of time". Did these 3rd- and 4th-year students not do 1½ months in their first and second years?

Answer: They did.

NH (objecting): They have already been away 7 years, so the total for the course so far is, in the case of a 3rd-year student, 10 months, and in the case of a 4th-year student 11½ months, which is more than the regulations say.

Answer (rattled): It's rather complicated. In some departments they take part in physical labour for longer periods than in other departments.

NH: When the 3rd- and 4th-year students return will they be exempt from labour for the rest of their course?

Answer: Yes.

NH: Have their courses been interrupted for 7½ months?

Answer: In a sense, they have been interrupted.

NH: Have they taken texts with them?

Answer: Yes.

(This reply conflicted with the evidence of my conversation with the 5th-year student.)

NH: Do the students who are now in Sinkiang –

Answer: There are no students in Sinkiang.

(The mention of this area aroused no objection from the 5th-year student.)

NH: Do they learn from teachers while they are in the countryside?

Answer: Yes. The peasants and the intellectuals get together. Students of biology get together with their Professors and lecturers in the countryside.

(Professor Wang then repeated the official explanation about breaking down barriers between peasants and intellectuals. His statement about the presence of teachers disagreed with what the 5th-year student had said.)

NH: Are the movements of the philosophy and history faculties to the countryside connected with the criticism of Yang Hsien-Chen, the philosopher and Wu Han, the historian?

Answer (after a long silence): The philosophy and history faculties have gone to the countryside just for work-study. There is no connection with Yang Hsien-Chen and Wu Han.

NH: Is the moving of the 3rd- and 4th-year students to the countryside connected with unreliable elements in the English department?

Answer: No. The Central Committee of our Party has decided on work-study and we think Peking University is behind what they have decided. All the departments except foreign languages departments are doing work-study (i.e. doing part-work, part-study).

NH (objecting): But what has happened to the 3rd- and 4th-year students is not connected with work-study.

Answer (after a lengthy silence): Apart from work-study, our students take part in socialist education. We hope that our society has solid foundations. But among them (i.e. students) there are some whose ideology does not conform with socialism. They don't know the nature or future of socialism very well. So although they are living in a socialist society their ideology is partly capitalist. Capitalist ideology leads to non-socialist remarks and acts. Therefore our Government thinks it necessary to carry out nation-wide socialist education. Even my theoretical understanding of socialism is not high, in spite of my practical experience, so those without practical experience will make remarks and acts not in line with socialism. Chairman Mao points out that their understanding (i.e. misunderstanding) is due to the historical background of our society. We believe that after being educated they will have lesser and lesser bourgeois ideology. According to Chairman Mao we resort to education, not to other more drastic means. We believe that people can be remoulded. That's why we think the teachers and students of Peking University have this responsibility to educate these people (i.e. peasants) in this time of our Government's need. When they are in the countryside they appear as labourers.

(Up to the end of this answer, the students had been the subjects as they are of the last sentence. The penultimate sentence was an obvious attempt to confuse.)

NH: How are they "remoulded"?

Answer: The peasants have undergone changes. You must know that the countryside was ruled by the landlords before the Liberation. Their exploitation of the peasants caused much suffering and there were rich peasants besides. We tell the peasants about the past. So when the teachers and students first go to a commune they write history for the peasants, not only pre-Liberation history but history about the area and the village. In these communes and villages many peasants used to be oppressed, and the students and teachers learn something particular about the village. From writing the history of the commune, they make their analysis and they teach the peasants.

NH: Are these the 3rd- and 4th-year students?

Answer: Yes.

NH: We have just been told that their ideology is limited, and they are now going to gain. Is that correct?

Answer (hesitantly): Yes. They have to raise the level of their understanding through writing history. They use these facts to educate the peasants and raise their own understanding of the past. Through them the peasants review their past deeds and learn what is right and what is wrong.

NH: If a student's ideology is unreliable, might he not be a bad influence on the peasants?

Answer: Ninety-five per cent have good consciousness.

NH (objecting): But this move is compulsory.

Answer: No, voluntary. The students are eager to go to the countryside.

NH: Why, then, do you require a medical certificate to be exempt? (*See* pp.196, 509.)

Answer: They do not need one to be exempt.

NH (objecting): But the 5th-year does.

Answer: A few days ago I lectured to my students and I said, "Students must take part in physical work but those whose health is poor are exempted."

(In other words, the students *did* need a medical certificate to be exempt.)

NH: Are the 3rd- and 4th-year students all in the same village as the peasants?

Answer: Sometimes. They do not live apart from each other.

(These last statements disagree with what the 5th-year student said.)

NH: Exactly why did the movement to the countryside begin in August 1965? Why not in January 1965, for example?

Answer: It was purely accidental. There is no particular reason.

NH: Didn't it have anything to do with the 4 checks?

(Sometimes called the 4 clearances, *ssu ching*, the four checks were the unpublicised campaign against anti-Party ideology, economics, organisation and politics. An examination of the transcript shows that what happened at Peking University was due to this unpublicised campaign. In that sense the unpublicised campaign *was* socialist education.)

Answer: The 4 checks *is* socialist education.

NH (objecting): But until now the 4 checks has been a rural policy to reform the ideology of the peasants, and not students.

(Sir Donald Hopson, the British Chargé d'affaires had said the previous day that the 4 checks were directed against peasants. The interrogation showed that they were directed against students. Any mention of the 4 checks always created an impression of panic.)

Answer: The students are educated through writing history. They make an analysis in terms of Chairman Mao's thinking, concretely.

NH: How do they make an analysis in terms of Chairman Mao's thinking concretely? Who guides them while they make their analysis?

Answer: They have studied Chairman Mao's thinking at the University.

NH: Are there any teachers with them to guide them?

Answer: Yes.

(This again disagreed with the 5th-year student.)

NH: How many hours a day are set aside for book guidance by teachers in the countryside?
Answer: It depends on the circumstances in the countryside. I cannot tell you definitely. (Under pressure.) One hour per day or one day per week.

NH: And these hours would be supervised by a teacher?
Answer: Sometimes they study by themselves.

NH: Have any students protested against this Party action?
Answer: So far, in Peking University I have never heard of any protest.

NH: If the ninety-five per cent are reliable, why do they need re-educating?
Answer (rattled): We think everyone needs educating because there is no end to our understanding (i.e. misunderstanding). For example, I am nearly 60, and I must still learn.

NH: I have compared the hours spent in political education with the hours spent in the teaching of English, and political education has not been a success in comparison with the teaching of English. Would you agree?
Answer: No.

NH (objecting): I am interested that you have such confidence in your students and I am surprised that they are not allowed to teach the peasants in this way.
No answer.

NH: Where are the 3rd- and 4th-year students?
Answer (under extreme pressure): In Hopei province.

NH: Are there any 3rd- and 4th-year students on the campus?
Answer: No.

NH: Where is the philosophy faculty?
Answer: In Szechwan province.

NH: Where is the history faculty?
Answer: In Hopei province, about 30 kilometres outside Peking.

Analysis
What are we to make of this? As we see from the sentence "Apart from work-

study, our students take part in socialist education", there are clearly two issues involved, and the socialist education policy is the nearer to the truth. According to a diplomat contact (i.e. Sir Donald Hopson), the socialist education policy was devised in 1962 to clean up the country ideologically, the background being the criticisms that had arisen in the three bad years, 1959–1961, and which could not be suppressed in those bad years. In 1961, this diplomat thought, the Party lost its grip, and it has turned on the screws since then.

What has happened to the 3rd- and 4th-year students is clearly a Party rather than a University affair. Note the word "directives" and the failure to contradict the question "Have any students protested against this Party action?"

Perhaps the most revealing sentences are: "According to Chairman Mao we resort to education, not to other more drastic means. We believe that people can be remoulded." Stalin *would* have resorted to more drastic means. The end of the paragraph from which these sentences are taken does not make it clear whether the students are doing or suffering the resorting and the remoulding, but it is quite clear that the students are the "people who can be remoulded", and the matter is clinched if we collate the two questions "How are they remoulded?" and "Are these the 3rd- and 4th-year students?"

Interpreting the word "remarks" in the phrase "remarks and acts" (which occurs twice) as applying to the students, we can glimpse the discontent among the students which presumably forms the background to the movement to the countryside.

On the subject of what the 3rd- and 4th-year students are doing, who does one believe – the 5th-year student or Professor Wang? Do they have no books at all, or are they studying? Do they live separately or together? Do they or do they not have teachers with them? Are they supervised by the peasants or are they writing histories for the peasants?

In conclusion, it should be emphasised (1) that the guide lied whenever this subject was approached; (2) that in China the Party and the collective wisdom of the people is always right, and the onus is on the individual to prove that they were wrong; and (3) that 7 months, with or without books, spent in doing other things than one's subject in the middle of a course that is generally regarded as being at least a year too long, is not the most ideal of ways to turn out brilliant and scholarly specialists. As for me, there is no doubt in my mind. And, thinking of the "remoulded" Shanghai capitalist I met who, between telling me about Cambridge University in the 1930s, mechanically spouted Chairman Mao, and thinking of the "remoulded" landlord I met on a Shanghai commune who, when jogged, mechanically spouted Chairman Mao, and thinking of their lesioned minds which, after a tremendous struggle, they have succeeded in giving to the Party, I shudder, and my heart goes out towards those voluntary work-study students who were 95% reliable.

5

Africa

Nicholas Hagger's main accredited articles on Africa in British newspapers
(in chronological order)

Libya's Young Puritans
The Times, 29 August 1970

A special correspondent reports on changes since the *coup*

Next Tuesday, September 1, the Libyan leader, Colonel Muammar al-Gaddafi, will have ruled for one year. He headed the *coup* that overthrew the Libyan monarchy of King Idris, who had ruled since the British left in 1951. Gaddafi, then a lieutenant of 27, was helped by a Revolutionary Command Council (RCC) of 11 other junior army officers of the same age. Most of these had been in the same class at school in Sebha (the first revolutionary meetings, according to Gaddafi, took place during school outings in the Suez crisis of 1956) and to many Libyans it seemed as though a group of students were staging an armed sit-in on the throne.

For more than three months after that the 12 Just Men wisely tried to remain anonymous, and their policies were understandably in doubt. They did have policies, however, and in the past year they have created an attitude of revolution which is truly remarkable. They have overthrown an old order; yet they have so far been able to avoid executions. At the same time they have created a spirit of constant and limitless revolutionary re-evaluation of the past, with everyone being called on to discuss things in true Arab style.

What were the RCC's motives? Suez started them off; they felt that the King had permitted aircraft to take off from the British base against Nasser and their Arab brothers (Gaddafi recently said this in a public speech) and that Libyan politicians had betrayed the Arab cause. They saw their leaders as "colonialist puppets" who had sold out to foreigners, who kept the Army weak to further their own pro-West line, and who had become rich and corrupted after Libya's oil revenues started in 1959.

The corruption in the Ministry of Petroleum was notorious. Oil company representatives seeking concessions frequently had to bribe minor officials, just for the right of seeing the official they wanted to negotiate with. And when they got to him, they had to pay huge sums in bribes to get the concession.

The RCC are cleaning up after what they regard as 18 years of graft. The principle of the queue has been instated in all Government offices, from the Ministry of Petroleum to the Ministry of Transport; paperwork has been reduced, not always successfully, so as to eliminate obstructing bureaucrats, the machinery of government has been overhauled, the old men have gone and have been replaced by new, inexperienced men. It is now ability and qualifications that count when applying for jobs, not bribes and names.

The RCC are also doing something about the past. In an attempt to recover money obtained illegally they have set up a People's Court with the declared purpose of trying "those responsible for political and administrative corruption in the old regime".

On the other hand, the trials have not so far begun, and many of the accused have been released from prison. So people are now beginning to feel that the trials may never take place.

In attacking the bad effects of the oil boom and restoring Libya to what they regard as her pre-1956 purity, the RCC have also made war on those two allegedly non-Islamic, Western influences: wine and women. For the past year there has officially been no alcohol in Tripoli, though illegal supplies have still been obtainable; and the four nightclubs have, until very recently, been closed.

Nonetheless, Gaddafi is very sensitive about the basis of his power. Officially, the September-1 affair is an "evolution, not a revolution", and at a think-in Gaddafi offered the following justification of his *coup*: "The September-1 Revolution is not a traditional *coup d'état*, a usurpation of power, a coveting of high positions or dignity, or a domination by the military over the Government. It was neither prompted by personal ends and narrow military reactions, nor represented a reflex action to the 1967 setback that befell the Arab nation. The September-1 Revolution was a natural phenomenon in logical harmony with the laws of nature, facts of life and the revolution of history."

When Gaddafi was asked by a student about three months after the *coup* when Parliament would reopen, he said: "Under the ex-regime there was a Parliament, but there was also corruption and no freedom. Therefore, Parliament is not necessary in a just and free society."

The Revolution has also given Libya's natural xenophobia a new momentum. It has its historical roots in the fact that there have always been alien rulers in Tripoli. The Phoenicians, the Romans, the Vandals, the Byzantines, the Normans, the Spanish, the Knights of St John, the Ottoman Turks, all had representatives who ruled from Tripoli.

The most recent invading power was Italy, which came in 1911. In the 1930s, thousands of Libyans are said to have died in Italian concentration camps. When the Italians surrendered Libya in 1945, there were only four

Libyan graduates.

All this has passed into the Libyan genes. Strangely the reaction has skipped a generation and for this the restraining influence of the British Military Administration (1945–51) and subsequently of the British-backed monarchy of Idris is the explanation. Libya's young puritans are very historically-minded. They are trying Libyans for corruption since 1951, and now they are fining the Italians for things that happened before 1945.

Recently the RCC confiscated all assets from all the 35,000 Italians and a handful of remaining Jews living in Libya. The decree mentions "all land and everything on it" and the RCC's public justification is that the Libyan people are receiving back "property usurped by the fascists, who came from over the sea to impose their tyranny".

The most wearying effect of the xenophobia is the stifling atmosphere of living under permanent scrutiny by the secret police. There is a new department within the Ministry of Interior for watching foreigners, and as the exodus progresses, foreigners can measure their rising social status by the increased attentions of the secret police.

This atmosphere has had its effect on the Libyans. They know it is not safe for them to visit Westerners now, they do not want to be seen dropping in, and so they stay away. A decree by Jallud, Gaddafi's deputy, modelled on the Egyptian legislation, has not helped matters. It imposes controls on all Libyans working in foreign embassies and companies, who now have to register all mail they send to or receive from, foreigners. One Libyan told me he would not be able to send me a postcard without the date and my name and the purpose of the card being recorded.

The Libyans' reaction against the colonialists has left them with a vacuum to fill, for they need help from someone. They have tried to fill a small part of it with the French, who are supplying *Mirage*s and trade delegations. But the French have a colonialist record in Tunisia, Algeria and Morocco, and they are not really trusted.

It is the Egyptians who have virtually taken Libya over. One of Gaddafi's slogans is "unity", and although he wants the impossible – the unity of all the Arabs – he is initially thinking of unity with Egypt and the Sudan. To Gaddafi, that means primarily Egypt. Gaddafi has supreme trust in Nasser's honesty. Since he first started talking revolution on those school outings, Gaddafi has idolised Nasser, and Libya is now in effect an Egyptian client-state.

There are at present thousands of Egyptian advisers, soldiers, even street-cleaners in Tripoli. As the British nurses and teachers move out, Egyptian nurses and teachers move in. There is no border between Libya and Egypt, and under a recent agreement, Egyptians can now own property in Libya.

All this is resented by the Libyan people, who dislike the Egyptians. All the Libyans I know believe the Egyptians think themselves superior, and they believe the Egyptians have no reason to be superior. They believe they lost the June war through cowardice, they are contemptuous of Egyptian tightness with money. This is a consequence of the fact that Egypt has a large population with a very low average wage and wartime domestic conditions, whereas Libya has a small population and her oil wealth. In small acts of protest and retaliation against the RCC, some bodies (like the university) have been dismissing Egyptians, who will presumably be reinstated by the RCC before the new academic year begins in September.

Libya under its Colonel from the Desert
The Sunday Telegraph, 30 August 1970

One year after the Revolution which ousted the conservative and pro-Western regime of King Idris, Libya's Colonel Muammar al-Gaddafi still survives as the nation's leader. I have been able to observe him, sometimes at close quarters, as he set about establishing a Socialist state, breaking old loyalties and forging new anti-Western links with his Arab neighbours.

Of desert origin and poor parents, he comes across as a lean, frail-looking, sincere man. His image is of a man of deeds rather than words, and he has a reputation for telling his hosts in other Arab states things like: "I haven't come here to attend banquets, I want action."

I remember his first visit to the University, about six weeks after the *coup*. He sat on a platform, surrounded by red-bereted armed guards, and answered questions put by the students for two hours. His rapport with the students was good, perhaps because he is only 28 years old himself. Question: "What is your economic policy?" Answer: "Oh, I have none." The joke was well received. But so oversimplified and frivolous were many of his answers that my interpreter said to me: "This man is too simple to be our leader."

Yet the next time he visited the University, to address a conference of Arab Ministers of Education, he made a visionary speech without so much as a smile. He can adapt himself to his audience, and perhaps that explains how he has kept the leadership in spite of his youth.

Gaddafi has cause to feel satisfied at present. One of his aims has been to end the period of economic exploitation, which began with the discovery of oil in Libya in 1959. He and his revolutionary colleagues were also quick to fold down the British and American military bases in the country.

By 1960 Libya had started to produce her own oil in large quantities, and now she is the fourth-largest producer in the world. Gaddafi feels that the oil companies do not pay enough for the oil, and the Revolutionary

Command Council, comprising Gaddafi and 11 other young officers, is trying to persuade the oil companies to pay more. Gaddafi has threatened nationalization if they will not agree. "Libya has done without oil for 5,000 years," he told a meeting of oilmen at the beginning of negotiations, "and if necessary, she can do without oil for another ten."

Libya's foreign policy is now dominated by the idea of anti-colonialist Arab unity. Like the youthful Alexander the Great, Gaddafi is a man of vision, and he believes in one Arabia, from Morocco to Iraq.

As a stage in this ideal, he has worked towards unity with Egypt and Sudan. The Arabs united can defeat all their enemies, including colonialist Israel – this is the theory. So Gaddafi has drawn up a war plan, which seeks to recapture Palestine by pan-Arab war without involving the Four Powers or the Security Council. Gaddafi has visited most of the Arab countries in connection with his war plan, and as if this is not enough for a young *coup* leader, he mounted two Arab summit conferences in Tripoli, one in June and one in July. Libya is now very much on the Arab map. She is now a symbol of Arab unity.

But Gaddafi is a dictator, and the RCC rules by decree. Many Libyans resent the continued closure of Parliament. The Press is muzzled, and journalists are intimidated with threats of execution.

Colonialism has been uprooted militarily, economically and historically, but in consequence there is in Libya a dislike of foreigners, and an intolerance of them, that is, as enlightened Libyans uncomfortably admit, very far from being civilised. Western lettering is being obliterated on street signs, gateposts and car number-plates. Alcohol is forbidden.

The Italian community has suffered most because of this intolerance. In their case, as with the few Jews left in Libya, the attitude has expressed itself in legislation. In a recent decree, the RCC has sequestrated all land and property, all furniture and cars, all bank balances owned by Italians and Jews, to compensate for the wrongs of the past.

But all nationalities have experienced hostile incidents. Even I was threatened with execution by one of the leading members of the Revolution at 4 o'clock one morning. But confrontations as violent as this are untypical. There have been deportations and threatened deportations – a British vicar was ordered to leave; trials in Arabic without a charge being specified, as happened to a British nurse; and numerous brushes with secret police from the new department in the Ministry of the Interior which keeps an eye on foreigners.

From the point of view of civilised Western values, the *coup* has not achieved all its promises of "Freedom, Unity and Socialism."

One of the greatest problems arising from the Revolution is the loss of hundreds of trained Western experts. It is impossible for Libyans to fill the gap. There are only one and a half million of them, and relatively few are educated. And of these, many have been purged for corruption. The result is that as Westerners leave, someone else must come in. And it is the Egyptians who are pouring in.

What of the future? The anti-Western line is hard to go back on, and the RCC look securely in control. So far the Revolution has been surprisingly moderate, as revolutions go, and it may be that the extremist phase is still ahead.

The war against racialism
The Times, 3 October 1970

The 120 members of the central committee of the World Council of Churches set up a Special Fund to combat racism in August, 1969, and empowered an international advisory committee of 16 members and ten consultants to advise it on the use of the fund.

The advisory committee had world-wide representation, but only five of the 26 involved were black Africans. Its recommendations were adopted by the 15 members of the executive committee on September 3 this year. There were no dissenting votes. The recommendations, disclosed here exclusively, set out the criteria for allocating the fund, as follows:

1   The proceeds of the fund shall be used to support organizations that combat racism, rather than welfare organizations that alleviate the effects of racism, which would normally be eligible for support of other units of the World Council of Churches.

2(a) The focus of the grants should be on raising the level of awareness and on strengthening the organizational capability of racially oppressed people.

(b) In addition we recognise the need to support organizations that align themselves with the victims of racial injustice and pursue the same objectives.
While these grants are made without control of the manner in which they are spent, they are at the same time a commitment of the Programme to Combat Racism to the struggle of these organizations for economic, social and political justice.

3(a) The situation in Southern Africa is recognised as a priority due to the overt and intensive nature of white racism and the increasing awareness on the part of the oppressed in their struggle for liberation.

(b) In the selection of other areas we have taken account of those places where the struggle is most intensive and where a grant might make a substantial contribution to the process of liberation particularly where racial groups are in imminent danger of being physically or culturally exterminated.

4 Grants should be made with due regard to where they can have the maximum effect; token grants should not be made unless there is a possibility of their eliciting a substantial response from other organizations.

On the basis of this criteria and after careful consideration the committee urgently recommends the immediate distribution of $200,000 (£83,000), out of a total of $278,769 received so far, as follows:

Australia

1 *Federal Council for the Advancement of Aborigines and Torres Strait Islanders*
An organization in support of land title rights of aboriginal peoples in Australia and especially concerned with legal action (criteria 2b). $10,000 (about £4,200)

2 *National Tribal Council*
Newly created organization by aboriginal people which aims at (a) a "grass roots" organizing campaign to establish local "tribal councils" as a means of effective political expression and (b) a national campaign of a political and educative nature, directed towards the white population and power structure (criteria 2a and 3b). $15,000.

United Kingdom

1 *West Indian Standing Conference*
A non-partisan umbrella organization consisting of 16 member organizations with 10,000 members total. The request is to enable this organization to promote solidarity among the black community with a view to create a strong "grass roots" black power base which could effectively protect them and thus combat racism (criteria 2a). $7,500.

2 Activities on behalf of Southern Africa in the United Kingdom (three arms of one activity) (criteria 2b):

(a) *The Africa Bureau*
An independent body with the aim to improve understanding in Britain about current events and problems in Southern Africa
– promoting British policies that will assist social and economic development in Southern Africa;
– opposing racial tyranny in Southern Africa;

- promoting the achievement of non-discriminatory majority rule in Southern Africa. $2,500.

(b) *Anti-Apartheid Movement*

An organization which earlier in 1970 was instrumental in organizing an effective national campaign of protest against the visit of an all-white rugby team from South Africa to Britain, and subsequently succeeded in getting the cricket tour to Britain cancelled. More recently active in trying to reverse the present Government's policy of lifting the arms embargo against South Africa. In close touch with African governments and liberation movements in Southern Africa. $5,000.

(c) *International Defence and Aid Fund*

The priorities of this organization are to provide legal defence for the opponents of racial discrimination in Southern Africa, material welfare for families of those executed, imprisoned, banned or banished for their political beliefs, and to assist in the education of political prisoners and their families. $3,000.

Netherlands

Angola Committee and Dr Eduardo Mondlane Foundation

The Angola Committee has over the past years increasingly influenced Dutch public opinion regarding racist policies in Southern Africa. The two organizations mentioned are now planning joint action in cooperation with similar organizations in western Europe under a new title "Foundation for the Promotion of Information about Racism and Colonialism". Aims are: research, documentation and information concerning Southern Africa in Dutch and English; audio-visual aids for schools and action groups; assistance to Portuguese deserters (criteria 2b). $5,000.

Japan

International Committee to Combat the Immigration Bill in Japan

Organization of Korean and Chinese minority groups working for change of the proposed new Japanese Immigration Bill which has racist overtones. The bill would put pressure of various kinds on aliens in Japan. As a result there is genuine fear that minority groups would lose their basic human rights (criteria 2a and 4). $2,000.

Colombia

Committee for the Defence of the Indian in Colombia

This committee supports Indian groups involved in studying the causes and processes which have produced the "Indian problem" in Colombia. (There are an estimated 500,000 Indians in that country.) These studies are part of a "conscientization" programme which will help the Indians to define and analyse the Indian culture and social life and to recuperate the Indian soul (criteria 2a and 3b). $15,000.

Zambia
Africa 2000 Project

A project by an organization in Zambia aiming at exposing and dismantling economic, political, social and racial structures in Southern Africa by which human beings exploit fellow human beings and replacing them by more just structures. This includes "conscientization" programmes, group work, consultations by black Africans from various parts of Southern Africa (criteria 2a). $15,000.

Southern Africa

Liberation Movements which in their struggle for the self-determination and for fundamental human rights of racially oppressed peoples are actually in control of liberated territory. These movements are requesting support from the churches in developing the necessary infra-structure in liberated territory (criteria 1, 2a and 3a).

Mozambique
Mozambique Institute of Frelimo

(Fronte de Libertacao de Mozambique). Frelimo claims to have control over one-fifth of Mozambique. The Institute is the educational and social welfare arm of Frelimo. It is now setting up the first development plan for free Mozambique which foresees among others the organization of agricultural cooperatives, the export of agricultural products (ground nuts, rye, cashew nuts, tobacco, rubber) and the organization of social, educational and health services. $15,000.

Angola

1 MPLA (Movimento Popular de Libertacao de Angola). $20,000.
2 GRAE (Governo Revolucionario de Angola no Exil). $20,000.
3 UNITA (Uniao Nacional para a Independencia Total de Angola). $10,000.

Each of these movements is in control of considerable parts of Angola (all three together claim over one-third of the country) and is in the process of developing emergency economic, educational, health and social welfare programmes, which are almost completely lacking.

Guinea-Bissao

P.A.I.G.C. (Partido Africano de Independência da Guinee e Cabo Verde)

This movement is probably in control of approximately two thirds of the country. Like the liberation movements in Angola and Mozambique it is in the process of developing economic, education, social welfare and health programmes. P.A.I.G.C. has already opened two hospitals and is in charge of school programmes for some 12,000 children. $20,000.

Liberation Movements in exile struggling for the self-determination and fundamental human rights of racially oppressed peoples. These movements are requesting support from the churches for programmes to counter propaganda of white *apartheid* regimes and to make known and inform international public opinion about the plight of their racially oppressed peoples (criteria 1, 2a and 3a).

South Africa
African National Congress (A.N.C.)
Movement created by Luthuli and active as an African political party inside South Africa until it was banned. Requests support for the launching of a "Luthuli Memorial Foundation" designed to inform world public opinion about alternatives to the present *apartheid* regime in South Africa and to do research (publications, audio-visual aids, etc.) and to assist victims of *apartheid*. $10,000.

South-West Africa (Namibia)
South West African People's Organisation (S.W.A.P.O.)
Requests assistance for (a) education of students in and outside Namibia; (b) issuing regularly an information bulletin on the situation in Namibian; (c) food and medical care to Namibians living in Zambia. $5,000.

Rhodesia
1   *Zimbabwe African National Union* (Z.A.N.U.)
    This movement requests support for its information service (a bulletin in English and in two local vernaculars); for financial assistance to wives and children of refugees, detainees and freedom fighters. There are many desperate welfare cases, including wives and children of African nationalists detained or killed by the Smith regime. The movement is also assisting a number of students with scholarships at African universities. $10,000.
2   *Zimbabwe African People's Union* (Z.A.P.U.)
    Requests support for relief on behalf of destitute families and dependants, several thousand mothers and children in Zimbabwe whose breadwinners are either in prison, concentration camps, or have been killed or are in military service for the liberation of their country. Relief includes paying school fees for children (primary and

secondary), providing food, accommodation, clothing, medical aid, etc. It also includes legal aid to prisoners. $10,000.

Opinion privately on the Council is that there is a risk in every donation to every charity. "If you give £500 to a South African refugee to help his family", one World Council of Churches member said, "he can go out and buy a few brenguns. Where do you draw the line?"

Pauline Webb, vice-president of the World Council of Churches, told me: "The sheer human needs are important. We've received a comment from Angola that the suffering haven't even tasted an aspirin. The plight of the suffering is so desperate that we have to take risks. All the liberation movements have given assurances that the money will be used for welfare means, and people are being naïve if they think that any arms the movements buy with our money will be a military threat to South Africa."

The theological justification for opposing institutionalised racism appears elsewhere in the report: "The Scriptures insist that righteousness includes justice. There can be no justice without equitable distribution of power.... God has revealed himself time after time as on the side of the powerless, not to endorse their powerlessness, but to secure justice. God calls men to love one another, but in our institutionalised world the closest approximation to love possible, is justice. We therefore recognise this demand for a sharing of power."

Portugal's African War
The Times, March 1972
(Version 1 of article paid for by *The Times*, but not used, 1 September 1971.
Version 2 not used, March 1972.)
(*See* p.362.)

Portuguese military bulletins admit that between 1 January 1970 and 30 June 1971 at least 651 Portuguese troops died in the three African colonies, against 4,969 guerrillas killed. Portugal has been called "the most underdeveloped country in Europe", and it has a largely peasant community. The key question is: how long will the Portuguese people continue to tolerate poverty at home so that 651 more soldiers can die in Africa?

The bulletins state that "terrorism" is decreasing in the two biggest colonies. In Angola, economically and strategically the more important, the Portuguese offensive of March–August 1970 led to proportionately fewer terrorist attacks on Portuguese troops, though intimidating actions against the local population increased. The December bulletin claims: "In 1970, the year the terrorists considered the year of victory, there was a systematic reduction of activities. We paralysed their activities, which were mainly revealed in raping people." Terrorism increased in February, the month of the battle of Caripandi, but increased 27 per cent in March, and in April and May it was 30 per cent and 38 per cent down for the same months in 1970. Statistics reflect the pattern:

	Portuguese	guerrillas
Jan–Sep 70		
killed	231	987
wounded	350	152
Oct 70–Jun 71		
killed	74	1,303
wounded		396

(NB: The Portuguese and Colonial Bulletin, following the Portuguese press, claims that 73 Portuguese troops died between January 18 and April 23, 1971 alone.)

In Mozambique, General de Arriaga's May–July 1970 offensive, "Operation Gordian Knot" led to a "reduction of subversion" and claims that FRELIMO had been smashed. Since then there have been two more offensives, in January and May, because of further guerrilla activity, so that the story reads:

	Portuguese	guerrillas
Jan–Apr 70		
killed	35	164
May–Jul		
killed or wounded	217	
killed		400
wounded		415
Jun–Dec		
killed	132	651
captured		1,804
surrendered		6,854

(During this period there were movements of 128,598 troops and military personnel, and 63,518 tons of equipment.)

	Portuguese	guerrillas
Jan–Jun 71		
killed	7	305
wounded	13	
captured		292

(The Portuguese and Colonial Bulletin, following the Portuguese press, claims that 82 Portuguese troops died between Jan 18 and April 23, 1971 alone.)

Nevertheless, the bulletins cannot hide the fact that, in spite of the Portuguese offensives, the liberation movements are continuing to put up stout resistance. The fighting may be down on 1970s figures, but the fact remains 147 guerrillas died in different parts of Angola last June, and 78 were put out of action in Mozambique last May, when Cabora Bassa and the rest of Tete province had to be brought under military rule. The bulletins admit that over the past 18 months fighting has taken place around a host of towns and villages in the North and East of Angola, and (particularly heavily) in the NE of Mozambique.

The bulletins are generally too insufficiently detailed to reflect the very specific *communiqués* of the guerrillas, which give tiny villages, numbers of trucks, identity cards of soldiers killed and serial numbers of weapons captured, etc. Occasionally, however, two interlock exactly and with surprising correspondence. One UNITA report about an ambush in January agrees exactly with the Portuguese account, while another in March quotes 15 Portuguese soldiers as being "wiped out" near the Lungu-Bungu river, whereas the Portuguese bulletin reports 15 "wounded".

The bulletins do not reflect the numbers of Portuguese the guerrillas claim to have killed. MPLA claim to have 'liquidated' 1,463 Portuguese in 1970, UNITA claim to have killed at least 440 (including 100 last May 1) over the 18 month period, and FRELIMO claim 1,835 killed between July 69 and June 70, together with 1,485 more up to last May. As the FRELIMO magazine remarks: "It remains merely our word against that of the Portuguese."

The Portuguese have anywhere between 130,000 and 180,000 troops strung round Africa, and their population is only 9½ million. Besides being a drain on manpower, the war is costing (estimates vary) between 41 per cent and 58 per cent of total Government expenditure. In 1971 Portugal will spend nearly £44 million on keeping its armed forces in Angola and Mozambique alone, a figure which will contribute to Portugal's trade deficit (£250 million in 1970). In fact, in 1970 Portugal imported from other countries over five times as much as she imported from her own colonies, and in her trade with the colonies (imports £93 million, exports £95 million) she had a surplus of only £2 million – which will cost getting on for £44 million to maintain this year in Angola and Mozambique alone.

The Portuguese are getting little out of the effort, save maintaining their empire and serving the interests of the settlers. In early 1969, the Minister of Defence was describing the situation in Mozambique as "frankly favourable" and that in Angola as stabilised, yet the liberation movements keep coming at them. In May there were reported to be 3,000–5,000 FRELIMO fighters, and the Portuguese estimate there are 6,000–7,000 guerrillas in Angola. (Other sources double this figure.) The Portuguese only control 60 per cent of Guinea anyway, and they face 5,000–6,000 guerrillas there. The guerrillas seem prepared for a long haul of five to 10 years.

For the future, Portugal has three options: to continue to fight "Operation Golden Fleece", which may lead to the big powers getting more involved, and another Vietnam; UDI for the white settlers (25,000 in Angola, 130,000 in Mozambique, and 2,000 in Guinea); or to create a multi-racial society on the lines of Brazil, one that allays African suspicions that they will merely "play football and dance the samba" while Portugal controls the politics and the economic situation. With the drift of history as it is, the colonies will have to be independent one day.

Church call to block finance for Angola
The Times, 4 March 1972

All this week, in a quiet retreat in the pine forest at Arnoldshain, near Frankfurt, some 60 members of church and action groups have been taking part in a symposium sponsored by the World Council of Churches.

Today they made their recommendations to the commission of the Programme to Combat Racism, which meets next month. If the commission agrees with recommendations, they stand to be approved by the central committee of the World Council in August.

They ask the council to fight the Cunene river scheme in Angola by opposing all forms of European financial and military involvement in Africa. In particular, they urge the council to press specific companies to leave Angola and Namibia (South-West Africa), and to withdraw church funds from certain European banks.

The council is also asked to block the establishment of a special relationship between Portugal and South Africa, to urge states to recognise land taken from Namibia as "plunder" which can be restored to the legitimate owners in national courts; to urge Nato countries to stop supplying arms and military training to Portugal; to work for international acceptance of the status of Portuguese deserters and those avoiding military service as political refugees; and to support all who oppose the regime inside Portugal.

The symposium was held under a resolution passed by the central committee of the World Council at Addis Ababa in January 1971, calling on members' churches "to discourage their governments and industrial commercial enterprises from supporting schemes like the Cabora Bassa dam and other such projects which entrench racist and colonial minority regimes in Africa".

The Cunene river scheme falls within this category. Rising in central Angola and flowing down to the Namibian border before turning west to the sea, the Cunene has long been dreamed of as a source of irrigation and electric power.

Ostensibly the scheme is admirably humanitarian. There will be 27 dams and hydro-electric plants at a cost of about $612m (about £235m). The greater part will be financed by Portugal and South Africa.

The first dam, at Gove in central Angola, was started in October 1969, and it is due to be finished this year. It will create one of the largest artificial lakes in the Portuguese colonies, exceeding even that of Cabora Bassa.

However, the political, military and strategic implications of the scheme go far beyond considerations of electric power and communications, and it is these that have led the action groups to make their recommendations.

Since 1960 the white population of Angola has increased by 119 per cent to 350,000 and that of Mozambique by 102 per cent to 150,000. The Cabora Bassa scheme will settle one million whites in Mozambique and the Cunene scheme half a million (Portuguese, South Africans, West Germans) in southern Angola.

Also, many of the Angolan nomads will be forcibly moved to restricted areas farther north, for more effective policing by the Portuguese army. Portugal and South Africa will thus be able to create a buffer territory of whites.

The scheme will supply cheap electricity to both the Kasinga mines in Angola and the Tsumeb mines in Namibia (the "jewel box of Africa"), which will benefit the Portuguese and South African Governments and the European and North American companies concerned – but not the Africans.

Action envisaged against banks and companies at present connected with the scheme includes the withdrawal of stocks and shares, boycotts and the exposure of future involvements in Angola and Namibia.

The World Council is being asked to appeal to the Roman Catholic Church to withdraw relevant bank accounts and to recommend that church links in Southern Africa should not support racism.

The instant rail track – with Chinese aid
Nicholas Hagger reports fast progress on a project vital to Zambia and Tanzania
The Guardian, 7 October 1972

A great track-laying machine suspended a length of railway line against the hot sun and lowered it towards the causeway of stones between two mountains. A Chinese in a blue suit and a yellow coolie hat blew a whistle, waved a flag and 30 African workmen leapt forward and prised the line into place with levers.

Others flicked nuts on bolts. Then, with a hoot and a roar, the track-laying machine edged forward and hoisted another length of line from its back and ran it along a girder so that it hung in mid-air.

"Six 12.5-yard lengths of line every five minutes 20 seconds," said the Chinese interpreter to the head of the railway formation team, Mr Chung, a greying commissar-like man with a large Chairman Mao badge on his lapel. "There are two eight-hour shifts every 24 hours, so we lay about two miles a day. We have only about 50 miles to go on this stretch now. The difficulties have been overcome."

The single-track, 1,150-mile long Tanzam Railway from Dar es Salaam harbour to the Zambian town of Kapiri Mposhi is central to the Tanzanian economy. China is lending money for it, and the repayments will be spread over 30 years from 1983. Tanzania finances the local costs of the railway, including the cost of feeding and paying the 20,000 Chinese "technicians" by buying Chinese goods.

There have been immense difficulties in the challenging second phase of the railway, the 98 miles between Mlimba and Makumbako. Broken escarpments rise from the low plains of the Kilombero valley to mountains as high as 6,000ft. and the railway has to cross precipitous valleys and quagmires and through 18 tunnels, one half-a-mile long. Tunnels have suffered from weathered rock, and mountain springs have poured through tunnel roofs.

I arrived at Lugema base camp around midday. After a Chinese lunch washed down with a lot of beer, I visited the Great Ruaha bridge, which was built in only 89 days, and watched a crane hoist wooden sleepers to a posse of bustling men.

I then went to Uchindile bridge, at one end of which the Chinese have moved a mountain. Two hundred African and Chinese workers swarmed over the base of the mountain like flies on a great Pyramid, cementing concrete slabs on the sloping earthwork walls with all the urgency of those five minute, twenty second deadlines.

After a night in a mud-hut in the Chinese camp at Mkera, I walked through Tunnel 13, squashing against the wall as the train trundled through. Stepping from sleeper to sleeper, I trudged a mile between two mountains, past several groups of Africans working flat out, and inspected the highest bridge, No. 25, which balances on two columns over 150ft. high.

During my tour I passed most of the bridges and tunnels between Mlimba and Makumbako, and I can confirm that all is proceeding well and tidily. The bridges and tunnels were all completed by July (though Tunnel 13 still leaks a ton of spring water a day at the exit), and the Chinese bridge teams have moved on to Zambia, where the bridge over the river Chambeshi is almost complete.

Track-laying started near Makumbako, and by September 23 had passed through 11 tunnels and reached near Iringa. Much of the stone-laying has been done, so the track-laying can go ahead at about two miles a day. With about 50 miles to go, the Mlimba-Makumbako stretch should be completed before the end of the year, unless the coming rainy season does disastrous things to the still exposed earth works near the bridges. China's first major overseas development project, it is claimed, is ahead of schedule.

The Tanzanian and Zambian workers clearly get on well with the Chinese, although the relationship is confined to work, for the Chinese keep themselves to themselves in the evenings. They have separate camps which they are "too busy" to leave, and though they have been admitting Tanzanians to the huts vacated by the experts who have gone to Zambia, they tend not to mix.

The African workers' conditions involve obvious hardship. They have to leave their women behind. "It is not fair on the Chinese if the Africans are not as celibate as they," is the official explanation of TAZARA, the railway authority.

Tanzania gets off the Peking gravy train
The Times, 18 October 1972

Tanzania will not be asking China for any more loans until the 1,150 mile long Tanzam railway – built with Chinese aid – is finished in 1976. Tanzania's new Foreign Minister, Mr John Malecela, apparently declined further aid during his visit to China last month, and this policy was confirmed by President Nyerere himself, when he said recently: "…China is not a rich country, and the railway is a huge undertaking, and there are other projects in the country which operate through Chinese aid. So really I think we require to see the railway out of the way before we discuss anything else with China."

One reason for this new reluctance to take Chinese money may be found in the 1967 Arusha Declaration: "Independence means Self-Reliance. Independence cannot be real if a nation depends upon gifts and loans from another for its development." Tanzania is genuinely grateful to China for building the railway, but she does not want to become dependent, and so in true non-aligned spirit she is now looking for alternative sources for the aid she so badly needs. Tanzania is at present receiving loans from Canada, West Germany and Scandinavia, which has started some Nordic agricultural projects near Mbeya.

Just as pressing may be Tanzania's feeling that already she is regarded in some quarters as a Chinese showpiece. Tanzania is at present very sensitive and bitter about the pro-Communist image she believes she has in the West.

As the Foreign Minister complained to me: "Tanzania is so much misunderstood in the West that accusations about Tanzania being a doorway for communism in Africa have almost become general assumptions. We are regarded as having become a communist country because we support the liberation movements, because of the railway, because we have nationalised banks, industries and houses, and because of the *ujamaa* villages."

In fact, as the recent policy of Africanizing jobs illustrates, and as many Easterners have learnt to their cost since nationalization in 1967, Tanzania is very much an "Africa-first" country, with a strong African identity. The communist presence must be understood in this context.

Similar African self-interest governs Tanzania's attitude to the Tanzam railway. Tanzania sees the railway – from Dar es Salaam harbour to the Zambian town of Kapiri Mposhi – as an opening-up of the interior which will bring modern life to the mud-hut villages in the bush, develop the potential of what could become good ranching land and improve communications for Zambia's coming entry into the East African Community. She regards the financial arrangements as very favourable: the Chinese loan of 2,865m Tanzanian shillings (about £170m) is interest-free, and when the repayments fall due in 1983, Tanzania's share will be less than £2m a year for 30 years. Meanwhile, Tanzania officially regards the Chinese goods which are ordered from Peking to pay for the local costs of the railway (including paying the 20,000 Chinese People's Liberation Army engineers) as commendably cheap. Although they are criticised for lacking durability, there is a Western alternative for most Chinese products in the supermarkets of Dar es Salaam.

To Tanzanians, the fact that the Chinese are the builders of the railway has always been almost incidental. Are not the Americans building the road beside it, and have not the Italians built a pipeline? Tanzanians say that the Chinese exercise no influence over the country but are present merely as "technicians". It is difficult to assess how much Chinese instructors go in for indoctrination on the railway, and the same can be said of the Chinese instructors in the freedom-fighter camps or the Chinese tank and infantry instructors who train the TPDF (Tanzanian People's Defence Force) following the withdrawal of the Canadian instructors at the end of their contract in 1970. But it is certainly true that the Chinese keep themselves to themselves.

Again, the *ujamaa* – literally "family" – cooperative system is a way of coping with a specifically African problem, the fact that the majority of the 14 million people in the vast rural Tanzanian mainland are scattered in small units. Based on President Nyerere's 1962 book, *Ujamaa – the Basis of African Socialism*, the system brings groups of 100–200 or more families together, the theory being that only if they live and work together can land be developed, incomes be raised, schools and hospitals be built, and economic use be made of tractors.

To official Tanzania, the Chinese commune system may have been an inspiration, but it is now an irrelevance. In practice, the *ujamaa* villages I saw were very different from communes. Most were like enormous shared allotments, for many of the villagers live outside the villages. They travel in and work from a few mornings up to six days a week, clearing the bush in teams, planting and growing maize, orange trees, cassava, etc. At the end of the year they share their produce in accordance with the amount of work each has put in. What you sow you reap, no work no profit – basically the spirit is capitalist rather than socialist. The system is still developing and it is possible that as more and more land is taken into *ujamaa* villages (which I was told already number between 2,000 and 3,000), one day all Tanzanians will be living on them.

Mr Malecela feels that Portuguese, Rhodesian and South African propaganda is partly to blame for misrepresenting his country's image, but he also speaks of a "barrier of understanding" which amounts to a generation barrier. Elderly Westerners, he says, cannot understand that all Africa must be free; Africans have tried to talk but nothing has been done, so they have resorted to armed struggle. The Organization of African Unity cannot obtain arms from the West, so it obtains them from the East. As a result, elderly Westerners see Tanzania, headquarters of the guerrilla movements, as a communist country. When they are asked to build the railway, they therefore refuse. So Tanzania again goes to the East and elderly Westerners are confirmed in their suspicions. And so it goes on until there comes a time when, no matter what caused the misrepresentation, the only way of untarnishing the country's image is to play down the connexion with China. Hence a strong motive for refusing Chinese cash.

Jumbe loyal to Karume
The Guardian, 30 November 1972

Aboud Jumbe, Zanzibar's President, is a very different leader from Sheikh Karume, both in style and personality. Formerly a teacher for 15 years, he gives his rare press conferences at the Afro-Shirazi Party (ASP) headquarters in a rational enlightened atmosphere far removed from Karume's emotional, highly charged, theatrical performances.

Nevertheless, Zanzibar doesn't change all that much. Jumbe is continuing Karume's policies – in fact, on April 10 he took an oath to do so and later even had it enshrined in Swahili on the ASP conference table.

According to Jumbe's translation the text says: "Mzee Karume was assassinated and buried. But what was assassinated and buried was his body only. He has left the Party and the Revolutionary Council behind. They are here, they will continue his policy. We shall endeavour to do that for ever and ever."

This "promise," as Jumbe calls it, helps to explain why, both in Zanzibar and on the mainland, Sheikh Karume still has undisputed place of honour on every wall. It also helps to explain why, in spite of Zanzibari suspicions of the mainland (acknowledged by President Nyerere of Tanzania), the union between Zanzibar and the mainland has not been shaken by the assassination of Karume.

Jumbe is continuing Zanzibar's brand of socialism. The promises of the nineteen-sixties involved giving farmers three-acre units of land and a share in the clove harvests, rehousing poor families in modern flats, handing out pensions to needy Africans, and making education and medication treatment free and equal for all. Zanzibar is back to normal again after the upheavals that followed the assassination. There is little obvious tension. No citizens carry arms.

Everywhere Africans talk without apparent fear, at least on subjects like rice and fish prices, which are cheaper than on the mainland, or free education. However, they do not offer political opinions. "You don't ask questions about Jumbe," a Zanzibari "guide" warned. "Here people work and sleep, that is all."

Critics will say that Zanzibar has not had freedom of political opinion since 1964; pro-Jumbeists will question this last, disparaging view of the Zanzibari people or attribute their silence to the investigations of Karume's murder, which Jumbe has just completed.

As a result, the 65 still held out of a total of 414 people arrested will soon be brought to trial. The 65 include Abdul-rahman Babu, together with members of the former Umma Party, and seven who came from the Persian Gulf.

The implication is that these seven were connected with the Sultan, who is in exile in Britain, and who, Jumbe believes, is "waging war" against Zanzibar. "We have complete evidence of the number of people he is sending to many Arab countries for military training," he told me, "with a view to coming one day and invading these islands."

In these circumstances, it is naturally difficult to open the island up even a little, but that is what Jumbe is now trying to do.

6

International Politics

Nicholas Hagger championed patriotic British causes, freeing Europe from Soviet occupation and delivering a Universalist World State. His initiatives and pro-Western, Churchillian principles and stance in international politics (encapsulated in 'The Heroes of the West', *see My Double Life 2*) were 'behind the scenes' and spread out over 50 years, but when drawn together are seen to have advanced the British cause, defended the West against Soviet expansionism during the Cold War and shaped the post-1991 world and a coming World State.

Aug 1960	Located the UK's most wanted enemy, Col. Grivas, in Greece.
Nov 1961–Jun 1962	Implemented Churchill's policy of reconciling Sunnis, Shiites and Kurds in Iraq.
Nov 1961–Jan 1962	Helped monitor Kaseem's military movements in Baghdad.
Jul 1965	Clinched Japanese loan to Bank of England.
Oct 1965	Helped plan Prince and Princess Hitachi's State visit to UK.
19 Jun 1966	Received a vision of enlightened world leaders in a World State's world government in the Cathedral of the Archangel in Moscow (described in 'Archangel'); now stood for a World State.
Nov–Dec 1966	Pressed for increase in Japanese funding of Asian Development Bank.
31 Oct 1966, 9 Jan 1967	Called for the removal of Mao.
19 Mar 1967	Discovered the Chinese Cultural Revolution while interrogating the Vice-President of Peking University.
3, 15 Nov 1968, 1969	Inspired a *coup* to keep Libya pro-Western after King Idris and was set to control Libyan oil.
24 Aug 1969	Wrote an article on the closeness of Libyan-British relations that appeared in English and Arabic in Libya – and triggered Gaddafi's 1-September Revolution.
5 Sep 1969	Planned date for pro-Western *coup* to be carried out by Col. Saad eddin Bushwerib and Ben

	Nagy for Muntassers.
Oct–Nov 1969	Arranged the defection to the UK of Viktor and his nuclear secrets, fending off attempt by the CIA to persuade Viktor to defect to the US.
1 Jan 1970	Knocked off Col. Gaddafi's peaked hat in defiance of Gaddafi's Revolution.
19 Feb 1970	First to locate Soviet SAM-3 missile transporter, near El Alamein.
27–28 May 1970	Defied Mohammed Barassi's terror-state threats of execution on behalf of Gaddafi.
24 Aug 1970–17 May 1973	Appointed as Edward Heath's 'unofficial Ambassador' to the African liberation movements and Chinese.
12 Sep 1972	Persuaded Tanzanian Minister of Foreign Affairs to move Tanzania away from the Chinese and back towards British and Western influence, and to invite Sir Alec Douglas-Home and Edward Heath to visit Dar and offer British aid.
20 Sep 1972	Outmanoeuvred the entire Tanzanian state to access restricted area of Chinese Tanzam railway by appealing to President Nyerere.

Notes and References

The narrative draws on files, letters, notes, diaries, pocket diaries, newspaper articles, booklets and other autobiographical material. These sources, including the *Diaries*, are in the Hagger archive. The notes are numbered within episodes rather than chapters.

Many of the quotations in the narrative are from Nicholas Hagger's *Diaries*, 1963–2013. To avoid overuse of notes, in the later episode there is sometimes only one note in each headed section. (In long sections there will be more than one note.) This note will list a succession of dates relating to *Diary* entries in the order in which they appear within the section. Some listings will therefore not be in strict chronological order. The important thing is that there is a source, written on the day on which they happened, for most of the events and reflections in the text, which do not just depend on my memory. Almost every word in *Diary*-based sections can therefore be sourced and verified by referring to the narrow band of dates listed in each note. Ideally, every sentence in such sections would have a sourcing note, but this is clearly impractical and the above solution is the above alternative.

There are separate notes within a paragraph for dates of more significant or evidential quotations, and for sources other than the *Diaries*.

Epigraphs
1. *The Times*, 'Have found secret of DNA, love Daddy', 23 March 2013, p.3.

Prologue: The Path and Pattern
1. Nicholas Hagger, *A Mystic Way*, introductory Note, pp.159, 776–77.
2. Tricia Moxey.
3. Michael Hanlon, 'Turing's flower theory blossoms', *The Sunday Times*, 28 October 2012.
4. It may be of interest to record that I had already outlined 21 pairs of opposites for an early draft of these two volumes, subsequently discarded, which I viewed as two spirals: 13 + 8. The first 13 would take me to the point of illumination, the 8 would cover the next 8 episodes and take me to the beginning of my writing career. Between them they would cover the birth of my outlook. I saw that the next 21 pairs of opposites would continue the first 21 within the two spirals, and cover the next 21 episodes and take me to the development of my outlook. The first 13 episodes of these would complete my development of the world, and the next 8 episodes would complete my new view of the world and take me to the end of my life, with a capacity to store memories to the end of my life. The last 12 are still ahead of me.

5. Letter from Asa Briggs to Nicholas Hagger, 20 October 1978; in the Hagger archive.

6. Two Libyan dissidents brought civil actions against an MI6 official and the ex-Foreign Secretary relating to rendition and torture allegations. See, for example, *The Independent on Sunday*, 21 October 2012, p.34.

PART ONE
Quest for the One
1. Origins

1. Leaflets and posters in the Hagger archive.

2. In the Hagger archive.

3. According to the Methodist Church Archives and History Committee (document in the Hagger archive) the Rev. Benjamin Broadley was born on 15 August 1833 at Ackworth, near Pontefract, Yorkshire. He trained at Richmond and then went to India. For 18 years he "rendered efficient service in our garrisons both abroad and at home". In 1876 he was transferred to an English circuit, Altringham, then in 1879 Glasgow, in 1882 Macclesfield, in 1885 London Westminster, in 1888 Sheffield (Norfolk Street), in 1891 Hull (Great Thornton Street), in 1894 Nottingham, in 1897 Liverpool Bootle, in 1900 Nottingham Wesley, in 1903 Tavistock and was superannuated in 1906 at Nottingham. He died on 24 October 1913. Letter from Rev. William Leary, Connexional Archivist of The Methodist Church Archives and History Committee, 16 June 1982; in the Hagger archive.

4. George Herbert Broadley's birth certificate – he was born on 11 March 1870 – gives his mother's name as Charlotte Broadley, formerly Harrison.

5. Margaret E. Broadley, *A Century of Change, 1896–1996*, booklet, p.5.

6. John Broadley I married Selina Nettleton (whose great-grandfather Joseph Nettleton was born in 1750).

7. Hagger, *Diaries*, 26 December 1976.

8. Margaret Broadley, *A Century of Change, 1896–1996*, p.6.

9. *Broadleys, East Grinstead 1896–1996*, leaflet compiled by John Broadley V and Margaret Broadley, 1996.

10. *Broadleys, East Grinstead 1896–1996*, leaflet compiled by John Broadley V and Margaret Broadley, 1996; Ruth Lawrence, 'Broadleys: Footsteps through time', *Sussex Living Magazine*, December 2012.

11. Statement in the Hagger archive.

12. *Broadleys, East Grinstead 1896–1996*, leaflet compiled by John Broadley V and Margaret Broadley, 1996. Also Margaret Broadley, in conversation with Nicholas Hagger.

13. Margaret Broadley in conversation with Nicholas Hagger.

14. Hagger, *Diaries*, 14 March 1996.

15. In the Hagger archive.

16. Will of George Herbert Broadley; in the Hagger archive.

17. Probate of the Will of George Herbert Broadley, 22 March 1927. For net value in 2011 terms, *see* MeasuringWorth.com.

18. Nicholas Hagger, *Awakening to the Light*, 3 August 1966, pp.320–321; conversation with Lucy on Bognor beach: "George bought Grannie [i.e. Elsie] out between 1931 and 1952 at £250 capital a year, bar a spell during the war."

19. Hagger, *Diaries*, 17 April 1987.

20. Perkins, Copeland & Co., Eastbourne, 'Trading and Profit and Loss Account and Balance Sheet for Broadley Brothers for the year ending 20 February 1949'; in the Hagger archive.

21. *Broadleys, East Grinstead 1896–1996*, leaflet compiled by John Broadley V and Margaret Broadley, 1996.

22. Notification from Barclays Bank, East Grinstead, dated 2 July 1940, setting out the purchase cost and the commission (£1.16.3d and contract stamp 2s.), which in all totalled £700. The envelope is postmarked 2 July 1940; in the Hagger archive.

23. Hagger, *Diaries*, 3 August 1966.

24. Hagger, *Diaries*, 9 October 1992.

25. Hagger, *Diaries*, 9 October 1992.

26. Norah Hagger's Statement to Essex Education Department, 28.6.1964 (prepared by Robert Hagger); in the Hagger archive.

27. Norah Hagger's Statement to Essex Education Department, *op. cit.*

28. Perkins, Copeland & Co., Eastbourne, 'Trading and Profit and Loss Account and Balance Sheet for Broadley Brothers for the year ending 20 February 1949'; in the Hagger archive.

29. *Broadleys, East Grinstead 1896–1996*, leaflet compiled by John Broadley V and Margaret Broadley, 1996.

30. In the Hagger archive.

31. Birth certificate of Cyril Hagger, 12 September 1906; in the Hagger archive.

32. *Kelly's Directory of Hertfordshire*, 1933, quoted in an email from Martin Hagger to Joanna Martin, 17 June 2000; in the Hagger archive.

33. In the Hagger archive.

34. In the Hagger archive.

35. *See* http://www.geni.com/family-tree/index/6000000009064302980.

36. Research by the late Mrs. Dell of Cambourne, Cornwall; in the Hagger archive.

37. W.P. Blockmans, *The Social and Economic Effects on Plague in the Low Countries, 1349–1500*, p.837, *see* http://www.persee.fr/web/revues/home /prescript/article/rbph_0035-0818_1980_num_58_4_3301.

38. Mrs. Dell's research; in the Hagger archive.

39. The Victoria County History's *A History of the County of Cambridge,*

http://www.british-history.ac.uk/report.aspx?compid=66669, para 15.

40. The Victoria County History's *A History of the County of Cambridge*, http://www.british-history.ac.uk/report.aspx?compid=66669, para 9. The information in the rest of this paragraph and in the next four paragraphs comes from the same source. *A History of the County of Cambridge and the Isle Ely*, vol. 5, 1973, 'Parishes: Bourn', pp.4–16.

41. Margaret Greenwood, *People from Bourn History*, Bourn-based booklet, 1999.

42. The arms were confirmed by William Camden, Clarenceux King of Arms to John Hagar, College of Arms Manuscript: Misc. Grants I/51, Camden II/45, Camden III/12 & Vincent 169/84. (Letter from Thomas Woodcock, Norroy and Ulster King of Arms, the College of Arms, 23 March 1999; in the Hagger archive.)

43. *Visitation of Cambridge made in AD 1575, continued and enlarged wth the visitation* (sic) *of the same county made by Henery St George, Richmond-Herald, Marshall and Deputy to Willm. Camden, Clarenceux, in AD 1619, wth many other descents added thereto*, edited by John W. Clay, F.S.A., London 1897, p.56, Hagger entry. *See* http://www.archive.org/stream/visitationcambr00brit goog#page/n10/mode/2up.

The word *'d'or'* is used instead of *or* in The Herald's Visitation of 1619: *Catalogue of the Heralds' Visitations; with references to many other valuable genealogical and topographical manuscripts in the British Museum, printed for James Taylor*, 2nd edition, London, 1825. *See* http://www.archive.org /stream/catalogueofheral00nicoiala#page/n5/mode/2up.

44. Letter from Thomas Woodcock, Norroy and Ulster King of Arms of the College of Arms, 23 March 1999; in the Hagger archive.

45. The Victoria County History's *A History of the County of Cambridge*, http://www.british-history.ac.uk/report.aspx?compid=66669, para 10 and note 72 citing V.C.H. Hunts. iii. 377; Mon. Inscr. Cambs. 13.

46. The Victoria County History's *A History of the County of Huntingdon*, vol. 2, 1932, 'Parishes: Waresley', pp.376–379, http://www.british-history.ac.uk /report.aspx?compid=42517.

47. RootsWeb's WorldConnect Project: Our Children's Ancestors and other Families, http://wc.rootsweb.ancestery.com/cgi-bin/igm.cgi?op=GET&db =rettheadley&id=120659. Also researched by the late Mrs. Dell of Canbourne, Cornwall.

48. Margaret Greenwood, *op. cit.*, p.6.

49. In the Hagger archive.

50. In the Hagger archive.

51. In the Hagger archive.

52. Research by Odense Central Bibliotek, Odense, Denmark.

53. DNA Tribes, February 2010.

2. The Call

Episode 1: Family and War

1.   Hagger, *Diaries*, 13 July 1991.
2.   London Hospital receipts; in the Hagger archive.
3.   Letter from Brett's Ltd of Streatham dated 26 October 1942, sending a cheque for £5.10.2d (4 weeks' rent at 29s. per week, less collection and postages); in the Hagger archive.
4.   Hagger, *Awakening to the Light*, 15 June 1966, p.304.
5.   Hagger, *Awakening to the Light*, 16 June 1966, p.304.
6.   Oaklands register for 1944, held at Oaklands School, Loughton.
7.   *Froebel Educational Institute, List of Former Students of the College*, booklet, December 1936; in the Oaklands School, Loughton archive. Miss Lord is listed as having trained in 1918–1921 and Miss Reid in 1923–1926.
8.   *See* Hagger, *A View of Epping Forest*, pp.85–90.
9.   *See* Hagger, *A View of Epping Forest*, p.94.
10. Announcement in *The Methodist Recorder*; in the Hagger archive.

Episode 2: Nature and School

1.   Deed of Partnership, Miss L.E. Lord and Miss M. Reid, 17 January 1948, the partnership being deemed to have commenced on 1 September 1947; in the Hagger archive.
2.   *See* Hagger, *A Mystic Way*, pp.16–18.
3.   Letters from Dr James; in the Hagger archive.
4.   *See* Hagger, *A View of Epping Forest*, pp.9–12, 18–23.
5.   For the Caracalla identification, *see* Nicholas Hagger, *A View of Epping Forest*, pp.38–39. For Professor Chris Howgego's Elagabalus identification (AD218–222), *see* R. McAlee, *The Coins of Roman Antioch*, 2007, p.296.
6.   Chigwell School report, spring term 1948; in the Hagger archive.
7.   Chigwell School report, summer term 1948; in the Hagger archive.
8.   Leaflet distributed at Speech Day, 1949; in the Hagger archive.
9.   *See* Hagger, *A View of Epping Forest*, pp.29–30.
10. Chigwell School report, summer term 1951; in the Hagger archive.
11. *See* mounted cuttings; in the Hagger archive.
12. *See* http://www.britishpathe.com/video/pegasus-win-amateur-cup.
13. Harold Orlans, *T.E. Lawrence, Biography of a Broken Hero*, p.55. *Also, Oxford Dictionary of National Biography*.
14. Nicholas Hagger's translation of *Caesar at Alexandria*; in the Hagger archive.
15. Letter from Capt. W.E. Johns to Nicholas Hagger, 24 February 1954; in the Hagger archive.

Episode 3: Archaeology and Politics

1.   Sir John Masterman, *The Double-Cross System*.

Episode 4: Literature and Law

1. Colin Wilson, *Dreaming to Some Purpose*, p.117.
2. Stephen Dorril, *MI6, Fifty Years of Special Operations*, p.16.
3. Peter Calvocoressi had been an RAF intelligence officer at Bletchley Park during the war, *see* Asa Briggs, *Secret Days*, pp.18, 22, 28, 91, 95, 123.
4. Hagger, 'Defence', *Right Wheel*, 1958; in the Hagger archive.
5. Letter from John Biggs-Davison to Nicholas Hagger, 4 March 1958; in the Hagger archive.
6. Letter from John Biggs-Davison to Nicholas Hagger, 12 May 1958; in the Hagger archive.
7. In the Hagger archive.
8. Letter from Colin Wilson to Nicholas Hagger, 31 May 1958; in the Hagger archive.
9. Letter from Nicholas Hagger to Colin Wilson, 4 June 1958; in the Hagger archive.
10. Letter from Colin Wilson to Nicholas Hagger, 6 June 1958; in the Hagger archive.
11. Letter from Nicholas Hagger to family, 21 August 1958; in the Hagger archive.
12. Letter of 1 March 1959; in the Hagger archive.

Episode 5: Wisdom and Intelligence

1. *The London Gazette*, 26 June 1959, p.4208 (*sic*), *see* http://www.london-gazette.co.uk/issues/41751/pages/4208/page.pdf.
2. Anon., 'A Visit by Mr T.S. Eliot', *Cherwell* 22 No.3 (11 February 1928), p.60. Quoted in David Bradshaw, 'The American Chaplain and the Modernist Poets: William Force Stead, W.B. Yeats and T.S. Eliot', *Worcester College Record*, 2011, pp.127, 129.
3. Christine Keeler, *The Truth at Last*, p.104. Claims that she first met Profumo in the Pinstripe Club (now the Kingly Club) are incorrect.
4. Richard Deacon, *A History of the British Secret Service*, pp.32–33, 36–37, 221.
5. For the Coroner's Report, *see* http://www.marlowe-society.org/marlowe/life/deptford3.html.
    In 1925 Leslie Hotson discovered the Coroner's Inquest Report detailing the circumstances surrounding the death of Marlowe, *see* http://www.themar-lowestudies.org/author-hotson.html.
6. Deacon, *op. cit.*, pp.32, 65, 74.
7. Keith Jeffery, *MI6: The History of the Secret Intelligence Service 1909–1949*, pp.91, 118–119, 237; Nigel West, *MI6, British Secret Intelligence Service Operations 1909–1945*, p.14; Deacon, *op. cit.*, pp.32, 221; *see also* http://www.pbs.org/wgbh/nova/venona/dece_maugham.html. Maugham was chief agent in Russia for the British and American Secret Services

during the weeks preceding the Bolshevik *coup* of 1917, *see* Rhodri Jeffreys-Jones, 'W. Somerset Maugham: Anglo-American Agent in Revolutionary Russia', *American Quarterly*, vol. 28, no. 1 (spring 1976), pp.90–106, published by the Johns Hopkins University Press, http://www.jstor.org /discover/10.2307/2712479?uid=3738032&uid=2129&uid=2&uid=70&uid=4 &sid=47698790192587.

8. Intelligence papers relating to T.E. Lawrence, 1916–1918 in National Archives, *see* http://yourarchives.nationalarchives.gov.uk/index.php.

9. *The Daily Mail*, 25 April 2013, 'Torment of A.A. Milne, reluctant wartime secret agent', p.33.

10. Christopher Hawtree, 'A Muse on the tides of history: Elisabeth Dennys', *The Guardian*, 10 February 1999.

11. BBC, *Arena: Graham Greene*, BBC News, 3 October 2004; Jeffery, *op. cit.*, pp.479–481; Stephen Dorril, *MI6, Fifty Years of Special Operations*, pp.120, 391, 547; Deacon, *op. cit.*, p.400. See also Robert Royal, 'The (Mis)Guided Dream of Graham Greene', *First Things*, November 1999, *see* http://www.firstthings.com/article/2007/01/the-misguided-dream-of-graham-greene-15.

12. In Kipling's novel *Kim* there is a description of the training of an intelligence agent that has been taken as autobiographical.

13. Jeffery, *op. cit.*, p.54. *See also* http://www.bbc.co.uk/scotland/arts/writingscot land/writers/john_buchan/.

14. Jeffery, *op. cit.*, pp.173–175.

15. Dorril, *op. cit.*, pp.228–229, 233, 246.

16. Dorril, *op. cit.*, pp.11, 51, 57, 59, 440, 477–81.

17. Dorril, *op. cit.*, pp.59, 477–478, 481.

18. Kenneth R. Johnston, *The Hidden Wordsworth*, pp.530–533, 616–617.

19. John S. Koliopoulos, *Brigands with a Cause, Brigandage and Irredentism in Modern Greece, 1821–1912*, p.59.

20. Copy of Nicholas Hagger's letter to Major Goulding, 14 July 1960; in the Hagger archive.

21. Letter from Major Goulding to Nicholas Hagger, 5 August 1960; in the Hagger archive.

22. Letters from Admiral Sir Charles Woodhouse to Nicholas Hagger, 21 November 1960 and 1 May 1961; in the Hagger archive.

23. Letters from Colin Wilson to Nicholas Hagger, 11 January 1961 and 22 February 1961; in the Hagger archive.

24. Colin Wilson, *Dreaming to Some Purpose*, pp.195, 263.

25. Letter of 27 November 1960; in the Hagger archive.

26. Exam papers; in the Hagger archive.

27. Civil Service Commission booklet, p.11; in the Hagger archive.

28. Civil Service Commission booklet, p.11; in the Hagger archive.

29. Receipt from Gresham Hotel dated 11.3.61; in the Hagger archive.
30. Letters from the BBC of 19 May and 5 June 1961; in the Hagger archive.

3. The Journey: Awakening
Episode 6: Marriage and Dictatorship
1. Barry Winchester, *Beyond the Tumult*, Introduction by Group-Captain Leslie G. Nixon, Foreword by Douglas Bader.
2. H.B.T. Holland, Oversea Service, An Experiment in Lay Responsibility', 1955, *see* http://onlinelibrary.wiley.com/doi/10.1111/j.1758-6631.1955.tb01762.x/abstract. The headquarters of Oversea Service is 2 Eaton Gate, London, SW1.
3. Pamphlet, 'An Introductory Course arranged by Oversea Service at Dunford College, Midhurst, Sussex from August 22nd–27th, 1961 for British Council going overseas'; in the Hagger archive.
4. *Observer Magazine*, 18 March 1979; in the Hagger archive.

Episode 7: Vitalism and Mechanism
1. Nicholas Hagger, *Confessions of a Rationalist*, early version of *The Tree of Knowledge*, awaiting publication.
2. Within Nicholas Hagger, *Becoming and Being*, awaiting publication.
3. Letter from Admiral Sir Charles Woodhouse to Nicholas Hagger, 15 October 1963; in the Hagger archive.
4. Letter from R.L. P. to Nicholas Hagger, 18 October 1963; in the Hagger archive.
5. 13 November 1963.

Episode 8: The Absolute and Scepticism
1. John Haffenden, *William Empson, vol. 1: Among the Mandarins*, pp.287–355.
2. "Visiting Foreign Professor" in two contracts dated 1 April 1966 and 1 April 1967, signed by "Tomoo Miwa, President, The Tokyo University of Education", and Nicholas Hagger; in the Hagger archive.
3. "Invited Foreign Lecturer" in contract dated 13 September 1963, signed by Tomoo Miwa, "President of Tokyo University of Education", and Nicholas Hagger; in the Hagger archive. Status amended to "Visiting Foreign Professor" in contracts dated 1 April 1964 and 1 April 1965, and subsequent contracts (*see* note 10.)
4. Frederick Tomlin, *T.S. Eliot, A Friendship*.
5. Tomlin, *T.S. Eliot, A Friendship*, p.233.
6. Tomlin, *T.S. Eliot, A Friendship*, p.233.
7. Nicholas Hagger: 'The Contemporary Literary Scene in England, The Missing Dimension', *The Rising Generation*, 1 July 1964.
8. Hagger, *Diaries*, 21 December 1963; *Awakening to the Light*, p.58.

9.   Letter from Edmund Blunden to Nicholas Hagger, 11 July 1966 and postcard of 10 August 1966, both signed 'E. Blunden'; in the Hagger archive.

10. Thomas Fitzsimmons, *Iron Harp*, University of New Mexico Press, 1999. *See* http://www.laalamedapress.com/books/ironharp.html.

11. Tony Rayner went on to become Professor of Agricultural Economics at Lincoln University. He died in 1990.

12. Hagger, *Diaries*, 9 July 1964; *Awakening to the Light*, p.78; *The Rising Generation*, 1 September 1964, p.5.

13. Hagger, *Diaries*, 23 November 1964; *Awakening to the* Light, p.105.

14. Hagger, *Diaries*, 10 December 1964; *Awakening to the Light*, pp.110–111.

15. Hagger, *Diaries*, 30 December 1964; *Awakening to the Light*, p.118.

16. Hagger, *Diaries*, 24 January 1965; *Awakening to the Light*, p.125.

17. Hagger, *Diaries*, 26 January 1965; *Awakening to the Light*, p.126.

18. Hagger, *Diaries*, 25 April 1965; *Awakening to the Light*, p.151.

19. Leon Stover and Bruce Kraig, *Stonehenge, the Indo-European Heritage*.

20. Hagger, *Diaries*, 24 June and 1 July 1965; *Awakening to the Light*, pp.168, 170.

21. Hagger, *Diaries*, 26–27 July 1965; *Awakening to the Light*, pp.177–178.

22. Hagger, *Diaries*, 26–27 July 1965; *Awakening to the Light*, pp.177–178.

23. Hagger, *Diaries*, 5 August 1965; *Awakening to the Light*, p.180.

24. Frederick Tomlin, *T.S. Eliot, A Friendship*, p.239.

25. Frederick Tomlin, *T.S. Eliot, A Friendship*, p.233.

26. Hagger, 'Reflections on T.S. Eliot's Poetry', *The Rising Generation*, 1 May 1965, pp.42–44.

27. Hagger, *Diaries*, 15 August 1965; *Awakening to the Light*, p.184.

28. Hagger, *Diaries*, 11 September 1965; *Awakening to the Light*, p.192.

29. Hagger, *Diaries*, 13 September 1965; *Awakening to the Light*, pp.192–193.

30. Hagger, *Diaries*, 14 September 1965; *Awakening to the Light*, p.193.

31. Hagger, *Diaries*, 22 September 1965; *Awakening to the Light*, p.195.

32. Hagger, *Diaries*, 5 October 1965; *Awakening to the Light*, pp.197–198.

33. Hagger, *Diaries*, 10 October 1965; *Awakening to the Light*, p.199.

34. Hagger, *Diaries*, 10 October 1965; *Awakening to the Light*, p.199.

35. Hagger, *Diaries*, 11 October 1965; *Awakening to the Light*, p.199.

36. Hagger, *Diaries*, 17 October 1965; *Awakening to the Light*, pp.200–201.

37. Hagger, *Diaries*, 18 October 1965; *Awakening to the Light*, p.201.

38. Hagger, Diaries, 5 November 1965; *Awakening to the Light*, p.205.

39. Hagger, *Diaries*, 20 January 1966; *Awakening to the Light*, p.326.

Episode 9: Civilizations and Communism

1.   Hagger, *Diaries*, 7 January 1966; *Awakening to the Light*, p.230.

2.   Letter from Emé Yamashita enclosing a letter of introduction to Mr Soma, 20 February 1966; in the Hagger archive.

3.   Hagger, *Diaries*, 13 February 1966; *Awakening to the Light*, p.246.
4.   Hagger, *Diaries*, 15 March 1966; *Awakening to the Light*, pp.259–260.
5.   Hagger, *Diaries*, 18 March 1966; *Awakening to the Light*, p.261.
6.   Hagger, leather-bound pale-blue notebook labelled China 1966, p.97; in the Hagger archive.
7.   Hagger, leather-bound pale-blue notebook labelled China 1966, pp.101–109; in the Hagger archive.
8.   Hagger, *Diaries*, 19 March 1966; *Awakening to the Light*, p.262.
9.   Hagger, *Diaries*, 20 March 1966; *Awakening to the Light*, pp.262–263.
10.   Hagger, *Diaries*, 29–30 March 1966; *Awakening to the Light*, p.269.
11.   Hagger, *Diaries*, 4 June 1966; *Awakening to the Light*, p.298.
12.   Hagger, *The World Government: A Blueprint for a Universal World State*, pp.167–168.
13.   Hagger, *Diaries*, 15 June 1966; *Awakening to the Light*, pp.303–304.
14.   Hagger, *Diaries*, 22 June 1966; *Awakening to the Light*, p.306.
15.   Hagger, *Diaries*, 3 August 1966; *Awakening to the Light*, pp.320–321.
16.   Hagger, *Diaries*, 27 August 1966; *Awakening to the Light*, pp.333–334.
17.   Hagger, *Diaries*, 27 September, 4 October and 25 November 1966; *Awakening to the Light*, pp.351, 355 and 281.
18.   Hagger, *Diaries*, 4 November 1995.
19.   Hagger, *Diaries*, 19 September 1966; *Awakening to the Light*, pp.346–347.
20.   Hagger, *Diaries*, 31 October 1966; *Awakening to the Light*, pp.368–369.
21.   Hagger, *Diaries*, 12 August 1966; *Awakening to the Light*, pp.325–326.
22.   Hagger, *Diaries*, 24 October 1966; *Awakening to the Light*, p.364.
23.   Hagger, *Diaries*, 24 October 1966; *Awakening to the Light*, p.364.
24.   Hagger, *Diaries*, 27 October, 10 and 17 November 1966; *Awakening to the Light*, pp.366, 374, 378.
25.   Hagger, *Diaries*, 23 November 1966; *Awakening to the Light*, p.380.
26.   Hagger, *Diaries*, 24 November 1966; *Awakening to the Light*, p.380.
27.   Hagger, *Diaries*, 24 November 1966; *Awakening to the Light*, pp.386–387.
28.   Hagger, *Diaries*, 23 November 1966; *Awakening to the Light*, p.380.
29.   Hagger, *Diaries*, 8 December 1966; *Awakening to the Light*, p.388.
30.   Hagger, *Diaries*, 14 and 19 December 1966; *Awakening to the Light*, pp.391, 392–393.
31.   Hagger, *Diaries*, 31 January 1967; *Awakening to the Light*, pp.413–414.
32.   Hagger, *Diaries*, 11 January 1967; *Awakening to the Light*, p.404.
33.   Hagger, *Diaries*, 19 December 1966; *Awakening to the Light*, p.393.
34.   Colin Wilson, *Dreaming to Some Purpose*, p.250.

PART TWO
Path through a Dark Wood
4. Way of Loss: Dark Night of the Soul, the Purgative Way

Episode 10: Establishment and Revolution

1. Hagger, *Diaries*, 10 April 1968.
2. Hagger, *Diaries*, 28 April 1968.
3. Hagger, *Diaries*, 28 July 1968.
4. Hagger, *Diaries*, 13 July and 23 August 1968.
5. Hagger, *Diaries*, 11 July 1968.
6. Hagger, *Diaries*, 21 July 1968.
7. Hagger, *Diaries*, 3–4 August, 2 September, 12, 17 October 1968.
8. Hagger, *Diaries*, 18 September 1968.
9. Hagger, *Diaries*, 12 October 1968.
10. Hagger, *The Libyan Revolution*, p.10.
11. Hagger, *The Libyan Revolution*, pp.12–13.
12. Hagger, *Diaries*, 15 November 1968.
13. Hagger, *The Libyan Revolution*, p.15.
14. Hagger, *The Libyan Revolution*, pp.19, 232.
15. Hagger, *The Libyan Revolution*, p.24.
16. For these newspaper articles, *see* Hagger, *The Libyan Revolution*, Appendix, pp.157–279.
17. Hagger, *Diaries*, 11 April 1969; *The Libyan Revolution*, p.29.
18. Hagger, *Diaries*, 13 April 1969; *The Libyan Revolution*, p.29.
19. Briggs, *op. cit.*, p.10.
20. Hagger, *Diaries*, 15 April 1969; *The Libyan Revolution*, pp.29–30.
21. Hagger, *Diaries*, 16 April 1969.
22. Hagger, *The Libyan Revolution*, p.31.
23. Hagger, *Diaries*, 30 May 1969.

Episode 11: Liberation and Tyranny

1. Hagger, *The Libyan Revolution*, pp.34–35.
2. For later confirmation of this view *see* Michael Herb, *All in the Family: Absolutism, Revolution and Democratic Prospects in the Middle-Eastern Monarchies*, pp.193–196.
3. Hagger, *Diaries*, 26–28 June 1969.
4. Hagger, *The Libyan Revolution*, pp.36–37.
5. *See* Hagger, *The Libyan Revolution*, Appendix, pp.261–268 for the article.
6. Hagger, *The Libyan Revolution*, pp.38–39.
7. The BBC, listening to a radio announcement, wrote Bushwerib's name as Bushweir. *See* http://news.bbc.co.uk/onthisday/hi/dates/stories/september/1/newsid_3911000/3911587.stm.
8. Hagger, *The Libyan Revolution*, pp.273–275.
9. Hagger, *The Libyan Revolution*, pp.275–279.
10. Hagger, *The Libyan Revolution*, Appendix, pp.171–176.
11. Alison Pargeter, *Libya, The Rise and Fall of Qaddafi*, pp.48–60.

12. See Thomas C. Reed and Danny B. Stillman, http://www.ndu.edu/inss/ Press/jfq_pages/editions/i51/30.pdf, quoted in Hagger, *The Libyan Revolution*, p.65.
13. Hagger, *The Libyan Revolution*, p.65.
14. Herb, *op. cit.*, p.195; quoting interview with Abd al-Mun'im al-Hawani in *Al-wasat*, p.188 (4 September 1995).
15. Herb, *op. cit.*, p.196; quoting John Wright, *Libya: A Modern History*, p.121.
16. Herb, *op. cit.*, p.195; quoting Fathi al-Dib, *Abd al-Nasir wa thawrat Libya*, p.11; and Salah El Saadany, *Egypt and Libya from Inside*, p.6.
17. Herb, *op. cit.*, p.196; quoting Fathi al-Dib, *Abd al-Nasir wa thawrat Libya*, p.11; and Salah El Saadany, *Egypt and Libya from Inside*, p.6.
18. Mohammed Heikal, *The Road to Ramadan*, p.70.

Episode 12: Purgation and Separation
1. Whitehead, Process 73: An event is "a nexus of actual occasions, inter-related in some determinate fashion in one extensive quantum", i.e. at a given time and place. [p.269]
2. Geoffrey Read in conversation with Nicholas Hagger. The view of time as a succession of events is touched on in Peter Hewitt, *The Coherent Universe, An Introduction to Geoffrey Read's New Fundamental Theory of Matter, Life and Mind*, pp.145–147.
3. J.D. Haines, article in *Retired Officer Magazine*, February 2001; quoted in http://groups.google.com/group/soc.history.what-if/browse_thread/thread/ 51484ef146. *See* also http://nationalaviation.blade6. donet.com/compo-nents/content_manager_v02view_na. Also: http://www.airforcemagazine .com/MagazineArchive/Pages/2008/January/%202008/0.
4. Isabella Ginor and Gideon Remez, 'The Tyranny of Vested-Interest Sources: Shaping the Record of Soviet Intervention in the Egyptian-Israeli Conflict, 1967–1973', *Journal of the Middle East and Africa*, 1, pp.1–24, 2010. In their research Ginor and Remez have found that the Soviet SAM-3 missile system was installed in Egypt in December 1969, earlier than previously thought.
5. Matthew Campbell, *The Sunday Times*, 23.9.2012; *Daily Mail*, 24.9.2012, http://www.dailymail.co.uk/news/article-2207382/Gadaffi-raped-school-girls-kidnapped-serve-sex-slaves-checking-emails-book-reveals.html.
6. Isabella Ginor and Gideon Remez, email to Nicholas Hagger, 12 February 2012: "You date your arrival in Egypt on the same day as the Israeli bombing of a factory – evidently the raid on Abu Za'bal on 12 February 1970 – and the SAM incident occurs a few days later. This makes it the earliest Western sighting we have found so far of the Soviet Air Defense

deployment in Egypt." Ginor and Remez published the prize-winning *Foxbats over Dimona: The Soviets' Nuclear Gamble in the Six-Day War* (2007) and in 2012 were working on a sequel, *The Soviet-Israeli War*, which, they said, would include details of this "important incident".

7. Tennyson, *Maud*, Part 1, section x, stanza 5.

8. Report in English-language newspaper on seminar held on 20 May 1970; in the Hagger archive.

9. *Luke* 9.24.

10. This reception was held on Thursday 28 May 1970, not Thursday 4 June 1970 as stated in *The Libyan Revolution*, p.82.

5. Transformation: the Illuminative Way

Episode 13: Ambassador and Journalism

1. Hagger, *Diaries*, 16 July 1970.

2. Hagger, *Diaries*, 18 July 1970.

3. Hagger, *Diaries*, 25 July 1970.

4. HH. *See* Hagger, *The Libyan Revolution*, pp.279–285.

5. For *The Times* and *The Sunday Telegraph* articles, *see* Hagger, *The Libyan Revolution*, pp.279–285: 'Libya's Young Puritans', *The Times*, 29 August 1970; and 'Libya under its Colonel from the Desert', *The Sunday Telegraph*, 30 August 1970.

6. Hagger, *Diaries*, 31 July 1970.

7. Hagger, *Diaries*, 17 August 1970.

8. Letter from Nicholas Hagger to Donald Maitland, British Ambassador to Libya, 30 June 1970; in the Hagger archive.

9. Letter from Donald Maitland to Nicholas Hagger, 14 July 1970; in the Hagger archive.

10. Letter from Douglas Hurd to Nicholas Hagger, 15 July 1970; in the Hagger archive.

11. Letter from Brendan Sewill to Nicholas Hagger, 22 July 1970; in the Hagger archive.

12. Most recently, Mark Edmonds, 'I finished off Bond in a flash', *The Sunday Times*, 14 October 2012.

13. Red notebook labelled J1 on front, p.1; in the Hagger archive.

14. Letter from Brian MacArthur to Nicholas Hagger, 22 September 1970; in the Hagger archive.

15. Nicholas Hagger, 'The war against racialism', *The Times*, 3 October 1970; in the Hagger archive. *See* Appendix 5, p.522.

16. Nicholas Hagger, 'Angolan Spider's Web'; in the Hagger archive.

17. Confidential circular signed by committee director of MPLA in Mexico, 12 June 1970; in the Hagger archive.

18. Hagger, *The Times Diary*, 14 October 1970, 'Quebec seeks Guerilla Manual';

in the Hagger archive.

19. Hagger, *The Times Diary*, 24 October 1970, no title; in the Hagger archive.
20. *John* 12.24.
21. Letter from the British Council to Nicholas Hagger, 24 May 1971; in the Hagger archive.
22. Hagger, *The Times Diary*, 7 May 1971, 'Black press'; in the Hagger archive.
23. Nicholas Hagger, 17 June 1971, *The Times*, 'Medical pressures to tighten the Abortion Act'; in the Hagger archive.
24. *The Times* remittance advice, 20 October 1971; in the Hagger archive.
25. For questions jotted down at the conference prior to being memorised, *see* the Hagger archive.

Episode 14: Illumination and Nationalism

1. Hagger, *Diaries*, 16, 23, 26 July 1971.
2. Hagger, *Diaries*, 26 July 1971.
3. Hagger, *Diaries*, 2, 8, 19 (365 days) August 1971.
4. Hagger, *Diaries*, 8 August 1971.
5. Hagger, *Diaries*, 9 August 1971.
6. Hagger, *Diaries*, 16 August 1971.
7. Hagger, *Diaries*, 19–21 August 1971.
8. Hagger, *Diaries*, 26, 27, 29 August, 2 September 1971.
9. Hagger, *Diaries*, 4, 5, 4, 7 September 1971.
10. Hagger, *Diaries*, 10 September 1971.
11. Hagger, *Diaries*, 10 September 1971.
12. Hagger, *Diaries*, 11 September 1971.
13. Hagger, *Diaries*, 12 September 1971.
14. Hagger, *Diaries*, 13, 14, 16, 25 September 1971.
15. Article in *Pravda*, 2 October 1971; in the Hagger archive.
16. Christopher Andrew, *The Sword and the Shield: The Mitrokhin Archive and the Secret History of the KGB*, p.417, *see also* http://www.scribd.com/doc/32581452/4/Part-2-After-Operation-FOOT.
17. Interview with Philby in *Kodumaa*, 13 October 1971; in the Hagger archive.
18. Hagger, *Diaries*, 3 October 1971.
19. Hagger, *Diaries*, 12, 13 October 1971.
20. Hagger, *Diaries*, 18, 12 and 25, 18 October 1971.
21. Hagger, *Diaries*, 22, 25, 27 October 1971.
22. Hagger, *Diaries*, 21 November 1971.
23. Hagger, *Diaries*, 16, 19, 20, 19, 20 December 1971.
24. Hagger, *Diaries*, 3 January, 2 February 1972.
25. Hagger, 'The Silence', line 1333.
26. Hagger, *Diaries*, 27 February 1972.
27. Hagger, *Diaires*, 29 February 1972.

28. Hagger, *Africa Confidential*, 16 June 1972, 'Portugal'; in the Hagger archive.
29. Hagger, *The Times Diary*, 13 December 1971, 'Roy Sawh to leave for Guyana'; in the Hagger archive.
30. Hagger, *The Times Diary*, 14 January 1972, 'Words in exile'; in the Hagger archive.
31. *Africa Confidential*, 4 February 1972, 'London: Still the Exiles' Mecca'; in the Hagger archive.
32. *Africa Features*; in the Hagger archive.
33. Hagger, *The Times Diary*, 7 February 1972, 'London Birth'; in the Hagger archive.
34. Hagger, *The Times Diary*, 7 February 1972, 'London Birth' (same article as in n.33) and letter from Bishop Abel Muzorewa to the Editor of *The Times*, 10 February 1972; in the Hagger archive.
35. Hagger, *Diaries*, 4 March 1972.
36. Hagger, *The Times*, 4 March 1972, 'Church call to block finance for Angola'; in the Hagger archive. *See* Appendix 5, p.530.
37. Hagger, *Diaries*, 6, 7, 8 March 1972.
38. Hagger, *Diaries*, 16, 17, 19 March 1972.
39. Hagger, 'The Silence', lines 1163, 1165.
40. Hagger, *Diaries*, 19 March 1972.
41. Hagger, *Diaries*, 2 April 1972.
42. Hagger, *Diaries*, 3, 6 April 1972.
43. Hagger, *Diaries*, 8, 9 April 1972.
44. Hagger, *Diaries*, 17 April 1972.
45. Hagger, *Diaries*, 17, 19, 22 April 1972.
46. Hagger, *Diaries*, 7, 15 May 1972.
47. Hagger, *Diaries*, 16, 19 May 1972.
48. *Genesis* 25.29–34.
49. Hagger, *Africa Confidential*, 19 May 1972, 'Rhodesia: ANC and others'; in the Hagger archive.
50. Hagger, *Diaries*, 17 March 1972.
51. *The Guardian*, 1 June 1972, p.2, 'South Africa makes a concession to the UN over Namibia', 'Nicholas Hagger adds'; in the Hagger archive.
52. Hagger, *Africa Confidential*, 2 June 1972, 'South West Africa'; in the Hagger archive.
53. Hagger, *Africa Confidential*, 2 June 1972, 'Tanzania'; in the Hagger archive.
54. Hagger, *Africa Confidential*, 14 July 1972, 'Rhodesia: What will the Africans do now?'; in the Hagger archive.
55. Hagger, *Africa Confidential*, 28 July 1972, 'Angola'; in the Hagger archive.
56. Hagger, *Africa Confidential*, 11 August 1972, 'Rhodesia: Distant Prospects'; in the Hagger archive.
57. Hagger, *Africa Confidential*, 11 August 1972, 'South-West Africa'; in the

Hagger archive.

58. Hagger, *The Times Diary*, 25 August 1972, 'Sawh point in black university row'; in the Hagger archive.

Episode 15: Meaning and Disenchantment

1. Hagger, *Diaries*, 2 June 1972.
2. Hagger, *Diaries*, 30 June 1972.
3. Hagger, *Diaries*, 2 July 1972.
4. Hagger, *Diaries*, 2 July 1972.
5. Hagger, *Diaries*, 13 August 1972.
6. Hagger, *The Times*, 18 October 1972, 'Tanzania gets off the Peking gravy train'; in the Hagger archive. *See* Appendix 5, p.533.
7. Hagger, *The Guardian*, 30 November 1972, 'Jumbe loyal to Karume'; in the Hagger archive. *See* Appendix 5, p.535.
8. Hagger, *The Guardian*, 7 October 1972, 'The instant rail track – with Chinese aid'; in the Hagger archive. *See* Appendix 5, p.531.
9. Receipts signed by John Temple for 136 Tanzanian shillings "towards share of cost of journey Dar es Salaam to Makumbako and return", 24 September 1972; and for 114 Tanzanian shillings "in completion of contribution towards costs of trip to Makumbako", 25 September 1972; in the Hagger archive.
10. Letter from J.S. Malecela, Tanzanian Minister of Foreign Affairs, to Nicholas Hagger, 22 November 1972; in the Hagger archive.
11. Hagger, *Railway Gazette International*, December 1972; in the Hagger archive.
12. Hagger, *Africa Confidential*, 20 October 1972, 'Tanzania: Internal Developments' and 'Zanzibar'; in the Hagger archive.
13. Hagger, *Africa Confidential*, 3 November 1972, 'Rhodesia: ANC and FROLIZI'; in the Hagger archive.
14. BBC talks requisition/contract, 24/25 October 1972, 'Interviewed by Pete Myers on Chinese and African living conditions on the Tanzam railway'; in the Hagger archive.
15. Hagger, *Diaries*, 6, 10, 12 November 1972.
16. Hagger, *Diaries*, 25 November 1972.
17. Hagger, *Diaries*, 25 November 1972.
18. Hagger, *Diaries*, 4, 9, 10, 20 December 1972.
19. Hagger, *Diaries*, 21 December 1972.
20. Hagger, *Diaries*, 12, 23, 24 January 1973.
21. Hagger, *Diaries*, 29 January 1973.
22. Hagger, *Diaries*, 2, 3, 7 February 1973.
23. Hagger, *Diaries*, 11 February 1973.
24. Hagger, 'Why I am an Existentialist'; in *Becoming and Being* and the Hagger archive. Also, Hagger, *Diaries*, 20 February 1973.

25. Letter from H.J. Blackham to Nicholas Hagger, 19 March 1973; in the Hagger archive.
26. Hagger, *Diaries*, 12 March 1973.
27. Hagger, *Africa Confidential*, 30 March 1973, '"*Blitz*" in Namibia'; in the Hagger archive.
28. Letter from Tadashi Sasaki, Governor of the Bank of Japan, to Nicholas Hagger, 23 March 1973; in the Hagger archive.
29. Hagger, *Diaries*, 23 April 1973.
30. Hagger, *The New Philosophy of Universalism*, pp.250–251.
31. Wilson, *op. cit.*, pp.297–298.
32. Wilson, *op. cit.*, pp.349–350.
33. Hagger, *Diaries*, 24 April 1973.
34. Wilson, *op. cit.*, p.275.
35. Hagger, *Diaries*, undated 14–27 December 1985.
36. Wilson, *op. cit.*, pp.59–61.
37. Hagger, *Diaries*, 30 April 1973.
38. Hagger, *Diaries*, 22 March (Dartford), 7 June (St Nicholas Hospital), 21 June (Windsor) 1973. The visit to St Paul's took place on 14 December 1972; *see* list of visits from Riverway, in the Hagger archive.
39. Hagger, *Diaries*, 5 September 1983.
40. *Encyclopedia of World Biography*, *see* http://www.notablebiographies .com/supp/Supplement-Fl-Ka/Granville-Christine.html.
41. Hagger, *Diaries*, 9 June 1979.
42. Hagger, *Diaries*, 13 May 1973.
43. Declassified memorandum of Henry Kissinger's talks with Chou En-lai, 9 July 1971, *see* http://www.gwu.edu/~nsarchiv/NSAEBB/NSAEBB145/ 09.pdf.
44. Declassified memorandum of Henry Kissinger's talks to Chou En-lai, 21 October 1971, *see* http://www.gwu.edu/~nsarchiv/NSAEBB/NSAEBB70/ doc12.pdf.
45. Declassified documents relating to President Nixon's visit to China in February 1972, *see* http://www.gwu.edu/~nsarchiv/nsa/publications /DOC_readers/kissinger/nixzhou/.
46. Henry Kissinger, declassified memorandum to the President, 15 November 1972, 'Sir Alec Douglas-Home's recent conversations with Chou En-lai'. *See* http://nixon.archives.gov/virtuallibrary/releases/jun12 /declass21.pdf.
47. Declassified memorandum of Henry Kissinger's talks with Chou En-lai, 14 November 1973, *See* http://www.fas.org/irp/world/china/memcon11 1473.pdf.
48. Hagger, *Diaries*, 27 July 1973.
49. Hagger, *Diaries*, 31 July 1973.
50. Hagger, *Diaries*, 15, 16 August 1973.

51. Hagger, *Diaries*, 16 August 1973.
52. Hagger, *Diaries*, 16 August 1973.
53. Hagger, *Diaries*, 17, 18 August 1973.
54. Hagger, *Diaries*, 19, 20 August 1973.

Epilogue: View of the Path – Episodes and Memories, Pattern and Unity

1. *The Times*, 'Have found secret of DNA, love Daddy', 23 March 2013, p.3.

Bibliography/Reading List

Addison, William, *Epping Forest, Its Literary and Historical Associations*, J.M. Dent, 1945.

Andrew, Christopher, *The Sword and the Shield: The Mitrokhin Archive and the Secret History of the KGB*, Basic Books, 1999.

Autobiography of William Butler Yeats, The, Macmillan, 1916; Collier Books, New York, 1965.

Biggs-Davison, John, *Africa: Hope Deferred*, Johnson Publications, 1970.

Briggs, Asa, *Secret Days*, Frontline Books, 2011.

Coleridge, *Samuel Taylor, The Notebooks of,* vols I–III, ed. Kathleen Coburn, Routledge & Kegan Paul, 1957–1973.

Deacon, Richard, *A History of the British Secret Service*, Taplinger Publishing Co., 1969.

Dorril, Stephen, *MI6, Fifty Years of Special Operations*, Four Estates, 2000.

Easton, Stewart C., *A Brief History of the Western World*, New York: Barnes & Noble, 1962.

Fitzsimmons, Thomas, *Iron Harp*, University of New Mexico Press, 1999.

Gibbon, Edward, *The History of the Decline and Fall of the Roman Empire*, vols 1–3, 1776, 1781, Allen Lane, The Penguin Press, 1994.

Ginor, Isabella and Gideon Remez, *Foxbats over Dimona, The Soviets' Nuclear Gamble in the Six-Day War*, Yale, 2007.

Haffenden, John, *William Empson, vol. 1: Among the Mandarins*, Oxford University Press, 2005.

Hagger, Nicholas, *A Mystic Way*, Element, 1994.

Hagger, Nicholas, *A View of Epping Forest*, O-Books, 2012.

Hagger, Nicholas, *Awakening to the Light, Diaries, 1958–1967*, Element, 1994.

Hagger, Nicholas, *Collected Poems 1958–2005*, O-Books, 2006.

Hagger, Nicholas, *My Double Life 2: A Rainbow over the Hills*, O-Books, 2015.

Hagger, Nicholas, *Overlord*, O-Books, 2006.

Hagger, Nicholas, *The Libyan Revolution, Its Origins and Legacy*, O-Books, 2009.

Hagger, Nicholas, *The New Philosophy of Universalism*, O-Books, 2009.

Hagger, Nicholas, *The World Government: A Blueprint for a Universal World State*, O-Books, 2010.

Heikal, Mohammed, *The Road to Ramadan*, New York: Quadrangle/New York Times Book Co., 1975.

Herb, Michael, *All in the Family: Absolutism, Revolution and Democratic Prospects in the Middle-Eastern Monarchies*, State University of New York Press, 1999.

James, William, *The Varieties of Religious Experience*, Fontana, Collins, UK, 1960.

Jeffery, Keith, *MI6: The History of the Secret Intelligence Service 1909–1949*, Bloomsbury Publishing, 2010.

Johnston, Kenneth R., *The Hidden Wordsworth*, W.W. Norton and Co., 1998.

Keeler, Christine, with Douglas Thompson, *The Truth At Last: My Story*, Sidgwick & Jackson, 2001.

Kelly's Directory of Hertfordshire, Kelly's, 1933.

Koliopoulos, John S., *Brigands with a Cause, Brigandage and Irredentism in Modern Greece, 1821–1912*, Clarendon Press, Oxford, 1987.

Masterman, J.C., *The Double-Cross System in the War of 1939 to 1945*, Yale University Press, 1972; Lyons Press, 2011.

Orlans, Harold, *T.E. Lawrence, Biography of a Broken Hero*, McFarland & Co, 2002.

Pargeter, Alison, *Libya, The Rise and Fall of Qaddafi*, Yale University Press, 2012.

Spengler, Oswald, *The Decline of the West*, George Allen and Unwin, 1932 and 1959.

Stover, Leon and Bruce Kraig, *Stonehenge, the Indo-European Heritage*, Nelson-Hall, Chicago, 1978.

Tomlin, Frederick, *T.S. Eliot, A Friendship*, Routledge, 1988.

Toynbee, Arnold, *A Study of History*, Oxford University Press, 12 vols, UK, 1934, 1939, 1954, 1961.

Underhill, Evelyn, *Mysticism*, Methuen, London, 1911 and 1960.

Victoria History of the County of Cambridge and the Isle of Ely, A, vol. 5, 1973.

Victoria History of the County of Huntingdon, A, vol. 2, 1932.

West, Nigel, *MI6, British Secret Intelligence Service Operations 1909–1945*, Weidenfeld and Nicholson, 1983.

Whitehead, Alfred North, *An Anthology*, selected by F.S.C. Northrop and Mason W. Gross, Cambridge University Press, 1953.

Wilson, Colin, *Dreaming to Some Purpose*, Century, 2004.

Winchester, Barry, *Beyond the Tumult*, Allison & Busby, 1971.

Wint, Guy and Peter Calvocoressi, *Middle East Crisis*, Penguin Books, 1957.

Index

Note: Page numbers for illustrations appear in italics. Titles of books where the author is not indicated are by Nicholas Hagger. Entries are mainly in alphabetical order but in some cases, where they describe a narrative, in chronological or page order.

meets Junzaburo Nishiwaki again
186, *186*
see also +A + −A = 0
mind and universe one 92–3
the One by Worcester College lake,
experiences 92–3
the One, experience of 160–1
oneness of the earth and the
universe 209–10
oneness of the universe, in harmony
with xxiii, 482
oneness with frosty stars, early
mystic experience, 43, 61
at one with everything 175
satori 173, 483
Second Mystic Life 490–91
accepting the One law of the
universe 383
beginning of 371
Flowing Light 373, 374, 401
golden light 483
Great Flow 368–70
Great Flow and acceptance of
events 384
illumination 373–5
images and visions 470
imagination 380
increased intensity 370
Inner Light 402
law of Nature, Law of the Seed
383–4
Negative Way 367–8
round white Light 483
spring 420
tidal flow of Light 380
transformation xxiii, 329, 380,
406
visions 375–80
visions, four raptures 401–4, 485
white Inner Light 399
white light 373, 374, 443
end of 406–7, 413

see also illumination
universe, in touch with 57, 60, 61
the universe, new view of man and
379
a visionary and a mystic 468
see also Dark Night; illumination
Mysticism (Underhill) 161, 213, 372,
373, 375
Mystic Peace 378
A Mystic Way xxiv–xxv
Mystic Way xxiii, 22, 132, 188, 293,
329, 446, 452, 453
Mythologies (Yeats) 332

Nairobi 436
Namibia 466
Namibia International Conference
408–10, 485
Narita, Professor and 25-course meal
168
Nasser, Col. Gamal 67, 69, 276, 277,
297, 299, 301, 484
nationalism xxxiii, 472
National Service 73, 92
Nature 35, 42, 51, 65, 75, 383–4, 481
hidden powers of 60
at one with 68, 303
seeing through soul 61
The Naughty Ninepins (Praeger) 30
La Nausée (Sartre) 210
Negative Way 367–8
neo-Baroque 88, 337, 466, 469
new centre 132, 465
new epoch 379
A New Philosophy of Literature xxiv, 166
The New Philosophy of Universalism 213,
384, 452
Newsweek 192, 200, 201
New Testament (Bible) 62
New World Order xxxiii
The New York Times 192, 200
Niarchos, Stavros 115

BOOKS

O is a symbol of the world, of oneness and unity. In different cultures it also means the "eye," symbolizing knowledge and insight. We aim to publish books that are accessible, constructive and that challenge accepted opinion, both that of academia and the "moral majority."

Our books are available in all good English language bookstores worldwide. If you don't see the book on the shelves ask the bookstore to order it for you, quoting the ISBN number and title. Alternatively you can order online (all major online retail sites carry our titles) or contact the distributor in the relevant country, listed on the copyright page.

See our website www.o-books.com for a full list of over 500 titles, growing by 100 a year.

And tune in to myspiritradio.com for our book review radio show, hosted by June-Elleni Laine, where you can listen to the authors discussing their books.

MySpiritRadio